Venezuela

THE BRADT TRAVEL GUIDE

Third Edition

Hilary Dunsterville Branch

Bradt Publications, UK
The Globe Pequot Press Inc, USA

First published in 1993 by Bradt Publications,
This third edition published in 1999 by Bradt Publications
41 Nortoft Road, Chalfont St Peter, Bucks SL9 0LA, England
Published in the USA by The Globe Pequot Press Inc, 6 Business Park Road,
PO Box 833, Old Saybrook, Connecticut 06475-0833

British Library Cataloguing in Publication Data
A catalogue record for this book is available from the British Library

Library of Congress Cataloging-in-Publication Data is available

ISBN 1 898323 89 5

Photographs
Front cover Scarlet macaw, *Ara macao* (Stephen Dalton/NHPA)
Text Hilary Bradt (HB), Paul Morrison (PM), Edward Paine (EP)
Wildlife illustrations Oliver Whalley
Maps Alan Whitaker

Typeset from the author's disc by Wakewing
Printed and bound in Italy by LEGO, Vicenza

Author

Hilary Dunsterville Branch is British by descent, American by birth and Venezuelan as a *re-encauchada* citizen (literally a 're-tread'). Travel was a way of life as she grew up in half a dozen countries with oil-company parents. She left her first job as a reporter, for *The Villager* in New York City, to return to Venezuela in an old Willys, advertising for a driving companion, Lou-Bette Herrick. But once in Caracas, the two continued south, with a pet ocelot, through the Andes to Tierra del Fuego. They eventually found a sponsor to make the circle back to New York via Alaska. Hilary wrote about it for *Life en Español* and Venezuela's English-language paper, *The Daily Journal*, where she later worked as reporter and news editor. For many years as editor of *Ve Venezuela* tourism magazine, as well as an orchid hunter with her parents, she explored the wilds of her adopted country – and admits there are many places as yet unvisited. Hilary and her husband Douglas Branch live in the coffee hills south of Caracas.

Her advice to travellers in Venezuela is: 'Take nothing for granted'. Flights, hotels and services are part of a young, rapidly changing industry and enthusiasm often outshines capacity. She hopes visitors will share their surprises, pleasant or not, with readers of the next edition, by sending her a card, or an email letter to Katraca@telcel.net.ve.

THE BRADT STORY

In 1974, my former husband George Bradt and I spent three days sitting on a river barge in Bolivia writing our first guide for like-minded travellers: *Backpacking along Ancient Ways in Peru and Bolivia*. The 'little yellow book', as it became known, is now in its sixth edition and continues to sell to travellers throughout the world.

Since 1980, with the establishment of Bradt Publications, I have continued to publish guides for the discerning traveller, covering more than 100 countries and all six continents; in 1997 we won the *Sunday Times* Small Publisher of the Year Award. *Venezuela* is the 152nd Bradt title or new edition to be published.

The company continues to develop new titles and new series, but in the forefront of my mind there remains our original ethos – responsible travel with an emphasis on the culture and natural history of the region. I hope that you will get the most out of your trip, and perhaps have the opportunity to give something in return.

Travel guides are by their nature continuously evolving. If you experience anything which you would like to share with us, or if you have any amendments to make to this guide, please write; all your letters are read and passed on to the author. Most importantly, do remember to travel with an open mind and to respect the customs of your hosts – it will add immeasurably to your enjoyment.

Happy travelling!

Hilary Bradt

Contents

LIST OF MAPS

Acknowledgements

My special thanks go to Paul Rouche and his wife Jocelyn Lespinasse whose passion for hiking the mountains of Venezuela gave me solid ground for writing this book. In the same way, Forest Leighty hiked the Avila and Sierra Nevada trails, Chris Stolley contributed the first version of sections on Cumaná and Margarita, as did Bill Quantrill on Roraima, and Mark Dutton, Peter Ireland, James Mead and Justine Freeth on the Paria Peninsula. I am also most grateful to Edward Paine and Jorge Vall for excellent photographs and reproductions.

Many readers provided valuable input for early editions. To name some: Florence Smith, Huw Clough, Oyvind and Helen Servan, Don Jacobs, Steve Whitaker, Sandrine Tiller, Lindsay Griffin, Andrea Bullock, Darren Kealey, Chris Sharpe, Michele Coppens, C Nacher, Edith Steinbuch, Julian Singleton, Tim Wainwright, Alison Vickers, Peter Weinberger, Sven Berge, Karen and John Whitehead, Barney Gibbs, Tracey and Paul Weatherstone, Harald Baedeke, Luke Tegner, Elizabeth Lung and Cliff Walker. For their help in improving the third edition of *Venezuela* I am indebted to Lt M J Bristow (Cambridge University Officers Training Corps), Philippa Budgen, Sheena Henderson, Susan Brodar-Lorenzato, Dr G Bucciarelli, Robin Gordon-Walker, Stuart McKamey, Peter Hutchison and Nicholas Ziegel.

If there is one person who provides constant inspiration – not only by exploring the country and sharing her love of its wilderness through her book *Birding in Venezuela*, but by defending Venezuela's great natural diversity through tireless work in the Audubon Conservation Society (SCAV) – it is Mary Lou Goodwin. I thank her for generous assistance.

Introduction

Venezuela is an excellent gateway country to South America, with some of the cheapest flights to the continent routed through Margarita Island and the capital, Caracas. Travellers may take one horrified look and flee from this disordered city. But Caracas has its devotees and it is always important not to judge a country by its capital. The largest Venezuelan cities are located near the Caribbean coast. Everything else is called the *interior*. Because 90% of Venezuelans live in the northern 10% of the land, much of the country remains delightfully free of urban blight, retaining local colour and traditions. There is some excellent backpacking in a variety of mountain scenery, from cloudforest to glacier, and in some splendid national parks. Away from the built-up coast, there are waterfalls, amazing birdlife, tablelands and savannahs – and a relative absence of international tourism. The exception is Margarita Island: a magnet for sun seekers, mainly from Europe and Canada.

This guide emphasises ecotourism and is not intended as a complete guide to every city and all hotels. It has grown in response to readers' suggestions and requests, describing places of greatest interest to the more adventurous traveller.

Part One

General Information

Background Information

FACTS AND FIGURES

The Republic of Venezuela is on the north coast of South America. Besides the Caribbean, its borders are Colombia in the west, Guyana in the east, and Brazil in the south. Its area of 916,445 km² (352,144 square miles) is larger than Spain + Portugal and UK + Ireland combined. The republic is divided into 23 states, a federal district (Caracas), and a federal dependency of 72 islands. Population: 23,700,000. Capital: Caracas, estimated metropolitan population 4,000,000; other major cities Maracaibo, Valencia, Barquisimeto, Maracay, Ciudad Guayana. Life expectancy: men 70 years, women 74. Birth rate: 2.9. Infant mortality rate: 21/1,000. Literacy: 90%.

The gross domestic product (1997) was $67,600 million, or $2,900 per capita; overall debt was $35,000 million. Out of a workforce of 8.8 million, 50% are in the informal sector. Of the remainder, 12% to 20% are unemployed, depending on who makes the estimates. Inflation, which stood at 103% in 1996, dropped in 1997 to 37%, and in 1998 to around 30%.

GEOGRAPHY AND CLIMATE
Geography

Venezuela lies between latitude 12° and less than 1° north of the equator. Terrain and climate extend from tropical sea level to icy Andean peaks, although most of the land is below 1,000m. The coastline is 3,000km long. The country may be outlined in three geographical regions: the coastal north limited by mountain ranges; the central plains and delta of the Orinoco; south of the Orinoco, the Guayana highlands and Amazonian forests.

The north coast, and many islands, are bordered for long stretches by semi-arid hills, interrupted by lush coastal valleys such as Choroní and Chichiriviche. The densely populated coastal region is limited by three major ranges. Rising in the west to over 5,000m, the Andes form the 'roof' of Táchira, Mérida and Trujillo states, before ending in Lara. These states are cultivated with coffee, fruit and vegetables. The Andean cordillera blocks the fertile basin of Lake Maracaibo, largest in South America, and still rich in oil after 70 years' exploitation. The central Coastal Cordillera extends from Falcón eastward to Miranda State and is capped by Pico Naiguatá, 2,765m. In the east, the Cordillera Oriental runs through Sucre State to the tip of Paria Peninsula.

The central plains, or *llanos*, slope from the Andes south to the Orinoco River. Including 40,000km² of the delta, this sparsely inhabited region covers a quarter of Venezuela. The Orinoco runs 2,800km to the Atlantic, third longest and most voluminous river in South America. It is navigated by container ships as far as the industrial centre of Ciudad Guayana. The upper llanos are extensively cultivated (rice, sorghum, corn, tobacco, oil palm). But the nutrient-poor lower llanos support mainly free-range cattle in Apure, Barinas and Guárico states, and pine plantations in eastern Anzoátegui and Monagas states, better known for their huge oil reserves. Annual rains flood vast stretches of Apure. In the remaining months of drought, wildlife concentrates in lagoons, palm stands and marshes.

South of the Orinoco are the Guayana Highlands and the rainforests of Bolívar and Amazonas. The two states total 418,000km² or 45% of the country, but have only 5% of the population. The extraordinary *tepuis*, or tablelands, are remnants of the Guayana Shield, one of the earth's most ancient formations. Its sandstones date to sediments eroded from the earth's crust 2,000–3,000 million years ago. Over a hundred *tepuis* rise above a rolling plateau; Auyantepui gives birth to the world's highest cascade, Angel Falls, 907m high. Although rich in forests, water and minerals such as iron, bauxite, gold and diamonds, the region had a very thin layer of soil. Forming the border with Brazil is Cerro de la Neblina, 3,040m, the highest peak in South America east of the Andes. The Amazonian forests continue into the Orinoco basin in an uninterrupted carpet. The Orinoco shares some of its water with Brazil via the Brazo Casiquiare, the only natural waterway to connect two major river systems.

Earthquakes are not uncommon in Venezuela. These are related to three main geological faults, all of which have had quakes of great magnitude (although rare): the Boconó system in the Andes, the San Sebastian or Caribe system in central coastal Venezuela, and El Pilar fault in the east. The last intense quake in Caracas was July 1967 on the city's 400th anniversary, and in Cumaná-Cariaco in July 1997. Buildings in Caracas are required to be built with earthquake-proof construction, and the Metro was designed to withstand severe quakes.

Climate

Venezuela has two main seasons, rainy and dry. These are called winter (*invierno*), May–June to October; and summer (*verano*), Nov–Dec to May. The hottest months are usually April and August when the sun is directly overhead. When it is gloomy and wet in Europe and the USA, it is the opposite in Venezuela. Torrential rains peak in June–July, when an umbrella gives about as much shelter as a sieve. But it rarely rains all day and clouds are dramatic and beautiful. In the high Andes snow may fall in July–September. Altitude, humidity and winds contribute to very variable temperatures. Margarita, at sea level, averages 27°C; Mérida at 1,645m, 19°C; and Mucuchíes at 2,938m, 11°C. When added to altitude, the daily highs and lows can swing 10–15°C, so that while the top of Roraima may be below 5° at night, heat at noon exceeds 20°C.

FAUNA AND FLORA

An extraordinary variety of fauna and flora thrives in a score of very diverse and well-defined ecosystems. Nine biogeographical regions have been described: Lake Maracaibo basin, enclosed west and south by mountains; the arid Coro system from the Guajira to Paraguaná peninsulas; the Andes; the central coastal cordillera to Paria Peninsula; islands and archipelagos; the Llanos; the Orinoco Delta system; and the region south of the Orinoco, made up of four biogeographical subregions. Many life forms are exclusive to the rainswept Guayana *tepuis*, or mesas, giving the name *pantepui* to their summit ecosystems. The *llanos*, or plains, are a spectacle of bird and animal life around waterholes in the dry season.

In the Andes when the moor-like *páramos* above 3,000m elevation come into bloom in October, many species of wildflowers create a tapestry of yellow, white, orange and blue. This is the only ecosystem in Venezuela where flowers in profusion may be compared with a meadow in northern climates. Indeed, many *páramo* species are now cultivated in Europe, such as the nasturtium, aster, clematis, gentian, befaria and calceolaria.

Mammals

Flying animals top Venezuela's list of 327 mammals: the diminutive bats account for over 150 species. They raise one baby at a time on milk from underarm teats. Only one lives off other mammals, the common vampire which is as widely distributed as its cattle hosts. Next most prolific is the rodent order, varying from mice weighing 10g to the capybara or *chigüire*, at 65kg the world's largest rodent. Manatee, up to 500kg, and Orinoco dolphins, 200kg, are easily Venezuela's largest mammals. On land the tapir is the biggest native (140–180kg), much pursued for food. Among the most fascinating of animals are the Edentata: sloths, anteaters and armadillos. The giant armadillo looks like a living fossil and, barring a magical reprieve, is headed for extinction through hunting. Like the 30 species of marsupials, they are among the most primitive mammals, all originating in South America.

Capybara

Birds

Birdlife, at the latest count 1,346 species, is amazingly varied – from the smallest hummingbirds (an incredible 97 species) to the reintroduced Andean condor. Ornithologists travel halfway round the world to track the harpy eagle, cock-of-the-rock, capuchinbird, sunbittern, bearded bellbird, violaceous trogon, spangled cotinga, paradise jacamar, and many other fabulous birds. As many as 250 species have been spotted around a single camp in Amazonas, 315 in the llanos, and a record of 578 in Henri Pittier National Park. In Caracas, at the Botanical Gardens, Avila Hotel or Parque del Este (home to some scarlet ibis), many beautiful birds are resident: orioles, tanagers, thrushes, flycatchers, heron, saltator, green jays, and noisy flocks of the city's escaped parrots and macaws.

Conservation

The main danger to fauna and flora in Venezuela, as elsewhere, is loss of habitat through annual burning, logging and development. Mining and agriculture contaminate rivers. Ministry of Environment investigations in 1997 showed that the western plains are being deforested by 3.8% a year. The area south of Lake Maracaibo suffers the worst forest destruction, 7.4% yearly. Studies are to cover the whole country.

Since the creation of its first national park in 1937, Venezuela has brought 141,043km² of wilderness, an area twice the size of the Republic of Ireland, into a system of national parks and natural monuments. These represent over 15% of the country and cover almost all ecosystems. But legal protection is one thing, and effective management another. Few parks have guards or rangers, and the National Parks Institute, Inparques, is small and understaffed. The Ministry of Environment appears unable to resolve conflicts embroiling parks in claims by ranchers, loggers, even the Ministry of Energy and Mines.

Although trade in wildlife is banned by international pact, an intense illegal traffic in thousands of parrots and songbirds finds an outlet via the Delta to dealers in Trinidad and Guyana. The Red Book of threatened fauna in Venezuela lists 28 mammals (11 endangered), including the giant armadillo, manatee, Margarita deer and monkey, giant otter, and spectacled bear. The Orinoco and coastal crocodiles are so rare that they are seldom seen in the wild. The Arrau river turtle, and five sea turtles, are all protected by law but like crocodiles their future is uncertain as, if they are not killed outright, their eggs are taken.

A BRIEF HISTORY
Early settlers
Venezuela has the distinction of being the part of the American continent where Columbus set foot. Contemporary mapmakers labelled it simply 'Terra Firma'. Columbus landed on Paria Peninsula on his third voyage of discovery in 1498. At first he thought that Paria was an island and named it Isla de Gracia, or Land of Grace, for its 'happy, amiable and hospitable' people. This easy-going state did not last long as disparate tribes were unable to repel the Spaniards who followed in the early 1500s, enslaving natives to dive for the pearls of Cubagua and Margarita islands. Once the oyster beds were stripped, the Conquistadors sought in vain for El Dorado. But traders and settlers, usually preceded by missionaries, created ranches and plantations, ports and towns. The earliest towns on the mainland were Cumaná, 1521, and Coro, 1527.

Towards independence
The Spanish colony's first stirrings of independence came in 1749. Then in 1806 Francisco de Miranda, sailing from New York and assisted by American volunteers, attempted to overthrow the ruling powers. Two of his three ships were captured; Miranda escaped but 63 Americans were imprisoned and their officers hanged. His second expedition proved somewhat more successful; he captured the town of Coro but then had to withdraw. In 1812 Miranda commanded the First Republic's revolutionary army, with even worse luck: the patriots were defeated and he was taken by Spaniards. Simón Bolívar then took up leadership (more about Bolívar in *Chapter 4*) and decreed 'War to the Death'. The turning point in the patriots' long struggle came when they captured Angostura (now Ciudad Bolívar) in 1818. With British recruits and fearless horsemen of the plains led by General José Antonio Páez, the ragged army then marched over the Andes to free Colombia in 1819. This led to the proclamation of the Republic of Gran Colombia, made up of present-day Venezuela, Colombia, Ecuador, Peru and Panama. Independence was sealed at the Battle of Carabobo on June 24 1821, and two years later the Spanish army was finally booted out of Venezuela.

A sovereign state
The union of Gran Colombia soon broke down and Venezuela declared itself a sovereign state before Bolívar died in 1830, his health broken by tuberculosis, his hopes shattered. Venezuela, already devastated by 12 years of Independence wars, was to be bled by continuous civil strife for the rest of the century. After the first president, strongman José Antonio Páez, came a series of despots and dictators. The best of these was Antonio Guzmán Blanco (1870–88), a liberal who

introduced free compulsory schooling at the same time as banning religious seminaries and putting up statues to Bolívar and himself. He liked to be addressed as the 'Illustrious American', although he imitated everything French as did most of Caracas society.

The 20th century

An illiterate Andean named Juan Vicente Gómez arrived in Caracas in 1899 with the army of another usurper, *caudillo* Cipriano Castro. In 1908 Gómez took power and held it for 27 years with cunning and great cruelty. He acquired vast properties and ran the country like one of his ranches. As those who disagreed with him were clapped into leg irons, the student-inspired opposition went underground or into exile, rising later to lead the country into democracy. Gómez, who died an old man in 1935, was followed by two transitional president-generals, Eleázar López Contreras and Isaías Medina Angarita. Medina was ousted by an army coup led by Marcos Pérez Jiménez in 1945. A member of this revolutionary junta, Rómulo Betancourt, prepared the first democratic elections in 1947, with universal suffrage for men and women over 18. These were won by popular novelist Rómulo Gallegos. However, a coup led by Pérez Jiménez ended Gallegos' presidency in eight months. PJ's dictatorship is known for splashy public works, highways from Caracas to the coast and to Valencia, huge low-cost housing blocks, hotels, a race-track, and the cablecar systems in Mérida and Caracas. However, Pérez Jiménez' dictatorship was tainted by corruption and the infamous National Security or secret police.

When Pérez Jiménez was overthrown in 1958 democracy returned. Rómulo Betancourt, leader of the Acción Democrática (AD) party, became the first democratically elected president to complete a term, 1959–64. He handed power over to Raúl Leoni, also of AD. The Social Christian party alternated in 1969 with President Rafael Caldera, the same man who 25 years later broke the two-party system by winning as candidate for splinter groups. Shortly after Carlos Andrés Pérez, 67, of AD won his second term in 1989 (first term 1974–79), rising prices led to an outbreak of riots and looting called 'El Caracazo'. Recession plus economic liberalisation prompted further social breakdown in the two coup attempts of 1992. Where force failed, law prevailed and Pérez was impeached by Congress in June 1993 on corruption charges. He was found guilty and sentenced to two years' imprisonment under house arrest. Ramón J Velásquez was chosen interim president for the remainder of Pérez' term. In the elections of December 1993, former president Rafael Caldera, 75, was returned to power by a coalition of 16 opposition parties under the banner of Convergence.

The present day

Now, desperate for change, the country seeks new leadership. Among independent candidates heading their own parties in the elections of December 1998 were ex-army commander Hugo Chávez who led a 1992 coup attempt; Irene Sáez, mayor of Chacao township and former Miss Universe; and Henrique Salas Romer, businessman and ex-governor of Carabobo State. Backed by 56% of the electorate, Chávez, 44, was voted Venezuela's president from 1999 to 2004.

GOVERNMENT AND POLITICS
Government

The president is elected by plurality vote for a term of five years and may not be re-elected for another ten years. He decides the members of his cabinet, mainly heads of ministries, and exercises considerable power. Since the decentralisation reforms of 1989 he no longer appoints state governors who are now elected directly, as are mayors and town councillors. Another overdue reform has initiated direct election of half the 210-member Chamber of Deputies, while the other half and all 57 members of the Senate are still chosen by party slate. Congress elects the 18 members of the Supreme Court of Justice, and civilian judges are selected by a judicial council. Vital reforms in the public sector, including the judiciary, social security and electoral systems, are being assisted by multilateral loans. The government, however, remains hampered by bloated bureaucracy.

After forty years, democracy in Venezuela is struggling with a structural crisis, having exhausted its statist model. The economy continues to be heavily dependent on oil. Although revenues and spending reached peaks in 1997, benefits are nowhere in sight and three-quarters of the population is sunk in poverty. Until the end of World War II, most families lived modestly, farming and raising livestock. There was little industry and nearly half of all Venezuelans were illiterate. But with growing oil exports people moved to the cities in search of the better jobs, education and health care offered under democracy. Arturo Uslar Pietri, an intellectual who has observed this evolution, sees the end result as 'the state does not live off the nation through taxation and other sources of revenue, but the nation lives off the state... The state has grown into a monster which must be dismantled'. The government employs 1.2 million people, over 13% of job holders. Handing out jobs and patronage in exchange for power – as access to wealth (legitimate or not) – has been entrenched since Spanish colonial days. Then, as now, influence peddling, commissions and kickbacks made efficient administration impossible. To such corruption, independent of the integrity of early democratic presidents, has been added gross mismanagement of very considerable income and resources.

The **Armed Forces** keep apart from politics, vowing to uphold democracy. The army, navy, airforce and national guard or Fuerzas Armadas de Cooperación (FAC) depend on conscription for some 80,000 servicemen and women. Career officers do not vote in elections, nor can they hold electoral office.

The economy

Venezuela's economy, overcoming bank failures, recession and inflation, saw growth of 5% in 1997, spurred by the opening of the oil industry to foreign investment, plus high oil prices. International reserves exceeded $17,000 million. The bulk of Venezuela's trade surplus of $6,800 million came from oil exports to the United States. The state steel mill was sold and the aluminium sector was to be next on the auction block. Venezuela is privatising seaports and airports, hotels, telephones, the Avila cableway, even state race-tracks.

However, the economy was hammered by a 30% slump in oil prices in 1998. Oil accounts for 70% of total exports, half of all government revenue, and over a quarter of gross domestic product. The state oil company Petróleos de Venezuela, PDVSA, has entered huge joint ventures in heavy oil upgrading projects and petrochemical plants. PDVSA's Refining Center in Paraguaná, with a capacity of 940,000 barrels per day, is the largest refinery in the world. PDVSA also owns refineries in Curaçao, six in the US including the Virgin Islands, 50% of a Swedish refinery and 50% of four refineries in Germany. Petroleum reserves total some 62,000 million barrels, gas reserves 240 trillion cubic feet, and deposits of heavy oil or bitumen 1.2 trillion barrels. Other natural resources are iron, bauxite, coal, gold and diamonds, wood, and hydropower. Venezuela is the top oil supplier to the US and has long been a close trading partner, importing food, machinery, vehicles and parts.

Unemployment is officially over 12%, while nearly half the workforce of 8,800,000 is in the informal sector. Thirteen percent of jobs are in the government,

51% in private services, 34% in industry, agriculture and construction, 1% in the state oil industry. Non-oil exports are led by iron ore, steel, aluminium, chemicals, textiles and paper. **Agriculture** accounts for exports of tobacco, beef, chicken, rice, coffee, cocoa and fruit, but fails to meet more than 40% of the nation's food needs. The single largest private conglomerate is Polar Enterprises which generates 2% of GDP excluding oil, with sales of over $1,870 million (1997) in food (Polar beer is the world's eighth largest in sales), beverages, supermarkets, distribution, aluminium. Polar has put $1,000 million into building a large fertiliser plant.

   Tourism attracts nearly a million overseas visitors. The industry now generates about $1,200 million. As one of the economy's most dynamic sectors, it is expected to show annual growth of 14% through the year 2000 and to create 80,000 direct jobs. In Caracas alone, four luxury hotels were to open in 1998, and in Margarita a dock for cruise ships is being built. About half of visitors come from Europe and 30% from the United States and Canada.

THE PEOPLE

Venezuela's indigenous peoples today make up scarcely 1.5% of the population and live mainly in remote or border areas. Most belong to the Carib or Arawak language families. The Guajiros or Wayúu (170,000) are the most economically competitive, raising cattle and running businesses in Zulia State. In the east, the Warao people (24,000) live precariously in the Orinoco Delta. In the far south of Amazonas State the Yanomami and related Sanema (15,000) face invasion of their forest privacy by goldminers. The Yekuana or Makiritare, Panare, Piaroa, Pemón and Kariña have seen little progress in securing their rights within Venezuelan, or *criollo*, society. The official policy has been to pressure these groups, and a dozen more, into joining mainstream culture. In plain language the state, at best, provides token health services; at worst it encourages invasion of indigenous lands, and allows violence by *criollos* to go unpunished. The Yekuana run their own bicultural schools and prepare young men as teachers with the aid of the state Fundación del Niño, not the Ministry of Education. The Yanomami are visited by sporadic health teams whose care cannot arrest severe diseases such as malaria, tuberculosis and hepatitis.

   Venezuelans today are 70% a racial mix of white, Indian and African blood. Blacks account for a further 8%, and whites 20%. Postwar immigration from Spain, Portugal and Italy was followed in later decades by over a million people from Colombia, then Ecuador and Peru, plus refugees from dictatorships in Argentina, Uruguay and Chile. About 25,000 United States citizens live in Venezuela.

   By the year 2000 Venezuela will have some 24.5 million inhabitants – one quarter under the age of 20. The rate of population growth is 2%. As most people (88%) today live in cities, with metropolitan Caracas absorbing one fifth of the population, the rise of urban violence is unsurprising. Crime and drug abuse are linked to lack of work and education in a society where 75% of students quit school by 15 or soon after.

   The success of macroeconomic plans has not been reflected in better jobs or a higher standard of living. While there is more foreign investment, debt is heavier. Social conditions have deteriorated as purchasing power declines: from 1995 to 1997 the poverty index rose from 31% to 69% of the population. The minimum wage was to be raised in 1998 to $200 monthly. But the critically poor (38%) who earn about $100 cannot afford milk, meat or cheese. By 1996 food consumption was already 30% lower than it was pre-recession. Recent years have seen a collapse in the public health system. State hospitals have had periodic shutdowns

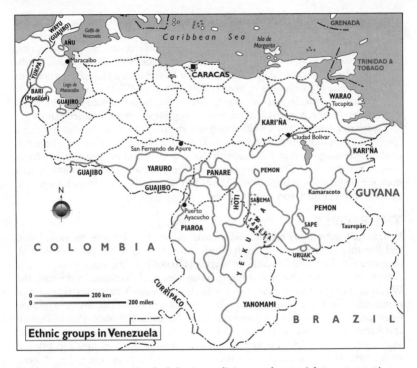

Ethnic groups in Venezuela

by doctors and nurses who lack basic medicines and materials to treat patients. Thirty percent of the population has no access to health services for geographical or economic reasons. Official figures for families lacking safe drinking water exceed 300,000.

Civil rights

There are 40 or more NGOs working in the field of human rights around Venezuela, including three devoted to Indian rights. Provea, the Venezuelan Program for Education-Action in Human Rights, reports yearly on civil rights as well as economic and social rights such as education and health (provea@derechos.org.ve). Provea trains teachers, lawyers and judges in the defence of human rights. Violence comes not only from criminals but also from law enforcers. Police made over 11,000 summary arrests in special operations in 1997, and 151 people were killed by state and police forces.

LANGUAGE AND RELIGION

Spanish is the official language. English is studied as a second language but few people can speak it. Along with Spanish, Columbus brought Catholicism to the New World. The Church was subordinated to the Spanish crown which collected tithes for supporting the clergy, authorised the building of churches and seminaries, and ordered that all communication with Rome be directed through Spain. Catholicism was the only legal religion, and worship of native gods or those of African slaves was suppressed.

Missionaries were the tireless explorers and pioneers of the 17th and 18th centuries, founding 350 settlements often under harsh and risky conditions. At the same time these Capuchins, Franciscans, Dominicans and Jesuits studied the languages of their converts including Carib, Arawak, Warao, Cumanagoto, Saliva, Jirajara, Achagua and many other tongues. Complete with schools, Catholic missions are still the founding force of remote communities such as Kavanayen, Wonken, Kamarata, Tucuco and Amacuro, as they once were in Tucupita, Upata, Guasipati and Tumeremo. Since the 1950s Evangelist missionaries have settled in Amazonas State.

In 1834 Congress declared freedom of worship. The Catholic Church had lost three-quarters of its clergy as well as property and prestige during the independence wars, as most churchmen – good monarchists – had opposed the revolution. On the other hand, among the patriots were Jewish families from Curaçao who now settled in Maracaibo, Coro, Puerto Cabello and Caracas.

A visit by the Pope leaves no doubt that the country is largely Catholic as hundreds of thousands cheer and wait all night to see him. But many people live with common-law spouses (30% of unions), practise family planning, treat abortion as a medical problem, and in general are nonobservers. Hundreds of poorer communities no longer have a priest. Indeed, the most vigourous religious groups today are the Evangelists, Baptists, Jehovah's Witnesses and pentecostal groups who have made thousands of converts in small towns all over the country.

Santería-like cults also have disciples. The pagan María Lionza cult is centred in Sorte, Chivacoa, where followers enter trances and observe rituals to figures of myth, religion and history. The pantheon is led by *Las Tres Potencias*: María Lionza, a forest spirit who rides a tapir, the black patriot Negro Felipe, and Indian chief Guaicaipuro.

EDUCATION AND CULTURE

State schools and universities are basically free. Public education is compulsory up to the ninth grade (*ciclo básico*), after which attendance drops sharply from 80% to 52%. Despite concerns over low budgets, rising enrolment and poor quality of primary education, great strides have been made over the past four decades. This is reflected in the rise of literacy from 60% to 90%. At the same time universities quadrupled from seven to 31, and were supplemented by more than 90 technical and university institutes offering three-year courses.

The **Universidad Central de Venezuela**, oldest and largest in the country with some 70,000 students, was founded as a royal seminary in 1721. The university city, begun in the 1940s, has been declared a National Monument as a working synthesis of art and architecture. It is one of the few modern examples of a large compound designed and built by a single architect, Carlos Raúl Villanueva. Next oldest is Mérida's **Universidad de Los Andes** (1810) which has some 35,000 students.

Public libraries are found in all cities and belong to the Biblioteca Nacional network. The head library, housing a big collection of periodicals, is located in Caracas' Foro Libertador. Playwriters and novelists continue a long literary tradition. Ballet, dance, opera and theatre companies all contribute to the nation's cultural life. Big annual and biennial events include international theatre, music, graphic arts, pottery festivals, and an Ibero-American art fair. A Latin-American music festival is sponsored by the Ateneo de Caracas, an arts centre with concert hall, theatre and gallery. Modelled on this cultural centre are *ateneos* around the country where recitals, lectures, art shows and classes are held, often free.

Venezuela is a nation of music makers. Throughout the plains and mountains, people make and play the native four-stringed guitar or *cuatro*, violin, maracas, harp and drums. Less common are the pan flute, bone flute and deer horn. Despite pop, salsa and foreign influences, there has been a resurgence of folk music. Traditional rhythms such as the *joropo*, *gaita*, *golpe* and *décima* are alive and well. At Christmas, no one can escape the characteristic music of Zulia State, the *gaita*, an insistent beat carried by local instruments such as the *charrasca* and drumlike *furruco*.

Practical Information

WHEN TO VISIT

Venezuela's climate, lacking hot and cold extremes, makes it seasonable year round for beach lovers and sightseers. Sunny spells often interrupt the pattern of rains. Even in wet months, for instance, the sun shines an average 7–9 hours a day even in Margarita. The hottest months are usually April and August when the sun is directly overhead. There are regional differences, too: rains are generally light in Los Roques and coastal areas such as the Paraguaná Peninsula, Coro, and Cumaná. The very best months are November to January when sunny skies are glorious and nights are brisk. Depending on special interests, travellers should plan for the dry season (November/December to April), or rainy (May/June to October).

Camping, climbing, hiking Dry season. Nevertheless, the tablelands of the Gran Sabana seem to have their own weather machine for churning up storms. The dry season is ideal in the Andes where hiking in mud and fog can be downright dangerous. Do not camp on beaches or islands in October–November when winds may drop, allowing tiny gnats to sting mercilessly all night.

Fishing Year round for deepsea fishing, December through April for river fishing, May to September for trout in the Andes.

Photography Go in the rainy season for lush vegetation, scrubbed skies and full waterfalls. Dry season visibility is poor for panoramas because of *calina*, dust and smoke in the air.

River travel Dry season, except for Angel Falls river trips made by operators *only* in wet season as navigation is faster and easier in high water. In general during the rains biting insects are torture on slow rivers like the Orinoco, Delta and the Llanos tributaries. Travel on the Caura and other swift 'black water' rivers is splendid in dry months when waters sparkle and sandbanks grow into beaches.

Wildlife Dry season. Animals are amazingly plentiful on the Llanos, or plains, when waterholes shrink. The number of wading birds is astounding. Birdwatchers should plan well in advance for the Llanos lodges.

Windsurfing Trade winds are strong most of the year on the Paraguaná and Araya peninsulas and Margarita's southern shore, El Yaque. If any period is slack it is October and November.

Note People allergic to bites of midges, mosquitoes and ticks should travel to the interior only in the dry season when insect pests are few, even in the Delta. As a general rule, they are not present at altitudes over 1,200m.

High/low seasons

School holidays count as high season: late July, August and September, Christmas to January 6, Carnival and Easter. The last two are peak beach times; late bookings for Margarita and coastal areas are obtained by sheer luck. Stay well away from the Margarita ferry at these times. As people start travelling a week ahead, keep clear of bus or plane stations until the holiday is half over. International flights are also not advised but if you must fly, start to check in 3–4 hours before departure as there are queues waiting for your seat. On the other hand, the general exodus to beaches means that big cities are at their best during such holidays.

Specialised tourism activities such as river fishing, birdwatching and windsurfing, which mainly attract foreigners escaping the northern winter, in general charge higher rates during the dry season.

TOUR OPERATORS

Much may be said for a good tour if your destination is remote. In wilderness areas operators provide all transportation and food, leaving you to enjoy the scenery. Guides are often biologists or ornithologists working with local people, so if you are a first-time visitor you can get a quick introduction to the country. Travel agencies in any city can book you on a tour to Canaima–Angel Falls, the Andes, Margarita, or Los Roques. For such major destinations advance reservations may not be needed in off-season. However, special tours, charters and expeditions require planning ahead.

Here are a few standard prices for 2-day/1-night tours including flights; costs are in US dollars per person based on double occupancy. Ciudad Bolívar–Kavac $240, Porlamar–Delta $285, Caracas–Los Roques $295, Caracas–Canaima $200. You should check whether the package includes the national park fee (Canaima $4, Los Roques $12) or 16.5% luxury tax.

The following are some of the agencies and operators exploring places off the beaten track. Others will be mentioned in the chapters covering their particular area. Agencies are usually closed at weekends.

Akanan Travel Edif Claret-mezz, Calle Laguna at Av Sanz, El Marqués, Caracas 1070; tel: (02) 2342103/2323, fax: 2373879; email: akanan@sa.omnes.net. Fixed monthly departures on 2- to 8-day treks to Auyantepui, Paraguaná, Paria, Colonia Tovar-Maya; river trips on the Akanán, Caura rivers; cycling to Canaima at Carnival and Easter. Logistics cover transfer by Toyota from (almost) anywhere to the field.

Alpiturismo Torre Centro-piso 1, Parque Boyacá, Av Sucre, Los Dos Caminos, Caracas; mailing address: Alpi Group, Apartado 70150, Los ruices, Caracas 1071A, Venezuela; tel: (02) 2831433/2836677, fax: 2856067; mobile: (016) 6225171; email: alpitour@compuserve.com. Around the Llanos, Amazonas, Andes by air, road and river. New lodges or camps not yet on general offer. Alpi is run by an avid fisherwoman and yachter, Linda Sonderman; ask her about peacock bass in Camatagua, Cinaruco. Alpi specialises in charters: crewed sailboats, yachts, houseboats; 4- to 30-seater planes.

Amazonair Capt Willi Michel, Edif Santa Eduvigis-local 1/2, 1ra Av de Santa Eduvigis, Caracas; tel: (02) 2836960, fax: 2832627. Wilderness camping by single or twin-engine plane in Bolívar, Amazonas and Apure states; also Los Roques, Caura River.

Bagheera Tours Oficina 86, CC Gran Sabana-piso 2, Paseo Caroní, Ciudad Guayana, Bolívar State; tel: (086) 529481, fax: 528767; email: bagheera@telcel.net.ve. Roraima treks, tours to Guri Dam, Gran Sabana, by car; into the Delta, and from Kamarata to Angel Falls by river.

Cacao Expediciones Calle Andromeda, Quinta Orquídea, El Peñón, Caracas; tel: (02) 9771234/2798, fax: 9770110; email: cacaotravel@cantv.net. Hiking up the Sierra Nevada, Auyantepui or Roraima; expedition from Cunucunuma to Río Negro, Brazil; departures every Saturday for Caura River-Para Falls. Own lodges in Choroní, and on the Caura, Orinoco and Ventuari rivers.

Kumeka Tours Av José Felix Sosa, Altamira Sur Ed Torre Británica M2, S3, L7; tel: (02) 2631219, 2632749; fax: (02) 2631219; email: kumekatours@cantv.net.

Lost World Adventures Edif 3-H, Of 63, Boulevard de Sabana Grande, Caracas 1050; tel: (02) 7611108/9024, 7635092; fax: 7617538. Phone in US (1800) 9990558; email: lwaccs@cantv.net. A US company with a Venezuelan branch. Arranges high adventure, hiking and biking in the Andes, to 'Lost World' summits, fishing in Guri Lake, sailing in Los Roques, diving in Morrocoy.

Montaña Adventure Apartado Postal 645, Mérida, Estado Mérida; tel: (074) 662867, fax: 661448; email: andes@telcel.net.ve. Andean pioneer in ecotourism, Montaña leads treks with porters and pack animals from pueblo to pueblo; birding from La Mucuy and the páramo down to the Llanos; paragliding, horseriding, biking. Also Gran Sabana tours, Roraima.

Orinoco Tours Torre A-piso 7, Galerías Bolívar, Boulevard de Sabana Grande, Caracas; tel: (02) 7618431, fax: 7616801, email: orinoco@sa.omnes.net. Avila range on foot or by jeep, Pittier National Park, wildlife lodges, by river into the Delta, up the Caura, or from Canaima to Angel Falls.

SBA Nature Expeditions tel/fax: (02) 2510990; email: sbanatureve@yahoo.com. Scientific and photo expeditions; Gran Sabana base camp (and airfield) for kayakers, cyclers, Roraima trekkers. Restored house in Choroní is centre for birdwatchers, hikers, scuba divers.

Turismo Colorama Local 53, CC Bello Campo-lower level, Av Coromoto, Bello Campo, Caracas; tel: (02) 2617732, fax: 2621828. Paria Peninsula, Playa Medina, Rio Caribe, Central Coast, Laguna de Tacarigua, Puerto Maya, Trincheras hot springs, Morrocoy.

Tour guides

Guides trained in biology, particularly ornithology, work with the **Audubon Society** of Venezuela; most speak at least two languages. Audubon is very active and has generated so much interest abroad that it runs an ecotourism agency, for members and nonmembers. For information about services, see section on *Environmental NGOs* in *Chapter 3*.

RED TAPE
Visas

Travellers to Venezuela should have a passport with at least six months' validity. Vaccination or health certificates are not a requirement, but the consul may ask for them. Nationals of the UK, much of Europe, USA, Canada, Australia, New Zealand and Japan do not need visas. Instead, airlines and cruise ships are authorised to issue them with 60-day **tourist cards** (*tarjeta de turismo*) on board, at no cost. Extensions for periods up to 60 days can be obtained in Caracas from the Dirección de Extranjería (DEX), Departamento de Turismo, 2nd floor (east stairs), Av Baralt and Este 8. Each 30-day *prórroga* (max 60 days) costs about US$20. You will need an early start, plus: photo, letter on legal paper (*papel sellado*) stating reason for extending stay, photocopy of air ticket, and ID card photocopy from the travel agent or person you are with. Allow two days. (The DEX office has been undergoing major restructuring for some time.)

For entry by land a **tourist visa** is needed. You can only obtain a multiple-entry tourist visa in your country of residence. Valid for one year, the visa costs up to US$30 depending on nationality, and your passport must be good for at least one year. The consulate may require a personal interview, and a bank or job letter as proof of financial solidity. Allow 2–3 days. In Britain: 1 Cromwell Rd, London SW7 2HW; tel: 0171 581 2776.

Despite financial solidity and an ongoing ticket, visa requests have been turned down by consulates in countries where the traveller is passing through, so be prepared. Border officials may not know the official requirements.

A **transit visa** (72 hours) is good for emergencies only, and cannot be extended at a DEX branch office, although headquarters in Caracas may grant an extra day so you can leave the country legally. Transit visas are good for passengers, airline staff and sailors who can prove imminent departure. **Transient visas** which allow you to work or study require health and 'good conduct' certificates, a sponsor or job, prior DEX approval, US$50, and a great deal of patience. Legally, your application should be made outside Venezuela. Because a *transeunte* needs a tax clearance to leave the country, this is not for you.

Your passport must be stamped by Immigration on entering and leaving the country. If the DEX office is not at the border itself, be sure to go to the nearest one in office hours. Make photocopies of the information page of your passport and your ticket in case of loss. Always keep your tourist card and passport on you as identity documents.

Travellers under the age of 18 unaccompanied by a relative are required to have a letter of authorisation signed by their parents or legal guardian, with a photocopy of their identity document.

CONSULATES

Consulates in the abbreviated list below are open to the public for visas on weekday mornings to 12.00 or 13.00, except where noted. (Please see *Chapter 10* for consular services in Porlamar, Margarita.)

Argentina Edif Fedecámaras, Av El Empalme, El Bosque; tel: (02) 7313159/3311; fax: 7312659. Mon–Fri 09.00–13.00, 13.30–16.00.

Australia Quinta Yolanda, Av Luis Roche at Trans 6-7, Altamira; tel: 2614632/0658, fax: 2613448. Mon–Fri 08.30–16.30.

Austria Torre Las Mercedes-p4, Av La Estancia, Chuao; tel: 9913863/3979, fax: 9599804.

Barbados Oficina 501, Edif Frailes, Calle La Guairita, Chuao; tel: 9916721, fax: 9910333. Mon–Thur 09.00–12.00, 13.00–16.00, Fri 09.00–15.00.

Belgium Quinta Azulita, Av 11 at Trans 6-7, Altamira; tel: 2633334/35, fax: 2610309. Mon–Thur 08.00–13.00.

Bolivia Av Luis Roche at Trans 6, Altamira; tel: 2633015, fax: 2613386.

Brazil Centro Gerencial Mohedano-p6, Calle Chaguaramos at Av Mohedano, La Castellana; tel: 2615505, fax: 2619601.

Canada Edif Omni, Av 6 between Trans 3 and 5, Altamira; tel: 264 0833, 2615680 (visas), fax: 2618741. Mon–Thur 07.30–11.00.

Chile Edif Venezuela, Av Venezuela, El Rosal; tel: 9535594/98, fax: 9531501.

Colombia Consulado de Colombia, Calle Guaicaipuro, opp CC Chacaito, El Rosal; tel: 9513631, fax: 9517056. Mon–Fri 08.00–14.00.

Cuba Quinta Marina, C Roraima near Río de Janeiro, Chuao; tel: 9916661/2911.

Denmark Torre Centauria-p7, Av Venezuela, El Rosal; tel: 9514618, fax: 9515278. Mon–Thur 08.00–16.00, Fri 08.00–13.00.

Ecuador Torre Este-p13, Centro Empresarial Andrés Bello, Av Andrés Bello; tel: 7815280, fax: 7827978.

France Calle Madrid at Av Trinidad, Las Mercedes; tel: 9936666, fax: 9933984.

Germany Edif Panaven-p2, Av San Juan Bosco at Trans 3, Altamira; tel: 2652827/0363, fax: 2610641.

Grenada Edif Los Frailes, Calle La Guairita, Chuao; tel: 9911237/9359; fax: 9918907. Mon–Fri 09.00–16.00.

Guyana Quinta Roraima, Av El Paseo, Prados del Este; tel: 9771158, fax: 9763765. Mon–Fri 08.30–15.30.

Holland Edif San Juan, Av San Juan Bosco at Trans 2, Altamira; tel: 2633622/3387, fax: 2630462.

Ireland Torre Cavendes-p11, Av Miranda, Los Palos Grandes; tel: 2860672, fax: 2866912.

Israel Ofic D, Centro Empresarial Miranda-p4, Av Miranda at Av Principal Los Ruices; tel: 2394511, fax: 2394320. Closed Tuesdays.

Italy No10, 6th Av between Trans 3 and 5, Altamira; tel: 2610755/1779.

Japan Edif Bancaracas-p12, Plaza La Castellana at Trans 2, La Castellana; tel: 2618333; fax: 2616780.

Norway Edif Exa-p9, Av Libertador, Chacao; tel: 2670044, fax: 2621506. Mon–Fri 09.00–15.00.

Peru Quinta No 1, Av 4 between Trans 3 and 4, Altamira; tel: 2664936.

Portugal Av 2, Campo Alegre; tel: 2672382/8989, fax: 2667052.

Spain Edif Bancaracas-p7, Plaza La Castellana at Trans 2; tel: 2660222/0367, fax: 2665745.

Suriname Quinta No 41 Los Milagros, Av 4 between Trans 7 and 8, Altamira; tel: 2612724, fax: 2612095.

Sweden Centro Coinasa-p2, Av San Felipe and Trans 2, La Castellana; tel: 2662968/5121, fax: 2668686,

Switzerland Torre Polar-p6, Plaza Venezuela, Los Caobos; tel: 7931608, fax: 7931419.

Trinidad and Tobago Quinta Serrana, Av 4 between Trans 7 and 8, Altamira; tel: 2615796/4772, fax: 2619801. Mon–Thur 08.30–12.00, 13.30–16.30, Fri 08.30–12.30.

Uruguay Torre Delta, Av Miranda, Altamira, near Altamira metro station, west exit; tel: 2611407.

United Kingdom Torre Las Mercedes-p3, Av La Estancia, Chuao; tel: 9934111/5280, fax: 9939989.

United States Calle F at Calle Suapure, Colinas de Valle Arriba; tel: 9772011, fax: 9770843.

Honorary consuls There are four honorary British consuls. **Maracaibo:** George Podolecki, tel: (061) 921355/5557, fax: 913487. **Mérida:** Robert Kirby, tel: (074) 66337, 712479. **Puerto La Cruz:** Ian Robinson, tel: (081) 812922/1011, fax: 814494/28. **Valencia:** Donald Martin, tel: (041) 238401/6096, fax: 234742.

GETTING THERE AND AWAY
By air
Arrival
Most visitors fly into Venezuela through the capital, arriving at the Simón Bolívar International Airport in Maiquetía on the coast. Whether you arrive in Maiquetía, or in Margarita, Barcelona, Barquisimeto or Maracaibo, if you are on a short visit try to reconfirm your return flight with the airline upon your arrival.

Departure
Reservations for international flights must be reconfirmed by phone or fax more than 72 hours in advance, for domestic flights 24 hours ahead. The airline should give you a locator (*localizador*) number which effectively proves reconfirmation. This is important even when your ticket is paid and already confirmed. Check-in times are two hours before international flights and one hour before domestic flights, but queues may form an hour earlier. Take these times seriously as latecomers – even with confirmed bookings – risk being bumped off overbooked flights, particularly at peak times.

When an airline does not embark a passenger confirmed on a flight, or on another flight within four hours, the passenger should receive meals, hotel and a free phone call to his/her destination. Regulations also make airlines responsible for damage caused by loss of checked luggage or delays in delivery.

Exit and airport taxes are usually collected by the airlines and you may pay in US dollars. Adults pay a total of $29 on international flights; children under the age of 15 pay $15.

Flights and tours from Britain

Prices for air travel vary greatly between low and high season. Flights in July, August and December, the most expensive months, cost as much as £570, compared with Iberia's flight to Caracas via Madrid for only £440 (September 1998). TAP (Air Portugal) and Avianca generally have good rates. Other airlines serving Venezuela from London are Air France, Alitalia, British Airways, KLM, and United via New York. Since the demise of Viasa which had the cheapest flights, new Venezuelan airlines are vying to fill the gap, with Avensa the most likely candidate for some European routes in 1999.

For flights the specialist travel agency for South America is **Journey Latin America**, 12 Heathfield Terrace, Chiswick, London W4 4JE; tel: 0181 747 3108 (flights) and 0181 747 3815 (tours); fax: 0181 742 1312; website: www.journeylatinamerica.co.uk. Some of the cheapest fares are to be found in London, and tickets can be sent to you in almost any city. A ticket bought in Venezuela will cost more than the same route paid for in the UK.

Trailfinders, 42–50 Earls Court Rd, London W8 6FT; tel: 0171 938 3366; net: www.trailfinders.com, offer cheap flights and a complete traveller's service – vaccination centre, library and insurance scheme. **STA Travel**, 6 Wrights Lane, London W8 6TA; tel: 0171 361 6262; email: enquiries@statravel.co.uk; website: www.statravel.co.uk, has six more branches in London and twelve outside, plus several university sites. Two other agencies worth investigating are: **Travelbag**, 373–375 The Strand, London WC2R 0JF; tel: 0171 240 3669; email: mail@travelbag-adventures.co.uk; net: www.travelbag-adventures.co.uk; and **Campus Travel** which has 45 offices in the UK listed on its website: www.campustravel.co.uk.

Adventure travel companies feature Venezuela in brochures with treks to Angel Falls and the 'Lost World' of Roraima. As an operator specialising in Venezuela, **Last Frontiers** offers organised tours all over the country. Besides flights, their main business is booking tailor-made itineraries for independent travellers. Enquiries: Last Frontiers, Fleet Marston Farm, Aylesbury HP18 0PZ; tel: 01296 658650; fax: 01296 658651; email: travelinfo@lastfrontiers.co.uk; net: www.lastfrontiers.co.uk. This agency was one of the first to have a website. It is continuously updated with travel information, flights and currency, and also has links to other sites of interest. (For other websites on Venezuela, see *Appendix 2*.)

Geodyssey is another knowledgeable company specialising in Venezuela. As well as treks and tours off the beaten track they provide individual service for people such as ornithologists who do not wish to join a group. They are at 29 Harberton Rd, London N19 3JS; tel: 0171 281 7788, fax: 0171 281 7878; email: enquiries@geodyssey.co.uk; net: www.geodyssey.co.uk.

Also worth contacting are **Gane & Marshall**, 98 Crescent Road, New Barnet, Herts EN4 9RJ; tel: 0181 441 9592; fax: 0181 441 7376; email: holidays@ganeandmarshall.co.uk and **Interchange**, 27 Stafford Road, Croydon, Surrey CR4 4NG; tel: 0181 681 3612; fax: 0181 760 0031.

Flights and tours from the USA

Travellers have been getting shuttle rates of US$300 round-trip from Miami to Caracas. American Airlines serves Caracas with seven flights daily from Dallas, New York and Miami. Continental flies from New York, Delta from Atlanta, and United from New York and Miami.

STA Travel, tel: 1800 777 0112, has five branches on the west coast as well as in New York, Boston and Cambridge.

A US company promoting Venezuelan travel, **Lost World Adventures** is run by a former resident who works closely with local specialists, from Andean climbers to yachtsmen. For enquiries: toll-free 1800 999 0558, tel: 404 971 8586, fax: 404 977 3095. In the UK, tel: 01522 681532; email: lwaccs@cantv.net.

Wilderness Travel of California is restarting treks to Roraima and Angel Falls led by local experts. For enquiries: 801 Allston Way, Berkeley, CA 94710; tel: 800 368 2794 or 510 548 0420, fax: 548 0347; email: info@wildernesstravel.com.

Members of the travellers' network sponsored by **Great Expeditions** get discounts on tickets and books. For information about the journal write to: Box 18036, Raleigh, North Carolina 27619; tel: 919 846 3600, fax: 847 0780.

Flights from Canada
In general flights from Canada are almost double the fare from New York. For ways to save money, the people who know are Travel Cuts, the Canadian student travel organisation based in Toronto; at 171 College St; tel: 416 977 3703, fax: 977 4796.

Flights from Australia
The best connection for Venezuela seems to be Sydney-Los Angeles-Miami by Qantas, and the cheapest ticket (two months) costs $2,587 in Australian dollars, or US$1,640 round trip between April and August.

Venezuelan airlines
Venezuelan international carriers are headed by Aeropostal and Servivensa, related to Avensa. For this pair, tel: 1800 AVENSA; or, in Florida tel: 305 381 8001. Servivensa flies daily to Miami, New York, Bogotá, Medellín, Lima, Quito, Panama, Aruba and Curaçao. Aeropostal serves Atlanta, Aruba, Curaçao, Barbados, Manaus, Miami, Santo Domingo and Trinidad. For more, see *Domestic airlines* on page 29.

Avensa's Air Touring Pass (ATP) covers both national and international flights on Avensa-Servivensa and may be bought from any authorised representative. (Residents of Caribbean and Central or South American countries are not eligible.) You buy a minimum of four coupons including international routes.

By boat
Caribbean ferry service
Windward Lines makes a weekly circle from **Barbados** to Venezuela, stopping at **St Vincent**, **Trinidad** and **St Lucia**. The round trip is not only scenic but cheap at US$158. The fare includes neither meals nor air-conditioned cabins (an extra US$10 per night). The vessel carries 250 passengers and 40 cars. It sails from Barbados on Sunday evening, spending Monday in St Vincent and Tuesday in Trinidad, to arrive at Güiria in the Gulf of Paria on Tuesday evening. It sails northward on Wednesday evening from Güiria, alternating every second week with Pampatar, Margarita. A special Trinidad–Venezuela service is laid on for Carnival. More information from: Windward Lines Ltd, #7, James Fort, Hincks St, Bridgetown, Barbados; tel: 809 4310449, fax: 809 4310452. For details, see *Chapter 9*, page 223.

Curaçao–Falcón ferry
Falcón Ferrys have reopened the long-closed route from **La Vela de Coro** to **Curaçao** and **Aruba** with the refurbished *Lusitania Express*, for many years a ferry in Scandinavia and Poland. It offers restaurant, bar, self-service cafeteria, money change, gaming tables, duty-free shops, air conditioning. The crossing takes 5–6 hours and costs US$85 first class, $65 tourist. Sailings leave Curaçao for Venezuela on Tuesday, Thursday and Saturday evenings; from Aruba on Wednesday and Friday evenings. You need only a valid passport. The charge for cars is US$100.

DRUGS

The frontier between Colombia and Venezuela carries more than ordinary risk because of drug running. People coming from Colombia may be searched so it's wise to have all medicines labelled and carry a copy of the doctor's prescription, along with copies of visa, passport and credit card. Do not carry dried herbs, even common ones, to avoid arousing suspicion. Officials are also sensitive to picture taking; try not to have rolls of exposed film. It is good policy to wear a clean change of clothes, have a reasonable amount of cash (not too much), and carry the telephone number of a contact in Venezuela. Keep to yourself and discourage casual friendships or favours at this time.

Colombian guerrillas operate on both sides of the border. Drug trafficking, smuggling and kidnapping are common in remote areas of Zulia, Táchira, Apure and Amazonas states. However, cross-border violence is not usually random but targets ranch owners or army posts, so travellers on main routes are in little danger.

Vehicles must have international insurance, and police certification. In Willemstad, Curaçao, tel: (599 9) 4656911; in Oranjestad, Aruba, tel: (297) 823888, 826182; in Coro, tel/fax: (068) 530520, 78517/37; email: ferry@telcel.net.ve. For details, see *Chapter 17*, page 396.

By bus

International coach lines link Venezuela with **Brazil**, **Colombia** and points south. Valid passport, visa and yellow-fever vaccination are required. Many travellers from Colombia fly to Cúcuta, take the bus to cross the border, then fly or bus from San Antonio del Táchira.

Expreso Internacional Ormeño Calle Sucre con Calle Nueva, San Martín, 2 blocks east of La Paz metro station, Caracas; tel: (02) 4714614/7437, fax: 4717205. Departures Monday and Friday at 16.00 on an 8-day South American route: Bogotá (30 hours), Cali, Quito (day 3), Guayaquil, Lima (day 4), Santiago (day 6), Buenos Aires (day 8). If you go all the way the most you pay is US$310 including hotels. Reserve a week in advance.

Ruta de América Esq Isleños, north on Av Fuerzas Armadas, Caracas; tel: (02) 4423723/1054/5739. Route covers Venezuela to Chile for US$365: Colombia, Ecuador, Peru. To reserve a week ahead: tel: 5459627.

Línea Caribe-Uniao Cascavel Puerto La Cruz terminal; tel: (086) 518669. Linking Puerto la Cruz and Ciudad Bolívar, the Caribe express buses leave at 17.00 on odd-number days via Santa Elena de Uairén for Boa Vista, Brazil, with connections to Manaus. In return, the Uniao Cascavel travels from Brazil to Puerto La Cruz; tel: (086) 519214. Fare: US$40.

HEALTH

with Dr Jane Wilson-Howarth

Venezuela is a sophisticated country. Urban hospitals are good; surgeons are excellent but this is a tropical country with some special health considerations. Preparations to ensure a healthy trip to the Americas require checks on your immunisation status; you'll also need to pack lotions and long clothes to protect you from insect bites and the sun. Tetanus immunity needs to be boosted ten yearly, polio ten yearly, diphtheria ten yearly. Yellow-fever is a must and immunisation against rabies and hepatitis A are also worth considering; for most travellers it's best to have immunisation against hepatitis A with Havrix or the new Avaxim; the course of two injections costs about £80 in the UK, or $32 in Venezuela but protects for ten years. Gamma globulin is an alternative if your trip is a spur-of-the-moment, short, one-off visit; it gives immediate but partial protection for a couple of months and costs around £5 but there are theoretical risks in using this blood-derived product. Typhoid immunisation is only about 60% effective; it needs boosting every three years unless you are over the age of 35 and have had four or more courses; such travellers do not need further immunisations. Immunisation against cholera is no longer required anywhere.

Parts of Venezuela carry a risk of malaria, yellow fever and some other insect-borne diseases; the riskiest regions are the Delta, Guayana or Amazon areas.

Travel clinics
It is wise to go – if you can – to a travel clinic a couple of months before departure to arrange your immunisations. As well as providing an immunisation service, travel clinics usually sell a good range of mosquito nets, treatment kits, repellents and malaria medicines.

United Kingdom
Berkeley Travel Clinic 32 Berkeley St, London W1X 5FA, tel: 0171 629 6233.
British Airways Clinics These are now situated in 30 towns in the UK and three in South Africa (UK tel: 01276 685040 for the nearest). They provide inoculations and malaria prophylaxis and sell a variety of health-related travel goods including bed-net treatment kits.
Fleet Street Travel Clinic 29 Fleet St, London EC4Y 1AA, tel: 0171 353 5678.
MASTA (Medical Advisory Service for Travellers Abroad), London School of Hygiene and Tropical Medicine, Keppel St, London WC1 7HT, tel: 0891 224100. This is a premium-line number.
Nomad Travellers' Store and Medical Centre 3–4 Wellington Terrace, Turnpike Lane, London N8 0PX, tel: 0181 889 7014.
Trailfinders Immunisation Clinic 194 Kensington High St, London W8 7RG, tel: 0171 938 3999.
Tropical Medicine Bureau This Irish-run organisation has a useful website specific to tropical destinations: www.tmb.le.

USA
Centers for Disease Control This Atlanta-based organisation is the central source of travel health information in North America, with a touch-tone phone line and fax service. Travelers' Hot Line: (404) 332 4559. Each summer they publish the invaluable *Health Information for International Travel* which is available from the Center for Prevention Services, Division of Quarantine, Atlanta, GA 30333; email: netinfo@cdc.gov; net: www.cdc.gov.
IAMAT (International Association for Medical Assistance to Travellers), 736 Center St, Lewiston, NY 14092, USA. Tel: 716 754 4883. Also at Gotthardstrasse 17, 6300 Zug, Switzerland. A non-profit organisation which provides health information and lists of English-speaking doctors abroad.

Australia
TMVC has 20 clinics in Australia, New Zealand and Thailand. For the nearest clinic, phone 1300 658844, or try their website: www.tmvc.com.au.

Brisbane Dr Deborah Mills, Qantas Domestic Building, 6th floor, 247 Adelaide St, Brisbane, QLD 4000 (tel: 7 3221 9066; fax: 7 3221 7076; email: dmills@tmvc.com.au).

Melbourne Dr Sonny Lau, 393 Little Bourke St, 2nd floor, Melbourne, VIC 3000 (tel: 3 9602 5788; fax: 3 9670 8394; email: melb@tmvc.com.au).
Sydney Dr Mandy Hu, Dymocks Building, 7th floor, 428 George St, Sydney, NSW 2000 (tel: 2 221 7133; fax: 2 221 8401; email: syd@tmvc.com.au).

Malaria

Seek advice on the best antimalarial tablets to take. For recorded information on malaria risk and prophylaxis phone (UK) 0891 600350. If mefloquine (Lariam) is suggested, start this two and a half weeks before departure to check that it suits you; stop it immediately if it causes vivid and unpleasant dreams, mood swings or other changes in the way you feel. Anyone who is pregnant, has suffered fits in the past, has been treated for depression or psychiatric problems or has a close blood relative who is epileptic should avoid mefloquine. The usual alternative is chloroquine (Nivaquine) and proguanil (Paludrine) – two tablets weekly of the former and two daily of the latter. Travellers to remote parts may wish to consider carrying a course of treatment to cure malaria. At present quinine and Fansidar is the favoured regime, but it would be best to take up-to-date advice on the current recommended treatment. Self treatment is not without risks and generally people over-treat themselves. If at all possible consult a doctor if you are taken ill since diagnosing malaria is difficult without laboratory facilities. Only two (*Plasmodium vivax* and *P. falciparum*) of the possible four malarial strains are found in South America.

The symptoms of malaria appear from one week to a year after exposure and may be no worse than a dose of flu initially but more often there is high fever, shivering, chills, profuse sweating, nausea and even diarrhoea and vomiting. In falciparum malaria there may be all this plus hallucinations, headache, numbness of the extremities and eventually fits or coma. Given prompt treatment, most people (99%) recover. A number of effective drugs treat malaria. Indeed quinine, derived from the Amazonian cinchona tree, was widely used from 1700, before the disease was understood.

No prophylactic is 100% protective but those on prophylactics who are unlucky enough to catch malaria are less likely to get rapidly into serious trouble. Whether or not you are taking malaria tablets, or carrying a cure, it is important to protect yourself from mosquito bites.

Other common medical problems
Travellers' diarrhoea

Travellers' diarrhoea is common amongst those visiting Venezuela, and the newer you are to exotic travel, the more likely you will be to suffer. Yet simple precautions against travellers' diarrhoea will also protect you from typhoid, cholera, hepatitis, dysentery, polio, worms, etc. Travellers' diarrhoea and the other faecal-oral diseases come from getting other people's faeces in your mouth. This most often happens from cooks not washing their hands after a trip to the toilet; yet if your food has been thoroughly cooked and arrives piping hot, you will be safe despite this. The maxim to remind you what you can safely eat is: PEEL IT, BOIL IT, COOK IT OR FORGET IT. This means that fruit you have washed and peeled yourself and hot foods should be safe but raw foods, cold cooked foods and salads are risky. And foods kept luke-warm in hotel buffets are usually dangerous. It is much rarer to get sick from drinking contaminated water but it can happen, so try to drink from safe sources. Water should have been brought to the boil, or passed through a good bacteriological filter or purified with iodine (add four drops of tincture of iodine and allow to stand for 20–30 minutes);

TREATING TRAVELLERS' DIARRHOEA

It is dehydration which makes you feel awful during a bout of diarrhoea and the most important part of treatment is taking lots of clear fluids. Sachets of oral rehydration salts give the perfect biochemical mix you need to replace all that is pouring out of your bottom but they do not taste so nice. Any dilute mixture of sugar and salt in water will do you good, so if you like Coke or orange squash, drink that with a three-finger pinch of salt added to each glass. Otherwise make a solution of a four-finger scoop of sugar with a three-finger pinch of salt in a glass of water. Or add eight level teaspoons of sugar (18g) and one level teaspoon of salt (3g) to one litre (five cups) of safe water. A squeeze of lemon or orange juice improves the taste and adds potassium which also needs to be replaced. Drink two large glasses after every bowel action, and more if you are thirsty. If you are not eating you need to drink three litres a day plus whatever is leaving you in sweat and down the toilet. If you feel like eating, take a bland, high-carbohydrate diet; heavy greasy foods will give you cramps.

If the diarrhoea is bad, or you are passing blood or slime, or you have a fever, you will probably need antibiotics in addition to fluid replacement. A three-day course of ciprofloxacin or norfloxacin or nalidixic acid are good antibiotics for dysentery and bad diarrhoea. These are far better treatment than the 'blockers' like Imodium or Kaopectate. Be careful about what you take from local pharmacies: drugs like chloramphenicol (sold as Chloromycetin, Catilan or Enteromycetin) and the sulpha antibiotics (eg: Streptomagma) have too many serious side effects to be worth the risk in treating simple diarrhoea. Do not take them!

chlorine (eg: Puritabs) is also adequate although theoretically less effective and it tastes nastier. Mineral water has been found to be contaminated in many developing countries and may be no safer than tap water. If diarrhoea strikes, see box for treatment.

Avoiding insect bites

Pack long loose 100% cotton clothes and a DEET-based repellent stick or roll-on such as Cutters, Off!, Autan or Jungle Jell (sadly vitamin B does not work). Keep this to hand at all times. Take a permethrin-impregnated bed-net or a permethrin spray so that you can treat bed-nets in hotels. Permethrin treatment stops mosquitoes biting through the net if you roll against it and makes even very tatty nets protective.

Night-biters Mosquitoes and sandflies may transmit malaria and leishmania (respectively) between dusk and dawn, so at sundown don long clothes and apply repellent on any exposed flesh. Malaria mosquitoes are voracious and hunt at ankle-level so apply repellent under your socks too. Sleep under a permethrin-treated bed-net or in an air-conditioned room.

Day-biters During days out in the forest, it is wise to wear long loose clothes with trousers/pants tucked into socks; this will help to protect you against the day-biting Aedes mosquitoes which may spread dengue and yellow fevers, and also against ticks and chiggers. Minute pestilential biting day-active blackflies spread river blindness in some parts of tropical South America; the disease is caught close to fast-flowing rivers where the flies breed. Eucalyptus-based natural repellents do not work against them.

Sandflies

These are very small biters which are most active at twilight but bite throughout the night. Some transmit leishmania, a protozoan disease causing painless tropical sores which, in extreme cases, grow to look like leprosy. Sandflies are able to penetrate mosquito netting but treating the net with insecticide keeps them out. Ceiling fans – if available – will help keep them off. Sandflies are the biggest problem in rainforests. Leishmania is reasonably common and is difficult to treat, so precautions against being bitten must be taken seriously. The severe and untreatable form of the lowland disease is called espundia.

Kissing bugs and Chagas' disease (trypanosomiasis)

Chagas' disease is a very rare disease in travellers although it is much talked about and occurs in Venezuela. It is a problem of the rural poor and those sleeping on floors in wattle-and-daub-type village houses. A hammock will help protect you, particularly if it has a built-in mosquito net; these are marketed in South America.

Flesh maggots

The Macaw or warble-fly lays her eggs on mosquitoes so that when the mosquito feeds the warble infants can burrow into the victim's skin. Here they mature to cause an inflammation which will need surgical removal. Now there's another reason to avoid mosquito bites!

Jiggers or sandfleas (niguas)

These are minute flesh-feasters, not to be confused with chiggers (see below). They latch on if you walk bare-foot in contaminated places (locals will know where), and set up home under the skin of the foot, usually at the side of a toenail where they lay a painful boil-like egg-sac. These need picking out by a local expert; if the distended flea bursts during eviction the wound should be dowsed in spirit, alcohol or kerosene otherwise it may become infected.

Ticks

Ticks transmit a variety of unpleasant infections in the Americas including Rocky Mountain Spotted Fever, but there is no Lyme disease in Venezuela. If you get the tick off promptly and in one piece the chances of disease transmission are much reduced. Manoeuvre your finger and thumb so that you can pinch the tick's mouthparts as close to your skin as possible and slowly and steadily pull away at right angles to your skin. This often hurts. Jerking or twisting will increase the chances of damaging the tick which in turn increases the chances of disease transmission. Once the tick is off, dowse the little wound with alcohol (local spirit, pisco, etc is excellent) or iodine. An area of spreading redness around the bite site or fever coming on a few days or more after the bite should stimulate a trip to a doctor.

The chigger, chivacoa or itch mite

Both ticks and these pestilential little mites can be kept off by applying repellent (even on your boots) and tucking pants/trousers into socks. Chiggers are related to little red harvest mites that run around in the summer in Europe. The American version is incredibly irritating and the itching stays with you long after the mite has gone. Eurax cream (crotamiton) or calamine lotion is most likely to help, plus exposing the itchy part and cool sponging.

Skin infections

Skin infections set in remarkably easily in warm climates and any mosquito bite or small skin-nick is a potential entry point for bacteria. It is essential, therefore, to clean and cover even the slightest wound. Creams are not as effective as a good drying antiseptic such as dilute iodine, potassium permanganate (a few crystals in half a cup of water) or crystal (or gentian) violet. One of these should be available in most towns. If the wound starts to throb, or becomes red and the redness starts to spread or the wound oozes, and especially if you develop a fever, antibiotics will probably be needed; flucloxacillin (250mg capsules four times a day) or cloxacillin (500mg four times a day). For those allergic to penicillin, erythromycin (500mg twice a day) for five days should help. See a doctor if the infection does not improve in 36–48 hours.

Fungal infections also get a hold easily in hot moist climates so wear 100%-cotton socks and underwear and shower frequently. An itchy rash in the groin or flaking between the toes is likely to be a fungal infection. This needs treatment with an antifungal cream such as Canesten (clotrimazole). If this is not available try Whitfield's ointment (compound benzoic acid ointment) or crystal violet (although this will turn you purple!).

Prickly heat

A fine pimply rash on the trunk is likely to be heat rash; cool showers, dabbing (not rubbing) dry and talc will help. If it's bad you may need to check into an air-conditioned hotel room for a while. Slowing down to a relaxed schedule, wearing only loose, baggy, 100%-cotton clothes and sleeping naked under a fan reduce the problem.

Damage from the sun

The incidence of skin cancer is rocketing as Caucasians are travelling more and spending more time exposing themselves to the sun. Sun exposure also ages the skin, making people prematurely wrinkly; cover up with long loose clothes, put on plenty of sun cream and wear a hat when you can. Keep out of the sun in the middle of the day and if you must expose yourself, build up gradually from 20 minutes per day. Be especially careful of sun reflected off water and wear a T-shirt and lots of waterproof SPF-15 suncream when swimming; also Bermuda shorts when snorkelling or you may get scorched thighs.

Heatstroke is most likely within the first week or ten days of arriving in a hotter, more humid climate. It is important to slow down and drink plenty and avoid hard physical exercise in the middle of the day, particularly at first. Treatment for heat exhaustion is rest in the shade and sponging, plus lots to drink.

Foot injuries

If you wear old plimsolls (sneakers) or jellies on the beach or riverside, you will avoid injury and are less likely to get venomous fish spines in your feet. If you tread on a venomous fish, soak the foot in hot (but not scalding) water until some time after the pain subsides; this may need 20–30 minutes' submersion in all. Take your foot out of the water when you top up otherwise you may scald it. If the pain returns re-immerse the foot. Once the venom has been heat-inactivated, get a doctor to check and remove any bits of fish spines in the wound.

Stingrays

There are plenty of venomous creatures in the sea but be aware that South America also boasts freshwater stingrays whose barbed tails inflict damage as well as dispensing venom. Piranhas and candiru fish are fine travellers' tales for scaring the uninitiated. Don't worry about them; stories are exaggerated to the level of fiction.

Risky sex

Travel is a time when we may enjoy sexual adventures, especially when alcohol reduces inhibitions. Remember the risks of sexually transmitted infection are high, whether you sleep with fellow travellers or with locals. About half of HIV infections in British heterosexuals are acquired abroad. Use condoms or femidoms. If you notice any genital ulcers or discharge get treatment promptly; sexually transmitted infections increase the risk of acquiring HIV. AIDS is known as SIDA in Spanish; in Caracas there is a SIDA hotline which functions on weekdays: (02) 5780644. HIV is not uncommon in Venezuela and it is most prevalent in areas visited by tourists.

Animal attacks

If you are venturing into the rainforest ask around about dangerous wildlife. And if you are sleeping out a net will keep off vampires as well as smaller biters. Any mammal can carry rabies and the disease is common in bats (especially vampires); village dogs must also be assumed to be rabid. Any suspect bites should be scrubbed under running water for five minutes and then flooded with local spirit or dilute iodine. A post-bite rabies injection is needed even in immunised people and those who are unimmunised need a course of injections. These should be given within a week if the bites are to the face, but if the bites are further from the brain the incubation period is longer and you probably have more time; make sure you get the injections even if you are far from civilisation. The incubation period for rabies can be very long so never say that it is too late to bother. Death from rabies is probably one of the worst ways to go!

Snakes rarely attack unless provoked, and bites in travellers are unusual. You are less likely to get bitten if you wear stout shoes and long trousers when in the forest. Most snakes are harmless and many of the highly venomous and brightly coloured coral snakes have such small mouths they are unlikely to be able to bite you unless you offer them an ear-lobe to nibble. Even those larger venomous species capable of harm will dispense venom in only about half of their bites; keeping this fact in mind may help you to stay calm. Most first-aid techniques do more harm than good; cutting into the wound is harmful and tourniquets are dangerous; suction and electrical inactivation devices do not work; the only treatment is antivenom. In case of a bite which you fear may have been from a venomous snake:

- Try to keep calm – it is likely that no venom has been dispensed.
- Stop movement of the bitten limb by applying a splint.
- Keep the bitten limb BELOW heart height to slow spread of any venom.
- If you have a crepe bandage, bind up as much of the bitten limb as you can, but release the bandage every half hour. Get to a hospital which has antivenom.
- NEVER give aspirin; you may offer paracetamol which is safe.
- NEVER cut or suck the wound.
- DO NOT apply ice packs.
- DO NOT apply potassium permanganate.

If the offending snake can be captured without risk of someone else being bitten, take this to show the doctor, but beware since even a decapitated head is able to dispense venom in a reflex bite.

Local snake antivenom (*suero antiofídico*) is effective against both the rattlesnake (*cascabel*) and fer-de-lance (*mapanare*); it should be administered by medical experts. In Caracas you will find such doctors at the Periférico de Coche Emergency Hospital and Clínica El Avila. Antivenom is sold by Biofar, UCV School of Pharmacy, tel: (02) 605 2705/2690.

Bilharzia or schistosomiasis

Bilharzia (*Schistosoma mansoni*) occurs only in Lake Valencia, Camatagua reservoir and some coastal rivers of the Litoral and Barlovento. It can be avoided by knowing a little about the parasite, which is acquired by bathing, swimming, paddling or wading in freshwater in which people with bilharzia have excreted. Getting out of the water within ten minutes and vigorously towelling yourself dry should reduce the risk to a minimum. Avoid bathing or paddling on shores within 200m of villages or places where people use the water a great deal, especially shores where there is lots of waterweed. Covering yourself with DEET insect repellent before swimming is also protective, but this may detract from the joy of bathing.

If your bathwater comes from a risky source try to ensure that the water is taken from the lake or river in the early morning and stored snail-free, otherwise it should be filtered or Dettol or Cresol added. Well water should be safe. Bathing early in the morning is safer than bathing in the last half of the day. If you think that you have exposed yourself to bilharzia parasites, arrange a screening blood test (your GP can do this) MORE than six weeks after your last possible contact with suspect water.

Further reading

Self-prescribing has its hazards so if you are going anywhere very remote consider taking a health book. For adults there is *Bugs Bites & Bowels: the Cadogan Guide to Healthy Travel* by Jane Wilson-Howarth, and if travelling with children look at *Your Child's Health Abroad: A Manual for Travelling Parents* by Jane Wilson-Howarth and Matthew Ellis, published by Bradt.

SAFETY

Always carry your passport (keep a photocopy separately). People found to be *indocumentado* are liable to be fined, imprisoned or at the very least harassed by officials. Carry your passport well hidden in a money belt or inside pocket, separate from your money. Buy a CANTV telephone card (*tarjeta*) and keep it with you.

Robbery is increasingly common in Venezuelan cities as jobs and money become scarcer. Keep your valuables hidden or locked in the hotel safe. Better still, carry theft and health insurance. When travelling by car, leave your belongings locked in the boot. Although this is no guarantee against professionals, 'out of sight' is good policy. Make it a rule never to go to lonely places, even in daylight in a group of three. Most crimes are street related and can occur at any hour of the day; in many cases the thieves are kids. Do not put up resistance.

Australian Consular Services publish leaflets for travellers such as *Backpacking Overseas, Missing Overseas* and *If You Are the Victim of Sexual Assault*, a case when the consul can give a wide range of assistance regarding the social, medical, legal and practical consequences.

WHAT TO TAKE

Common sense will tell you what to pack: if it's a coastal holiday with swimming and snorkelling, take lots of sunscreen, a mask and snorkel, and clothes that protect areas prone to sunburn – shoulders, base of neck and thighs. Also take old trainers to protect your feet against coral or sea urchins.

If you are backpacking in the Andes, remember temperatures may drop to freezing at night, and be alternately cold and hot during the day. You will need rainwear and layers of clothes — two thin wool sweaters will be more practical than one thick one (unlike some Andean countries, there are no great sweater bargains to be had in Venezuela). You'll need all the usual backpacking gear: light tent, stove (Bluet Gaz is available in cities), 3-season sleeping bag, thermal wear. Decent mountain gear, although expensive, can be found in sports shops in Caracas and Mérida.

Those travelling to the hinterland and on rivers should take or buy a fine-mesh mosquito net (the self-standing sort is unavailable in Venezuela), malaria pills, cotton-mix clothes, a warm blanket for chilly tropical nights, and plastic bags to waterproof clothes. Cameras and lenses are kept water-free with clingfilm. The best insect protection is a long-sleeved shirt and long socks (spray socks and cuffs). A hat is essential for river travel and savannah walking.

Everyone should have a rain poncho (cheap, plastic), torch (flashlight) for dodgy electricity supplies, earplugs (for noisy hotels or buses), strong needles and thread or dental floss for repairs, reliable matches or lighter, a large supply of tea which is regarded in Venezuela as a drink for sick people (or, shudder, a teabag is dangled in a cup of hot milk), and a knowledge of Spanish or at least a good phrasebook and dictionary. Carry a basic first-aid kit, plus items mentioned in the *Health* section (above).

For photographic film see page 39.

MONEY

The currency unit is the *bolívar*. Notes under Bs1,000 are being replaced by coins of Bs10 to Bs500. As of 1999 Bs1,000, 2,000 and 5,000 notes will be supplemented with new bills, Bs10,000, 20,000 and 50,000. In January 1999, the bolívar was valued at Bs567=US$1, Bs890=£1. US dollars are widely accepted; other hard currencies may be much more difficult to change. Before changing money, count your notes in full view of the teller to avoid 'losing' a bill. Always change money (dollar bills, never pounds) before leaving major cities. It is useful to carry some small-denomination dollar bills for emergencies. US$ travellers' cheques can be exchanged in *casas de cambio* in most, but not all, cities and you may be asked to produce your cheque purchase slip.

Banks

Banking hours are Mon to Fri 08.30–15.30 (with some exceptions such as in Caracas' new Sambil mall, open 365 days). Banks may work Saturdays around Christmas. Besides national holidays, they take off several religious feastdays, closing on the Monday after: January 6 – Three Kings, March 19 – St Joseph, June – Ascension Day, June 29 – St Peter, August 15 – Assumption, November 1 – All Souls' Day, December 8 – Immaculate Conception.

Most banks will not change dollars except for clients, and when they do accept travellers' cheques they may put a limit of $200 and require proof of purchase. However, many have automatic tellers or cashpoint machines. The Banco Union is said to give fast confirmation of cards.

Credit cards

In cities credit cards are useful, but in smaller towns many hotels and restaurants are not affiliated because they are charged a 7%–10% commission. Visa is the most widely used and is serviced by 17 banks; tel: 800 12169. MasterCard is represented by 11 banks; tel: 800 12902, (02) 5087444. For

American Express, call Corpbanca: (02) 2060333, loss 2062795/96. Diners is the least accepted; tel: (02) 2022121/2424. Although cash advances from abroad by credit card should take less than a day in Caracas, this service may be unavailable in the 'interior'.

Electronic transfer

Italcambio provides electronic transfer of funds: your Moneygram from abroad goes by computer to an authorised bank or agency for pickup. Italcambio has branches in Valencia, Maracaibo, Maturín, and four in Caracas; tel: (02) 5635833, 2637110. Western Union calls its electronic transfer service Money in Minutes – as fast as the sender can inform the recipient. The name on the transfer must be the same as on the recipient's passport, and the recipient should know in advance how much is being transferred. Zoom couriers offer this service in forty Venezuelan towns and ten Caracas agencies. For information: (02) 2427111/0144; email: gzooveme@true.net.–

Prices

Readers should note that while the Venezuelan bolívar devalues (to the advantage of hard-currency travellers) local prices rise versus the US dollar. For this reason more fares and prices are quoted in US dollars rather than bolívars.

GETTING AROUND
By air
National flights

Various discounts are offered on domestic flights, starting with 50% for children aged 2 to 10 or 12 years. Most discounts are designed for residents qualifying as families or students and holding a national identity card, but try anyway. The exception seems to be discounts for senior citizens, 60 or 65 years of age, depending on the airline. Aeropostal offers 50% off for travellers over 60, except during Easter and Carnival. Among other discounts: students 15%, early purchase (30 days) 20%, weekend travel 50%. To apply for discounts have ready a photocopy of your passport and student ID.

Routes on Avensa's Air Touring Pass (ATP) may not be repeated in the same direction, but otherwise travel is unlimited, including international routes such as Aruba and Curaçao. Canaima bookings are tied to lodging at the Hoturvensa camp.

Charters are widely used for business and tourism. Some charter lines: Aeroejecutivos, (02) 9917942, fax: 9935493; Amazonair, (02) 2836960, fax: 2832627; Helicópteros del Caribe, tel/fax: (031) 552339; Renta Avion, (02) 7931072/2537, (095) 620742, fax: 628414; Roques Air, (02) 9521840/6210; Rutaca, tel: (085) 24010, fax: 25955; (031) 551838, fax: (031) 551643.

Domestic airlines

New, competitive airlines are led by Aeropostal, and Aserca, now 70% owner of Air Aruba. Aside from domestic routes, many give international service. All those listed below serve Caracas (Maiquetía), except for Aeroejecutivos, Oriental, Sasca. Caracas phones (02) are followed by the Maiquetía airport phones (031) where available.

Aereotuy (TUY) Edif Gran Sabana, Boulevard de Sabana Grande No 174, Caracas; tel: (02) 7635035/5072, 7618043/6247, fax: 7625254; Porlamar (095) 630307/67. Scheduled flights to Maturín. Tour flights to Canaima, Kavac, Los Roques, Porlamar. Overseas to Tobago, Grenada.

Aeroejecutivos (AE) Base Aérea Francisco Miranda, La Carlota, Caracas; tel: 9917942, fax: 9935493. Barcelona, Los Roques, Porlamar.

Aeropostal-Alas de Venezuela (VH) Torre Banco Lara, Av Principal, La Castellana, Caracas; tel: 800 AVION (28466), (02) 2646422, fax: 2678166; 3552828. Barcelona, Barquisimeto, Maracaibo, Maturín, Porlamar, Puerto Ordaz, San Antonio. Overseas to Aruba, Atlanta, Barbados, Curaçao, Manaus, Miami, Trinidad, Santo Domingo.

Air Venezuela (VZA) Oficina 42-A, Torre A, Galerías Bolívar, Sabana Grande, Caracas, tel: 7612988/5584, fax: 7618740; 3442560/2945, traffic 3552355. Barquisimeto, Cumaná, Maracaibo, Mérida, Porlamar, Puerto Ayacucho.

Aserca (R7) Torre Taeca, Calle Guaicaipuro, El Rosal, Caracas; tel: 800 VUELO (88365), 9532719/1448, fax: 9537228; 3551016. Barcelona, Barquisimeto, Maracaibo, Las Piedras, Maturin, Porlamar, Puerto Ordaz, San Antonio, Valencia.

Avensa (VE) Piso 25, Torre Humboldt, Av Río Caura, opp Concresa, Caracas; tel: 800 AVENSA (283672), 9078000, 2847756, fax: 5630225; 3551810. Barcelona, Barquisimeto, Coro, Maracaibo, Mérida, Puerto Ayacucho, San Antonio, San Fernando, San Tomé. For international routes, see Servivensa.

Avior Express (3B) Aeropuerto de Barcelona, Cumaná; tel: 800 28467, for east Venezuela 800 78827, 2384622, fax: 2341024; 3552767, fax: 3552941. Barcelona, Barinas, Carúpano, Cumaná, Guanare, Porlamar, Mérida, San Felipe, San Tomé, Valera.

Laser (LER) Torre Bazar Bolívar-p8, Av Miranda, El Marqués, Caracas; tel: 800 23732, (02) 2356979, fax: 2355566; 3552750. Maracaibo, Porlamar.

Línea Aérea IAACA (LAI) Quinta No 87, Av Avila, Bello Campo, Caracas; tel: 2632719/3615, fax: 2634661; 3552322. Acarigua, Barinas, Barquisimeto, Carúpano, Ciudad Bolívar, Maracay, Maturín, Porlamar, Valencia, Valera.

Oriental (ORT) CC Le Petit Galerie, Av 4 Mayo, Porlamar, Margarita; tel: (095) 612019. Cumaná: airport, (093) 612019. Barcelona, Cumaná, Maracaibo, Mérida, Porlamar, Santa Bárbara.

Rutaca (RUT) Edif Rutaca, Av Jesús Soto, Aeropuerto de Ciudad Bolívar; tel: (085) 25955, 24010, fax: 25955; 3552767, fax: 3551643. Anaco, Barcelona, Maturín, Porlamar, Puerto Ordaz. International: Boa Vista, Trinidad.

Santa Bárbara (BBR) CC Salto Angel, Av 3Y San Martín con Calle 78, Maracaibo; tel: 800 72682, (061) 922090, fax: 927977. Coro, El Vigía, Maracaibo, Mérida, Paraguaná, Santa Bárbara, Valera. International: Aruba, Barranquilla.

Sasca (Servicios Aéreos Sucre) Aeropuerto de Cumaná; tel: (093) 671150, (014) 9930639. CCM, Local 215, Porlamar, Margarita; tel: (095) 627156/4255. Serves Cumaná-Porlamar. Tours to Canaima, Delta, Grenada.

Servivensa (VC) (Sister company of Avensa) Piso 25, Torre Humboldt, Av Río Caura, opp Concresa, Caracas; tel: 800 283672, 9078000, 2846679, fax: 5630225. Barquisimeto, Canaima, Cumaná, Las Piedras (Paraguaná), Maturín, Porlamar, San Antonio, Santa Elena de Uairén, Valencia. International: Bogota, Curaçao, Lima, Medellín, Miami, New York, Quito, Panama.

By road
Buses
Buses go from the capital to all points of the country. Each town has its connecting lines and station, called the *terminal de pasajeros*. Fares are not expensive, ranging from US$12 to San Fernando de Apure, $26 to Maracaibo or San Cristóbal, up to $40 as far as Santa Elena de Uairén (22 hours). It is always best to travel at midweek or buy your bus ticket, *boleto*, a day ahead (tickets for Fridays are scarce) or even three days in advance of holidays. The best advice for travelling during holidays is to wait until they are half over.

You will find coaches listed in the telephone directory under Expresos, Líneas de Autobuses, or Uniones. *Expresos* are fast, comfortable and air conditioned, but so cold you need a sweater or blanket at night. They have smoked windows making it difficult to see out. *Ejecutivo* buses are fancier, and have reclining seats, snacks and toilet. You cannot open the windows and must not touch the curtains so as not to interfere with air conditioning and video screening. There are three large executive lines running between the capital and the country's largest cities: Maracay, Valencia, Barquisimeto and Maracaibo in the west; Puerto La Cruz, Cumaná, Maturín and Ciudad Guayana in the east. Aeroexpressos Ejecutivos, Expresos Camargüi and Peli Express each have their private terminal. Consult *Chapter 4*, page 83.

Note Never travel without passport or ID papers. Bus passengers are open to hassle from police or army searching for drug carriers and illegal immigrants. Mask your anger; flattery is more effective.

Por puestos

Long-distance *carritos* or taxis for which you pay by the seat leave (often near a bus terminal) as soon as they fill up. Routes have set fares but you can hire all the seats of a *por puesto* for a journey; this is called a *viaje expreso*. The cost is almost double the bus fare but it saves time and may be more comfortable. Also *por puestos* will stop to let you go to the toilet, a need at times imperative.

In cities, owner-operated *por puestos* have grown into small buses providing most of the urban transport.

Taxis

The other word for a taxi in Venezuela is a *libre*, meaning available. Every district has its *línea de taxi* (see telephone book), operating during the day. Officially, taxis are to install meters, but until this happens negotiate a price before getting in. Rates have risen with inflation but are not exorbitant: a short ride costs US$5; a long one, $10; Caracas–airport, $20. Taxi drivers do not normally expect tips. Radio-taxis provide reliable service day and night; phone ahead to request wake-up and a car for the airport.

In view of high car-rental rates, travellers report that combining taxi and bus service is flexible and economical for a morning's tour. No parking, no car theft. Negotiate the cost before setting out, on a basis of the car, not per passenger.

Car hire

Half a dozen small and large rental companies compete at every airport. All require credit cards and stipulate that drivers be over 21, or 25 for jeeps. Any 4x4 *vehículo rústico* is nearly double the cost of a small car, already a stiff US$65 per day/$400 a week. Some local firms in Margarita or Ciudad Bolívar may offer better rates than big companies so check them out. Ask about charges for additional driver, sales tax, returning the car to a different city and insurance, particularly for car theft. The advantage of working with a large franchise is a greater supply of cars, not better service. You must still check basic points such as tyres, brakes and belts. When you reserve a car from abroad and the chosen model proves unavailable, the company must assign you a better model at no extra cost. Budget is the only firm giving unlimited free mileage. Petrol (gas) is relatively cheap.

Call any agency for a quote: **ACO**, (02) 9911054/8511, fax: 9930762; **Budget**, 800 28343; **Dávila Tours**, (074) 660711; **Dollar**, (02) 9526502/7035, fax: 9532834; **Hertz**, 800 43781, fax: (02) 9530192; **Margarita Rentals**, (02) 923797, (095) 626966; **Oriental**, (095) 612667; **Rojas**, (02) 2858316.

Automobile club

If you need advice on driving conditions, insurance, rules, or vehicle documentation, the automobile association can help. The **Touring & Automóvil Club de Venezuela** (TACV) is affiliated with international groups such as the

AAA and RAC and extends its services to their members. Among services are 24-hour towing, coverage of hotel bills and transfers resulting from car accident or theft, assistance with documents, legal matters, and licence renewals. TACV provides international licences for Venezuelan drivers and the triptych for border crossings for cars with Venezuelan plates. Offices in Maracaibo, tel: (061) 970350; San Cristóbal, tel: (076) 442664/75; and Caracas, piso 15, Torre Phelps, Plaza Venezuela, tel: (02) 7819743/7491, fax: 7819787.

By metro
Caracas opened its first metro line in 1983 and now has three lines, with more being built. Plans have been announced for a 9.5km extension to Los Teques which would bring total length to 50km, east to west, by the year 2002. For more information, see *Chapter 4*. Maracaibo is now engaged in building a metro system.

By train
The first leg of a national electric rail system, from Caracas to Charallave/Cúa, is supposed to be ready by 2001. Work is well advanced on tunnels allowing the train to climb 625m in altitude; there remains a 6.8km tunnel. The $900 million system, being built by an Italian, French and Venezuelan consortium, will operate with 13 Japanese-made trains, each with four cars, travelling at 120km per hour. Studies are already complete for a second stage linking Cúa with Maracay/Valencia and Morón on the coast where a cargo line serves Riecito Mines in Falcón State. At present the only passenger train in operation links Puerto Cabello with Barquisimeto. It was built in the 1950s, at a time when there were still old lines running between Caracas and Valencia, and Caracas and La Guaira.

ACCOMMODATION
The government classifies hotels by the star system. If you have a complaint, this should be directed to the consumer protection institute, Indecu, Edif Norte-piso 7, Centro Simón Bolívar, Caracas; tel: 800 43328.

Hotels distinguish between two kinds of double rooms: *habitación doble* meaning twin beds, and *matrimonial* with a double bed. Many economy hotels offer only double beds, adding an extra single bed or cot where wanted. Cheap hotels and *pensiones* normally provide a room with dim lighting, indifferent mattress and bathroom with cold shower. However, they can also be clean, humble and owner maintained. Other places may turn out to be *hoteles de cita*, also known as 'mataderos' (slaughterhouses), where guests by the hour are preferred. The higher the price, the better and more discrete are such hotels, providing adequate accommodation at a pinch.

In towns and cities
All cities and most towns have a range of hotels from first class to the anonymous hostel. Caracas has the highest rates and the price categories below make allowances for this, also for low/high season changes. For example, while a reasonable hotel in Caracas may cost $50 double, in Mérida you would expect to pay $35. This does not reflect on the quality which may actually be better in a smaller hotel. During high season, city hotels, if anything, are likely to lower their rates to attract cash-strapped Venezuelans (such offers are not always open to foreigners). High season or *temporada alta* normally parallels school vacations: Christmas, Carnival, Easter and July–August. To secure a reservation, make a deposit to the hotel's bank account and fax them the bank slip. It is a good idea to reconfirm reservations.

The **international** chain hotels such as the Hilton, Inter-Continental or Melia catering to businessmen charge upwards of US$200 double. All have swimming pools, nightclubs, shops and five-star facilities, but they are often in locations inconvenient to public transportation. Dropping steeply but still high priced in local terms are the better hotels with rates of $70–140 a double. The middle range provides the best combination of good quality, price and location for around US$35–70. **Economy** hotels charge anywhere from $17 to $34. **Budget** lodging is considered to be $16 and under for the purposes of this book.

Hotel rates usually, but not always, include taxes in the room price.

In the country

Country lodgings may be the beautifully kept extension of someone's farm, a converted home, an old colonial house given new life, or just 'rustic' rooms which means basic, a step up from primitive. *Posadas*, guesthouses or inns (some do not provide meals), may be small and economical, or quite exclusive and upscale with full meals. But they are always different and there's usually a story behind each. *Posadas* are multiplying in the Andes where tourism is expanding fast. A *pensión* or *residencia* is a low-cost place in town for roomers (often workers), where little space is left for travellers. If your target is an intimate inn away from the main street, consult the updated *Guide to Camps, Posadas & Cabins* by Elizabeth Kline, writer and publisher, who researched over 400 lodgings. The *Ecotourism Guide to Venezuela*, a Miro Popic publication covering national parks, far-out lodges and *campamentos*, is also most useful. In wilderness areas *campamentos* and *hatos* (ranches) often provide first-class lodging; rates include meals and excursions.

Resort hotels

Margarita Island, specifically Playa El Agua, comes closest to being a beach or holiday resort where new hotels and holiday homes are springing up in growing numbers. Mérida State, now with 3,990 guesthouses and hotels (guest capacity 11,330), is *the* mountain resort area, attracting not only Venezuelan holidaymakers but many young hikers and climbers from abroad.

However, what is generally meant by a resort hotel is a large, luxury hotel providing international-class facilities at international prices.

Camping

A *campamento* is not a site for camping. Such facilities are almost unknown outside a few national parks, and camping is still a do-it-yourself affair. You are reasonably safe away from main roads, in the Gran Sabana, the Llanos, Andes and parks. But beaches near towns attract robbers. Where possible, ask a local dweller for permission to camp; this will usually give you protection. Do not leave your tent unattended. Do bring plastic bags to pick up rubbish; your good deed will reflect well on all campers.

Short tropical days mean that camp must be made early; the sun sets at about six in the evening (an hour later in July). And normally a roof or tarpaulin is needed in case of rain.

EATING AND DRINKING
Eating

'*Buen provecho*' means '*bon appétit*' and in Venezuela it's a courteous address on entering a dining room. Venezuelan cooking is simple and tasty, relying on seasonings such as bay leaf, coriander and garlic rather than hot peppers.

VENEZUELAN FOOD

Some local dishes, drinks and better-known tropical fruits and vegetables:

aguardiente	colourless alcohol (firewater), often anise flavoured
apio	yellow root (arracacha) like turnip or swede; good in soup
arepa	cornmeal griddle bun, staple in much of Venezuela in place of bread. When filled with cheese, chicken, shark... called a tostada
asado	pot roast, usually muchacho asado, rump
batido	juice of freshly blended fruit such as mango, lechosa (pawpaw) sometimes with added water and sugar.
cachapa	pancake of grated sweetcorn
cambur	banana; (fig) easy job, often bureacratic. Policamburista, person holding various such jobs
caña	alcoholic drink, especially aguardiente, firewater
carne en vara	side of beef roasted on a spit
casabe	cassava, flat dried bread of grated *yuca* (manioc) root, the staple grown by forest people (from the Carib)
empanada	turnover filled with cheese, chicken or meat, made of cornmeal and cooked in oil, like the *pastelito* made of wheat flour. Sold as quick snacks at half the price of an *arepa*
guarapo	pressed sugarcane juice
hallaca	maize dough with chicken stuffing, wrapped and boiled in banana leaves, traditional at Christmas
hervido	soup made with a base of beef (*res*) or chicken (*gallina*) stock, carrots, potatoes, onions, pumpkin and roots such as yuca and yam. When made with both beef and chicken it is *cruzado*. When made with fish, it is usually called *sancocho*.
jojoto	an ear of fresh maize
lagarto	pot roast of shank
mondongo	tripe, *callos* in Spain
nata	thick salty cream used in place of butter
queso de mano	fresh white cheese, also *queso guayanés*
tajadas	fried slices of ripe plantain
tequeño	hot fried cheese-stick in pastry
teta	name (meaning teat) now used for a homemade ice frozen in small plastic bag
tostones	thin rounds of green plantain, fried like potato crisps
tuna	cactus with spiny, plate-shaped 'leaves'; its edible fruit. Tuna fish is *atún*
yuca	manioc. Varieties of this root, whether 'sweet' *yuca dulce*, or 'bitter' *yuca amarga*, all have poisonous properties when raw. Roots should be well boiled, or the juice expressed, as in the making of cassava, *casabe*

Local dishes

Try the national dish called *pabellón*, which combines *carne mechada* (shredded beef), tasty fried *tajadas de plátanos* (sliced cooking bananas), and black beans – the *caraotas negras* so cherished by Venezuelans. On the coast, sample excellent fish such as *pargo* (red snapper), *mero* (grouper) or *carite* (kingfish). Trout from the

Andes, shipped frozen to Caracas, is quite good. Grilled steak and sausages are served as *parrillada* accompanied by fried yuca. Avoid *bistek* which is tough fried meat, not to be compared with beef steak. Most towns have chicken rotisseries preparing inexpensive *pollo a la brasa*. Variety is added by many reliable Italian, Spanish and Chinese restaurants. Not only McDonald's, but Wendy's, Burger King and other American franchises provide fast food. For formal dining, see *Chapter 4*, page 75 and 84.

The universal rib-sticker is a bowl of *hervido*, a stew of hen, beef or fish with chunks of onions, maize and roots such as *yuca* (manioc), *ñame* (yam) and *ocumo* (dasheen). Although these roots are called *verduras*, there is little green in the national diet. Vegetarian travellers soon become eager to eat anything rather than roots. Most city dwellers rely on beans and rice (and spaghetti). Other staples vary regionally: in the centre, maize; in the Andes, potatoes; in the east and south, manioc. *Casabe* is made of bitter manioc, grated, pressed and dried (the poisonous juices become harmless when cooked); it qualifies as the early native invention of preserved food, and no Indian will travel without a supply. Too bad it has little food value and less taste.

Snacks

Satisfying popular foods in Venezuela are almost made to order for travellers. *Arepas* are a national staple. These hot maize buns make a nutritious meal-in-a-snack when stuffed with cheese, meat, avocado, chicken or any of a dozen other fillings. Another good snack is the *cachapa*, a pancake made from grated corn-on-the-cob, usually served with fresh white cheese. Such cheese is called *queso de mano* in the Guayana region where it is made and *queso guayanés* in Caracas, and it is truly excellent. Another delicious creation, invented in Los Teques, is the *tequeño*, a cheese finger fried in dough. *Hallacas* are a savoury Christmas speciality of maize flour and olives with chicken or pork, all wrapped and cooked in banana leaves like a *tamal* and ready to travel. *Empanadas* (fried turnovers) are the cheapest of popular snacks, a bit greasy. When they're made with wheat dough instead of maize, they are called *pastelitos*. A great nutritious pack snack is the guava bar, sold in supermarkets as

COFFEE FOR ALL TASTES

Coffee drinking is an art cultivated by Venezuelans. And Venezuelan Arabica coffee compares well with the best in the world. In the shops a pound of coffee costs the equivalent of $3.30. The owner of the remotest farm or mining camp is proud to share hospitality, often a tiny cup of coffee. Over a wood fire the cook prepares *café de olla*, bringing the coffee, sugar and water to a boil and letting the grounds settle to make a basic, rewarding brew. In towns or pueblos, drip coffee or *café colado* is traditional for its smoothness. Strong Italian-style coffee is called *café de máquina* and is popular in cities where espresso machines are installed in every coffee bar.

A *Caraqueño* when ordering coffee does not just ask for *un café* but a certain kind or colour. Black can be *negro, negrito*; long or short – *largo* or *corto*; strong – *fuerte, cargado*; bitter – *amargo, cerrero*; weak – *suave, claro*; thin – *guayoyo*; weak and sweet – *guarapo*. Plain coffee with milk is *café con leche*; when it is more milk than coffee it is sometimes called a *tetero* (baby's bottle). Coffee can also be served darker or lighter brown – *marrón*, or *marrón claro*. Or topped with whipped cream in a rich *capuchino*. If you like coffee laced with rum, ask for a *café bautizado*.

bocadillos de guayaba. The bar is pure fruit and sugar. You can buy tins of delicious guava shells in syrup, *cascos de guayaba*, a treat when served with cream cheese.

Drinking

Discover the dozens of fresh fruit juices called *batidos* (with some sugar and water depending on fruit), liquefied on the spot – pineapple, mango, tangerine, guava, grape, even 3-in-1 made of carrot, orange and beetroot. *Batidos* are made in all places selling *arepas* and in most grilled chicken and low-cost restaurants. Bakeries sell processed juices (sometimes fresh orange juice), chocolate milk and, also in a carton, *chicha*, a rice/milk drink which is sweet, soothing and custardy.

PUBLIC HOLIDAYS
National holidays

Venezuelans take holidays seriously. Families migrate to the coast during peak beach vacations (January–April). Traffic is frantic, roads are clogged, bus and plane terminals are mobbed. If you are travelling during these periods, wait for people to leave the city and then you may find transportation. On New Year's Day, you cannot get s bus or anything to eat. Even gasoline (petrol) stations are closed.

If a red-letter day falls on a Thursday or Tuesday, many people make a *puente* (bridge) to take a four-day weekend. This makes appointments difficult to keep. In December, government offices close early, working roughly 07.30 to 15.30. From December 15–18 on, rule out any idea of business until schools open again after January 6, *Los Reyes Magos*, the day when the Three Kings bring children presents. Work does not begin in earnest until January 15. The same applies to the days before Carnival weekend and the pre-Easter week when many businesses are shut. Banks are the major exception, working full hours except on the legal holidays listed below; see section on *Money* (page 28), for more bank holidays.

January	1	New Year's Day
Carnival		Mon–Tues before Lent
Easter		Holy Thursday, Good Friday
April	19	Proclamation of Independence
May	1	Labour Day
June	24	Battle of Carabobo
July	5	Independence
July	24	Bolívar's Birth
October	12	Columbus Day (Día de la Raza)
December	25	Christmas Day

Feast days and fairs

Pueblos honour their patron saints with processions, masses, and street dances deeply engrained in folklore. In many cases these fiestas are three-day affairs fuelled by rum. Citywide *ferias*, lasting one to two weeks, celebrate a saint's day with religious, cultural and sports events. Below is a partial list, with major events in bold.

January	2	*Virgen de Coromoto*, Patroness of Venezuela; masses at the National Sanctuary south of Guanare.
	6	*Los Reyes Magos*, Three Kings Day; San Miguel de Boconó turns out for a Romería and bottle dance.
	14	**Feria de la Divina Pastora**; Barquisimeto's weeklong festival for the Divine Shepherdess.
	20	**Feria de San Sebastián**; San Cristóbal opens a two-week fair of music, sports, bullfights.

February	2	*Los Vasallos de La Candelaria*, the Vassals of Our Lady of Candelaria; Mérida State.
Feb/March		*Carnival*; street parties, parades in many towns, the best in Carúpano, El Callao. Mérida City celebrates Carnival with the ten-day *Feria del Sol*. On Ash Wednesday *El Entierro de la Sardina*, The Sardine's Funeral, enacted in Macuto.
March	19	*San José*, St Joseph's Day; fiestas, bullfights in Maracay.
March/April		**EASTER** *Semana Santa*. Holy Week in Caracas opens on Palm Sunday with blessing of palm leaves in Chacao, and open-air mass in Plaza Caracas, 11.00. On Wednesday evening, Nazarene procession from the Basílica de Santa Teresa to Plaza Caracas. The Passion of Christ is acted out on Good Friday at Plaza Caracas, at El Hatillo's church, and in many, many pueblos, especially Ureña, Táchira. In Puerto Cabello the Blessing of the Sea takes place on Easter Sunday at a huge sunrise Mass by the marina. Easter ends on Sunday afternoon with the *Quema de Judas*, burning Judas' effigy.
May	3	*Velorio de Cruz de Mayo*; altars to the May Cross coincide with planting and the Southern Cross in the sky; widespread, especially in Puerto La Cruz and the east.
	15	*San Isidro Labrador*; in Mérida State – Apartaderos, Jají, Lagunillas, Tovar.
June		**Corpus Christi**, celebrated on the 9th Thursday after Holy Thursday. Rites by devil dancers in fantastic masks in Naiguatá, San Francisco de Yare, Chuao.
	13	*San Antonio*; in El Tocuyo, Quíbor, Sanare, the complex Tamunangue dances and mock battles.
	24	*San Juan*; 3 days and nights of African drums at the feast of St John the Baptist in coastal towns such as Choroní, Puerto Maya, Chichiriviche, Chuspa, Curiepe.
June	29	*San Pedro y San Pablo*; a costumed folklore play in Guatire.
July	25	*Santiago Apóstol*, St James the Apostle; Caracas honours its patron with a cultural festival. Religious processions in Mérida: Ejido, Jají, Lagunillas.
August	8	*Nuestra Señora de las Nieves*, Our Lady of the Snows, patroness of Ciudad Bolívar's *Feria del Orinoco*.
September	8	*Virgen del Valle*; patroness of seafarers inspires masses, processions in Valle del Espíritu Santo, Margarita, and the blessing of fishing craft in Margarita, Puerto La Cruz and eastern Venezuela.
	8	The day of Nuestra Señora de Coromoto, Guanare. The Indian chief's conversion by the Virgin is acted out in Chachopo, Mérida.
	24	*San Miguel Arcángel*, Archangel Michael; drums and dances in Puerto Maya, Jají, Mérida.
November	18	*Feria de la Chinita*; Maracaibo goes all out for the Virgin of Chiquinquirá, known to devotees as La Chinita, in a big festival: parades, races, music, folklore.
December	25	*Navidad*; Christmas masses on the Eve, at midnight *Misa de Gallo*, the Cock's Mass.
	27–29	*San Benito*; costumed dancers fete Venezuela's black saint in Zulia and Mérida states: Dec 27 Sinamaica, El Moján; Dec 28 Gibraltar, Bobures, Palmarito; Dec 29 Mucuchíes, Timotes.
	28	*Día de Los Inocentes*, Innocents' Day, recalling the slaughter of infants by Herod. It is a day for practical jokes, in the same vein as April Fool's Day (not observed in Venezuela).

SHOPPING

Shopping malls are called *centros comerciales*. Bright and modern, their shops are well stocked with the latest clothes and computers. Puerto La Cruz, Maturín and Valencia have many new malls. In Caracas three luxury malls opened in 1998 including the Centro Sambil, said to be South America's largest with over 500 shops, banks, cinemas, a bowling alley, an aquarium, and even a space simulator for kids. Centro Sambil opens for business until 21.00, 365 days a year – a revolution in a country where commerce has always shut down for lunch and there's no business on Saturdays.

However, to buy leather shoes and bags don't go to a shopping centre for reasonable prices. Try the older, downtown areas. Such districts are also best for gold and silver jewellery: in Caracas, facing the Capitol; in Ciudad Bolívar, on the Paseo Orinoco. Shoemakers and shoeshops congregate in La Carlota district of Caracas, where you can find all sizes and discounts on leather shoes, bags too.

Cities rely on supermarkets for most fresh produce. But the traditional covered markets thrive on stalls of fresh fish, eggs, meat, vegetables, beans and rice; they are usually closed after noon. These big marketplaces in Barcelona, Cumaná, Mérida, Porlamar and other towns are great for buying locally made chocolate and tobacco, as well as enamel plates, low-cost cotton clothes and some crafts.

Venezuelan coffee and chocolate are excellent for gifts and travelling. Chocolate bars made by Savoy and La India do not melt as readily as the Swiss or American variety, so they travel better.

Crafts of collection quality, especially Indian basketry, are made by the Warao, Yekuana, Panare and other peoples. Beautiful and curious wooden benches in the tradition of Yekuana jaguar seats come in a whole tropical bestiary of carved armadillos, tapirs and monkeys. The Guajiro Indians make bags and tapestries of exuberant colours. Guajira women wear long flowery robes called *mantas* which are sold in Zulia. Naïve paintings and sculptures from Mérida and Trujillo are both typical and charming. In Lara State, weavers make blankets and rugs, woodworkers turn fine bowls in semi-precious woods, and potters make pre-Columbian reproductions.

ARTS AND ENTERTAINMENT
Visual arts

Caracas leads the active national arts scene with big events such as the Ibero-American Art Festival (FIA) every July, the national painting and graphics salon, and the Americas Pottery Biennial. Many private galleries and five museums put on shows of international quality. There are art museums in eight other cities, representing styles from traditional, naïve and indigenous to the most modern. Some contemporary painters, graphic designers and sculptors of international repute are Marisol Escobar, Luisa Richter, Alirio Palacios, Alirio Rodríguez, Mateo Manaure, Jacobo Borges, Santiago Pol and Alvaro Sotillo. Jesús Soto, who won France's *Grand Prix de l' Esculture* in 1995, and Carlos Cruz-Diez are leaders of the kinetic art movement. For the many galleries and museums, check *The Daily Journal*.

Film makers are active despite budget cuts. Releases in 1998 were to include work by directors such as Carlos Azpúrua, Manuel de Pedro, Iván Feo, Oscar Lucien, Antonio Llerandi, Mariana Rondón and Julio Sosa Pietri. Films from abroad are released in their original language with Spanish subtitles. Tickets cost $3–4, with half price on Monday nights in many cinemas. Children under 14 may only go to afternoon showings of class A films. Theatre, ballet, and opera companies are an essential part of cultural life. An International Theatre Festival brings first-rate groups from many countries to Caracas in July every second year (1999, 2001...).

Music

International events include the **A Tempo Festival of European Music**, the biennial **Alfredo Rugeles Festival of Contemporary Latin American Music**, and a festival of Latin American popular/jazz music. Other festivals combine excellence and local colour each year in El Hatillo (Oct–Nov) and Colonia Tovar (March). Caracas is home to five full orchestras, plus three youth orchestras and many chamber groups. The Teresa Carreño Cultural Complex is a modern structure adorned with kinetic 'rain' by Jesús Soto. This performing arts centre is named after the country's first great concert pianist, famous in Europe until her death in 1917. Teresa Carreño is followed today by such renowned pianists as Carlos Duarte, Gabriela Montero and Arnaldo Pizzolante. Other acclaimed musicians are guitarists Alirio Díaz and Antonio Lauro, harpsichordist Abraham Abreu, cellist Paul Desenne, and harpists Pedro Castro and Carlos Orozco.

PHOTOGRAPHY

Bring plenty of film. Supplies in small towns may be sketchy, or old – particularly in those shops open when you run out. Kodacolor is everywhere, and Fujicolor is available, while Agfa is not common. Slide film is found only in specialised photo shops – and sometimes not even then. Fast colour printing service is standard in cities, but developing *diapositivas* (slides) takes up to a week.

MEDIA AND COMMUNICATIONS
Media

The nation's newspapers are led by *El Universal* and *El Nacional* followed by several other papers in Caracas and a strong regional press. Caracas has the only paper in English, *The Daily Journal*, which is strong on international news, sport and culture. *Business Venezuela*, one of the nation's best magazines, covers a wide field from the stock market to tourism. It is published monthly in English by the Venezuelan American Chamber of Commerce. Certain newsstands carry foreign papers, and all sell a range of international magazines.

Television is held to be more of a necessity than a luxury by most Venezuelan families; even homes without an oven or refrigerator will have a set. There are four or five private channels and a government channel, as well as satellite and cable services. The lives of soap opera characters are subjects of daily discussion; the soaps, called *telenovelas* or *culebrones* (long snakes), seem to be on morning, noon and night. Videos use the American image system. As this is incompatible with higher European resolution, British cassettes cannot be played on VCR equipment in Venezuela. The number of radio stations approaches 100 (AM and FM).

Postal services

An address with the word *apartado* is a post box, not an apartment. Outsiders have a hard time realising that letters take a fortnight or longer for delivery (and some never arrive). Allow a month for a letter exchange and be pleased if it takes less. Unless sending a small book, do not mail packages to Venezuela. The stamps cost as much as the contents and, if the parcel arrives, the receiver must not only make one or more trips to Customs, but pay duty on it. No-one uses letter boxes, except in large hotels. A minimum airmail letter costs US$1 in stamps (you pay sales tax). Use registered post, *correo certificado*, for important letters.

Other services at main post offices include: EEE Express Special Delivery between major cities, with proof of delivery and low rates, tel: 800 26378; and EMS Express Mail Service with courier despatch to five continents, again low rates. The larger Ipostel post offices are open Mon–Fri 08.00 to 18.00; smaller ones may close at midday. The central Caracas *Correos* at Esquina Carmelitas is open every day. For services such as philately and poste restante, see *Chapter 4*, page 83.

Telegrams

There is little urgency about delivering telegrams, losing the point of sending them. However, some people send telegrams locally because they are faster than letters. They can be used to request audiences with officials, for example. For sending a telegram by telephone, ring 800 46220.

Telephone

Venezuela's telephone company CANTV was partly privatised when a consortium led by GTE bought 40% in 1991. It is now spending $350 million on a three-year plan to prepare for the end of its monopoly on national line service by the end of the year 2000AD. CANTV has installed many new card phones but they are often out of order (an *'error de tarjeta'* message indicates the telephone is failing). The best place to find a functioning phone is in a hotel, or a metro station. The CANTV phone cards, *tarjetas magnéticas*, are sold at many newsstands for Bs2,000 and Bs5,000. When your card is running low, in order to avoid being cut off press simultaneously '*' and '#'.

National calls

Make it a rule when speaking to first give your name and a phone contact as a backup. The person answering may not understand English, or the line may be weak and your voice hard to hear, so leave explanations for later.

Using the telephone directory can be frustrating because people in rented flats may be under the landlord's listing for many years. Subscribers are listed by their surname (father's) plus initial of the second surname (mother's). Remember that in the Spanish alphabet CH is a single letter which follows C, just as LL comes after L, and Ñ after N. The Caracas directory no longer lists outlying towns such as La Guaira or Macuto. Volumes covering the entire country are hard to find: consult Caveguías, Torre Caveguías, Ibarras to Maturín, N of Av Urdaneta, Caracas, or ask at a CANTV *Centro de Atención Comercial* if they will let you look at the office set.

Access to long-distance direct dialling requires one '0' for national service. Dial 100 for the national operator and 103 for information. Numbers transferred to new exchanges may be verified anywhere in Venezuela by ringing (02) 5310333. This is an automatic service: you have only to enter the digits (with area code) of the number you wish to check.

International calls

In Venezuela you may dial abroad direct from card phones in major hotels, metro stations and shopping centres. Dial 00 for international access, or 122 for operator assistance, *Larga Distancia Internacional*. Phone rates are expensive, but reduced rates to Europe begin at 16.00 including Sundays; economy rates, even lower, apply from 20.00 to 07.00. For most of North and South America, reduced rates begin after 18.00 and economy rates after midnight.

All cities and major airports have a CANTV Communications Centre where operators place your call while you wait. Calls may be charged with MasterCard, Visa and Diners. For ATT direct service to the USA: 800 11120. The international dialling code for Venezuela is +58. When ringing from abroad, omit the '0' in Venezuelan area codes. The phone company offers a **collect call system**, '*Venezuela Directo*', allowing people abroad to reverse the charges by making the call through a special operator. For example, the telephone access for British callers is

0800 890058; for Canadians, 1800 4636564; for callers from France, 0800 990058; Germany, 0800 25800; Spain, 900 990581.

Cell phones
Cell phones are widely used to fill in for a lack of telephone lines (and for security reasons). There are now over a million Venezuelan users. Service is provided by rival companies TelCel, a BellSouth/Cisneros joint venture with local investors, and Movilnet, a unit of CANTV. Calling a *teléfono celular* on 014 (TelCel) or 016 (Movilnet) will be expensive as charges are based on long distance, so your phone card will not last long. Be prepared to ring two or three times no matter what the computer lady says. (If the phone is busy, you may get a message that it is 'out of the area, off', but this is not always the case, so try again.) You may hire a cellular phone with a credit card. Call Rent-a-Phone, tel: (02) 5034328/29; or Phontell, (02) 2674893, 2652798.

Fax
Principal post offices offer a public fax service at low cost. Also, the CANTV Communications Centres have fax machines for sending and receiving, again at low cost compared with private services such as Mail Boxes etc.

Internet and email
New post offices in Caracas first offered electronic mail service on an experimental basis in 1998, providing Internet links to the public at prices about half the commercial rate, and making available email addresses, transmission and reception. For information, send an email letter to: iptalta@cantv.net.

In several cities Internet services are springing up to offer email addresses, web pages, training courses, and computer work-stations. Competition should reduce the high charges, at present $8 an hour on Internet and $20 for a half-day at a computer station.

Couriers
Private mail and parcel services provide quick delivery; ask for the pickup or service point nearest to you.

Nationwide
Aerocav tel: (02) 2050122, for pickup 2050777; cargo and correspondence.
Aserca tel: 800 39773, new service by an airline with offices in major airports and cities.
MRW tel: 800 30400; parcels to 35kg; also urban, overseas (free student plan).
Zoom tel: (02) 2427111/0144; email: gzooveme@true.net; plus letter service to US Mail in Miami.

International
DHL tel: 800 34592, 800 34575; Torre Seguros Sudamérica, tel: Av Miranda at Av Venezuela, El Rosal; desks at Hilton Hotel (02) 5712322, and Tamanaco (02) 2087293; for electronic updates on deliveries: www.dhl.com.
FEDEX tel: 800 33339, for pickup (02) 2053333. UPS works through Transvalcar, tel: (02) 2416454/8819, fax: 2419249.

MAPS AND INFORMATION
Maps
Some folding maps of Venezuela and Caracas are sold through bookshops (*librerías*), but their quality is poor. Much better are the country maps produced and

sold at service stations by oil companies (Lagoven, Corpoven). Although these became unavailable when the national oil industry was restructured in 1998, they may well be reissued by PDV. Kevin Healey's excellent *International Travel Map of Venezuela,* which has been used to check many of the maps in this guide, can be obtained from the publishers at PO Box 2290, Vancouver BC V6B 3W5, Canada; tel: 604 687 3320; fax: 604 687 5925. It is available in Venezuela from the Librería Alemana, Centro Perú, Av Libertador, 1½ blocks west of Av Principal de El Bosque, Caracas; tel: (02) 7630881, fax: 7625244, and in the UK from Stanfords, 12–14 Long Acre, London WC1; tel: 0171 836 1321.

The *Guía Vial de Venezuela* edited by Miro Popic is a 250-page spiral-bound road atlas with practical information (in Spanish), including restaurants, hotels and mechanics, for most towns. It's very clear and good quality, but expensive and gives no distances (km) between towns.

The Environment Ministry, through the Dirección de Cartografía Nacional, maps the entire country. Regional and state maps, on a scale of 1:100,000 and 1:25,000, are sold for about $5. If the originals are unavailable Cartografía will make you photocopies. Cartografía headquarters are in Edificio Camejo, Calle Este 6 opp Av Norte 1, Caracas; tel: (02) 4081115/1219, fax: 5420374. This is a five-floor building east of Plaza Diego Ibarra and the Twin Towers of Centro Simón Bolívar. As all these government offices are under repair, when last visited Cartografía was working behind hoarding. Hours: 08.30–11.30, 14.00–16.00. Cartografía maps are also sold from a Metroguía outlet in La California metro station, southeast corridor; tel: 219496/9265. Hours: 08.30–19.00; Sat 10.00–14.00.

Tourism

Corpoturismo is the state bureau in charge of tourism. Its headquarters are on 37th floor, Torre Oeste, Parque Central, Caracas; promotion and information, tel: (02) 5078815/16, fax: 5738983. For brochures or posters (*afiches*) take a written request to Promoción & Información on Tuesday or Thursday, tel: 5741513.

All your touring and transportation questions in Venezuela are answered in two travel-industry handbooks published monthly in Spanish. They are the travel agents' bibles, listing all flights in Venezuela and on-going connections, hotels, tours, agencies and car hire. *Guía Aérea y Marítima (GAM)*: Centro Parima-p10, No 83 Av Libertador, Chacao, Caracas; tel: (02) 2630283/3977, fax: 2633972. *Gaceta Aérea*: Res La Carlota, Av Libertador at Las Acacias, Caracas; tel: (02) 7935183/5377, fax: 7821164.

Mérida has its own tourism corporation, CORMETUR, Av Urdaneta at Calle 45, by the Mérida airport; tel: 800 63743, (074) 680814, fax: 632782; email: cormetur@cormetur.com. For information about Táchira State, there is the Corporación de Turismo de Táchira, (076) 565956, fax: 562421. For Margarita: Cámara de Turismo del Estado Nueva Esparta, Av Santiago Mariño at Calle Amador Hernández, Porlamar; tel: (095) 635644, fax: 635922. Also, Pro-Margarita, Centro Tradimat-mezz, Av 4 de Mayo, via Los Robles; tel: (095) 640264, fax: 634448; email: promar@enlared.net.

BUSINESS

Venezuelans are early risers and by 07.00 the day's first rush-hour builds into a jam of people going to work. Business hours vary, with most companies starting at 08.00. But almost all close at lunch for one to two hours. People used to work half-day on Saturdays (*sábado inglés*); but that went out with the *locha*, a 12½ cent coin. For what goes on behind the scenes in business, consult people in the know.

The Venezuelan American Chamber of Commerce is a highly organised group of more than 4,500 US and Venezuelan businessmen. VenAmCham publishes a *Business Guide to Venezuela*, and an excellent monthly magazine, *Business Venezuela*. The chamber runs an electronic Infocenter providing all sorts of data; services for subscribers include market studies and partner search. For more details, see *Chapter 4*, page 79.

Venezuela's vital statistics are available in CD Rom, diskette or paper form from the Oficina Central de Estadística. OCEI's Centro de Documentación is in Edif La Salle, Av Boyacá at Av Principal de Maripérez, Caracas; tel: (02) 7821156/7815412, fax: 781138; email: ocei@platino.gov.ve; net: www.ocei.gov.ve. Open weekdays 08.30–16.00.

CULTURAL DOS AND DON'TS

Venezuelans are a proud and generous people who react quickly to a slur on their cultural identity. Simón Bolívar, as their highest role model and Liberator of a great deal of South America, is honoured everywhere. If you find yourself in Plaza Bolívar, respect must be extended to Bolívar's statue. Don't cross in front carrying bulky packages, or loiter in beach clothes. Respect for Bolívar also extends to his printed likeness. The editors of one newspaper were made to recall all copies because a currency devaluation report was illustrated with a banknote torn in half through Bolívar's face.

To disrespect someone is to *faltarle el respeto*, a grave wrong. Although a uniformed official may be overstepping his authority, be careful in word (and looks) when addressing representatives of the law: never demean their position or dignity. (They are always in the right.) You could begin: '*Con todo respeto, oficial...*' To the charge of '*faltó el respeto*', the only defence is to say it was unintentional, '*Perdón, fue sin intención*'.

Social graces are important. When people meet, the custom is to enquire about the welfare of the entire family before getting down to business. Be complimentary first, make your complaints later, and try to find the other person a way out of any difficulty he has caused you without losing face.

Latin men are very sensitive to slights. Flattery may not get you everywhere, but it will go a long way. Try not to be *antipático*, disagreeable or negative. If there is nothing good to say about a road block, a missed plane, or an outboard engine that fails, try to be sympathetic to the traffic policeman, the overworked employee, or the sweating mechanic. They all have families and problems. You can begin to defuse any situation if you offer a juice, coffee or drink.

GIVING SOMETHING BACK

While travel opens one's eyes to major problems, there may occur to you some practical ways on a local level that you can show appreciation for the country's hospitality. For example, children are everywhere, playing in city streets, or offering flowers by Andean roads. One traveller donated inflatable globes to remote schools, another took frisbees on a Gran Sabana trek. If carrying gifts is not possible, you can buy paper and pencils at a bookshop (*librería*) on the way. That's the place to get materials for kites, *papagallos* – tissue paper, string and glue (*papel de seda, pabilo, cola*) – if you are headed for windy places like hills, beaches, or rivers.

By supporting groups which are already committed locally, you help to advance a plan of action. Below are five programmes now under way. For more details, see the sections (in bold face) of corresponding chapters in the book.

A **Centre for Indigenous Self-Development** – CEPAI in Spanish – supports cooperatives in Amazonas State where seven ethnic groups not only make crafts and raise honey bees, cacao and coffee, but also do the planning. The Sanema, a subgroup of the Yanomami, harvest 10,000kg of honey a year on the upper Paru River, using genetics to keep African bees from colonising the hives. Products are sent to Puerto Ayacucho and from there to Caracas where CEPAI has a crafts shop. Tel: (048) 214956, Apartado Postal No 9, Puerto Ayacucho, Estado Amazonas. Also, see *Chapter 4*, page 81. Caracas: tel: (02) 4811398, fax: 4824001; Quinta Etey, Av Monte Elena No 03-10, El Paraíso, Caracas 1020.

From El Dorado the **road to Brazil** passes through the Imataca Forest Reserve. Settlers, many of whom are from Guyana and speak English, struggle with malaria and mercury-polluted water from gold-mining activities. Far-flung communities lack medicines, school books, clothes and farming equipment. Even a football (plus pump) would give these needy people a positive lift. **Padre Adriano Salvadore** at Km 67 is working on a clean water supply. See *Chapter 12*, page 280.

'We can use help with logistics, and with solar and computer equipment,' says Marcus Colchester who heads the Forest Peoples Program of the **World Rainforest Movement**, a British NGO he set up some years ago. Those who see, as he does, that protecting forests protects their people too, can join a move to 'Save the Caura'. The **Caura River** is targeted by a state power plan to divert half its waters to feed Guri Dam. The area is home to the Sanema and Yekuana people who are now mapping their ancestral lands using GPS techniques. See box on page 292.

The goal of **Tierra Viva** is to help sustainable growth through environmental education. Their work in schools, communities and companies in the basin of Lake Valencia earned first place in 1998 among projects submitted to the United Nations Development Program, Alliances for Reduction of Poverty. As part of Tierra Viva plans for **Henri Pittier National Park**, visitors now have a map detailing park ecosystems. Tierra Viva needs volunteers for a Delta project tackling serious health and educational problems. Fundación Tierra Viva, tel/fax: (02) 9512601, (045) 51406; email: tierraviva@compuserve.com. Also see page 49 and 318.

In **Margarita**, the endemic parrot population has tripled as a result of dedicated care by members of **Provita**. They have worked with local people for a decade to protect the *cotorra margariteña*, until it has now been declared Margarita's Regional Bird. Provita raises parrots from eggs for later release in the wild. However, a subspecies, the *ñángaro*, is in critical state, with fewer than 200 birds. And Provita's 11 years of environmental education in Mérida have not yet persuaded locals to stop hunting the Andean spectacled bear. See also pages 48 and 185.

National Parks and Special Interests

NATIONAL PARKS

Venezuela has an impressive 43 national parks and 20 natural monuments including the major table mountains (*tepuis*). All told, these cover about 141,000km^2 or over 15.5% of the country. They are administered by the Ministerio del Ambiente y Recursos Naturales Renovables (MARNR), through the Instituto Nacional de Parques, known as Inparques. Enquiries about parks may be addressed to: Dirección de Parques Nacionales, Av Rómulo Gallegos, Santa Eduvigis, Caracas, tel: (02) 2854106/5056, fax: 2853070. Hours are Mon–Fri 08.30–12.30, 13.30–17.00 (except in December, 07.30–15.30). The office is a few steps east of the Parque del Este metro station, north exit. For information ask for the reference library, *biblioteca*.

Permits

People planning a scientific, filming, caving or diving (*submarinismo*) **expedition** in a national park should request special permission in writing 60 days in advance. Write to the Director of Parques Nacionales (see above) stating your objectives, group members plus their passport numbers, and Venezuelan affiliations. Other enquiries may be directed to Inparques Regional Offices, listed below.

Canaima permits good for three days cost US$4, paid upon landing. There is no area designated for camping in Canaima, so it's best to consult with the park ranger, *guardaparques*. Tourists taking the highway through the Gran Sabana pay a Canaima park fee of less than US$1 per day. Until park regulations are published, no permits are being issued for *tepui* expeditions. In the meantime, people still trek to Roraima with normal permits.

The marine and coastal park of **Morrocoy** is restricting overnight stays to the islands of Cayo Sal, Paiclá, Sombrero and Cayo Muerto; the permit costs $2. For information, ring 800 84847 (VIVIR).

Ordinary **hiking** permits are issued for a small fee at ranger posts, or *puestos de guardaparques*; you need only present a passport or ID. If you are overnighting, request a *permiso de pernoctar*, which costs about $2 and applies to parks with shelters called *kioscos* and areas designated for tents. Exceptions to this are Dinira, Guaramacal, Guatopo, Laguna de Tacarigua, Sierra Nevada, and Yacambú Parks. More expensive are El Guácharo ($12§), Los Roques ($12), Mochima ($16), and Henri Pittier ($16). Two parks – Guatopo and El Avila – have very low-cost dormitories. These sleep 30 people and, as they are booked months ahead, a written request for reservation must be directed to Inparques in Caracas; tel: (02) 2391886, 2371779.

Travel in **Amazonas State** is restricted beyond La Esmeralda because the Alto Orinoco Biosphere Reserve is located in southern Amazonas. Direct all enquiries to the headquarters of SADA-Servicio Autónomo para el Desarrollo Ambiental de Amazonas: Base Aérea, La Carlota, Caracas; tel: (02) 9917853.

National Parks and Natural Monuments

Fishing permits

Seasonal permits for sport fishing (*pesca deportiva*) are issued by local parks offices in Laguna de Tacarigua and Los Roques. The permit specifies each species' limit and minimum size; sport fishermen follow the catch-and-release practice. For information about fees, which vary by boat and by park, enquire at Regional Offices listed below. For rivers and lakes outside the parks, permits are issued by Pesca Deportiva, Ministerio de Agricultura y Cría, 10th floor, Torre Este, Parque Central, Caracas; tel: (02) 5090375.

Inparques regional offices

Amazonas Edif Funeraria Amazonas-PA, final Calle La Guardia, Barrio Unión, Puerto Ayacucho; tel: (048) 214771, fax: 213715.

Anzoátegui Parque Andrés Blanco, Paseo Colón, Puerto La Cruz; tel: (093) 314873, (081) 677777, fax: 678973.

Apure Edif Pasquali, Calle Bolívar opposite Palacio Los Barbaritos, San Fernando de Apure; tel: (047) 25530, fax: 413794.

Aragua Zoológico Las Delicias, Maracay; tel: (043) 413933, fax: 419909. For Henri Pittier NP: Las Cocuizas Recreational Area, Maracay-Choroní road.

Bolívar Edif CVG, piso 1, Av Germania con Andrés Bello, Ciudad Bolívar; tel: (085) 27722/23, fax: 29908. For **Canaima Park (west)**, tel: (086) 613151; **Canaima Park (east)**, Campamento Aponwao, Km 139, road to Santa Elena; **Canaima Park (south)**, Alcabala Guardia Nacional, San Ignacio de Yuruaní, road to Santa Elena. Emergencies, tel: (085) 27723-CVG.

Capital Region Inparques, Av Rómulo Gallegos, Caracas; tel: (02) 2371779, fax: 2379752;

NATIONAL PARKS (Total area 129,805km²)

	Area (km²)		Area (km²)
Aguaro-Guariquito	586	Macarao	150
Archipiélago Los Roques	221	Mariusa	3,310
Canaima	30,000	Médanos de Coro	913
Cerro El Copey	71	Mochima	949
Cerro Saroche	323	Morrocoy	321
Chorro El Indio	170	Páramos Batallón La Negra	952
Ciénaga del Catatumbo	2,500	Parima-Tapirapeco	34,200
Cinaruco-Capanaparo	5,844	Península de Paria	375
Cueva de la Quebrada del		Río Viejo	682
Toro	49	San Esteban	435
Dinira	420	Sierra de Perijá	2,952
Duida-Marahuaca	2,100	Sierra de San Luis	200
El Avila	818	Sierra La Culata	2.004
El Guácharo	627	Sierra Nevada	2,764
El Guache	167	Tapo-Caparo	2,050
El Tamá	1,090	Terepaima	186
Guaramacal	210	Tirgua	910
Guatopo	1,225	Turuépano	700
Henri Pittier	1,078	Yacambú	146
Jaua-Sarisariñama	3,300	Yapacana	3,200
Laguna de la Restinga	189	Yurubí	237
Laguna de Tacarigua	391		

NATURAL MONUMENTS

Abra Río Frio	Las Tetas de María Guevara
Cerro Autana	Loma de León
Cerro Platillón	María Lionza
Cerro Santa Ana	Meseta de la Galera
Cerros Matasiete-Guayamurí	Morros de Macaira
Chorrera de las González	Morros de San Juan
Cueva Alfredo Jahn	Pico Codazzi
Cueva del Guácharo	Piedra del Cocuy
Laguna de las Marites	Piedra La Tortuga, La Pintada
Laguna de Urao	Tepuis (25, in all 10,698km²)

Guatopo, tel: (014) 9344729; **Laguna de Tacarigua**, tel: (034) 711143.
Carabobo Antigua Estación, Plaza Los Enanitos, Av Paseo Cabriales, Valencia; tel: (041) 574609, fax: 591917. For **San Esteban Park**, Quinta Asturias, Calle Principal Tejerías, Puerto Cabello; tel: (042) 615503, fax: 590530.
Falcón Jardín Xerófito de Coro León Croizat, Intercomunal Coro-La Vela; tel: (068) 78582, fax: 78451. For **Cerro Santa Ana**, Inparques, Santa Ana, Paraguaná Peninsula. For **Sierra de San Luis**, (068) 611076. For **Morrocoy**, Tucacas, tel: 800 84847, (042) 830053/69.
Guarico Edif MARNR, Av Principal del Centro, Calabozo; tel: (046) 713523.
Lara Av Los Leones facing Centro Comercial Las Trinitarias, Barquisimeto; tel: (051) 541448, fax: 542366.
Los Roques Autoridad Unica Los Roques, Ministerio del Ambiente, Torre Sur, piso 19, Centro Simón Bolívar, Caracas; tel: (02) 4081167/69. Superintendent in Gran Roque, tel: (014) 2024970.

Mérida-Trujillo No 5-44, Calle 19 con Av 5-6, Mérida; tel/fax: (074) 529876/8284.
Miranda See Capital Region.
Monagas-Delta Parque Andrés Eloy Blanco, Carretera Vía Sur, Maturín, Estado Monagas; tel/fax: (091) 417543.
Nueva Esparta (Margarita), Quinta Bi-Yzarak, Calle Paralela, El Poblado, Porlamar, Margarita; tel: (095) 48237, fax: 48553.
Sucre Parque Guaiquerí, Av Arismendi, Cumaná; tel: (093) 311570, fax: 314873. For **Paria**, Inparques, Av Principal Campo Claro, Irapa.
Tachira-Barinas Parque Metropolitano, Av 19 de Abril, San Cristóbal; tel: (076) 465216, fax: 470183. For **Páramos Batallón, La Negra**, Vivero MARNR, Bailadores; tel: (075) 70029.
Yaracuy Parque Leonor Barrabás, Av Los Baños, San Felipe; tel: (051) 44553, fax: 44424.
Zulia MARNR, Cabecera Puente sobre el Lago, Sector Punta de Piedra, Maracaibo; tel: (061) 619355, fax: 619298. Also, MARNR, Av San Francisco, San Francisco, Maracaibo, (061) 619298. For **Ciénaga Juan Manuel**, Oficina MARNR, Machiques, Carretera Machiques-La Fría; tel: (063) 730955.

ENVIRONMENTAL NGOS

Environmental organisations vary from small groups to associations of over 1,000 members. What they have in common is the goal of guaranteeing a better quality of life for future generations through study and protection of Venezuela's biodiversity. A directory of these nongovernmental organisations was published by Econatura.

Amigransa Apartado 50460, Caracas 1050; tel: (02) 9876716, 9927296; Friends of the Gran Sabana contacts in Caracas are Alicia Garcia and Maria Eugenia Bustamante.
Econatura Torre B, piso 12, Centro Plaza, Av Miranda, Los Palos Grandes, Caracas; tel: (02) 2849056/8189, fax: 2847489; email: 73070.2660@compuserve.com. Priorities: research grants for undergraduate and postgraduate students, training for park guards, resource management, and conflict-solving in national parks.
Fudena Oficina 611-A, Trans 2 at Av Principal, Los Cortijos de Lourdes, Caracas 1071; tel: (02) 2382930/1761/1720, fax: 2396547; email: fudena@reacciun.ve. Priorities: community participation for better use of natural resources; protection of sea turtles and the Orinoco crocodile, releasing young into the wild. Fudena manages protected areas such as Cuare Wildlife Refuge.
Fundación Proyecto Paria Calle Ribero No 50, Río Caribe, Estado Sucre; tel: (094) 61883; (02) 7617328, fax: 7625030. Priorities: projects contributing to social welfare and conservation on the Paria Peninsula.
Provita Oficina 105, Nivel 0f-1, Edif. Catuche (entrance via USB-Edif Tajamar), Parque Central, Caracas, tel: (02) 5762828, fax: 5761579; email: provita1@telcel.net.ve. Priorities: protecting habitat and species including manatee, spectacled bear and Margarita parrot. Provita publishes *Biología de los Psitácidos en Venezuela*, and the *Libro Rojo de la Fauna Venezolana* (Red Book of endangered species), and is making an inventory of endangered flora. For information, and wildlife posters and T-shirts, write to Apartado 47552, Caracas 1041A, or send email.
Sociedad Científica Amigos del PN Henri Pittier Apartado Correos 4626, Maracay, Estado Aragua; tel/fax: (043) 453470; email: eafb@telcel.net.ve. Priority: cloudforests, their study and importance. Members made the Andrew Field nature walk through the Rancho Grande cloudforest.
Sociedad Conservacionista Audubon de Venezuela La Cuadra mall in CC Paseo Las Mercedes, opp Tamanaco Hotel, Caracas, tel: (02) 9931727/2525, fax: 9939260; email: crodner@reacciun.ve. Priorities: action and studies in defence of ecosystems such as

wetlands and the Gran Sabana; camping and hiking trips (these are not free) to mountains, plains, parks. The society publishes *Mamíferos de Venezuela*, bird lists, and *Birding in Venezuela*, and sells books on Venezuela, travel, and ecology, as well as maps and nature T-shirts. The Audubon gets so many requests for travel assistance that they operate an Ecotourism agency in their headquarters: Apartado Postal 80450, Caracas 1080A; tel: (02) 9923268, fax: 9910716; email: 104706.3053@compuserve.com.

Sociedad Conservacionista de Aragua Vereda 6 Sector 2, Urb. Caña de Azúcar, Via El Limón, Maracay, tel: (043) 831734. A watchdog for Henri Pittier and regional parks; library, environmental education programmes.

Sociedad Conservacionista de Guayana Edif San Luis-local 1, Av Las Américas, Puerto Ordaz; tel: (086) 222179, fax: 223025. Alternate energy, farming programmes among Pemón communities. Watchdog group documents mining, logging and other environmental problems in the Gran Sabana area.

Sociedad Conservacionista de Mérida (SOCOME) Apartado 241, Mérida; tel: (074) 523404, 401556, fax: 401503. Priorities are training for environmental teachers, and cloudforest conservation.

Tierra Viva Oficina 2-A, Edif Gañango, Av Bolívar at Calle Arismendi, San Joaquín, Estado Carabobo; tel/fax: (045) 51406, Caracas (02) 9512601; email: tierraviva@compuserve.com, tierraviva@cantv.net. Priorities: environmental education projects involving schools, communities and companies; creation of regional environmental centres to improve local quality of life. See also page 325.

SPECIAL INTERESTS, SPORTS

Phone contacts are given for the groups appearing below, unless they are operators already listed in *Chapter 2* under *Tour Operators*.

Bicycling

Cycling treks, either from La Paragua to Canaima, or the Morros de San Juan in Aragua, are on **Akanan Travel**'s calendar once a month, except January and March. In the Andes, consult **Montaña Tours** who use a support vehicle to carry cyclists' camping gear over the *páramos*, even crossing to Los Nevados. Mérida bicycle trails are also led by Chucho Faría, a local guide and mountain biker. He can be reached nights on tel: (074) 636491.

Birding

Read the practical *Birding in Venezuela* by Mary Lou Goodwin available from **Audubon** (see page 48), and checklists for various national parks, and head for the *monte* on your own. If needed, Audubon's ecotourism service will draw up an itinerary based on interests and season, with hotels, guides, car rental and permits. Among the local expert guides, Chris Sharpe is an English birder who may be contacted on tel/fax: (02) 749701; email: rodsha@true.net.

Caving

Venezuela has over 1,500 caves, two more than 10km long. For information on speleology and spelunking, the people to contact are the **Sociedad Venezolana de Espeleología** who do fieldwork and publish an annual scientific bulletin. They meet Wednesday nights at 20.00 in Edif Yorako (sótano), Av Caurimare opp CC Caroní, Colinas de Bello Monte, Caracas. For information, contact members Francisco Urbani, tel: 9780621, email: furbani@sagi.ucv.edu.ve; Carlos Bosque, email: carlosb@usb.ve; or Wilmer Pérez who has more English, email: chico_wilmer@yahoo.com. Write to Apartado 47334, Caracas 1041A, or phone (02) 746436, 2429001, 9868630.

Climbing

Mérida is the place to find mountaineers, rock climbers, and the **Federación Venezolana de Montañismo & Escalada**, tel/fax: (074) 521665. The federation has a calendar of courses and competitions. Member groups meet in Barquisimeto, Caracas, San Cristóbal, Trujillo and Valencia. Other mountaineers: **Grupo Andino de Rescate** (GAR), tel: (074) 444666; **Asociación Merideña de Andinismo** (AMA), tel: (074) 526806. In Caracas, **Rocademia**, a rock-climbing school, works out in La Guairita; tel: (02) 5767714; instructor Andrés Lizardo leads climbs in Mérida.

Diving

Mike Osborn, a three-star NAUI instructor in Morrocoy National Park, has been telling people for years about Venezuela's submarine world. He leads underwater photography sessions, dive tours, and open water and advanced diving courses. Ask him about Las Aves Archipelago. Address in Tucacas: **Submatur**, Calle Ayacucho No 6; tel: (042) 830082, fax: 831051.

Two recommended dive schools which also rent equipment are: **Sunset Diver Academy**, tel: (02) 2431307, (016) 6252105; and **Sesto Continente**, tel: (02) 749080, fax: 743973. The latter holds theory classes in Caracas, and practice in Los Roques where they have a dive base.

Chichiriviche Divers provide a centre for courses, tank fills, equipment rental and boat trips in the village of the same name west of Maiquetía; reservations, tel: (02) 2412318, (016) 6239551. Also in Chichiriviche the **Diver's Center** offers technical dives and classes: Quinta Diver's Center, Av Río de Janeiro, Chuao; tel: (02) 921229; email: diversc@telcel.net.ve. In Puerto La Cruz call the **Scuba Divers' Club** in the Bahía Redonda Marina; tel/fax: (081) 635401. In four intensive days you can become a PADI certified diver; instruction in wreck diving, night diving, rescue. In Mochima, Rodolfo Plaza's dive base is called **Campamento de Buceo Mochima**; he offers dive packages and an intensive course for CMAS certification, plus lodging. For information, tel/fax: (02) 9612531, (014) 9296020; email: faverola@cantv.net.

Hiking

In its seven decades the **Centro Excursionista Caracas** has trekked most of Venezuela's best trails. Walkers of many nationalities go out on Sundays, often to the Avila; they meet Saturdays at 14.30 in the park at Calle Yare by Chivacoa, San Román, Caracas. For monthly programmes, ring Olga González, (02) 2374077, or Juan Carlos Roncayolo, (014) 9196742. Another multinational group is **CECODA** – Centro de Conservación y Defensa del Ambiente (Sabas Nieves). For information about projects and hikes, call Juan Carlos Guardia: tel: (02) 2865448, fax: 2662117.

In Mérida, learn about high Andes hiking through the **Asociación Merideña de Andinismo**, tel: (074) 526886, or similar groups listed at tourism information booths. A highly knowledgeable hiker is Rosita Pavón, tel: (074) 448608/632277.

Paragliding

Interest in paragliding or parapenting rides high on great glides from mountaintops to valleys and beaches. An excellent professional school with 400 graduate students is **YCC Escuela de Parapente**, Edif Grano de Oro, Calle Bolivar, Chacao, Caracas; tel: (02) 2639357/1772, fax: 2650134; email: yccadventur@cantv.net. It offers radio-guided student flights, tandem flights, and pilot accreditation courses. Victor Delon, David Castillejos and Alejandro

González answer queries. In the Gran Sabana, Roberto MacGregor and Emilio Coraleiro in Santa Elena de Uairén make Kukenan flights; tel: (088) 951720. In Puerto La Cruz: Alex Popov, (016) 6822855.

To take advantage of Mérida's fantastic launch points, contact champion paraglider Leopoldo Turco, tel: (014) 2051460; or José Alvarrón at **Guamanchi Expeditions**, (014) 9745331. A French paraglider, Simon Vacker, tel: (074) 529565, leads crosscountry flights, 30km in tandem, 70km for radio-guided pilots; also 5- or 8-day courses. For details, see *Chapter 16*, page 363.

Sailing, yachting

Located in El Morro, Puerto La Cruz, is a young sailing school, **Escuela de Vela Américo Vespucio**, based in the Centro Marino de Oriente (CMO); tel: (081) 677011, 631819; fax: 678550, 631021; other contacts, Humberto Constanzo (014) 9803088; Maleles Jiménez (016) 6801830. The same CMO phone and fax: numbers apply for the **Asociación Náutica** which represents all the marinas, boatyards and marine services in Puerto La Cruz, Vemasca in Margarita and Navinca in Cumaná. The **Asociación Nacional de Marinos Deportivos** holds classes for yacht skippers; enquire in Caracas, tel: (02) 7629344, fax: 7629347; also in the Bahía Redonda Marina, El Morro.

Windsurfing

Local and foreign windsurfers gather on three main shores where conditions year-round are world class: Adícora, the Paraguaná Peninsula; Araya on the Araya Península; and El Yaque on Margarita's south coast. Enthusiasts are found at the local hotels and supply stores: there are eight clubs, six shops and 12 hotels in El Yaque; bilingual contacts in Adícora are Carlos Cornielles at **High Winds**, and Nicolas Hardinghaus at the **Náutico Moustacho** centre. For more information, see *Chapters 8* (Margarita), *9* (the Oriente coast) and *17* (Falcón State).

Part Two

The Guide

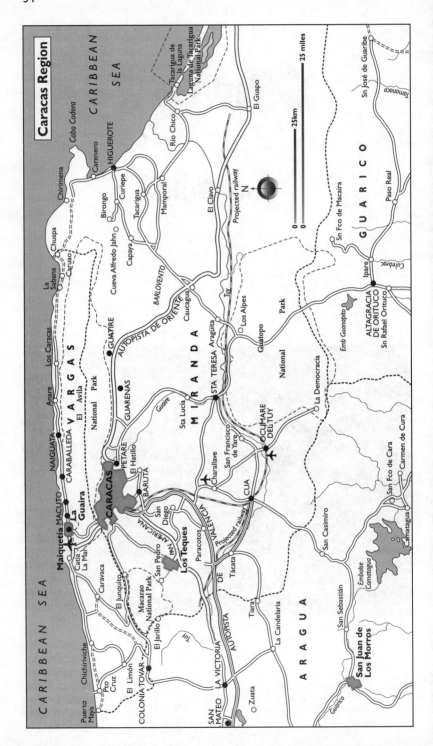

Caracas Region

Caracas

4

Some people see Caracas as a crazy sprawl, others admire its air of sophistication; some say it's not a city at all but a once-fertile valley ringed by *ranchitos*, while yet others swear by the sunny climate and superb mountains. Like most big cities – and the metropolitan area is heading for 4,500,000 inhabitants – Caracas has its good and bad points. A passing acquaintance is necessary as it is the hub of many air and road routes and the starting point for tours to beaches, plains, the Andes, nature preserves and even Amazonian jungles.

Not a place for walkers, Caracas is an inconvenient city. Its topography goes from long and narrow to high and twisty, with bottlenecks everywhere. Traffic jams are infamous. Mail is slow (never rely on letters within the city), telephones are frustrating, and bureaucracy prevents you from getting anything done in one visit. On weekends banks, travel agencies and most post offices are closed; if you want an air ticket, you must go to the airport.

MAIQUETIA AIRPORT
The airport for Caracas is in Maiquetía on the coast (30km from midtown Caracas). It is known as Maiquetía Airport (MIQ), although officially named Aeropuerto Internacional Simón Bolívar.

International terminal
The international terminal is handsome and modern. However, there are complaints about poor loudspeakers, aggressive porters, and lack of lockers for checking luggage. The lack of an information desk or central point for meeting friends can certainly complicate life. It is a good idea to decide in advance where to meet, for instance at a certain airline counter, or a booth in the main concourse such as Italcambio or Corpoturismo (see *Money* and *Hotels* overleaf).

Airport services
Catering In place of a passenger lounge there are fast-food restaurants on the upper level and a big observation terrace over the runway. Well hidden in the basement is the low-price workers' Cafetín where you can get a hot meal as well as fresh juices and espresso coffee, from 05.30 to 24.00. To find it go down in the lift one floor to the basement (Nivel 1), or take the stairs from the rear corridor opposite the Sheraton booth.

Assistance Among airport services are a round-the-clock passenger assistance number, tel: (02) 3551225/27; and medical assistance and ambulance (02) 3551331. A Metropolitan Police booth is open day and night at the east end of the main hall, tel: (02) 3551482. The airport switchboard number is (02) 3551111.

Airline counters These are located to the far east and west of the hall, separated by Customs. They are open at flight times only. Avensa has an information booth at the hall's west end, open every day, 06.00–24.00. Legally, airlines should post a list of departing passengers in a place visible to the public, two to three hours ahead of scheduled departure. This is seldom done.

Car hire Booths are in the main hall. Agencies require a credit card, a foreign or international licence, and a minimum age of 21 (25 for 4x4 vehicles). Avis, Budget, Aco and Hertz are open daily 06.00–23.00 or midnight, closing earlier on Sundays. Dollar works 08.00–21.00, Sun 14.00–21.00.

Hotels/travel Corpoturismo, the state tourism agency, is located midway in the hall, on duty daily 7.00–24.00; tel/fax: (02) 3551060/2598. It provides travel information and makes bookings for selected two- to five-star Caracas hotels, one week minimum with one night's deposit. The Macuto Sheraton, a coastal resort (35 minutes by car), has a booth open every day 09.00–24.00; tel/fax: (02) 3552219. The Eurobuilding, a luxury hotel in Caracas, also has a desk. Travel agencies are led by Turismo Maso and Viajes Union, open 05.00–24.00 except holidays.

Money Italcambio is the busiest of three exchange services and should be open 24 hours every day; tel: (02) 3551176/1081. The Banco Industrial de Venezuela teller, next to the Customs exit, is on duty 08.00–24.00 every day (no money change). Upstairs, the Banco de Venezuela opens weekdays 08.30–15.30; it has a cashpoint for Visa, MasterCard, Cirrus, SuicheB. A Banco Mercantil automatic teller serves Cirrus and Mastercard.

Telephones The area code for Maiquetía, formerly 031, is now the same as Caracas, 02. The CANTV Communications Centre on the upper level is open daily 08.00–20.00; it also offers fax and photocopy service; AT&T, MCI, SPRINT; USA DIRECT with credit card. Buy the CANTV card (*tarjeta*) for public phones here, or at automatic card dispensers (Bs5,000) in the main hall. For postal service look for Ipostel Correos in the main hall.

Taxis and buses A system of taxi tickets regulated by the airport allows you to pay (at your destination) according to a zoned map of Caracas. Rates for a *taxi autorizado* are also posted outside the central doors marked TAXI. Pay porters $1 or less for each piece of luggage; however, tipping taxi drivers is not customary. A $2–3 surcharge for night rate applies between 18.00 and 06.00. Taxis will want to charge much more for luxury hotels; to avoid this, pick a general area, not a hotel. Authorised fares run at about $18 to San Bernardino-Chacaito in Caracas, $20 to Prados del Este-Cafetal, and $22 to El Hatillo. The rate for Macuto is $8 and for Caribe/Caraballeda $10.

Por puesto vans (pay-by-the-seat cars and minibuses) go to Caracas for around $2 a seat. If you are going to Macuto or another hotel along the coast to the east, which is called the *Litoral*, you may catch a *por puesto* from the main road – during the day and avoiding rush hours. Walk from the upper airport concourse through the parking lot to reach the highway. Macuto is an old-fashioned seaside town with many economy hotels. (See *Chapter 6*, page 127.)

The blue and white airport buses charge about $1.50 Maiquetía–Caracas. They park outside the main hall. Once in Caracas many passengers switch to the metro at Gato Negro station on Av Sucre. The airport bus terminus is west of Parque Central, on Av Sur 17 beneath Avenida Bolívar; UCAM tel: (02) 5751879. For the metro, walk 1½ blocks to the Bellas Artes station on Av México. Bus service begins in Caracas at 04.00, running until 19.00. The terminus is also the starting point for some airport *por puestos*.

Departure

Even if your ticket is paid and flight confirmed, it is important to reconfirm by phone or fax. To avoid the risk of being bumped off over-sold flights, you must reconfirm more than 72 hours in advance of international flights, 24 hours before domestic flights. Request a localiser number (*localizador*) to secure reconfirmation. International passengers pay exit and airport taxes of $29; children under 15 pay $15.

To be safe, be at the airport three hours before international flights on weekends or holidays when the airport resembles the annual sales day at Marks & Spencer's. Allow 1½ hours for the drive from midtown Caracas. Be prepared for heavy traffic on weekends when beach-goers may cause blocks at tunnels (one is 2km long) on the 17km tollway or *autopista*. Torrential rains or accidents can produce serious hold-ups.

National terminal

Airport buses also serve the national terminal. This building is 300m east of the international terminal and they are linked by a free circle bus. When taking a domestic flight soon after arrival in Venezuela, it is simple to walk to the national terminal if you are not heavily loaded.

As national flights can also be overbooked, it is wise to reconfirm your flight two days ahead of departure. You are asked to be at the airport one hour before flight time but at peak periods, including long weekends, two hours are better. On domestic flights, passengers pay a small airport tax but have to stand in a special queue to do so. If you are going standby, get a standby number from the desk at the far left of the main hall.

Services include car rental, a bank, automatic tellers, coffee bars and travel agency desks such as Canaima Tours, sharing with Helicópteros del Caribe, tel: (014) 9300122, tel/fax: (02) 3552339.

Charters are widely used for business and tourism. Tour flights to destinations such as Los Roques may depart from the original one-floor *terminal viejo*.

Satellite airports

Some charter lines flying to Los Roques, Amazonas and the Llanos use private airports in the Tuy Valley, south of Caracas. The Aeropuerto de Caracas 'Oscar Machado', tel: (02) 5724321, fax: (02) 5521587, is on a flattened hill some distance from Charallave, about one hour's drive from Caracas. It has a restaurant, telephones, shops, and taxis, but no public transportation. The Aeropuerto Metropolitano in Ocumare, tel: (039) 255060, is 45km south of Caracas. No public transportation, but it is close to the town of Ocumare.

GETTING AROUND

In Caracas, north always points to Mt Avila, so set your internal compass by the mountain. Look up – the tower on the Avila is the Humboldt Hotel, linked by a cableway to the city; both remained closed in 1998. For information, tel: 7816324 (see next chapter, *Teleférico*). Local maps are posted in all metro stations. The Caracas telephone directory has a city map in sections at the back of the yellow pages. It starts in the north, reads east to west, and works south to El Hatillo.

The city's heart is the old sector around Plaza Bolívar. All streets started here in colonial times when Caracas was laid out in *cuadras*, or blocks. A fifth part of a block was called a *quinta*, the name used today for a house and garden. Streets began at the Plaza Mayor (Bolívar) where today the cathedral still divides east from west and north from south. Avenida Norte (0) goes uphill from the cathedral to the Pantheon; sometimes it's called Boulevard Simón Bolívar. Downtown addresses are commonly located by the nearest corner or *esquina*. Every corner has a name and a story. The Central Post Office is at Esquina Carmelitas named after a Carmelite convent; El Conde Hotel is on Esquina El Conde where the cacao-wealthy Counts of La Granja once lived.

Caracas marked its 400th anniversary in 1967. Today the city overflows its valley, stretching from Caricuao in the west to Petare in the east. Major arteries parallel the Guaire River that separates the city's northern and southern parts (creating notorious bottlenecks). Travellers who stay north of the Guaire will find it easy to reach scores of places to stay and eat in the Centro, in Sabana Grande (midtown), and Altamira (the east). Please see map of Caracas main roads, pages 62–3.

South of the Guaire, the districts of Las Mercedes and Chuao offer nightclubs, many good restaurants, shopping malls or *centros comercialies* (CC), office blocks, and four major hotels. Further south are residential suburbs such as Cafetal, Caurimare, San Román, Santa Fe, Prados del Este, and the townships of Baruta and El Hatillo.

Main districts
Taxis
New taxi services in Caracas include Coventaxis, equipped with digital meters and telephones enabling the client to call out; tel: 800 TAXI1, 800 81111, day and night. Dejota Services offers hourly rates and airport reception, tel: 5611715, (014) 9269699. Other Caracas numbers for 24-hour service: Astrala 818138/5672, Taxi Movil 5770922/3344, Taxitour 7939744, Taxiven 9850296, Teletaxi 7529122/4146, Unitaxi 7612513/6948, Utac 5750053/1231.

Buses
The bus system in Caracas was privatised by default years ago as municipal buses fell into disrepair, and owner-operated *por puesto* cars covered their routes. These cars, in which you pay by the seat (place or *puesto*), have grown into efficient minibuses. Each line's route is painted on the side of the bus, as 'Carmelitas–Petare', 'El Silencio vía Autopista'. A list of fares is posted near the driver, who may collect as the passenger gets off, or on, if the person has the fare ready. Short rides are less than Bs200 ($0.40), while extra-urban routes are double. There are no tickets or conductors, and you may get on and off by the same front door. Buses do use bus stops, although people will board a bus at any traffic light. And there's the rub: traffic jams are frequent, and at rush hour the bus queues are horribly long. Then you wish you were on the metro.

There is no map of city bus routes, except for the Metrobus (see below).

The metro
The efficient underground system, South America's longest and still growing, is the saviour of Caracas, making up for chaos above ground (no smoking, please, and officially no suitcases). It's fast, and it makes people smile, restoring their faith that something works. Also it makes crossing the city, 40km from Propatria in the west to Palo Verde in the east, fun and fast. The first eight stations of Line 1 opened in 1983; Line 2 (Caricuao–El Silencio) was completed in 1988 and Line 3 (Plaza Venezuela–El Valle) in 1994. Work has begun on the first section of Line 4, paralleling Line 1 for 5.5km between Capuchinos and Plaza Venezuela. Target date for completion is 2002. The second half of Line 4 will continue east to Parque del Este by way of Bello Monte, Las Mercedes and Chuao.

The metro operates daily 05.30–23.00. Stations are clean and well signposted with area and route maps. There are shops and occasional art shows – but no public toilets. For metro-linked cultural events and other information, contact CAMETRO, Edif Miranda B-7, Multicentro Empresarial del Este, Chacao, Caracas 1060 (public relations, tel: 2082746/2630).

A *multiviaje* ticket is good for ten rides anywhere. Keep your ticket after going through the turnstile because you need it to get out. When you are buying ask about transfers, *boletos integrados*, which cover four stations plus a **metrobus** ride. These buses link the subway with outlying districts such as San Bernardino, Cafetal, El Hatillo, even Guarenas.

Warning People riding the metro escalators have had necklaces and wallets taken. A frequent ruse involves two men, one ahead who trips or bends down in front of the victim, the other snatching the valuables.

EXPLORING CARACAS BY METRO
Colonial history, museums, theatres, cafés, shops and parks are all reached by Line 1 of the metro. With a few exceptions, this is the best way to see the city's points of interest. Museums (and some parks) close for maintenance on Mondays. Exceptions to this are the Boulton History Museum, the Concejo Municipal, and the Botanical Gardens.

Historical sights
Start at the **Capitolio station** and walk to places famous as settings of Simón Bolívar's birth, boyhood and burial. The houses where Bolívar lived reveal an era whose traces have all but vanished in Caracas. This intense, passionate young man, who gave his ideals, energies, fortune and ultimately his health to his country, still means a great deal to Venezuelans. A town is not a town until it has a Plaza Bolívar, as you will inevitably see.

The Capitol
First, enter the restored Capitol; show your passport to guards at the west gate. Its original dome, brought from Belgium in 1891, was replaced in the 1960s by a cupola of Venezuelan aluminium. Visitors are shown the ceremonial Salón Elíptico. This oval hall, where the Declaration of Independence lives in a locked casket, is noted for Tovar y Tovar's canvases of the Battles of Carabobo, Junín and Boyacá, painted in Paris and later glued in place. The next hall has a huge triptych by Tito Salas showing Bolívar on Monte Sacro, crossing the Andes, and on his deathbed. When Congress is in session you may request permission to visit the chambers of Deputies and the Senate facing Avenida Universidad. These '*hemiciclos*' were built in 1874 in a record 114 days. The Capitol's ironwork was brought from England.

Souvenir and watch shops crowd along the pedestrian pavement north of the Capitolio; you can get a $5 'unisex' haircut in the glass-roofed Pasaje Capitolio which goes through to the next street. (If you detour here, you will arrive in two blocks at the Correos de Carmelitas post office on Av Urdaneta, once the splendid residence of the Counts of Tovar. Opposite is the Banco Central de Venezuela which displays Bolívar's sword and jewels, and Venezuelan coins dating from the 16th century. The 1880s Miraflores Palace housing the President's office is west on Av Urdaneta. Photographs are not permitted.)

Plaza Bolívar
Plaza Bolívar, or the Plaza Mayor as it was in colonial days, was laid out by Spanish founder Diego de Losada. Every year Caracas celebrates its founding date, July 27

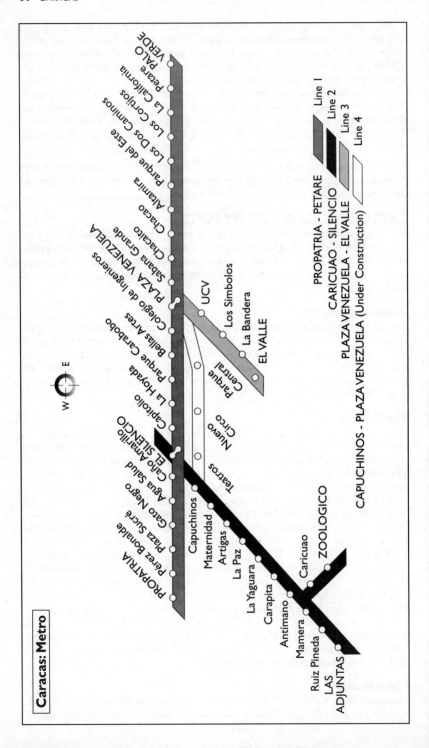

Caracas: Metro

1567, with international festivals of theatre and music. But not in the plaza; that's for the Martial Band concerts, a tradition here since 1864. The band is martial in name only, the players wear T-shirts for Sunday concerts at 5pm. The shady square, today almost domestic with its habitués, children, pigeons and squirrels (and sometimes sloths), had many guises before it became Plaza Bolívar in 1883. It was the Plaza de Armas where rebels were hanged, later a marketplace, a bullfight plaza, and in republican times the Plaza La Constitución. The famous equestrian statue of Bolívar by Adam Tadolini is a copy of one in Lima. It was cast in Munich and shipped in pieces, but the brig foundered in Los Roques and the boxes had to be fished out of the sea. The statue was finally unveiled in November 1874 by President A Guzmán Blanco who had a 'time box' containing coins, documents and a map sealed into its base.

Anticlockwise around the Plaza are: north, the **Federal District Government House**, where occasional art exhibits are open to the public; west, the **Casa Amarilla**, seat of the Foreign Ministry, once infamous as a 17th-century royal prison and later a presidential residence; southwest corner, **Edificio La Francia**, nine floors of wholesale and retail jewellers offering great buys in gold and silver jewellery sold by the gramme; south, the **Concejo Municipal**, or Town Council, tel: 5459920. It houses the Museum of Caracas, Raul Santana's miniatures of 1930s daily scenes, and paintings by Emilio Boggio. Free Sunday concerts are given in the Concejo's Patio de Los Leones. Ask to see the Concejo's handsomely restored Santa Rosa Chapel, famous as the 'cradle of Independence' because Congress declared Independence here on July 5 1811. The chapel served as seminary in the 17th century and the University of Caracas in the 18th century.

The cathedral

The Caracas Cathedral, on the east of Plaza Bolívar, has had many lives since the city was founded. It began as a mud-walled chapel dedicated to St James or Santiago, patron saint of Spain and Caracas. The church that replaced it was destroyed by earthquake in 1641, rebuilt with a belltower but again damaged by the 'quakes of 1766 and 1812. After this the belltower was left as it is today without the top level. Inside you can see amazing treasures gathered by the Cathedral, not the least being various gilded altars, paintings by Rubens (*Resurrection*), Murillo (*Presentation of the Virgin*) and Michelena, whose *Last Supper* was his unfinished last work. There are eight elaborate side crypts with altars. That of the Bolívar family holds marble tombs of Bolívar's Spanish bride who died when Simón was 18 (he never remarried), his father who died when Simón was two and a half, and his mother who died when he was nine.

Be sure to visit the **Museo Sacro** beside the Cathedral, open Tue–Sun 10.00–17.00; there's a small fee. Once an episcopal college, it was built over a church cemetery in 1884 to sidestep a law banning seminaries. Stoop through massive walls to the dark ecclesiastic gaol; the osarium behind has been excavated 2.5m deep, and 12 sealed niches hold remains of early church leaders. Beyond a green patio the little Café Sacro serves elegant sandwich & salad lunches Tuesday to Friday. Exhibitions are held in the gallery, and recitals are given every Saturday or Sunday at 11.30; also at 16.00, often free. A gift shop, El Vitral de Caracas, gives on to the plaza.

Bolívar's tomb and birthplace

Bolívar's remains, brought from Colombia where he died penniless in 1830, were buried in the cathedral crypt (after an emotional funeral, see below, *Iglesia de San Francisco*). Walk six blocks north to see the **National Pantheon**, where his remains were enshrined in 1876. Every 25 years the President of the Republic

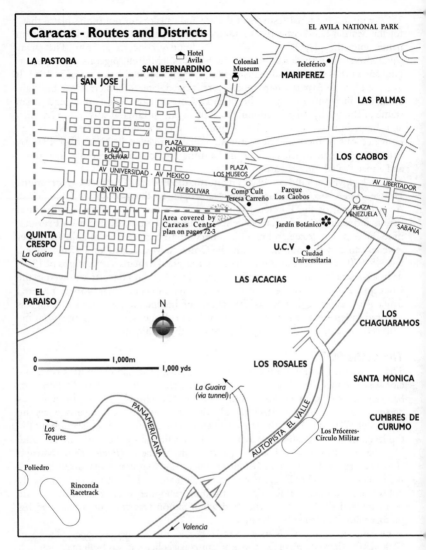

Caracas - Routes and Districts

EL AVILA NATIONAL PARK

LA PASTORA

Hotel Avila
SAN BERNARDINO

Colonial Museum

Teleférico
MARIPEREZ

SAN JOSE

LAS PALMAS

PLAZA CANDELARIA

PLAZA BOLIVAR

LOS CAOBOS

AV UNIVERSIDAD - AV MEXICO

PLAZA LOS MUSEOS

AV LIBERTADOR

CENTRO

AV BOLIVAR

Comp Cult Teresa Carreño

Parque Los Caobos

PLAZA VENEZUELA

Area covered by Caracas Centre plan on pages 72-3

Jardín Botánico

SABANA

QUINTA CRESPO
La Guaira

U.C.V
Ciudad Universitaria

EL PARAISO

LAS ACACIAS

N

LOS CHAGUARAMOS

0 ———— 1,000m
0 ———— 1,000 yds

LOS ROSALES

SANTA MONICA

La Guaira (via tunnel)

PANAMERICANA

AUTOPISTA EL VALLE

CUMBRES DE CURUMO

Los Teques

Los Próceres-Círculo Militar

Poliedro

Rinconda Racetrack

Valencia

opens the casket below the monument by Pietro Tenerani to verify that the Liberator's remains are undisturbed. One of the five people buried with Bolívar in the central nave is his Irish aide-de-camp, Daniel O'Leary. Ceiling paintings are by Tito Salas. In all, 138 founding fathers and national figures are interred in the Pantheon. Two empty tombs await the remains of Francisco de Miranda who died in a Spanish prison and Antonio José de Sucre, assassinated in Colombia. Tradition has it that when the original church (completed the year of Bolívar's birth) was destroyed in the 1812 earthquake, part of a pillar rolled downhill to the Plaza where, in smashing the gallows, it gave the revolutionaries a moral boost.

Around the Pantheon's plaza, called the Foro del Libertador, are: the restored 19th-century **Casa de Bellard** and colonial **Casa Santaella** housing a tiny crafts shop, La Tiendita, tel: 5647490, open Mon–Fri 14.00–17.00, weekends

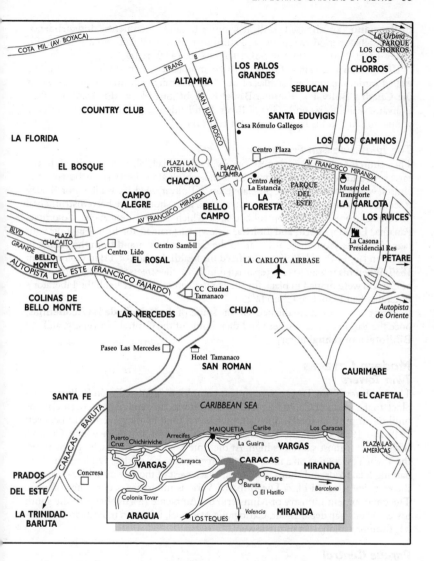

09.00–13.00; the concrete **National Archives** building, and, south, the **Biblioteca Nacional**, headquarters of the national library system. The Hemeroteca, tel: 5641215, or periodicals collection, has a well used reading room, open Mon–Sat 09.00–16.45, where you can consult magazines from around the world... Africa, art, astronomy... the first newspaper printed in Venezuela (1808), even the world's smallest newspaper according to Guinness, the thumbnail *Colosso* published in Altagracia de Orituco. The gallery of the Centro de Fotografía is also under the library roof; hours are Mon–Fri 09.00–16.30.

The **Casa Natal** on Plaza El Venezolano, Esquina San Jacinto, is the house where Simón Bolívar was born on July 24 1783, fourth child of a patrician couple. Reconstructed after neglect by later owners, the Casa Natal is a tourist 'must', a block east and south of Plaza Bolívar. Here, and next door at the **Museo**

Bolivariano, are housed Bolívar's uniform and documents, Independence memorabilia, period weapons and furniture; tel: 5459828. Hours: Mon–Fri 09.00–12.00, 14.00–17.00; Sat–Sun 10.00–13.00, 14.00–17.00.

(If you plan a detour to Quinta Crespo another day, visit at the same time the walled gardens, patios and stables of the Bolívar family's summer home known as the **Cuadra Bolívar** at Esquina Bárcenas, eight long blocks due south of Plaza Bolívar. Near the erstwhile Guaire River, farmlands and riding paths once offered young Simón and his friends space for conspiracy.)

The Iglesia de San Francisco
This church, opposite Congress on Av Universidad, also figures in Bolívar's career. Founded as a monastery in 1575 and rebuilt after the 1641 earthquake, the church was the setting for the proclamation of Bolívar, aged 30, as Liberator. Today it seems miraculous that so young and slight a man should have been instrumental in freeing from Spanish control the area which is now Venezuela, Colombia, Panama, Ecuador, Peru, and Bolivia, a new state named for him. Fighting with ragged patriots, from the Caribbean to the Chilean border and from the Pacific to the boundary of Brazil, Bolívar sacrificed his health; he died of TB in Colombia in 1830. When his remains were repatriated in 1842, the streets, houses and churches of Caracas were draped in black for the biggest ceremony ever held: the Liberator's funeral at San Francisco Church.

Next to the church are the neo-Gothic spires of the **Palacio de las Academias**, once the San Francisco convent and then home of the Central University, and the **Biblioteca** or central library.

Modern Caracas
Twin Towers
The 30-storey Twin Tower government complex or Centro Simón Bolívar rises a block to the south of Capitolio metro station. It was the symbol of modern Caracas until outstripped by the Parque Central towers. Built by the government between 1949 and 1958, the Twin Towers spelled the end of an era in which Caracas' skyline was at most six floors high. At the time South America's tallest structures, the Twin Towers rest on a massive reinforced quake-proof slab. Underground are parking lots, roads and shops. The open space west of the towers is Plaza Caracas; the east side is called Plaza Diego Ibarra. Various ministries occupy the complex. The environment ministry or Ministerio del Ambiente (MARNR) is in the south tower. Their map department, Cartografía Nacional, is located in Edificio Camejo-p1, Esquina Colón, east of the towers.

Parque Central
This is a concrete enclave where, it was advertised, 'nothing resembles the past'. Metro station **Bellas Artes**. You may not be attracted to the idea of seven 44-storey condominiums, plus two 56-storey towers, but the development is undeniably conspicuous. (In contrast, the hills directly to the south are covered with *ranchitos* – some rented, some better built than others. Nearly half of all Caraqueños live in precarious conditions of hygiene and security in such districts called *barrios*.) The government-built complex, started in 1970 and finished in 1986, has a daily traffic of some 60,000 people in its schools, supermarkets, cinema, convention halls, offices and five museums, of which the **Museo de Arte Contemporáneo** and **Museo del Niño** (see below) are of real importance. Other museums include: Museo del Teclado (tel: 5720713), a recital hall and collection of keyboard instruments dating from the 17th century, in Edif Tacagua-mezz, west of the Children's Museum;

Museo Audiovisual, mainly a video library with booths for projections in Edif Catuche, Nivel Bolívar; and the Museo Criminológico, tel: 5719001, a small showcase of weapons and forgeries, run by the Centre of Criminological Studies of Simón Bolívar University, Edif Tajamar, Level Oficina 1, Room 118.

Parque Central's glass-sided octagonal towers are the tallest in the country. Among government offices in the East Tower is the Agriculture Ministry (MAC), tel: 5090111/21, responsible for sport fishing permits, 10th floor, tel: 5090276/375. The penthouse is occupied by the Ministry of Transport and Communications. The MTC has an information service, tel: 5091711; road condition enquiries, tel: 5091601. In the West Tower are: Cordiplan, the Mines and Energy Ministry with a library on the 2nd floor, tel: 5075080, and Corpoturismo, information tel: 5749553/3091, library 5078796. To get permission to photograph the view from Mindur's 53rd floor mirador, ask at the Centro Simón Bolívar's office in Sótano 1.

Metro art on Line 1

The metro is a showcase for work by many of Venezuela's leading artists. You can combine culture and communications along Line 1 where murals, stained glass windows and sculptures of many schools enliven the stations. Some stations stage exhibitions and concerts.

If you are travelling west from the centre, note Marisol Escobar's bronze tribute to the hero of tangos in her 'Monument to Gardel' in the **Caño Amarillo** station. Every year on June 24, the day he died in 1935, admirers of Carlos Gardel give a tango festival in his honour here. Quinta Santa Inés, declared a National Monument as the 1884 residence of president Joaquín Crespo, is being restored here by the Instituto de Patrimonio Cultural. It was built in 1884 near the terminus of the Gran Ferrocarril de Venezuela linking Caracas and La Guaira.

A giant steel serpent and hummingbird by a team of artists, Sanabria, Silvestro and Zamalloa, grabs attention outside the **Gato Negro** station. This is the station for visiting the Parque del Oeste and its Jacobo Borges Art Museum and sculpture garden. Striking an apparently impossible balance near Catia's Plaza Sucre station in Catia is Rafael Barrios' 'Levitation', a tower of five iron cubes. The Catia Boulevard and **Plaza Sucre**, like the Sabana Grande Boulevard, are urban renewal gifts from the Metro company to the pedestrians of Caracas.

La Hoyada station has an exhibition hall for art and orchid shows. Among works commissioned for this station is a stained glass window by Mercedes Pardo. On a lower plaza stands one of Francisco Narváez' last works in Cumarebo stone blocks. This stop is linked by a passage under Fuerzas Armadas Avenue, allowing you to walk south to the Nuevo Circo Bull Ring. Since 1919 it has been the scenario for bullfights and circuses, ice skating, boxing, folklore and political events. Line 4 of the metro is to stop here. There is a museum nearby on Parque Vargas: the Carlos Cruz-Diez Museum of Prints and Design, tel: 5727876, fax: 5721476.

At the **Parque Carabobo** station, a ceramic bas relief by Rita Daini, portraying 'Caraqueños in the Metro', makes a gentle comment at the station's entrance. From this stop it is an easy walk north to Plaza La Candelaria. The tomb and chapel of saintly doctor José Gregorio Hernández, whose good works treating the poor ended in one of Caracas' early traffic fatalities in 1919, draws many visitors to the Iglesia de La Candelaria. The parish has long been home to Basques, Canary Islanders and Galicians. It is famous for small, crowded Spanish restaurants and tasca bars where beer flows freely. As lively as this area is by day, it has a reputation of being unsafe at night.

Two stops further east, at **Colegio de Ingenieros** station, Lya Bermúdez' scarlet 'bat wings' loom over the platform. East again, at **Chacaito**, are Soto's

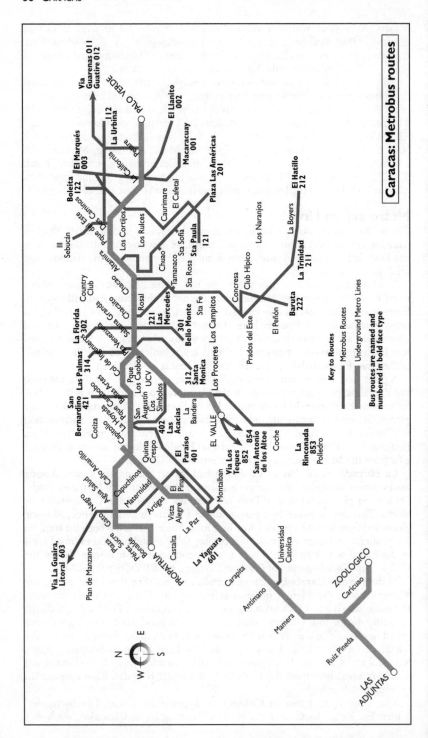

Caracas: Metrobus routes

Key to Routes

━━━ Metrobus Routes

━━━ Underground Metro Lines

Bus routes are named and
numbered in bold face type

'Vibrant Cubes' of suspended blue and black tubes, Teresa Casanova's steel boxes and, underground, Beatriz Blanco's lively 'Human Silhouettes'.

Museums and galleries

Get off at the **Bellas Artes** station for the cultural area called **Plaza Los Museos** (Plaza Morelos): Museums of Fine Arts and Sciences, National Gallery, the Ateneo Theatre, Teresa Carreño Cultural Complex, Hilton Hotel, and Parque Central, the Sofía Imber Museum of Contemporary Art. Except where noted, museums are open Tue–Fri 09.00 and Sat–Sun 10.00–17.00.

The **Museo de Arte Contemporáneo Sofía Imber** (Museum of Contemporary Art), tel: 5771659, is located at the northeast corner of Parque Central beside the Anauco Hilton. MACCSI displays some of the continent's finest exhibitions (Tue–Sun 10.00–18.00). Its permanent collection includes Botero's 2m fat cat in bronze, and works by Maillol, Calder, Moore, Picasso, Léger and many top-notch Venezuelans including Gego, Marisol and Soto (whose kinetic pieces are also found in the nearby Estudio 1, Edif Mohedano, Nivel Lecuna). MACCSI also has an excellent reference library of art books and audiovisuals, a classy gift shop in Sótano 1, and a small restaurant in the main entrance garden.

The **Museo de los Niños** (Children's Museum), tel: 5733434/4112, has a tri-colour building all of its own within Parque Central. This is a popular hands-on museum of fun and learning for children (over six years of age), often full at holiday time. Entrance is $1 for children, $4 adults; hours Wed–Sun 09.00–12.00, 14.00–17.00.

Facing the circular Plaza de los Museos at the entrance to Los Caobos Park (just east of the Caracas Hilton) is the neoclassical **Museo de Ciencias Naturales** or Natural History Museum, tel: 5775786, which puts on imaginative new exhibits with computer-animated displays ($1.00). Across the plaza is the **Galería de Arte Nacional**, tel: 5781818. Well-lighted rooms surround a green patio and pool where recitals are held on Sunday afternoons. The Cinemateca Nacional is here, too. The National Gallery was designed by Carlos Raul Villanueva, a Venezuelan architect whose career began in the 1930s with this museum and ended in 1976 with the adjacent four-storey **Museo de Bellas Artes**, tel: 5711819. The Fine Arts Museum is actually in Los Caobos Park; in the rear is a pleasant sculpture garden.

The Fundación John Boulton, tel: (02) 5631838, 5644366, runs a fine, small **Museo de Historia** and library on the 11th floor of Torre El Chorro at the southwest corner of Esquina El Chorro, Av Universidad. Metro station **La Hoyada**. Collected by the family of British merchant John Boulton (1805–75) are rare china, portraits, and 19th-century Venezuelan documents, including books owned or read by Bolívar. Don't miss engravings of Liberator-inspired fashions in Europe, a double-tiered cape, *pantalon americaine* tights, and the 'Bolívar hat'. Mon–Fri 08.30–11.30, 13.30–16.30.

A short ride north of the Bellas Artes station by taxi or metrobus is the **Museo de Arte Colonial**, or Quinta Anauco, tel: 514256, fax: 518517. One of Caracas' most enjoyable museums, the colonial house dating from 1797 is located on Av Panteón in San Bernardino. Explore the Marquis of Toro's gracious residence, kitchen, stables and even a bath fed by a stream. Some evening recitals and Christmas carols are presented free. Tue–Sat 09.00–11.30, 14.00–16.30; Sun 10.00–17.00; small admission charge. Visits are guided and you must arrive early.

The **Transport Museum**, tel: 2371261, is reached by a pedestrian bridge from Parque del Este's east parking lot. Its collection of railroad steam engines, old cars and planes opens to the public on weekends 09.00–17.00, other days for schools. Metro: Parque del Este. Further east, Petare station is the stop for the Petare Museum of Popular Art and the Galería Tito Sala – see page 73.

Caracas - Parque Central

Theatres, cinemas, concert halls

In the Bellas Artes vicinity, opposite the Caracas Hilton, there is a splendid performing arts centre, the **Teresa Carreño Cultural Complex**, tel: 5749033/44; box office 800 67372; advance reservations, Tickexpress, tel: 2062951/52. The Sala Ríos Reyna seats 2,500 and has a full calendar of concerts, opera and ballet. The Venezuelan Symphony Orchestra plays here on Saturdays at 10.00, and the José Félix Ribas Philharmonic on Sundays at 11.00. Next door, the **Ateneo de Caracas**, tel: 5734400/4600, houses a concert hall, Rajatabla Theatre, art gallery, cinema, library, bookshop and cafeteria.

The theatre of the **Casa del Artista**, tel: 5747996, 5734948, in Quebrada Honda is a short walk from the Plaza de Museos, by way of Av Libertador; take the first right. You pass an extraordinary mosque with a concrete minaret. It is named after a Saudi Arabian sheik, Ibrahim Al Ibrahim, who came for the 1993 opening. The host was President Carlos Andrés Pérez whose idea it was to donate the land.

The area's two art cinemas are: the **Sala Margot Benacerraf** at the Ateneo, and the **Cinemateca Nacional**, tel: 5761491, in the Galería de Arte Nacional, Tue–Sun at 18.30 and 21.00; children's films on Sunday at 11.00.

Midtown: university, cafés, shops

Sixty years ago Caracas ended at the coffee hacienda of Los Caobos, now a popular park (although not safe at lonely times or places according to joggers who have been mugged). In the days when Sabana Grande was a 'big savannah' used for horse racing, a railway linked Caracas with the eastern villages of Chacao and Petare.

Today, you approach on the metro by way of the **Colegio de Ingenieros** station. Outside, a Peruvian food fair sets up stalls of *anticuchos* and *ceviche* on Sundays by the little Church of Santa Rosa. At the station's north exit on Av Libertador, the telephone company, CANTV, has an art gallery and theatre open to the public. Around the corner west of CANTV, the large public **Guaicaipuro Market** overflows on surrounding streets every Tuesday, Thursday and Saturday morning. Fresh fruit, vegetables, fish, Chinese slippers, shirts...

The circular Plaza Venezuela and its fountain which mark midtown are actually located three blocks west of the metro station. Artist Carlos Cruz Diez was happy to use the plaza's large ventilation duct for one of his striped 'Fisicromías'. You can't miss Alejandro Otero's 16m-high steel windsails, or the blue and white bars of a Jesús Soto rig suspended from Torre Capriles.

Cross over the *autopista* bridge from Plaza Venezuela to the **Jardín Botánico**, on the right before the university gates. Like the university, the 150-acre botanical gardens once belonged to Hacienda Ibarra. You will find lilies, cacti, orchids, and 265 species of palms growing here. Open Mondays, and every day, 08.00–17.00 (free). There is a Botanical Institute, tel: 6053981, with a large herbarium.

The **Central University of Venezuela** occupies a large campus of 26 buildings called the Ciudad Universitaria (in which police are not allowed). Saunter with some of the 62,000 students, or go to a concert at the 3,000-seat Aula Magna where the Municipal Symphony Orchestra plays every Sunday when the UCV is in session. Its ceiling has acoustic clouds by Alexander Calder, great friend of architect Carlos Raúl Villanueva. The university city is compared with Brasilia as unique in Latin America for its integration of architecture with art – some sixty frescos, murals, stained glass windows and sculptures. Works by Léger, Arp, Laurens, Kandinsky and Pevsner are accompanied by Venezuela's Narváez, Soto, Otero, Manaure and Poléo.

The **Plaza Venezuela** metro station marks the west end of the pedestrian haven called Boulevard de Sabana Grande (also Av Abraham Lincoln). Watch Caracas go by... the shoppers, salesmen, office girls, urchins, chess players, hookers... and motorcycle cops. Day and night the boulevard is a stage to sidewalk café devotees. Open till 02.00, the Gran Café is king of cappuccino coffee. Its marquee, alongside several competitors, is near the old Cine Radio City.

The district known as **Sabana Grande** encompasses three stations, Plaza Venezuela, Sabana Grande and Chacaito, serving an area famous for good, reasonable restaurants and hotels. Explore Av Solano López for Italian pasta houses and Spanish tascas. As many as 20 moderate hotels are located between Av Las Acacias in the west and Las Delicias de Sabana Grande/Chacaito in the east.

The boulevard ends in Chacaito at the large paved Plaza Brión. Here the Centro Comercial Chacaito has a supermarket, nightclub, underground cinemas, English books at Librería Lectura, French books at La France, art and computer supplies. You can get fast colour developing at Foto Print beside the Papagallo's tables.

Within walking distance of Chacaito are the upscale dining and clubbing districts of El Rosal and Las Mercedes. At the first traffic light on Av Miranda, turn south. On your left, pricey restaurants line Av Tamanaco, the first street in El Rosal. On your right are popular places such as McDonald's, Arepas Misia Jacinta, and several *criollo* restaurants west on Av Pichincha. For Las Mercedes, continue under the *autopista*; restaurants line most of the streets leading to the Rio Guaire (not a nice river but wild parrots roost in trees on its banks). Paseo Las Mercedes shopping centre and the Tamanaco Hotel are at the end of Avenida Las Mercedes.

East Caracas – Parque del Este, Petare

The Caracas Country Club starts where Chacaito (and the Federal District) ends; in the 1930s its huge trees and golf links really were in the country. Today, they provide some relief from East Caracas' office blocks. The metro tunnels below Av Miranda to **Chacao** station. Walk north and east three blocks to the Church of San José and square where the former village of Chacao, named after an Indian warrior, was founded in 1768 as the centre of plantations. At first the crops were wheat and sugarcane. Then the owners of Hacienda Blandín and Hacienda La Floresta introduced coffee, and together drank the first cup of home brew in Venezuela in 1786. From that date, coffee went on to become an important export crop.

Chacao's shops offer economical shoes, jeans and shirts, and on Thursday mornings the Chacao market comes to life on Calle Cecilio Acosta. Chacao is also the station for the Metro offices: 7th floor, Edificio Miranda-B, Centro Empresarial del Este, Av Miranda.

Caracas' super shopping complex, the **Centro Sambil**, was opened in 1998. From the Chacao metro station, west exit, walk south a block on Calle Elice to Av Libertador; turn left 1½ blocks. Touted as Latin America's largest shopping-plus-recreation mall, its 540 shops and banks are certainly the height of fashion and, what's more, they work every day until 21.00 including Sundays and holidays. In addition there are cinemas, bowling lanes, an art museum, aquarium with sharks, a space simulator and robotland – and the branch of an art museum, **Museo Jacobo Borges**.

From the next station, **Altamira**, walk two blocks up Av Luis Roche for the cultural centre called **Casa de Rómulo Gallegos** (CELARG), tel: 2852990/2721. There is a busy programme of art exhibitions, films and lectures, as well as a top notch restaurant, Vizio's. A few steps from Plaza Altamira is the **Centro de Arte La Estancia**, tel: 2086945/6622, on the south side of Av Miranda opposite 1st Avenue of Los Palos Grandes. The large walled property was part of Hacienda La Floresta, a late 18th-century plantation where the first coffee was grown in Venezuela (together with Hacienda Blandín). Bought by Petróleos de Venezuela, the restored house was opened in 1995 as an exhibition and information centre specialising in design. The gardens, as lovely as ever, have a small restaurant. For information and multi-lingual guides, tel: 2086922/45; Tue–Sun 09.00–16.00.

Record, photo and gift shops and a supermarket occupy three floors of the big Centro Plaza mall on Av Miranda, northeast of La Estancia. On the mezzanine there is a CANTV Telecommunications Centre, open Mon–Sat 08.00–20.00. You can make overseas calls there, send and receive faxes and buy telephone cards.

WILD AND ESCAPED PARROTS ADOPT CARACAS

If parrots like Caracas, all is not lost. Every time a band of large, loud yellow-headed parrots crosses the eastern sky early in the morning, their squawks and trills recall the rivers and forests of Amazonas. That's where this *Amazona* genus belongs, not in the capital where space is haggled over by some four million people.

Many parrots, including foreign species and other escapees from houses, have found their niche in Caracas. Watch for the Amazon parrots at dusk when, two by two, flocks of 30 or more settle for the night in Las Mercedes in trees lining the Guaire River, little more than a sewer. After all, the trees are not natives either; many are African tulip trees.

A small, brilliant green cloud settles in a *mamón* tree at a busy corner in Las Mercedes – it is a flock of tiny parrotlets (*Forpus passerinus*), the kind people used to sell in the market. A macaw screeches above a construction site – the big red bird is perched on a crane, calling for its mate. In San Bernardino, late every afternoon a pair of green macaws descends by an apartment block to roost in royal palms.

During the day these parrots fly off to feed on the Avila range or in Parque del Este where more parrots live. In season, mango trees and palms provide them with food in Caracas. Not all the parrots are naturalised. Some are migratory, like the maroon-faced parakeets (*Pyrrhura emma*) which visit when palm nuts are ripe, and the brown-throated parakeets (*Aratinga pertinax*) which may flock by on their way to a greener part of the range. These parakeets hollow out nests in large termite mounds on trees, cohabiting peacefully with the insects.

(Metrobuses leave from the Altamira station, north side, for the districts of Chuao and Cafetal, stopping at the pricey shopping complex called Centro Ciudad Comercial Tamanaco. The British Embassy is in Torre Las Mercedes nearby. The CCCT has a hotel, offices, banks, cinemas, and supermarket.)

Parque del Este, at the station of the same name, is by far the city's greatest park. The gates open at 05.30 for joggers and at 08.00 for the public; closing whistle at 17.30. It's officially Parque Rómulo Betancourt after the president who in 1961 asked Brazilian landscape architect Roberto Burle Marx to transform this old coffee hacienda. The 200 acres of walks, lawns and woods brim with people on Sundays, and are closed on Mondays for clean-up (but open to joggers). Storks, egrets, parrots and sloths breed freely here. There is a monkey island, a giant otter pool, a snake house, jaguar pit, anaconda moat, aviary and a lagoon with scarlet ibis. There is a replica of Columbus' ship, the *Santa María*, an acoustic shell for outdoor shows, and the **Humboldt Planetarium**, tel: 2649198. The Navy runs sky programmes on Saturday and Sunday at 13.00, 14.00, 15.00. The stars are beamed by a 3-ton mechanical Zeiss machine with 200 separate projectors, in fact a 1952 classic bought by dictator Marcos Pérez Jiménez. Run by the Navy, night courses are given in astronomy and navigation. Adjoining the **Transport Museum** (see page 69) are the administrative headquarters of the Instituto Nacional de Parques.

South of Los Dos Caminos station, at the foot of Av Principal La Carlota, is **La Casona**, the presidential residence. High walls screen from sight the converted 18th-century plantation house. It was the centre of a sugar hacienda owned by the Marquis of Mijares which ran from La Carlota airport to part of Los Dos Caminos. La Casona is open to guided visits on Wednesdays. Ring Protocol for reservations, tel: 2867822; no children under nine. You are shown part of the seven gardens, large art collection and antiques.

The metro passes under the drab industrial zones of Los Ruices, Los Cortijos and Boleita to reach La California district and its big shopping centre, Unicentro El Marqués. The next station is **Petare**, last stop but one on Line 1. Leave the Caracas sprawl behind as you walk up the hill crowned by **old Petare**, a village founded in 1621. For a change its plaza is not named Bolívar but Plaza Sucre. The Town Council is on the north side. The handsomely restored pink church is called **Dulce Nombre de Jesús**; it was built in 1760. Signs point you to a beautiful colonial house, once the home of patriot Lino de Clemente, Bolívar's uncle, and now the **Petare Museum of Popular Art** on Calle Lino de Clemente; open 10.00–18.00 except Mondays. The museum's concerts and art exhibitions are well attended. The **Galería Tito Salas** is between Clemente and Guanche, open Tue–Fri 09.00–16.00, Sat–Sun 11.00–15.00; evening films. Also on Lino de Clemente are the small **Cesar Rengifo Theatre** and the **Lira Cultural Centre**.

In Petare, a statue of the Cristo de la Salud heads a religious festival on the last Sunday in September, a tradition begun in 1868. In that year, people were struck by yellow fever and turned for help to Christ on the Cross; miraculously the plague ended.

Caricuao Zoo

Z for zoo adds a postscript to this tour by metro. To reach the Caricuao Zoo you have to go to the opposite end of Caracas on Line 2. In the zoo's 1,200 acres live many native animals and birds without bars, some in mixed groups. Deer wander through woods and overhead are spider and howler monkeys. Wading birds, free to come and go, enjoy ponds. There is an African section with giraffes and rhinos, too. Hours Tue–Sun 09.00–16.30.

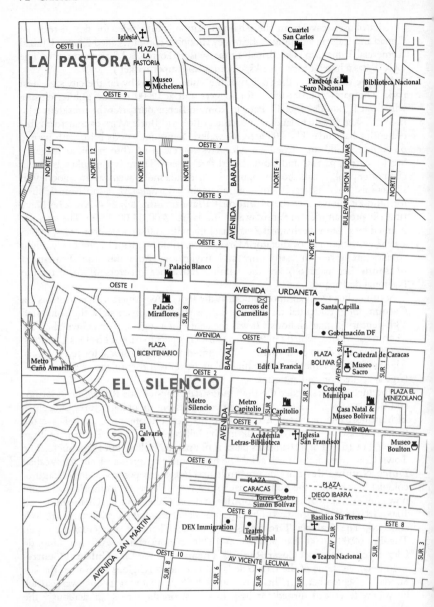

WHERE TO STAY

The area telephone code for Caracas is (02)

Upper range

Hotel rates vary enormously, with international chains charging US$200 to $300 a night, nearly double the rate of expensive local hotels. During low business periods such as Christmas and Easter, however, some may promote weekends at half price. Caracas boasts four new luxury hotels with five-star services: multiple restaurants, nightclubs, pools and gym, shops, fax/computer

Caracas Centre - El Centro

rental, business centre and convention facilities. Some, like the Eurobuilding, have an adjoining tower of full service apartments which are called suites. Watch for the opening of the Humboldt Hotel and casino atop Mount Avila, targeted for 1999.

The following hotels are keyed with an initial: **(I)** international (5 star), US$150 and up; **(H)** high rates, about US$70 to $149. All on this list have a pool.

Altamira Suites (H) East Trans 1, Los Palos Grandes; tel: 2852555/2244, fax: 2855574; e-mail JOO10909-9@cantv.net. 250 suites, 2 tennis courts.

Avila (H) Centre Av Washington, San Bernardino; tel: 5553000, fax: 5528367. 117 rooms; gracious 4-storey hotel amid gardens near the mountain.

CCT Best Western (I) East/south Ciudad Comercial Tamanaco, Chuao; tel: 9028000, 800 46835, fax: 9596697. 200 suites in big shopping/office complex.

Continental Altamira (H) East Av San Juan Bosco, Altamira; tel: 2619091/6019, fax: 2622163. Good location, best rates, 75 rooms.

Embassy Suites Hotel Caracas (I) East Campo Alegre at Av Miranda; tel: 9532490/8448, fax: 9530423. 224 condominium suites to be opened in 1999.

Eurobuilding (I) East/south Calle La Guairita, Chuao; tel: 9021111, 9590433, fax: 9072069/2189. 253 rooms, 247 tower suites, 37 bungalows.

Four Seasons (I) East Av Miranda at Plaza Altamira. Deluxe hotel of 212 rooms; services shared by adjacent condominium suites. To open in 1999.

Gran Meliá Caracas (I) Midtown Av Casanova; tel: 7628111, 800 Meliá; fax: 7623737. Luxury hotel and convention centre topped by a heliport, opened by Sol Meliá of Spain in 1998. 432 rooms with fax-modem lines, bar, jacuzzi. Top five executive floors have fast check-in lounges, and business and computing support. Apartments (236) have private office, kitchen, 24-hour room service. Convention facilities offer 25 salons for 30 to 1,250 people.

Hilton Caracas (I) Centre near Parque Central; tel: 5035000, fax: 5035003. 905 rooms and suites, convention facilities for 5,000. By metro, museums, Teresa Carreño cultural complex.

Residencias Anauco Hilton Parque Central; tel: 5734111/6333, fax: 5737724. Apartments fully equipped for 1–5 persons; use of Hilton reservations, pool, tennis courts.

Lido (I) East Av Miranda at Calle Naiguatá, El Rosal; tel: 9525040, fax: 9522944. Deluxe hotel with 92 rooms, 10 suites, opening Sept 1998. No pool.

Paseo Las Mercedes (H) East/south Las Mercedes shopping mall; tel: 9910033/77, fax: 9930341. 197 rooms in nightlife, dining area; near Chuao.

President (H) Midtown near Plaza Venezuela, Sabana Grande; tel: 800 77374, 7088111, fax: 7826144; email: president@cantv.net. 165 rooms and suites.

Tamanaco Inter-Continental (I) East/south Las Mercedes; tel: 9097111/65, fax: 9097116; email: caracas@interconti.com. Now owned by Bass Plc brewers of UK: 600 rooms/suites, convention facilities for 2,000. Tennis courts. Opp Paseo Las Mercedes mall; also near CC Ciudad Tamanaco.

Medium to budget hotels

A sampling of hotels is listed here. The letter **(G)** stands for good, with rates of approximately US$36 to $70 a double; **(E)** for economy, $17 to $35; and **(B)** for budget, $16 and under. The nearest metro station is added in bold type. Budget hotels (more at southern end of Av Las Acacias and Calle El Colegio) often do not accept credit cards.

Taxes are usually included in rates but, to be sure, do ask.

Altamira (E) South of the plaza; tel: 2674255, fax: 2671926. **Altamira.**

Atlántida (G) Av La Salle; tel: 7933211, fax: 7813696; email: JOO16048-@cantv.net. Fifty rooms; airport transfer, tours. **Pza Venezuela.**

Broadway (E) Av Casanova, east end; tel: 9511922, fax: 9516939. **Chacaito.**

Bruno (E) Av Sur Las Acacias; tel: 7818444, fax: 7815223. **Pza Venezuela.**

Campo Alegre (G) Calle 2 Campo Alegre; tel: 2655558, fax: 2621243. **Chacao.**

City (E) By Torre Previsora; tel: 7935785/1735, fax: 7826354. **Pza Venezuela.**

Coliseo (G) Av Casanova; tel: 7627916-19, fax: 7617333. **Sabana Grande.**

Conde (H) A block west of Plaza Bolívar; tel: 811171-76, fax: 8620928. **Capitolio.**

Condor (E-G) 3rd Av Las Delicias, tel: 7629911/15. **Chacaito.**

Cristal (E) Sabana Gde-Pasaje Asunción; tel: 7619131, fax: 7632118. **Pza Venezuela.**

Cumberland (H) Av 2 Las Delicias; tel: 7699961-67, fax: 7626606. **Chacaito.**
El Cid (G) Av San Felipe, La Castellana; tel: 2632611, fax: 2635578. **Altamira.**
Escorial (E) Calle Colegio; tel: 7619621; fax: 7627505. **Pza Venezuela.**
Jolly Inn (E) Av Solano opp the Tampa; tel: 7623665. **Pza Venezuela.**
La Floresta (G) Sur Plaza Altamira; tel: 2631955, fax: 2621243. **Altamira.**
Las Américas (G) Bello Monte, south of Av Casanova; tel: 9517133/7798, fax: 9511717.
Small swimming pool. **Chacaito.**
Lincoln Suites (H) Av Solano; tel: 7627575, fax: 7625503. **Sabana Grande.**
Luna (E) C Colegio, Av Casanova; tel: 7625851-57, fax: 7625850. **Pza Venezuela.**
Mara (B) Esq Pelota, Av Urdaneta at Norte 3; tel: 561500. **La Hoyada.**
Mari (B) Av Casanova near C Humboldt; tel: 9511476/3252. **Sabana Grande.**
Montpark (G) South of Av Casanova; tel: 9510240/0611, fax: 9517437. **Chacaito.**
Montserrat (G) Plaza Altamira south; tel: 2633533, fax: 2611394. **Altamira.**
Nostrum (E) Metrobus 221 to Av Orinoco, Las Mercedes; tel: 927646. **Chacaito.**
Odeon (E) Av Sur de Las Acacias; tel: 7931322/45. **Pza Venezuela.**
Pent House (E) Av San Felipe, La Castellana; tel: 2661039. **Altamira.**
Plaza Catedral (G) Plaza Bolívar; tel: 5642211, fax: 5641797. **Capitolio.**
Plaza Palace (G) Las Delicias; tel: 7624821/29, fax: 7626375. **Sabana Gde.**
Plaza Venezuela (E) Av La Salle; tel: 7817811/7344. **Pza Venezuela.**
Renovación (E) Av Este 2, La Candelaria; tel: 5710133, fax: 5778910. New pleasant hotel,
walking distance from museums. **Parque Carabobo.**
Savoy (G) Av 2 Las Delicias; tel: 7621972-79, fax: 7621971. **Chacaito.**
Shelter Suites (G) Libertador opp Sambil; tel: 2653866-69, fax: 2657861. **Chacao.**
Tampa (G-H) Av Solano; tel: 7623771-79, fax: 7620112. Patronised by many foreigners
for good services, Rugantino Restaurant. **Pza Venezuela.**
Terminus (E) Av Sur Las Acacias; tel: 7829210, 7931885. **Pza Venezuela.**
Savoy (G) Av 2 Las Delicias, tel: 7629961-69, fax: 7625549. **Chacaito.**
Waldorf (E) Esq Puente Anauco; tel: 5715543, fax: 5768996. **Bellas Artes.**

WHERE TO EAT

Free-spending Caraqueños eat out a lot and the capital is famous for its many
restaurants. Places are constantly opening, changing owners, remodelling.
Executives talk business over the table, favouring classy restaurants in eastern
Caracas – easy to spot by the fancy cars parked three deep. There, lunch or *almuerzo*
may linger past 15.00, and dinner or *cena* does not get going until 21.00 or 22.00.

Inflation has pushed prices way up in Caracas and many restaurants compare
in cost with the UK or USA. Lunch menus are more reasonable. As a guide to
price levels, restaurants listed below are keyed: (H) high, US$21–30+; (G) good,
$13–20; (E) economic, $7–12; and (B) budget, $6. These prices refer to food only.
Some places may make a small charge per setting. Some will not serve water,
unless bottled.

Ten percent for service is added to the bill or *cuenta*. It is customary to leave an
extra tip for good service.

Serious diners and swingers are urged to get the *Caracas Gastronomic Guide* by
Miro Popic, an excellent and updated reference with clear maps. It describes night
spots, and lists museums and cinemas. Popic keeps up with standards of cuisine,
good or bad, in over 600 restaurants.

Dining by metro
Downtown

Restaurants cater mainly for office workers; no high prices, no haute cuisine here.
Closed on Sundays, except for Les Grisons and Plaza Mayor.

For Arabian food try one of two upstairs places on Av Este 2, E of Plaza Bolívar: **Beirut**, 3½ blocks, Esq Salvador de León **(B)**; **Kafta**, one block, Esq San Jacinto **(B)**. Best choice for vegetarians.

On either side of the Cathedral are the international restaurants: **Café del Sacro** in the Museo Sacro, beautiful light lunches, Tue–Sat **(E)**; **Les Grisons**, top of Hotel Plaza Catedral with view over Plaza Bolívar; Swiss dishes, too **(E)**. **La Terraza**, Esq Gradillas a San Jacinto, 2nd floor on south side; good food attracts business lunchers **(E)**.

For seafood try **Municipal**, behind the Teatro Municipal near Av Baralt; traditional **(E)**. **Plaza Mayor**, Av Norte near Plaza Bolívar; pizzas on ground floor, standard dinners downstairs **(E)**.

Venezuelan cuisine can be sampled at **Atarraya**, 19th-century house on Plaza El Venezolano; *arepas* at the bar **(B)**, full courses in dining room **(E)**. **Dama Antañona**, in 150-year-old house two blocks north of the Cathedral, Av Oeste 3; in the best tradition **(E)**. El Tablón de la Cátedra, a block south of Plaza Bolívar; simple, clean **(E)**.

La Candelaria

In this little Spanish district food, especially seafood (the finest), is important. Now run by third and fourth generations of families are many small, crowded and lively restaurants; squeeze in where you can and join the waiting queues. It is three blocks to Plaza Candelaria from the **Parque Carabobo** metro. Within a block or two of Iglesia La Candelaria, in any of a dozen restaurants, you can eat well and heartily. Choose a speciality of the day: *fabada*, fish steak, shrimp, squid, stuffed peppers, lamb, rabbit.

Behind the church: **Achuri** is the place for irresistible *tapas* **(E)**; in the cul-de-sac are **El Aldeano**, small and friendly **(E)**, and **El Pozo Canario**, with some Galician and some Canary dishes **(E)**. Down from the church: **La Tertulia (G)**, and **La Cita (G)** on the corner have long queues matching great food. **Bar Basque**, down Av Sur 15, has six tables and excellent family cooking **(G)**; opposite is the renowned **Guernica (G)**. On Av Este, a block east of Plaza Candelaria, are two small *tascas* with good, open kitchens: **Mallorca (E)**, and **Akelarre (G)**; and across the street is the traditional **Las Burgas**.

Sabana Grande

From Plaza Venezuela to the Sabana Grande and Chacaito metro stations, there are some 60 restaurants. Two are rated very good by Miro Popic: **Chez Wong** and **Urrutia**. This informal scene is now changed by elegant places in the 5-star Gran Meliá on Avenida Casanova: **La Champagne**, the Japanese **Sumire**, **Ostería Prosciutto**, and **L'Albufera** with Flamenco performers.

The best choice for taboule and falafel may be **El Arabito**, a block west of the Meliá on Avenida Casanova at C Villa Flor **(E)**. Go up Villa Flor for good vegetarian fare prepared by an Indian restaurant, **Delicatesses Indú**; closed Sunday. More inexpensive Syrio-Lebanese places compete on the next street west, Calle El Colegio, up towards the Boulevard.

At the west end of Sabana Grande Boulevard the famous **Gran Café**, on the corner of Calle San Antonio, serves the hungry from 07.00 to midnight: Caesar salad costs $5, pabellón $8, red snapper $10. Another traditional spot, **Jaime Vivas**, three doors down on Calle San Antonio, makes satisfying criollo dishes **(E)**.

For good Italian and Spanish food walk one block up to a street of restaurants, Avenida Solano López. Start at the west with Italian places, and move east to Spanish tascas. **Da Guido**, in the first block, has had a devoted following since the

60s **(E)**. Farther along is the **Sorrento**, still popular for good budget food. In between is a spot recommended for Chinese-inspired cuisine: **Chez Wong (G)**.

Crossing Av Los Jabillos you come to a colourful Italian standby, **Al Vecchio Mulino (G)**. The **Rugantino** at Hotel Tampa has a reliable kitchen and live music at night **(G)**. Opposite is **El Lagar**, first of the convivial *tascas* where people crowd in for Spanish food and drink **(E)**. The **Kiribay** has opened a clean, white place **(B)** at Calle San Gerónimo where José Reyes makes his own pasta and ten kinds of *pasticho* (lasagne); open 07.30–19.00.

Passing the church you will find more Spanish restaurants open from midday to midnight: **La Cazuela** down C Los Apamates **(G)**, **Rías Gallegas (G)**, and the place preferred by locals, **Mi Tasca (E)**. **La Quintana**, opposite, has charm and good Spanish dishes **(G)**. **Urrutia**, on the corner of C Los Manguitos, is known to have the best Spanish cooking, and you're lucky to get in **(G)**. **La Huerta** is also a good choice, again Spanish, at the corner of Las Delicias, Av 1.

Finally, **Le Coq D'Or**, a little French restaurant which has kept up its standards since the 60s, is still going; Calle Los Mangos, down from Av Solano **(E)**. Closed Sunday evening and Monday.

Chacaito to El Rosal

Chacaito is a crossroads with many places to eat economically around the plaza.

El Papagallo, the Kite, is a good meeting spot in Centro Comercial Chacaito because it opens on to Plaza Chacaito; sandwiches and meals at any hour **(E)**. Other places in the mall include a *simpático* Spanish *tasca*, **El Mesón del Rey (G)**; and an Italian restaurant underground, **Il Forchettone (E)**.

Cut south to Av Pichincha for **El Portón**, known for traditional Venezuelan cooking **(G)**. Turn right at El Portón for Caracas' first and still the best Japanese restaurant, **Avila Tei (H)**. Another Japanese culinary success is **Sushi Delivery** in Torre Oxal, Av Venezuela, half a block east of Pichincha; there are tables in the patio where you can eat your choice.

Misia Jacinta, at the corner of Av Las Mercedes and Av Tamanaco, stays open 24 hours serving *arepas* after the cook has gone home **(B)**. However, once you cross east into El Rosal proper, low-cost places are elbowed out by upscale restaurants on Av Tamanaco such as: **Barba Roja**, seafood; **Chocolate**, Spanish cooking and music; **Arizona Grill**, T-bone and french fries; **Dena Ona**, seafood.

Las Mercedes

For a detour to restaurant-studded Las Mercedes, now the night-life centre of Caracas, continue straight down the avenue and under the *autopista*. If you were to eat at a different restaurant every week, it would take more than a year to sample the fare here. Perhaps the most fun is to pick one of several outdoor cafés clustered around California and Orinoco streets, such as the **Mondo**, **Costa Café** or **Bermuda Union**. The once charming district of Las Mercedes suffers from overcrowding, neglect and a loss of quality: the only restaurant now rated as excellent is the **Japanese Taiko** on Calle La Trinidad near Río de Janeiro. To pick a good restaurant or a night spot to suit your taste, dip into Miro Popic's thorough *Caracas Gastronomic Guide*.

La Castellana, Altamira, Los Palos Grandes

In this classy area, served by the Altamira metro stop, there are over 70 restaurants, not including cafés and night spots. Below are some old favourites, some new tastes.

First, a few budget places: **Chipi's Deli**, Plaza La Castellana; all sorts of sandwiches and dogs. **Da Ricci**, Av 2 near Trans 1, Los Palos Grandes. Big servings **(E)**; Italian.

El Coyuco, Av 3 at Trans 3, Los Palos Grandes; grilled chicken. **El Mundo del Pollo**, Av Blandín, La Castellana; grilled chicken, steak **(B–E)**. **El Presidente**, Av 3 between Trans 1 and 2, Los Palos Grandes; best 3-course menu **(B–E)**.

American **Lee Hamilton**, Av San Felipe, La Castellana; great salads, roast beef – no stinting **(H)**. **Weekends**, Av San Juan Bosco at Trans 2; Tex-Mex food, salad bar, brunch; dancing, bands **(E–G)**.

Criollo **Carbón & Leña**, Trans 4, Los Palos Grandes; parrilla, black beans **(E)**. **Medellín**, Av 3 at Trans 4; Colombian dishes **(E)**.

French **Le Petit Bistro de Jacques**, Av San Felipe, La Castellana; top rated **(H)**. **Le Bistro de La Torre**, Torre Británica, Sur Av Roche; best at night, Mon–Fri only (G). French-Asian **Cathay**, CC Las Cúpulas, Av 2 and Trans 4, Los Palos Grandes; the height of food fashion **(H+)**.

German **Fritz & Franz**, San Juan Bosco, Trans 3; bratwurst, sauerkraut **(G)**.

Indian **Royal Tandoori**, Edif Plaza, Av Andrés Bello, Los Palos Grandes, half block from Av Miranda; simple outdoor tables, nice change **(E)**.

International **Café La Estancia**, Centro de Arte La Estancia, Av Miranda, a block E of Plaza Altamira; breakfast and light lunch in lush garden **(E–G)**.

Italian **Casa Vecchia**, Av Mohedano, La Castellana; busy **(G)**. **Da Pippo**, Av San Felipe, a block east of Plaza Castellana; ample and fast **(E)**. **Da Franca**, Av 1 near Av Miranda, Los Palos Grandes; standard **(E)**. **Il Padrino**, Av San Juan Bosco, a block south of Av Miranda; busy old-time cellar **(E–G)**. **L'Operetta**, C El Bosque, La Castellana; a mansion where everything is classy **(H)**. **Vizio**, Casa Rómulo Gallegos, Av Roche, Altamira; worth the price **(H)**.

Japanese **Hatsuhana**, Av San Juan Bosco, Altamira; great style **(H)**. **Sakura**, Av 1 above Trans 1, Los Palos Grandes; six tables, take-out **(G)**.

Mediterranean **Caffe Vlassis**, Trans 3 at Av 2, Los Palos Grandes; Mon–Sat. Moroccan, Greek, Italian, French, Spanish, Lebanese **(G)**.

Seafood **Altamar**, Trans 3, between Av Roche and San Juan Bosco; good quality **(G)**. **El Barquero**, Av Roche at Trans 5, Altamira; crowded **(G)**.

Steak **Carrizo**, Av Blandin, La Castellana; smoky old favourite **(G)**. **La Estancia**, Av Principal, south of Plaza Castellana; best beef from Zulia **(G)**.

Thai **Samui**, Av Andrés Bello near Av Miranda, Los Palos Grandes; exotic **(H)**.

El Hatillo

For restaurants in this area south of Caracas see end of chapter.

WHAT TO DO

The Friday edition of *El Universal* newspaper is sold with a magazine, *Brújula*, that is a complete guide to what's on in Caracas. It covers concerts, theatre, art galleries, museums, festivals and events. *The Daily Journal* publishes a page of cultural events, and also lists churches. Check these pages for theatres and cultural centres such as the Ateneo de Caracas, Casa Rómulo Gallegos (CELARG), Centro Cultural CorpBanca on Plaza La Castellana, as well as the Museo de Arte Colonial and the Museo Sacro which often have recitals at low cost.

Drama and music

Plays in English are staged at the Caracas Theater Club, Calle Chivacoa, San Román, tel: 9610011.

Among concerts held at regular times and places are:

Friday Concert at 20.00, Universidad Simón Bolívar, Sartenejas (Baruta) except during vacations.

Saturday Concert at 18.00, sponsored by the Gran Mariscal de Ayacucho, Sala José Félix Rivas, Complejo Teresa Carreño. This is followed by a concert at 20.00 by the Philharmonic Orchestra.
Sunday Concert at 11.00 by the Municipal Symphony Orchestra in the Aula Magna, Universidad Central de Venezuela; no concerts during vacations.

Bicultural groups

Organisations where English, French or German is the first language all have libraries. Cultural activities of general interest to travellers include lectures, films, recitals, music, jazz and dance events, often free.

Alliance Française Quinta Wilmaru, Av Mohedano at Trans 1-2, La Castellana, tel: 2676458/3156, fax: 9413673. The popular Alianza Francesa has a branch in Chacaito, Edif Centro Solano, at the corner of Av 3 de Las Delicias, tel: 7631581.

Asociación Cultural Humboldt Av Jorge Washington at Juan Germán Roscío, San Bernardino, tel: 5526445/7634, fax: 5525621; metrobus route 421 from Bellas Artes. ACH has a theatre, multimedia library, and a replica of Alexander von Humboldt's 19th-century study. German studies and scholarships are sponsored by the Goethe Institute. There is a quarterly magazine, *Encuentros*.

British Council 3rd floor, Torre Credicard, Av Principal del Bosque, N of Beco in Chacaito; tel: 9529965/9757, fax: 9529611; website: www.britcoun.org/venezuela. There is a branch in Maracaibo. The institute sends to England students in economics, law, science and technology, and aids nine Latin American countries including Cuba with English teaching.

Cámara Venezolano Británica de Comercio 11th floor, Torre Británica, Av Luís Roche, a block south of Plaza Altamira Sur; tel: 2673112, 2613396; fax: 2630362; email: britcham@ven.net. Here you will find knowledgeable people, and a yearbook of members around the country.

Centro Venezolano Americano NW end of Av Principal, Las Mercedes, tel: 9937911, fax: 9936812; email: cva@ccs.internet.ve. The CVA cultural and teaching centre keeps a library of periodicals up to date in architecture and arts, computing, ecology, management and many more specialities. Branches at Esquina Mijares downtown, and in La Trinidad.

Venezuelan American Chamber of Commerce Torre Credival, Av 2 Campo Alegre, half a block from Centro Lido on Av Miranda; tel: 2630833, fax: 2631829; email: venam@venamcham.org. Their complete guide, *Living in Venezuela* ($50), covers excursions, entertainment, health, schools. Large membership forms a powerful body promoting business through high level seminars and publications. An Information Centre offers electronic data and business services at the Hilton; tel: 5779879, fax: 5767256.

SHOPPING
Shopping centres

Shopping and window shopping are popular Caracas pastimes. The first big *centro comercial* (CC) or shopping centre was the **CC Chacaito**. Two more on metro Line 1 are **Centro Plaza**, two blocks east of the Altamira station, and the **Unicentro**, at La California station. Others in more distant districts follow the same formula: cinemas, banks, shops, restaurants and supermarket. Caracas sports three new shopping centres: the **Centro Lido** on Av Miranda in El Rosal/Campo Alegre; the **Centro San Ignacio** on Av Blandín in La Castellana; and **Centro Sambil** on Av Libertador, two blocks southeast of the Chacao metro.

Centro Sambil advertises that it is the largest shopping and recreation centre in South America. Besides having 540 shops and banks, it was designed for entertainment. Open-air concerts are held in the rooftop amphitheatre. There is a branch of the Jacobo Borges Art Museum, a marine aquarium full of sharks, a 24-

lane bowling alley that converts into a discotheque at weekends, and for the kids a space travel simulator, robotland and fun fair. All businesses in the mall stay open until 21.00, 365 days a year.

Specialist shops
Camping supplies

Bluet Gaz ($3) is distributed in Caracas and other cities through *ferreterías* as well as sports and camping shops. Ironmongers also sell plastic sheeting in 3m width, and rope or *mecate* for slinging hammocks. **Marumen Store**, Trans 3 between Av Roche and San Juan Bosco, Altamira, tel: 2618134, fax: 2611428. From fishhooks to sport sandals, Goretex boots, Nikko packs, mosquito nets, sleeping bags from 3lbs, kayak oars, stoves, unleaded gasoline. Marumen sells maps and guidebooks, and their people are members of climbing and fishing groups. For quality mountain gear go to **Verotex**, 2nd floor, Edificio Arta, tel: 9513670; at the southeast exit of Chacaito metro. Owner Evelyn, known as 'la Alemana' to climbers, imports the best rope, tents, boots, sleeping bags and backpacks; also has some rental gear.

Beco in Plaza Chacaito is a large department store with branches in Valencia and Barquisimeto. Their camping section has gear designed for beach and river holidays: Coleman lamp/cooker $50, small sleeping bag $30, cotton hammock $20, two-person tent $50, Nikko packs from $75, fishing rod $30. A textile chain, **Bazar Bolívar** (Sabana Grande, Chacao, California Norte), sells cheap sleeping bags (usually small), OK for lowland camping.

Rye bread kept in a paper bag will last a week or longer if you air the loaves occasionally. **Panadería Amistad**, Av Rómulo Gallegos, tel: 352771; opposite Centro Comercial El Trébol, Dos Caminos metro; best time is 13.00. Ask for rye (*centeno*), either *pan sucre* or *pan camerún*; also *pan integral*, whole wheat. **Panadería Steinbuch**, Calle Barrialito 28, Baruta; look for a blue door (no name) down the last left side street as you leave Baruta to the south; best time Tue–Sat 10.00–11.00. Ask for *pan negro*, or *pan integral*. In Caracas this 'pan Baruta' is found at 15.00 in **Supermercado Veracruz**, Las Mercedes, opposite the PDV gasoline station below the Tamanaco Hotel. The **Boston Bakery**, Av Roche near Plaza Altamira, tel: 2632457, makes wholewheat/nut loaves; Mon–Sat 07.00–20.00, Sun to 13.00.

A good source of dried food – mushrooms, soups, noodles, tea – is **Koc Chai**, Av Gloria at Calle El Empalme, El Bosque, tel: 7312070; four blocks north of Av Libertador; open every day 10.00–18.00. Enthusiasts of wasabi, buckwheat noodles with tempura and roasted seaweed should check out the Japanese shop: **Lotte Market**, Av 2 near Trans 3, Los Palos Grandes; tel: 2852957; open Mon to Sat 08.30–13.00, 14.40–19.30.

Fishing, sports

Other shops in the Chacaito area may be useful: **El Baqueano**, downstairs at Beco's, Plaza Chacaito; **Tortuga Sport**, downstairs at Centro Comercial Unico, Plaza Chacaito, tel: 9520292-3; **El Cador**, Av 3 de Las Delicias, near the Boulevard de Sabana Grande, tel: 7621623.

The **Wind Center**, Av 2, Los Palos Grandes near Av Miranda, tel: 2859057, specialises in mountain bikes (Marin, Cannondale), watersports and accessories such as sunglasses. They have a busy bicycle repair shop.

Hammocks, crafts

Artisans from the Guajira, the Andes, Ecuador and Colombia have a permanent crafts market, the **Mercado Guajiro**, in Paseo Las Flores off Plaza Chacaito west;

look for steps down to the left off the boulevard, near Kuai Mare bookshop. A variety of hammocks come in single size (*individual*) or double *(matrimonial)*. Those of woven cloth are called *hamacas*; the open fishnet ones are *chinchorros*. Compare the plain cotton hammocks with the more costly Indian-made *chinchorros* of *moriche* palm fibre – beautiful but heavy (they must be packed dry to prevent rot). Hand-knotted *chinchorros* in nylon thread are the lightest and last forever. Check the stalls, and bargain a bit.

Sotavento (tel: 9935814) is worth the walk from Chacaito for beautiful Warao basketware and carved animals brought from the Delta; your money goes back to individual craft workers. The shop is on the corner of Calles California and Jalisco (first right off the Principal de Las Mercedes), behind the service station. They also represent many potters and woodworkers of Quibor, Lara State.

Pro-Venezuela is a shop bursting with souvenirs and crafts on the Gran Avenida west of Plaza Venezuela metro, tel: 7923638; open Mon–Sat 08.00–19.00. By far the biggest crafts centre is **Hannsi's** near Plaza Bolívar in El Hatillo (see page 85), on the southern outskirts of Caracas. Occupying a pair of houses, it is the most complete craft centre of all. El Hatillo buses start west of Cine Broadway in Chacaito; or take Metrobus 212 from Chacao.

The **CEPAI Centre** receives Indian goods direct from seven ethnic cooperatives in Amazonas State, at Quinta Etey on Av Monte Elena, El Paraíso; tel: 4811398, fax: 4824001. It's way off the metro route but you could combine a taxi trip with a visit to the Cuadra Bolívar, or the market in Quinta Crespo. Prices marked by the Indians are fair, and you have the satisfaction that purchases support the communities' goal of self-development. They plant and process cacao, raise bees for honey, make *seje* palm oil and collect *chiquichiqui* palm fibre, as well as practising traditional crafts. Hot pepper sauce, forest honey, Brazil nuts, Curripaco brooms, Yekuana benches and Yanomami baskets pass through El Paraíso for distribution to shops.

Phone ahead in the morning to check on hours and the latest shipment; stock is low at times. CEPAI stands for Centre for Education, Promotion and Self-Development of Amerindians. It is staffed by volunteers and supported in part by wellwishers in Spain and the USA who believe that indigenous peoples should take the lead in planning ecologically sound projects in Amazonia.

In Centro Plaza's section of small shops, called the Villa Mediterránea, you can find stylish showcases of wooden toys, puzzles, carvings, paintings, and selected Indian crafts: **Galería Terráquea**, Local 29; **Las Pleyades**, Local 49; and **Tierrazul**, Local 100. For getting to Centro Plaza, see *Telephones*, page 80.

T-shirts

Best places to buy *franelas* with nature and local themes are the **Sociedad Conservacionista Audubon** and **Provita** (see *Chapter 3, Environmental Groups*). Also **Para Ti Diseños**, Calle Unión, south of Boulevard Sabana Grande, although their designs are rather stylised.

Books

Books about the 'Lost World', Andes, colonial architecture, flora, fauna and travel, and some maps, are stocked by the **Audubon** shop; tel: 9932525, La Cuadra minishops, ground floor, CC Paseo Las Mercedes. Lavishly illustrated coffee-table books, in English or German, are found in hotels and good bookstores. In Plaza Chacaito, try **Librería Lectura**, basement of CC Chacaito, tel: 9522240; Lectura is two doors from **Librería La Francia** where not everything is in French. North by way of Av Principal del Bosque and west on Libertador 100m, is the **Librería Alemana** in CC El Bosque, tel: 7630881; German, Spanish books, guides and maps.

Thousands of English books at fair prices are found in a new book centre: **Read Books**, Plaza Urape by St Mary's Anglican Church, San Román, tel: 9915562; fax: email: readbooks@cantv.net.

In Altamira, the **American Book Shop**, tel: 2635455, Av San Juan Bosco, just north of Plaza Altamira, sells books in English.

Tecni-Ciencia Libros, tel: 9590315, has a very large and varied stock including guide books: Nivel C-2, CC Ciudad Tamanaco, Chuao; and Centro Lido, tel: 9751841, Av Miranda, El Rosal.

Photos

Same-day colour printing is done on the premises by photo labs in various shopping centres such as Centro Plaza in Los Palos Grandes, and Centro Comercial Chacaito. At the other end of Sabana Grande is **Foto Profesional**, tel: 7621964, by the Gran Café. For black-and-white developing, look up the **Instituto Fotográfico** behind Teatro Las Palmas, Callejón San Camilo, tel: 7936515. For passport photos: **Pronfot**, downstairs at nivel 4, Centro Plaza, Av Miranda, Los Palos Grandes, tel: 2831511. They also do your colour work.

MONEY

Exchange houses Money change agencies, or *casas de cambio*, are generally closed at weekends. **Italcambio** agencies are the exception, working half day. *Casas de cambio* are the best places for changing foreign currency and travellers' cheques. A few convenient ones are:

Cambios Caracas Parque Cristal-mezz, Av Miranda at Av 3, Los Palos Grandes.
Italcambio Four agencies, open Mon–Fri 08.30–17.00, Sat 08:30–12.30. Located in: Edif Abril, Esq Veroes, Av Urdaneta and Edif Camoruco, Animas a Platanal, Av Urdaneta (both city centre); Edif Adriático, Av Casanova (Sabana Grande); Edif Belmont, Av Roche, near Plaza Altamira Sur (Altamira).
La Moneda Edif San Germán, Av Solano López west, Sabana Grande.
Multicambio Edif Seguros Adriático, Av Miranda at Plaza Altamira west.
MVS Cambios Av Solano López at Calle Los Manguitos, Sabana Grande.

Electronic funds Electronic money transfer is provided by **Italcambio** which offers MoneyGram service, and **DHL** and **Zoom** couriers which represent Western Union's Money in Minutes. Zoom's head office is in La Urbina, Calle 11 at Calle 5, tel: 2427111/0144; email: gzooveme@true.net. Some Zoom branch addresses: Av Principal de Bello Campo, south end; Torre Capriles, ground floor, Plaza Venezuela; and Suploficina, Plaza Venezuela metro station, SW exit to Torre Lincoln.

For information about bank services and credit cards, please refer to *Chapter 2, Money*.

COMMUNICATIONS
Telephones

CANTV operators will place your call at the Centro de Telecomunicaciones, two blocks east of the Altamira metro station: Centro Plaza-mezz, Av Miranda, Los Palos Grandes; open Mon–Sat 08.00–13.30, 14.00–19.30. Calls may be charged with MasterCard, Visa and Diners. You may also call direct from there, or from card phones in principal hotels, metro stations and shopping centers.

The same centre will receive faxes at 2862261; information 2856788.

Postal services

The central *Correos* at Esquina Carmelitas is open every day 08.00 to 18.00, Sat–Sun to 17.00; tel: 800 26378 for enquiries, 800 64367 for complaints. There is a philately department on the corner, Mon–Fri 09.00–16.00. The poste restante address is: Lista de Correos, Ipostel, Carmelitas, Av Urdaneta, Caracas 1010. Other Ipostel branches are closed at weekends; the smaller post offices may close at midday.

Email, fax

The post office, Ipostel, has launched an inexpensive public Internet service, not only transmission and reception, but also email addresses. The first to have this service was the Altamira office on Av Miranda at 1st Av, Los Palos Grandes; email: iptalta@cantv.net. Ipostel provides fax services at main post offices only.

Various Internet services are now available, providing beginners and adepts with computers, email transmission, and courses. The Webcenter is in Torre Banco Lara, Av San Felipe at Av Principal La Castellana; tel: 2614151, fax: 2646081; email: info@webcenter.com.ve. The cost of an hour on the Internet here is US$8, half-day at a computer station $20. Webcenter also does copying and digital publishing. Internet Para Todos offers slightly cheaper electronic services: Local 143, CC Paseo Las Mercedes by the supermarket, near Hotel Tamanaco; tel: 924155, fax: 926905.

Long-distance buses

Long-distance lines serving eastern Venezuela leave from the Terminal de Oriente. This modern, well-organised bus station is on the Guarenas highway, 3km beyond Petare. Local buses take passengers from the Petare metro stop to the terminal.

In place of the old Nuevo Circo depot, torn down in 1998, coaches serving western Venezuela leave from La Bandera Terminal, south on Av Nueva Granada (metro line 2 from Plaza Venezuela). Here you will find facilities geared for 25,000 passengers daily, with electronic arrival/departure boards.

Some coach lines use private terminals. Two lines with widely spread routes are: Aerobuses de Venezuela, Alcabala a Isleños, Av Fuerzas Armadas; tel: 4423723/1054, 4725739; Rodovías, Boulevard Amador Bendayán and Av Libertador, Quebrada Honda; tel: 5776622 .

Buses to La Guaira and the *Litoral* or coast now use a terminal near the Caño Amarillo metro stop. The Carcaguaili buses to Macuto-Caraballeda wait on Av Oeste 2, a block west of Av Baralt; they run from 04.30 to 23.00. Buses to El Junquito (Colonia Tovar) wait on Av Sur 9 at Av Lecuna, leaving hourly from about 05.00.

Express lines

Ejecutivo coaches with air conditioning, VHS, toilet, reclining seats, give nonstop service to major cities. Their terminals in Caracas are listed below.

Aeroexpresos Ejecutivos Av Principal de Bello Campo; tel: 2663601/2214, fax: 2669011. Twenty-seven departures daily to Barquisimeto, Maracaibo, Maracay, Maturín, Puerto La Cruz and Valencia.

Expresos Camargüi Calle Sucre at Calle Nueva, behind Bloque de Armas, San Martín; tel: 4717437/4614/7205. Executive and normal buses cover eastern Venezuela: Cumaná, Carúpano, Maturín, El Tigre, Puerto Ordaz.

Expresos Occidente Transversal Los Bucares, behind Telares Los Andes, El Cementerio; tel: 6322335/2670. Super 'BusCama' (bus-bed) service gives you VHS, snacks, toilet, deeply reclining seats. Service to east and west.

Peli Express Zona Rental de Plaza Venezuela; tel: 7940818/1442. To Puerto La Cruz: four departures daily, two on Sat–Sun; 'executive' fare $17, 'Peli' class $20 with lunch. To

Valencia: five departures daily, two on Sat–Sun; $8. Peli is moving early in 1999 to a lot in the Museo de Transporte, opposite the east end of Parque del Este.

BEYOND THE CITY
El Hatillo

Caracas has spread south to this old village where houses are painted every colour of the rainbow, and none is over two floors high. A little cattle farm or *hato* in the 16th century, it grew very slowly into a hamlet around a plaza (elevation 1,150m) and chapel. The church, Santa Rosalía de Palermo, was built in 1784. Today El Hatillo is the seat of a wealthy township that has permitted so many upscale developments in the hills that the village is besieged, its valley as fragile as a teacup in a traffic circle. Everyone who is anyone, it seems, wants to live near El Hatillo and the adjacent Lagunita Golf Club.

An international music festival fills the plaza and cultural centres for ten days in Oct–Nov. Religious processions mark three days of fiestas honouring Santa Rosalía, September 4, and at Easter when the tiny Capilla de El Calvario (across the high street), opens for observances.

You can stroll through the pleasant plaza, have a *cachapa*, ice-cream or coffee, browse in boutiques, curio and craft shops. The pioneer souvenir place, Hannsi's, gathers crafts from all over Venezuela, and shoppers from around the world, at No 12 Calle Bolívar up from the church, tel: (02) 9635577/6513. Open 09.00–19.00, Sunday from 10.30 (closed for lunch Mon–Fri 13.00–14.30). You are invited to meet El Hatillo's weaver family, the Muro sisters, whose loom – *telar* – is in a tiny room by steps down from Calle 2 de Mayo, east end. Los Aleros on the southwestcorner of Plaza Bolívar has shops with copper and pewter imports; at the back is an amazing Spice Market selling cinnamon, coffee, seeds, grains and nuts of all sorts. You can also get tattooed in El Hatillo: Manuel at the Balinese Tattoo shop, south on Calle Bella Vista, does body piercing, too.

Getting there

City buses to El Hatillo leave from Av Humboldt near the Chacaito metro station: walk two blocks west on the boulevard passing the Cine Broadway. The route ends at Plaza Sucre in El Hatillo. Metrobus route 212 from Chacao goes to El Hatillo.

Eating out in Hatillo

The village is a haven of inviting, airy little restaurants: Japanese, Swiss, Thai, Italian, Venezuelan, even Antillean. Competition has kept prices quite reasonable, ranging from US$8 to $18 without alcohol. Restaurants are crowded at weekends. Hours are normally midday to midnight from Tuesday to Sunday, except where noted below.

Use Plaza Bolívar as a hub for exploring. On the southwest corner and down Calle Rosalía are three of El Hatillo's oldest restaurants, best of their specialties. **Das Pastelhaus**, tel: 9635486, is famous for cakes, mousses of chocolate or *parchita* (passion fruit), pizza diavolessa and calcetone on the attractive terrace **(E)**. **L'Arbalette**, tel: 9636496/7278, is a Swiss-French restaurant of fine repute, good value **(G)**. Here, too, is **La Gorda's**, tel: 9637476, where Señora Ninette runs the oldest village restaurant, known for typical *criollo* dishes; lunch only, plus Sunday brunch **(B–E)**.

Mauricio's, tel: 9630789, occupies the roof of Los Aleros crafts centre; specialties are fondue and Swiss-French dishes **(G)**. **Hatillo Grill**, tel: 9611356, on the west side of the plaza, has a surprisingly large, airy patio for sizzling steak; open Monday **(E)**. At the top of Plaza Bolívar turn left and you will see **Padrísimo**

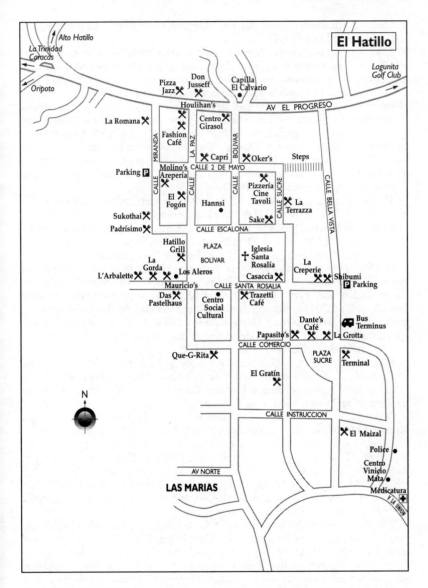

Taquería, tel: 9610553, at the bend of Calle Miranda; it's a *simpático* Mexican place with six tables and a two-way view; stick to the tacos **(E)**; open Monday. Next door is an intriguing place, **Sukothai**, tel: 9635698, where ginger mixes with mango and hot sauce, Thai style, is cooled by visions of a shady banana grove; no lunch on Tue–Thur **(G)**.

On the plaza's southeast corner is **Trazzeti Café**, tel: 9611165; pizza, pasta and Polar beer on the terrace **(B-E)**. Overlooking Calle Rosalía east of the plaza is **Casaccia**, tel: 9611652/1755, a polished Italian restaurant of fine cuisine, candlelight and white cloths **(G)**; open Monday. Go east another block to two small, pleasant places open on Mondays: **La Creperie**, tel: 9637243, creations with salmon, cream and leeks, also luscious desserts **(E)**; and **Shibumi**, tel: 9634509, plenty of Japanese rolls, sashimi and shrimp **(G)**.

Sake, also Japanese, is in a house above the street, uphill at No 8, Calle Sucre, tel: 9611342; its terrace is stylish and the food sought after; open Monday **(G)**. Opposite it is **La Terazza**, tel: 9635551, an Italian trattoria with good pasta **(E)**.

Plaza Sucre is El Hatillo's other plaza, entirely shaded by a big silk-cotton or ceiba tree. Local bus routes end here. People crowd into the **Terminal Restaurant** for plain, hot lunch and cold beer **(B)**. Popular **La Grotta**, tel: 9635425, bakes serious pizza in wood-fired ovens **(E)**. Next on Calle Comercio, by El Hatillo's former cinema, is **Dante's Café**, a cavernous bar and pizza parlour which fills up at weekends **(G)**. A tranquil spot with eight tables, **Que-G Rita** at 10 Calle Comercio serves home-cooked breakfasts for $5 and *chupe*, a filling Andean soup, for $6; closes at 16.00.

The metal stairs to **Papasito's** Mexican-Peruvian terrace, tel: 9637964, are on the corner of Calle Sucre **(E)**. Half a block down Sucre you will find the Antillean restaurant, **El Gratín**, 9637492; try their roti, curries and crab; closed lunchtime Tue–Thur **(G)**. **El Maizal**, two blocks south of Plaza Sucre on Calle Bella Vista, serves snacks of blackberry juice and hot *cachapas* of fresh corn **(B)**.

Not forgetting restaurants at the entrance to El Hatillo, there are another dozen places between the high road, Calle El Progreso, and Plaza Bolívar. Two cling to the road's left side: **Pizza Jazz**, tel: 9634753, in the Minicentro **(E)**, and **Don Jusseff**, (061) 6339117, offering Arab take-out food **(B)**. At the traffic light you can't miss the fancy **Centro Gastronómico Girasol**, tel: 9611434/39; breads, pastries, cold cuts and imported delicacies; an air-conditioned *tasca* bar-restaurant upstairs, and lunch tables on a noisy terrace **(G)**.

Houlihan's, tel: 9637945, a brass and wood pub on Av Progreso, enjoys air conditioning, a good kitchen, and jazz-rock-salsa bands at night **(G)**; open Monday. In the same building is **Fashion Café**, tel: 9637945, with a showroom upstairs; pizzas from a wood oven, plus small daily menu **(E)**.

Down Calle Miranda a few paces you can see the thatched roundhouse of **La Romana Hatillana**, tel: 9611816, open Monday. This is a loud Llanos-style place where pork and beef roasted on a spit are sold by the kilo ($20); harp and cuatro groups play Thur–Sat nights. In the next block, **Molino's Café & Arepería**, open daily 08.30–22.30, provides quiet breakfasts and Venezuelan dishes **(B)**. Another Venezuelan budget spot is **El Fogón del Hatillo**, second floor, above Calle La Paz; their speciality is the *hallaca*, a meal wrapped and cooked in banana leaves; *arepas*, *criollo* breakfasts; open 08.00–20.00 except Monday.

The **Capri**, tel: 9612655, is upstairs on Calle 2 de Mayo; in an open kitchen the lady of this small friendly spot, Señora Ita Bettin, makes her own pasta and tortelones; salads, chops **(B)**; open Tue–Thur 10.00–14.00 only, Fri–Sun also at 16.00–20.00. **Pizzería Cine Távoli**, tel: 9610515, on the next block, combines good pizzas and films, old and new. On Calle Bolívar, a Spanish pub with three eating areas, **Oker's**, tel: 9632249, serves potato omelettes, fish and cured ham; busy bar at night **(G)**.

Miranda's Parks – Avila, Tacarigua, Guatopo

EL AVILA – CARACAS' MOUNTAIN

If Caracas had no *cordillera*, the city's character would
be as flat as its (former) Guaire River. The coastal range
soars to a sparkling 2,765m (9,071ft) at Naiguatá Peak.
Much of the range comprises the Avila National Park,
separating the capital from the Caribbean. The park stretches
86km from east to west and covers an area of 850km², a great
part of it wild. The changes in climate, fauna and flora as you go
up are fascinating. Some 200 kinds of birds and 130 mammal and reptile species
live here. Although most walkers can spot hummingbirds, hawks and lizards,
there have been cases of campers who have fled from terrifying roars, only to
learn later that their 'jaguars' were in fact howler monkeys. Howler monkeys like
hot country and they are rarely seen on the Avila, perhaps because like many
animals they do not live on the Caracas side, preferring the wilder Caribbean
slopes. This would be true of capuchin monkeys and many other species. The list
of species includes ocelot, margay, racoon, armadillo, grison, agouti, spiny rat,
and the more common foxes, rabbits, deer, and skunks. Besides monkeys, many
animals have prehensile tails and are found in trees, such as the porcupine,
tamandua or honeybear (anteater), sloth, six kinds of opossum, climbing rats,
and of course, squirrels. Even the tayra, a large member of the weasel family,
climbs trees after its prey.

With its well-marked trails, shelters, ranger stations and Los Venados visitors'
centre, the Avila offers more facilities than all other parks. There is even an ice-
skating rink in the cable-car terminal – which may reopen by the third millennium.

The Avila is an oxygen maker, and Caraqueños walk up for the exhilarating air
as well as magnificent views. The first ascent of the Pico Oriental, 2,637m, was
made in 1800 by Alexander von Humboldt and Aimé Bonpland, aided by 80
porters and peons cutting a trail up the Sabas Nieves route. Naiguatá was first
climbed in 1872 by a group including German painter Anton Goering and British
traveller James Mudie Spence. In his book, *The Land of Bolívar*, Spence said that
from the peak he could see as far as Los Roques Archipelago and the plains of
Guárico.

Today, hikers in good training do the Naiguatá route and return the same day.
In a race to the Pico Oriental and back to Caracas, winners took less than 70
minutes, and a 68-year-old was clocked at 95 minutes. However, most mortals find
Avila Peak, at 2,153m (7,054ft), a tough day's challenge. You can plan short walks
from various points along Boyacá highway, known as the Cota Mil for its 1,000m
elevation.

Start early even on short walks because the sun gets hot by 09.00 and the lower
slopes are almost without shade. The Avila's paths are steep enough to set your
heart pounding so they make good training for any expedition. Most flatlanders

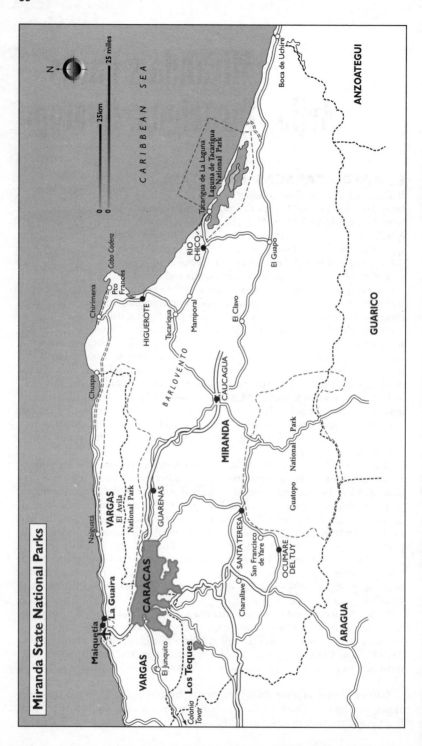

Miranda State National Parks

will find walking down the mountain a worse strain than going up, as rest stops do not restore weak knees and ankles. The dangers of falling are real.

Permits and maps

Park rangers at guard posts, *puestos de guardaparques (PGP)*, issue hiking permits at token cost. Children under 12 need not have a permit but should be accompanied by an adult with one. A trail map is sometimes available at the guard post, but to be sure it's better to buy one at the Audubon Society bookshop, open Mon–Fri (see *Chapter 3,* page 48), or at the Librería Alemana in Centro Perú, Av Libertador, El Bosque, tel: 7630881, open Tue–Sat. There is a colour map which includes the coastal side of the mountain, although trails are not shown in detail. A complete park map including coastal trails accompanies a useful book (in Spanish), *Guaraira Ripano Sierra Grande* by Jesús Pereira and fellow hiker Pedro Aso. They outline 64 hikes, from $1/2$ to $2^{1}/2$ days.

Organised walks

A good way to explore the park safely and enjoyably is to join a walking party. There are various *centros excursionistas*, informal groups of usually mixed ages and nationalities who are only too pleased to show newcomers 'their mountain'. Members of the **Centro Excursionista Caracas** meet on Saturday afternoons to plot hikes. Their base is the Green Zone shelter, Calle Chivacoa, in San Román district near the Tamanaco Hotel. For information, ring Olga González, tel: (02) 2374077, or Juan Carlos Roncayolo, tel: (014) 9196742. Another group of Avila walkers is called **Cecodeca**, formerly the Centro de Conservación Sabas Nieves. Their notice is usually placed at the Sabas Nieves guard post. Cecodeca organises hikes and jeep excursions to Galipán. For information, ring Juan Carlos Guardia, tel: (02) 2865448, or Florencia Sulbarán, tel: (02) 5417164.

Remember The Avila is a big, bold mountain and careless walkers can come to grief when straying from paths, walking at dusk or in mist. The park guards' job is to bring you safely down in case of accident, but they cannot do this speedily if you are not on a trail. Do not attempt short cuts; do not run downhill.

Campgrounds

Campgrounds, as listed below, are those with a sanitary facility (flush toilet). There are many places in the park flat and clear enough to serve as a campsite. As the park is heavily used, it is very important that human waste be properly buried and other refuse packed and carried out. The park is generally fairly clean considering the number of visitors. The campsites that follow are listed in the west-to-east direction.

Los Venados A large number of campsites available, many with kiosks that are handy in case of rain. *Caballeros* (His) and *Damas* (Hers) sanitary facilities available. This area is very heavily visited at weekends and on school holidays such as Christmas, Carnival, Easter and summer.

Mirador La Zamurera A number of campsites with a sanitary facility (not always operable). This is reached by the start of the Traverse trail. The PGP La Zamurera area just above Mirador has considerable additional space. See *Traverse of the Park*, page 102, for directions.

PGP Papelón A number of campsites in areas below the PGP. A sanitation facility (stand-up type but it flushes).

PGP Chacaito Few sites but with relatively new (hopefully clean) *Caballeros* and *Damas* facilities. Sabas Nieves, the next PGP to the east, is a frequent choice by trekkers overnighting in Caracas. There is shelter and water above the PGP.

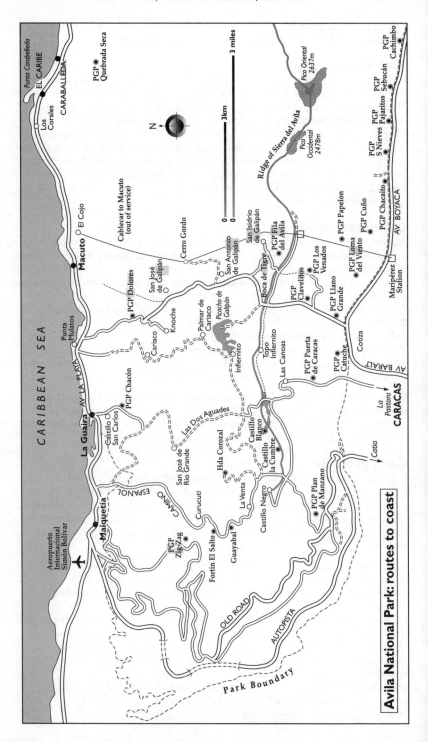

Avila National Park: routes to coast

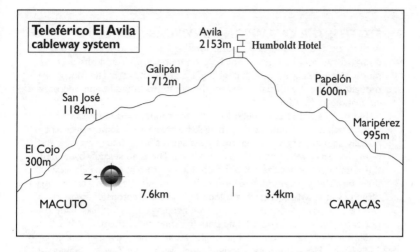

PGP Sebucán Relatively few sites and it is difficult to return to Caracas from here without a vehicle. The PGP can be reached from the Avenida Boyacá expressway going west just past the Sebucán entry. There is only space to park one vehicle.

The *teleférico*

The cableway provides a less strenuous way of seeing the park, but it has not worked for some years. The hours used to be 08.00–21.00 and, if your Spanish is adequate, you can telephone (02) 7816324 to check status of operation. A contract for operating the Hotel Humboldt and cableway was signed in May 1998. The plan is to reopen the *teleférico* and recreational areas including skating rink and restaurants first, and later the Humboldt Hotel and a casino – to be Caracas' first and only casino. Only then will the cableway on the Caribbean side be repaired.

The hotel and *teleférico* were built by dictator Marcos Pérez Jiménez, who was overthrown nine months after they were opened in 1957. Extremely popular with Caraqueños, the German-built *teleférico* carried up to 3,000 people a day on the 15-minute ride to Mount Avila at 2,105m elevation (3.4km). The luxury 14-floor hotel operated by the Sheraton chain had an English pub, German beer hall, Italian café, Japanese restaurant, ballroom with heated marble floors, and heated indoor pool. Entertainers at the revolving discotheque included salsa stars Celia Cruz and Tito Puentes. But with only 70 suites the hotel was never profitable and closed in 1971. Then a government hotel school took over until the *teleférico* was shut down for cable replacement in 1977. When reopened ten years later, it worked for little more than a year before giving up again.

Roads

Six roads and 4WD tracks to the coast cross the western half of the park. The first is used by buses, cars and heavy trucks.

1 The toll road or **autopista**.
2 Its predecessor, the Old Road or **Carretera Vieja**, is still in use but is narrow, precipitous and slow. (There used to be a parallel railway; trains took two hours to reach La Guaira and were abandoned in the 1950s.) In Caracas, it starts to the right of the *autopista's* Catia access, north of Avenida Sucre. The 27km make an hour's exciting drive to Maiquetía, if you like hairpin curves. But walkers are warned of holdups and muggings near the *barrios* at either end.

SLOTHS, THE CHAMPION SURVIVORS

A sloth on the ground is helpless, looking like a moth-eaten doormat trying to swim as its legs cannot hold up its belly. In fact sloths do have moths living on algae in the fur (giving it a greenish cast). The moths are thought to be beneficial, causing the sloth to scratch and increase circulation to the skin.

Normally a sloth has no need to come to ground, living in forests where tree branches touch and the only thing to be crossed would be a river (they actually float and swim). When motorists see a sloth painfully crossing the road, the driver will often stop to lend a hand. This is done safely by holding the sloth firmly under the armpits from behind, so that its long claws with their terrible grip cannot hook on to the rescuer. Rescued *perezas* are often put in town squares; if you look high in the treetops of some Plaza Bolívar you may a see sloth scratching, or sleeping curled in a ball. They are not early risers and stay curled up until the sun warms them.

Sloths wear a bemused half-smile at all times, even if upset or frightened. How do they survive? Very well, thank you. Leaves of various trees give them both water and food which they digest in a many-chambered stomach. Curiously, sloths cover over their faeces, coming down from their tree to do so. While clinging to the trunk they have been seen to open a hole at the tree's base with their stumpy tail, and defecate in it.

They are not as slow as believed and given a few moments will disappear into the canopy, camouflaged by the fur algae. Their fur, growing from the belly to the back, sheds rainwater while they eat upside down. Their feet are adapted for hanging, having hook-like claws instead of free toes. The common Venezuelan sloth has three toes, and their grip is like iron. Males use these as a terrible weapon in territorial fights, and a struggle can end in the death of one rival.

Sloths make almost no alarm cry, grunting softly or hissing. They appear to see poorly, and locate each other with a high thin whistle. The young are born singly and ride clasped to their mother's chest for several months. If a baby is separated from its mother, or falls out of the tree, it stands a poor chance of finding her again. As William Beebe observed, the babies are able to walk upright on branches before learning to hang upside down.

Hunters in Venezuela shun sloths as having more mat than meat, and even boys think it unsporting to kill so sluggish an animal. Zoos don't want sloths because they do not adapt well to captivity. However, a clue to this mystery lies in the umbrella-leaved cecropia or *yagrumo*, a tree often preferred by sloths. These trees have hollow stems colonised by ants. Apparently it's not freedom that sloths pine for in zoos, but something lacking in their diet akin to formic acid (a fatty acid found in ants).

3 The **Camino de los Españoles** is a historic Spanish road between Puerta de Caracas (La Pastora sector) and the coast. In 1608 the township began laying cobblestones with Indian labour from plantations. The job was to cost 100 pesos but money raised was insufficient, so the paving stopped halfway. Later, a toll was charged to cattle owners who were blamed for the road's deterioration. Parts of the cobbled surface survive. The road is driveable in parts. Relatively low (1,500m) and 'civilised', this unpaved, 20km route to Maiquetía is interesting because of the remains of Spanish forts, Castillo Blanco and Castillo Negro, and ruins of the ancient inn at La Venta. The Maiquetía end is in very bad shape.

4 Splitting north from the Spanish road at Castillo Blanco is another colonial *camino*. Known as **Las Dos Aguadas**, the path crosses over the ridge to Gato Negro where it picks up a rough track and descends through San José de Río Grande, coming down at Castillo San Carlos, altitude 300m. This Spanish fort above La Guaira, built in 1768–69 by Conde Roncale, has been handsomely restored. It is a 20-minute walk from here to the sea.

5 From Las Dos Aguadas fork a **trail** climbs east along the ridge to Topo Infiernito, where pine woods stand by the ruined walls of a house. From Infiernito a wooded mule track leads down to the abandoned groves of Hacienda Cariaco, an hour's walk, 780m elevation. A path from here continues to Punta Mulatos on the coast. Not for jeeps.

6 There is a **paved access road** which starts in Cotiza at the top of Avenida Peñalver, San Bernardino district. People bound for Los Venados campsite and visitors centre take this road (cars may drive to Los Clavelitos PGP which has parking space). To avoid uphill strain take one of the *por puesto* jeeps going to Galipán; they leave from Cotiza. The main route (paved) continues climbing to the cablecar terminal and Humboldt Hotel. A jeep road forks north at Boca de Tigre, and descends to the sea by way of San Antonio de Galipán, San José de Galipán (starting point for the route to 'Doctor Knoche's mausoleum') and PGP Dolores. The 10km from Galipán to Punta Mulatos are being paved. This 15km walk takes groups most of the day.

WALKS AND HIKES IN THE AVILA RANGE
The Spanish road
Paul Rouche
Rating Not difficult, but long, so keep a good pace.
The *Camino de los Españoles* is recommended for its 18th-century forts, the ruins of Hacienda Corozal with its elegant palm trees, the charming colonial house at Guayabal and the sea views from La Venta. This route, about 20km long, crosses the park's western edge to Maiquetía; see map on page 90.

Access
Calle Norte 10 leads from Miraflores Palace to the old part of town known as La Pastora, specifically La Puerta de Caracas, historic gateway to the city. *Por puestos* run up the Calle Real El Polvorín, and are worth the small price to get you up the stiff hill through a *barrio* of unsavoury reputation. It is now not safe to walk here unaccompanied.

The trail
Rising from the last house, the road is asphalted only in part and is used by the occasional battered pick-up. The first 'fort' is a recent pastiche, home of a Spaniard. But near his 'castillo' is the first of 14 crosses built along the historic road as a Via

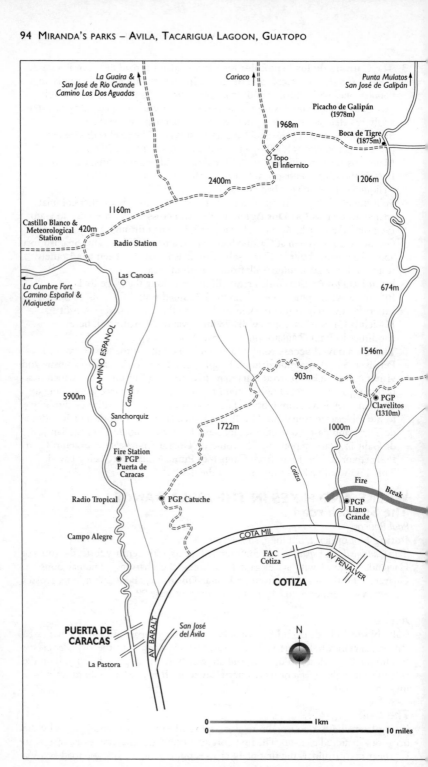

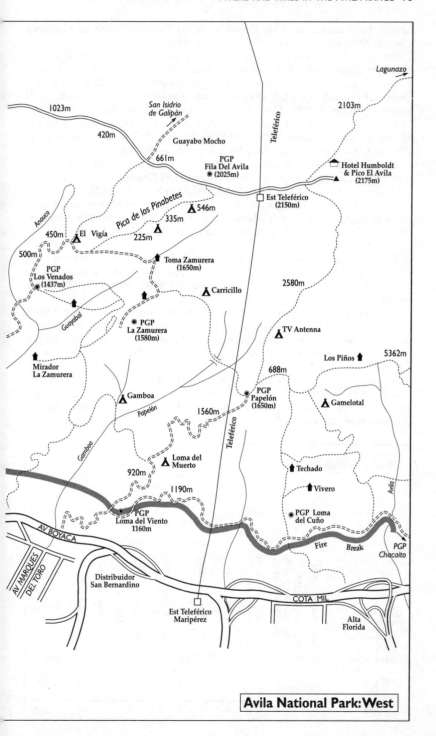

Avila National Park: West

Crucis. Each Easter, the faithful walk from La Pastora Church to Maiquetía Church, praying at each cross. The pilgrimage takes 12 hours.

Remains of the colonial cobbled surface are seen on the left just before the Puerta de Caracas guard post; altitude 1,370m; distance 2km. The road goes up at a steep incline for another 0.5km to **Campo Alegre**, passing Radio Tropical's tower and a chapel on the left; altitude 1,460m. The way continues north by small farms; it flattens briefly. Make no right turns, keep straight on. At 1,470m 'travellers are accustomed to halt near a fine spring known by the name of Fuente de Sanchorquiz,' reported Alexander Humboldt in 1799. He also noted that the Caracas–La Guaira road takes three hours by mule, or five on foot.

The road dips, and you will see on the right a tree and shrine enclosed in a concrete wall and then on the left the entrance to **Las Canoas**, a house where you can beg water. Continue up; at 1,500m the road levels out and in 1km comes to a crossroads; go left. (The right fork towards the radio transmitter in turn divides into four ways, of which one heads up to Infiernito and Galipán Peak, and another, 0.8km, to the ruins of Castillo Blanco, a small fort built in 1770.) The toughest part of the road is now over.

You are on the downslope, with the cliff on the left. At the next two crossroads, 1.5km, take the left both times, descending. (To the right in 100m is the way to La Cumbre Fort, also called Castillo San Joaquín or Castillo del Medio, 1784. Look for the old well.)

Continue west (left) 300m along the **Loma del Viento**, or windy hill, to a triple crossroads: the left is a jeep road to Caracas and PGP Plan de Manzano; centre is the Via del Medio to the nearby ruins of Castillo Negro and Castillo La Atalaya; and, on the right, the Spanish road. Keep going down. Distance from Puerta de Caracas: 8.5km.

Very soon you will pass another path coming down on the right from La Cumbre Fort (a five-minute hike). Keep left here and also left at the next fork (right for Hoyo de La Cumbre and Gato Negro communities). Shortly, a view of the sea opens up ahead; there are houses on the right. The altitude here is

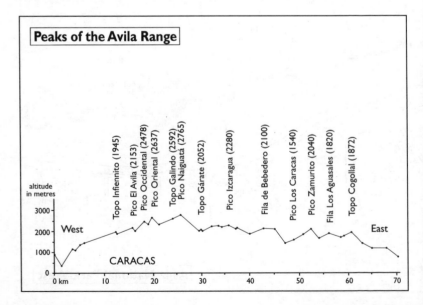

1,330m. The remains of once-famous La Venta are at 1,190m elevation. Describing this colonial inn, Humboldt wrote that La Venta 'enjoys some celebrity in Europe and the United States for the beauty of its surrounding scenery... The spectator beholds at his feet Cabo Blanco, the village of Maiquetía with its cocoa-trees, La Guayra, and the vessels in port.' Today it's a good spot for a campsite if you carry water: breezy, some shade, no close neighbours. Distance to Maiquetía: 8.2km.

Twisting down, the colonial road passes an entrance to Corozal, an interesting old coffee hacienda (right 1.4km) whose palm trees are seen from far above. Next reference point is **Guayabal**, 950m. Another former inn, this simple, attractive colonial house is among the very few old structures still in use, 7km from Maiquetía. From here down, the road has little shade. In less than 1km you reach the small, partly restored **Fortín El Salto**, c1650, which used to have a drawbridge across a 10m crevasse (the *salto* or leap), now filled in. The road continues steep and stony and in about 20 minutes you can see in the west the asphalted Old Road to La Guaira. At 630m elevation, the remains of walls on the right are all that is left of **Torquemada**, a colonial way-station. (Just below, a path leads left to the Old Road, a 30-minute walk.)

The last open stretch drops fast to the community of **Quenepe** which clings to exposed slopes. From here it is 10 minutes' walk to the coast. Or you can take a *por puesto* down. The Caracas–Litoral buses go along the coast road.

Remember In dry weather, water and a hat are essential; in the rainy season, May to December, a hat and waterproof. For camping, a tent, hammock, or light sleeping bag. Biting insects are not likely to bother you at La Venta.

The Fila Maestra and Naiguatá Peak
Paul Rouche
Rating Very strenuous
This is a rugged two-day hike for backpackers carrying rain gear, tent and cold-weather sleeping bag. Day temperatures may be hot but the drop at night is dramatic. Distance is about 30km. The steep gradients are compensated for by an aviator's view of Caracas, the Caribbean and cloudscapes, and by changes in vegetation from tall tropical forests to páramo flowers and shrubs.

Access
Take the 'San Bernardino' bus to the top of Avenida Peñalver, or the *por puestos* which go up Calle Real de Cotiza past the police barracks (*cuartel*) and Luis Razzetti Hospital, stopping 200m from the park. If you have a jeep you can drive as far as Los Clavelitos PGP (see map on page 94). Cotiza is also the starting point for the Toyotas which give *por puesto* service to Galipán. Or, should the cablecar up the Avila be working, you can shorten the climb by several hours.

The park road starts at 960m altitude, passes under Boyacá Avenue (the Cota Mil) and begins to ascend steeply after the Llano Grande guard post. There is parking space at **Llano Grande** as well as at the next ranger station, **Los Clavelitos** PGP; distance 2km; altitude 1,310m. Two ways lead up: the right via Los Venados campsite with its lawns and shelters, the left (faster) to **Boca de Tigre** and the ridge road. Hikers will find good signposts.

The trail
The jeep track to Boca del Tigre on the ridge climbs steadily through woods to 1,880m elevation, about an hour's hike (not counting rests). Here one trail goes to the west (left) to El Infiernito and returns to Puerta de Caracas, one goes north to

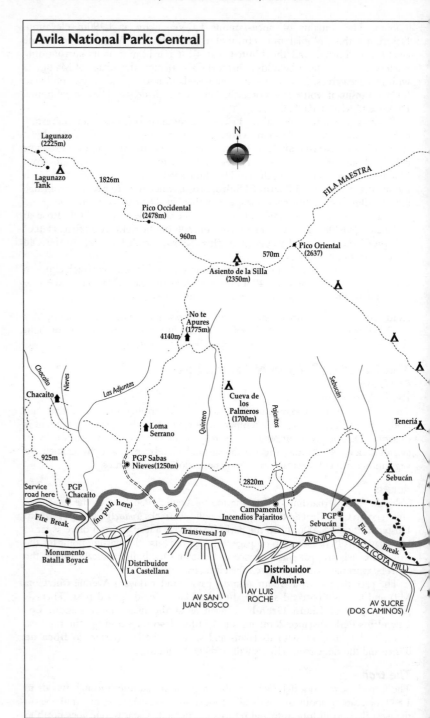

Avila National Park: Central

N

Lagunazo (2225m)

Lagunazo Tank

1826m

FILA MAESTRA

Pico Occidental (2478m)

960m

570m

Pico Oriental (2637)

Asiento de la Silla (2350m)

No te Apures (1775m)

4140m

Chacaito

Nieves

Las Adjuntas

Chacaito

Loma Serrano

Cueva de los Palmeros (1700m)

Quintero

Pajaritos

Sebucán

Teneriá

925m

PGP Sabas Nieves(1250m)

2820m

Sebucán

Service road here

PGP Chacaito

(no path here)

Campamento Incendios Pajaritos

PGP Sebucán

Fire Break

Fire Break

Transversal 10

AVENIDA BOYACA (COTA MILL)

Monumento Batalla Boyacá

Distribuidor La Castellana

Distribuidor Altamira

AV SAN JUAN BOSCO

AV LUIS ROCHE

AV SUCRE (DOS CAMINOS)

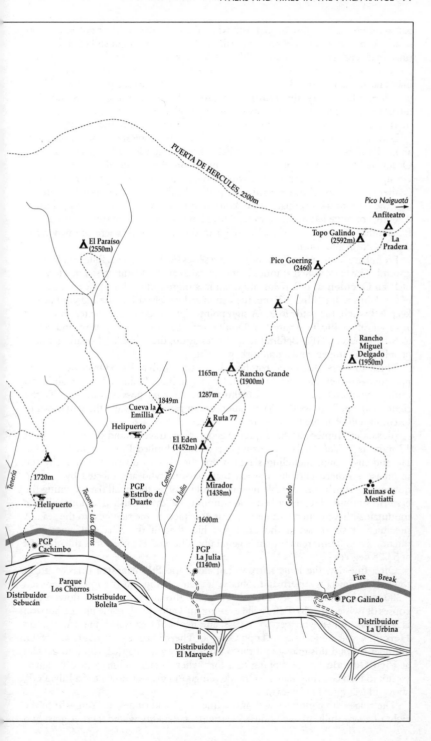

San Antonio and San José de Galipán, while the ridge road to the right brings you in about an hour to the *teleférico* terminal. No longer as steep but still climbing, the ridge road reaches 2,025m at PGP **Fila del Avila**, where the path from Los Venados joins up. The cablecar terminal is at 2,150m altitude. Besides food and drink, gilded lilies and souvenirs are sold here. If you need water, there's a tap near the cable. If you need shelter, try the **Humboldt Hotel** lobby, a strange brass-and-glass intrusion among the mountain mists. It is very cold up here and the wind fierce. Go no further unless the day is young and you have good visibility and footing.

Leaving the concrete path (and the ridge) by some stone steps down to the left, about 100m before the Humboldt Hotel, take the trail east to Lagunazo and Pico Occidental (see map on page 98). Ten minutes on, the way divides at a watertank. Go up to the left, a sharp incline with boulders giving way to gentler, moorlike gradients. The next choice is really one path: take the left for the shorter route, or take the right to the Lagunazo water collection tank if you need to fill up; altitude 2,200m; continue left of the cascade. Above here is a grassy spot suitable for a tent. It's another ten minutes of rocky ascent to the ridge itself where the panorama unfolds north and south.

From here to the West Peak the way is a series of short ascents followed by level ground. The path, which at times branches, takes about 40 minutes. The elevation of **Pico Occidental** is 2,478m, although it is more rounded than steep. The trail onward dips to the **Silla**, 2,350m, the seat or saddle separating east and west peaks: keep left where the paths fork. (A sign points right or down for shelter and water at a spot called 'No Te Apures' or 'Don't hurry', because it's very steep, and below to Sabas Nieves PGP.) Before the trail rises again, there is a level clearing where people have camped, and a trail fork; go right.

Thick, low (and often wet) bamboo shades the climb to **Pico Oriental**. Several not-quite-so-steep variants of the path lead right, but all join up later. In about 50 minutes you reach the crown at 2,600m, where there is a possible campsite. To the right are the peak 'proper', 2,637m, another campsite, a cross and the trail down to Cachimbo PGP above Los Chorros in Caracas.

Alexander Humboldt, that supreme geographer, traveller and writer who spent 18 months in Venezuela measuring everything, climbed Pico Oriental in 1800. He and his group, including slaves, were the first to do so. Standing by the immense northern cliff, he warned that 'persons who are affected by looking downward from a considerable height' should stay on the small flat crowning the eastern summit. He described the summit as 'distinguished among all the mountains I have visited by an enormous precipice on the side next to the sea... A precipice of six or seven thousand feet like that of the Silla of Caracas is a phenomenon far more rare than is generally believed.' He measured the gradient at 53.28 degrees.

On a fine day, the long, narrow trail along the **Fila Maestra** (master ridge) towards Naiguatá is superb and solitary. It seems to dip and rise forever between 2,300 and 2,500m, or at least for three hours, through sub-páramo flowers and copses of twisted shrubs. Before the evening mist and clouds come up, the horizon is limitless. When you get to a pass among boulders called the **Puerta de Hercules**, you are halfway to Topo Galindo. There is a grassy campsite at 2,550m altitude. Beyond this grassy spot the ridge is rocky and exposed, rising to 2,592m at **Pico Galindo** before dipping to a fork where a sign points east to Naiguatá (south to Pico Goering, Rancho Grande refuge and the way down to La Julia PGP, above El Marqués in Caracas).

The ridge path continues with more fine views and campsites. You skirt to the right of a *topo* (hilltop) and come to La Pradera, 2,590m, where there is grass and water; a rocky overhang offers some shelter. Another marked crossing points east to Naiguatá (south to Galindo PGP, above La Urbina in Caracas).

From La Pradera, the trail to Naiguatá is well trodden. It starts gently, passes rock formations with names such as the Devil's Plates and La Arepa, rises and comes to a sea view on the right. Two forks follow closely: stay left at the first and right at the second. In ten minutes you reach the **Amphitheatre**, a protected vale at 2,630m where there is space for tents and rocks for shelter. Up the trail a path detours to the left to a spring called Manantial Stolk. **Pico Naiguatá** is only ten minutes on, reached by a narrow, eroded path up an incline to 2,765m. A cross of metal pipe that can be seen from Caracas stands on the top. The view is an unforgettable 360° of city, mountainscape, and sea.

At least three trails continue on from the peak: one to Naiguatá town on the coast, others to Santa Rosa and Gárate. They are less trodden, however, and better crossed with a guide.

The descent from Pradera to La Urbina in Caracas has two interesting stopping places. The first stage, rocky and wooded, comes down in an hour to a sign pointing east to Rancho Miguel Delgado where a shelter once stood by a creek. Good campsite (five minutes from the path, 2,000m). Return to the main path. Ten minutes on, a fork to the left diverges to the ruins known as **Hacienda Mestiatti**, 1,580m; the trail rejoins the main path half an hour downhill.

Count Adolfo Mestiatti, a cousin of King Vittorio Emmanuelle, was born in Italy in 1860 and came to Venezuela in 1897 with the job of settling Italian peasants. Legend has it that the count, a famous gambler, was booted out of Italy for leaving his bride (chosen by the king) at the altar in favour of a card game. When the immigration scheme failed, the count stayed, using his family allowance to buy the coffee hacienda – and gamble. He cut down the coffee trees and planted onions which were so profitable that for years he was content to pay deforestation fines to the *jefe civil*. His comfortable, carpeted home was ransacked after his death in 1935.

The ruins are on the right (ignore tracks to the left leading to Quebrada Caurimare): the path crosses a creek, a low wall and the overgrown foundations of the house. You can see ruins of other buildings once used for coffee processing. Further on, there are steps down to the left. The way down continues to the right, passing through two small walls. The vegetation, now mostly bracken, offers no shade. Back at the main path (1,540m) the descent is a wearing series of zig-zags following a waterline down an exposed flank. Keep the electricity tower on your right: go right at the junction with a jeep road; almost immediately turn left for **PGP Galindo**, 970m. The path brings you out at La Urbina Norte by the Terrazas del Avila apartments.

Remember Although the weather may appear dry, afternoons on the mountain often bring rain. Altitude and cold over 2,000m increase the hardship and risk of exposure. Water sources are few and far in the dry season, January to April. Also, remember when climbing to look before using handholds: snakes live in woods up to 2,000m; others prefer to sun themselves on hot rocks. The park guard posts are in theory equipped with snake serum; in case of snakebite do not drink coffee or alcohol which speed up blood circulation.

La Cueva de los Palmeros

Facing east, a 5m cross of aluminium stands atop a rock named 'Diamond' on the Pico Oriental. At sunrise, it reflects the rays and can be seen from east Caracas. At the foot of the cross is a sign placed by the Palmeros de Chacao, devotees of the Holy Cross. Their custom is to trek up four days before Palm Sunday to gather leaves of the *palma bendita* or wax palm (*Ceroxylon klopstockia*) in the headwaters of two streams, the Pajaritos and the Seca, under Pico Oriental. Among great ficus trees (strangler figs) at 1,620m elevation, the *palmeros* set up camp. The nearby Cueva de los Palmeros, a cave among the boulders of Quebrada Quintero, is the setting for an altar with crosses and rosaries, lighted by candles. On the Saturday before Palm Sunday, the palm bearers descend and are welcomed by Chacao residents at the Sabas Nieves exit from the park. The procession arrives at the church about 10.00, greeted by crowds and fireworks.

The most direct route to reach the Cueva de los Palmeros, says Rosswaag, is from Transversal 10 in Altamira (by Tarzilandia Restaurant). At a fork above **Sabas Nieves PGP** you will find shelter and water. From the left enters the trail looping up from Chacaito PGP. Go up to the northeast over Loma Serrano. On the steep climb to **No Te Apures**, where there is another *refugio* (shelter), you go through cool forests with orchids, ferns and heliconias. A path leads west from No Te Apures (1,800m) to a waterhole. Shortly after this, you need to take a trail east to **Quebrada Quintero** and, beyond, **Pajaritos**. The trail is not marked, however, and is easily lost. Walkers not familiar with the area should take a guide or get in touch with the Centro Excursionista de Caracas.

The main route, continuing up to the Silla, is in part that taken by Alexander Humboldt, the first to climb the Avila's Pico Oriental in 1800, the first to measure its altitude, and the first to calculate the height of Caracas.

Remember You can avoid getting ticks by tucking the legs of your trousers inside your boots or socks and, before walking, spraying everything with repellent. Since the bites of even the microscopically small harvest mites or *chivacoa* (called 'chiggers' by Americans and 'bête rouge' by Britons) can itch for weeks, this is a good practice. It doesn't work, however, if you sit down on the trail. Think of the cooler regions where there are fewer pests, and keep moving.

Traverse of the park
Forest Leighty

There is a 'low level' route through the park, from Los Venados in the west to Los Palos Grandes district in the east, which traverses the park without ever descending completely to Caracas. This traverse is 17km in length and has elevation gains estimated to equal a climb of 580m.

The trail goes from Los Venados (1,432m) to PGP Papelón (1,615m) to PGP Chacaito (1,310m) to PGP Sabas Nieves (1,360m) to near PGP Los Palos Grandes; and then descends to Caracas at Altamira. All of the park's guard posts offer possible points of entry or exit. Each section of the trail will be given a brief description in the west-to-east direction as described above, with an indication of where an east-to-west traveller might have a problem.

The best route from **Los Venados** starts from the parking area, passing alongside the museum. Follow the signed trail toward La Zamurera and immediately enter a pleasant forest with a number of kiosks. Soon the trail takes a semi-natural staircase alongside a small cascading stream. After about 100m of elevation gain, a small waterfall is passed and the trail reaches a junction. To the right is the **Mirador La Zamurera** camping area and on a clear day one would want to make the brief detour down to the Mirador as it has an exceptional view of Caracas. To the left, the traverse trail goes up a short stretch of jeep road for about 60m of elevation gain to where the jeep road makes a sharp left, and the signed trail to **Papelón**, relatively level, goes to the right. It is a forested area and there is, in addition, a waterfall near where the trail passes directly under the *teleférico*.

Alternatively, one can start from the Los Venados parking area via the jeep road that is the start of the Los Venados–*Teleférico* (Los Pinabetes) trail, continuing on the jeep road past the Pinabetes trail until the bend where the trail leaves the jeep road. However, this route has more uphill stretches to negotiate, and is less scenic than the route via La Zamurera.

At PGP Papelón the traverse trail crosses the San Bernadino (*teleférico*) route which goes steeply up and down at this junction. The traverse trail leads east at the lower edge of the PGP and continues on a level course for about a kilometre. (In the first section from the PGP there are two trails leading downward which should be avoided as they are not well maintained.) This level area is forested with pines, hence its name of Los Pinos. As the trail approaches the deep Quebrada (Chacaito Gorge), it turns steeply down and in less than two miles drops 300m to reach **PGP Chacaito**. Ignore a spur trail to the west about a half mile before the PGP (when coming up this is to the left; continue straight up, north).

The trail continues past the front of the PGP Chacaito and traverses back into the Chacaito Gorge staying at about the 1,200m level. About 1km into the gorge, the trail enters a heavily forested area and switchbacks down about 45m in elevation to cross another small cascade and bears to the east to join the Sabas Nieves (Pico Oriental) trail just above the upper camping area. Total elevation gain from the Chacaito stream is 213m. (In the reverse direction, after leaving the upper Sabas Nieves camping area, the traverse trail goes to the left while the Pico route goes upward.) This section of the trail with the dense forest and cascading streams is one of the nicest in the park.

The trail continues downward past Sabas Nieves and descends the jeep-quality road toward Caracas. After some 150m of elevation drop, there is a trail going down off to the left, just past where the road goes under high-tension lines. If this cut-off is missed (easy to do), continue down the road until meeting a very small stream. Take the trail upward to the left of the stream. Continue upward, in the stream as necessary, until an obvious exit leads right from the stream and up to a very broad trail. The traverse trail continues, passing a cascade, up to an electricity tower where a trail heads left and climbs 305m to a water source but no campsite. The traverse trail goes around below the tower and soon comes to a junction; go right. After a very short descent there is a trail leading horizontally to the left away from the descending trail.

This next portion is little used and not in great condition (very narrow in spots). After less than a mile, a **cascade** is reached which is 30m or so high and just misses being a free waterfall. There is a small, not too smooth, campsite at the cascade. The trail continues upward to a junction. Here, instead of descending to Caracas at Altamira, take the path onward and upward. You soon come to a campsite with piped water, and thereafter to the abandoned **PGP Los Palos Grandes**, the end of this traverse. It is straight downhill to Campamento Incendios Pajaritos on the Boyacá expressway or Cota Mil. At the bottom you will find no way to cross the highway. On Sunday, however, the Boyacá Expressway is closed until 13.00 for pedestrian and recreational use. On a weekday, entry to Campamento Incendios Pajaritos can be made by taxi.

If you are planning to hike from east to west, the entry trail leads to the right of Campamento Pajaritos (at the rear of the parking area), down, and across the stream and then up.

LAGUNA DE TACARIGUA
Beach, wetlands, scarlet ibis

This national park of 39km² is an important wetlands area on the coast east of Higuerote. Visitors are rewarded with the unforgettable sight of perhaps the largest gathering of scarlet ibis anywhere. The *corocoros* live in the lagoon's mangrove swamps where they nest late in the rainy season. Since Inparques prohibited cars some years ago, the park is now wonderfully peaceful. On one of the longest Caribbean beaches, the sandy coast stretches for many kilometres without houses or towns. Sadly, the beach receives onshore currents bringing endless plastic flotsam, a problem with no easy solution because the beach is 95km long and as soon as one part is cleaned up, the sea deposits more rubbish.

Access

The drive from Caracas by way of Río Chico takes about 2½ hours. The first hour drops you down to Caucagua where a sign points left to San José de Río Chico/Higuerote. Through avenues of pink poui (flowering in May) the road

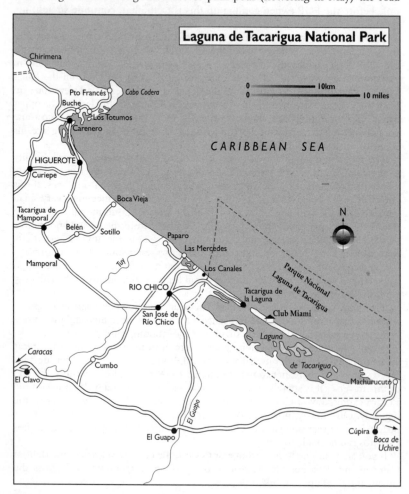

Laguna de Tacarigua National Park

reaches an area rich in cacao. At harvest time you can see the cacao beans or *almendras* spread to dry outside houses in the town of **Tacarigua de Mamporal** where cultivation was begun in 1764. Go straight on (do not turn left). Trees form a living green tunnel shading the way on to Mamporal. At **Río Chico**, once the terminus of a railway built for cacao and now a holiday centre, go straight on for **Tacarigua de la Laguna**, about 12km northeast. Approaching this fishing village, you will come to a triangle at a road bend; turn north (left) for the little port on the sea. For the pier on the lagoon and the Inparques offices, keep straight on (right) about 400m to Las Tablitas district. Buses to Tacarigua de la Laguna leave from Higuerote-Rio Chico, or from el Guapo on the Oriente highway.

Tacarigua Lagoon

The national park was created in 1974 to protect the wetlands, lagoon of 28km by 5km, and sandbar between the lake and the sea, from pressures by vacation developments, overfishing, and contamination. This area between the Guapo and Cúpira Rivers was later enlarged to include 20km^2 of sea. The lagoon's exit to the sea is a channel through the sandbar. In the dry season when the channel closes, vehicles used to cross the bar and drive on the beach all the way to Boca de Uchire. To the great benefit of the park, cars have been banned by Inparques.

The lake's fertility as a breeding ground (12.5km^2) comes from freshwater streams mixing with saline water from the opening and closing of the sea outlet. Fish enter to lay eggs in the brackish water during the rains, little shrimp swim out to sea, and tides stir up nutrients that are eaten by oysters clinging to mangrove roots. The mangroves trap sediments and form islands. Nearly 200 species of local and migratory birds thrive in this ecosystem including osprey, great black hawk, pelican, frigate bird, cormorant, egrets, herons, ducks, plovers, sandpipers, parakeets, kingbirds, oriole blackbird and mockingbird, down to the tiny bananaquit.

Scarlet ibis cover the sky in an amazing spectacle. For over an hour they fly in from all parts of the lagoon to roost at dusk together. There must be thousands. When you think no more can settle in the chosen mangrove, a glance into the sunset shows hundreds more homing in to the same *dormidero* or roost. For months all the *corocoros* will use this roost, then abruptly switch to a different part of the lake. The breeding season is August to December when fewer *corocoros* may be viewed. The boatmen who show visitors around like to start soon after 17.00 to be at the *dormidero* early and not disturb the birds.

The coastal crocodile, all but wiped out by hide hunters, is breeding again in the brackish lake. Mammals in the park live mainly in the south, a drier, sandy shore, but whether they are doing as well as the ibis is not so obvious. Elusive local dwellers include the crab-eating raccoon, crab-eating fox, ocelot, capuchin monkey, Virginia deer, capybara, paca (*lapa*) and agouti – the last four are preyed on by poachers.

The Laguna de Tacarigua still faces big problems. Commercial fishing is banned, but local fishermen are allowed in the lagoon and some use prohibited methods. It is the Guardia Nacional's task to catch offenders but illegal hunting continues. Road construction has changed natural drainage. The Guapo River's diversion into the lake has led to the formation of a delta that is advancing at a rate of 1km per year. Sewage and agricultural runoff are continued threats.

Permits, 'paseos'

At the two small Inparques buildings, you pay a parks permit; in 1998 $1 daily per tent, $3 daily to park a motor home, adults $0.50. From Friday through the weekend, you will find boats waiting at the pier to take you into the lagoon; the charge for a *paseo* of about three hours is $8 a person. During the week you should allow time to hunt up a boatman in nearby Las Tablitas, whose name comes from early driftwood huts. Teodoro Rivas, Remigio and Hector do amiable duty as launch captains and tour leaders. Teodoro will also take sports fishermen on the lagoon and pick up the appropriate permit which costs non-residents $8 a day; tel: (034) 711012.

Where to stay and eat

Located 7km from the lagoon mouth, the modest beach hotel **Club Miami** makes a convenient no-frills base for exploring the park. The people are friendly and the hotel has withstood time and salt winds since it was built by Russian emigrés in 1951. Access is by way of the lagoon, a 25-minute ride; boatmen charge $6 a person round trip, paid on return. The main two-storey house serves as restaurant. Somewhat newer, 12 double-triple rooms on two floors are clean and comfortable; fans, semi-salt shower water. Half a dozen rustic cabins for two or four people await renovation. The beach, planted with coconut palms, has shelters and chairs. Price, $35, includes breakfast and supper; you can order lunch, or bring an ice chest with drinks and snacks. The operators are Ecoposadas, Quinta Tropitone (2nd floor over furniture shop), Av Orinoco at C Londres, Las Mercedes, Caracas; tel: (02) 9935866/1695, fax: 9928984.

Ivan Pastuch, a Ukrainian who emigrated in 1948, rents rooms in the house he built not far from Inparques. For $4 you get a barebones room, shared shower and also the right to use kitchen and refrigerator; in Caracas, tel: (02) 8726908. Teodoro Rivas, the *lanchero*, will find rooms with beds or hammock space in **Las Tablitas** where he lives.

In Tacarigua, the **Posada de Carlos** offers eight basic rooms, overpriced at $10; it is run by Carlos Colmenares from a wheelchair; on Transversal 2, in the east sector of La Boca near the Eveba canning plant. In the pueblo, first settled in 1780, there are various places selling beer, and fish. Restaurants such as **El Pelao** roast *lebranche* from the lagoon; go right 3 blocks for the large Restaurant Poleo.

MINIATURE ORCHIDS IN MICRO-HABITATS

Plants and insects compete for every habitat in the tropics, no matter how small. A single large tree may have a variety of microclimates: a sunny, breezy canopy, branches with filtered sun and moisture, lower levels with little air circulation and light. Tiny orchids may cling to twigs and leaves in treetops, or hide among mosses on a trunk kept damp by a waterfall's vapour.

These secretive plants have jewel-like flowers, some as small as a capital O. You can really appreciate their colours only under a microscope when each pinhead flower glows. Wherever orchid species abound, the number of orchids with small flowers far outnumbers the large-flowering ones. (The larger extreme is a *Phragmipedium* with 2ft petals.)

Microscopic orchids are in a class by themselves, say collectors who try to duplicate the micro-habitats. *Notylia norae* was mentioned in the Guinness Book of Records as the world's smallest orchid plant, several fitting into a thimble. But its collectors, Nora and Stalky Dunsterville, found many smaller flowers in the rainforests of Guatopo, the cloudforests of Pittier Park, and even on Andean páramos.

Iguana Camping is a genuine place for tenters worth checking out by travellers on the highway from El Clavo to El Guapo, as there is a road from here to Río Chico, 22km. About 25km east of El Clavo, there is a pink wall and gate on the right. This is a pretty spot for tents in the heart of lush Barlovento, where José Baptista (he speaks English) runs a little restaurant by a sparkling stream and natural pool. There are plans for guest rooms.

In Río Chico a convenient stopping place (except on weekends) is the new hotel and restaurant **Coma y Comente**, tel: (034) 74480, 74231; Calle Libertad near the town's northeast exit and Higuerote–Tacarigua de Laguna road. Forty air-conditioned rooms with double bed on two floors, $40, extra bed $10; avoid rooms over bar, restaurant, patio parking. Live bands on weekends.

A good halfway choice is the older, quieter **Campomar**, located on the road to Higuerote, 4km from Tacarigua de Mamporal, tel: (034) 74625, fax: 74214, in Caracas (02) 9512721/0665. It is a spacious, well maintained hotel with pleasant pool, restaurant, 100 air-conditioned rooms; double bed $22, with two extra beds $34; ask to see the suites with jacuzzi. Bungalows for two to five people, $24 to $42. Higuerote itself is the centre of beachgoers' hotels.

GUATOPO NATIONAL PARK
Rainforest south of Caracas

Few people except birders stop to explore Guatopo's dense forests despite their amazing wealth of plant and animal life in Miranda State, quite close to Caracas. If you could glide like a swallow-tailed kite, **Guatopo National Park** would be just 50km south of Caracas. As it is, the drive from Caracas takes two to three hours.

Access

If you are going by bus from Caracas, take the Altagracia de Orituco line. If you are driving, follow the Autopista de Valencia out of Caracas until the second exit, for Charallave, then head east through Santa Teresa where the road crosses the Tuy River bridge and winds into the park; a 30km climb leads to a fork called Los Alpes del Tuy where there is a cafeteria. Traffic for Caucagua and the east coast goes left; for the park, and Altagracia de Orituco (55km), right. It is 10km south to **La Macanilla**.

The park

As the highway to Altagracia curves through the park drivers slow down, thankful for the cool green canopy and dapple of sun and shade. They may notice that as the elevation rises, great trees, philodendrons and orchids replace bamboos. Luckily most people explore no further and much of Guatopo's 1,224km² remains untouched wilderness. Because this part of the **Serranía del Interior** (highest point Cerro Azul, 1,450m) is the first to catch storms sweeping over the plains, yearly rainfall may exceed 3m. Its rivers and reservoirs are vital to Caracas and nearby industries; the Taguaza alone supplies 20,000 litres/second. Guatopo is bounded by the factories of Santa Teresa in the north and the burnt hills of Altagracia de Orituco in the south.

In July–August flocks of 50 or more swallowtail kites can be seen on forays, snatching insects from treetops and jostling branches to dislodge caterpillars. Birdlife in Guatopo is particularly varied. And noisy. You hear belligerent hummingbirds, chattering parrotlets, chachalacas in raucous chorus, large colonies of oropendolas gossiping in hanging nests, and even military macaws screeching at dusk. Birder Mary Lou Goodwin's list includes the crested guan, macaw, toucanet, tinamou, collared trogon, jet antbird, golden-headed manakin, king vulture, as well as euphonias, tanagers, honeycreepers and many more.

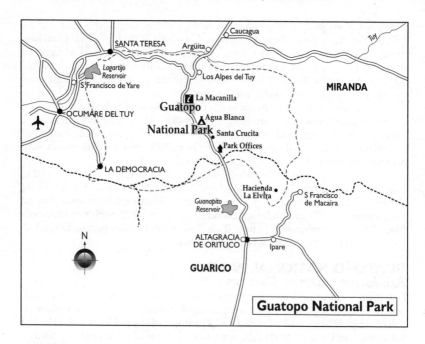

Guatopo National Park

Guatopo is one of the country's few parks with adequate visitor facilities. The guard at La Macanilla Information Centre will explain camping regulations and point out nature trails such as the one to La Guzmanera. (He lives here, so he's disposed to be chatty.) Recreation areas close at 15.00 on weekdays and 16.00 at weekends. As camping areas are all on the highway, a route increasingly taken by heavy trucks, the absence of park guards at night makes camping inadvisable at Santa Crucita and Quebrada Guatopo.

The first and main recreation area, **Agua Blanca**, is 12.8km south of La Macanilla. An old *trapiche* or sugar mill has been restored. The mountain river has been dammed for swimming; there are changing rooms, toilets, and picnic shelters with grills. Kiosks provide food at weekends. Speak to the park rangers about renting one of the old wooden cabins (sleeping five) if you have your sleeping bag or blanket. A communal kitchen and inexpensive bunk beds in Campamento Los Monos must be reserved in writing and paid for in Caracas, along with the nominal parks permit: Parques Nacionales, Av Rómulo Gallegos, tel: 2391886, 2371779. (See *Chapter 3, Permits.*)

Santa Crucita, 1.5km south, has a picnic area, toilets, large grassy grounds for tents and caravans, and a lagoon (not for swimming). Here and at Aguas Blancas, Audubon's bird list includes maroon-faced parakeets, collared trogon, orange-bellied euphonia, various tanagers and, in the magenta-flowering *pomagás* or Malay apple trees (Oct–Nov), a host of jacobins, plumeleteers, violet-headed hummingbirds, golden-tailed sapphires and purple honeycreepers.

The park administration HQ are at **El Lucero**, 5.4km beyond Santa Crucita (ask here about visiting Hacienda La Elvira). Here you will find more picnic areas. And shortly after this is **Quebrada de Guatopo**, near the south end of the park, with its own pretty camping area, clear stream, and changing rooms.

A small research station in the park HQ provides a base for visiting biologists who study foxes, bats, rodents and monkeys. Seldom seen are larger mammals such as deer, puma, anteaters and tapirs, but they are all here, as well as capuchin monkeys, tree porcupines and sloths. The same goes for snakes, both harmless and poisonous, so look where you put your hands and feet.

Hacienda La Elvira Mary Lou Goodwin reports that the restored colonial coffee hacienda on the park's southeast rim is 'an exceptionally lovely place' well worth a visit. You should overnight in **Altagracia**; Hotel Amazor, tel: (038) 341577, offers good food and plain rooms at No 16 Calle Pellón. To reach Hacienda La Elvira take the Ipare road east of town then turn north towards San Francisco de Macaira. The entrance to La Elvira is 13.8km up this road, on the left. The gate may be locked if there is no park guard on duty, so probably it's best to check first at the park HQ in El Lucero. The main building dates from the 1700s and there is a huge coffee-drying patio. Camping is permitted, or you can sling hammocks.

La Guzmanera Trail
Paul Rouche
At last report this easy 9km trail, with its beautiful, cool vegetation, had not been cleared for some time and so was overgrown in places. The main part follows a cart track built 125 years ago; it parallels today's highway along the west side of the mountain. Start at **La Macanilla** Information Centre. Park guards request that you report in here in case of accident. You can obtain a permit and check the map in the small museum.

Opposite La Macanilla (altitude 530m) steps ascend the bank leading to a water tank. Go left without passing the tank, along a path which rises, crossing La Macanilla creek several times. In about 45 minutes, the path reaches the ridge called Fila La Macanilla (650m). It continues along an old cart track, clear and wide, at times level, at times up and down.

If you don't linger, you will emerge at the same highway within 1½ hours, at a spot known as El Danto (tapir); altitude 400m. From there, it is 4km back to La Macanilla PGP, or some 8km south to Agua Blanca.

Remember Although the wettest months are said to be October–December, thunderstorms are common from June on. During the rains, frequent landslides make an already slow road precarious. Unless you plan to camp, make an early start.

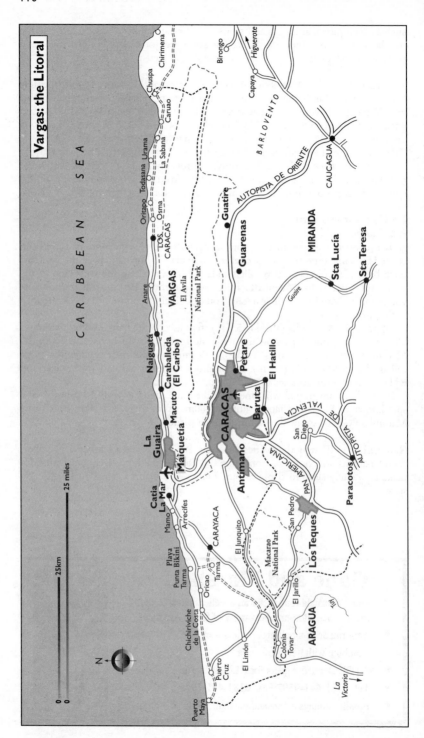

Vargas: the Litoral

Vargas: the Litoral, Beaches and Colonia Tovar

VARGAS, A NEW STATE

A new state was created by Congress in 1998: Vargas, Venezuela's 23rd state. Once the Federal District and then Vargas District, it covers the coast from Puerto Maya in the west to Chuspa in the east, an area of 1,930km², much of it mountainous parkland. La Guaira is the capital. Vargas has a population of approximately 400,000.

Vargas State rises to summits of the Cordillera de la Costa: Naiguatá peak (2,765m) in Avila National Park, and Codazzi peak (2,425m) in the west. Its boundary parallels a large part of the road to Colonia Tovar where trails wind among cloudforests and German-style inns. Colonia Tovar itself is located in Aragua State. However, the town is economically tied to the capital region and is a favourite mountain retreat of Caraqueños. From the road to Colonia Tovar, three mountain routes descend north to the coast: to **Puerto Cruz** and **Puerto Maya**; to **Chichiriviche**, and to **Carayaca**.

For regional tours, see page 138.

COLONIA TOVAR TO WESTERN COVES

Peasants from the Black Forest in Germany settled Colonia Tovar in 1843. Almost totally isolated, for the next century they farmed, planted coffee and clung to the customs and language of the Schwarzwald (see box on page 116–17, *A Hard Life for Pioneers*). Taking a mule trail down to La Victoria in Aragua, settlers traded coffee for cloth and tools. Finally, prosperity arrived with the opening of a road to Caracas in the 1950s, paved as late as 1963. Since then, the population has grown from 1,500 to 8,000.

Colonia Tovar

Colonia Tovar, with its inns and hearty food (no night clubs or golf course), makes an ideal base for walkers and campers, set among orchards, blackberry brambles, pines and palm trees. Except for the Avila National Park no area has as many wooded paths. The average temperature is 16°C, dropping at night to 8°C. Campers will need good sleeping bags and rainproof gear.

Getting there

First, avoid heavy traffic by choosing a weekday. Although the distance from western Caracas to Colonia Tovar is only 54km, the road winds up from industrial Antímano through crowded *barrios* and it can take an hour and a half. On Saturdays and Sundays day trippers throng **El Junquito**, 27km, a market town, in search of rural delights such as strawberries and cream, crackling (*chicharrón*), and sausages (*chorizos*). When you add fog or rain to the traffic, the queue of cars slows to a crawl.

Por puesto vans or small buses to El Junquito leave Caracas daily from 05.00

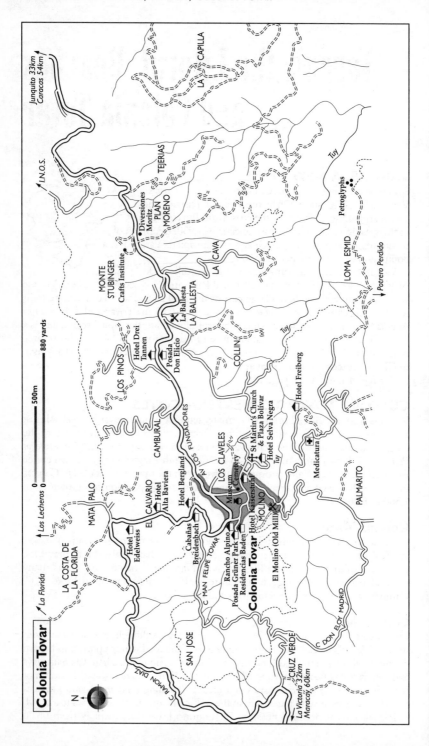

through to early afternoon; they park by the corner of Calle Sur 9 and Av Lecuna. Change buses in El Junquito for Colonia Tovar. Once past El Junquito, traffic thins; the ridge road winds on for another 19km to arrive at an archway marking the Aragua State border. Colonia Tovar is 8km to the left. Through the town, a paved road winds over the mountain to La Victoria, 34km. Served by *por puesto* jeeps this route is dramatically steep as it descends 1,250m in elevation, and is never crowded.

On the way into Colonia Tovar you'll pass **Charcutería Tovar**, makers of pickles, knackwurst, smoked sausages and all kinds of picnic goodies. Also on the right, 4km on, you will see Colonia Tovar's new **Crafts Institute**, a splendid training centre built with German backing. There are dormitories for 40 students, a library, a sales- and show-room, and workshops for wood turning and cabinet making. The land was donated by Veba Oel of Germany; and the complex was designed by Venezuelan Dirk Bornhorst and built by the government.

At weekends sightseers are elbow-to-elbow in the town's narrow streets. But during the week the restaurants and small hotels give great value for money. The bread is German, the jam homemade, and the strawberries and vegetables garden fresh.

Where to stay
The area telephone code for Colonia Tovar, formerly (033), has been changed to (044)
Set among hilly flower gardens, many small hotels and inns or *posadas* provide bed and breakfast for two at about US$30–36. A few offer rooms or apartments without food. All have private bath and hot water, except where noted. Reservations with bank deposits are required for weekends when inns may stipulate two days minimum stay; most do not accept credit cards.

On the entrance road
Posada Don Elicio, La Ballesta sector, tel: 551254, fax: 551073; in Caracas (02) 2840464, fax: 2842429. This luxury inn comes highly recommended for its antique decorations, view, gardens, playground, terrace tables and excellent food. Eleven rooms and a cottage for two to four guests, double $100 per couple, triple $45 per person; breakfast and dinner included. **Drei Tannen**, tel: 51264; on the right above the road; nine nicely kept rooms and suites for two to five guests, attended by owner Rudolf Klampferer; hearty breakfasts home-cooked by Frau Klampferer; $40.

In the village
Rancho Alpino, tel: 551470, fax: 551439; on the right as you turn down Calle Museo from the high street; six doubles run by a restaurant; sausage, egg and cheese for breakfast; $36 for two. **Residencias Baden**, tel: 551151; on a street turning sharp right off upper Calle El Museo; eight plain apartments with kitchen, double room, fireplace, nice view; no TV, no food; $20. **Posada Grüner Park**, tel: 551520, tel/fax: 551983; end of the same street; seven large rooms and three apartments with kitchen in a new building made to look old; prices from $16 for a double bed to $34 for an apartment; no food service. **Kaiserstuhl**, tel: 551132; Calle Bolívar, a block above the church, is a handsome structure with two restaurants, terrace dining; 21 rooms for two to six people; $36 a double, $10 extra person; breakfast. **Selva Negra**, tel: 551415, fax: 551338; below the church to the right, is Colonia Tovar's first and leading 3-star hotel; spacious grounds, four rooms and 40 heated units in well-appointed, carpeted bungalows for two to five people, $60 to $90, without breakfast; very good restaurant. **Hotel Freiburg**, tel:

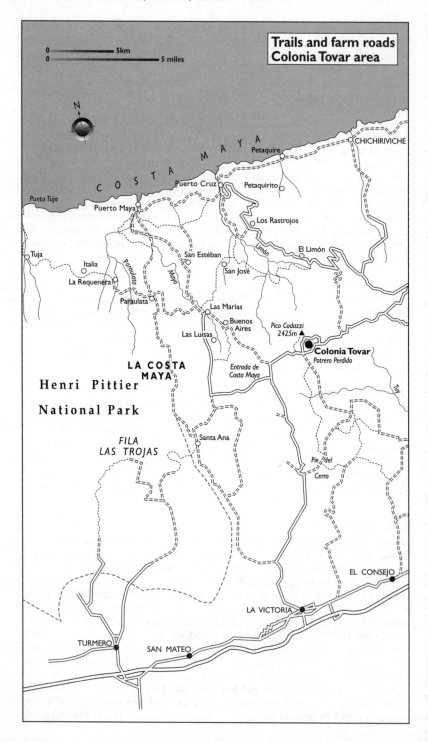

551313, fax: 551983; located 700m beyond El Molino restaurant and the Tuy River bridge, southeast towards the Medicatura. A valley setting of neat lawns and flowering shrubs for cottages with 14 comfortable rooms, two to four guests; $44 with breakfast for two. Large, reasonable restaurant, open midday to 21.00.

Upper sector
Bergland, tel/fax: 551229; on La Victoria side of Tovar, six heated cabins in garden for two to five guests, 15 new double rooms, $56–76; with breakfast Mon–Thur. **Cabañas Breidenbach**, tel: 551211; three new houses with 13 units nicely furnished for two to six guests, the larger ones with kitchen; $32–50, no food. **Alta Baviera**, tel: 551483; farther up same road, a German-style house, restaurant and terrace with great view; 24 rooms, six comfortable cottages for up to five guests; double $56, cottage $64; breakfast included. **Edelweiss**, tel: 551260; 100m up same road, 19 pleasant rooms and suites for two to four guests; double bed $52, suite for five $90; breakfast included.

Tour services
Rustic Tour, an agency on Calle Codazzi (high street) near the service station, makes jeep tours to the beach, mountains, El Jarillo, and petroglyphs of Potrero Perdido; tel: 551908. The longer tours to Puerto Maya, Puerto Cruz or Chichiriviche cost $40 a person including lunch. For information about apartments, cabins, camping, paragliding, mountain biking, estimates for transfers anywhere by car and tours of Tovar, call Ulrich Tal at **Trans-Colonia Tovar**, Regenwald Tours, above Novedades Burkheim, on Calle Bolívar, tel: 551662, (014) 9335109. Their jeeps are red striped with black.

In Caracas, contact **Turismo Colorama** (see page 15) for tour information: tel: (02) 2617732, fax: 2621828.

Colonia Tovar on foot
Walk along the high street, Calle Codazzi, from the service station (and another arch). Besides souvenir and crafts shops you will find a bank, bakery and supermarket. More large crafts places line Calle Museo, descending at the street's end. Relics of the past can be seen on weekends in Nestor Rojas' private **Museum of History and Crafts**, Calle Museo on the left. The display includes immigrants' contracts and belongings, farm tools, pieces of the original forge, a printing press and mill, even a petroglyph. Rojas, who owns the Residencias Baden, knows about local petroglyphs, as does Ulrich Othmer of the Freiburg Hotel.

At the first corner downhill, go left and pause at the **cemetery**; it has a lovely view over the church and valley below. Among the graves you can trace the colony's growth: wooden crosses for early leaders such as mayor Alexander Benitz (d.1865) and botanist Karl Moritz (d.1866) who planted the cypress still growing here; and marble mausoleums for later prosperous residents.

Follow Calle Bolívar down to the **St Martin's Church**, named after the colony's (and founder Martín Tovar's) patron saint. During the *fiestas patronales* on Nov 11 and nearest weekends, the statue of St Martin, brought from Germany by the colonists, is taken out in procession. The church's black timbers, raised in 1862, make it unique in Venezuela, although the rebuilt tower has some painted 'beams'; the wall and windows next to the bell tower are original. Inside, you will see the twin naves once separating men from women. Jacob Ruh who constructed the church later took up coffee growing and built two warehouses, one with a tavern, on opposite sides of the high street; look for shops with pitched roofs and porticos at the south end.

A HARD LIFE FOR PIONEERS

Venezuela needed farmers to work the land after devastating Independence wars. Don Martín Tovar, a congressman and supporter of immigration, put up a 60,000 peso loan to back a colony of Germans. His nephew, Manuel Felipe Tovar (later president of the country), set aside a mountain tract west of Caracas. Two foreigners were key to the settlement's success: Agustín Codazzi, an Italian geographer, and a young engraver from the Kaiserstuhl, mapmaker Alexander Benitz whom Codazzi met in a Paris printshop. Together they visited sites in Venezuela at the government's request. Codazzi returned to France to hire the emigrants' ship and buy food and equipment such as a printing press and sawmill. Benitz signed up land-hungry peasants and craftsmen; he also signed on as an immigrant himself. On January 11 1843, both Benitz and Codazzi sailed aboard the *Clemence* from Le Havre with the emigrants, in all 392.

Things did not go well. On the 52-day voyage to La Guaira several lives were lost to smallpox, giving rise to a three-week quarantine on board. Luckily, Codazzi had the quarantine switched to a landing near Choroní. Next, the settlers shouldered their gear up the cordillera and over to Maracay. There they were welcomed with a big barbecue by the president of Venezuela, General José Antonio Páez. Páez offered some wagons to take women and children to La Victoria, starting point for the trek up to Tovar. Skirting chasms and tripping over roots, the colonists, who now numbered 374, finally arrived on April 8 at a clearing where a few dismal huts stood among burnt stumps. Each settler was indebted for two hectares of this wilderness (children under one received one hectare), as well as for the voyage, food and gear.

The timbered houses opposite the church are among Tovar's oldest: the **Jahn House** where mapmaker Agustín Codazzi lived, and the 1846 **Benitz House**, now the Muuhstall café. Alexander Benitz, guiding spirit of the colony, had a brewery (the first in Venezuela), printshop and store in his house, the oldest one surviving.

Below the church down Benitz street is the **Selva Negra**, Colonia Tovar's pioneer hotel founded in 1936. Carlos Breidenbach, a descendant of the original families, is the carpenter who made the hotel's large house with beautifully worked wood, and continued its expansion including the many cottages around the grounds. His workshop, Carpentería Codazzi, is 150m down the road from the Kaiserstuhl. Where the road crosses a little river (the Tuy headwaters), stands the **Old Mill** with its 1860 waterwheel, today a backdrop to El Molino Restaurant.

Music festival Colonia Tovar, along with concert halls in Caracas and Aragua, stages a yearly International Festival of Chamber Music, held about the third week in March. Musicians and singers from Germany, Italy, the United States, even China, join Venezuelan chamber groups. The Selva Negra, Freiburg and other local hotels offer settings for foreign and Venezuelan musicians.

Jokili at Carnival The jesters traditional in Germany, *jokili*, are central to Carnival in Colonia Tovar. They wear red costumes with bells, and carved wooden masks. The *jokili* have their own society and meeting place, the Jokili Heim, not far above the Edelweiss Hotel.

To Codazzi Peak

You have only to ask at the Alta Baviera or Edelweiss hotels for paths uphill: to strawberry fields near the INOS watertanks, to the chapel of the Virgen de los

The debt was interest free and could be paid off in work. There were typesetters, carpenters, a blacksmith, shoemaker, tailor, baker, brewer (who made the first beer in Venezuela), barrel-maker and teacher. Classes began on the fourth day for some 80 children under the age of 14. As their leader and later mayor, Benitz helped the colonists tackle hardship, disease and isolation. He was named chief justice replacing Codazzi, who had unwisely brought in soldiers to enforce the colonists' labours.

Desertions soon depleted the colony and among the first to go were the teacher, doctor and typesetter. The *Colonia Tovar Bulletin*, in German and Spanish, ceased publication. The priest from La Victoria came only once a year. Remote and unprotected, the colony was sacked during civil wars. A project to open a road to Caracas failed. And the colonists worsened their isolation by banishing members who married outside and confiscating their lands. This led to inbreeding and cultural poverty. Illiteracy, once only 5%, grew to 40%.

However, new immigrants arrived and there were still leaders. One mother gave classes in reading and writing; her daughter helped a Swiss physician for two years, then treated the sick herself; botanist Karl Moritz led Bible studies and gave horticulture lessons. Coffee growing brought some degree of prosperity. But, even in the 20th century, teachers and priests sent from the outside world could not endure Tovar's rigidity. It was not until 1942, when Colonia Tovar became a township and Spanish became the official language, that land could be bought by anyone and colonists could marry freely. Finally, with the opening of an earth road to Caracas in 1950, Tovar's mulish isolation ended. Caraqueños 'discovered' Tovar.

Dolores named for an image the settlers brought from the Black Forest, or to the woods by an area called Los Lecheros. **Codazzi Peak**, 2,425m, is the highest point in this part of the Cordillera de la Costa. It has a television relay tower on top. Take the road leading out of town towards La Victoria. In about 3.5km, where a cross stands by the road, go right (left for Capachal). Less than ten minutes up, where the road goes over a brook, look on the left for a path leading through bamboos. The walk through woods and shrubs to the top takes half an hour. The view can be breathtaking when clear: east to Naiguatá Peak above Caracas, north to the sea, west as far as Lake Valencia.

The peak and surrounding 117km^2 have been declared **Monumento Natural Pico Codazzi**. Its cloudforests feed the headwaters of the Chichiriviche, Limón, Tuy and other rivers. The protected area was designed as Venezuela's first 'ecological corridor', linking Pittier National Park in Aragua State with Macarao National Park in Miranda.

To the petroglyphs

During his field trips in 1844, naturalist Hermann Karsten found the way to a set of boulders known as the **Piedras de Los Indios**. These petroglyphs were made by Indian artists long before the arrival of Europeans. Ask for Potrero Perdido; it's a good walk of some 14km round trip. Start downhill (east) from the church. At the first fork turn right (left circles back to the main highway at La Ballesta) on a steep concrete road passing the Evangelist chapel. If you hear a grinding noise opposite, it is Enrique Collin's mill at work. He makes the wooden waterwheels himself.

Cross the bridge over the upper Tuy; continue along its banks a way. After climbing through coffee farms and gardens, the sandy path comes to a spring and bridge; head left at the junction (right goes back to Tovar). Views open over the valley as the jeep road leads east through woods and fields to a community called **Potrero Perdido** (5km from Tovar). The Piedras de Los Indios are about 2km further east. Follow a track leading uphill; at a spot with a fine open view, look for a pair of pine trees on the left. The trees help to locate the flat boulders on the right which may be hidden by long grass. Unfortunately, someone has painted the petroglyphs white, probably to photograph the incised designs.

LONGER HIKES IN THE REGION
Costa Maya circuit
Paul Rouche

This is a strenuous circuit with links to the sea. By following this rough jeep route used by farmers you can make a circle, returning to about 1km from the starting point. Descending the Caribbean slopes, locally known as the *Costa Maya*, the road drops from wonderfully cool cloudforest to coffee plantations and, lower, sunny banana and bean plots. The route is important because several stretches give access to longer hikes (two days) down to the sea at Puerto Cruz, Puerto Maya, and even Cepe-Chuao in Henri Pittier Park. With a very early start, you can complete the circle described below in one day. However, the return is a stiff haul uphill from 680m elevation to over 2,000m.

Access

The entrance is by a farmhouse called La Pollera on the paved road between Colonia Tovar and La Victoria. La Pollera is 7.5km from Tovar and 1.1km north of a crossroads signposted **Entrada de Costa Maya**. *Por puestos* leave Colonia Tovar hourly for La Victoria. In La Victoria *por puestos* leave from Calle Sur Libertador between Calles Páez and Rivas Dávila.

The trail

Leading west, the asphalted entrance by **La Pollera** becomes a jeep road penetrating cloudforest at an altitude of 2,150m. After crossing the ridge, 2,250m, the trail begins a long northwest descent. The way is superbly misty and green, with dripping tree ferns, epiphytes, palms and rushing brooks. Within half an hour you'll see a huge rock on the left (possible shelter); 15 minutes further, a clearing (campsite). Keep straight on at a crossroads lower down (right for the distant farm of La Llanada); altitude 1,650m.

For another hour and a half the road continues down, with fine views of coffee hills and planted valleys. Before **Hacienda Buenos Aires**, a trail comes in on the left from Portachuelo (a much longer route). Buenos Aires is an old tile-roofed house with a *patio de bolas*; altitude 1,060m. Take a left fork below. You have been walking some 2½ hours downhill and can now start the circle back. At **Quebrada Las Minas** – instead of entering Las Marías, a community on the east bank where the path to Puerto Cruz starts – take the left road, fording the river's 8m bed. There are no problems crossing except after a storm (rainy season June–Sept); altitude 680m.

Now begins the return climb on a jeep road which ascends from Puerto Maya to join the Colonia Tovar road at the Entrada de Costa Maya. There are a few houses in small *caseríos* (hamlets). Keep to the left (right, for Puerto Maya, 4–5 hours north). The hamlet of **Las Luisas**, at 900m, has a small grocery and medical dispensary. The road continues up steeply through coffee plantations without branching. At 1,250m there is a *bodega* or country store called Las Mercedes; at

1,360m, in **Portachuelo** there is another shop where you can buy tinned sardines, crackers or soft drinks. This part of the ascent has been a hard walk of nearly two hours but the road is wide and the tree canopy ever thicker and cooler.

The stage above Portachuelo is, if anything, more strenuous. However, there is a fine mountain brook in half an hour. The final ascent to the ridge takes 1½ hours (without stops). A wayside cross at a fork, **La Cruz**, marks the left turn eastward (right for Santa Ana and a rutted jeep track down to La Victoria). The altitude is 2,100m.

The hike's last stage (1½ hours) is known as **La Entrada**, or 'The Entrance' to Costa Maya although you are leaving. This is a thickly wooded area often swathed in mist. Most of the road is asphalted. If you are short on time, you may be lucky enough to hitch a ride with a farmer to the main highway; from there it is 8.5km (left) to Colonia Tovar, or 24km (right) down to La Victoria.

Down to the sea

From the Costa Maya circuit, roads and paths lead to the sea: east to **Puerto Cruz**, north to **Puerto Maya**, and west to **Punta Tuja** (pronounced 'Tooha'). Serving coffee plantations and farms, the roads are adequate for 4x4 vehicles. The best road is that to Puerto Maya made recently for laying a power line.

Fishermen in Puerto Maya are willing to spin visitors over to Puerto Cruz or to Punta Tuja. It takes only half an hour by sea; the cost per boat is roughly $100. In order to avoid walking back up the mountain, it is advisable to contract a boat to pick you up on a certain day (you pay on return).

West to Punta Tuja

This walk continues on from the circle route above and follows jeep roads for the first 3½ hours. From the vicinity of Las Marías (farthest point on the previous hike), the walk takes 6–7 hours.

The way starts on an asphalted road (do not enter Las Marías, down to the right). At the first crossroads (left to Las Luísas), continue to Quebrada Las Minas, altitude 680m, and take the road left, downhill. This will bring you to the community of **San Antonio**; pass the country store and take the right fork, descending sharply to **Rivera** (15 minutes). Bear left (west) at the crossroads for **El Carmen**, altitude 800m (20 minutes). Keep on the main road; the last part rises steeply to **El Deleite**, 950m (30 minutes).

The second hour is spent on the walk to the school of La Paraulata by an earth road with minor ups and downs. It intersects twice with other jeep tracks (go left at the first, right at the second) before crossing the **Paraulata River**, about 5m wide; stop here and look for a beautiful double cascade and pool, 30m on the left. In less than 15 minutes there is a main crossing where the jeep road Monte Oscuro–La Victoria enters from the left; keep right for the **Escuela de Paraulata**, altitude 1,000m (1 hour).

From here it is easy walking on the main road to the next *encrucijada* at **Paraulata** (25 minutes); take the left hand (right goes to Río Central and Puerto Maya). There are two inferior *bodegas* in La Paraulata; for small purchases you're better off buying at the shop run by a Spaniard, Sr Domingo, in **La Requenera**, altitude 750m. On the way there (35 minutes) you pass coffee groves, scattered houses and the San Isidro Chapel. The next stage to the road's end (passing a house called Italia) is again an easy walk; altitude 850m (40 minutes). From here a trail continues west-northwest.

The trail crosses cultivated plots and many small ravines. In about 15 minutes it climbs steeply to a ridge at 1,030m, then descends to a ravine (seven minutes); go right here at a crossing, then left at a fork by a boulder, uphill a little. The next boulder, altitude 950m, is large enough to provide shelter (five minutes). The way climbs to another ridge at 1,050m and a high point where you can at last see the sea.

The downward trail becomes a broader path or *camino*; it dips and rises, leading through dry stream beds and lovely open woods (40 minutes). A view of the sea to the right signals the final descent to the **Tuja Valley**, altitude 600m (30–35 minutes). (The path continues left to **Cepe** and **Chuao**; if you need water follow it to a stream, four minutes.) For the sea, go right. It is still another hour's walk, crossing the Tuja five times, to reach **Punta Tuja**. The tiny rocky bay is almost uninhabited – there are two houses, one belonging to a fisherman, the other to a Guardia Nacional post.

East to Puerto Cruz
The way to Puerto Cruz is wilder and less frequented than the route to Puerto Maya. However, once you are in Puerto Cruz there is the possibility of hitching a ride to Colonia Tovar (there appears to be no public transportation as yet). To simplify notes of this five-hour descent through beautifully shady woods, start at the lower part of the **Costa Maya circuit** (see above).

At **Quebrada Las Minas** (do not cross the ravine), take the right-hand road into **Las Marías**, altitude 700m, and look for the path to Topo El Paraíso, altitude 950 (30 minutes). There follows a long stretch of fine rainforest; the trail nowhere divides. Magnificent old trees shade the ridge or **Fila La Virginia** (one hour) before the trail dips to the huts of **San José** (25 minutes). Ask the *campesinos* there for the mule path (*camino de recua*) to Río Grande (the Limón River); this descends through a handsome, open deciduous forest to a crossroads (20 minutes), go left (right is for Riítos and Hacienda El Limón). The last stage down is by a road so old that erosion over the centuries has carved it into a canyon of almost vertical walls with the **Limón River** at the bottom, altitude 100m (40–45 minutes). Cross the river, about 4m wide. Mule drivers once rested here before starting on the way up.

Follow the river left. It is a 45-minute walk, crossing seven times the clear waters which tumble among huge boulders, before the track emerges at the main road. There remains nearly 3km to **Puerto Cruz**, a fishing village and a small, pretty bay with a nice beach. On weekends and holidays the beach attracts a fair number of visitors and you can buy beer or soft drinks, and fried fish.

From Puerto Cruz, there is a rough road crossing west to **Puerto Maya** and another even more tortuous paralleling the coast east to **Chichiriviche**. They are used by a few 4x4 vehicles and pickup trucks.

Costa Paraulata trek
The beautiful forests of Pittier National Park in Aragua State are reached by back country roads from Colonia Tovar. There is a hike somewhat similar to the Punta Tuja route (see above) leading to the bay and gorgeous beach of *Cepe*. This 3-day excursion, mostly downhill, is offered by Viva Trek Tours who drive the first 50km in a 4x4 vehicle, then continue on foot for seven hours down the trail. From Cepe, fishing boats take you to either Puerto Colombia or Puerto Cruz. For dates and rates, ring Douglas Pridham, tel: (016) 6320050, fax: (044) 551683, (016) 6320050.

COLONIA TOVAR TO THE SEA BY CAR
If exploring by car, remember to fill up before leaving because there are no services on the paved roads to the sea. From the gasoline station and arch before Colonia Tovar, the descent winds through cool forests down to coffee groves shaded by *bucares*, the immortelle trees whose bright coral blooms are so vivid in February and March. On the coast are the villages of Puerto Cruz, Puerto Maya and Chichiriviche.

El Limón to Puerto Cruz

This road has more twists than a snake so allow four hours for the round trip if you plan on returning to Colonia Tovar. The distance is 43km to the tranquil little bay of Puerto Cruz. The route is dramatically beautiful as clouds roll down forested flanks to steep valleys, and mist outlines vines, orchids and bromeliads on huge trees. Halfway down is the coffee hacienda of **El Limón**; there are few other communities, and no restaurants, although people in Puerto Cruz prepare fried fish for weekend visitors.

Staying in El Limón

Retired archaeologist Luis Laffer and his wife Margarita have built a small house with a simple guest room. Look for a sign on the right, 'Rooms-Zimmer & Museo de Petroglifos', 20km from the arch at Colonia Tovar. Drive up the grassy entrance. Their home is shaded by huge trees and surrounded by flowers and birds. Margarita also rents two units providing clean but basic shelter (tin roof, shower, cooker) at $20 a weekend. You pay the same whether you stay the whole weekend or not. Bring food for your stay because supplies are scarce, and the Laffers' larder consists of rice, beans, yuca and coffee.

The house, which is also a museum, has a wealth of books, sound recordings and anthropological relics. Laffer, a Hungarian who speaks four or five languages, has spent much of his life recording and cataloguing the native music of Venezuela, from Barlovento to Sinamaica. In El Limón his project is cataloguing the area's many petroglyphs. He can take you by jeep to visit some of the bigger, more remote *piedras pintadas*. Alison Vickers found her stay in El Limón 'a weekend simple in accommodation and food, but rich in company'.

Puerto Cruz

This remote fishing village offers a crescent beach of fine sand and some trees for hammocks. Aside from fishermen the bay and beach are largely deserted from Monday to Friday. Local ladies make fried fish at weekends when the regular beach-lovers arrive by car.

A very stony, tortuous jeep track crosses the sun-baked promontory east to Chichiriviche in about 30km; not recommended as there is no help if your jeep comes off the 'road'. Another track leads west to **Puerto Maya**; it's 16km and, although a lot better, may take 40 minutes to drive. Much more fun is to park your car with Señor Branco and hire a fishing boat; this takes only 25 minutes to Puerto Maya and costs as little as $12 round trip if you have a group of six, or can join a party.

Puerto Maya

The village is on an even smaller cove at the boundary of Henri Pittier National Park in Aragua State. The road from Puerto Cruz has been graded in preparation for paving and is now quite good. However, the sea crossing is faster (25 minutes) and more fun. As you skirt the coast in a small boat under cliffs sculpted by the surf, you slip into another time, one framed by the sea, steep headlands and the rising cordillera walls. A dozen open boats are moored in the bay; on the sand fishermen mend nets. Under coconut palms a street doubles as a basketball court; school is out and children are everywhere. It is the week before Good Friday, villagers are putting up stalls and everyone looks forward to the holidays, to sales of beer, drinks and fish, but more exciting, to new faces. In Puerto Maya, everyone seems to be related, it's like one big family. Houses are placed wherever their owners decided; all belong to villagers (although some have been sold to outsiders). No Plaza Bolívar, no founding date. Two small *abastos*, groceries. One policeman. One chapel, always open.

As a fishing community Puerto Maya until recently had few land visitors; there is still no link with mountain cultures such as Colonia Tovar. These are black people and they live well off the sea. The price of fish is high in La Guaira, less than two hours away, and that is where the fishermen go to sell their catch, refill, buy clothes and supplies, or seek hospital care. New fibreglass *lanchas* are bought in Tacarigua de la Laguna where they are made.

The women meanwhile tend maize, yuca, pigs and chickens. Descendants of African slaves, the people of Maya laugh, dance, play the big drums and drink quarts of alcohol at Carnival and traditional fiestas such as San Juan, a three-day affair around June 24, and the *fiestas patronales* honouring Archangel Michael on September 24.

The Río Maya rushes between boulders on its way to the sea. Walk up beside the river to fine pools for splashing; Pozo de los Perros has a torrent chasing over rocks. Mountain water from the Maya is pumped through a pipeline east to supply Catia and La Guaira. The villagers see this as fair because in return they get electricity.

Beaches, snorkelling

Fishermen know the best places to snorkel and when not working their nets will take you to bays further west such as Tuja, Cepe or Chuao which have no roads. Make arrangements with stalwarts such as 'El Embajador' Primo Hugo, Marinero, Cacayo or Venancio.

Where to stay/eat

You can pitch a tent on the beach or rent a village house with kitchen, bathroom and beds; ask for Señor Eufemio. On the seafront a two-room house with fans, fridge, kitchen, double bed and three bunks is rented by Ana Maldonado and Gabriel Salazar; enquiries through Sobeida who will arrange cleaning and cooking. The cost is $17 per person including one meal. Reservations in Caracas, tel: (02) 6312967, 6618086.

The **Gua-K-Maya** is a weekend home at the beach's western edge, converted by the Lemoine family into a comfortable *posada* (no phone) with eight doubles and triples with fan, some with shared bath. The package includes breakfast and dinner and the food is plentiful; lunch and special dishes such as lobster, sushi, are extra. In Caracas, **Eco Posadas** offer a 3-day/2-night package at $120 a person, and can arrange car transfer from Caracas, $140 return trip for four, or a van for up to 12 people $180. Tel: (02) 9931695/5866, fax: 928984. In the evening you may call owner Carlos Lemoine, tel: (02) 9790323. If you wish to go by launch (25 minutes) from Puerto Cruz, a service provided by Chencho (who also guards your car), this will cost $50 round trip, shared by up to six passengers; you pay on return.

There is a little restaurant, **La Negra**, run by Señora Maritza who prepares *pargo* (snapper), *mero* (grouper), paella and shellfish. Alternatively, buy your fish from the fishermen.

Chichiriviche de la Costa

To avoid confusion with the bigger beach town of the same name in Falcón State, it's best always to add 'de la Costa'.

Start from the Colonia Tovar arch down towards Puerto Cruz and take the second right after 10km (the first fork goes to Carayaca). You will want to go slowly over the next 25km to take in fine views of farms, forest and sea. On the last stage, a protected watershed, ferns and heliconias proliferate by the road; there are few dwellings. Because this part is not paved and crosses the tumbling Chichiriviche River many times (some concrete aprons but no access ramps), a car with ample clearance is best. The road and river, which even has hot springs, come out at a growing beach community on a clean crescent bay enclosed by promontories. The village, church and coffee-drying patio of Chichiriviche proper are set back 1km from the sea. There is good fried fish to be had.

Stands of immense mahoganies shade houses behind the beach. At the east entrance there is a well stocked food and liquor shop called **La Parada**. But no public transportation stops here. In order to continue to Catia or Maiquetía, you must have a car or else hitch.

Scuba diving

Excellent underwater banks give Chichiriviche growing fame as the best diving area on the *Litoral*. Fishermen will take you out to Banco Los Arenales, Los Barriles, and Noche y Día. One group, **Chichiriviche Divers**, (see page 50) has built a two-storey dive centre: at the large *Bienvenidos* (welcome) sign near the entrance to the beach you will see a red brick structure by the Kiosko Virgen del Valle. This is the dive centre where you can take courses, rent equipment, fill tanks, arrange a launch or stay overnight; tel: José Antonio Rodriguez, (016) 6239551, or tel: (02) 2412318. Another group, the **Diver's Center**, has an operations base for technical dives and classes. They will provide students a place to stay. In Caracas: Quinta Diver's Center, Av Río de Janeiro, Chuao; tel: (02) 921229; email: diversc@telcel.net.ve.

Whales have been sighted off this coast. The sperm whale is more or less resident, while the humpback comes from the north in winter. Twenty humpbacks were seen only 200m off shore in October 1996. When this happens, you can approach in a fishing boat for a closer look.

Along the coast

Hikers can explore west of Chichiriviche. A few trucks take this coastal track all the way to Puerto Cruz, 17km, but it is steep, tricky and low-gear most of the way. Near **Petaquire**, 8km, you pass Peñon La Petaca, a rock five storeys tall. At the beach where the Río Petaquire joins the sea there is a cliff with a cave. As you hike upstream, at one point the river vanishes into a hole among boulders, emerging as a cascade in a cave. This outing is perhaps best done by fishing boat as the road is largely shadeless and hot. Fisherman were charging about $6 round trip per person to Petaquire in 1998. For $100 you could contract the boat for a day's outing, for instance to **Punta Tuja**.

Where to stay/eat

Hotel El Montero, a block from the beach at the east entrance, tel: (014) 9296310, tel/fax: 8620436; a modest German-run hotel with ten rooms, double bed $60; also two cabins for six with refrigerator. Restaurant, pool, tasca, good value. Owner Bruno Sponsel will arrange excursions with fishermen. **La Posada de Loli** is located on the right at the village's east entrance. Loli's is one of the first houses you see, two floors with lime green trim and parking lot; seven rooms, with private bath $9 a person, shared bath $7. Loli, a stocky Spanish blonde, also cooks up a storm: breakfast $4, lunch or supper $7. For reservations ring Loli's daughter, Elda, tel: (02) 9450541.

Look around the beach for signs saying 'room for rent', *se alquila habitación*. You may have to hunt up the person in charge in the pueblo itself as few Chichiriviche residents live by the beach.

Coast road to Maiquetía

Heading east from Chichiriviche by a graded, unpaved road, the next community is **Oricao**, 12km. As there is a private beach club in Oricao, the bay is no longer

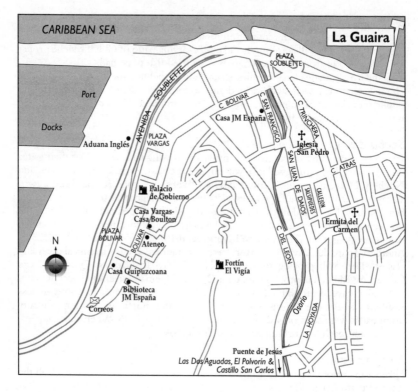

primitive although legally you have access to the 300m beach. The lovely grounds have five pools, 150 rooms in cottages, and parking for 1,000 cars.

Continue 4km east to a fork. (Take this turn for a southwest route to Colonia Tovar, or a southeast one to **Tarma**, 2km, and **Carayaca**, 5km. From Carayaca yet another road rises up to the Junquito–Tovar road, 30km.) The coast road is scenic, although rocky and arid, and there are some beaches for swimming: Punta Tarma, Playa Paraiso Shangrilá, and **Bikini**, a large breezy beach with a restaurant. Beyond this point, however, swimming is not recommended. Soon after Arrecife and the crowded, hilly road through Mamo, you enter the urban disorder of **Catia La Mar** and the highway to Maiquetía.

LA GUAIRA, HISTORIC PORT

The coast from La Guaira eastward is called the *Litoral Central*. The sea approach to this coast is striking. You get the full impact of the coastal range plunging from over 2,500m elevation in the Avila National Park down to the sea, leaving a strip only wide enough in places for three streets. This is where the old town of La Guaira hides, behind the docks and modern highway. As the port lacks a naturally deep harbour, it was made by dredging to handle a constant flow of ships, mostly containers bringing wheat, chemicals, paper, glass and some vehicles for the capital region. But La Guaira is no longer the country's busiest port, now moving only 1.6 million tons (Puerto Cabello handles over three times this). Caribbean cruisers stopped coming to La Guaira during the low season, finding Puerto La Cruz and Margarita more attractive. Indeed, Vargas State faces a big job to put new life not only into the port, but into its capital, the historic town which has survived as a remarkably intact unit.

Tours

Jesyka Travel has an office in the Gran Caribe (Meliá) Hotel in Caraballeda, tel: (02) 3948534/5555, ext 609. They take groups in 4x4 vehicles up to Avila National Park and the flower growers in San Antonio de Galipán. Request a guide speaking English, French or German. The cost is $60 per person, or $55 from Caracas where this tour starts. A minimum of four passengers is required for this tour and others to Colonia Tovar or the wilder eastern coast and beaches such as La Sabana; 2 days/1 night $155. **Pérez Travel** also offers coast tours with multilingual guides, $70 per person; in Caracas: tel: (02) 7628575 ext 556; Hotel Lincoln Suites, Sabana Grande; and tel: 5763432, Edif Anauco Hilton, Parque Central.

Buses

The distance from Caracas to La Guaira is some 36km (about 50 minutes). Take almost any *litoral* bus from Caracas to the coast, except those for Maiquetía and Catia La Mar (west). The buses leave from a terminal near the **Caño Amarillo** metro station. Buses of the Carcaguaili line serving Macuto queue two blocks west of the National Capitol at Esquina Solís, Av Oeste 2 (if they haven't moved to a permanent terminal). *Por puestos* also go to La Guaira and Maiquetía from Avenida Sucre at the **Gato Negro** station. Before buying your metro ticket to Gato Negro, ask for a *boleto integrado* for metrobus route 603 to La Guaira and the Litoral Central. This bus goes as far as Macuto and Caraballeda.

Historic centre

La Guaira's origins as a port date to 1567 when Diego de Losada founded Caracas in a valley some 24km over the mountains. La Guaira (*huayra* means 'hot wind') was officially founded in 1589 by Diego de Osorio as the main port for the Province of Venezuela. For over a century it was exposed to attacks by pirates the likes of Amyas Preston who went so far as to sack Caracas in 1595, and Henry Morgan who sacked La Guaira in 1669. As late as 1680 the French pirate Gramont landed one night, looted and burned the port, and only retired when faced with 2,000 soldiers. This at last prompted the construction of military forts.

La Guaira rises up steep streets to these colonial forts along the 16th-century Spanish road, *Las Dos Aguadas*. In the early 1600s work was begun on the definitive route, now known as the *Camino de los Españoles*, that starts about 2km east in the old part of Maiquetía. Still standing are the 17th-century **Polvorín** or powderhouse; **Fuerte El Zamuro** or El Vigía, visible from Plaza Soublette; and the **Castillo San Carlos**, not visible from the town, with its own eagle-eye view of the port from 2km higher than El Vigía (the Lookout). The Castillo was constructed in 1768–69.

A look around the old sector's charming streets is fun. They are quiet during the day and lively at night when people are home from work, gossiping beneath the street-lamps and slanging *politicos*, while kids play basketball. The houses are so close on Calle Salsipuedes that you can touch both sides at once; its name means 'leave if you can'.

The imposing **Casa Guipuzcoana**, largest civil structure of the colonial era, faces the coast road. Now the seat of government offices, it dates from 1734 when it was built as headquarters for the Guipuzcoana Company, a royal trading monopoly run by Basques who exported cacao and indigo and brought back guns, tools, wine and cloth. Rife with corruption and abuses, the Guipuzcoana was hated by the native citizens, the *criollos*. For the next 200 years the three-storey building was a customs house. Finally restored in the 1970s, its patios, balconies, and tall rooms are open during office hours.

Directly behind is Calle Bolívar. On this street are the grandest houses. Iron gates, shut at sundown, stood at either end of Calle Bolívar and protected its prosperous citizens for over a century. The east gate stood by the Guipuzcoana's warehouse, now restored as a public library, the **Biblioteca José María España**. Doubling as a cultural centre, the pleasant library has three floors for reading, reference and children's activities, with a terrace at the top overlooking the port. The young librarian will find you books on La Guaira's history, pirates and famous men. Next door, a yellow and green building housing a school used to be a red-light port of call for sailors, the Muchinga Bar.

Walking east you pass the former Curaçao Trading Company post, newly painted as the home of the Lions' Club and Bolivarian Society.

In the street's 19th-century heyday, the big shippers, importers and suppliers lived on balconied second storeys above spacious, tall offices and depots, some with doors you could enter by horse and wagon. Those restored to date are: the **Ateneo del Litoral** occupying a large house with wooden beams which was the mansion of José María Vargas, a doctor who became Venezuela's second constitutional president in 1835; now serving as coastal nucleus of the Simón Bolívar University; and the adjacent house, continuing the same balcony, for 140 years the seat of **Boulton & Co**. There are plans to reopen the house as a centre for Caribbean history studies. Lancashire merchant John Boulton arrived in the late 1820s as a young man, starting up an import-export business which is still going strong today.

On the north side, 19th-century warehouses once the headquarters of shipping agents crumble with neglect. Ferretería El Ancla has gone to dust. However, a building extending through to Av Soublette is today the fashionably remodelled **Palacio de Gobierno**. Plaza Vargas, also between Calle Bolívar and Soublette, stands in need of new trees and benches.

Across the highway you see large grain silos painted in kinetic stripes (designed by Carlos Cruz Diez). They dwarf a solitary house with a wrap-around balcony, the **Aduana Inglés**. In payment of an 1864 loan of £1.5 million, the English La Guaira Harbour Company was given financial control not only of La Guaira, but of all the major ports in Venezuela. The debt was finally paid off in 1938.

A colonial house at No 9 Callejón San Francisco (three blocks east of Plaza Vargas, and 50m uphill) bears the name of martyr José María España. He was a pre-Independence rebel who escaped the Spaniards but returned to his home here two years later, and was captured, hanged and quartered by the Spaniards in 1799. Across the *arroyo* (what's left of the Río Osorio) is the church of **San Pedro Apostol** which has a fine golden pulpit and carved retable dating from the 18th century. The church itself, like all La Guaira's major buildings, was destroyed by earthquake in 1812, killing 600 worshippers at Holy Thursday services. Continuing uphill, you find the narrowest street of all, Callejón Salsipuedes. Above it, left, is the pretty, restored **La Ermita del Carmen** which was destroyed in 1812 two years after it was finished, and rebuilt in 1863.

Residents of La Guaira caution visitors not to walk alone beyond La Ermita in view of assaults by gangs of youths. However, you could ride in one of the *por puesto* jeeps that go up the hill. The views are spectacular. For **Fuerte El Vigía**, take the right fork above the Polvorín.

MACUTO

Macuto, a small seaside town with a nostalgic air, seafood restaurants, and small hotels, makes a convenient base for travellers arriving or leaving by air. Some 10km from the airport, it is on bus and *por puesto* routes to Caraballeda (Caribe). To return to the airport get a *por puesto* for Catia la Mar and ask for the *Entrada Aeropuerto Nacional*, or *Internacional*, $0.50. A hotel taxi will cost $16.

Presidential seaside resort

Macuto shone for many years as the resort preferred by presidents, starting in the 1880s when Antonio Guzmán Blanco was so taken that he made a plaza and bathing houses (he also built a railway from Caracas, opened in 1883). His residence, **La Guzmania**, is still in presidential use but all you can see are armed guards and high walls next to the Plaza de las Palomas. Pigeons were brought to the plaza a century ago by poet Andrés Mata, founder of *El Universal*. In the 1950s dictator Marcos Pérez Jiménez built them fancy cotes. The mayor's office provides them food. This a mixed blessing as inflation's grip has put most Venezuelans on a meatless diet – except in Macuto where the pigeons are vanishing into cooking pots.

President Joaquín Crespo built a residence in 1888 on Calle La Guzmania, west of the plaza; it was last occupied by a school. After Crespo died Juan Vicente Gómez, who was to become Venezuela's longest-ruling dictator, came to take the sea air and completed the Crespo mansion. Gómez also built the **Hotel Miramar**, height of fashion in 1928. Designed by Alejandro Chataing who was also responsible for Caracas' Teatro Nacional and Nuevo Circo, it saw splendid banquets and balls as a part of Venezuela's only luxury beach resort, but was allowed to fall into disrepair under democratic governments. A local library now functions in one corner.

Like the Miramar, Macuto's elegance has faded. Although favoured by Caraqueños until the 1950s, its public beach became inadequate. Today the plastic awnings of cafés and hotels give colour to the **Boulevard Macuto** but often as not they shelter punters filing out racing forms. Busloads of beachgoers have replaced the high-society bathers of railroad days.

At the east end of Macuto near Hotel Las Quince Letras (count the letters) is the **Castillete de Reverón**, once the isolated seaside home and studio of Venezuela's inspired painter, Armando Reverón (1889–1954). By 1921 he had been to Paris and returned to Venezuela, to the white-hot light of Macuto where he spent his last 34 years. A recluse, too poor to afford much paint or canvas, the 'wild man' of Venezuelan art used charcoal, even sacks, and took as model his companion Juanita. Other models he made, stuffing life-sized rag dolls. He also made his 'castle' and most things in it out of found materials, bamboo, river stones, split palm trunks, driftwood. An **art museum** has been built in concrete beside the Castillete. To get there, walk east along Av La Playa for 15 minutes from the Plaza de las Palomas. You will come to Callejón Colón by Hotel Las Quince Letras. The Museum, tel: (02) 3341452, is open Tue–Fri 09.00–17.00, Sat–Sun 10.00–18.00. By car you follow the Intercomunal highway past Macuto and turn seaward at the first left; there is a signpost.

Where to stay

The telephone area code for the Litoral, formerly (031), has been changed to (02)

Macuto's hotels are convenient, reasonable and some have the attraction of pleasant seaside restaurants. Several cheaper hotels are near the Plaza Las Palomas; more modern ones are at the west end between Av Alamo and the sea. Unless noted, all rooms have bathroom. Using the same price guide as Caracas hotels for a double room, **(B)** represents budget hotels, $16 and under; **(E)** = economy, $17–35; **(G)** = good hotels, $36–69; **(H)** = high, $70–149; and **(I)** = international, $150 and up. High-season rates during school holidays may shift the key upward, for example B–E.

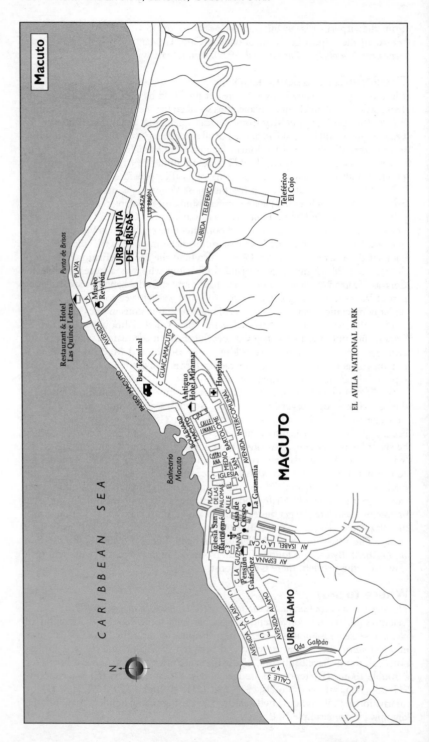

Alamo district

As you approach Macuto from La Guaira, the first sector is called Alamo. There are reasonable hotels and many restaurants on or near the coast road, Av La Playa, but there is no public beach. **Macuto (G)**, tel: 3341410/310, fax: 3341854, Calle 3; 77 rooms, suites, with air conditioning, good rate for triples; restaurant, pool. **Posada de Hidalgo (E)**, Av La Playa at Calle 3, tel: 3341138; a mansion emblazoned with coats of arms; the draw here is the Spanish restaurant in the hotel, plus seaside service. **Santiago (G)**, Av La Playa at Calle 2, tel: 3344118, fax: 3341754; 84 rooms and suites (four people $75), air conditioning, laundry; tennis court, no beach but pool with Avila view, waterfront seafood restaurant. **Alamo (B–E)**, Av La Playa at Calle 1, tel: 3341236; same management for 40 years oversees 30 spacious rooms with air conditioning, TV, no hot water; parking, good seafood restaurant.

West of Plaza Las Palomas

Pensión Guánchez (E), tel: 3341256, a block west of La Guzmania, Av 2 between Calle La Guzmania and Av Alamo (no name plate). Built as a second residence by President Crespo (1884–86), this handsome white mansion was later occupied by President Castro, dictator Gómez and others down to the Guánchez sisters who opened a now famous inn with tall ceilings, breezy porch and wooden shutters. Fourteen spacious rooms with fan, some with shared bath. Meals are not included; busy kitchen serves home-cooked breakfast, lunch, dinner. **La Alameda (B–E)**, C Isabel la Católica, next to the Iglesia de Macuto, tel: (016) 6263710; remodelled colonial-style house with ten rooms, fan, hot water, TV; run by Señora Lola. **Isaibel (B)**, C Isabel La Católica, tel: 3344910; 35 simple, air-conditioned rooms, no hot water, same rate for single or double bed, extra bed $4.

East of the plaza

Plazamar (B), tel: 3344271, on the plaza at Calle del Medio beside the Contraloría; is a quiet, family-run old hotel on two floors, 22 rooms with fan, TV, no hot water. The **Tojamar (E)**, tel: 3344559, Calle Regenerador, is a block east behind the Contraloría; a well-managed refurbished hotel with parking, restaurant, 22 air-conditioned rooms, twin beds, restaurant. **Corona (B)**, tel: 3344631, Calle Iglesia (no church any more), two blocks east of plaza and one up; 100-year-old house where owner Cesar Andrade and his daughter have 18 rooms with fan and TV, around a tiny orchid-scented patio; *criollo* food, coffee next door. **Riviera (E)**, tel: 3344313/1332, Calle San Bartolomé at Callejón 9; a family hotel with parking, good Spanish restaurant, 30 rooms on three floors, air conditioning, TV, hot water. **Sandra (E)**, tel: 3344727, Calle Santa Ana at a semi-plaza; a bright new orange hotel on 2nd floor, 14 air-conditioned rooms, modern but smaller than old hotels. **Colonial (E)**, tel: 3341462/552, Calle Santa Ana at pedestrian boulevard; not colonial but decent, 28 rooms for one to four people, air conditioning, TV, hot water. **Diana (B-E)**, tel: 3341553, Callejón 9 at the boulevard, beside Antiguo Miramar; parking, 34 air-conditioned doubles, outdoor café; noisy. **Mar Azul (B-E)**, tel: 3344522, at corner where Av La Playa turns south past Antiguo Miramar; facing the sea, a renovated four-storey hotel with parking, 42 rooms, TV, hot water, Las Brisas seafood restaurant. **Las Quince Letras (G)**, tel: 3341551, fax: 3341432, email: 110130.302@compuserve.com; a businessman's hotel on Av La Playa, eight floors, 79 rooms with seaview, air conditioning; pool, restaurant, plus popular seafood restaurant at the water's edge. The best beach is in Camurí Chico, 1km east.

Where to eat

Spanish seafood restaurants on Av La Playa in the Alamo district are a good choice, led by the **Posada del Hidalgo (G)** inside the hotel, then the **Alamo (E)** and

Santiago Hotel (E), where waiters thread through the traffic to serve seaside tables. The Santiago is open from 08.00 to midnight. The **Pensión Guánchez (B)**, Av 2 La Guzmania at Av Alamo (a block before this becomes the Intercomunal), has a dining room known for ample servings – ask prices of the daily menu (not printed) – and don't overlook hearty *criollo* breakfasts. Hours are: 08.00–10.00, 12.00–15.00, 18.00–21.00.

On the east side, **Las Quince Letras (E)**, Av La Playa about 1km from Plaza Las Palomas, has been the traditional seaside spot since the 1950s. It is run by the hotel which also owns the **Terraza Oriental (E)**, a small, air-conditioned *tasca* preparing Spanish food and fish. The Terraza serves tables by the sea, next to the Quince Letras.

CARABALLEDA–CARIBE

Avenida La Playa parallels the *Litoral Central* for 4km to Caraballeda, dotted by breakwaters and beaches with public facilities, *balnearios*. Such beaches are overcrowded on weekends and holidays when cars stream down from Caracas. After Macuto comes the large public beach of **Camurí Chico**, 1.5km, with changing rooms and soda fountains. Respect the signs saying PROHIBIDO on unused beaches: these mean dangerous currents. The next residential area, 2km, is **Los Corales,** merging with the resorts of **Caraballeda** and **Caribe** in a string of shops, billboards, restaurants and hotels. The public beaches in town are **Playas Lido, Alí Babá, Caribito and Bahía del Mar** on the west side; and **Laguna Beach**, **Playa Escondida**, entered by a lane between the Macuto Sheraton and Gran Caribe hotels, **Playa Los Cocos** and **Tanaguarena** to the east.

Caraballeda was the first site settled on the *Litoral*, in 1558, by Spaniards, or rather a *criollo*, Francisco Fajardo, son of Margarita Island's Spanish governor and a Guaiquerí chieftain's daughter. He had inside information from his uncle Naiguatá who had scouted the coast with him, as well as from chief Guaicamacuto. But ten years later when Diego de Losada needed a port for Caracas, Fajardo's settlement had been abandoned, so Losada founded it again. Guaicamacuto, shortened to Macuto, became the name of that settlement, first an Indian mission, then officially founded as San Bartolomé de Macuto on August 24, 1740. The date is marked still as Macuto's *fiestas patronales*.

Buses

The Carcaguaili line from **Caracas** turns around near the Meliá to return to Caracas. Buses run from 04.30 to 23.00; the fare is less than $1. In Caracas, the terminus is two blocks west of the Capitol, at Esquina Solís on Av Sur 8, opposite the Liceo Fermín Toro. Local *litoral* buses also stop a block from the Meliá where they turn around for **Catia La Mar**. *Por puestos* serving this route park on the next street east and charge about $0.50 to let you off at the **Maiquetía airport**, Terminal Nacional or Internacional.

Where to stay

The telephone area code for Caraballeda, formerly (031), has been changed to (02)
The five-star beach resort hotels are: the 543-room **Macuto Sheraton**, tel: 800 SHERA, 3944300, fax: 3944317, in Caracas tel: (02) 9595833, fax: 9596615; and the adjacent **Gran Caribe** (formerly the Meliá), tel: 3945555, fax: 3941509, with 252 doubles and 38 suites.

A few blocks east of the Gran Caribe on Av La Playa is a white walled corner house, **Hotel Tamacuro (E)**, tel: 3941325; 22 rooms with double beds, some twin beds, air conditioning, hot water; near Los Cocos beach.

Canadians were the first foreign tourists attracted to this 'sophisticated ocean playground' which they call simply **Caribe**. Many patronise small aparthotels such as the Golf Caribe and Avila Caribe which are not on the beach (apartments cost some $100 a day).

Two nearby moderate hotels on Boulevard Caribe, with air conditioning and hot water, are: the **Fiore (G)**, tel: 3941743, fax: 3948724; Restaurant La Gran Paella, room service, laundry, 34 rooms; and **Royal Atlantic (G)**, tel: 3941361, pool, restaurant, 20 rooms, slightly cheaper. Opposite is the **Costa Azul (E)**, tel: 3940174; three floors over a liquor shop; air conditioning, all rooms have double beds; noisy, badly run. **Mar y Cel (E)**, tel: 3942174, Esq Miami, Av Costanera; is small and often full. Old, with basic bed and shower, is **Hotel Tu y Yo (E)**, tel: 3940729, Av Costanera, Los Corales sector; 14 rooms and two cabins for beachgoers. **La Costanera (E)**, tel: 3943560, Av La Playa near Playa Lido, has air-conditioned motel rooms around central parking. **Litoral Palacios (E)**, tel: 3942070, Av La Playa, Playa San Luís sector; 18 air-conditioned rooms on three floors. Nearest beach for swimming is Alí Babá.

Where to eat

At the **Macuto Sheraton** you can enjoy pizza baked in a wood oven by the pool **(E)**, or go for broke at the **Sevilla (H)**, rated with three stars for fine French cuisine. Or go local. Follow the street in front of the hotel, Avenida Norte, to its end at the Marina Mar. On a pier is the thatched **Ranchocaribe (E)** where you are surrounded by yachts and served by waiters in sailor suits.

Go west along Avenida La Playa from the Boulevard Caribe; after 500m you come to **La Gabarra (G)** in Los Corales where you are greeted by a pet monkey, a generous menu, good service and air conditioning. The **Palmarejo (E)** is another traditional spot a bit further on, preparing rabbit and specialities such as conch and quigua. Continue west to Playa Lido. Here a big breezy restaurant, **El Farallón (E)**, serves a standard menu plus seafood, inside and outside at tables on the broad sea wall. There used to be a tunnel to the old Hotel Farallón across the road. Another economical choice is the **Mar y Cel** *tasca* by the hotel on Av Costanera.

Deep-sea fishing

This coast has some of the best marlin fishing in the world, half an hour from port where underwater mountains provide ideal baitfish habitat. These famous La Guaira shoals are 16km long and 6km wide. The peak months for billfish are: blue marlin, February to May; blue or white marlin, September through November. There is good fishing year round for sailfish, yellowfin tuna, wahoo, snook, tarpon, bonefish, kingfish. The **La Guaira Billfish Shootout** is an international event held annually at the end of April. As for all sport fishing in Venezuela, standard practice is catch, tag and release.

Caraballeda is the charter centre for yachting and fishing (*pesca de altamar*). The **Caraballeda Yacht Club**, tel: 3940271, by the Sheraton, is a good place to charter vessels for deep-sea fishing, and for cruises to Los Roques Archipelago or anywhere else you want to go. If you have a party of at least four, and are sure of your sea legs, a holiday to tropical islands can be surprisingly reasonable on a fully crewed motor-sailer for four passengers: daily rate of $450–550 includes boat, crew, tackle, food and beer. **Yachting Tours**, tel/fax: 3940591, or 3944300 ext 188, is based in the Macuto Sheraton. Ask them about nighttime swordfishing. **Venezuela Marlin Safari** operates from the Gran Caribe (Meliá), tel: 3948868, 3945555 ext 385; fax: 3944078; email: marlinsafari@

cantv.net. They will show you how to catch billfish, or take you on a big fish marathon from 09.30 to midnight. The cost of a ten-day fishing cruise to Los Roques for four is $2,000 a person.

Gigi Charters operates an upscale base two blocks west of the Macuto Sheraton where a large air-conditioned house goes through to a private dock in the Caraballeda Marina. The clubhouse accommodates 26 guests in style; cost per person is $80 a day with breakfast. Their yachts take four fishermen at $500–600, or maximum five in a 43ft yacht, $750. Gigi lays on full service cruises to Los Roques for beaches and bonefishing. For information, tel: 944689, fax: 948970; or in Caracas tel/fax: (02) 2429740; email: gigifish.com.ve.

NAIGUATA

On the rugged coast beyond Caraballeda seafood restaurants roadside stops such as **Carmen de Uria**, although bare of niceties, serve really fresh fish at modest prices. Worth the trip. Approaching Naiguatá, 13km, what you see first are the towers of a private marina and beach club, Puerto Azul and Playa Azul. The town itself lies east of the Naiguatá River. There are four streets paralleling the coast, and one of the *Litoral*'s best and longest public beaches with 1km of clear sea, palm trees, clean sand, and almost no bathers during the week. Fishing and tourism are the main sources of livelihood. Fishing boats pull in to the beach to sell their catch for the day's lunch.

Franciscan missionaries arrived here in 1690 and the settlement was formally founded in 1710 as San Francisco de Asís de Naiguatá, named (like Naiguatá peak on the coastal range) after an important Indian chieftain who lived in the mid 1500s. Naiguatá accompanied Francisco Fajardo on three explorations of the coast. But when the Indian inhabitants got to know the Conquistadors better, they made a plan in 1568 to wipe out the new settlement of Caracas. Among the leaders who answered the call by Guaicaipuro of the Teques people were the chieftains Baruta, Chacao, Guaicamacuto and Naiguatá. Their plan failed because Guaicaipuro was late and the Spaniards rallied early.

Where to stay/eat

The area telephone code for Naiguatá, formerly (031), has been changed to (02)
Doña Mar (B), tel: 3372938, Av José María Vargas, east end of beach, has basic but passable lodging in 18 rooms with fan, some with shared bath, for two to five people; only two rooms with sea view. **El Balneario (E)**, 71070, at the west end of the beach, opposite the town pool; is a white house with 11 rooms and double beds (you can request an extra bed).

The open-air **Kiosko Indio Coromoto** serves a low-cost daily menu with fresh juice and beer, at 15 tables on the beach. **Sifón Naiguatá**, facing the beach, offers standard fried fish and salad for more money.

A culinary surprise, the **Camurí Alto Restaurant School** is run by the Universidad Simón Bolívar, not far from Naiguatá. The USB's Nucleo del Litoral occupies the restored **Hacienda Camuricao**, a truly lovely setting for fine dining at minimal cost. A wine list accompanies the daily menu. There are ifs and buts: the restaurant is open only for lunch, Tuesday to Thursday, during part of the year; reservations must be made a week in advance and $4 per diner deposited in a bank account. For information, ring 3372911. The entrance gates to the USB Nucleo del Litoral are on the right, 2.5km east of Naiguatá passing the modern *balneario* of **Playa Los Angeles** (and before reaching Club Camurí Grande).

Hacienda Camuricao, its cobbled road, old cacao and coffee drying patio, and sugarcane mill or *trapiche* are well worth visiting. An aqueduct once fed a waterwheel and small refinery. The hacienda dates from at least 1622. Central buildings have been restored including the beautiful colonial house, elegant in its simplicity of white walls and columned porch. The hacienda house and grounds are open Mon–Fri 09.00–12.00, 13.00–16.00.

As part of its work the University has begun an ambitious project to link the *Litoral*'s grade schools with the Internet, recycling standard computers no longer used by companies and instructing teachers and students in their use.

Devil dancers

Naiguatá's street celebration of **Corpus Christi** is famous for its devil dancers in horned masks and costumes painted red and gold. Corpus Christi, a religious observation, is always on a Thursday, the ninth after Holy Thursday, frequently in early June. Members of the Corpus society vow to dance for a certain number of years, often as payment for a promise. Women may be devil dancers in Naiguatá, unlike in celebrations in Chuao and San Francisco de Yare. Symbolically, the dancers show the power of God over the devil as they advance upon the church, are turned away, and finally are blessed and attend mass at noon. Drums fuel the dance, plus infusions of anise-flavoured firewater.

After Corpus Chrsti comes the three-day **Fiesta de San Juan** around the day of St John the Baptist, June 24, celebrated with drums and dances throughout the coastal towns of Aragua and Miranda states.

The **Entierro de la Sardina** or 'Sardine's Burial' closes **Carnival** on Ash Wednesday with a mock wake complete with mourning widows, devil and policeman. Masks and costumes make fun of political leaders as people escort a large papier maché fish to the beach. Music led by the Naiguatá Sardines group keeps dancers going until the fish is thrown into the sea, and Lent begins. This picturesque custom is also observed in Macuto.

LOS CARACAS

The coast is splendidly wild as the road hugs a narrow shore between surf and cliffs to the 'vacation city' of Los Caracas. This workers' resort is at the end of the paved road (45km from La Guaira). The aging holiday complex, a model of architectural and natural beauty when opened by dictator Marcos Pérez Jiménez in 1955, was designed by Carlos Raúl Villanueva, architect of the University City and Fine Arts Museum. It still receives some 20,000 visitors a weekend but facilities limp along, awaiting promised overhaul. The National Training and Recreation Institute (Incret) office is at the entrance, tel: (02) 3379030; to look around the very large complex, consult the wall map. In a green park of 125 acres, trees shade 170 bungalows, unadorned but clean, providing kitchen and beds for six for about $30. There are 200 rooms in four hotels, an immense saltwater pool, five restaurants and cafés, a supermarket and a chapel. It's open to anyone, although school holidays are not the time to go. Reservations are taken only in Caracas: Incret, Av Lecuna, Esq Pinto a Miseria; tel: 5417044/7922.

Por puesto service

On Fri–Sun two lines go to Los Caracas from La Guaira, and from Caraballeda near the Gran Caribe Hotel. Also, five *por puesto* lines cover the distance from Caracas.

Toyota vans give *por puesto* service between La Guaira and Chuspa for $3. The line starts on Av Soublette at the parking lot of CADA supermarket (facing Timotes Restaurant), two blocks west of Plaza El Consul opposite La Guaira's passenger terminal. There is a stop at Los Tiburones Restaurant west of Macuto (3km from Plaza del Consul). The daily bus service from La Guaira is cheaper, slower, and can be quite an experience, chickens and all.

EAST TO CHUSPA

To take the road along the coast, now paved in part, ask the guards at Los Caracas for the way to Osma. It leads over the headland to surprisingly untouched beaches and the villages of Todasana, La Sabana, Caruao, and Chuspa, reaching the Chirimena–Higuerote highway in some 66km (about two hours). This route has the advantage of making a circle back to Caracas.

The last service station is in Los Caracas, so fill up before leaving. The coast is lush and beaches are empty on weekdays. If the road is ever paved, as announced, this is bound to change in a flash. There are plenty of potholes, and a 4x4 vehicle is recommended during the rainy season.

A growing list of inns and guesthouses in Osma, Todasana, La Sabana and Caruao offer accommodation from basic lodging to spacious new rooms with private bath; most have fans which cool you at night, and cold water, no hardship on a tropical coast. They work on a cash basis as the nearest bank is in either Higuerote or Caraballeda. It's best to arrive on Friday or before because weekends are busy.

Small restaurants or *comedores* will prepare fish and rice if you arrive in good time, otherwise you may have to rely on a picnic. Few shops sell fresh fruit although oranges, bananas and mangoes seem to grow everywhere.

The first hamlet is **Osma**, 10km. A left turn at the creek leads to Osma beach (nothing special), but nearby are good snorkelling reefs and other beaches, even a nudist beach you can reach by a steep path. Ask Max. **La Posada de Max (E)** has a pool, *tasca*-restaurant, 35 rooms with fan, private bath, double bed; extra beds $4 each. You can call Max and his wife during the week, tel: (032) 3833878/562, (014) 9362937.

On the way to **Oritapo**, you pass the entrance to **Fundo La Mantuana (E)** at Km17: a large property with saltwater swimming pool near (not on) beach, with space for riding horses, and hiking to cascades. The new houses are fashioned in colonial style with red tiled roofs; 18 rooms, fan, private bath. The price includes two meals a day. Reservations and bank deposit required, tel: (02) 3344793, 3945929, (02) 9526906. Ask about deep-sea fishing and watersports. The picture-postcard bay of Oritapo (19km) has a rocky beach, summer homes and a small river. Beside the river there is a little restaurant, **Posada de Oritapo**, where you can get fried fish and beer, and fruit juice.

Todasana

Todasana is 22km from Los Caracas. The **Egua Hotel and Restaurant (E)**, (016) 6232179, was one of the first opened on this route, beside the little river where fishing boats moor. You can negotiate with the *capitán* of almost any open boat to take you to deserted beaches. The Egua has 29 plain rooms with bathroom and fan; shade trees but no view. In the village proper **El Sabor de la Costa (B)**, tel: (02) 9878479, 2346643, began as a little restaurant (breakfast, dinner) and added five rooms upstairs, with shared bath. Ask Carolina about excursions.

Todasana's beach, **Playa Grande**, is 1.5km further on. The long curving bay has some seagrape trees for shade or you can rent a parasol. At weekends there's a stall with fried fish and salad. The sea can be fairly rough from January to March but surfers love it and this is the best camping time. Bathers arrive in jeeps complete with icebox and music. There are public toilets. Gustavo Izaguirre has a house on the beach with two budget rooms for rent; he will share his kitchen.

Approaching La Sabana, there are various tracks on the left leading to the sea and a lagoon. Just before a small bridge look for the track to Playa Paraíso, a beach which is cleaned every day by the people who rent beach chairs, and sometimes sell food.

La Sabana

On a bluff above the sea at Km 31, La Sabana is the largest town and one of the prettiest on this coast, sparkling with flowers and paint. There is a church, hospital, pharmacy, police station, grocery, bakery, restaurant, and hammock maker. Coconut-shaded sands, where kiosks sell drinks and fried fish on holidays, extend from La Sabana east to a bay 2km long. The sea may be rough in windy weather, but the beach is deserted more often than not and you can camp. Signs of a new beach resort threaten tourism development soon.

La Posada de Sofía (E) is on Plaza Bolívar, Calle 5 de Julio. Here Señora Ana María and Carmen Lilitha manage ten simple rooms which they rent with or without meals: two people with breakfast, $28; four people, $42; plus dinner, $40/$70. Transfer from Caracas on request: tel: (014) 9340329, (02) 4518871, 8624869. Some villagers let pleasant rooms; try Juan Escobar, Calle 5 de Julio.

The sunny Aloe Spa (G) overlooks the long bay from a hill between La Sabana and Caruao. Above their aloe, or *sábila*, plantation Andrés and Beatriz Berman have crafted a two-storey house with hardwood balconies as a centre for meditation or just relaxation, plus a guesthouse for ten people. The weekend plan includes all meals, yoga and tai chi, and a visit to hot springs; while optional plans offer steam room, and treatments by a therapist including hydrotherapy, aromatherapy, and reflexology. The Bermans prepare vegetarian fare (or fish if you prefer) and do not drink or smoke. You can ask Beatriz (in English) about mud baths, honey, aloe or mint masks, and mountain treks; tel: (014) 9340545; in Caracas EcoPosadas, (02) 9931695, fax: 928984.

Caruao

With its cobbled entrance at Km 37, Caruao is a clean pueblo on the beach of a verdant coast backed by mountains. This seaside community is preferred by weekenders who have built vacation homes. You can buy basic supplies and ice. For the beautiful, often empty, beach, turn left at the church. There is a police station but one wonders what they do for a living as thieves rifle outsiders' cars at will (see below). The Caruao public telephone number is (02) 3132002.

Ask the way to the clear mountain river called Aguas Calientes that tumbles over rocks down five pretty cascades. People swim in deep pools such as El Pozo del Cura. The 2.5km jeep track starts to the east, the second right turn after the 'Granja Venezuela' sign. Halfway, a left fork goes to the Universidad Simón Bolívar Parque Forestal, an experimental garden planted with fruit trees and 150 palm species by Capt Harry Gibson. Keep straight on to the river.

Note Almost every report about the Pozo del Cura mentions bands of young *malandros* or petty thieves who clean out your car and clothes like lightning; better to park in the village and walk.

Where to stay

There is a choice of small places. Next to the police station on tiny Plaza Bolívar is Posada Caruao Mar (B), a converted summer home with three spotless rooms, with fan and bath, for two to five guests, owned by Señora Rosa Echarri. The price includes breakfast. For reservations (a must) or transportation tel: (02) 3372635, (02) 818069/2491, 5729429; they also rent a little house by the beach next to the social club. The Audubon can make reservations for you. This coast is a good birding area; there are military macaws, oropendolas, violetears, trogons, jacamars, manakins...

The Posada de Josefa Ugueto (B) on the boulevard has a miniscule restaurant and 13 basic rooms, with fan and private bath, clean, but mostly facing the social club – where weekends are a long, loud party. Josefina has a reputation of being the best cook in Caruao, starting with fried fish, of course. To get messages to Josefa you could try Caruao's public phone, (02) 3132002. The **Posada de Andrea (B)** run by Eusebio is on the far side of Caruao; four rooms with bamboo furniture, fan, private bath, double and single bed; meals can be arranged.

Campamento Aventura Caruao (E) is run by Omar, a doctor who devotes his weekends to ecotourism. The camp house can sleep up to 20. Higher on the forested mountain by the Río Grande, Omar has a two-bedroom house for 15 guests. Package of 3 days/2 nights includes all meals, excursions to rivers and beaches, and transfer from Caracas. Reservations in Caracas, tel: (02) 6812639, 4326747.

Posada Aguamiel (E), 4km beyond Caruao, is the largest guesthouse hereabouts, a modern structure with terraces seen from the road, plus three cottages; indoor restaurant and thatched outdoor *caney*, game rooms, gym. The *posada* has 20 rooms with fan and bath (no hot water); cottages have double and twin beds. Breakfast and dinner are included. For information, ring Carlos Avendaño: (014) 9340349.

Chuspa

Chuspa, 43km from Los Caracas, is the last seaside village before the road cuts across the headland. The beach is on a broad, lovely bay. The village has clean streets and a seafront walk or *malecón* with trees and a statue of Francisco Fajardo who made a settlement here in 1555. Later inhabitants, descendants of slaves who worked on cacao plantations, turned to fishing. Their catch is sold at the Centro de Acopio by the ice house at the river's outlet where fishermen haul in small boats. On work days (note early closing on Fridays, dubbed *'pequeño sábado'*) and on Saturdays until noon, you can buy fish at half the Caracas price. A restaurant by the sea serves fried fish. Ask here for the cost of a *lancha* to take you to Playa Caribito where there is no road, so no people.

On this coast the big fiestas are the **Tambores de San Juan** on June 24 or closest weekend, and September 8, the day of the **Virgen del Valle**.

Cool and green, the road leaves the beach and winds on through tall forest. It passes the river and community of **Aricagua** to arrive in 16km at the community of Pueblo Seco. From here it is 6.8km to the paved highway.

CHIRIMENA TO CARENERO

For **Chirimena**, 7km, turn left at the junction. Houses crowd this fishing village's best beach but there's another beach on a small cove at the east end by the river. Waves can be rough and many surfers come here.

To continue to **Chirere**, get directions for the dirt road to El Banquito, another good beach. In 2km you arrive at **Hotel Playa Chirere (G)**, where gardens and spacious bungalows overlook a swimming pool, and a path leads down to the sea. There are 14 rooms with private bath, hot water, air conditioning when the generator works at night; extra bed or just mattress can be provided. The Swiss couple Pedro and Teresa who made this miniature resort are also excellent chefs. For information ring them from 17.00 to 20.00, tel: (014) 9340258. Prices include breakfast.

Back at the highway turn south. If you go left at the fork and sign for Puerto Francés, you will be headed towards more beaches on Cape Codera. The road passes El Mirador de Buche which has a restaurant and pier for shuttle boats to Buche Island. The next turn-off, right, is for **Los Totumos**, a long beach whose shallow, clear waters and prevailing winds are a target for windsurfers. There are food stands at weekends. The road passes oil storage tanks and then veers to the cape's north side, crossing a hot landscape of deciduous trees to the lovely bay of **Puerto Francés**, no longer uninhabited, but for most of the week the beach is yours.

Carenero

Carenero, 4km south on the highway, means a place for careening, hauling boats on land to scrape the hull. It was once a port of importance for exporting cacao and was the terminus of a railway from El Guapo. Today Carenero is the home of yacht marinas (try their restaurants) and boat services. There is a weekend shuttle service to the mangrove canals and Buche Island (15 minutes) from various *embarcaderos* near the Capitanía del Puerto; you pay by the person including return.

Where to stay

The area telephone code for Caranero is (034)
There are clean lodgings at a place called **Villa Golefa (G)**, Calle Leo, tel: 230037, opposite the public beach 2½km along the Carenero–Higuerote road. It is the Familia Di Bari's immense house with 16 air-conditioned doubles, ceiling fan, private bath and swimming pool, all behind a high wall. The villa has private mooring on a mangrove canal at the rear.

If you continue to **Higuerote** you will find high-rise apartments and more hotels. The bay is shallow and boring and the beach is brown with silt but safe for swimming. There are two expensive resorts. Among lower-cost lodgings, there is the old **Hotel Barlovento** on the unappealing beach; tel: 230457/161; swimming pool, restaurant; and the **Posada El Palmar**, Calle La Iglesia, tel: 230382. Motel-style **Posada El Mar** on the bay has a restaurant, 230384.

Buses and *por puestos* go frequently to Caracas, about 130km.

La Tortuga tours

Carenero is the base for yacht tours to **La Tortuga Island** which lies some 90km from the coast equidistant from Carenero and Puerto La Cruz. Little visited, it has white beaches, green waters, coral reefs and an airstrip. The catamaran and yachts below provide meals, national brand drinks, snorkelling and fishing gear. Víctor Mercader who built and captains his 11m catamaran, the *Realidad Aun*, has two double beds and a single aboard, with deck shower and a good kitchen. The trip out takes 12 hours (overnight), return with tail wind eight hours; best months are Jan–Apr. Víctor is a diver; he knows the good reefs and can arrange scuba gear rental. The cost per day for minimum 4–5 days is about $130 a person. Víctor speaks a bit of English and French. In Caracas ring Carlos Leiva, Outdoors Ecotours, tel: (02) 2669466, fax: 2650257.

Yachts of 36ft have two cabins, bathroom, kitchen, desalination plant, 245hp diesel engines and the latest navigation gear. A 3-day/2-night plan is recommended at a daily rate of $200 per person. English, French and Italian are spoken. For information in Caracas: Chang Lei Travel, tel: (02) 9935205, fax: 9935705.

Barlovento

You won't find **Barlovento** on road maps; it is the common name for the region inland from Higuerote renowned for lush cacao and fruit plantations. It is also a famous centre of traditional black culture and folklore. Many inhabitants are descendants of Nigeria's Yoruba tribe. There are old songs about Barlovento: *Tierra ardiente y del tambor/ tierra de las fulías y negras finas/ que llevan de fiesta su cintura prieta/ al son de las curvetas/ qui–ta qui-ta qui de las minas...*

The big two-man *curveta* and smaller *mina* drums of Barlovento call visitors to the pueblos of Curiepe, Birongo, Chuspa and Caruao on the **Fiesta de San Juan**, June 24 and nearest weekend, and **San Pedro y San Pablo**, June 28. The street dances are non-stop day and night, the rum also. It's quite an experience; the drums' throbbing seems to go right through you. **Curiepe** is 8km west of

Higuerote (there's an access road north of Carenero, too). **Birongo**, another 10km further along the same road through shady cacao hills, is an apparently uneventful village of slave descendants. But it has a lively reputation for *santería* rituals; people come long distances to consult famous *brujos* or witchdoctors.

On another track, shortly before Birongo there is a sign for Marasmita; take this for the **Cueva Alfredo Jahn**, one of Venezuela's largest caves with 4km of galleries and an underground river. It is above the left bank of the Birongo River, altitude 210m. Although declared a natural monument, it is little visited. (See *Chapter 3*, page 49).

REGIONAL TOURS

Circuits of the Litoral Central in 4x4 vehicles, from Caracas or Macuto to La Sabana and Higuerote, are arranged by Jesyka Travel (see page 125). These can be day tours or overnight with lodging at one of the local inns. For information in Caracas about these and Tacarigua Lagoon, ring María Cariani (she speaks English) at **Turismo Colorama**, tel: (02) 2617732, fax: 2621828, lower level Centro Comercial Bello Campo, west of Plaza Altamira.

The Marine National Parks

THE ROBINSON CRUSOE EXPERIENCE

There are three island groups where you may stay on uninhabited beaches: **Los Roques**, 135 to 166km north of La Guaira; **Morrocoy**, offshore **Tucacas** and **Chichiriviche** in Falcón State; and **Mochima**, between Puerto La Cruz and Cumaná. All have been declared national parks in view of their fragile ecosystems of coral, salt flats, mangrove swamps and marine communities.

In all cases campers must be self-sufficient. Water will be the main problem; bring a supply of plastic gallon jugs, sold by supermarkets, good grocers (*abastos*) and even bakers. In dire need, a large plastic sheet or tent fly-sheet can catch dew. Secondly, take enough food for emergencies as even if you are near a beach visited by food vendors they may not show up on weekdays. Just as important is sun protection. After 10.00 newcomers should wear an old shirt even when snorkelling, and slather sun block on the top of feet and back of knees as they burn quickly. Sunshade can take the form of a sheet, bin liner or tent; you'll need nylon cord for anchoring these in the wind. Hammocks are only practicable on the few islands that have palm trees or mangroves.

Try to plan your stay between long weekends and school vacations when even remote beaches get invaded. Also, avoid the windless months of November–December and part of January, when tiny biting midges make camping after sundown miserable, not to say impossible as they pass through the finest netting. There are many cases of fishermen rescuing campers who have spent the whole night in the water to escape *puri-puri*, 'no-see-ums'.

PARQUE NACIONAL ARCHIPIELAGO LOS ROQUES

The park comprises about 50 named islands and a further 200 or so banks, islets and coral reefs. The archipelago curves 36km east to west, and 24.5km north to south, an extension of 2,250km² of islands and sea which was declared a National Park in 1972. Gran Roque, the main island, lies some 166km north of La Guaira. All the islands except Gran Roque which has a hill of 130m are low-lying, with fine coral-sand beaches. Some have mangrove trees giving a little shade. The shallow central lagoon is crystal clear and has wonderful corals for snorkelling with water temperatures of 24° to 28°C. Barrier reefs in the east and south drop off into ocean water 500–1,000m deep. Los Roques' beauty is such that after a week surrounded by turquoise water, reefs and birds you may not want to leave. Pelicans wheel and plummet in formation down the sun like kingfishers, and gulls bob in rows in the water facing the wind.

The islands' odd names come largely from old English mapmakers who turned the Indian *cayo* into 'key'; these names were then borrowed back into Spanish. *Espenquí* means Spanish Key, *Lanqui* Long Key, *Sarquí* Salt Key, *Nordisquí*

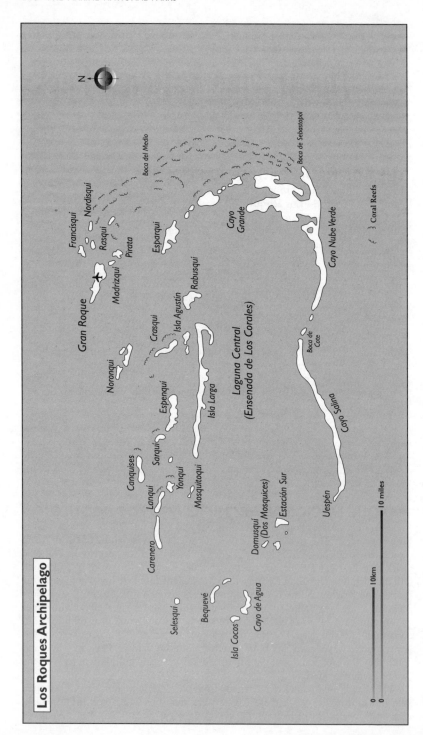

Los Roques Archipelago

Northeast Key, *Selesquí* Sails Key, *Esparquí* Spar Key, *Rabusquí* Robert's Key, *Domusquí* Domain Key. *Uespén* was once West Point and *Cayo Mosquito* was once Musket Key. *Madrizquí* is different; it was called Namusquí or Rataquí until the 1960s when a man named Juancho Madriz got a 100-year concession to develop the island for tourism. He died in 1972 but heirs sold these rights to some powerful Caracas families who built weekend houses. Besides this key, inhabited islands are Gran Roque, Francisquí with its tourist camp, Isla Fernando (a fishing settlement), and Dos Mosquises (Domusquí) where a biological station functions.

The archipelago is home to over 80 species of birds from petrels, pelicans, frigate birds and flamingos to canaries. The migratory visitors arrive in October. Selesquí, Bequevé, Canquises and Cayo Bobo Negro are noted for birdlife. There are black lizards but no snakes and no native land mammals except for a fishing bat. Four turtle species are all on the endangered list, the most persecuted being the green turtle (*Chelonia mydas*). During laying season the females are easily captured on beaches by fishermen who also steal the eggs. Fishermen coming from Margarita, 300km east, for the lucrative lobster season have now been banned. Their custom was to stay in temporary shelters called *rancherías* from November to April.

The beautiful queen conch is also protected. It is now illegal to sell or eat conch (*botuto*) due to overfishing. Huge mounds of harvested conch shells line many islands. Valued as high-protein food conches have been part of island diet since prehistory. Archaeologists Marlena and Andrzej Antczak have found tools, spoons and ornaments made of shell, evidence of a thousand-year-old 'conch culture'. Their excavations show that groups who came from the mainland for fishing used empty conches to gather rainwater. The conch piles they left at the water's edge are today well inland, a measure of island growth.

Marine biological station

The Fundación Científica Los Roques operates a biological station on **Dos Mosquises** in the southern archipelago. There are breeding tanks where green turtles and other endangered species are raised for release in the archipelago. The station's biologists were the first to raise queen conch larvae in captivity. Visitors are welcome on Saturdays, Sundays and holidays. Dos Mosquises is the only island aside from Gran Roque with an authorised airstrip. Prior permission to land should be requested from the foundation in Caracas, tel: (02) 2639729, fax: 2613461.

Gran Roque

The main island is roughly 3.5km long by 1km at its widest. It is the only island in the archipelago which is formed not by corals but by igneous rock; the highest point is 130m. The archipelago's single town, also called Gran Roque, has some 1,800 inhabitants, half of whom are native Roqueños. Records say a woman named Gabriela Estrada began the settlement on Gran Roque in 1906. Some of the fishermen who came from Margarita each season returned with their families to stay. Still, in 1987 there were only 807 people in the archipelago, a quarter of them Margariteños staying temporarily. In the next ten years the population doubled as the islands entered the tourism market. As everything must be brought from the mainland, it is little wonder that supplies and services seem way overpriced. Commercial fishing is prohibited in the park, so even your fish dinner comes from La Guaira.

Gran Roque is the park and fisheries headquarters for the archipelago. On the six streets of sand are a Guardia Nacional post, Plaza Bolívar, primary school, medical dispensary, food shop, telephones and one vehicle, the rubbish truck. With

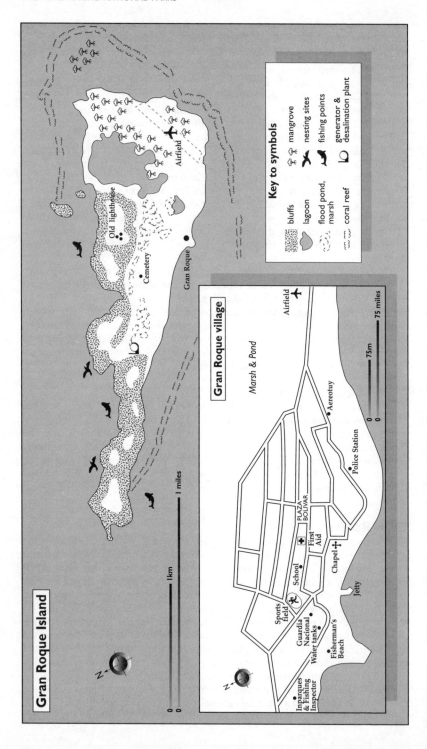

Gran Roque Island

Old lighthouse

Airfield

Cemetery

Gran Roque

0   1km

0   1 miles

Key to symbols

mangrove

nesting sites

fishing points

generator &
desalination plant

bluffs

lagoon

flood pond,
marsh

coral reef

Gran Roque village

Marsh & Pond

Airfield

Aereotuy

Police Station

PLAZA
BOLIVAR

First
Aid

Chapel

School

Jetty

Sports
field

Guardia
Nacional

Water tanks

Fisherman's
Beach

Inparques
& Fishing
Inspector

0   75m

0   75 miles

the aid of a Spanish cooperation agency, Gran Roque has become the first Venezuelan town to classify its solid waste for recycling; materials collected are taken to the mainland. Water and electricity are erratic although the island has a desalination plant and generator.

Once on Gran Roque you can negotiate with local fishermen for a *peñero* ride to a coral isle. You make a single agreement for boat hire including the return. Take time to shop around as there are no price controls and some fishermen ask what the traffic will bear. Among prices current in 1998: Francisquí $6, Madrizquí $7, Crasquí $12–16, and Cayo de Agua $24. Roqueños can tell you which islands have the best coral for snorkelling.

Permits

The National Parks Institute here is under the Environment Ministry's **Autoridad Unica Los Roques**, tel: (02) 4081167/69. No fishing is authorised except for the traditional rod-and-reel. Spearfishing is prohibited. Scuba diving currently requires a permit from Inparques whose headquarters are at the pueblo's west end on the beach. All arriving visitors should pay the parks fee at the Inparques office on the landing strip: $6 for residents, $12 non-residents.

Flights and tours

Air is the way to go, although it is not impossible to find a small fishing boat to Los Roques. The crossing against sea currents takes some 12 hours and the diesel engines stink and roar without relief. Ask at the Muelle de Pescadores in La Guaira which *capitán* is due to leave next. Most skippers pull out at midnight. The Wednesday and Saturday supply boats to Gran Roque leave about midnight of the previous day.

Air travel is expensive for the 30-minute flight from Maiquetía but reservations can be made through any travel agency. The small airlines offer day tours at about $40 more than the flight, that is $150 inclusive. For better value ask for a tour lasting two or three days. Most flights leave from the national terminal in Maiquetía. All passengers must carry an identity card, or passport and tourist card.

Aereotuy (LTA) is the largest company, tel: (02) 7618043/6231, fax: 7625254; Edif Gran Sabana, No 174 Boulevard de Sabana Grande, Caracas; in Porlamar, (095) 630307/67, fax: 617746. Daily flights in turbo-prop aircraft, $110 round trip: 08.30, 17.00; on Saturdays also at 07.00. If you take the flight out at 17.00, or return at 09.10 the next day, the one-way ticket costs only $35. From Porlamar: at 06.00 with return at 18.00, $90 one way; and at 17.00 with return at 07.10 the next day, $65 one way. Once paid for, day tours cannot be changed and are not refundable in case of cancellation. The cost of a 2-day/1-night tour is $300–360 depending on whether it includes standard or 'superior' lodging. Prices are higher on Fri–Sat and school holidays, Aereotuy's high season or *temporada alta*.

Aeroejecutivos Tel: (02) 9917942, tel/fax: 9935493; Porlamar, (014) 9131638; email: info@aerojecutivos.com.ve. They fly DC3s in fine style: from Porlamar at 07.30 returning at 17.00; from Maiquetía's Terminal Viejo at 08.30, returning at 17.00; round trip $100. Tours from 2 days/1 night, $240.

Rutaca Tel: (02) 3551838, fax: 3551643; Porlamar, (095) 691346, fax: 691245. Weekend flights in 19-seater Brazilian planes: Saturdays at 07.00 and 08.30, Sundays at 08.00 and 12.00; round trip $100 (20% discount for residents); charter flights any day at 10.00. Offices in the national terminal are open daily 07.00–12.00, 14.00–18.00.

Chapi Air Tel: (02) 3552786/1965, daily flights in nine-seater twin engine Cessnas at 07.00 and 09.00, returning at 16.00 and 18.00; fare is $100. Chapi offers day tours and stays of two days (or more) at a small *posada* for $250 (20–25% discounts on fares and tours for residents). Desk in the national terminal is open 06.30–19.00.

Warning It is not uncommon for departing passengers to be kept waiting on the airstrip by Aereotuy and other lines. As Gran Roque has no landing lights you may find yourself leaving the next morning. Do not plan an escapade to Los Roques just before your international flight.

Camping

While camping is permitted on certain islands, others are 'off limits' as totally protected. Areas where camping is allowed start on Gran Roque, on the beach by Inparques headquarters. A camping permit is issued free of charge here, and at the little office on the airfield. Several islands are designated for camping. The closest are Madrizquí and Cayo Pirata (you can walk between them over the coráls) where lobster fishermen corral their catch; and Francisquí, two isles joined by a sand bar, with an ocean beach on the north and a lagoon for swimming. Los Noronquises and Crasquí lie southward, 30 and 40 minutes away by boat. There is a *ranchería* of fishermen on Crasquí's south coast with boats pulled up on the sand. The park guard on Crasquí issues 3-day permits at no charge.

No facilities are provided for campers, and no fires are permitted. Bring a cooler of food, drinks and limes, and ask the *peñero's* crew for the favour of a fresh fish (try a trade with limes or onions).

Where to stay

The area telephone code for Gran Roque is (014)
The whole village is full of guest rooms. Most of the humble fishermen's houses have been done over as *posadas* with two to five rooms; they number over 60 and jostle elbow-to-elbow on five streets. There is not enough fresh water to cover demand, so service frequently dries up; guests are reminded to economise. Air conditioning and hot water are rare as the sea breeze is constant and the water never cold.

Prices are quoted per person, based on double occupancy for 2 days/1 night. This does not include air ticket. Rates may go up during school holidays. **Economy** pensions charge $40–60 (cash only) per person with breakfast and dinner, and perhaps a ride to the closest island. **Moderate** inns charge about $60–100 (cash again) for all meals and hopefully they take you out to a different beach. **Expensive** ones are over $100 and you get to visit more distant islands. If you are economising and have no reservations, enquire about *media pensión* which means check-in at 15.00, check-out before lunch.

Then there are **inclusive** packages for around $360 with flight, all meals, national brand drinks, daily beach excursions (with parasols, chairs, masks and flippers), and bilingual guides. It is important to check which islands are visited to avoid snorkelling in the wake of a dozen other oglers on Francisquí.

Except where noted, the *posadas* on the abbreviated list below have fan, shared bath, and cold water. However you go, an ice-chest with fruit and drinks is a great beach addition.

Upper range

Italian fishermen and scuba divers have discovered Los Roques. They are swept straight from Maiquetía to classy new lodges charging $130 and up; all services, private bathroom. (See also *Fishing.*) The first-rate **Pez Ratón Lodge** operates a fleet for fishermen. The three-room lodge with rooftop dining is owned by Elena Battani, tel: 9293305; in Caracas, (02) 9750906, fax: 9750305. She also has the handsomely furnished **Mediterraneo** nearby: library, roof terrace, six rooms, a large water tank and own generator; good service, good value. The **Arrecife** offers six modern rooms with private bath, optional air conditioning, fishing boats, and Italian-speaking staff; tel: 9374489, fax: 9285471. Angelo Belvedere runs the **Acuarela**'s 10 attractive rooms; tel: 9323502; in Caracas (02) 7815756, fax: 7937117. Antonela owns the 2-room **Malibu**, tel: 9126349, on Gran Roque's 4th street; you can ask for basic rate (bed & breakfast), at about half price. The **Tintorera**, another Italian oriented place, is a comfortable house with patio; you pay $90 which is value for money. In Caracas ring Gente de Mar, tel: (02) 9532707/605, fax: 9536677; email: marinero@sa.omnes.net. Ask about airport reception.

Aereotuy is the biggest operator with 65 good and 'superior' rooms, offered as part of inclusive packages: **Las Palmeras** and **Natura Viva** on Plaza Bolívar, the **Macabí** near the church; the costlier **Posada La Plaza**, and on the beach **Vistalmar** where a restaurant serves all Aereotuy guests.

La Corsaria, east on third street, is one of the newer places, done up by Carolina Pacanins in startlingly rich colours; large living area with 'executive' fridge, nine rooms with safe, louvred doors, private bath; tel: 9300796; in Caracas (02) 9936373, fax: 9937855. Inclusive package from $300. The latest luxury addition is a beautiful colonial-style house, **La Farola del Mar**, built towards the lighthouse.

Alexandra Harth, who speaks English and German, made her **Posada La Quigua** on the fourth street from the sea with teak beams, ceiling fans, six doubles and triples, private baths. Fisherman Guayo takes you to a different island each day; tel: 2051524; in Caracas, (02) 9634504.

Moderate
Roque's Air, Land & Sea represents various modest *posadas*: **Cinco Reales**, **Flamingo**, **La Rosaleda**, **La Marimba**, **Las Tinajas**. All provide breakfast, box lunch, dinner, and beach excursion. In Caracas: PH2, Edif Pichincha, Av El Bosque at Plaza Chacaito; tel: (02) 9521840, fax: 9525923.

Albacora Lodge is east of the medical dispensary. Tibisay and Igor rent seven plain rooms with private bath. Between them they speak English, Italian, French and Portuguese. They provide meals and excursions in their own boat; longer trips, bonefishing at extra cost; tel: 9125252.

Bora La Mar on the sea is a vine-draped restaurant with four rooms, private bath, two or three meals. No beach excursion included. Marta Agusti, the chef, also owns **La Rosaleda**. Tel: 9257814, in Caracas (02) 2385408.

Gremary, one of the oldest inns on Gran Roque, has 11 rooms, some with private bath; *criollo* cooking; tel: 9278614, (02) 3372765. **Paraíso Azul**, near playground, two rooms with private bath, two shared; two meals included, but beach transfer extra; tel: 9268343. English and Italian spoken.

Piano y Papaya, behind the church; an Italian couple has five doubles with private bath, one meal included; tel: 9144423, in Caracas (02) 2433628.

Economy
Doña Carmen's Posada was among Gran Roque's first 30 years ago and Carmen is still at the helm; two plain rooms with private bath, sea view; four more on the patio; daughter Dalia cooks *criollo* breakfast, dinner. Beach excursion $6; tel: 9382284. **El Botuto**, west near Inparques, seven rooms, private bath; breakfast and ride to island beach; tel: (016) 6375521, Caracas (02) 2861079. **Posada del Recuerdo**, Plaza Bolívar north, five basic rooms; tel: 9364709, in Caracas (02) 7614861/5861. **Roquelusa**, west sector; four spartan rooms with private bath, one shared; breakfast and dinner (no beach excursion); tel: 9238245.

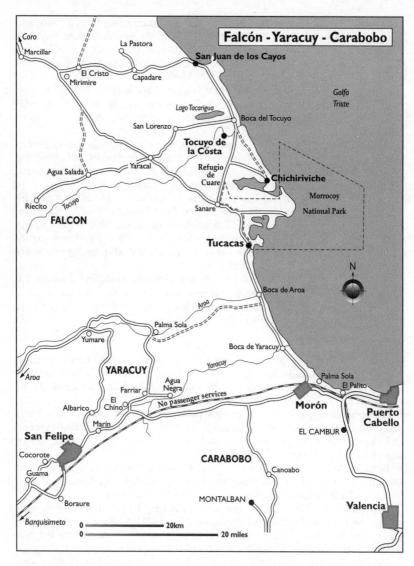

Falcón - Yaracuy - Carabobo

Coro
Marcillar
La Pastora
San Juan de los Cayos

El Cristo
Mirimire
Capadare

Golfo
Triste

Lago Tacarigua
Boca del Tocuyo

San Lorenzo
Tocuyo de
la Cósta

Agua Salada
Yaracal
Refugio
de
Cuare
Chichiriviche

Morrocoy
National Park

Riecito
Tocuyo
Sanare

FALCON

Tucacas

N

Boca de Aroa

Aroa
Palma Sola

Yumare
Boca de Yaracuy

YARACUY
Yaracuy
Palma Sola
El Palito

Aroa
Agua
Negra

Farriar
No passenger services
Morón

Albarico
El
Chino
Puerto
Cabello

Marín
EL CAMBUR

San Felipe

Cocorote
CARABOBO
Canoabo

Guama

Boraure
MONTALBAN
Valencia

Barquisimeto
0   20km
0   20 miles

Island lodging

Campamento Francisquí, just northeast of Gran Roque, is a house with five doubles and triples, four have private bath, rented as part of a standard package including flight from Maiquetía, boat transfer, meals, excursions; Francisky Tours, tel: (02) 7940693, fax: 7939609.

On the sea

Crewed yachts and sailboats are the very best way to explore the archipelago. If you have a group of four, or even two, sailing prices give better value than Gran Roque's *posadas*. The food is much superior, the beaches, too, and the crystalline water has no equal. Most cruises start from Gran Roque; the flight is a separate cost. Linda Sonderman who runs Alpiturismo suggests fishing/diving cruises in 35ft to 52ft craft, luxury 76ft sailboat with four cabins, or air-conditioned 54ft yacht. Such cruises may provide snorkelling, surfing and waterskiing, all meals and national drinks, for around $160 a day per person (four to six people). Alpi Tour, tel: (02) 2831433/1733, fax: 2856067.

The *Sula Sula*, a 42ft GibSea craft, carries up to six passengers in four cabins, at a rate of $120 a day each. This includes all meals, national drinks and Chilean wine. For information, ring Captain Fernando Martínez, tel: (014) 2046285; in Caracas, tel/fax: (02) 7511712. The *Bicho*, a 51ft sailing craft captained by Arnaud Dely, has 85HP engine, telephone, GPS. Including all food and drink, cost for a group of six in three cabins with double beds, hot water is $700–800 per day depending on the season; in Caracas, tel/fax: (02) 9784092, (016) 6223818; email: ttmjp@true.net (Transporte Turístico Marítimo Jean-Pierre).

For information about other sailboats, their captains and chefs, there is a group called **Explore Yachts**: Oficina 11a, Edif Saule, Av Miranda, Chacao; tel: 2632606, fax: 2634091; email: explore-yachts@usa.net.

Aereotuy operates a 76ft touring yacht, the *Antares III*, which has six air-conditioned cabins with bathroom. Weeklong cruises start in Maiquetía or Porlamar and cost $1,250 or $1,079 per person based on double or triple occupancy, and including insurance and bilingual guide. The rates for a week's 'live aboard' scuba cruise are $1,500 and $1,287; Sesto Continente provides all equipment for $85 a day.

Scuba

The diving is spectacular at Cayo Sal where caves in vertical walls sprout multicoloured sponges, and among corals and fishes of the clear Boca del Medio. At the south entry, Boca de Sebastopol, you can see manta rays and sharks. An abundance of tropical fish, and very few people, await divers in Los Roques.

Sesto Continente has a centre for tanks fills, dives and courses on Gran Roque by the Inparques headquarters. A dive permit costs $12. Divers must have accreditation from PADI, NAUI or similar group. Or you can take a starting course ($80), or open-water diver certificate ($350); price includes diving equipment and boats. Park rules limit dive groups to ten accompanied by a divemaster. Divers may not touch or stand on corals. For health reasons divers should not take plane flights until 12 hours after their last dive.

Sesto Continente rents equipment in the line of regulator, wetsuit, fins. Tanks and weights are included in the price of scuba packages which run about $80 a day. You can also hire a boat with captain and fuel. Dive packages, including flight from Caracas, pension on Gran Roque, all food and equipment, are about $230 a day; tel: (02) 7311507, tel/fax: 743873/9080.

Fishing

Shallows between the archipelago's islands provide excellent bonefishing. Serious anglers pay $200 to $300 a day and come thousands of miles to catch (and release) these lightning-fast fish, called in Spanish *pez ratón* and *macabí*. Fishing is good all year, particularly June–December. The sport fishing licence from Inparques costs about $15 a day.

In Gran Roque, certain *posadas* give fishing services, catering to the many Italian enthusiasts. The **Pez Ratón Lodge** has a fleet including skiffs, fibreglass *peñero* or open fishing boat with outboard, and a deep-sea craft. The young couple, Tibisay and Igor González at the **Albacora Lodge**, have two boats and make bonefishing or deepsea expeditons to the southern archipelago. (For phones, see *Where to stay*,

Morrocoy National Park

San Juan de
Los Cayos

Cayo Borracho

Caribbean Sea

Cayo Sal

CHICHIRIVICHE

Cuare Gulf
Wildlife Refuge

Cayo Peraza
Cayo Muerto
Cayo Pelón

Playa Varadero

Playa Larga

Cerro Chichiriviche

Mayorquín

Cayo
Sombrero

Cayo
Pescadores

Las Luisas

Morrocoy

Lizardo

Punta Tucacas

Coro, Sanare

Bahía
Morrocoy

Boca Grande

Playa Norte

Caño León

Boca Seca

Playuelita
Playuela

Isla de
Pájaros

Playa Mero

Paiciá

Bahía
de
Tucacas

Playa Ánimas

Boca de Suánchez

TUCACAS

Morón

Marina
Tucacas

Punta Brava

page 145.) The owners of the **Arena Blanca** and **Terramar** inns have a sailboat and offer deepsea or bonefishing plans; tel: (014) 9374489, fax: 9285471.

PARQUE NACIONAL MORROCOY

The mangroves, channels, coral keys and bays making up this national park of 320km² were rescued from runaway development in 1974 by a government determined to preserve the fragile ecosystems. The keys (*cayos*) are low-lying islands formed by corals and shell debris which curve from Tucacas in a line around the headland to Chichiriviche. Among the two dozen named keys are Punta Brava, Animas, Paiclá, Los Pájaros, Pescadores, Sombrero, Sal and Borracho. Home to frigate birds (they nest on Isla de Pájaros in December–January), spoonbills, flamingos and scarlet ibis, here is a region easily accessible for the backpacker. However, when the trade winds flag (Nov–Feb), tiny biting gnats make camping a torture at night. Look for a hotel! You will find a choice in **Tucacas**, 250km from Caracas, and **Chichiriviche**, 37km farther, both waterfront towns on the park.

Luxury hotels, condominium apartments and marinas have shot up in the area as more people from Lara and Carabobo states turn to the coast for weekends. These developments are found on the coast by Tucacas and Chichiriviche. There are now about 3,200 hotel rooms, and double the number of private vacation units. International tourism has grown, too, and charters fly Canadians direct to Valencia, bound for Morrocoy.

Then there is a pilot 'ecotourism' project for sustainable tourism, backed by the state government and the Inter-American Development Bank, at a site called **Playa Norte** on the coast towards Tocuyo de la Costa. It is said to be a low-profile, low-density, high-quality development.

Tucacas

Right on the Falcón State coastal highway, Tucacas has marinas, a diving centre, travel agency, bank, food, liquor shops (plenty of these), and new hotels, both luxury and basic. Tourism growth has brought a wave of Portuguese, Chinese and Arab businesses in the shape of video clubs, supermarkets, restaurants, tascas, bakeries and *areperas*.

The town is still scruffy but is taking steps to pave streets, improve schools and plazas, and restore what little remains of its past as a mining port. A railway, Venezuela's first, once carried copper and gold ore to the docks from the English-run Aroa mines. Tucacas today ships mainly fruit and vegetables to Aruba, Bonaire and Curaçao. To reach the Terminal Marino, walk down Avenida Libertador and go left on Av Marina (below Submatur), passing a colonial building restored as the Ateneo de Tucacas.

Morrocoy's keys

You don't have to take a boat to reach the park and a beach – just walk down the main street, cross the bridge, and you are on Punta Brava, the first and largest of Morrocoy's islands. The **Inparques** office is at the bridge; tel: (042) 830069, fax: 830053. Cars pay a small parks fee; no charge for people. It's a hot kilometre farther to the beach, so those on foot should go early. Punta Brava's beach and huge parking lot draw crowds at weekends. However, it is pleasantly empty from Monday to Thursday. There are hammocks slung from some palm trees and camping is permitted.

Camping

For camping on uninhabited keys you must follow a set of regulations requiring advance reservations through Inparques. Due to overuse (inadequate facilities), camping is restricted to four islands: Paiclá, Sal, Muerto and Sombrero, the farthest and biggest with a maximum capacity of 688 campers. You call 800 VIVIR (84847) to request a reservation, then deposit Bs1,000 per night for each camper, 12 years and older, at the Banco Unión or Banco Industrial de Venezuela. When you have the deposit slip, call 800 84847 again with the number (save the deposit slip to pick up your reservation in Tucacas). Within 48 hours, you must reconfirm (same phone) or your space will be cancelled. If you are already in Tucacas, check with Inparques to see if there is space, and make the deposit at the Banco Unión. Campers may not light fires or consume alcohol.

Launch service to the *cayos* is provided by a boatmen's cooperative. Walk down Avenida Libertador past Submatur, and turn left on Av Marino to the **Embarcadero** and pier. The ticket is round-trip; you tell the boatman to pick you up at a certain hour and day. Prices are posted and the fare per boat (up to eight people depending on gear) is regulated according to distance, from about $35 for the closest island, Paiclá, to $70 for the farthest, Cayo Sombrero.

Cayo Sombrero has many palms to sling hammocks from, and excellent beaches, the far side having most wind to blow away insects. The sea inside the reef, named La Piscina or pool, is ideal for swimming and snorkelling. The beach is cleaned every day and has many toilets. Bring large containers of water and a load of food, although at weekends you can buy fried fish, soft drinks and luscious coconut ice-cream. Boatmen will bring you more food or water if you stay on.

Palm trees, white beaches and clear sea. Add channels through the mangroves and flocks of flamingos, and for many it's a picture of paradise.

But underwater you see evidence of man-made disaster in dead corals. Officially, no-one was blamed for noxious chemicals that swept through the park, turning corals white in the space of a week. The spill in late 1995 probably came from a government petrochemical plant or oil refinery along the coast, but the mystery chemical was not identified as it vanished with the currents. The good news is that, three years later, some coral communities are showing clear signs of recovery.

Diving

How has diving been affected by Morrocoy's disaster? Mike Osborn, who has been diving professionally in the park for 20 years, must go to more distant keys, Cayos Norte y Sur and Cayo Medio, to observe healthy coral. On the other hand, Morrocoy appears to have more fish than before as a result of abundant algae, and birdlife is thriving.

Mike's small dive shop, **Submatur**, is at No 6 Calle Ayacucho, near the bottom end of Avenida Libertador; tel: 830082, fax: 831051 (night). The centre fills tanks, sells a range of good gear, rents other equipment, and gives diving tours and courses. Mike is a licensed NAUI instructor and underwater photographer. A 4-day open-water diving course covers theory, eight dives, boat and equipment for $330, and entitles you to a PADI certificate. A day's diving with all equipment runs to $70 a person, and a 2-day/1-night diving package with food and lodging costs $144. Mike is working with the captain of the *Kulkuri*, an 80ft sailboat, taking divers (and companions) on dive cruises to the uninhabited Archipiélago de Las Aves, 160km north. The cost, with all equipment, is $130 a day.

Dive Inn Morrocoy is a fully equipped dive centre in the marina at Morrocoy Coral Reef Resort. Dives from their 30ft boat cost about $65 with tank and equipment. Courses are given at the resort and in open water (PADI certificate). Equipment rental, too. For information ring Super Class Tours, tel: (02) 2854103/2430, fax: 2834644; email: supercla@telcel.net.ve.

Getting there

A car can cover the 250km from Caracas in just over three hours. From the Valencia terminal, buses and *por puestos* go frequently on the Morón–Coro route, dropping you at the entrance to Tucacas in 1½ hours. Coro is another four hours' ride.

From the highway, Avenida Libertador runs down to the shore. Tucacas' small hotels are found on or near Libertador which ends at a bridge from the mainland to the first of Morrocoy's islands, Punta Brava. 'Budget' prices may increase at holiday periods.

Where to stay/eat

The area telephone code for Tucacas is (042).

Hotels

The **Centro Turístico Said III**, on the highway's west side, is a motel, gaudy but serviceable; tel: 831830; 36 rooms and 11 bungalows for six. **La Gran Posada Morrocoy** is announced in the same fantasy vein by a sort of lighthouse; tel: 831067, behind the cemetery: swimming pool, restaurant; 12 air-conditioned rooms with bath; $60 per double with breakfast and dinner.

The **Hotel Gaeta** is at No 34, Av Libertador; tel: 830414; four storeys, 32 doubles with bath, air conditioning, TV, $36; fills up fast at weekends. Go right at Av Silva and Libertador for the **Manaure Hotel**, tel: 2830286/466, an older hotel with pleasant pool, restaurant, and 45 renovated rooms with hot water, air conditioning, $50 a double with breakfast.

Posada Johnathan, budget, a row of rooms behind owner Marco Soto's house, turn right midway on Av Libertador at Pollo Sabroso; double/triple with fan, bath; quadruple with air conditioning. **Hotel Otidalymar**, across Libertador on Calle 5 de Julio at Bermúdez, is a three-floor block of decent rooms with fan and bath. **Hotel Las Palmas**, tel: 831493. At No 5 Av Libertador there is a small sign announcing *'Habitaciones'*. This is the only sign put up by its owner Carlos, but you will see foreign travellers around. He has 12 basic rooms, most with private bath; his kitchen is open for cooking. **Hotel La Suerte** is a few steps more above Licorería La Suerte. Upstairs over its parking lot are breezy simple budget rooms with beds on raised platform with bath and fan; some with air conditioning. **Hotel La Esperanza**, next to Restaurant La Esperanza, is on the left at No 6 Av Libertador; rock-bottom rates are given by Norbert, the German manager, for doubles with two double beds.

Hotel Punta Brava, Av Marina, tel: 831469, is close to the island shuttle Embarcadero, to the left past Submatur. The 17 small rooms have been renovated with blue paint, hot water, air conditioning, TV; double $35.

André Nahon, a Belgian dive instructor, puts up travellers in **Submar Inn** by his home near the state highway, tel: 831754; six budget doubles and triples, or hammocks; kitchen privileges, barbecue grill, garden.

Posada Balijú, Calle Libertad, tel/fax: 831580, (014) 9430807. On the last right-hand street before the bridge to Punta Brava. Ask for *'la Posada de Pepe'*. Pepe is owner José Jelambi; his home is an attractive base for exploring the marine park as, surprisingly, it opens on to a jetty on the bay. Twelve air-conditioned rooms with hot water are part of an $80 package including very good food (breakfast, dinner) and boat to islands.

Resorts

Among resorts with pools, tennis, watersports and all services is the quite reasonable **Morrocoy Coral Reef**, entrance on the Falcón highway; tel: (042) 830301, fax: 830491; in Caracas, (02) 9536048, 9530448. On the bay are 304 rooms in attractive two-storey units. For around $60 per person in a double room, an off-season package includes meals, snacks, domestic beverages, and daily island excursion in a catamaran.

Sun Way Morrocoy, Falcón highway at Km 58, advertises as a 5-star resort with gardens, pool, gym, 215 rooms and suites. Low-season price goes down to $40 per person in double room; 12.5% tax not included. In Tucacas, tel: (042) 830001, fax: 830005.

Caribbean Marina and Beach Club is a vast new resort occupying 21ha near Boca de Aroa. You can see its 700m pier, with the marina and boat storage for 700 craft at the end. On land, there are townhouses grouped around artificial canals and lake, a dozen seven-storey apartment blocks, supermarkets and restaurants. To give the resort its due, a sewage and water treament plant recycles waste and the water recovered goes to new plantings.

Restaurants

In Tucacas there are economical roast chicken places and *areperas* such as **La Arepa Pelá**, midway on Av Libertador, where a filled *arepa* (*tostada*) and fresh juice costs $2.50. **Restaurant Varadero** at Hotel Punta Brava (see above) has air conditioning, stained glass, and reasonable prices for seafood specialities such as butterfly shrimp from Boca de Aroa. Another place for seafood is Restaurant Tito's, Calle Sucre, east of Av Libertador (midway).

What to do
Hammocks Local craftsmen make hammocks that are ideal for beaches as they are knotted of coloured nylon string: lightweight, strong, pretty and unaffected by water. They cost $30 and up, depending on size and adornment. Rows of these hammocks are displayed along the Falcón highway, some 10km west of Tucacas near the Cerro de Chichiriviche.

Cerro de Chichiriviche A paved road skirts these limestone bluffs, paralleling the Bahía de Morrocoy. It starts at Km 71 on the Falcón highway and continues to the communities of Las Luisas, Morrocoy and Lizardo. Where it ends, a trail continues around Tucacas Point to Mayorquines opposite Cayo Sombrero. There are caves here with remains of Indian pottery. The dry headland is covered with thorny scrub where wildlife includes crab foxes, ocelots and monkeys. The road offers few facilities apart from the private marinas of La Canoa, Morrocoy and La Cuevita. One or two rather exclusive guesthouses are on this route: **El Paraíso Azul**, tel: (042) 830929, with a splendid view of islands and canals; **Villa Mangrovia**, tel: (014) 9415176, long known for gracious hospitality; and **La Acacia**, tel: (014) 9431601, in Lizardo. They provide all meals, lodging and excursion by boat to island beaches. Make a note of La Acacia, home of Julieta and Carlos de Valdés: five large rooms in a wonderful house of wooden beams, tile roof, tall ceilings, a terrace where birds come to banquet and excellent food, for $60 a day.

Yaracuy River As your boat heads up the Río Yaracuy you soon wind among forests of buttressed dragon's blood trees and pink poui, banks of reeds and bird-of-paradise into a wilderness inhabited by crocodiles, capybara (*chigüire*), capuchin and howler monkeys. This fascinating trip of 3–4 hours is conducted by William Romero who lives southeast of the bridge at **Boca de Yaracuy**. His house is by the water tank at the settlement's end. He charges about $15 per passenger in a 14-person boat. Submatur will make arrangements. The Yaracuy marks Falcón's border, 20km east of Tucacas.

Las Aves The islands lie to the north some 160km, roughly equidistant between Los Roques and Bonaire. Separated into Las Aves de Barlovento and Las Aves de Sotavento, they are uninhabited except for a National Guard post. Few people remember them unless a ship runs aground there or a pirate wreck is discovered. In 1998 an American shipwreck salvager, Barry Clifford, announced the discovery of a sunken fleet of 18 French warships and pirate vessels that hit the reefs of Las Aves on May 3, 1678. 'It was like a shipwreck graveyard,' Clifford said. A conch fisherman showed him the place, littered with cannon in 9m of water. The ships belonged to a force of 35 vessels on their way to attack Curaçao. Some 500 men were drowned, but as many as 1,200 got to shore. Those who survived insects, disease and hunger were taken prisoner by the Dutch three months later.

Chichiriviche
On the park's northern access are plentiful hotels in what is not so much a town as a launching point for people going to islands such as Pelón, Peraza, Cayo Sal, Cayo Muerto and Cayo Sombrero. Chichiriviche, unlike Tucacas, a town without a beach, faces the sea and has a sandy shore. The 12km causeway to Chichiriviche crosses tidal flats of the Cuare Wildlife Refuge where wading birds are spectacular in the rainy season. As long as there is water flocks of flamingos may be seen feeding – as many as 6,000 have been counted. At dusk scarlet ibis, roseate spoonbills, parrots and egrets fly in to roost in mangrove swamps.

MONAGAS
Above left: *Cuevo del Guácharo (Oil-bird cave), Caripe* (HB)
Above right: *Cashew fruit for sale on the roadside* (HB)
Below: *Evening view of Caripe* (HB)

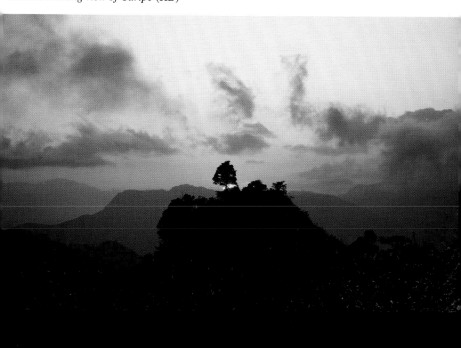

THE ANDES
October in the Sierra Nevada de Mérida. Espeletia, *in the daisy family, have velvety frost-resistant leaves. The tallest variety are known as* frailejones.

ANDEAN CHURCHES
Left: *A church built in the traditional style in Los Aleros, a reconstructed village* (EP)
Right: *Jaji, a restored colonial village southwest of Mérida* (EP)

THE LLANOS
Above: *Hato Piñero; note the hide for birdwatchers in the background.* (HB)
Below: *Llaneros, the cowboys of the Llanos. Mules have more stamina than horses and a greater resistance to disease.* (HB)

Ringed by wind-blown rubbish, pot-holed and largely deserted from weekend to weekend, Chichiriviche is an unplanned village which grew into an unplanned town. The land is so flat that it floods with the first rains, sewers back up, and seaside hotels are awash. Despite this, new hotels, fancy summer homes and highrise resorts continue to appear.

Two high streets mark the main districts: **Playa Norte** to the left of Avenida Zamora, a shopping street with supermarket, bank, travel agency and bus station ending at the shore; and **Playa Sur**, east of the road leading to the Fábrica de Cemento. This avenue forks right from Zamora at the Garza Hotel.

The Banco Industrial de Venezuela on Avenida Zamora does not cash travellers' cheques, but the travel agency, Varadero Tours, will change dollar cheques and bills.

Getting there

Chichiriviche is reached from **Valencia**, **Puerto Cabello** or **Barquisimeto**. From the latter get a bus from the terminal on Carrera 24 and Calle 42 to San Felipe, and cross the road to catch the bus for Morón and from Morón to Tucacas/Chichiriviche. Buses to/from Valencia run from 06.00 to 18.00, passing Morón. If you are coming from Coro, change at the Sanare fork for the Valencia–Chichiriviche bus covering the last 22km. The bus station in Chichiriviche is on Av Zamora.

Varadero Tours on Avenida Zamora will arrange transfers by car to Valencia and to **Caracas** (Maiquetía airport).

Where to stay

The area telephone code for Chichiriviche is (042)

Hotels and *posadas* change their rates with the season: higher during school holidays mid-July to mid-September, and New Year, Easter and Carnival weeks. Hotel operators can often get you economical launch service to the *cayos*.

Hotels

The rival 3-star hotels on Avenida Zamora, midtown, are the **Mario**, tel: 86811-15, 114 rooms, and **La Garza**, tel: 86048/126, 75 rooms. They have air conditioning, pool, transport to beaches (La Garza includes breakfast and dinner). The old-established **Parador Manaure** is a more moderate hotel on the left, Vía Fábrica de Cemento, tel: 86452/121, fax: 86569; pool, restaurant; 24 air-conditioned rooms, hot water. The Manaure owns **Suites Roca Dura** across the street which also has a pool. Most of the 18 apartments and some suites have a kitchen; they sleep four for $45, six for $60. Ask for rates including two meals. On this road you come first to the **Vaya Vaya**, tel: 86304, fax: 86779; it's a moderate, pleasant two-floor hotel with plenty of greenery; single or double; guests may use Hotel Mario's pool.

At the foot of Avenida Zamora is the **Capri**, tel: 86026, a small Italian-run hotel, nothing special but its 19 air-conditioned rooms are convenient and economic, and it has a good restaurant. Ask across the street at the Panadería **El Centro** for budget rooms with fan: the baker will take you round the corner to a two-storey hostel painted brown; take the windy side or nothing.

With waves lapping at a little jetty, the old **Hotel Náutico** on Playa Sur is poised for exploring the *cayos*; you can walk there along the shore. The hotel has no TV or air conditioning, but has radio communication with Caracas. Twenty rooms are rented as part of an economical plan with two meals and launch service. In Caracas, ring Sun Chichi, tel: (02) 9597866/8335. The Náutico's waterfront neighbour is the ageing **Hotel and Restaurant Playa Sur**, tel/fax: (042) 86033. Chichiriviche's pioneer hotel, it was founded in 1950; 19 rooms with fan, breakfast and dinner, about $35 a person.

Guesthouses
The **Alemania** is a good *posada* in the southern sector, left side along Vía Fábrica de Cementos, tel: 86979. It is in the two-storey Casa Mi Lucero; garden, balcony, ample living room, six clean doubles with fan and private bath, $15. **Casa Manantial**, tel: 86262, near the beach on a street leading left from Vía Fábrica de Cemento opp Coral Suites, is a modern *posada* with pool and restaurant; 12 air-conditioned rooms for four, private bath, $30. The **Villa Gregoria**, Calle Mariño, a block north of Zamora; tel: 86359; has 11 renovated rooms with fan and private bath, at $14 a double bed.

With kitchen
América Mía Guest House, Av Zamora, tel/fax: 86547, has five apartments in the Banco Industrial building. Each has two bedrooms sleeping four to five people; bedrooms may be let separately, sharing the bath and kitchen, at a cost of $8–10 a person. This is a good place to find your feet as the multilingual owner Enrique Castro knows a lot about local tours, island trips and diving. He offers a dive tour complete with an open-water dive course leading to PADI certificate, and a car from Maiquetía airport.

The **Villa Marina** in Playa Sur, Calle Negro Primero at Vía Fábrica de Cemento, provides 40 moderate apartments by the day or week; tel: 86205/441, fax: 86503. Gardens, snack bar and swimming pool; 100m walk to the Embarcadero for rides to the islands. **Residencias Jaiba Mar**, tel: 86172, is off Vía Fábrica de Cemento; watch for their sign on a left street; it's a two-storey house with terrace and one kitchen for four units, each sleeping four or more, with air conditioning and private bath.

Launches
There are two points where boatmen rent launches. The cooperative posts a list of islands and prices at Embarcadero Sur on the beach two blocks before Hotel Náutico. Embarcadero Norte is north of Av Zamora by the Malecón or concrete seawalk. Boatmen can tell you which island has food stands. Instruct the boatman when he should bring you back. You pay by the boat, capacity eight passengers. It is $20 round trip to the closest cayo, Isla Muerta (large beach, good snorkelling at south end). Cayo Borracho is the only island said to have no *plaga* (biting midges).

Diving
Scuba and snorkelling gear may be rented from the **Centro de Buceo Caribe**, Playa Sur, tel: (043) 86150; and **Varadero Tours**, Av Zamora, tel: (042) 86754, fax: tel: (042) 86754. Varadero handle all kinds of water sports, day tours to caves and petroglyphs, and a sailing tour to Las Aves. Pierre-Claude, a Swiss diver and PADI instructor, gives dive courses and takes divers out to reefs; Calle El Sol, Sector Sur, tel/fax: 86265.

Cuare Wildlife Refuge
The Golfete de Cuare, its wetlands and salt flats, together with the limestone bluffs and forests of Cerro de Chichiriviche, and five offshore keys, make up this refuge, Venezuela's first. The area of 113km² is home to some 315 species, a third of these

wading and water birds. Its wetlands provide feeding grounds for flamingos which have been seen in bands of 4,000–7,000. They are also one of the last holdouts of the coastal crocodile. Among problems that affect the wildlife refuge is land invasion by ex-Chichiriviche families who have sold out their houses to tourism, as Morrocoy Park grows more popular year by year.

PARQUE NACIONAL MOCHIMA

Venezuela's second (1973) marine park covers 950km², roughly three-fifths of it sea and islands, the rest coast, headlands and mainland. Mochima National Park stretches from (but not including) **El Morro de Barcelona** in Anzoátegui State east to **Punta El Peñón** near Cumaná in Sucre. The park, taking its name from deep fjord-like Mochima Bay, was decreed to halt inroads by vacationers building cottages wherever they pleased on coasts and islands. Many such illegal constructions were not demolished until 1990.

The coastal drive offers stunning views of coves, bays and islands in the blue Caribbean as the road crosses promontories east of Punta Colorada. (For beaches west of Playa Colorada, see *Chapter 9, Puerto La Cruz*.) Major groups of islands such as Picuda Grande, Islas Caracas and Venados are extensions of a sunken mountain range whose valleys now form the Golfo de Santa Fé, Ensenada Tigrillo and Bahía Mochima. The sea, protected by large headlands and peninsulas, is very calm. Beaches are white, sandy, but not numerous.

Santa Fe (coast)

One of the beaches most prized by travellers is that of Santa Fe, a little fishing port east of Punta Colorada, equidistant between Puerto La Cruz and Cumaná. Get off the bus at the gas station on the highway and walk through the town (uninteresting) to the sea. The people's banner is conservation and they clean the long beach as well as the village daily. As a result of this initiative, Santa Fe has become a target for backpackers. Fishermen will take you in open *peñeros* to any beach in Mochima; they charge by the person, not by the boat. Dive services, a shop, and very reasonable diving tours are run by Italian Ricardo Puzzi at the Siete Delfines. He is a professional PADI instructor (and now owner of the hotel).

Where to stay/eat

Many homes keep a room for tourists (you have only to ask), and there are several economical guesthouses on the beach. Go towards the sea and turn left at the last street which ends on the shore where fish trucks park to load; the restaurants and inns are along the beach by foot.

Residencia Los Siete Delfines and restaurant has a balcony overlooking the beach and sea, and 11 plain rooms, clean, with private shower, double $12 including breakfast. The atmosphere is relaxed and travellers trade trips and tips. They have a tel/fax: for reservations, (093) 314166.

José Vivas who built the Delfines went on to make **La Sierra Inn** next to it on the beach, tel: (014) 9933116. It has nine large doubles at $15. A fenced rear lot provides parking; you enter by way of the street behind. José, a wonderful cook, is the man who launched Santa Fe's eco movement. He also has the **Posada Los Delfines**, a seven-room inn on the main street of Santa Fe. Rooms are cheap, bathrooms are shared, but everything is clean. Double or triple $6.

The **Café del Mar**, tel: (093) 210029, is an informal beachside restaurant which has a dozen ample, pleasant rooms, all hand-built by a young German, Mathías; double with bath, fan and seaview $10; without $8. Good food.

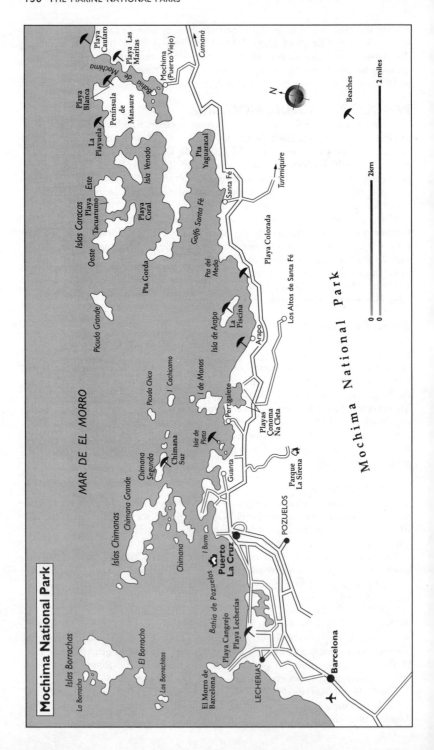

Mochima Bay and port

Before the beautiful highway reaches Cumaná, a fork on the left winds down 5km to tiny Puerto Viejo de Mochima. (*Por puestos* are the only public transportation; they come from Cumaná.) Every turn gives a lovely panorama. The village has two main streets, a public telephone, school, medical dispensary, marine biological station, a cock ring and a little church. By the dock are two restaurants. There is a dive centre.

The fishermen's cooperative is called Asotumo, and you may try the public phone (see below, *Where to stay*) to contract a launch, or just show up in the morning. Shuttle service to beaches starts at 06.00 on weekends. A price list is posted by Asotumo. You pay by the seat according to distance and once you land on a beach that's it, until the hour agreed for your pick-up. Ask for a copy of the Inparques map showing bays and beaches.

Mochima Bay, clear and gentle, has no waves. The first proper beach is **Las Maritas**, small and overbuilt. It has food and beer stalls, paved 2terraces and palm-roof shelters which fill up quickly. Near the open sea the next beach, **Playa Blanca de Guagua**, is bigger and better, also with food service although no umbrellas or jetty. You just jump off the boat on to the sand with your cooler, tent or hammock. If you need extra ice or food, your ferryman may oblige by bringing it on his next round.

Once out of Mochima Bay there are good beaches around the headland: west to **Playa Manaure** and around Manaure Peninsula to **Islas Caracas**; east to **Playa Cautaro, Cautarito** and **Puerto Escondido, Cachimena**. These and others further east are also visited by bathers from Cumaná, 30–40 minutes by speedboat.

Where to stay

The public phone, (093) 321588, may be rung to contact villagers with economical rooms and *casitas* OK for people spending the day on the beach. Kitchens are primitive. Ask for Indira, or Eucaris, Lía, La Negra, Milagros... In any case, bring your hammock. There are rooms for rent by the passenger pier or *muelle* (ask for Señor César), but the best choices are along the Avenida Principal.

Walk down the Avenida Principal to the end on the bay where **Posada Gaby's** second-storey terrace extends over the water; 14 simple double rooms with private bath, four with air conditioning at $10. They offer a plan with lodging, meals and transfer to the best beaches; for information, tel: (093) 310842, 322938. On your walk check on *Habitación* signs: owner Señor Otilio rents rooms in **Villa Vicenta**. Señora Milagros lives beyond the school on the right; she runs various rooms and simple but passable houses for up to nine people. No phone, but messages may be left at the Villa Coral in Cumaná; ring Emilia, (093) 513282. The three-bed **Casa de María** is rented by Señora María who lives by the school.

Dive centre

Divers may rent equipment or get tanks filled at the **Campamento de Buceo Mochima**. This centre is run by Rodolfo Plaza who organises 8-day diving 'camps' in August–September. Rodolfo provides instruction, insurance, scuba gear, lodging and boats to the best diving places all year. A $300 dive package includes lodging and a CEMAS course for international diving certificate. The camp has space for 10 people. Rodolfo offers a **rafting tour** on the upper Neverí River; $40 including transfer from/to Mochima; $50 with lodging. For information, in Caracas, tel: (02) 9296020, fax: (02) 9612531.

Margarita Island

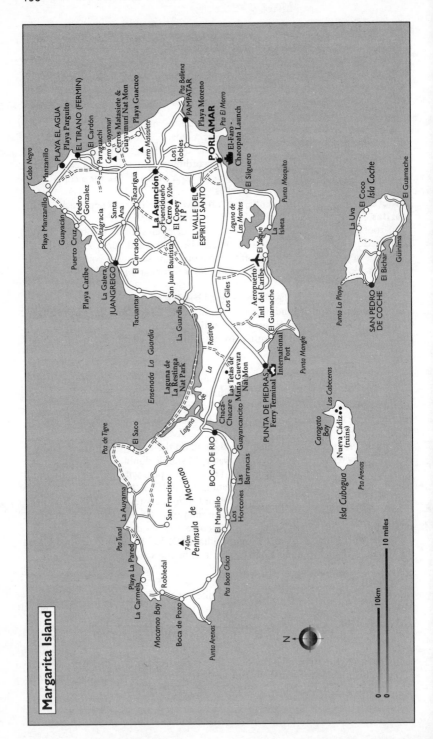

10km

10 miles

N

Cabo Negro
Manzanillo
PLAYA EL AGUA
Playa Parguito
EL TIRANO (FERMIN)
El Cardón
Guayacán
Playa Manzanillo
Pedro Gonzalez
Puerto Cruz
Santa Ana
Altagracia
Paraguachi
Cerro Guayamurí
Cerros Matasiete &
Guayamurí Nat Mon
Playa Guacuco
Pta Ballena
PAMPATAR
Playa Moreno
Pta El Morro
El Faro -
Chacopata Launch
PORLAMAR
Los Robles
Cerro Matasiete
La Asunción
Fuentidueño
Cerro 920m
El Copey
N P
EL VALLE DEL
ESPIRITU SANTO
Tacarigua
El Cercado
La Galera
JUANGREIGO
Playa Caribe
San Juan Bautista
Tacuantar
La Guardia
El Silguero
Punta Mosquito
Laguna de
Los Marites
La
Isleta
El Yaque
Los Giles
Aeropuerto
Intl del Caribe
El Guamache
La
Restinga
Ensenada La Guardia
Laguna de
La Restinga
Nat Park
Pta de Tigre
El Saco
Laguna de La
Chacare
Las Tetas de
María Guevara
Nat Mon
Guayancancito
PUNTA DE PIEDRAS
Ferry Terminal
International
Port
Punta Mangle
Punta La Playa
Pta Tunal
La Auyama
San Francisco
BOCA DE RIO
740m
Península de Macanao
Las
Barrancas
El Mangillo
Los
Horcones
Carogato
Bay
Nueva Cádiz
(ruins)
Los Cabeceras
Playa La Pared
La Carmela
Robledal
Macanao Bay
Boca de Pozo
Punta Arenas
Pta Boca Chica
Laguna de Macanao
Isla Cubagua
Pta Arenas
El Coco
Isla Coche
El Guamache
La Uva
SAN PEDRO
DE COCHE
El Bichar
Güinima
0
0

Margarita

PEARL OF THE CARIBBEAN

Margarita, 'Pearl of the Caribbean', was first famous for its oyster beds. Columbus, however, knowing nothing of such fabulous wealth, christened the island Margarita in honour of Margaret of Austria, Princess of Castille, not after the Greek word for pearl. He sighted the island in 1498 but did not land there. The island's first inhabitants, Guaiquerí and Carib Indians, called it Paraguachoa, 'abundance of fish'. Though Margarita has few pearls left today, its people love the sea. Fishermen, renowned as the country's best, still sail colourful wooden peñeros, although there are modern deep-sea fleets, too. Early in the morning you can see them unloading their catch on the shores of many bays. Boatyards and a sardine cannery are among the few traditional industries; but today, the island's 300km shoreline offering over 30 white beaches is the banner of a vigorous tourism industry.

Unlike continental Venezuela which has long rainy periods, on Margarita the sun shines an average nine hours a day almost all year. Day temperatures hover at 28°C, with the cooler months of December to March dropping to 20–21°C at night. And, most appealing to sea lovers, water temperatures average 26°C. Moderate rains fall in July–August and November–January.

Lying in the Caribbean 38km north of Cumaná, Margarita is the largest of Venezuela's 72 tropical islands. It measures 67km from east to west and 33km north to south, covering 934km². Part of the Lesser Antilles chain, Margarita is formed by two islands linked by a narrow strip called La Restinga. The western half, **Macanao Peninsula**, is beautiful but arid and so has fewer people. A vehicle is a must for getting around Macanao.

South of Margarita are two islands, Coche and Cubagua. The trio, together with a small archipelago lying northeast, Los Frailes, make up **Nueva Esparta State**, whose capital is La Asunción, a quiet town. Porlamar, the main city, is on the island's southeast coast. Most of Margarita's population of 320,000 is concentrated around Porlamar, the business and shopping hub.

Margariteños today are a blend of the original Indian inhabitants, the Guaiqueríes, with Spanish settlers and, later, Negroes. They are largely Catholics devoted to their patroness, La Virgen del Valle.

The island population doubles during peak holidays. Water is a problem, but development is made possible by a pipeline bringing fresh water from the mainland. *Tinajones*, large earthenware water vessels, are a legacy from the time when everyone carried water from a well or spring. It is only below El Copey mountain that enough rain falls to sustain limited agriculture.

The choice of honeymooners, Margarita is the country's most important tourism centre, both national and international. During the high seasons (July–September and December–April), visitors throng hotels, roads and beaches.

Package tours may repel some travellers, but '*Margarita sí vale la pena*' – Margarita is worthwhile. The island is compact and varied, its beaches are many and beautiful, restaurants are plentiful and good, nightlife is busy. Villages are clean and well cared for, plazas are filled with trees and houses overflow with plants: Margarita is mostly arid and people have learned to appreciate greenery. (Elsewhere in Venezuela you can spot a Margariteño's house by its plants.) It is a centre of craftwork – pottery, hammocks and straw hats. There are restored colonial forts and churches to explore.

Also of importance to first-timers in Latin America, Margarita is a good place to acclimatise. You will find many people eager to speak English of sorts and services have been honed by experience with foreign visitors. As you arrive at the airport, pick up folders listing hotels, travel agents and car rentals.

History
In 1499 Spaniards found the source of the pearls adorning the natives – oyster beds off **Cubagua**. The first shipment of 80lb of pearls to the Spanish court opened fortune hunters' eyes and the rush was on. Pearls represented 40% of all New World riches transported to Spain between 1500 and 1530. The first European town in the Americas was **Nueva Cádiz**, founded on Cubagua in 1528 after many years of settlement. But ruthless exploitation reduced not only Cubagua's pearls but indigenous divers. Enslaved natives were fed on oysters and forced to work until they died from exhaustion, blood gushing from mouth and nose. The alternative to this ugly death was sharks, attracted in great numbers. Mainland natives, enraged by slaving raids to replace the dead divers, attacked Cubagua. By 1541 when an earthquake and tidal wave devasted Nueva Cádiz, the pearl beds had been picked clean as bones. Pearl fishing had moved to Coche and Margarita where settlements such as El Valle were founded as early as 1529. Pearl beds were further damaged through a concession given in 1823 to an English company using dredges. In the early 20th century Puerto Fermín saw some pearling activity and later divers with helmets were successful in gathering almost 5 million karats (1943). Banned in 1962, pearling today is allowed in season, January–April, every other year.

During the colonial era a string of seven forts was built to protect Spanish interests. Two have been restored: **San Carlos Borromeo** in Pampatar and **Santa Rosa** in Asunción, both of which withstood pirate attacks and later assaults by royalists and patriots.

Margarita and Cumaná, on the mainland, were strong supporters of separation from Spain. Simón Bolívar landed on the island in 1816 to begin his third campaign. Margariteños still speak with pride of their part in the patriot victory and the role of heroine Luisa Cáceres de Arismendi. Imprisoned in Santa Rosa fortress, this 16-year-old gave birth (her baby died), was sent to Spain, escaped, and later returned to a free Venezuela and to her husband. Freedom fighters earned the name Nueva Esparta (New Sparta) for their state. Today two dates are marked as islandwide holidays: May 4, the day patriots declared Independence', and July 31, the Battle of Matasiete, 1817.

In the 1970s Margarita was declared a **free port** and exchanged peace and isolation for imports and shoppers. However, economic recession and a free market policy have eliminated many bargains for Venezuelans. Instead, currency devaluation has attracted foreign investors. International tourism is on the rise, led by Brazilians and Canadians, and large luxury resorts now sprawl over some of the best beaches.

Perhaps it comes as no surprise that today security is a major problem. The island, once so quiet it had no jail, has built a prison on Macanao Peninsula.

GETTING THERE AND AWAY
By air
Caribe International Airport
Officially known as Santiago Mariño (tel: (095) 691442), this is situated in El Yaque, 20km southwest of Porlamar. Built in 1970, it has two terminals, national and international. The airport was the first in Latin America to be privatised. Travellers will find money exchange desks, snack bars, information booths, and a duty-free shop (with more interesting goods than you can get in Porlamar). Car rental agencies are in the international section. Waiting-room telephones do not accept coins; you buy a phone *tarjeta* (debit card) at a booth or bookstand for a fixed sum: Bs2,000 or Bs5,000.

Taxis from the airport are plentiful but not overly cheap. An information booth in the national terminal supplies a list of rates to all parts of the island; also, check the Cámara de Turismo leaflet. To Porlamar, the current fare is $12; no tipping required. A low-cost airbus goes to Porlamar, but there are no regular buses from the airport to other towns. Minibuses leave from the airport entrance and go when full. From downtown Porlamar, look around Plaza Bolívar for the *carritos por puesto* to the airport.

International flights
Margarita is a point of direct entry into Venezuela. Aeropostal and Avensa, now starting up international routes, will help to fill the gap left when Viasa folded. At present most flights are charters. Scheduled flights include: Aeroperu from Lima, Aereotuy from Grenada and Tobago, Aeropostal from Aruba, Barbados, Curaçao, Dominican Republic and Trinidad. Allow two hours before international flights.

National flights
Be there at least an hour before departure to queue for your flight. Even reconfirmation of booking may be of no use if you arrive late, although there are many competing lines with special offers. Servivensa (the most expensive at $70), Laser, Air Venezuela and Aserca provide nearly 30 flights daily to Caracas. Other lines such as Oriental, Avior, LAI and Rutaca compete to serve eastern Venezuela, Barcelona, Cumaná, Carúpano, Maturín and Puerto Ordaz (Ciudad Guayana): $40. Aeropostal, Air Venezuela, Aserca and Laser go to central and western Venezuela, with two daily flights to Mérida, four to Valencia, ten to Maracaibo except at weekends ($90).

Charter lines such as Aeroejecutivos, Sasca (17 seater STOL craft) and Rutaca fill in for destinations like Canaima and Güiria. Aereotuy makes tours to Angel Falls, Kavac, La Blanquilla, Los Roques and the Delta.

By sea
The ferry terminal is in **Punta de Piedras**, 29km west of Porlamar. *Por puestos* and small buses go regularly between the two. Punta de Piedras is a small fishing town; many *peñeros* tie up at the dock. At the end of the beachside Paseo María Guevara is Edimar, La Salle's marine research station. As well as higher studies in marine biology, oceanography, fish farming and navigation, La Salle sponsors a fishing school and nautical high school.

Ferries
Conferry A million people go to and from the island yearly aboard Conferry's six vessels which link Puerto La Cruz and Cumaná, carrying not only passengers and cars but nearly all the island's food, cement, steel and building blocks. Every Easter

week Conferry takes some 33,000 people and 7,800 vehicles including large lorries to Margarita. Curiously, when the bridge over Maracaibo Lake in the west was built in 1963, it gave the island a big boost as the four lake ferries were acquired for Margarita duty. A sorely needed new ferry terminal is under construction.

The large Norwegian-built ferries carry 1,500 passengers and 160 cars; there is air-conditioned first class with seating both inside and out. Travellers should appraise the various ferry services. Although the crossing is quicker from Cumaná than Puerto La Cruz, service is worse. First class allows you on the upper deck, while tourist passengers are cooped up at the stern of the ship over two dark, noisy engines. On all Conferry tickets, there are 50% discounts for children aged 2–7 and adults over 65 (you need a photocopy of passport or ID card).

Conferry's new *Margarita Express* halves the crossing time to Puerto La Cruz from four to two hours. The 500-passenger vessel makes three round trips during high season, two in off-season. Fare $23 adults; $40 car, $50 for pickup trucks and 4x4 vehicles, $12 for motorbikes. The air-conditioned ship offers reclining seats, bar, cafeteria, stewardess service and snacks.

From/to Puerto La Cruz: about 4 hours; four to six sailings daily according to season. Fares about $6 tourist class and $9 first class. Cars $20, 4x4 vehicles $22, motorbikes $5.

From/to Cumaná: 3½ hours; two sailings from Cumaná, 07.00 and 16.00; return 11.30, 20.00. Fares $8 tourist class. Cars $10, 4x4 vehicles $21, motorbikes $5.

Even with **prepaid car reservations** (see below), drivers should be at the terminal two hours before sailing time, more at peak seasons. Cars without reservation join the queue four hours in advance. For enquiries, ring Conferry, tel: 800 33779 (FERRY).

Tickets can be bought in Punta de Piedras, tel: (095) 98440, 98148, fax: 98261; daily 07.00–21.00 (exceptions are December 25 and January 1, 6.00–10.00 – two sailings only). In Porlamar, tel: (095) 612935/6780, fax: 614364; Calle Marcano near Bella Vista Hotel, weekdays 08.00–12.00, 14.00–17.00. In Puerto La Cruz, Los Cocos Terminal, tel: (081) 677847/8332, fax: 677090; daily 07.30–21.00 hours, tickets by order of arrival. In Cumaná, Terminal de Ferries, tel: (093) 661903, tel/fax: 311462. In Caracas, Edif Banhorient, Av Casanova at Las Acacias, tel: (02) 7828544, 7819711, fax: 7930739; weekdays 08.00–11.30, 14.00–17.30; prepaid car reservations. Your reservation is confirmed upon depositing the full sum into a certain bank and faxing the copy to Conferry: 614364. Credit cards and travellers' cheques are not accepted.

Gran Cacique III This hydrofoil takes passengers from **Puerto La Cruz**: 2½ hours, sailings daily 06.30 and 14.00, returning at 10.30 and 18.00. Air conditioning (cold); deck access for first-class passengers, $15; tourist $7.50.

Tickets, in Punta de Piedras, tel: (095) 98072/399/430; daily 05.00–13.00. In Puerto La Cruz, Terminal *Gran Cacique III*, Los Boqueticos, tel: (081) 630935, 677286; daily 06.00–14.00.

From Cumaná: the *Gran Cacique II* hydrofoil crosses to Margarita in 2 hours, at 07.00 and 14.00, returning at 11.00 and 18.00. **Tickets** are bought at time of sailing, in the Terminal de Ferries, (093) 320011, 312589; first class $12, tourist $10. All luggage must be checked; you may carry on only a small bag. This is a smoke-filled cavern with blaring TVs.

Naviarca ferry Vehicles, cargo and passengers. From **Cumaná**, about 4 hours, two sailings daily at 12.00–13.00 and 15.00–16.00 whenever a load is full. The open-deck *chalana* carries 56 cars and lorries, 200 tourist passengers. You sit in a rumbling cave below the car deck; on deck is uncomfortable due to spray and engine exhaust.

Coche Island ferry Conferry's vessel, the *María Libre*, goes daily from Punta de Piedras. From/to **Coche**: 1 hour; weekdays to Margarita at 06.00, returning at 17.00; weekends from Coche at 06.00 and 18.00, return 08.30 and 19.30. Fare $1.75 adults. Cars $8, 4x4 vehicles $9, motorbikes $6.

Chacopata launches The Empresa Naviera Turismo Chacopata runs a daily passenger service between Porlamar and Chacopata, a fishing village on the northeast end of the Araya Peninsula, Sucre State. The *lanchas* leave from Chacopata at 05.00, 07.00, 11.00 and 13.00; from Porlamar at 08.00, 10.00, 13.30 and 15.30. In Porlamar, look for their small office on Paseo Rómulo Gallegos beside the Muelle de El Faro; open 07.00 to 16.00. The launch schedule varies on Fridays and Mondays.

(For more information, see *Chapter 9, Araya Peninsula*.)

Windward Islands ferry This ship makes a weekly circuit of the Lesser Antilles, Venezuela–Barbados. It departs for Trinidad at 18.00 every other Wednesday (alternating with Güiria) from the Muelle de Pampatar. All destinations require valid passport and continuing ticket. Ask about departure tax from Venezuela. For reservations call Unitravel in Porlamar, tel: (095) 617491, 630278, fax: 618297; Calle Cedeño at Santiago Mariño.

Cruise ships

The first ship to visit Margarita on a regular cruise circuit was the *Seawind Crown* (Antilles line) which docked at El Guamache International Port in 1998. Margarita's modern seaport also receives freighters. Located only a few kilometres from the Ferry Terminal at Punta de Piedras, the International Port is securely walled. The fishing village of Guamache is halfway to the road, its multi-coloured houses facing the sea.

Preparing to compete as a Caribbean port of call, Margarita is building a cruise dock in Porlamar, at the foot of Boulevard Guevara.

GETTING AROUND
Information and tours

Points of interest are never far away: from Porlamar it is 9km to Pampatar, 12km to La Asunción, 23.5km to Manzanillo (beyond Playa El Agua), 25km to Juangriego, and 40km to Boca de Río on Macanao Peninsula. Porlamar buses go to all these places.

The state **Corporación de Turismo** office is in the Centro Artesanal, Los Robles, about 3km northeast of Porlamar; tel/fax: (095) 622514/3638; email: corpotur@enlared.net

When you arrive at the airport, check the **information booth** in the national terminal's main hall and ask for a Porlamar map; Margarita give-away maps are often out-of-scale fantasies made for car drivers, but they do for a start. There is a full colour guide, *Margarita La Guía*, tel: 638487/812, published in English, German and Spanish, with lists of airlines, couriers, pharmacies and credit card agents. Their separate Margarita map is the best around. Look for a free copy in bigger hotels and agencies. Most pamphlets available at kiosks are half advertising. Exceptions are some free bilingual papers such as *Mira!*, tel: 613351, giving the 'independent traveller's alternative' in English, and covering beaches, food, entertainment.

If you have time for a mainland tour, go to any agency in the big hotels: they all handle destinations such as Angel Falls.

Boat trips

Many agencies in Porlamar, Playa El Agua and Juangriego offer day tours. They promote sailing, catamaran and fishing trips to Coche, Cubagua or Los Frailes. **Octopus**, one of the most important, is located at No 31 Av Bolívar, Porlamar, tel: (095) 611535, 634851. Catering to Europeans, the firm provides a complete dive service and all marine sports. Octopus has a base in the Hilton and desks in other hotels, notably the Dunes.

Other agencies specialising in watersports include **Delphin Swiss Tours** in Playa de Agua, tel: 48646/70; and **Enomis'** in the Dynasty Hotel, tel/fax: 622977.

Buses (por puestos)

Porlamar's **Terminal de Autobuses** is in the Centro Comercial Bella Vista, Calle San Rafael (ten blocks north of Calle Igualdad) near Av Terranova. Buses from the Terminal de Oriente in Caracas run at night and stop at the Conferry terminal in Puerto La Cruz. Unión Conductores Margarita leaves daily at 17.00 for Porlamar, boarding the night ferry and arriving in Margarita before dawn. Cost is $9.00 for the bus plus $11 for the ferry ticket.

Carros por puesto and 'microbuses' traverse the island. They are cheap and go almost everywhere but without a schedule. Many do not work after 21.00 and there is a small additional charge on Sundays. In towns, all you have to know is where the stops are; on roads you can wave a *por puesto* down. Some lines serving El Valle and La Asunción circulate around Plaza Bolívar in Porlamar; those going to Pampatar, the Margarita Hilton and Playa Moreno move up and down Av 4 de Mayo and Av Santiago Mariño respectively. Buses are frequent and have their routes painted on the side.

Starting points in Porlamar of some lines are:

Aeropuerto Plaza Bolívar, north side.
Asunción Calle Fajardo at Marcano.
El Valle Av Miranda at Marcano.
Ferry Terminal Calle Maneiro at Mariño, until 23.00.
Juangriego (via Santa Ana), Av Miranda between Igualdad and Marcano.
La Restinga and Macanao Peninsula Calle La Marina between Arismendi and Mariño, until 18.30.
Pampatar, Playa Moreno Calle Fajardo between La Marina and Maneiro.
Playa El Agua, Guacuco entrance Calle Guevara near Marcano, until 19.00.
San Juan and Fuentidueño Calle Libertad between Maneiro and La Marina.

Car hire

Renting a car is a good way to see Margarita and to identify places you wish to revisit. At the airport, some 12–15 agencies have desks in a new oval building; many are open until the last flight arrives. You will find rates are less expensive than on the mainland. There are two general plans, one without *kilometraje* or mileage and one with 150km included in a higher price. Maintenance may be a problem; people have reported changing cars three times in one day on Margarita because of breakdowns.

In response to such frustration, Helga Pfeifer started her own rental agency with new cars and a repair shop. She now has 30 Suzukis. Contact **Baveca Rent a Car**, Av 31 de Julio, La Mira near Playa El Agua, tel: (095) 48875.

Taxis

A good alternative despite rising fares, taxis can be hired by the trip, *viaje*, or by the day. An excursion by taxi will cost you (and three more) around $85 to make a circle of Pampatar, La Asunción, Juangriego, La Restinga and Playa El Agua. Air-conditioned taxis charge extra. Ask at the airport for a list of taxi rates. At night it will be hard to find a taxi to take you to out-of-the-way places. There is a surcharge of 30% after 21.00 and roughly 10% on Sundays and holiday. Tipping is not customary. Fix the price before getting in and pay after the ride.

Some lines serving hotels post their fares; the cabs are usually parked behind the hotels. The taxi line at the **Bella Vista Hotel** is good, likewise the **Margarita Hilton** line, tel: 623333. Another is the **Asociación Civil Taxis Concorde**, tel: 619078/619557, Calle Cedeño at Av Santiago Mariño. Use these fares to compare taking a taxi ride to La Restinga, say, with hiring a cab to spend four hours at the beach and returning.

BEACHES AND WATERSPORTS

Various circuits beckon you to explore Margarita and its many beaches on your own (see below, *East Coast, North Coast, Macanao*). All beaches are public property and in theory you can visit even those at luxury resorts. Carry little cash and don't leave your belongings unattended; take with you photocopies of your passport and tourist card for identification. Nude bathing is illegal but topless bathers have been seen at Playa Caribe, El Agua and even at the Margarita Hilton. When beach-going, especially on Macanao Peninsula which is mostly arid and shadeless, bring water, sunblock and some kind of shelter.

Windsurfers go to beaches on the tradewind side (southeast, east): El Yaque and Playa El Agua, and Punta Arenas on Macanao Peninsula. **Bodysurfers** work out at Playa Parguito and El Tirano.

Warnings Swimmers should avoid the sea near heavily populated areas. Water quality from Pampatar Bay to Porlamar is questionable; currents wash contaminants westward to El Silguero and La Isleta beach.

Among small shade trees in secluded coves you may find the poisonous manchineel tree, called *manzanillo* after its green 'apples'. Stay away: its stiff leaves, milky sap and even smoke from its burning wood are toxic.

PORLAMAR

Founded in 1536 as Pueblo de la Mar, Porlamar is Margarita's only real city and today has some 330,000 inhabitants. Its free port status acquired in the 1970s drew huge shopper interest. Many Venezuelans go to stores on Av 4 de Mayo and elite boutiques on Santiago Mariño, although prices are no longer competitive. There is a purchase tax on many goods. Shops and banks in Porlamar traditionally close on four local holidays as well as national ones: May 4 – Margarita's Independence declaration; May 31 – Free Port labour day; July 31 – Battle of Matasiete; September 8 – Virgen del Valle.

Consulates

The growing number of consulates in Porlamar reflects the rise of international tourism: **Canada**, tel: 613475, 640086; **Denmark**, tel: 637143/3002; **France**, tel: 618431; **Germany**, tel: 615212, 616175; **Holland**, 641658, fax: 641460; **Italy**, tel: 610213; **Spain**, tel: 615446/35; **Switzerland**, 628682/5672; **United Kingdom**, tel: 624665, (014) 9951276.

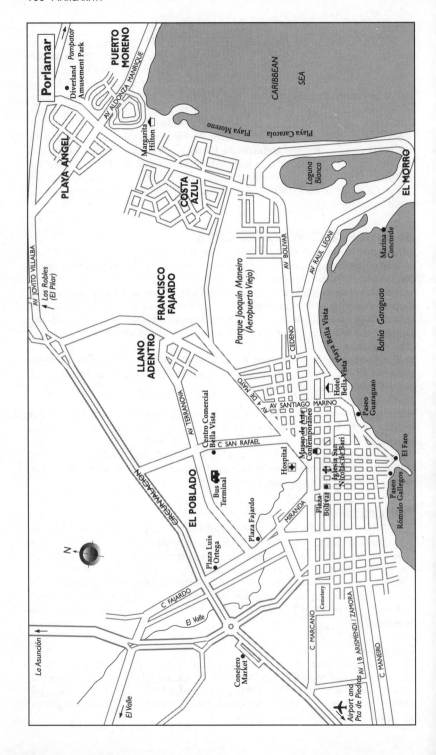

Porlamar

PUERTO MORENO
Diverland Pampatar Amusement Park
AV ALDONZA MANRIQUE
PLAYA ANGEL
Margarita Hilton
Playa Moreno
Playa Caracola
CARIBBEAN SEA
COSTA AZUL
EL MORRO
Laguna Blanca
AV JÓVITO VILLALBA
Los Robles (El Pilar)
FRANCISCO FAJARDO
AV BOLIVAR
AV RAUL LEONI
Marina Concorde
Parque Joaquin Maneiro (Aeropuerto Viejo)
Bahía Garaguao
LLANO ADENTRO
C CEDENO
Hotel Playa Bella Vista
AV CIRCUNVALACIÓN
AV TERRANOVA
Centro Comercial Bella Vista
AV 4 DE MAYO
AV SANTIAGO MARINO
Bella Vista
Paseo Guaraguao
C SAN RAFAEL
Hospital
Museo de Arte Contemporáneo
EL POBLADO
Bus Terminal
Iglesia San Nicolás de Bari
El Faro
Plaza Fajardo
MIRANDA
Plaza Bolívar
Plaza Luis Ortega
Paseo Rómulo Gallegos
N
C FAJARDO
El Valle
Cemetery
C MARCANO
La Asunción
El Valle
Conejero Market
C MANEIRO
Airport and Pta de Piedras AV J B ARISMENDI / ZAMORA

What to see and do
In Porlamar
Basilica of San Nicolás de Bari The Basilica, in the shape of a cross, is on the east side of Plaza Bolívar. Religious images include a replica of the black Virgin of Montserrat, patroness of Cataluña, Spain. A marble plaque bears the text of Porlamar's founding. Processions on December 5–6 mark the feast day of San Nicolás.

Museo de Arte Contemporáneo Francisco Narváez Situated at Calle Igualdad at Díaz; tel: (095) 618668. Open Tue–Fri 09.00–17.00; weekends 10.00–16.00; free cultural events on Friday evenings. The museum has rotating shows of contemporary Venezuelan art, lectures, concerts and film series. There is a collection of paintings and sculpture by **Francisco Narváez** who was born in Porlamar in 1905 and died there in 1982. Narváez made many monuments in Caracas and Porlamar, including one on Boulevard Guevara near Plaza Bolívar, and the delightful fountain La Ronda, of four children dancing, pigtails flying, near the Bella Vista Hotel.

Paseo Guaraguao A bayside promenade, also called Paseo Rómulo Gallegos, goes to a small lighthouse built in 1896, the **Faro de Porlamar**. Steps form an amphitheatre here for folklore spectacles. From the pier daily launches leave for Chacopata. At the foot of Boulevard Gómez is a single-storey building, the old *Aduana* or customs house. The large dock for cruise ships is to be built where the fish market operated, at the foot of Boulevard Guevara.

Mercado Municipal Conejeros The public market is on Porlamar's northwest outskirts by the Circunvalación highway. Well organised, about a hundred booths sell just about everything. The main building with its bright yellow panels houses fruit, vegetable and fish stands. Crowded stalls offer perfume, sandals, souvenirs and cotton imports. Prices are reasonable. Surrounding the market are *licorerías* selling low-priced alcohol. You can eat outside cheaply at stands where women fry *empanadas* (turnovers) of white cheese, chicken or shark, *cazón*. Or you can follow hustlers inside: they show you to one of various budget restaurants where the food is hearty and the boss is the lady serving the *hervido*.

Caserío Fajardo Also known as El Poblado or the village, this is an old district of simple tile-roofed houses along Calle Fajardo in northwest Porlamar. South of Plaza Fajardo the street is called Avenida Miranda. Restored homes, some revealing the original adobe bricks, show what El Poblado looked like when sugarcane grew by the Río El Valle. You can take a *carrito* there from Plaza Bolívar.

Ultralight flights
In operation for 12 years, Sistema Aéreo de Promoción (SAP), tel: 619137/617632, flies Quicksilvers, an ideal way to photograph the coast. Prices are said to be low for the Caribbean and include insurance. Flights go from Porlamar's Aeropuerto Viejo, north side of Parque Joaquín Maneiro, on Mon–Thur, and from Playa El Agua Fri–Sun.

Where to stay
The area telephone code for Margarita is (095)
Every kind of accommodation is available from luxury resort-style hotels down. Here is a sampling of hotels in central Porlamar.

Expensive

In the Porlamar area, only a few resort hotels have a beach: the Bella Vista, María Luisa, Margarita Hilton, and Marina Bay. But there is still plenty of room on the open beaches of Playa Caracola and Playa Moreno (not a patch on crescent bays such as Manzanillo, however). The 1990s saw the rise of many new resorts between Porlamar and the Hilton. Prices range from $60 a person to over $100. With pools and transportation to beaches, these have taken pride of place from the original (1955) resort hotel, the **Bella Vista** on Av Santiago Mariño, tel: (095) 617222, fax: 612557. But the Bella Vista's 314 rooms are convenient and sought after at $60 a double.

Margabella Suites, tel: 639960, fax: 619246, at the foot of Av Santiago Mariño is a seafront option west of the Bella Vista, with rooftop restaurant, 90 rooms and suites with kitchenette and pool; double $65. The **Stauffer**, tel: 613222, fax: 618708, Av Santiago Mariño at Calle Patiño, offers 100 rooms and transfer to beaches; $60 double or single.

Among the classiest of hotels, the **Margarita Hilton** is held to be the island's best for its top service and facilities; tel: (095) 624111/3333, fax: 623941, in Caracas (02) 5034114; 280 rooms, pool, gym, spa, popular yoga centre, karate and all water sports. The beach has lifeguards, shelters, parasailing. Classes and equipment for scuba diving, waterskiing and windsurfing are laid on by the Centro Náutico Octopus. The 5-star **Marina Bay**, tel: 625211, nearby in Costa Azul, has 170 rooms, pool, tennis and gym. The hotel has made a public walkway to Playa Moreno and has built breakwaters, planted palms, and installed a floating bar for guests. The luxury **Margarita Dynasty**, tel: 621622/411, fax: 625101; email: dynasty@enlared.net; is in Costa Azul near the Hilton. The resort has 127 studios for two, 16 suites with kitchen for two to four people, solarium, pool and shops.

Kamarata Beach Resort is an attractive, good apart-hotel on Av Bolívar, Sector Costa Azul, tel: 624311, fax: 620955; 40 suites ($65) with kitchen for four to seven people, poolside bar, tasca, restaurant, 500m from beach.

Finally, there is a low-profile, low-cost beach hotel in Puerto Moreno at the north end of the Hilton's bay (and why pay more for the same beach?), known by its former names of **Valu Club** and **Decameron**. The (today) **Viosmare Beach**, tel: 622633, fax: 622778, via Playa El Angel (en route to Pampatar), is a series of two-storey units built in the 1970s around a pool. The dining room is at the water's edge where at one time a Señor Angel had a restaurant. Renato Lombardi is the owner; he charges about $25 a day with food.

(The 27-floor Margarita Concorde on Punta El Morro remains closed. The adjacent public **Marina Concorde** is the base of pleasure boats such as the *Viola*, sailing at 09.00 every day for Cubagua, and another yacht going to Coche.)

Moderate

There are comfortable hotels in the $20–35 range around Av Santiago Mariño; an extra bed adds $3–4. **Hotel Boulevard**, tel: 610522, fax: 632184, on Calle Marcano between Guevara and Gómez; has 44 rooms and hot water. The **Nueva Scandinavia**, tel: 642662, fax: 635121, on Calle Marcano near Narváez, has 22 rooms, hot water, jacuzzi, restaurant, and is proud of Nordic management. The **Flamingo City**, tel: 639786, fax: 645564, Av 4 de Mayo at Santiago Mariño; has 40 rooms with hot water and fridge. **Howard Johnson Tinajero**, tel: 638380/89, fax: 639949, Calle Campos between Cedeño and Marcano; has 66 suites for two to four (plus two children free) with kitchen, jacuzzi, laundry, gym, pool; guests use the Mandinga's beach. Follow Calle Marcano east for the hotels below; most are on or near Av Raúl Leoni and the Guaraguao beach. They include: **Imperial**, tel:

614823, fax: 615056. **Hotel Evdama**, tel: 610075, fax: 618573; hot water in suites only. The **Daisy Suites**, tel: 619922, fax: 616595, Calle Fermín, 30 rooms with fridge. A block east on Av Raúl Leoni is the **María Luisa**, tel: 637940, fax: 635978; more expensive, double $45.

Economic

Approaching Plaza Bolívar hotels charging $12–16 a double include: **Hotel Torino**, tel: 610734, Calle Mariño, a block north of the España; **Hotel Central**, tel: 614757, Boulevard Gómez; **Hotel Italia**, Calle San Nicolás, tel: 633010; the **Brasilia**, tel: 634947, Calle San Nicolás; and **Nuevo Paraíso**, tel: 639652, below Plaza Bolívar on Calle Velásquez. There is an economic seafront hotel, the **Tama**, tel: 611602, at the foot of Calle Campos east of the Bella Vista; popular with Germans for its low rates, good restaurant-bar.

As you move east towards Av Santiago Mariño, accommodation rises in service and cost. The modern **Contemporáneo**, tel: 633068, is on Plaza Bolívar, Calle Mariño. Hotels on Calle Igualdad charge $16–19 for a double with air conditioning. Among these are: **Porlamar**, tel: 630271; **La Opera**, tel: 611642; **Evang**, tel: 616868; **Canada**, tel: 615920. Two blocks east of Santiago Mariño is the 17-room **Colonial Margarita**, tel: 639823, Calle Fermín, up from Calle Marcano (Av Raúl Leoni).

Budget

For those watching every penny, there are old downtown hotels towards the bay for about $10 a double with bath, some with air conditioning. The renovated seafront **Hotel Malecón**, tel: 642579, corner Calle Arismendi, promises a better future with a top-storey restaurant; air-conditioned double $12. Also near the waterfront is the clean, acceptable **Hotel España**, tel: 612479, Calle Mariño 6-35; with fan and shared bath; good-value restaurant.

Where to eat

Margarita, tourist mecca that it is, abounds in restaurants. Food ranges from the humble *arepa* to lobster, with prices in accordance. Menus are often posted at the door. For local, affordable meals, go for *comida criolla*, grilled chicken or pizza. Some suggestions in the moderate range in Porlamar follow.

Ana's Café on the rooftop of Edificio Avensa, Av 4 de Mayo, is modern, chic and breezy; closed Sunday. **El Chipi**, Calle Cedeño at Av Santiago Mariño, is an old standby where lobster tops a menu in French, Italian and English; typical dishes include *sancocho de pescado* (a seafood soup) and *rueda de carite* (kingfish steak). **Dino's Grill**, Calle Igualdad, serves economical lunch both indoors and in the garden; steak and seafood at night.

The **Cueva del Pescador**, Calle Fermín between Cedeño and Marcano, is a quiet tasca with good food at good prices. **Rigoletto** on Calle Malavé at Patiño serves its own *pasta al dente* and wood-oven pizza. Opposite, don't miss the **Heladería Italiana 4D** where ice-cream flavours are made daily.

Seafood The seafront **Bahía**, Av Raúl Leoni by the Bella Vista beach, is one of Porlamar's busiest restaurants; lobster and paella dishes show why people come (or is it to hear owner Galo sing?). The **Cocody**, also near Playa Bella Vista, has a romantic terrace setting for French dining, and owner Jacqueline sings, too. Near the Bahía and with access from the beach, **Rancho Mandinga** is an upscale place known for shrimp dishes. **Martín Pescador**, Av 4 de Mayo, has a fine reputation for very fresh fish; open Sunday evening, closed Tuesday.

Nightlife

Porlamar hums at night; clubs and bars are said to stay open until the last carouser leaves. It is a dynamic, changing scene with new spots opening frequently. Bingo is big locally, and casinos are the hot spots, popping up everywhere, although now they are being regulated under new laws. There are casinos in the Stauffer Hotel, open 24 hours, the Margarita Suites, Flamingo Beach, Hilton and Marina Bay. The big MGM casino is on Avenida 4 de Mayo.

The night person will find a variety of bars and discotheques on Av 4 de Mayo such as the **Subsuelo** (underground) in Galerías Fente, **Buccaneers** disco and grill, and **Gardfield** pool and bar. The **Chalet** is a Scandinavian restaurant and bar on Av Rómulo Betancourt at Av 4 de Mayo; live music and grillfest on Saturday nights. The flashy glass/chrome **Gran Pirámide** is on Calle Malavé, a block east of Santiago Mariño. At the bottom of this street is the very popular **Mosquito Coast**, behind the Bella Vista Hotel. Famous for its live entertainment, Mosquito Coast has a casual rattan atmosphere, plays a mix of old and new Latin and American beats 'driving you to dance', serves Tex-Mex food, and offers Margaritas at half price till 22.00. **El Punto** and the **Village Club** are also good spots for dancing.

Popular bars include **Brandy's** on Calle Malavé, **Gator's**, a meeting place for Canadians on the same street, **Cheers**, an American-style pub with food and beer on Av Santiago Mariño, and the **Flamboyant** at the Margarita Hilton.

ROUTE TO PAMPATAR

On the way to Pampatar, 10km east, make a detour to Los Robles to see its early colonial church. Go via the Circunvalación highway and Los Robles traffic circle where there is a shopping mall and a crafts centre by the highway. The Centro Artesanal Los Robles is a collection of shops selling Venezuelan clothes, food, crafts and birthday piñatas. The state **Corporación de Turismo**, Corpotur, has its office here.

Los Robles You can see the beautiful white colonial church of El Pilar in Los Robles, a 200m walk from the crafts centre up Route 2. On October 12, the feast day of Nuestra Señora del Pilar (also a national holiday, *Día de la Raza*), the little statue of 'La Pilarica' heads a procession around the pleasant village. A replica of one in Zaragoza, Spain, 'La Pilarica' is said to be of solid gold (she is kept in a bank) and was the gift in 1504 of Queen Juana La Loca, daughter of Fernando and Isabel of Spain. In pedestrian streets around the church cars are replaced with plants and benches; children swarm through the Plaza de La Concha with its small Venus in a shell.

Diverland The amusement park, also known as Isla Aventura, is near Pampatar via the Circunvalación. Touted as South America's biggest, the park has 16 attractions including a giant ferris wheel, roller coaster and water toboggan (take your swimsuit). Diverland's pool opens at 11.00 on weekends; the amusement park opens nightly at 17.00 during peak seasons of Easter, summer (July 15–Sept 15), and Christmas (Dec 15–Jan 10). The rest of the year the park is closed Mon–Tue. A single entrance charge covers unlimited use of all facilities; adults $5, children $3.50 (high season).

Pampatar

Old houses with tall doors and window grilles, decorative friezes and wrought-iron locks line the entrance to Pampatar. One of the oldest towns on Margarita, indeed in the Americas, Pampatar displays its share of history. Founded in 1535 on the island's deepest harbour, the 'Royal Port of Mampatare' was often attacked by marauders. In the 16th century pirates destroyed **La Caranta fort** on the eastern bluff; its ruins have a magnificent view of Pampatar's well kept plazas, long palm shaded bay, colourful fishing boats and sailboats from around the world. You can hire jet skis or contract a fisherman to take you out in his *peñero* around the point, about $20 for half a day. Swimmers are recommended to use the clear, unpolluted waters east of Pampatar such as **Playa El Terminal** below La Caranta fort.

Pampatar is the port of call for the **Windward Islands** ship, overnighting here on alternate Tuesdays; for information ring the agent David Hart, tel: 623527. He has a couple of guest rooms with fan and shower he can rent in an old house.

Where to stay/eat
The area telephone code for Pampatar is (095)
The **Aparthotel Don Juan**, tel: 623609, on Av Almirante Brion parallel to the beach, has rooms for two and suites for four, with kitchen; $19, $25. The **Posada La Bufonera**, tel/fax: 669977, also on Brion, has 20 rooms with fridge and cooker; $40 for one to four people. A good choice among moderate hotels is **Los Chalets de La Caranta** with its excellent, reasonable seafood restaurant at the bay's east end, Calle El Cristo, tel: 621214, (02) 7817509; 12 bungalows each sleep six and have kitchen facilities. Budget lodgings include the **Casas Vacacionales Manolo** in La Caranta district, tel: 78471; and **Casitas Vacacionales Trimar**, Calle Almirante Brion, tel: 621657, which has a restaurant facing the sea; about $20 for five people. **Villas de Pampatar** on Calle Cateo, Urb El Paraíso, tel: 622922, offers comfortable villas at $45 a double, but is rather far from the beach. Two new resorts in La Caranta are the **Hippocampus Beach**, tel: 621510/3090 and **Flamingo Beach**, tel: 622350, both on Calle El Cristo. The Hippocampus takes full advantage of its hillside view over marvellous Pampatar Bay; double $45. The Flamingo Beach has a fine reputation for facilities with beach, pool, tennis courts, gym and sauna, boutiques, disco, seafood grill, and free transfers to Porlamar; 170 rooms, double $55.

Every morning on Pampatar beach lunch stands serve up the morning's catch, fresh *pargo* (red snapper) or *carite* (kingfish), with rice and *tajadas* (plantains) on the side, all for about $3. Get your order in before the crowd appears at noon. *Empanadas de cazón* (shark turnovers) are the speciality at stalls in front of Fondene. The Luna Marina Restaurant on Pampatar Bay makes traditional Margarita dishes.

What to see
The **Castillo de San Carlos Borromeo** is Pampatar's pride. Burned in a Dutch attack, the seaside fort was rebuilt in 1664–84 complete with moat, now dry. The fort's star shape, like the one in Cumaná, is a fine example of Spanish military architecture. Among historical events portrayed in paintings is the imprisonment of Margarita's heroine Luisa Cáceres in 1816. Open daily 08.00–17.00; entrance free.

The church across the plaza from the fort is the **Iglesia de Santísimo Cristo del Buen Viaje**. Margarita's fishermen attribute great powers to the imposing altar crucifix for which the church was built in the 18th century. They say that when the ship which was transporting the crucifix to Santo Domingo stopped at Pampatar, the vessel attempted to continue its voyage and failed repeatedly until the statue was left in Pampatar.

The **Casa de la Aduana** or Customs House is a handsome two-storey structure. It is famous because it was here in 1817 that Margarita received the name of Nueva Esparta citing the islanders' heroism in the struggle for independence. It is now an art museum; exhibitions are held in ground-floor rooms around a cool courtyard. Open weekdays 08.00–12.00, 13.00–16.30. Fondene, the Foundation for Development of Nueva Esparta, tel: (095) 622494, has its headquarters here, providing tourism information and maps of the island (at a cost).

EAST COAST: GUACUCO TO EL AGUA

From Pampatar a road swings to the east coast, bypassing Punta Ballena. The first fork, marked 'Apostadero-Lagunamar', leads to a landscaped complex called *Margarita Lagunamar*, often touted as the island's premier resort. Its 300 acres include a kilometre-long beach and saltwater Gasparico Lagoon, six restaurants, pools, water slides, bowling lanes, tennis courts, health spa, theatre and convention centre. A marina is nearing completion, also a Gary Player golf course. For information tel: (095) 620711, fax: 621445.

Playa Guacuco is at the end of the next turn-off. This fine 2,000m beach, close to Porlamar and La Asunción, is popular as one of the few with changing rooms and showers (by a poorly guarded parking lot). Guacuco has chairs and parasols for rent. Palm trees provide shade and the sea is fairly shallow, not too rough. At beachside restaurants the thing to eat is guacuco soup, made from the little clams (*chipi chipi*) that people dig up right on the beach.

In Playa Guacuco the **Tamarindo Guacuco**, tel: (095) 422727/3181, (014) 9950140, rates as a 4-star complex of 33 tile-roofed cottages by the sea, plus 25 doubles in a central building, with restaurant, disco, gym and two pools; double $146 with meals. In Caracas, (02) 2646466, fax: 2641176.

A narrow white strand stretches north for 5km forming what is eastern Margarita's longest beach. Here, the road runs between hills and the sea. At the bluffs of Arena Cernida or Ranchos de Chana, the coast road turns inland between **Cerro Matasiete** (680m) on the south and **Guayamurí** (480m) on the north, to join the main route at La Fuente. (Turn south at this crossroads for a *cocada*, icy coconut elixir, at El Caney de Mocho or a plate of grilled meat and chicken at the well-known Restaurant Aguamiel.) **La Fuente** has a good private crafts museum and shop, Arte Guayamurí, with lots of Venezuelan native arts. The same owner has another crafts shop by the church in Paraguachí.

Continue north on the old road for La Rinconada and its big new baseball stadium. At the Dome of La Asunción, Venezuelan professional basketball teams fight out the national championship (March–July). Margarita's team, the Guaiqueríes, has won several times.

Paraguachí (La Plaza) is an old settlement with magnificent trees. People come to see the restored 1599 remnants of **Iglesia de San José**, namely the sacristy and dome to which three naves were added in the 19th century. The French privateer Marquis de Maintenon, who encrusted in the church tower two faience plates (long gone), spared Paraguachí in 1677 when he burned and plundered many settlements.

For **Playa El Cardón**, a beach on a wide bay, take the old road out of Paraguachí northeast. The beach stretches north 1.5km from the rocky bluff of the **Karibik Playa Cardón Hotel**, and you can drive along it to Puerto Fermín. The hotel has a great view of El Tirano Bay from its terraces, and offers 3-star comfort in 50 rooms and suites, double $25; pleasant restaurant, two pools, steps down to a tiny beach; car rental agency; for information, tel: 48624/726; fax: 48242.

Follow the beach north for 2km to the rocky headland of **Puerto Fermín**. Here fishermen bring in the catch every morning and later take tourists out to see the birds on **Los Frailes Archipelago**, some 15km distant. The village has character, a shady plaza, and some typical restaurants, as well as two classier places: the

Marymonte on Calle Marina, and the seaside Trattoria al Porto serving excellent Peruvian and Italian dishes.

To this day, Fermín is known as 'El Tirano' after Lope de Aguirre, a widely feared tyrant who seized the island briefly in 1561. Descending the Amazon from Peru, the infamous Aguirre terrorised Margarita, murdered the governor and went on to more killings before he himself was beheaded and quartered in Barquisimeto.

Playa El Tirano, a crescent lying north of Puerto Fermín, has good rollers for bodysurfing. The road here turns into gravel but you can reach the headland, Cabo Blanco, and cross over to **Playa Parguito** (southern part only). A favourite eatery is low-cost **El Caballito del Mar**, or Sea Horse, run by Mamá María at the south end of Playa El Tirano by the bridge.

Parguito's high, rolling breakers are famous among surfers, and international competitions are held here. The serious surfers study Internet satellite images of ocean currents and the reports on Atlantic storms, so they can anticipate the big waves. Coconut palms and sea-grapes give spectators shade and you can rent chairs and umbrellas. Restaurants and food stands serve inexpensive seafood. A new resort, the Cimarrón Club Suites, now sprawls between the sea and hills.

For **Playa El Agua**'s lovely, 4km-long white beach continue on Route 4. Direct *por puestos* zoom in from Porlamar, 23km, as well as the No 3 bus from 4 de Mayo Avenue. At peak times, crowds have trouble getting through the cars. The most visited of Margarita's beaches, palm-shaded Playa El Agua brims with beauty and biceps, kids and matrons, Germans, Italians and locals. There are many restaurants and you can safely start with the chef's suggestion at the Varadero; there's live music at night. At weekends you can find an alternative by walking to the south end and down to quieter **Playa Parguito**.

Warning Playa El Agua's constant breeze raises breakers good for surfing, but rollers can be treacherous and bathers are safer staying within their depth.

A grass landing-strip for ultralight planes runs by the road at the north end of Playa El Agua. SAP offers 15-minute flights at weekends for $30; tel: 617632, or 623519. You are given film to shoot aerial photos of Cerro Guayamurí and five beaches. A ride to Porlamar takes 40 minutes.

Playa del Humo, the next beach being developed, lies just north of Playa El Agua. There are already large hotels such as the 300-room Portofino Mare on the way.

From Playa El Agua, the road to the pueblo of Manzanillo veers left and begins the western half of this circuit, where crescent beaches lie at the foot of hills (see *Northwest Coast* below).

Where to stay
Paraguachí
A short distance past the Paraguachí turn are the fenced **Residencias Paraguachí**, tel: 48452; four plain white cottages with two air-conditioned bedrooms for five, hot water, equipped kitchen; $26.

Puerto Fermín
Hostería Casa Maya, tel: 48187, (014) 9950079; two doubles with fan and shared bath, and two with air conditioning, hot showers, in a fine old house restored by Swiss chef Andreas; $25/$30 with breakfast. **Hostería Marymonte**, tel: 48066, fax: 48557, behind the restaurant on Calle Marina: small pool, nine comfortable

new bungalows for two with big bathrooms and hot showers, is run by the French couple who make dining a delight.

Out of town

North of the Puerto Fermín turn, the **Hotel Golf**, tel: 48120, is on Route 4; 36 rooms, lovely garden, pool and the excellent Beach Haus Restaurant. A young German couple, Andrea and Rudi, liked Margarita so much that they returned here to build. There are small, friendly inns on the **Aricagua** road above Playa El Tirano (this road runs west of the highway which it rejoins at El Agua). Bed and breakfast are offered by **Oasis** at the Aricagua junction, tel/fax: (095) 48194. A favourite among Germans, pricey and comfortable, Oasis has a small pool and bar. Owner Gaby Braun provides refrigerators and strongboxes in every room. **Los Tinajones** is far enough up the mountain to have a cool breeze and good view. Bar, small pool, mountain bikes for rent; 7-day package with breakfast, $195; other meals may be arranged. Contact is through Isla Azul, Porlamar, tel: 637747/6044, fax: 615521.

Playa Parguito

The French owners have spared no details on gardens, pool and the eight **Villas Cabo Blanco**, tel/fax: 48631, (014) 9950290, a block from the beach. Tiled floor, kitchen, air conditioning, ceiling fan, hot water in houses for four to eight people; $50 to $90 high season.

Playa El Agua

Here choices are varied, from 4-star to good small lodgings.

Canadian Dan O'Brien and his Dutch wife Trudy offer two attractive places, **Trudel's Garden Vacation Homes** for two to four adults (and two children), and a B&B, **Casa Trudel**, tel/fax: 48735, in La Mira above Playa El Agua; king-sized beds with breakfast for $45 double. Trudy serves light supper by request and is known as an excellent cook. The spacious vacation homes, on Calle Miragua 200m from the beach, have fully equipped kitchens; cost for one or two people $40; three or more, $50.

Hostería El Agua, tel: 48935, is a budget choice run by Sarah Studer, two blocks from the beach, 15 rooms with fan, fridge for one to three people, laundry. **Shangrila**, tel: (014) 9952388, is on the main road (vía Manzanillo), a 5-minute walk from the beach. A garden wall hides 11 rooms with air conditioning and hot water; double $35 with breakfast; restaurant open 16.00–23.00. **Residencia El Agua**, tel: 491975, on Calle Miragua, a block from the beach, has five plain cabins for six and two with doubles, $15 and $7.

The **Miragua Village**, tel: 491823, (016) 6285599, gives good value right on the beach; 50 rooms in cottages with air conditioning and hot water; restaurant, pool, gardens; $50 double with breakfast. Small and intimate, the **Eden Tropical Resort**, Calle La Miragua, tel: 48637, fax: 48750, has 24 apartments for four with kitchen, central air conditioning, pool and jacuzzi; double $50. The hillside **Casa Marina**, tel: 48839, on Calle La Miragua by Route 4, has 70 rooms on four floors, seaview terraces, open-air restaurant and pool.

Golden Paradise, tel: 491577, fax: 491177, Boulevard Playa El Agua, has 90 air-conditioned rooms with hot water, refrigerator and strongbox; double $55; pool and beach. **Las Palmeras**, tel: 491635, fax: 490377, set in gardens two blocks above the beach; 46 air-conditioned rooms, $60 double; money exchange, pool. **Playa El Agua Beach Hotel**, Av 31 de Julio, La Mira, tel: 616701/48601-10, is one of the top resorts here although 800m from the sea; double $125, all services, tennis and water sports included. In Caracas, (02) 5637715/85, fax: 5636645.

EL VALLE AND CERRO EL COPEY

Of three roads linking Porlamar and La Asunción, roughly 12km apart, the west one goes to El Valle, and from there to Parque Nacional Cerro El Copey. This road winds through the beautiful range of La Sierra to Santa Rosa Castle in La Asunción; great views of Porlamar and the east coast.

La Virgen del Valle

People come from all over Venezuela to see La Virgen del Valle and her neo-Gothic shrine, 2.5km from Porlamar's Circunvalación road. She is the *patrona* of Margarita and of all fishermen and sailors who commend themselves to her before going to sea. She has the allegiance of the navy and is present on all its vessels. The twin-spired **Santuario de la Virgen**, pale pink and white, was built in 1909 on the site of earlier churches. Visitors must wear below-knee-length skirts or trousers; shorts are banned.

El Valle del Espíritu Santo got its lofty name in 1529 from settlers inspired by the heavenly valley. It was Margarita's first capital until 1594 when Asunción took over. According to local lore, in the 16th century the Virgin's image was found by a Guaiquerí Indian in a mountain cave. However, Father Nectario María writes in his history that the people of Cubagua ordered the image of Mary from Spain. They received it in 1530 but, after a tidal wave destroyed Cubagua in 1541, the image was taken to El Valle where many Spaniards relocated.

The obvious devotion paid to the Virgin is amazing to see on September 8, her fiesta and a statewide holiday. To Margariteños, weeklong celebrations are the year's most important event. Do not even think of taking a car beyond the village entrance; go in on foot. Under the shade of Plaza Mariño's big *samán* trees, hawkers of religious artefacts form a kind of flea market. Busy shops lining Plaza Mariño sell souvenirs, food, hammocks, crafts and clothes.

You may visit the **Museo Diocesano** beside the church for a small fee. Heaps of coins, rings and jewellery given by grateful pilgrims show why the sanctuary is so rich. Gold miniatures represent favours granted: a leg, hand, breast or eye healed; a car, house, boat or pig saved or won.

Cerro El Copey National Park

Park signs on the high point of La Sierra road direct you to this cool and moist retreat. *Por puestos* will let you off in front of the Guardia Nacional post; it is a short walk to the *mirador* or lookout, complete with picnic shelters and grills. There are some attractive trails and the park warden, Isidro Salazar, is happy to talk (in Spanish) about his domain. Named for the waxy-leafed copey tree (*Clusia* family), the 7,000 hectare park is home to the *mono mandarín*, capuchin monkeys whose mysterious presence on the island has never been accounted for. This is a good place to see cloudforest with its tree ferns, bromeliads (air plants), orchids, mosses, vines and elegant mountain palms. Closed to traffic, the park road is a walk of about one and a half hours from the lookout up to the peak known as **Las Antenas** for its communications repeater towers. At 920m elevation, you are on the highest spot in Margarita and the view to Juangriego is tremendous.

Castillo de Santa Rosa

The restored fortress stands between the park and La Asunción, 0.9km. Open daily 08.00–18.00, except Monday 08.00–15.00. The fort's beautiful view overlooks La Asunción, Cerro Matasiete and the distant sea. When it was built in 1682 Santa Rosa was linked to Asunción's church, monastery, and Governor's house by a kilometre-long tunnel (closed). The moat and drawbridge have also disappeared.

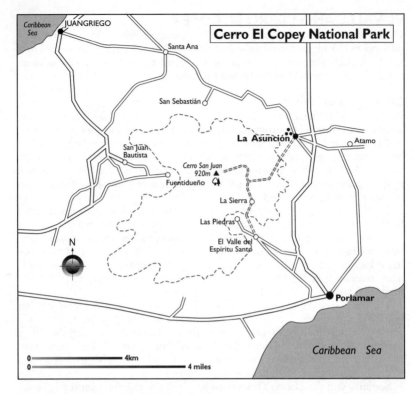

Period weapons are on display, as well as heavy iron balls once attached to leg irons. Behind the kitchen is a 'bottle' dungeon whose only entrance is a hole in the ceiling.

As a teenage bride in 1815, patriot Luisa Cáceres de Arismendi was imprisoned in Santa Rosa. Captured by royalists on September 24, the day before her 17th birthday, she was held hostage for her husband, Juan Bautista Arismendi, commander of Margarita's defence forces. Four months later she gave birth to a daughter in her cell; the baby died. The cell is seen today with its original wooden rafters, tiled floor and lamp. Luisa was transferred to prisons in Pampatar, on the mainland, and then in Spain where she got help in escaping. Both she and her husband are buried in the Panteón Nacional in Caracas. Her statue, along with that of Simón Bolívar, graces Asunción's large shady plaza, variously called Plaza Cáceres or Plaza Bolívar.

LA ASUNCION

Founded in 1565 in a fertile valley, the capital of Nueva Esparta State is a peaceful little town full of great trees and charming houses.

In Asunción there is a modern private hospital, the Centro Médico Nueva Esparta, tel: (095) 421711/420011, fax: 420833; Sector El Dique. The clinic has a good reputation for facilities and emergency attention as well as several medical specialities.

Where to stay

Hotel Ciudad Colonial, set in walled gardens on Calle Margarita at Noria, tel: (095) 41311; pool, buffet, snack bar, suites for four with air conditioning, kitchenette; about $10 a person. It opened in 1995 and so far has no competition.

What to see

The **Cathedral** of Nuestra Señora de La Asunción, begun in 1570, is Venezuela's oldest and among the first in the Americas. Its classic rectangular design and strong, stark lines set Venezuela's colonial style along with the Cathedral of Coro (1583). Inside, two rows of massive columns rise solemnly. Outside, the bell tower is unique, the last example surviving from the 16th century; the bells themselves are now in the plaza. In mid-August the feast day of Our Lady of the Assumption is celebrated with a procession and special mass.

Dating from the late 1700s, the building at the corner of Calles Independencia and Fermín once housed the Casa Capitular or government seat. Today it is the **Museo Nueva Cádiz** with a library and varied historical collection including archaeological finds from Cubagua, site of Spain's first town in South America, Nueva Cádiz. There is a statue of the tyrant Lope de Aguirre (remember the film *Aguirre, Wrath of God* by Werner Herzog starring Klaus Kinski?) who terrorised the island in 1561. An excellent relief map of Margarita occupies the patio. Open 09.00–18.00 except Monday; entrance free.

Casa de La Cultura A modern, colonial-style building facing the cathedral on Calle Fermín displays replicas of pre-Columbian pottery made by local artisans. Open weekdays 08.00–20.00, Sat 08.00–15.00, Sun 08.00–12.00. Such replicas can be bought at Cerámica El Cercado near Santa Ana.

Casa Juan Bautista Arismendi A block west of the museum on Calle de Independencia is the colonial house where patriot Arismendi was born in 1775. A collection of family portraits and belongings is on view. The Centro Bolivariano and its library function here. Open 09.00–17.00.

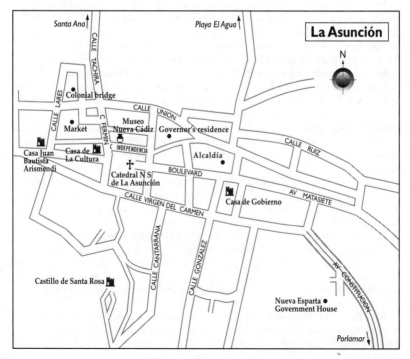

Casa de Gobierno Before housing the State Legislature, this 16th-century building was variously a Franciscan monastery, a prison and later a hospital. It faces the **Palacio Municipal** (Alcaldía), or town hall. At the corner of the Casa de Gobierno is a sundial, 'Relox Equinoca Inferior', in use ever since it was placed there in 1612 by a far-sighted governor who also built the bridge.

Puente colonial Built in 1608 and in use until the 1970s, the stone bridge north of Calle Unión is now part of a children's park; walk one block west of Calle Fermín. The bridge's name '4 de Mayo de 1810' recalls Margarita's declaration of Independence. For more than 350 years it formed the north entrance to La Asunción. The old market, complete with gargoyles, faces the bridge.

SANTA ANA AND CRAFT VILLAGES

From Asunción, the road to Santa Ana rises first to El Mirador de Portachuelo, a lookout with splendid sunset views of Juangriego. But, if you have a car, it is worth starting out early as nearly every village from Santa Ana to Fuentidueño appears to be the centre of a different craft. The first, **Tacarigua**, is a popular stop for *chinchorros*, open-weave hammocks deriving from fish-net techniques (see box below).

Santa Ana, founded in 1530 as La Villa del Norte, has beautiful trees, plazas and colonial houses. Its handsome church, built between 1748 and 1769, has a magnificent bell tower with outside stairs. Now declared a national monument, the church secured its place in history on May 7 1816, when Simón Bolívar proclaimed the Third Republic here. The chair Bolívar used is by the baptistry. Parish records list the marriage of Luisa Cáceres to Juan Bautista Arismendi on December 4 1814.

Many old houses remain around the church. The former Arismendi residence stands at No 3 on the south side; Bolívar and Mariño also stayed there. The Casa de Cultura and a restaurant, Casa Antañona, occupy other colonial homes. In front of the church, Plaza Francisco Esteban Gómez honours Santa Ana's hero of the battle of Matasiete in 1817. His home, a few steps west, is conserved as a museum.

Miniature tables and chairs are made in Santa Ana, also hammocks.

Four roads fan out from Santa Ana. To the north (via Pedrogonzález) are the remains of Fortín España. Look for its obelisk; from here you can see as far as Macanao Peninsula. In **Pedrogonzález** people make and sell fibre bags called *mapires*. **Altagracia**, on the northwest road, is known for leather-soled sandals, or *alpargatas*. The road west to Juangriego goes through the village of La Vecindad, another hammock centre. Cotton hammocks made here are sold all along the road to Juangriego.

Head south to **El Cercado**, 1.5km, where the craftswomen are among Margarita's best potters – and have been for generations. You can see many primitive kilns and chose a water jar, jug, flower pot, griddle (*anafre*) or portable furnace. Ask for the house of Vicenta, a local *ceramista* who made the Virgen del Valle figure in the Margarita Hilton; she fires a variety of pots at home.

El Maco is on this road; signs for *calzados* announce home-made shoes. Then comes **Los Millanes** where practised hands roll cigars for Margarita's smokers, including many women of the older generation; ask for Señora Leonidas or Ismelda. The tobacco comes from Sucre State and the cigars are said to compare well with Havanas, at a much lower cost.

San Juan Bautista lies another 8km and many curves down the road. The 16th-century town has a colonial church and two plazas honouring native sons Antonio Díaz and Vicente Marcano. Some villagers weave palm hats from date and

HAMMOCKS: BOON TO TRAVELLERS AND SAILORS

The first navigators to the New World brought back a great native invention used all over the tropics: the hammock. English ships soon saw the advantages of hammocks below decks and sailors have been swinging ever since. Hammocks are the only traditional furnishings of Warao houses (see *Chapter 10*). In their language *hanoko* means 'the hammock's place' or house and in all probability it is the origin of our word. In Venezuela two basic kinds are distinguished: the *hamaca* made of woven cloth and the *chinchorro* which, like the fishnet it is named after, is usually knotted. Most hardware stores sell pre-cut lengths of *mecate* or rope for slinging hammocks.

The open weave of the *chinchorro* makes a very cool, comfortable bed, but if you are looking for a hammock to take travelling, remember that bugs and cold air pass easily through the holes. What is a delight in the daytime on the beach may be a misery at night. Less elegant, but more rough and ready and less costly (most *chinchorros* are handmade), is the normal hammock of solid cloth. These too are very comfortable if you remember to get one wide enough to allow you to sleep on the diagonal with a relatively straight back. A warmer hammock that you can partially wrap around you will allow you to carry a lighter bedroll.

A hammock is almost a must for the overland traveller in tropical Latin America. They are used in all the warm areas and allow you to sling your bed up off the (wet, buggy, crawly) ground, and sleep anywhere there are two points to hang it from. You will see them everywhere. Every trucker carries his sling under the chassis to wait out the inevitable delays of Latin American travel.

coconut leaves; others now make wooden furniture, and gold, silver and pearl jewellery. When it comes to religious days, especially the **Feast of St John** on June 24, the town turns out in force to celebrate.

Fuentidueño is an old community by a spring above San Juan. Walk up Calle Bolívar from San Juan's Plaza Marcano; cross a small, clear stream and follow it uphill to a tiny village of steep streets. Generations of Fuentidueño's women have made a sweet from papaya (*lechosa*) called *piñonate*, as well as hats of braided date leaf that are sold as far away as Maracaibo.

There is a special place, built to honour crafts as the language of legends, dignity and history, called **Tacuantar**, south of Juangriego on the coast road. This minivillage took Pepe (José) García seven years to build. He made half a dozen red-roofed houses and piled into them his lifetime collection of baskets, weaving, pots, woodwork, sculptures and paintings from around Venezuela, calling the whole a workshop, '*Así con las Manos, Tierra, Agua y Fuego*'. Then he put in a restaurant for visitors. Many pieces are not for sale, such as the Simón Bolívar collection. Pepe, who is a self-taught potter from the Canary Islands, fires his pieces in an open blaze; the religious images sell well. His shop in Porlamar, Los Makiritares, is on Calle Igualdad near the Bella Vista Hotel.

JUANGRIEGO

Legend says that this charming town takes its name from a Greek called Juan who, wounded and left here by fellow pirates, was taken in and cured by fisherfolk. He took to the sea again but always returned to see his friends.

Juangriego may become Margarita's second most important town with a population of 15,000, if it keeps growing faster than Asunción. Juangriego fringes a magnificent broad bay whose sunsets and fishing craft attract ever more visitors. Boats with eyes painted on the prow (to help fishermen return home) throng the bay at sunrise. The day's catch is sorted on shore; some fish go to distant markets, some are set to dry on poles in the sun, others are sold on the spot. More picturesque than Porlamar and Pampatar with their huge posh resorts, Juangriego is a growing tourism centre with free-port shops.

Fortín La Galera commands a splendid hilltop view of neighbouring bays. Little is left of the fort which was taken by royalists and burned in 1817. Blood made the water red in the lagoon behind the fort, earning its name Laguna de los Mártires.

The best beaches are north of Juangriego, by way of Calle Los Mártires: **La Galera**, lying between the Fortín and the Gasparosa cliffs; and the clean, beautiful sands of **Playa Caribe**. You can rent parasols and chairs.

Where to stay/eat
The area telephone code for Juangriego is (095)
Lodgings are divided between large apart-hotels on the outskirts with swimming pools, and plain hotels downtown. While a group may afford a 'villa', single travellers can find inexpensive options in waterfront hotels (mostly with fan and private bath; no credit cards). Some are: the **Gran Sol**, Calle La Marina, tel: 530736; **Hotel El Fortín** and restaurant, tel: 530879; and the **Nuevo Juan Griego**, tel: 532409, also with restaurant, done up by a Dutch couple. A block from the beach is the inexpensive **Hotel El Yare**, tel: 530835, where they speak English; doubles and a few suites with kitchen.

Laguna Honda Inn, tel: 531150, is a guesthouse at the east entrance to Juangriego. Run by Englishman David Lamble and his wife Esther are seven air-conditioned rooms around a patio; single or double with breakfast, $30; restaurant with good food and wine. Under French management is **Hotel Patrick's**, Calle el Fuerte, tel/fax: 534089, with bar-restaurant; 14 rooms; view of bay from top floor; double with shower, hot water, $20. **Posada de Clary**, Calle Mártires, tel: 530037, 530297, is a modest family-run inn; 15 rooms and seven *cabañas* at about $10 for one ot three people; busy restaurant.

In the same direction (via Altagracia) are the two four-storey buildings of **Catame Suites**, Ampliación Juangriego, tel: 531016, tel/fax: 530516; 90 apartments, double $30; small pool, bicycle rental. A new hotel nearby is the comfortable **Villas Castilla Mar**, tel: 532503, fax: 532232; Caracas reservations, tel: (02) 9591802, fax: 9594736; 50 apartments in two-storey houses, pool, snack bar. There are other, bigger apart-hotels such as **Villa El Griego** on Calle Pica Quinta, tel: 531507, fax: 530258; 50 houses and 168 nice studios with balcony, eight pools for adults and kids, disco for dancing; double $45.

There are cottages for rent in **La Galera**, which also has pleasant beachside restaurants, each with outside and inside tables, and two watersports agencies renting Sunfish, waterskis, kayaks and sailboards. On the way you will find three sets of economical bungalows. The **Posada del Sol**, tel: 530354, has 20 clean, basic cabins sleeping five; all have kitchen, air conditioning and cold water. The **Cabañas La Galera**, tel: 530151, comprise ten cottages with kitchen, and two bedrooms with double bed plus three singles. **Chalets Flamingo**, tel: 530341, is a motel-like row of old two-bedroom units, with stove and fridge.

Juangriego's restaurants are mainly uncrowded and reasonable. There are breezy seafood places on La Galera Bay, and air-conditioned ones on Calle Los Mártires such as **Da Aldo's** Italian house, **El Carpacho**, and **Shien Ling** whose cook escaped from Caracas to open the first Chinese restaurant here. **Patrick's Bar-Restaurant**, Calle El Fuerte, has meat and fish, grills, pizza; French run; tel: 534089. Other moderate to cheap choices on the beach are the **Viña del Mar** with traditional Arab fare, near the outdoor tables of the Fortín's good restaurant. This is the place to be. Also try the **Viejo Muelle**'s beach bar, if only to listen to the musicians; good food too.

NORTHWEST COAST

The west road goes to beaches as good as Playa El Agua, without its crowds. The smaller bays by a wonderful clear sea are indeed more beautiful and have few bathers during the week. The first one north of Juangriego, **Playa Caribe**, is formed by a kilometre-long pair of U-shaped beaches without trees but with dunes (**Playa Arenas**), shells and an emerald sea. Among many open-air restaurants the best is Mosquito Beach, or Churuata de Bernardo, offering chairs, sunshades, showers and bathrooms.

Playa Boquita's idyllic, deserted sands lie southeast of Playa Caribe's rocky headland. Look for a dirt track which leaves the main road and runs down to a long treeless shore. Bring a parasol and water; sometimes there is a refreshment stand. At low tide you can walk over rocks to a tiny island; at high tide swimmers should be on guard against treacherous surf.

The next bay north, **Bahía de Plata**, has been taken over by a 'tourist city' of holiday homes with beach club and restaurants. **Hotel La Ceiba** has 28 fully equipped bungalows, and its neighbour **Las Dueñas Beach Resort** has 109 suites with kitchen in three-storey units around a large pool where a novel parasol cools off swimmers. Transportation is provided to lovely **Playa Las Arenas**. Reservations for La Ceiba and Las Dueñas, tel: 56122/312, fax: 56114.

Playa Zaragoza curves around a splendid bay in the lee of Zaragoza Point; the sea is transparent, cool and calm. There are no palms but beach chairs and sun roofs are available; water skiing and jet skiing, too. **Pedrogonzález** is the fishing hamlet on this beach (1.5km from the main road). Lots of bright paint and a new seaside boulevard have made the village quite picturesque. One of the two boulevard restaurants, the **Tic Toc**, enjoys some fame for Venezuelan dishes, many created by Beatriz, the chef in this old house. Beside Don Pedro's restaurant at the roundabout, be sure to ask for Horange, who makes colourful scale model boats. At No 11 Calle Marina, tel: 818119, Mme Bourdais rents two seafront apartments, each $30.

Just north, **Playa Puerto Cruz** is a spectacular crescent of white sand and blue-green water. Many rate it as the island's finest, fanned by breeze and shaded by palms. However, the surf can be very rough and swimmers are warned of a dangerous undertow. A 5-star 'club style' resort, the 240-room **Dunes Hotel**, tel: 621461, 632910, lies behind the beach. Its apartments in colonial-style cottages are modern and very comfortable; good restaurants, night-lighted tennis courts, gym, massage, infirmary; double $110 all inclusive.

Playa Puerto Viejo is within walking distance of Playa Cruz, less than 2km if you like scrambling over a rocky promontory. This cove, one of Margarita's loveliest, has fine white sand, shallower and calmer water than Playa Cruz, rocks to fish from, trees and a good breeze. The small beach is overpowered by the 312-room **Isla Bonita Beach and Golf Hotel**, tel: 657111, fax: 639068. The resort has five desalination plants to water an 18-hole golf course, and pools. It is operated by Occidental Hotels.

Guayacán and **Playa Manzanillo** are the last northern bays on the ring road before it turns east to Playa El Agua. Hidden by hills, Guayacán is a lively fishing village where almost all the inhabitants are related. It is at the bottom of a steep road; the sea is usually calm and there are trees, and kiosks selling beer and soft drinks. In the same area is **Playa Escondida**, a hidden beach. Bring food and drink and, of course, a hammock as there are trees. The way to Escondida goes down from **Punta Ausente** where you leave the main road at the same place as for Guayacán; you turn to the right into a tiny path. Park your car if it's not a jeep (but do not leave it overnight) and walk down for 10 to 15 minutes. You come out to a dry river bed; follow this for ten minutes to the playa.

On **Playa Manzanillo** there is a fishing village where fishermen mend nets, and can sell you fresh fish, also served in the informal restaurants. The white beach is on a generous bay with good swimming, parasols and chairs, getting more popular as Playa El Agua fills up. From here you can explore beaches around Cabo Negro (Black Cape) by hiring a *peñero* after the morning's catch has been unloaded. Speak to one of the captains, Omar, Octavio and Raúl. They will quote you a price for taking up to 20 persons to Los Frailes, or to closer beaches such as Caricare or Puerto Príncipe in **Bahía Constanza** which is recommended for its clear, tranquil waters. The price will depend on how long you want to spend there.

WEST TO LA RESTINGA

Twin conical hills called **Las Tetas de María Guevara**, 130m, rise near the coast. How they got named after a woman's breasts is part of Punta de Piedras' history. María Guevara did exist. She was born in Cumaná in 1801 and in her twenties married a Margariteño. Having some property, she invested in his fishing fleet in Punta de Piedras. Under her management a well was dug, houses were built for fishermen from Juangriego and the little port grew to be the most important on the island. The enterprising lady, who died there at age 85, unwittingly left her name as homecoming sailors use the hills as a landmark. Ironically, María Guevara's breasts were said to be small. In 1974 the hills were declared a natural monument, along with Laguna Las Marites and Cerros Matasiete and Guayamurí.

La Restinga National Park

Bridging east and west, La Restinga National Park occupies a narrow isthmus (a *restinga* is a sandbar) between what once were islands. Its attractions are broad: 10,700 hectares of sea, shore, lagoons, channels and tangled mangroves. A boat trip through the channels to the beach is well worthwhile. The park entrance is 36.5km from downtown Porlamar where a *por puesto* line runs until 20.00. Línea La Restinga starts near the waterfront, Calle Mariño between La Marina and Maneiro. Avoid going on Sunday if possible as return transportation is scarce in the afternoon.

The embarkation pier, **Embarcadero El Indio**, is 350m from the road. At the pier's entrance you pay a park fee of $1. Scores of *lanchas* wait their turn here; note the name and number of yours. Each boat takes 5–6 passengers to the beach, via a longer or shorter tour through fascinating mangrove channels, some so narrow you can touch the trees on either side and see oysters clinging to tangled roots; the price per boat, ½ to 1 hour, is $14–20, paid on return. At the far dock by the *balneario* you set a time for the same boat to pick you up, or have the boatman wait an hour. There are clean restrooms; ask a waiter for the key. Souvenir stands sell crafts and open-sided restaurants offer food and shade, so that's where most people go. Check prices as the closest restaurants are reported to charge more.

Sweeping in a long crescent to either side of La Guardia Bay, the bar enclosing the lagoon forms an oceanic beach 10km long; the swimming is good. A layer of shells covers the beach and in clam season people scoop up bucketfuls of guacucos at the water's edge: good for seafood broth, as well as eating fresh like oysters.

As the return trip goes straight to the Embarcadero, you might negotiate a price with your boat captain to see more mangrove channels or go out to sea via Boca de Río (where most of the *lancheros* live).

MACANAO PENINSULA

Across the bridge from La Restinga Lagoon is the 'other side' of Margarita, a rugged semidesert land. Surprisingly, what looks like wasteland supports varied wildlife: snakes, lizards, foxes, rabbits, the occasional deer and feral goats. Look carefully at the tops of cacti and you will spot songbirds and finches. You may even see flocks of rare Margarita parrots, a species that mates for life and nests in the same hollow tree year after year (see below, *Margarita Parrot Festival*).

A good road of 68km circles the peninsula. Macanao is served by the Línea La Restinga which goes to scattered fishing villages as far as Robledal and San Francisco (see above, *La Restinga National Park*). There are plans (fortunately unrealised) to 'transform' Macanao into a sort of Las Vegas-style resort. At present accommodation is as scarce as water. But people are friendly and an adventurous traveller with good Spanish (the local dialect is strong) could sling a hammock in one of the boat shelters found in every coastal community. If you are not in a hurry you can find someone to prepare you fried fish or *sopa de pescado*. Remember to carry a water container, good shoes, a hat and sun block (the important thing here is protection). Macanao is surrounded by beaches, largely shadeless.

Boca de Río

Macanao's only town, Boca de Río is the home port of a large deep-sea fishing fleet. Its name really should be Boca de La Restinga as it is at the lagoon's mouth. The fleet, which also anchors in Chacachacare, is known throughout the Caribbean and northern Atlantic, pursuing grouper and red snapper as far as Suriname and even Brazil. Margarita is an important centre of wooden boat building and Boca de Río is a good place to see ship carpenters at work. The trawler-sized boats called *tres puños* are handmade to a design which has varied little in centuries.

Steps lead from the port's boulevard down to the water. Smaller wooden boats, *peñeros*, dock here.

Models made by local carpenters of Margarita's fishing vessels are on view at the fine new **Museo Marino**, plus displays of marine species, corals, fishing gear, nets, traps and knots. A salt water aquarium and a pool of sharks get lots of attention. Entrance fee is $1.50. The two-floor museum, its stark white walls and red-tiled roof conspicuous on the waterfront, is the pride of Boca de Río, Fondene and the Universidad de Oriente. Students rescued and cleaned the skeleton of a 14-metre whale which died on Cubagua. The university's research institute and School of Applied Marine Science are based in Boca de Río.

As you might expect in a town which lives from fish, this is what the few restaurants serve. Everyone knows the **Restaurante Fríomar** and its owner Cucho who proudly makes (and invents) island specialities: omelettes of *erizo* (sea urchin), fish sun dried and then grilled, and *arepas* and turnovers filled with *chucho* (ray). As you go through Boca de Río after crossing the bridge, the traffic route leads you west to the Fríomar.

Between Boca de Río and the far end of the peninsula, the coast road passes by sun-bleached villages such as **El Horcón** and **Manglillo**. Fishermen haul their boats under makeshift shelters to do repairs in the boat's shade. They mend nets and rest during the day, and go out to sea at night. One sign of impending tourism is a resort named **Laguna de Macando** going up near Punta Arenas named Laguna de Macando. At present, however, the traveller is delightfully on his, or her, own.

Boca de Pozo and Robledal

Of the two villages on broad Macanao Bay, Boca de Pozo is the larger. Houses, school, clean streets, a big shady plaza and a new church all show the success of its fishermen. A new pier and refrigerated warehouse stand between the villages, 2km apart. You can see the big boats at anchor when fishermen come home from high seas tours lasting as long as a month. They make sure to return for the festival of **San Rafael**, October 24–30. To drums, *cuatros* (four-string guitars) and fireworks, the image of San Rafael heads a procession from Boca de Pozo to Robledal, and back again after five days. Celebrations include dancing, bicycle and sack racing and greased-pole-climbing.

There is a gasoline station in Boca de Pozo, and a recommended B&B with restaurant in Robledal. **L'Auberge L'Oasis** on Calle El Tanque by Robledal beach is truly an oasis. Macanao's first inn is the enterprise of French Canadians Patricia and Santiago Lucque who built their home with six guest rooms and balcony overlooking tranquil Macanao Bay. They also run a French-Venezuelan restaurant, relying on fishermen to bring the day's special. The price of bed and breakfast for two people is about $30. For information, tel/fax: (095) 915339; in Montreal ring Yvon, tel: (514) 6466293.

Beaches

Punta Arenas is Margarita's westernmost point, 27km from Boca de Río and 6km south of Boca de Pozo. Bordered by dunes, with a blazing white beach of 1.5km and seashells brought by ocean currents, Punta Arenas is attracting windsurfers and watersports. It is hot. There are three trees, a few houses, and some tables on the sand where **Arminda's restaurant** does more than fill a need: the grilled fish is succulent and Arminda may have lobster in season, November to April.

The wild coast north of Robledal has isolated beaches used by campers with cars who bring their own food, water and shade. You see jeep tracks cutting off the road through scrub to **Playa Carmela** or La Mula. **La Pared** (The Wall) beach is conveniently close to the road, at the foot of a bluff 8km from Robledal. No services, but there is a **Parador Turístico** on top of the bluff where the owners prepare fried fish, squid, maybe a lobster, with rice and fried plantain. And you can watch a fantastic sunset over the sea.

There is a fishing community at the next northern beach. You follow a track of about 1km to the small point of **El Tunal**. The beach stretches for over 2km. Again there is no shade or facilities; the breakers are rough on this bit of unprotected coast. On the east side of Punta El Tunal is another, longer beach, **La Auyama** (the pumpkin), also close to the road.

About 1km east of the crossroad for San Francisco de Macanao, you may see a sign and a jeep track on the left for **Arenas** (at this point the main road veers SE to Boca de Río). The jeep track follows the coast around the large headland of **Punta El Tigre**, rejoining the paved road 10km before Boca de Río. Punta El Tigre encloses La Guardia Bay and is part of La Restinga National Park. On this side is the beach called **El Saco**. During the week you'll have the beaches of Macanao to yourself.

Hato San Francisco The people you may have seen riding horses along a beach come from this ranch in a valley between the hills of Macanao and Guaranao. José Enrique Salazar has opened his fine stables to visitors. You can not only hire horses but swim in a thermal pool and enjoy lunch with a view. For a day tour, ring Ana Cecilia, tel: (016) 6950408.

Margarita Parrot Festival

On the first Saturday in June, the people of Macanao make merry. This is the day honouring the yellow-shouldered Margarita Parrot with music and dance in Boca de Río. Schools, theatre groups and tour operators join in. The little parrots are not there, however; they live on the mountainsides. A few years ago their fate was in doubt as numbers of the *Amazona barbadensis* dwindled to 700. Worried conservation groups began a study and found that the birds' isolated habitat was raided by locals in search of chicks for the pet trade. To reverse this, Provita biologists devised a double plan, first raising fledglings for return to the wild and secondly raising the parrot's public image. Their plight became a public cause and, as Magariteños love parrots, they made it offically Nueva Esparta's state bird. The Parrot Festival celebrates the increase of *cotorras margariteñas*, which now number over 2,000.

Provita's work on Margarita continues, with the support of conservation groups and the Salazar family who own much of Macanao including the nesting grounds in San Francisco. A second endangered parrot, known locally as the *ñángaro* (*Aratinga acuticaudata*), is down to fewer than 200 birds. It lives *only* in La Restinga National Park. If you have enjoyed these wilderness areas and wish to lend a hand, you may contact Provita in Boca de Río: Adriana Rodríguez or Daniel Carrillo, tel: (095) 93707; email: provita2@telcel.net.ve.

THE SOUTH: EL YAQUE

El Yaque is 5km directly south of the airport by way of a fork as you approach the terminal. It is the only village before the road ends at Laguna de Las Marites. Hotel operators and guests cross from El Yaque to Coche Island in half an hour by launch. Another way to cross is by fishing boat from La Isleta, a village on the east side of Las Marites.

The international reputation of El Yaque comes not from beach lovers but from **windsurfers**. There seem to be a lot of them as El Yaque's growth rate is phenomenal. Where there were three hotels four years ago, there are now 12, plus eight windsurf clubs. The bay is calm and wide, the sea less than waist deep for 300m out, and the trade winds blow steadily at 25–35kph (slacking a little in Sept–Nov), qualities made to order for windsurfing. **Margarita Wild Winds Foundation** promotes the wonders of El Yaque, which is today firmly on the world circuit of windsurfing regattas. The major event in El Yaque is a regatta in late May; windsurfers from 15 countries take part. El Yaque's Colette Guadagnimo took the South American championship in Peru, 1998, and Carlos García was placed fourth in the tough Open class; Rufino Lucero of Sucre won the junior championship.

Where to stay

Lodgings seem to be run exclusively for windsurfers by windsurfers, including some Venezuelan champions. Prices given are for the high season, generally November to March, with low-season rates from 25% to 40% cheaper. All accommodation below has air conditioning and private bath, unless noted. Boards and sails can be rented at surf hotels and schools. El Yaque is great for learning how to waterstart and jibe because of its shallow water and sandy bottom.

The first, and best, hotel is the four-floor **California**, tel: (014) 9951907, fax: (014) 9950908; email: calfort@enlared.net; net: www.elyaque.com. Run by owner Michel Emery who speaks English, French and Spanish, the hotel, restaurant and pool with jacuzzi are above the beach, set among gardens and palm trees; 46 large rooms and a panoramic suite have telephone, room safe and balcony over the sea;

$40–60 per person with full breakfast; discounts on windsurf classes and equipment rental. Free daily transport to Porlamar. The hotel also operates 10 split-level 'villas' with kitchen, hot water, balcony and parking in **Las Brisas del Yaque**, tel: (014) 9956504, at the end of the main street; $120 for four to six people. Courses and rental of French and German equipment at the California Beach Club.

The **Windsurf Oasis**, tel: (016) 6818641, pension style, has eight good double rooms with hot shower, $45; on the beach near the California. A surf shop on the street parallel to the beach, **No Work Team**, tel: (014) 9952698, rents five simple rooms with shared baths for two to three in a rear house; good value at $15 single, $20 double. The place is popular with Germans, French and Italians.

The beachfront **Hotel Restaurant El Vigía**, (014) 9372148, offers a busy restaurant doubling as a night spot with music, dancing, and the Margarita Windsurf Club: eight plain triples at $25; more being built. **Los Surf Pirata**, tel/fax: (016) 6950190/91, has 11 budget-class rooms with shared bath, $15, in a walled beachfront complex including restaurant.

El Yaque Paradise Hotel and **Windsurf Paradise** are managed by windsurf champion Carlos García, tel/fax: (014) 9952183, 9952182. On the beach, Windsurf Paradise has 53 rooms with hot water, gym, solarium, jacuzzi, pool table, tennis court, restaurant and car rental. El Yaque Paradise, 300m from the beach, has 26 rooms with balcony, mini bar, restaurant and beach service. Rates, $38–55 per person, double occupancy, include breakfast. The two hotels run a windsurf school and duty-free surf shop. As good wind and water conditions extend to Coche, Paradise guests are taken by hotel launch to the island, with the possibility of alternating their stay at the **Coche Speed Paradise** at no extra cost. The crossing takes half an hour. Surfers do the 13km run downwind.

Laguna de Las Marites

The road stops just beyond El Yaque at the lagoon's mouth. You can arrange for a fishing boat to explore the lagoon, or use El Yaque windsurf clubs which offer tours and water skiing. Las Marites Lagoon and mangroves, 9km^2, were declared a Natural Monument in 1974 to protect fauna including the coastal crocodile. Briny channels and dense mangroves like those of La Restinga are the habitat of many birds such as herons, pelicans, frigate birds, ibis and migratory flamingoes. From Porlamar another access road turns south to **Playa El Silguero** (don't trust the quality of seawater). There is a modest hotel here, the **Oasis Silguero**. The road ends at La Isleta, a drab village where fishing boats can be hired. Fishermen cross regularly to San Pedro on Coche Island.

COCHE

On Coche, an island that appears to be like Margarita 30 years ago, time is no longer standing still. Its hot sun, dazzling beaches, and turquoise water at 27°C are too much for developers to resist. So plan a trip there soon, while sands are untracked. Coche is about 11km long by 6km wide, and its highest point rises 60m.

Coche's 9,200 people live from the sea and process enough salt to cure fish. Shrimp and crayfish farms produce enough for export. The island has water piped from the mainland, telephones, an asthma clinic, good roads, almost no traffic, and an airfield of 1,200m. **San Pedro** is the chief town and district seat. Roads link San Pedro to the fishing communities of El Bichar and Güinima which have deepwater harbours on the west coast, El Amparo and Guamache in the south, and Zulica, Piedra Negra and La Uva and Playa El Coco on the east coast. To get to El Coco, you follow a canyon road through cliffs.

Although arid, Coche must have once had trees as its name means 'deer' in Indian tongue. That changed with the Spanish conquest; now you will see goats if anything, and the only trees are those planted and nurtured by hand. Important pearl beds were exploited in the 1500s and today there is still a small production from eastern banks.

Getting there

From Margarita's airport, it is a hop by airtaxi to Coche. There has been no regular service since Aereotuy stopped its flights. Ferries run daily from Punta de Piedras (see *Ferries*, page 163) to San Pedro on Punta El Botón. Alternatively, from Porlamar you can catch a *por puesto* on Calle La Marina for La Isleta where fishing boats leave for Coche every evening as late as 23.00, taking locals and all their purchases, and returning the next morning.

Where to stay/eat

Hotel Isla de Coche, tel: (095) 991315/1431, fax: 991132, is on the island's northwest point. Around a pool are gardens, buffet, bar and 24 rooms with fan and air conditioning. A double costs $104 with breakfast and dinner. Activities include snorkelling, diving, mountain-biking and excursions to solitary beaches. There is windsurfing gear and an instructor, also watersports.

Constant trade winds provide excellent windsurfing on the north coast and the opening of a hotel for windsurfers was definitely by design. The **Coche Speed Paradise**, tel: (014) 9952182/83, (014) 9952726, is part of the Paradise group of El Yaque. Guests arriving at Margarita's airport are taken by boat from El Yaque to Coche in 30 minutes. The hotel has 48 air-conditioned rooms with kingsize beds, refrigerator, terrace, gardens, pool and restaurant; double $80 in low season, $100 in high (Nov–Apr), including breakfast, El Yaque transfer, and activities: tennis, mountain biking, diving, fishing, windsurf lessons, and a 3-hole putting course.

If a spell on the beach makes you hungry, ask the way to **El Oasis** in Valle Seco, tel: 991423, run by Elis Pérez and his wife who started out with a shelter for weekends and in time planted trees and built an oasis with a swimming pool. Elis has become an expert cook, bus driver and tour guide. Your best choice on Calle La Marina, right on the sea in San Pedro, is **El Bohío de Doña Carmen**. Helped by her son, Doña Carmen prepares most of her dishes with seafood; excellent cream of crab. Another inexpensive restaurant, **El Pescador de La Isla**, draws people to El Bichar to eat at the seaside.

CUBAGUA

Cubagua's 22km² were not always a desert. Archaeologists have uncovered remains of native cultures 2,800 years old on Punta Gorda: potsherds, conch tools, wood fires. Its last few trees were cut by camps of pearl fishers. Today you can discern the foundations of Nueva Cádiz, Spain's first city in the Americas, swim or go scuba diving. Researchers from the Universidad de Oriente and La Salle Foundation work on the island.

Pearling sounds romantic but it was a cruel form of mining, exterminating human lives along with oyster beds. Spaniards discovered the pearl banks in 1499 and in the next three decades Cubagua declared pearl harvests exceeding 11 tons, a fifth of which went to the Spanish crown. In 1519 drinking water was supplied by Cumaná and the settlement grew into a town of 1,000, formally founded as Nueva Cádiz in 1528. By this time, however, pearls were on the decline and settlers were leaving. A tidal wave swept the 'island of Satan' clean on Christmas Day, 1541.

Day trips

Tour agencies offer sailing and diving trips but do not always go to the ruins. These are comfortable tours providing food and drinks, and perhaps some fishing along the way. Boats leave from the marina at the Margarita Concorde.

In Punta de Piedras you may find a fisherman willing to make the all-day trip for about $50 total. It is a 20km round trip in an open *peñero*, and can be wet and cold returning in the afternoon chop. Take a polythene sheet or poncho to keep cameras and yourself dry. Carry water and food, as well as full sun protection, as there is none on the island; there is no shade but lots of wind and reflected sun.

The yacht *Viola Festival* has for several years made day tours to Cubagua, leaving the Marina Concorde at 09.00. Passengers get a light breakfast on board and picnic lunch on Cubagua Island, plus open bar. Walk to the ruins, swim, snorkel, or jet-ski (additional cost); for reservations, ring Viola Turismo, (095) 630715, fax: 638402. The Centro Náutico Octopus runs a 40ft yacht, the *Rumba II*, which regularly visits Cubagua one day a week, Los Frailes two days, and Coche three days. As on the *Viola*, food and bar are included. Scuba diving (one immersion) is an option at extra cost; information, ring Octopus, tel: (095) 611535, fax: 618258. The *Don Gregorio* is another 40ft yacht leaving from the Marina Concorde; the yacht first visits a beach on Coche for the morning and spends the afternoon at Cubagua; buffet on board, music, drinks on the two-hour return crossing.

The Oriente Coast

ANZOATEGUI STATE

Visitors to Anzoátegui can expect more colonial churches in Clarines (particularly fine), Caigua and El Pilar, more beaches – urban in Puerto La Cruz, uninhabited in Mochima – and oil. The massive presence of petrochemical plants has altered the coast permanently in Jose, 15km from Píritu. Jose (originally spelled Hoces) is the site of the Eastern Cryogenic Complex. Using Venezuela's huge natural gasreserves, an MTBE (methyl-ter-butyl-ether) plant, the world's second largest, makes additives replacing lead in gasoline, for export. Thousands of kilometres of pipeline link the complex with eastern fields. Offshore loading terminals also handle exports of Orimulsion, Venezuela's patented boiler fuel made out of water and heavy oil from the vast Orinoco tar belt.

Coal, cement, farming and tourism also support Anzoátegui's growth, reflected in the urban complex of Barcelona–Puerto La Cruz. Two-thirds of the state's 1.2 million inhabitants live in the linked cities.

Unare Lagoon marks Anzoátegui State's western border with Miranda, separated from the Caribbean by a largely empty beach stretching west and east as far as eye can see. Views over the shallow lagoon and its avian visitors, herons, cormorants, scarlet ibis and flamingos, reward drivers headed for the *Oriente*, or the Eastern coast, as they wind over the steep Morro de Unare (*morro*, a promontory). This mountain has been a sailors' beacon since Amerigo Vespucci put it on his 1499 map.

Píritu

The road detours around a second large lagoon, **Laguna de Píritu**, and returns to the sea. Make a stop at the restored **Iglesia de Píritu** standing in imposing isolation, much as it has since its massive walls were raised in the 1700s. The town of Píritu is below, and 5km further at the sea is **Puerto de Píritu**, a fishing village and holiday town where there are a number of moderate hotels near a generous beach. Don't miss the early morning fish market on the beach, west by the lagoon; you can breakfast on *empanadas*, or *arepas* toasted over coals, and when these finish, roasted fish.

Where to stay

The area telephone code for Píritu is (081)

Beach homes and small hotels dot the 21km sandy bar of Laguna de Unare between Boca de Uchire and El Hatillo. You get best value at the **Posada Oro Verde**, 7.5km from El Hatillo, tel: (016) 9817988; email: sintequi@saomnes.net. Owner Heinz Eckert and his daughter tend what amounts to a small resort set in gardens with a little zoo, pool, 15 rooms for two to four, four bungalows for six (some air conditioned), and a restaurant on the beautiful beach. Price per person,

Barcelona Area

$45 single, $40 double, includes full board. You can make excursions to the Unare River, to Puerto Píritu's fish market, nearby islands, or hot springs. For information, tel: (02) 9799086, fax: 9798412.

In Puerto Píritu, the best known hotel is the moderate **Casacoima**, a block from the beach, tel: (081) 411511-13, fax: 411970; it has two pools, restaurant, and 35 rooms. For a good guesthouse, ring Rosa Virginia, tel: (081) 413769/2963, who has eight rooms with fan, private bath and cold water, in her fine old home, **La Coromotana**, Calle Las Flores, a block from the beach; with or without breakfast. Ask the way west to **Posada Beach**, tel: (014) 9811951, located on Calle La Colina (Hill Street), not on the beach: ten rooms with cold water and private bath (five with shared bath); $10.

Barcelona
The quiet old state capital (pop 278,000) merges with newer Puerto La Cruz, brasher and more expensive in every way. Barcelona, founded in 1671 on the Neverí River, rose as the colonial administrative, church and economic seat of the region, exporting cacao, cotton, and salted beef from the plains. The two-storey Aduana El Rincón, once a colonial customs house, can still be visited north of the city although mangroves now swallow its former access. Barcelona's many green plazas and proudly restored colonial buildings make it a pleasant city.

Getting there and away
By air Barcelona's International Airport, also gateway for Puerto La Cruz, is about 2km south of downtown by the *por puestos* on Avenida 5 de Julio. The new international terminal has many services (free medical attention) but car rental

agencies are in the national terminal. Seven flights daily to/from Caracas by Aeropostal, Aserca, Avensa and Avior, $60. Barcelona–Porlamar is flown by Aeropostal, Avior, Oriental, and Rutaca, $31. Aeropostal, Aserca and Laser serve Maracaibo; Rutaca and Aeropostal go to Ciudad Guayana; Aserca goes to Barquisimeto, Paraguaná, San Antonio, Valencia. An air taxi line, Sasca (Servicios Aéreos de Sucre), tel: (093) 671180/2016, offers day tours to Canaima, $160, and Los Roques, $132.

By bus The big Terminal de Pasajeros is down Calle 4 (San Carlos), two blocks after it intersects with Av Fuerzas Armadas. There is frequent service to Caracas, 310km, 4½ hours; east to Cumaná, 92km/2 hours, and on to Carúpano; south to Ciudad Bolívar, 295km/4 hours, and on to Pto Ordaz. Some lines are: Aerobuses de Venezuela, tel: 666257; Tierra Firme, tel: 667534; Expresos La Guayanesa, tel: 666612. Local buses to downtown Puerto La Cruz go east on the Intercomunal or Vía Alterna. Just outside the station, *por puestos* leave for Santa Fe. For Mochima take the Cumaná *por puesto*.

Where to stay
The area telephone code for Barcelona is (081).
Barcelona's hotels are older and cheaper than those of Puerto La Cruz. Best is the moderate **Hotel Oviana**, Av Caracas near Av Country Club, tel: 761671/4147; apart-hotel with restaurant. The **Barcelona**, 5 de Julio and Calle Bolívar, tel: 771065/76, has 70 rooms, slightly cheaper at $20 double. The older **Neverí** costs less; it overlooks the river and Puente Boyacá on Av Fuerzas Armadas at Av Miranda, tel: 772376; this is a bus route (noisy). These hotels are air conditioned.

Basic lodgings in the centre are $7–12 and may have shared bathrooms and fans (often preferable to rackety air conditioners). **Hotel Canarias'** pleasant, clean rooms surround the patio of a colonial house, Carrera 13 (Bolívar) and 5 de Julio, tel: 771034. **Hotel Plaza** by the Cathedral on Plaza Boyacá, tel: 772843, occupies a two-storey house at least 200 years old which has fallen on hard times; lumpy mattresses; some of the 26 rooms have air conditioning and private bath, double $11; without $8. **Hotel Cultura**, Carrera 14 near 5 de Julio, is another budget place.

What to see
The main business street, Avenida 5 de Julio, runs south-north through town (and on to the Rincón Aduana). In its vicinity you will find many inexpensive places to eat. The government seat, **Gobernación del Estado**, is a pyramidal structure layered with greenery opposite Plaza Miranda. The tourist board, Coranztur, is on the ground floor, tel: (081) 741121/3646. Gardens extend south to spacious Plaza de la Raza while on the east side of 5 de Julio magnificent royal palms and pink poui trees (*apamate*) announce a trio of plazas: Plaza Miranda, Plaza Tricentenaria, and Plaza Bolívar.

The story behind the stark ruins of the **Casa Fuerte** across from Plaza Bolívar is one of heroism, defeat and death. Patriots took over the former Franciscan monastery as a stronghold. When a royalist force of 4,300 occupied the city many families took refuge in the Casa Fuerte, defended by 1,400 men under General Pedro María Freites, aged 27, and William Chamberlain, Bolívar's young British aide-de-camp. The fall of the Casa Fuerte on April 7 1817 and the tragic fate of Chamberlain and his companion Eulalia was told and retold in poems and even a play in Europe. One version says that Chamberlain called for a priest, married Eulalia, put a bullet through her brain and then went to give his life on the ramparts. There were few survivors.

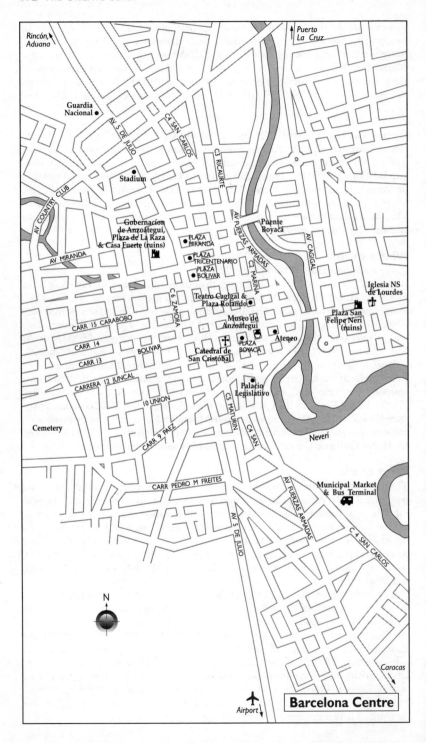

Rincón,
Aduana

Puerto
La Cruz

Guardia
Nacional ●

AV 5 DE JULIO

C4 SAN CARLOS

C3 RICAURTE

Stadium ●

AV FUERZAS ARMADAS

Puente
Boyacá

AV COUNTRY CLUB

AV CAGIGAL

Gobernación
de Anzoátegui,
Plaza de La Raza
& Casa Fuerte (ruins) ■

PLAZA
MIRANDA ●

AV MIRANDA

PLAZA
TRICENTENARIO ●

PLAZA
BOLIVAR ●

C3 MARINA

Iglesia NS
de Lourdes ✝

C6 ZAMORA

Teatro Cagigal &
Plaza Rolando ●

Plaza San
Felipe Neri
(ruins)

CARR 15 CARABOBO

Museo de
Anzoátegui

Ateneo ●

CARR 14

BOLIVAR

CARR 13

Catedral de
San Cristóbal ✝

PLAZA
BOYACA ●

CARRERA 12 JUNCAL

10 UNION

Palacio
Legislativo ■

Cemetery

CARR 9 PAEZ

C5 MATURIN

C4 SAN

Neveri

CARR PEDRO M FREITES

AV FUERZAS ARMADAS

Municipal Market
& Bus Terminal 🚌

AV 5 DE JULIO

C 4 SAN CARLOS

N

Caracas

Airport ✈

Barcelona Centre

Barcelona's historic centre is **Plaza Boyacá** between Carreras 12 (Juncal) and 13 (Bolívar). The city's founding square honours an independence battle in Colombia and its local hero, José Antonio Anzoátegui. The Cathedral, erected on the plaza in 1748–73, has a glowing gilded altar screen. The church is famous for the embalmed and robed remains of Italian Crusader San Celestino, venerated as having miraculous powers. Celestino is Barcelona's third patron saint; his feast days and procession are on May 3 and 4. Across from the Cathedral is the Palacio Municipal or Alcaldía, a handsome town hall erected in 1858.

On the south side of Plaza Boyacá stands a single-floor house said to be Barcelona's oldest (1671). Restored complete with colonial kitchens, it was once a private residence with a back door leading to the river; later a club and maternity hospital; and now the **Museo de Anzoátegui**. Its historical collection scarcely fits and there are plans to move it to more spacious quarters. Next door is the birthplace of Diego Bautista Urbaneja who in 1819 was president of Venezuela's Third Republic. Opposite on Calle 4 stands the two-storey birthplace of Pedro María Freites (1790–1817) who led the ill-fated Casa Fuerte defence. Three blocks east, the **Ateneo Miguel Otero Silva** occupies another restored colonial residence, donated to the city by the family of the novelist (1908–85) who was born there.

Yet another colonial home with tall caned ceilings and massive wood doors is now a shop crammed with crafts from all over Venezuela, the **Gunda Arte Popular**, Carrera 13 towards the river. It is opposite the post office, Ipostel. The colonial bridge over the Neverí, Puente Bolívar, is westbound only but you can walk over if you are interested in the ruins of **San Felipe Neri**, a church destroyed by an earthquake in 1812. In the surviving apse an altar has been built, La Gruta de Nuestra Sra de Lourdes.

Walk up Calle 2 to **Plaza Rolando**, named after the statesman who in the 1890s built both the lovely church and the fine theatre on the plaza, **La Ermita del Carmen** and the **Teatro Cagigal** with its splendid gold curtain and 300 crimson seats. This is an area of many once-stately homes awaiting renovation.

The big covered **Mercado Municipal**, where you can find stalls of clothing and hot food as well as fresh fish and vegetables, is about a kilometre south of Plaza Boyacá, next to the **bus terminal**.

Lecherías and El Morro

Barcelona's city limits include the beach and suburb of Lecherías and a peninsula pointing north into the Caribbean: **El Morro de Barcelona**. A road climbs to the Mirador del Morro at the top; go up for a great view of city, sea, and islands called 'drunkards', Los Borrachos. There is a luxury hotel, the Vista Real, and several condominiums on the way up. On the Morro's west side the city has reconstructed a small colonial fort, **Doña Magdalena**, in a new park with a cultural centre, scene of jazz festivals.

At the foot of the isthmus is the Punta Palma Hotel & Marina, Playa de Lecherías, a popular beach although water quality is dubious, and the pioneer marina, Club Náutico El Morro (which is public). The shopping centres and hotels of Lecherías line wide streets to the south.

Complejo Turístico El Morro

The showcase El Morro Tourist Complex, including the peninsula, is a stunning project said to have inspired the creators of Cancún. Thirty years ago sailing enthusiast Daniel Camejo envisioned a vacation city in neglected salt flats. Today canalside homes, hotels, shops, marinas and golf courses have brought Camejo's

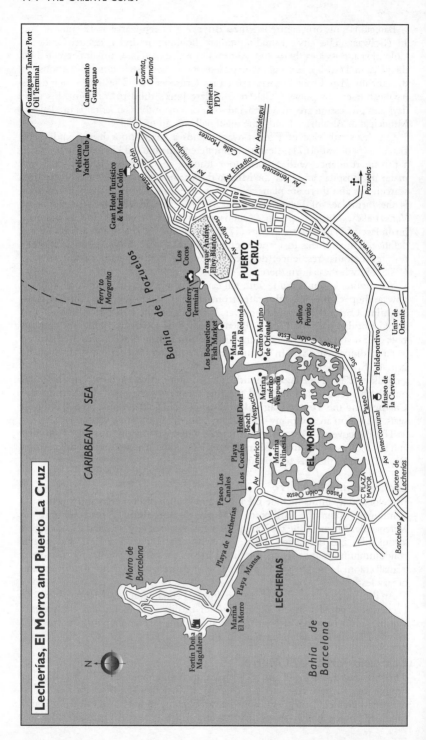

Lecherías, El Morro and Puerto La Cruz

CARIBBEAN SEA

Guaraguao Tanker Port Oil Terminal

Campamento Guaraguao

Guanta, Cumaná

Refineria PDV

Pelícano Yacht Club

Colón

Paseo Colón

Av Municipal

Calle Montes

Av Estadio

Av Anzoátegui

Av Venezuela

Gran Hotel Turístico & Marina Colón

Pozuelos

Av Congreso

Bahía de Pozuelos

Los Cocos

Parque Andrés Eloy Blanco

PUERTO LA CRUZ

Ferry to Margarita

Conferry Terminal

Los Boqueticos Fish Market

Marina Bahía Redonda

Centro Marino de Oriente

Salina Paraíso

Av Universidad

Univ de Oriente

Paseo Colón Este

Polideportivo

Museo de la Cerveza

Hotel Doral Beach

Marina Américo Vespucio

Marina Américo Vespucio

EL MORRO

Paseo Colón Sur

Av Intercomunal

Playa Los Cocales

Av Américo Vespucio

Marina Polinesia

CC PLAZA MAYOR

Paseo Los Canales

Playa de Lecherías

Paseo Colón Oeste

Barcelona

Crucero de Lecherías

Morro de Barcelona

Playa Mansa

Marina El Morro

LECHERIAS

Bahía de Barcelona

Fortín Doña Magdalena

N

dream to life. There are diving, island touring and yacht charter services (see below, *Watersports*). Playa Cocales and Los Canales are the best beaches in Puerto La Cruz, with palm trees and soft sands. Along Avenida Costanera, a broad pedestrian boulevard, showers have been installed for bathers and joggers. Southwest on Paseo Colón Sur is the entrance to a large shopping centre with cinemas, the Plaza Mayor.

The complex lies between the two cities that provided the land, and lives independently of either; it is not detailed on maps of Puerto La Cruz or Barcelona. The land and water development encloses 20km of navigable canals dredged to give access to the bay and depends on 20 pumps and a sewage treatment system (not always adequate). On the main channel the Américo Vespucio marina has slips for 80 yachts, and there is a shipyard for complete yacht overhaul, the Centro Marino de Oriente (CMO); this is the country's most modern yard with a 70-ton travel lift, shop and restaurant. The condominiums of the CMO, and of the new Bahía Redonda Marina with 150 slips, are reached by road via Puerto La Cruz.

Where to stay in El Morro
Facilities in the tourist complex are mostly resorts vying for dollars. Exceptions are the modest **Hotel El Marino**, tel: (081) 692463, above the former Gran Cacique ferry terminal; it has 18 convenient rooms at moderate price, and open-air restaurant on the channel; access is by way of Los Boqueticos, Puerto La Cruz. The **Maremares**, a 5-star resort, is a canalside complex of pink stucco villas in gardens, with a 9-hole golf course, two tennis courts, convention rooms and day-care centre, and 493 rooms. Guests ride in electric carts to the spa, 3,000m^2 lagoon-pool, marina, and the boats to island beaches; tel: 811011, fax: 813028; in Caracas tel: (02) 9590148, fax: 9590172.

Hostería El Morro, west on Av Américo Vespucio, has access to La Costanera and Los Cocales beach; 279 rooms in two-storey units, pool, restaurant; tel: 811312/4157, fax: 814226. First-class **Doral Beach** is on Av Américo Vespucio, tel: 816629/3252, fax: 814344; in Caracas, Corp L'Hotels: (02) 9594113/0291, fax: 9591516. Eight restaurants and bars, pools, tennis, water sports. The hotel is promoted as South America's largest, capable of lodging 4,000 guests in 1,312 doubles and suites (32 villas, 600 apartments).

The **Vista Real**, tel: 813144/1511, fax: 811878, on top of El Morro peninsula is a pricey set-up with great view, but windy and isolated. **Punta Palma**, tel: 811413/1211, fax: 818277, at the foot of El Morro isthmus, has its own marina, pool and beach, also tennis; 180 rooms and suites over the sea.

More hotels are found in Lecherías: the smaller **Venus** and **Saturno**, tel: 862802; and **Hotel Teramum**, Av Principal Lecherías, tel: 810411.

Puerto la Cruz
Puerto La Cruz took on life as an oil terminal as recently as 1939. Before then it was little more than a few bayside huts of mostly Margarita fishing families. The cross of its name stood by alkaline springs, the Pozo de la Santísima Cruz, that once flowed near Plaza Bolívar. The cross is now kept in the **Iglesia de la Santa Cruz**, two blocks west of Plaza Bolívar.

Yet the bay's potential was long known. In 1878 James Mudie Spence wrote (*In the Land of Bolívar*) of his search for a coaling station as Barcelona's port was inadequate. He began sounding the coast and hit upon a place with sufficient depth: 'It had good anchorage for a thousand vessels and was situated within 4½ miles of the capital. This was on the eastern side of a small peninsula named the Morro de Barcelona.' Spence gave his report along with a painting by Ramón Bolet of the future port with railways and telegraphs to President Guzmán Blanco who said, 'In time it will no doubt become the centre of commerce for the eastern section of the republic.'

And so it did. At the turn of the century coal from the mines of Naricual was brought by train and shipped from **Guanta**, today the region's busy commercial port. One of the world's largest oil ports, **Guaraguao**, functions east of Pozuelos Bay, behind fences so there is little to be seen. Pipelines feed heavy, medium and light crude in a totally automated system loading several ships at a time with as much as 70,000 barrels of oil hourly. The refinery and old oil camp complete with tree-lined streets, school and club may be visited with permission.

The area's third impetus came from tourism. Puerto La Cruz has funnelled most of Margarita's visitors through its ferries since 1959. And the opening of the 5-star Meliá Hotel in 1974 launched the town as an international destination.

Getting there and away

By air Barcelona's airport serves Puerto La Cruz. Some airlines also have offices in Puerto La Cruz. For American Airlines, tel: (081) 673333/0766, 817713; Avensa/Servivensa, tel: 671301-05; KLM-ALM, 667931; Rutaca, tel: 675681, 672830; United Airlines, tel: 666744, 672422. Various travel agencies can also make bookings.

Helicópteros de Oriente (Helior) has an office in Puerto La Cruz: Of.2-22, Novo Centro, Av Stadium, tel: 673211; also near the exit of Maremares Hotel, El Morro; tel: (081) 811011 ext 1062, fax: 675169. The charter charge is by the hour.

By ferry Conferry provides the sea link to Margarita. (For ferry data, see *Chapter 8*, page 162). Conferry's schedule varies according to high or low season. The terminal, tel: (081) 677221/847, is off Paseo Colón opposite Parque Andrés Eloy Blanco. These big ferries cross in 4½ hours; 6–8 sailings daily.

By bus The large Terminal de Pasajeros is located three blocks south of Plaza Bolívar on Calle Juncal. Coaches and express lines serve the same destinations as from the Barcelona terminal. To Caracas it is 5 hours by bus, 4 by *por puesto*; to Ciudad Bolívar, 5 hours; to Maturín 3 hours; to Cumaná 1½ hours. Frequent buses and *por puestos* to Barcelona run from Av 5 de Julio/Calle Juncal.

Línea Caribe buses go from here to Puerto Ordaz, continuing service to Boa Vista in Brazil on coaches of the Uniao Cascavel; departures at 17.00 on Mon/Wed/Fri, $50. For information in Puerto Ordaz, tel: (086) 519248/8669.

Aeroexpresos Ejecutivos run direct coaches between Puerto La Cruz and Caracas. Their office, tel: (081) 67885/7955, is in the Conferry Terminal; departures at 07.00, 11.30, 15.30, midnight; $15. Also one direct coach goes to Maracay and Valencia, at 23.30. This rapid service offers numbered seats, air conditioning, toilets and video; fine at night, but no daytime appeal as windows are closed and curtained. (See also *Chapter 4*, page 87.)

Where to stay

The telephone area code for Puerto La Cruz is (081)
Many hotels are on or near the Paseo Colón. For a decent double room prepare to pay $15 and up (more on peak holidays); a single costs almost the same as a double. The partial list below does not include apartment hotels which require a week's stay at holiday times, 2–3 nights during off-season.

There are various expensive choices for $85 and up. At the top is the only hotel on the beach, the former Meliá which is now the **Hotel Turístico de Puerto La**

Cruz, tel: 653611, fax: 653117; 220 rooms, pool open to non-guests, tennis courts, car rental and ferry agencies, dive shop and adjacent marina; double with breakfast is $130–170 according to the season. The 25-floor **Rasil**, a Cumberland hotel, is on Paseo Colón, ten blocks west, tel: 672422, fax: 673121; 337 rooms, pool and all services; in Caracas ring (02) 7611622, fax: 7616681. The **Caribbean Inn**, Calle Freites at Honduras, tel: 674292, fax: 672857; 102 rooms and terrace pool. **Cristina Suites**, tel: 674712, fax: 675058, is a 4-star alternative seven blocks south.

In the middle range, the **Sorrento**, an economical business hotel, has 82 rooms on Av 5 de Julio between Maneiro and Freites; tel: 686745. The **Hotel Riviera** at Paseo Colón 33, tel: 672111, fax: 651394, has 74 doubles in the $40 range. Its competition are the **Gaeta** on Paseo Colón, tel: 651211, fax: 650065, 50 rooms, and the **Gaeta City**, tel: 672092, fax: 674717, on Calle Maneiro four blocks away, with 44 rooms. Also in the 3-star range is the **Senador**, Calle Miranda at Bolívar, tel: 673985, fax: 652338.

Several low-price older hotels cluster between the Paseo and Plaza Bolívar; some have even cheaper rooms, not air conditioned. The **Neptuno**, Paseo Colón at Juncal, tel: (081) 685413, fax: 653261 has five floors, 31 rooms at $15 double, and recommended rooftop restaurant. Its neighbours are the **Montecarlo**, tel: 685677; and **Margelina**, tel: 687545, also known for its dining room. On Plaza Bolívar are the **Europa**, tel: 688157, a notch up in quality and price; and the **Hotel Rey**, tel: 686810. Rooms at nearby **Hotel Diana**, Paseo No 99, tel: 650017, start at $12.

Where to eat

Around Paseo Colón are some of the city's best and busiest restaurants, at least 20. Seafood is a good choice here although not cheap.

For a reasonable *criollo* brunch, go to Perriven, Av Bolívar at Arismendi. The **Casa Pueblo**, Calle Carabobo a block from the Paseo, also serves good Venezuelan dishes. **Pastelería Fornos** on the Paseo opposite the Coranztur module bakes excellent bread and pastries throughout the day. Next to the old favourite **Parador del Puerto**, on the Paseo at Calle Buenos Aires, the **Dulcería Arabe** has the reputation for the tastiest coffee in town and amazing Arab sweets. By the bus station is an Arab restaurant, **El Faraón**, Calle Juncal 61.

Two blocks further west on the Paseo, hotel restaurants are recommended as reliable and moderate: the **Neptune**'s rooftop restaurant, and the **Margelina**'s Italian dining room. Several pizza and pasta houses are nearby. For French food, wine and music, try the **Chic e Choc** at Paseo Colón 113.

If your budget is pinched, sample the tacos or burritos sold by **Taco To Go** carts. Or have an *empanada* (turnover) filled with *cazón* (shark), or *pabellón* (black beans-beef-plantain); these are served day and night at several kiosks in the Conferry Terminal. At lunch ask for fried fish or a *sancocho de pescado*, a soup to raise the dead. Stalls at Los Boqueticos fish market offer a variety of good, inexpensive seafood dishes; they serve from 07.00 to 16.00.

What to see

Lining the breezy Pozuelos Bay is **Paseo Colón**, centre of town life. At its east end is the former Meliá Hotel. From the bronze statue of Colón (Columbus) and the Cross in an oval plaza, the shore boulevard runs a dozen blocks to the Hotel Rasil's concrete tiers. Paseo Colón continues west another kilometre, passing the Conferry Terminal and **Parque Andrés Eloy Blanco** where it leaves the shore to go southwest around El Morro Tourist Complex.

By day visitors and locals gather at the Paseo's benches and bandstands, pastry shops and open-air restaurants; they read, lie about on the sand (the sea is not clean

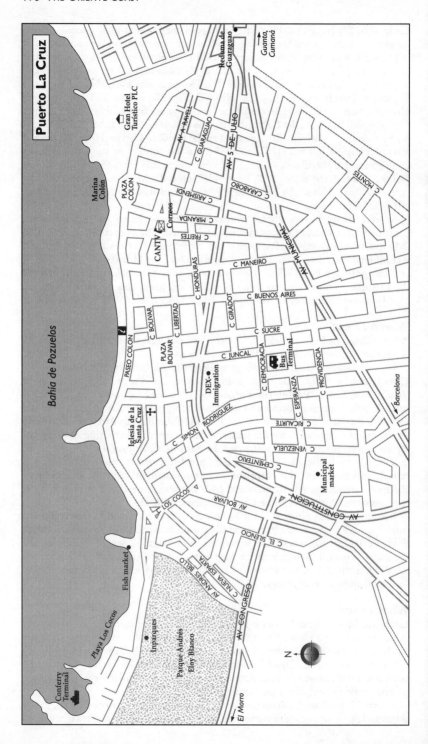

Puerto La Cruz

enough for swimming), or set out in boats for island beaches. At night street vendors sell crafts, souvenirs, toys, cassettes, paintings and sandals. Bars light up and people of all sorts and nationalities stroll in the cool evening.

Fishermen bring their catch early in the morning to the waterfront **fish markets** of Los Cocos and Los Boqueticos. Los Cocos is just west of the Rasil; Los Boqueticos is about 1km beyond the Conferry Terminal.

A city with a short past, Puerto La Cruz has no historic monuments and few tourist attractions. One exception is **Pozuelos**, once a separate village, now a quiet suburb about 1km south of the Intercomunal and Vía Alterna highways. Named for its springs whose luxuriant greenery announced water to passing sailors and explorers, Pozuelos is on a steep hill with a wonderful view of the bay at the top. A mission was founded in 1681 to resettle Indians and a little church was built, dedicated to Nuestra Señora del Amparo. A colonial painting of the Virgin stands over the altar.

Beer fans write home about the **Museo de la Cerveza** and its fine collection of labels, flasks and barrels dating to the Middle Ages. You will even find a paean by Bridget, the Irish saint. The museum is in a building next to Distribuidora Polar Oriente, Las Garzas, south side of Av Intercomunal.

Festivals

Carnival is celebrated with dances in clubs, street parades on the Intercomunal, steel bands, and plenty of vigour and liquor. This four-to-five-day *'super-bonche'* ends with Carnival Tuesday. Hotels are fully booked, restaurants crowded, and pickpockets overactive.

The **Cruz de Mayo** is a spring festivity heralding the appearance of the Southern Cross constellation at planting time. Altars are decorated on the eve of May 3 in many homes, and the observation begins with a *velorio* or vigil, and songs. Puerto La Cruz celebrates with a festival around the cross on Paseo Colón, drawing processions with altars from various parishes. Singers begin the give and take of *contrapunteo* couplets sung to music called the *galerón*.

September 8 honours the **Virgen del Valle**, patroness not only of Margarita but of all eastern Venezuela. As many Lecherías families come from Margarita, they celebrate in a big way. Fishermen adorn boats with flowers, figurines and banners hailing the Virgin. After a priest says mass, scores of boats sail along the coast towards Puerto La Cruz. The flower-decked leading *peñero* bears the Virgen del Valle, and fishermen chant prayers and hymns. On shore a procession lets off fireworks.

Watersports

Regattas are drawing foreign sails to Puerto La Cruz's top attraction: 700km^2 of calm waters locally called the **Sea of El Morro**. In the hurricane season marinas such as the Bahía Redonda quickly fill up with visiting sailboats.

Puerto La Cruz is the country's biggest watersports centre with over seven marinas and yacht clubs. The newest, **Bahía Redonda**, is a world-class marina with not only 150 full service slips, but a swimming pool, hot showers and communications centre, tel: (081) 677810. To reach the marina, follow Paseo Colón past the ferry terminal and at Redoma Los Cerezos go west to Los Boqueticos, and the Centro Marino de Oriente. Enquire about charters, both sail and motor.

Some other marinas are: the Pelican Yacht Club; Club Náutico El Chaure in the oil terminal; the Guanta Marina; Hotel Punta Palma's marina; and the pioneer **Marina Club Náutico El Morro** at the isthmus of El Morro peninsula, tel: (081)

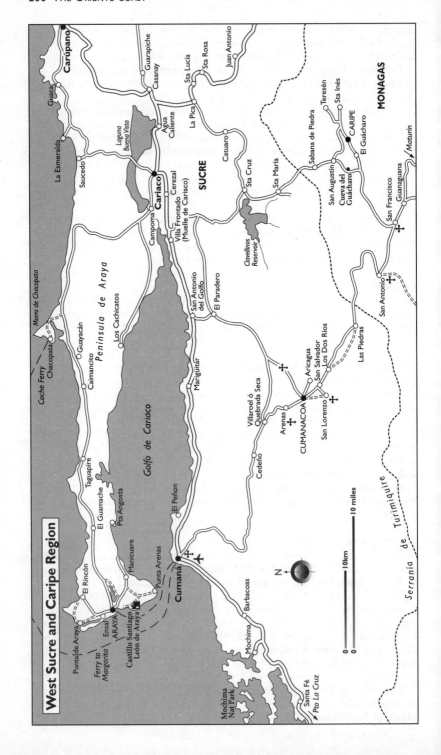

West Sucre and Caripe Region

Carúpano

Guaca
La Esmeralda
Saucedo
Guarapiche
Casanay
Sta Lucía
Sta Rosa
Juan Antonio
Laguna Buena Vista
Agua Caliente
La Pica
Teresén
Sta Inés
Catuaro
Sabana de Piedra

MONAGAS

Cariaco
Villa Frontado (Muelle de Cariaco)
Cerezal
Campoma
SUCRE
Sta Cruz
Sta María
San Augustín
CARIPE
Cueva del Guácharo
El Guácharo
Maturín

Morro de Chacopata
Coche Ferry
Chacopata
Guayacán
Caimancito
Los Cachicatos
Península de Araya
San Antonio del Golfo
El Paradero
Clavellinos Reservoir
San Francisco
Guanaguana
San Antonio

Taguapire
El Guamache
Pta Angosta
Marigüitar
Aricagua
San Salvador
Los Dos Ríos
Las Piedras

El Rincón
Manicuare
Punta Arenas
El Peñón
Villaroel ó Quebrada Seca
Arenas
CUMANACOA
San Lorenzo
Cedeño

Punta de Araya
Ferry to Margarita
Ensal
ARAYA
Castillo Santiago León de Araya
Cumaná

Golfo de Cariaco

Mochima Nat Park
Mochima
Barbacoas
Santa Fé
Pto La Cruz

Serranía de Turimiquire

N

10km
0
10 miles
0

810332. Now up for sale by the city, it has a restaurant, marine shop, forklift service and some space for visiting yachts. The **Marina Américo Vespucio**, El Morro Tourist Complex, tel: (081) 87911, is also public. Anyone can use its restaurants and marine shop. Among agencies there offering yacht rental, day cruises, deep sea fishing and island hopping tours are: Yates Comerciales, tel: 813393; Tayana Charters, tel: 812798; Horisub, tel: 812501, scuba gear, tank fills and rental. Rasi Tours, tel: 811295, takes groups of six to various islands for the day with lunch and beer; also arranges sailing and waterskiing.

By the former Meliá Hotel, the **Marina Gente de Mar** or **Marina Colón**, tel: (081) 691517/8, offers visiting yachtsmen launching service plus fuel and ice; closed Wednesdays for maintenance. **Explosub**, tel: 653611 ext 3347, has a dive shop in the former Meliá and on the beach; they fill tanks and rent masks, scuba equipment, boats, wind sails, Sunfish; open 08.00–17.00 daily. Explosub can give you Mochima tour information.

In Guanta, just east of Puerto La Cruz, there is a marina with full dive services: **Lolo's Diving Centre**, tel: (081) fax: (081) 656636.

A sport seaman's school is operated in Bahía Redonda by the Asociación Nacional de Marinos Deportivos. Courses prepare candidates for licences as yacht captain. A sailing school, the Escuela de Vela Américo Vespucio, is based in the Centro Marino de Oriente, tel: 677011, 631818, fax: 678550.

Diving

The **Scuba Divers Club**, tel/fax: 635401, is a complete dive centre (rather than a club) offering school, equipment and boat rentals, and tours within Mochima National Park. It is based in the Bahía Redonda Marina, Av Tajamar (near the former Gran Cacique terminal). Divers who go out with them must have certification. Beginners can start with a day's theory and safety. If you have done this elsewhere, get a referral form from your instructor. The open-water course entitling you to PADI certification takes a minimum of four days. Including all equipment, wetsuit, and snacks, a day's diving (two immersions) costs $75. Ask about prices for more days/people.

Information and tours

The state tourism body, **Coranztour**, has a module on the Paseo Colón, open daily. However, you may get more help from the tiny Sotillo Municipal office at the Paseo's eastern end.

Local tours are announced everywhere in free flyers and what's-on publications. The *Caribbean Queen*, a pleasure boat, takes passengers on excursions around islands, stopping at beaches and providing lunch; tel: (081) 817816, 817272. For Margarita, Angel Falls and further afield, try hotel agencies or Viajes Venezuela beside the Riviera, Viajes Atlantic on Plaza Bolívar. (For beach and Mochima tours, see *Island beaches* below.)

The post office and telephone centre occupy the same building on Calle Libertad at Freites. CANTV is open 24 hours a day.

Inparques has offices in the Parque Andrés Eloy Blanco, tel: (081) 678973. If you need a camping permit, request it in writing, make photocopies of your passport, and be patient.

As a measure of its growth Puerto La Cruz has several consulates: **Belgium**, tel: (081) 663134; **Colombia**, tel: 651348, 688391; **Denmark**, tel: 687297/5710; **Holland**, tel: 814262; **Italy**, tel: 23890, fax: 691943; **Norway**, tel: 674722; **Spain**, tel: 650821/328. In the event of passport loss, notify also the Immigration authority, DEX, Edificio Oriente, Av 5 de Julio and Calle Juncal.

Island beaches

Although urban beaches may be clean, the sea is not because currents carry pollutants from ports and cities. There is hope for Puerto La Cruz, however, as a German firm is helping to construct a better sewage system.

The truly beautiful beaches are on the islands and coasts of **Mochima National Park** (see *Chapter 7* for map and eastern Mochima). A dozen islands lie within easy reach of Puerto La Cruz. Although arid and hilly they are surrounded by clear waters where groups of dolphins play. Coral reefs invite snorkellers and divers. Some popular beaches have food stands, shelters and toilets.

At the east end of Paseo Colón the boatmen's cooperative called Transtupaco has a stand, tel: 679093. Their 16 *peñeros* equipped with roof, life jackets and radio are on call every day from 08.30. You buy a numbered ticket; the price of $5 includes a return trip at 14.30 or 16.00. They take you to the beaches of El Saco and El Faro on the Chimanas. Other *embarcaderos* for beach excursions are on the bay near the Coranztur tourism office. Weekends are crowded. If you prefer to explore various islands, consult the Explosub people at the former Meliá Hotel beach; their dive shop offers tours, too.

As fishermen work their nets at night many boats are available for hire during the day. These *peñeros* unload their catch every morning; you can find the captains near Los Cocos and Los Boqueticos fish markets, respectively east and 1km west of the Conferry Terminal. They do not have a service cooperative so you may need to haggle.

The **Borracha** and **Chimana** island groups lie some 11km and 6km north of Puerto La Cruz. La Borracha has good reefs; **Playa de Guaro** is on the west side. Chimana Grande has protected beaches called **Puinare** and **El Saco** (most popular), and a well-run restaurant. Chimana Segunda has **El Faro**, a quiet beach (with restaurant) where snorkellers enjoy clear waters.

Drive along the coast east of Puerto La Cruz for more island hopping. **Isla de Plata**, named for its silver-white sand, nestles between the headlands of Guanta and Pertigalete. Crystal waters, reefs, umbrellas and food stalls attract plenty of bathers on weekends. A 10-minute shuttle service runs 07.30–16.30 from the Embarcadero Pamatacualito; $1.50 round trip. Service is less frequent during the week. *Por puestos* to **Pamatacualito**, about 10km, leave from Plaza Bolívar (south side) in Puerto La Cruz; the Isla de Plata *peñeros* tie up between La Baritina (barite unloading docks) and Marina Pamatacualito.

If you wish to camp overnight, consult the ferry cooperative first; they will need to know your transportation and food requirements. However, be advised that an island is no guarantee against robbery. The boatmen who rotate ferry duty can take you to other islands and beaches: Isla de Monos, Ña Cleta, Conomita and La Piscina.

Near the Pertigalete headland is **Playa Santa Cruz**. Above this beach is a comfortable little hotel surrounded by flowers, **Chez Frederic et María**, tel: (014) 9803751, (014) 9322159. They have built a pool, restaurant (good food), and have 12 rooms, some with fan, some air-conditioned, at $30 for single, double or triple. Ask them about a boat ride to islands or the beautiful beaches of **Conoma** and **Conomita** around the steep headland.

Fishermen in Valle Seco just beyond Pertigalete will take you to **Conoma, Conomita** (ten minutes), **Ña Cleta** (five minutes) and **Isla de Monos** (18 minutes) which has a small beach and beautiful corals. A narrow road descends from the highway to the community of Valle Seco. Agree on a price per boat round trip, *ida y vuelta*.

Arapo and **Arapito** islands, where vendors ply *empanadas*, beer and cold soft drinks, lie opposite the very popular mainland beaches of **Playa Arapito**,

Vallecito and **Colorada**, 23–26km from Puerto La Cruz. Between the islands is La Piscina, the 'swimming pool', famous for its mirror-like translucent water. Off Arapo, northwest, is a rocky pelican perch, **Isla de Pájaros**. Boatmen in Playa Colorada or Arapito charge about $15 per boat (five passengers) to these islands, returning at an agreed hour.

The ample crescent beach of **Playa Colorada** is on the coastal highway (now Sucre State). It is known for reddish sand, coconut palms for slinging hammocks, informal restaurants, and weekend crowds. You can overnight in your tent or hammock for a fee; although security is questionable, many people do camp out over Easter. Or, across the road, walk uphill to the German-run **El Tucusito** or Villas Turísticas, tel: (081) 691950, which has a restaurant, small pool, and six caravans with two bedrooms, kitchen, and air conditioning; 12 smaller suites for two to three persons; $40, $30 a day. In Caracas, tel: (02) 9521393/1826.

A French Canadian couple, Jacques and Lynn, tel: (016) 6818113, have conditioned two houses about eight blocks from the beach as bed and breakfast pensions, seven rooms for one to four guests; with fan or air conditioning, hot water, and some private baths. About $17 for two.

La Tortuga Island, thirty minutes by private plane from Barcelona airport, is an uninhabited island lying 90km northwest (not in Mochima Park). Espartaco has built a bare-bones camp here with tents. He arranges overnight excursions for about $190, full day $140. Bring your swimsuit and sunblock; the island provides luminous sea, white beaches and, with luck, fish for the barbecue. For information, ring Ma-Ci-Te Turismo, tel: (081) 652050/1512, fax: 688528.

SUCRE STATE

To most Venezuelans the 'Oriente' stands for Sucre's long Caribbean shore stretching from Mochima National Park (see *Chapter 7*) east to Paria Peninsula. Cumaná's airport is being enlarged to bring jets direct from Europe as it makes an excellent hub for travel to Margarita, Monagas State and the Orinoco Delta.

The area has much to offer: quiet beaches, the famous Guácharo Cave, forests, mountains, and rural towns whose residents will treat you as a person. Dialects vary from the rapid accents of Cumaná's fishermen to the English and French influence of patois in Güiria. Daily life revolves around fishing and farming. Coconut plantations fringe the bays of Paria; water buffalo are at home in wetlands; huge trees shade lush cacao groves beyond Carúpano; sugarcane blooms in the rich valleys of Cariaco and Cumanacoa. Mangoes are so abundant that in season they cover the ground.

Cumaná
Chris Stolley

The state capital, Cumaná, is a major tuna port and canning centre. The city is at the outlet of the Manzanares River which divides it roughly east and west. A walk through Cumaná's small centre will not lead you to believe that this city is home to 300,000 people (half under 20 years of age). Most inhabitants live in outlying *barrios* and their daily comings and goings have produced a serious transportation crisis. For the traveller, however, the concentration of activity downtown offers unlimited opportunities for people-watching.

History

Cumaná claims to be the continent's oldest Spanish town (1521) and certainly it was the most important native community on the coast, home to the Cumanagoto Indians. The discovery of pearl beds off Margarita made Cumaná an important supply centre for water and slaves to support the pearling, and Franciscan missionaries arrived in 1515 attempting to protect the Indians. What followed were 54 years of massacres as Cubagua's slavers came back, Indians turned against monks, and Spaniards sent punitive expeditions.

In 1569 Cumaná received its first permanent settlers and in the 1660s two forts, San Antonio de la Eminencia and Santa María de la Cabeza, were constructed. These forts and the whole city were destroyed several times by earthquakes, in 1684, 1797, 1853 and 1929. San Antonio has been partially restored, but of Santa María there remains little. Cumaná joined the Captaincy General of Venezuela in 1777, and during the war for independence from Spain in the early 1800s played an important part, being taken and retaken a number of times. Sucre State is named after native son Grand Marshal Antonio José de Sucre who fought with Bolívar and liberated Ecuador, Peru and Bolivia. He was Bolivia's first president.

Getting there and away

By air The airport is about ten minutes east of town. From the airport to town you will need to take a taxi; do NOT walk out to the highway to flag a ride. To get to the airport, take a taxi from Plaza Miranda or a *por puesto* that goes from the river east of the plaza. The *por puesto* stops at the airport only for outbound passengers.

Servivensa flies Caracas–Porlamar–Cumaná daily ($61); Oriental, Avior and Air Venezuela make a total of five flights daily (four on Sunday). Air Venezuela has the lowest Caracas fare, $41, and also flies daily except Sunday to Mérida. There are six flights a day from Margarita to Cumaná by these lines, $28–42. Avensa/Servivensa tel: (093) 671518; Oriental tel: 672097/1191.

By ferry Ferry and launch services go separately to Margarita and to Araya. (For details see *Chapter 8*, and *Araya* section below.) Remember that ferry schedules are

HAND-ROLLED CUMANA CIGARS

In a world where a real Cuban cigar can cost as much as an elegant meal, and many of the rest are made with an outer wrapper (if not part of the insides as well) of chemically treated paper, Cumaná is an oasis in a desert of mediocrity for the tobacco lover. Hand-rolled cigars, called *puros* or *tabacos*, are a traditional speciality of Cumaná, a home-based industry of long standing mostly carried out by older women. Their way of smoking cigars (you can see it done with cigarettes as well) is with the lit end inside the mouth. Try it if you dare.

Follow your nose to the various *fábricas* along Calle Rendón on the sea side of the river, just south of Av Bermúdez, a main shopping street. My favourite is **Tabacos Guanche**, Calle Rendón 48 (heading towards the sea on Av Bermúdez go left one block at Bar Stalingrado), run by Canary Islander Jaime Acosta Paiz. Señor Acosta has an international as well as a local following, although his production is small. He is a patient man, as fits his profession, and will sometimes treat buyers to a tour. This is for good Spanish-speakers only. 'The best I have smoked in 20 years,' said the publisher's father when presented with a box by his loving daughter. Prices start at about $10 per box of 25 in a simple paper box. If one so desires and has time to wait, orders can be placed for big *ejecutivo* cigars with personalised rings in an elegant wooden box also handmade by Señor Acosta.

not written in stone, so be flexible. The ferry terminal is at the foot of Av El Islote, several blocks down from the Mercado Municipal. A *por puesto* leaves from Plaza Miranda between the two bridges. It is better not to walk if you are alone or carrying anything as the waterfront can be a dangerous place for the unfamiliar and anyone with anything to lose.

By bus The Terminal de Pasajeros is on Av Las Palomas, another dubious area. It is open all night when many long-distance coaches arrive. Reservations are made by buying your ticket two days in advance. Buses fill up, especially on Fridays and Sundays; long weekends and major holidays are next to impossible. Coaches to Caracas, $9, and also to Ciudad Bolívar, $7, go through Puerto La Cruz. For Guácharo Cave, take the Caripe bus at 07.30 or 12.00, $3. Service to Carúpano, 2½ hours, and Güiria, 4½ hours, throughout the day.

Ask about *carros por puesto* if you are in a hurry. You can choose one with good tyres and a seat with leg room (or buy all the seats and have lots more space). There are various routes served only by *por puesto*, such as Cumaná–Cumanacoa–Maturín. This is a beautiful 3-hour trip through the Turimiquire mountains and on to the plains of Monagas, the Delta. *Por puestos* to Mochima and to Santa Fe park a block north of Redoma El Indio.

Where to stay
The area telephone code for Cumaná is (093)
At the far west are three resort hotels: the four-storey **Cumanagoto**, tel: 653355/2011, fax: 652043; has 166 rooms in spacious beachside park, with shops, tours and watersports. The new **Barceló Nueva Toledo**, tel: 519595/9991, fax: 519974, is a member of the RCI time-sharing system. A low-season plan including meals and national brand drinks costs $110 for two people. The hotel is 300m from the beach. **Los Bordones**, tel: 513111/5630, fax: 515377; is on the beach; it has all services including disco, pools, and dive shop; 115 rooms on eight floors.

Among good hotels, away from the centre, is the 3-star **Minerva**, tel: 662712/03, fax: 662701, on Av Perimetral Norte past the Marina Cumanagoto. It has a view over the gulf and Araya, 122 rooms and suites, and a small pool. Near Los Uveros beach is the **Gran Hotel**, tel: 510218/0671, fax: 512677, Av Universidad (2km south of the Redoma del Indio); pool, restaurant, 50 rooms with air conditioning, double $40. On the shore to the south along Av Universidad are quiet hotels, some *posadas*. The *uveros* or seagrape trees shading a 3km promenade lend their name to one of the country's longest public beaches: **Balneario Los Uveros**. Playa San Luis is one sector. The hotels have high fences on the beach with gates that are locked at dusk. Two modest ones are the **Villamar**, tel: 652411, two floors with restaurant near beach; and **Hotel Caribe**, tel: 514548/6101, pleasant blue and white cottages with kitchen for two to four people; windsurfing, diving.

Something new in Cumaná is **Bubulina's Hostal & Restaurant**, tel/fax: 314025, on the restored colonial street between Iglesia Santa Inés and the Manzanares River. Two fine old houses, one with an excellent Venezuelan restaurant, have been joined to give six rooms with double beds and six with twin beds, with TV, air conditioning, fan, private bath and hot water; $40 including breakfast for two.

On Calle Sucre between Plaza Bolívar and Iglesia Santa Inés there are small, friendly and inexpensive hotels charging about $8 for a double with fan and private bath: the **Italia**, tel: (093) 663678; **Vesuvio**, tel: 314077; **Cumaná**, 310545; and **Astoria**, tel: 662708, which has air conditioning.

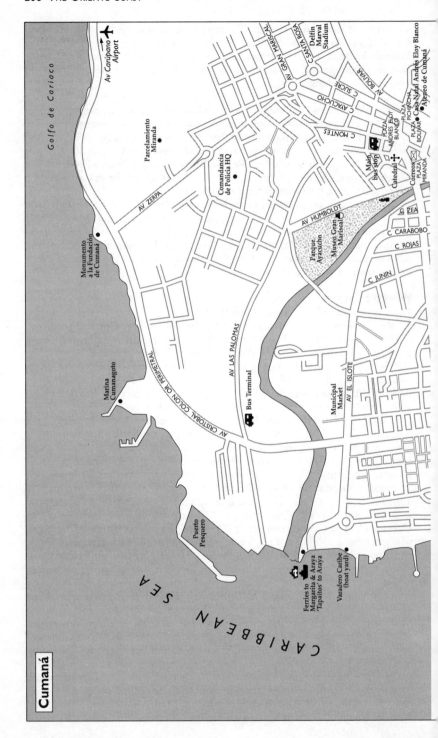

Cumaná

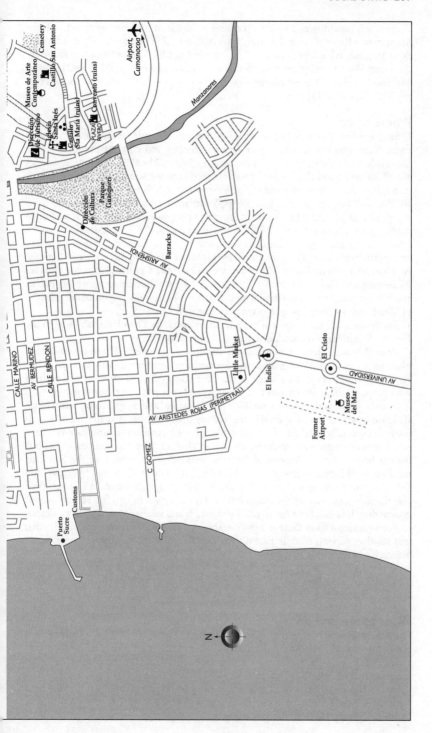

Another downtown area of economical hotels is on the west side of the Manzanares River. Facing the river: **Dos Mil**, tel: 323414, double $8; and the six-floor **Regina**, tel: 322581, air-conditioned double $20. Also in this price range are the seven-floor **Guaiquerí**, two blocks west on Av Bermúdez, tel: 310821; **Hotel Mariño**, tel: 322311, four blocks west on Av Mariño, 75 rooms; and the **Savoia**, tel: 312855, fax: 314379, west on Av Perimetral, 49 rooms.

Where to eat

Cumaná offers the Venezuelan standards of *parrilla, pasta, pollo, pescado*: grilled meat, pasta, chicken and fish. *Parrillas* vary in class and cost. At the top ($11) is **Vitorio's** on Av Arístides Rojas (Perimetral), close to Hotel Savoia, where you can get all-around good food. I prefer a street *parrilla* at the south end of Calle Sucre, past Iglesia Santa Inés, in front of the Plaza Rivero. It is very popular and rightly so. You will be served, on a base of *bollitos* (maize), *yuca* (manioc) or *ocumo chino* (taro), grilled steak and two kinds of sausage with *guasacaca* sauce. Top it off with a *parchita* juice (passion fruit), and the bill will be about $3.50. Best deal in town.

For the sweet-toothed, Cumaná has a special treat. Exquisite Italian-style ice-cream, fruit ices and cakes are offered by **Helados La Barquilla** at two locations: Av Gran Mariscal by Banco Mercantil, and behind the Centro Comercial Gina on Av Bermúdez. The fruit is true to life, there are exotic flavours to please any palate, and the *torta castillo* is a guaranteed diet destroyer. Personally recommended by the publisher who insisted on going twice in one day.

For homemade pasta and brick-oven baked pizza, try **Don Pietro's**, next to the Parque Ayacucho. The outdoor tables are quiet and relaxing.

Pollo en brasa, chicken barbecued on a spit, is everywhere. There is one special place to get your chicken grilled over a wood fire and served with an *arepa pelada* (ground whole corn): at the edge of the Mercadito (see below) there is a woman who prepares them afternoons and evenings. A bit hard to find but worth it.

Pescado – fish, and *mariscos* – shellfish (note: '*marico*' and by extension '*marisco*' are slang for 'gay') are the basic food in this fishing town. Be sure that all seafood is well cooked, especially shellfish. Raw (as in the popular ceviche) or undercooked they can transmit unpleasant diseases, including cholera. Try the nationally famous **Mercadito**, a noisy collection of 20 or so seafood restaurants; take the San Luis minibus to El Indio, a cement statue of an Indian holding a fish, said to be the only fish not consumed in Cumaná. Try the *hervido* or *sopa de pescado*, an inexpensive chunky fish soup with all the bones left in. This is a meal in itself and a mainstay of coastal diet. It is excellent for an uneasy stomach and when recovering from illness.

For vegetarian food there is a good restaurant on Av Bermúdez by the Alcaldía, and another serving Middle East dishes, *comida Arabe*: the **Cleopatra** next to the Supercine on Avenida Perimetral.

Venezuelan cuisine is tops at **Bubulina's Restaurant**, in a restored old house on Callejón Santa Inés west of the church. Here you can dine on *asado* pot roast, *apio* cream soup, fish with a flourish of coconut milk, orange and passion fruit.

What to see and do

Cumaná's historic core is conveniently compact. The centre is **Plaza Bolívar** and government buildings. At the northwest corner of the plaza is the Bar Jardín Sport, a delightful open-air bar beneath shady trees that has become somewhat of an international traveller's mecca and communication centre. Here you can listen to the *rocola* (jukebox) blare out Latin hits of the past 30 years while you beat the heat with an ice-cold Polar or fruit *batido* and watch the action in the plaza. Local hustlers abound. Be cautious, but enjoy it.

The birthplace of beloved poet **Andrés Eloy Blanco** (1896–1955) is on the west side of Plaza Bolívar. The restored house where his grandparents and parents lived conserves the period furniture, kitchen, and 200-year-old piano which is still used for recitals. Hours are 09.00–12.00, 15.00–20.00; closed Sunday morning. The **Ateneo de Cumaná**, tel: 315245, on the plaza's east side next to the Government House, has an active cultural programme and a crafts shop.

Looking up from the plaza to the only high spot around, you see the fort, **Castillo San Antonio de la Eminencia**. Follow the signs from Plaza Bolívar (or take the steps up from Calle La Luneta behind Iglesia Santa Inés, two blocks south). Sharing the spectacular view over sea and port, the new **Museo de Arte Contemporáneo** (MACC), opened in 1998 at the foot of the fort, adds a dynamic dimension with terraced sculpture gardens and an open-air café. It is the focal point of Cumana's International Art Bienniel, next celebrated in the year 2000.

The **Iglesia Santa Inés** is dedicated to Cumaná's first patron saint, named in 1572 after settlers beat off a dawn Indian attack. The second patron, St John the Baptist, earned the honour when **Walter Raleigh**, fresh from an expedition up the Orinoco, failed to take Cumaná and was forced to exchange his prisoner, Trinidad governor Antonio de Berrío, for English casualties. That was on St John's Day, June 24, 1595. The church that you see, raised after the disastrous earthquake of 1929, is the last in a series begun in 1637. Alongside and up the hill are the inconspicuous ruins of **Santa María de la Cabeza** fort (1673). Continue to Plaza Rivero; in front you will see a crumbling stone wall, all that remains of the 17th-century **Convent of San Francisco** that served once as Cumaná's first university and ended as a soap factory. Resist temptation to wander up into the old section of town on the hills behind; it is a tough area. The rest of Cumaná is built on filled swamp. If you visit in the wet season you will note that some parts of the city simply have no drainage.

Museums

The equestrian statue and museum of the **Gran Mariscal de Ayacucho** are in Parque Ayacucho, two blocks from the Cathedral. The museum's ground floor displays portraits, weapons and relics of Antonio José de Sucre, Cumaná's most famous son, born in 1796. His Spanish father was governor of the Province of Nueva Andalucía and Guayana, and Antonio José began military training at the age of ten in the fort of San Antonio de la Eminencia. Before he was 16 he had joined the patriot army of Francisco de Miranda. A brilliant general and strategist, his victory at Pichincha in 1822 liberated Ecuador. Then in 1824 he won the Battle of Ayacucho which brought independence to Peru, earning him the title of Grand Marshal. The following year he thrashed royalists in Alto Peru and on the creation of Bolivia was elected president, proving to be an able administrator. Perhaps he was too able. Opponents of Bolívar's design to unify the liberated countries into Gran Colombia saw an enemy in Sucre, also. Attempts were made on Bolívar's life in Colombia, and in 1830 Sucre was ambushed and killed there. He was 35. The museum is open Mon–Fri 09.00–12.00, 15.00–18.00; weekends 16.00–21.00.

Museo de Arqueología e Historia, Calle Sucre No 25, has a display of archeological finds from Sucre State. It is followed by a cultural centre in the birthplace of José Antonio Ramos Sucre, then the tourist board offices, tel: 671022; they may have a map, or *plano*, of the city. As most of Cumaná does, these all close for a long lunch of 2½ hours.

The **Museo del Mar**, 1.5km south of town, on Av Universidad, occupies the former airport terminal. A coelacanth takes the place of honour in this museum. Collected by the oceanographic institute are some 10,000 specimens of crustaceans, fish and reptiles; exhibitions cover the continental drift, red tides and Venezuelan fishing craft. Hours are 08.30–11.30, 14.30–18.00, closed Monday.

Other attractions

Music Music is everywhere, from the solitary wanderer singing to the accompaniment of his *cuatro* (a four-stringed guitar), to groups of children drumming on discarded tins, to blaring 'minitecas' wheeled around town by sellers of bootleg cassettes. It is perfectly acceptable to dance as the mood strikes, whenever and wherever. For those who like a little more structure, popular *discotecas* are **La Tasca** on Calle Bolívar just down from Plaza Bolívar, and the **Acuario**, all flash, on Av Universidad. **'Un Café Llamado Deseo'** on Calle Sucre, just past Iglesia Santa Inés, offers an outdoor bar with live music provided by the house band.

Mercado Municipal The big market on Avenida El Islote is a must – by far the best public market in all the Oriente, large, open and well organised. Wander through the airy main building where fruits, vegetables and meats are sold, and around back to the '*playa*', the part where the trucks unload and vendors sell directly to the public. In this section you will find the freshest produce and best prices. You will have the opportunity to choose a live chicken and deliver it to be killed and plucked, get your hair cut, select some handmade cigars (a local speciality), buy shoes and clothing at the lowest prices around, eat and drink all manner of interesting things, and generally be dazzled. By the main parking entrance is an *artesanía* (crafts) section that sells pots, hats, birds, herbs, handmade furniture, a good variety of hammocks and souvenirs in general. It's open every day till noon, but best and busiest at weekends. During market hours almost all minibuses stop here. Look for the 'Mercado' card on the windscreen. All the local colour you can handle and then some.

Yacht marina The Marina Pública Cumanagoto on Av Perimetral offers an opportunity to rub shoulders with the yachting set and perhaps hitch a ride or secure a crew position. The marina has a coffee shop open to the public until midnight, **La Marina Café**, and a restaurant, **El Navegante**. The pharmacy has a used-book exchange with titles in English, Spanish, French and German. To enter the slip area you will need your passport, an invitation from someone with a boat, and a pass from the office. It is best to leave the bulk of your gear at the hotel and wear clean clothes.

Beaches Cumaná is known for its long beach and tranquil sea but they are unfortunately polluted by sewage and agricultural chemicals from the Manzanares River. This does not stop the Cumaneses, however, and on weekends and holidays they flock to the seaside. The main beach is **Playa San Luis** on Avenida Universidad reached via 'San Luis' minibuses. Dedicated beachgoers might like to walk west past Hotel Los Bordones to some quieter and (hopefully) less polluted shores. Observe standard security precautions.

Rio Cancamure When you need a break from the heat and bustle of the town, a dip in a cool river may provide the cure. Close to Cumaná is a small river, the Cancamure. Its upper reaches are beautiful and clean, although muddy after rain. This popular bathing area half an hour from town is served by the San Juan de Macarapana *por puesto* which leaves from Las Cuatro Esquinas, Av Arismendi, near El Cuartel (a military enclave). Spend the day, or the afternoon, and watch the iguanas playing in the coconut palms. The road runs beside the river and there are picnic shelters with tables, small shops in which to buy basics and on the busier days hot *empanadas* (turnovers), *tortillas* (omelettes), chicken and pork. Weekends and holidays bring crowds. Stop into the Bar Campo Lindo for a cold beer and a game of dominoes or *bolas criollas*, the Venezuelan game of bowls.

ARAYA PENINSULA

Araya is a long desert peninsula across the Gulf of Cariaco from Cumaná. Beaches on the Caribbean side are of broken shells with generally rough water. Swimming is best on western and gulf shores. The gulf is very deep and the water is cooler than one would expect, a welcome contrast to blazing sun. These depths are an important breeding ground for fish, and Araya's inhabitants are by and large fishermen.

Araya's industry is salt, mainstay of the town of Araya. People come daily from Cumaná to join the Arayans in salt exploitation. The *salinas* have been worked since 1499 when they were known as the world's richest and they still produce 500,000 tons a year. Seawater is evaporated from the salt, and the evaporation lagoon is an other-worldly pinkish mauve which must be seen to be believed. When you cross from Cumaná to Araya by ferry or launch you will see a mountain of salt off to the north. On work days, 06.00–14.00, you can ask at the Ensal offices about seeing the salt works. In one of the old salt pans a shrimp farmer is doing quite well breeding sea shrimp for export. The pink colour of evaporation pools comes, in fact, from microscopic shrimp. If you take the road north of the town to Punta Araya, you get a good view of the rectangular salt pools.

The same winds that dry the salt now make Araya an off-the-beaten-track destination for **windsurfing**. Winds are strong but with onshore/sideshore direction, not easy for beginners. Adepts use the beach near the fort.

The fort of **Santiago León de Araya** dates from 1622 and was built to protect the salt pans, mainly from the English and Dutch. Construction of this massive *castillo*, whose partly restored ruins may be visited just south of the town, took 47 years working largely at night to avoid the day's heat. You will see the fort as you approach Araya by sea. It is an easy walk from the village and has a good (but shadeless) beach.

If you plan to explore Araya's wilder beaches take good shoes for the rugged terrain and ubiquitous cactus. There's no shade; full sun protection is called for. Take a hat and carry water. Araya's roads are generally rough and unmarked, with very little traffic. Wildlife away from the road is surprising: lizards and snakes, birds perched on cactus tops and feral goats everywhere. There are foxes and rabbits as well but these are more difficult to see. The lagoon near Chacopata, about 50km east of the town of Araya, is known for its bird life, especially flamingos.

Getting there and away

By road *Por puestos* from Araya village go south to Punta Arenas and Manicuare, but no further. The main peninsular road runs along the north coast (the circle to Cumaná is 180km). Although there's no through bus, there are regular *por puestos* between Cariaco and Chacopata. Starting from Cariaco, the peninsular road goes via Campoma. Here a left fork leads along the Gulf of Cariaco's north coast. For Araya, the scenic, often solitary road heads north to a dramatic coastline of rocks and cliffs. The only turn-off is the 3km road to Chacopata, an unkempt village on Araya's northern point. From this fork the road goes west 50km to the pueblo of Araya, passing communities of subsistence fishermen: Caimancito, Taguapire, El Guamache.

Chacopata–Margarita boats A passenger boat service crossing from Chacopata to Margarita is gaining popularity. Like a *por puesto*, the boats of all sizes leave when they are full, until mid afternoon; the fare is $4 for the 1–2-hour trip. This service is used mainly by residents of eastern towns who take a *por puesto* from Cariaco or Carúpano. Drivers leave their cars by a Guardia Nacional post. *Peñeros* can be contracted to go to Coche Island, 40 minutes away.

By ferry Araya is accessible from Cumaná, 5km (1hr) by Naviarca's inexpensive open car ferry from the main dock at the foot of Av El Islote that serves the Margarita ferry and launch. Sailings are variable: morning (earliest at 06.00, often with a waiting queue), noon and afternoon on weekdays, and once on weekends at about 09.00. As the ferry goes when it fills up, on arrival check demand for the return so as not to get left high and dry. For information call Naviarca, tel: (093) 315577/2642.

By launch Passenger launches make trips throughout the day for about $1 from the ferry terminal. They are known as *'tapaitos'* which refers to their roofs or *tapas*. Most go to the port of Araya, and you can ask to be dropped on the way at **Punta Arenas**, a community with ample beach and pensions (see below). Others go to **Manicuare**, a gulf village known for its pottery, but it has nowhere to stay and the beach is nothing special. At holiday times you may find there are no *tapaitos*.

If your needs require other services, you can make a deal with the owner of a *peñero*, the wooden fishing launches with outboard motor to be seen everywhere. Your negotiations will be in the strong local dialect, a challenge for anyone and prohibitive for marginal Spanish speakers. You may be asked for money up front to buy gasoline for the trip. This is normal. If you are arranging for a pick-up as well as drop-off, do not pay in advance for the pick-up. In all dealings of this nature, as with taxi drivers, get an eyeball-meeting, hand-shaking agreement, or look for someone else. This will avoid misunderstandings and possible police intervention.

Where to stay
The area telephone code on the peninsula is (093)
Basic lodging, little more than fan, shower and bed, may be found in **Araya** village for about $8 a *matrimonial* (double bed). To find the six-room **Hospedaje de Petra**, tel: (093) 71335, ask on the street towards the Alcaldía. **Maita's**, tel: 71240, is near Malariología beyond the Alcaldía, six rooms. **Posada Guacamaya**, tel: 71087, is by Plaza Bolívar. **Posada Helen**, tel: 71101, near the fort, has 15 simple, clean rooms with private bath; single or double bed $10, triples $12.

Posada Araya Wind, tel: 71442, near the fort, is an attractive new magnet for windsurfers who park their 'sails' at the inn's shelter; 12 comfortable rustic rooms with fan and cold water, $10; some have private bath, $12.50. Restaurant.

In the village of **Punta Arenas** there are pensions offering beds, hammocks, meals and a quiet, slow pace; ask the launch to leave you directly on their beach. Facilities are 'rustic', with fan and shared bath, plus meals, for about $20. Most owners will arrange excursions on Araya, Margarita or the mainland. Multilingual Carlos has six spartan rooms for $20 per person with all meals at his **Posada Villa Arenas**. As there is no telephone, make arrangements through Caracas (02) 7612290. **Posada Shailili-Ko** has been here the longest: Arquímedes Vargas has made five quaint rooms and a small pool, set back in the village; two meals.

Churuatas Taguapire is the upscale alternative on the north coast, halfway to Chacopata. Overlooking, but not on, the beach it is an attractive layout of thatched bungalows and restaurant open to sea breezes, with pool, stables, courts for volleyball and *bolas criollas*. The idea is to offer Margarita travellers a trip by yacht to Araya. Plans cost $45 per person for lodging, three meals and horse riding; or $190 with a visit to Araya's beach, salt lagoons, and round-trip Margarita transfer. For information: tel: (014) 9958750; in Margarita, tel/fax: (095) 533739.

On Araya's south coast near Los Cachicatos, **Medregal Village** takes full advantage of the Gulf of Cariaco with its own beach and jetty, catamaran, pedal and motor boats, equipment for windsurfing, waterskiing, diving and snorkelling (and an instructor) – plus an amphibian ultralight. Twelve air-conditioned rooms have terrace and sea view. French chef Christian Protche makes this hotel an exceptional choice anywhere, no less than amazing on a back road 80km from the nearest town. With full meals, the price is $48 per person (double occupancy) to $39 (four persons); for 3-day/2-night package with return flight from Caracas for two people: $392. Tours, and boat transfer from San Antonio del Golfo, tel: (014) 9930700; in Caracas (02) 2632297, fax: 2631474.

EAST SUCRE STATE
The route to Paria Peninsula
The road leaving Cumaná follows the sheltered Gulf of Cariaco on one of the loveliest drives in the country. On tranquil shores there are three seaside places worth checking for a day's rest. Just before Marigüitar are the jetty, beach, pool and tennis court of the Swiss-managed **Maigualida Complex**, tel: (093) 91070, fax: 91084; two modern buildings have ten rooms with air conditioning and hot water at about $30 double, and four apartments with kitchen, $40. The big open-sided restaurant serves good, moderate food. Two kilometres west of San Antonio is **Balneario Cachamaure**, tel: (093) 93045, fax: 663616, set in a grassy park with coconut palms where **hot springs** feed a pool open to non-guests (small fee). There are shower facilities, shelters for camping and the grounds are fenced; 24 basic state-built *cabañas* (kitchen but no pots), four people $30. More hot sulphur springs are found in the sea at the west entrance to San Antonio; there's a concrete path (or look for people standing in the sea). An old house on the plaza in town serves as the **Hotel San Antonio del Golfo**, run by an Italian.

There are popular thermal pools beyond Cariaco to Casanay, a good choice being **Balneario Los Cocoteros**, (094) 319240, which has a restaurant; ask for a new air-conditioned room with hot shower, $20 for four.

Cariaco, an agricultural town of 15,000 people at the end of the gulf, bore the brunt of Venezuela's worst earthquake in thirty years on July 8, 1997. The quake of 6.9 on the Richter scale split streets, flattened most homes and buildings, and left over 70 dead, many of them school children. Cumaná and Cariaco are on not one but two active fault systems.

Carúpano
On a lovely bay 55km from Cariaco, Carúpano has a long history as trading and shipping centre for the Paria region. From the port it sends over two thirds of Venezuela's cacao crop to Europe and Japan, and tons of salted fish and shark. Carúpano also enjoys certain fame for rum distilleries: **Real Carúpano** made on Hacienda Altamira, Macarapana, and **El Muco** in town; you can visit El Muco's installations.

With a population of less than 100,000, the town has pleasant streets with well-kept old houses. A block from the shore drive, the sector around the old plaza and church of Santa Rosa de Lima has been renovated; a two-storey colonial house is now the **Museo de Historia de Carúpano**. A fine 19th-century building, **La Casa del Cable**, has also been restored by the Fundación

SUGAR, A BITTER-SWEET INDUSTRY
Chris Stolley

Sucre (which does not mean sugar) has two large sugar-producing areas, the wide valleys around Cumanacoa and Cariaco. In these towns are located big sugar refineries or *centrales azucareros*. Sugarcane has been planted on a large scale here for several hundred years, and remains of old water operated mills with their adjacent rum distilleries can still be seen. Sugar production is a difficult business as the world price is low. Even with Venezuela's inexpensive labour, competition is stiff. Cariaco's *Central* is privately owned and its owners have not found it profitable to buy all the local cane, a situation which has caused much distress and many confrontations.

Sugar production is an environmental disaster in all its aspects. A monoculture, cane is chemically fertilised and pesticided: a soil destroyer. Land retired from cane production is so exhausted as to be good for little else. Fertiliser and pesticide residues are washed into local water systems. The Manzanares River passing through Cumanacoa is heavily polluted and all ground water is affected as well. Prior to harvest the fields are burned to clear off the sharp-edged leaves and drive away snakes and insects. In the refineries, bagasse (the dried remains of pressed canes) is burned to provide heat for reduction of the juice. Smoke and ash from these processes produce an intense respiratory irritation known locally as 'Cumanacoaitis'. It is a vicious cycle, difficult to break because of massive dependence on this one crop.

Raw sugar loaves called *papelón* (conical) or *panela* (brick) are made on a small scale at numerous operations dotted around the countryside. The cane is pressed in a *trapiche* or heavy mill powered by a large displacement 'one lunger' diesel engine. The cane residue or *bagazo* (locally corrupted to 'gabazo'), dried in the road, provides fuel for the reducing process. This is generally a series of three deep iron basins set atop a stone base, mouth at one end to receive dry *bagazo*, chimney at the other. The raw juice called *guarapo* is poured into the first kettle. When the master stirrer and mixer decides it has reached the proper consistency, he dips it into the next kettle, usually with an aluminium hard-hat attached to the end of a long pole. After the final consistency is reached, the concentrated syrup goes into a cooling trough hollowed out of a solid log. It is then ladled into conical moulds made of fired clay. The sugar cools rapidly and is shaken out of the mould and wrapped in dry cane leaves for shipment and sale. The entire operation resembles scurrying slaves attending a dragon breathing fire at one end, expelling smoke at the other and with steam rolling off its back, all accompanied by the roar of the mill and motor. The final product has a rich brown colour and, freshly made, the better quality *papelón* will have a flavour not unlike maple sugar.

Proyecto Paria as a cultural centre. It is on Plaza Bolívar, 14 blocks southwest of Plaza Santa Rosa de Lima. In between, modern shops and office buildings are centred around Plaza Colón.

The town is famous for its **Carnival** celebrations, a week-long *bonche* with street dances, parades and costumes including figures from folklore such as the donkey-and-rider, followed on the next weekend by a last gasp called the Octavita. Hotel reservations are a must at this time; some charge what the traffic will bear. Other popular festivals celebrate the feast of **Santa Inés** on January 21, and the **Día del Carmen**, July 16, when the Virgin's statue is brought by sea from Guaca, escorted by fishing boats.

There are various travel agencies, among them **Venezuela Evasión**, Av Independencia 172, tel: (094) 319577/127, fax: 319403. For Playas Medina and Puy Puy: **Encuentro Viajes**, Carúpano airport, tel: (094) 315241/9932, fax: 312067. The offices of **Corpomedina**, Wilfried Merle's Paria development company, are on Plaza Santa Rosa de Lima, tel: (094) 312283/9724. Ask about the Río de Agua buffalo ranch, a cacao hacienda. Corpomedina has recently opened a guesthouse in town, La Colina (see below).

Getting there and away
By air The airport, 1.5km west of town, brings in tourists from Margarita and Caracas; LAI flies daily to Caracas, Porlamar, Ciudad Bolívar and Maturín. Carúpano is within easy reach not only of the Gulf of Cariaco, Araya and Paria Peninsulas, but also of the famous Guácharo Caves (see *Chapter 10*).

By bus The bus station is midway on Av Perimetral. There are frequent departures for Caracas (8–9 hours) and points west on the way, Cumaná, Puerto La Cruz; east to Güiria (2½ hours); and south to Ciudad Bolívar (6 hours). *Por puestos* to Río Caribe leave from El Kiosko restaurant, Av Perimetral, east. The line to Chacopata leaves from Av Perimetral, west, opposite the Mercado Municipal.

Where to stay
The area telephone code for Carúpano is (094)
European tourists, particularly Germans, are coming to Carúpano where there are now excellent places run by German/English-speakers. **Posada Nena**, tel: 317624, fax: 317297, is on Playa Copey, a broad beach 2km west of Carúpano; it has restaurant service in a thatch-roofed garden shelter (or borrow the grill for a beach barbecue); nine double and triple rooms with hot shower; double $20, triple, $26. Owners Volker and Minerva will rent you a bike or arrange a trip to Paria, Guácharo. **El Colibrí**, tel: 323583, is on Av Sur; ring owners Polly and Gunter Hoffmann for directions. Rather than a guest house, the Hoffmanns have built three two-floor houses around a pool enclosed by gardens and a wall; full kitchens, also palm-thatched restaurant; everything tops. The price is $60 for two, $75 for three.

The best city hotel is the **Victoria**, tel: 311554/3910, fax: 311776, Av Perimetral just before the port; it has a restaurant, small pool, 53 air-conditioned rooms on five floors, double $32. On the street above is **Posada La Colina**, tel: 320527, fax: 322915, a well-appointed 17-room guesthouse with sea view, small pool and restaurant, $38 for a double with breakfast. **Hotel María Victoria**, tel: 311170, a block west of the Victoria, has air-conditioned rooms at half the price.

The downtown **San Francisco**, tel: (094) 311074, fax: 315176, Av 4 Juncal 87A at Calle 11, and **Hotel Lilma**, tel: 311341, fax: 312424, Av 3 Independencia near Calle 12, charge $24 and $32 a double. Two blocks farther on Independencia is the **Ecuador**, tel: 313455, cheaper, with private bath.

Where to eat
Before you leave Carúpano, try the local cured sausages, *chorizos carupaneros*, which are sent all over Venezuela. **La Colina** has a restaurant by the pool, and an air-conditioned *tasca* indoors, both recommended. You can eat inexpensively on the beach at the **Café Boulevard** and the restaurant opposite, **Frente al Mar**, by the

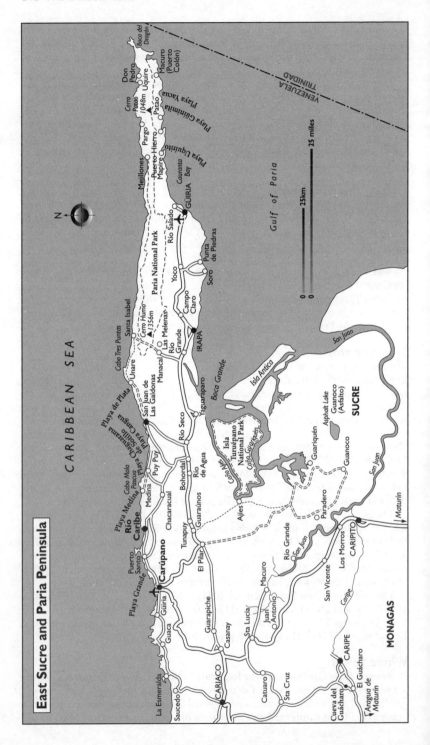

East Sucre and Paria Peninsula

port. The open-sided **El Kiosko** is perhaps the best known restaurant for its location on Av Perimetral at the foot of Av Independencia; it serves lots of seafood. **Trattoría La Madriguera** by the Plaza Santa Rosa serves the best Italian food. The **Lilma Restaurant** in the hotel has a reputation for good fish dishes, Spanish style. Among inexpensive 'luncherías', three on Av Juncal towards Plaza Bolívar serve Arab fare.

Río Caribe and Paria's north coast

From Carúpano two routes lead to Paria Peninsula. Most *por puestos* to Güiria go south and east via El Pilar, a total of about 160km. The route to Río Caribe passes picturesque fishing villages and beaches.

Along the lovely Caribbean coast 12km beyond Carúpano, a headland called **El Morro de Puerto Santo** juts into the sea. On either side of the narrow isthmus are bays: the colourful Puerto Santo fishing fleet anchors to the west; El Morro village where ship builders can be seen making *peñeros* separates the palm shaded eastern bay. Swimmers here are warned of strong undertows.

Río Caribe is 5km on. The old fishing port is gaining popularity among travellers for its charm and many *posadas*. It has some century-old houses, shady avenues, three plazas, two banks and a church. St Michael's, built soon after the settlement's founding in 1713, was rebuilt in 1919. At one time a rich centre of cacao exports, Río Caribe funnelled production from haciendas on Paria's southern drainage which receives more rain than the north. In the mid 1800s many immigrants from Corsica settled in the area and began coffee and cacao cultivation, acquiring large properties. Their names today are familiar among statesmen and doctors: Pietri, Luciani, Massiani.

The harbour shelters a very large and colourful fishing fleet. The fishermen who unload their catch by the Hotel Mar Caribe are able, and usually willing, to take you along the coast to Playa Caracolito, Chaguarama de Loero, Playa Medina (20, 30 and 45 minutes), or beyond.

Nature and wildlife excursions of one or more days are arranged by Cristina Castillo of the Papagayo (she speaks German) to the marshes and rivers of Caño Ajíes in Turuépano National Park; also to beaches without roads. In Río Caribe there is an office of the Fundación Proyecto Paria, Calle Rivero No 50, tel: (094) 61883; email: fppcarcs@telcel.net.ve. The Club Med people have targetted Playa Medina.

Where to stay

The area telephone code for Río Caribe is (094)

Río Caribe has good variety of *posadas*; many townspeople rent rooms so you can live with a family. Unless noted, guesthouses come with fan, cold water and shared bath, and accept only cash.

The best is **Posada Caribana**, tel: 61162/242, on No 25 Av Bermúdez, where Gonzalo Boulton has impeccably restored a colonial house; 11 comfortable rooms around a traditional patio, air conditioning or fan, private bath, hot water; per person, including breakfast, $65; with all taxes, meals and beach excursions by boat, $85 double occupancy (discounts for Venezuelan residents). Caribana will arrange tours around Paria, and pick up guests from the Carúpano airport, $10 round trip. For information in Caracas, also for Playa Uva, tel: (02) 2633649, 2659145, fax: 2639455. **Playa de Uva**, on a small, wild beach, is a charming *posada* with three rustic houses hidden among trees, 12 rooms with private bath, and restaurant.

A country alternative, **La Ruta de Cacao,** is 2km from Río Caribe, a big property where María Otilia rides horses and rents two rows of rooms with tiled roof and private bath, at $12–15 per person including breakfast. You can ride to hidden beaches on horseback, or visit cacao plantations. Airport pick-up.

Cristina Castillo's **Pensión Papagayo** (no sign), tel: 61868, faces the school on Calle 14 de Febrero, Plaza del Liceo, in one of those old houses whose charm is all interior, with patio and garden; four rooms and use of kitchen; $5 per person. **La Posada de Arlet**, 61290, is at No 22 Calle 24 de Julio where Arlet Scossa (who speaks five languages) offers tours, mountain bikes, and eight rooms with private bath, double $15, with breakfast $20. Señora **Ana Espín** lives at No 28 Av Bermúdez, tel: 61134; she has three rooms around a patio to rent for $8–10. Share the kitchen and family life.

At **Posada Cendal**, tel: 61079, on Calle Crispín Quijada, Luis Francisco and Antonieta have converted their second storey for guests, with two rooms, big breezy terrace and kitchen. **Posada San Miguel**, No 83 Calle Zea, tel: 61894; in a two-floor house, has 15 plain rooms with air conditioning, private bath and use of kitchen; double bed $10, two double beds, $14.

The single-storey **Hotel Mar Caribe**, tel: 61491/61494, which annexed a former colonial maize mill on the waterfront, provides 50 colonial-style rooms around a pool, double about $28 with breakfast; its kitchen has a reputation for good 'Riocaribeña' cooking. The other hotel, **Evelín**, tel: 61759, No 39 Av Bermúdez, has air conditioning; double bed $18.

To San Juan de Las Galdonas

There is no road from Río Caribe eastward. To reach the beautiful bays you must first take the southeast Bohordal route through lush cacao and coffee hills where Spanish moss (here called 'English beard' or *barba inglés*) festoons great trees. From this main road, four smaller ones branch northeast. Turn at Km 3 for Playa Caracolito, at Km 6 for the solitary beach of Chaguarama de Loero; at Km 18 for Playa Medina and Puy Puy; and at Km 25 for Playa Cangua and San Juan de Las Galdonas.

About 11km from Río Caribe in the pueblo of Chacaracual is **Hacienda Bukare**, a lodge opened by Billy Esser on a working cacao hacienda; tel: (014) 9940054. Bukare serves as a base for birdwatching tours to Paria Peninsula and treks to Cerro Humo and Caño Ajíes; also excursions to north-coast beaches by car and boat, and to the south coast as far as Macuro. The hacienda house has a restaurant, bar, and four large comfortable rooms with balcony, bath, hot water; each with capacity for four. Spacious grounds, swimming pool. For prices and airport transfer, contact Mareaje Tours, Av Bermúdez, Río Caribe, tel/fax: (094) 61543.

Campamento Bambusal gives good value at a sumptuously green hacienda, on the right, along the highway (passing the Playa Medina fork): 11 impeccable rooms with private bath in a great thatched house, river for swimming, all Paria excursions; per person (double occupancy), $36 with meals. For information, ring José Zapirain, tel: (093) 671344, fax: 671777.

The way to **Playa Medina** and **Puy Puy** forks left at Km 16. **Posada de Angel** in Medina village (6km) has 19 rooms with hot shower, and a big restaurant with hearty *criollo* food, $20 per room and transfer to beach. **Playa Medina** is 3km farther by a left fork, tucked in a lovely half-moon cove between two promontories. The cape on the right was named Cabo de Mala Pascua by Columbus when a storm drove him into the bay in 1498. The old hacienda of stately coconut palms will be the base of a Club Med. (Thames Investment holds shares in future hotels of 364 and 200 rooms.) In the meantime, under the palms there are eight charming cottages of rammed 'tapia' walls, red-tiled roofs and cane ceilings, and a beachside restaurant. Packages with all meals, drinks, and car from Carúpano are about $85 a person per night (discount for nationals). For other plans, with tours of a cacao plantation and water buffalo ranch, ring Encuentro Viajes (see *Carúpano*, page 215); in Caracas, Turismo Colorama, tel: (02) 2617731, fax: 2621828.

From the Medina's left fork, a rough road goes east 6km, ending at **Puy Puy**'s near perfect beach: a kilometre of soft golden sand where you can camp for $1 under palm trees. At the far end there are a couple of general stores. The sea is a little rough and the waves can get big enough for bodysurfing, but watch out for strange currents. There is an economical restaurant, plus 18 reservation-only cabins for two to four; $58 per person with all meals, or $25 for a double, no food. This is another development by Corpomedina (see page 215). You can stay in the pueblo of Puy Puy where Doña Paula has four rooms at $10, but it's 4km from the sea.

Return to the main road. At the next left in 7km, head back to the coast on a rough jeep road. This route to San Juan de Las Galdonas is not as good as the one east of Bohordal. But it passes Playa Cangua, and Querepare beach (where there is a camp), on the way. **San Juan** is a fishing village with a long beach stretching at the foot of a mountain, and a welcome from **Posada Las Tres Carabelas**, tel: (014) 9940346; 15 simple rooms with bath, some with a sea view, double $12. Their terrace restaurant's staple is fresh fish. Excursions by sea and on foot to Paria National Park can be arranged. Civilisation has arrived in San Juan in the shape of cassette players, those boom boxes that deny sleep, and, worse, narcotics. The old smuggling route between Paria and Trinidad has become drug highway, affecting lives along the way in San Juan. Travellers should take precautions against robbery, especially by young people.

The unpaved road ends in another 22km at **San Juan de Unare**. Beyond, fishermen can take you to still more remote beaches (see below, *Santa Isabel*). To return, take the better road from San Juan de Las Galdonas, 24km south to the main Carúpano–Güiria route.

Carúpano to Güiria

The road rises to verdant hills where cacao trees thrive in deep shade. You can see the beans drying in the sun around El Rincón and El Pilar. On the stretch east from El Pilar, there are two water-buffalo ranches. Turn right in 5.5km towards Guaraúnos to visit the camp of **Vuelta Larga**. At weekends, drop in for a sizzling lunch of roast buffalo served by Claus and Mayra Muller.

Finca Vuelta Larga The home of Claus Muller and his family is Campamento Vuelta Larga, 600m from the highway. His large *finca* (farm) and nature reserve lie 12km beyond, stocked with water buffalo from Australia. The wetlands are wonderful in late afternoon when parrots return to roost. From an observation hut on stilts you can see cayman, turtles, capybara, jabirú and many other water birds. Claus supports conservation programmes through ecotourism. He runs 1–5-day river trips by canoe with outboard motor, providing all camping gear and food, at a cost of about $70–77 a day. Mangrove fringed rivers such as Caño La Brea teem with wildlife including scarlet ibis, kingfishers, giant otter, Orinoco crocodile, and, if you're very sharp-eyed, manatee.

Claus also leads hikes in Paria Park and over Cerro Humo to Santa Isabel where there is a beach shelter; walking time about six hours. From Santa Isabel hikers return by sea to Carúpano. Together with the International Council for Bird Preservation and Pro Vita, the Vuelta Larga Foundation carries out environmental education work encouraging sustainable agriculture outside Paria Park. (Climate deterioration is evident in Paria, now hotter and drier with less cloud cover.) Projects include a honey farm and medicinal crops.

Claus speaks German and English, as do his sons who lead excursions. His address is No 8 Calle Bolívar, Guaraúnos, Estado Sucre; tel/fax: (094) 69052, 67292, best after 18.00. In Caracas, **Roymar Viajes** make reservations combining Vuelta Larga and four national parks: Mochima, Paria (beach), Guácharo and Turuépano, tel: (02) 5765655/5281, fax: 5766992.

The camp's palm-thatched buildings, with vents in the roof taking the place of fans and large windows of fine netting, are cool and mosquito-free. Claus has made many innovations besides a solar oven and a latrine that uses natural airflow. Lodging includes eight rooms, some with private bath, and two cabins; $77 per person with all meals. Spend the night and in the early morning take a walk by the marsh, habitat of an astonishing array of birdlife.

There are cacao plantations south of Guaraúnos, and then the horizon opens to marshes. A road continues to Ajíes, on Caño Ajíes which forms the northern boundary of Turuépano Park. These marshes and *caños* are the habitat of 160 different birds, including ten species of hawks and falcons, four kites, eight kinds of woodpecker, the great potoo, little tinamou and hoatzin.

Río de Agua The Corporación Bufalina de Paria station is 16km farther. The ranch may be seen on tours sold by Corpomedina (see page 215). There is an airstrip and guests can fly in direct from Carúpano. The property's 1,000 hectares stretch across floodplains to Caño Ajíes. Wilfried Merle, who like Claus Muller came to Paria over 35 years ago, introduced the first water buffalo, with much hard work and notable success. He dredged many kilometres of canals to allow navigation, and made electric fences with solar panels. Mozzarella cheese is one of the benefits of this industry, now also prospering in the Llanos.

Bird and buffalo watching, fishing, and river trips on Caño Ajíes are major attractions. Solar power, a biogas plant fed by buffalo manure, and water pumped by wind power support a camp of five Indian-style dwellings with bath and twin beds, plus a great cone-roofed dining shelter.

PARIA NATIONAL PARK

Paria National Park covers 375km² of the northern slopes and crest forming the backbone of Paria Peninsula. A few fishing hamlets dot bays at the foot of the coastal range which rises almost straight from the sea. Highest peak is **Cerro Humo**, 1,356m. This is an area of superb cloudforest, remarkable because it grows as low as 800m elevation. Many palms, tree ferns, lianas, epiphytes and huge buttressed trees thrive in drenching conditions created partly by condensation recycled by the forest itself. These mountains are described as once forming part of a 'forest island' which included Trinidad and as such are the refuge of endemic species. The scissor-tailed hummingbird, Venezuelan flower-piercer, white-throated barbtail, spiny rat and black nutria live here only. Chris Sharp has compiled a list of the birds of Paria Peninsula. On hikes to Cerro Humo and Cerro El Olvido near Macuro, he has seen more than 225 species. Chris is a birding guide and trekker; for information, ring tel/fax: (02) 749701, email: rodsha@true.net.

However, only half Cerro Humo is legally protected, and there are only half a dozen *guardaparques* or rangers to patrol the entire park. The forest is affected by farm clearing, especially in the south where villages are expanding.

The area is targeted for development. Under the name of Christopher Columbus Project, oil companies hope to export a yearly 4.6 million tons of liquefied natural gas. Offshore fields on the Caribbean side will send gas to Mejillones, then across the peninsula to a plant on the gulf side.

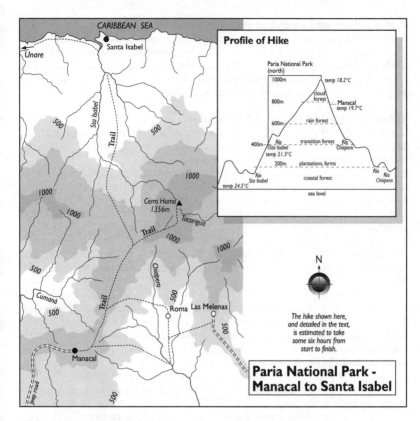

Profile of Hike

Paria National Park
(north)

1000m — temp 18.2°C
cloud
forest
800m — Manacal
temp 19.7°C
600m — rain forest
400m — Rio transition forest Rio
Sta Isabel Chispero
temp 21.3°C
200m — plantations, farms
Rio Rio
Sta Isabel coastal forest Chispero
temp 24.5°C
sea level

N

The hike shown here,
and detailed in the text,
is estimated to take
some six hours from
start to finish.

**Paria National Park -
Manacal to Santa Isabel**

Manacal to Santa Isabel
Mark Dutton, Justine Freeth, Peter Ireland and James Mead

There is some good hiking around Cerro Humo, using Manacal as a base. The village is on the top of a ridge. Of the 30 families, 25 are evangelicals, and the others think they are mad. At night, the light outside the evangelist church flashes in the mist instead of a bell; there is a two-hour service every night. If you want to see how hard these farmers work, ask to go with someone to their *conuco* or plot. They grow maize, roots such as *ñame* (yam), *ocumo* (dasheen), *yuca* (cassava) and *mapuey* (cush-cush), and bananas and plantains.

Ask the *comisario* if you can camp, or possibly stay in the school. Nights are cold enough for a sleeping bag in your hammock. Food in the village shop is limited to basics: sardines, spaghetti, sugar, wheat and cornflour. Or with some advance notice, ask a señora to cook up some yams or yuca; or perhaps a *dumplín* which is a great wheat arepa. The villagers are not set up for tourism in any way but are very generous. If they do not charge you, be prepared with presents: good string, scissors, lighters, cigarettes, pencils, paper, or whisky (everyone has rum). [Publisher's note: if bringing presents choose them with care. Anything that increases consumer awareness for goods normally unobtainable may ultimately do more harm than good. Giving sweets to children, for instance, will create little beggars and cause tooth decay. Give to the adults to whom you owe a debt of gratitude and play with the children. This gift will last in terms of goodwill.]

Getting there and away The *por puesto* to Río Grande de Irapa on the Güiria route should leave you at the entrance road (left) to Manacal; specify 'Manacal arriba de Río Grande' so as not to confuse it with another Manacal beyond Irapa. Only 4x4 vehicles can make it to Manacal, otherwise it's a three-hour hike up to 800m elevation. One or two vehicles go up each day. If you can catch a ride, it may be possible to pay the driver to go all the way (about $5).

Hikes to Cerro Humo and Santa Isabel

You will need a guide for hiking, not only because the way is not always clear, but because of accidents or snakes (the nearest hospital is in Carúpano). Cipriano is a good guide (about $5 the day); or ask the *comisario*.

The trail to Santa Isabel first leads to towards Cerro Humo and Roma, another high village on the south slope. Keep on up the ridge. After the turning for Roma, you come to a cleared area with views north and south, as far as Irapa and the Delta. You have to step over a large stone before re-entering cloudforest. At a high point, 1,000m, a tree on the path is marked with an E and a K. The K is for the path to Santa Isabel. The E stands for Entrada or entrance to Cerro Humo. This path drops before a final ascent to the peak (3 hours). The top is a cleared plateau with a surveying point, though trees tend to obscure the view.

From the K, the left path to Santa Isabel makes a steady descent to the sea, crossing beautiful streams as you pass through primary forest, then cultivations. Before you reach the village you have to wade through the Río Santa Isabel; idyllic pools shaded by the forest are just large enough for swimming. The whole walk takes about six hours.

Santa Isabel, above the river mouth, is used to tourists. It has a paved main street, normally covered in fishing nets with fishermen repairing holes. The atmosphere is different from that in Manacal; the people seem more industrious. Boats come into the river to unload. The sea here is rough and there are sea-urchins on the rocks. For swimming it's best to stick to the river. Or continue on a path which drops into the next cove east, with a long deserted beach. To stay in Santa Isabel, ask for Mayra's house which has a fantastic view of the sea and a small island. Mayra provides a very inexpensive bed or hammock, and a meal of fried fish, rice and *plátanos*.

To leave, you can take a boat to Unare (1¼ hours); price is negotiable. You get fantastic views of forest coming down to the beach. It is possible to arrange for a boat to drop you off on such a beach for a day or so. Unare is at the end of the jeep road on the north coast and there are *por puestos* to Río Caribe.

Güiria

Wooden lattices, fretwork and some slate-tiled roofs give Güiria a Caribbean flavour. This is a sizeable fishing port with an ice plant for the modern trawlers which fish the rich **Golfo de Paria**. To have a look at the bay, walk down from the church on Plaza Bolívar; the new international port with its docks is on the right. North of the docks are yards where ships are repaired and built of wood. On the beach wooden boats are drawn up and repaired. A kiosk has a few tables serving economical fried fish, *arepas,* and *hervido*.

Getting there and away

There is a small airport within walking distance of town but scheduled service has been suspended for some time. All travel to Macuro and points on the south coast of Paria Peninsula beyond Güiria is by boat.

By bus From Caracas' Terminal de Oriente, Expresos Güiria and Los Llanos stop in Barcelona and many other towns en route to Güiria (700km, 12 hours), $14. Many buses travel at night, and the next day at 07.30 return to Caracas. Buses stop at Plaza Sucre where the highway enters town, six blocks from the bay. *Por puestos* run between Carúpano and Güiria (2 hours).

By boat The international port on the south end of the bay handles larger vessels such as the **Windward Lines ferry** which carries 250 passengers and up to 40 cars. A weekly maritime service by Windward Lines is providing a 'bridge' between Venezuela and the Antilles. The agents are Acosta Asociados, Calle Bolívar 31, opposite Banco Unión; tel: (094) 81233, 820058, fax: 81679. The ferry leaves Güiria at 23.00 every second Wednesday (alternating with Pampatar) for Trinidad, arriving there at 06.30 Thursday. The air-conditioned ship continues up the Lesser Antilles cruising at night (13.5 knots) and calling in at St Vincent, Barbados and St Lucia before completing the circle back to Venezuela. Fares range from US$60 one way to Trinidad ($80 return), up to $108 to St Lucia ($174 return), not including restaurant or porters. Tickets are cheaper when bought on board, and there's a discount for seniors. Forty cabins offer twin berths at $10 a night per person. There is a port tax and an exit tax. You should have a passport, and ongoing ticket for the islands.

The *peñeros* going to Macuro pull up near a kiosk at the left end of the bay. They mostly leave by mid-morning, after the daily market, but you should start queuing before 08.00. No service on Sunday. The 30km trip takes almost two hours and a *puesto* costs about $10. There is infrequent service to Paria's north-coast villages.

For boats to the **Orinoco Delta**, ask fishermen who is going to Pedernales, more than twice the distance (and cost) of Macuro. This is an oil base at the outlet of the Pedernales River, an arm of the Delta reaching Tucupita.

Where to stay
There are several cheap hotels at $10–12 for a double bed: the **Plaza Hotel** on Plaza Bolívar is perhaps the best, with air conditioning, and its restaurant is OK. Family-style rooms (two air-conditioned, eight with fans) are rented out by Leonor de Smith, **Hotel Oriente**, Calle Pagallos. **Hotel Gran Puerto** tel: 81343, Calle Pagallos at Bideau, has small rooms and a cold showers. Up a notch are: **Residencia Gran Puerto**, Calle Vigirima south of Plaza Bolívar, tel: 81085, with fan or air conditioning; and **La Posada de Chuchú**, tel: (094) 81266, on Calle Bideau, a block from bus line offices; restaurant and nine air-conditioned rooms, hot water, TV.

Macuro
Near the peninsula's tip, closer to Trinidad than to Güiria, is Macuro, also called Puerto Colón in honour of Columbus' only landing on the American continent. On the 500th anniversary, August 5 1998, Macuro was declared capital of Venezuela for one day and President Caldera led the speeches. Promises had been made to build a dock, cobblestone the streets and improve public services. But what people saw was a refurbished reading room with a plaque crediting the Spanish Embassy and cooperation agency. President Caldera promised a boat repair yard, and a 48-passenger launch (to be maintained through fare income). An international youth delegation, Ruta Quetzal, donated 2,000 books and maps for the library, and offered an ambulance launch financed by Unesco.

The names in Columbus' log are still in use: the Indians called the land Paria and their village Amacuro, now shortened to Macuro. Columbus' ships passed from Trinidad, which he named for its triple peaks, through straits roaring with tides of sweet water; he called the straits Serpent's Mouth and Dragon's Mouth. Columbus at first named Paria *Isla de Gracia*, 'island of grace', because he was so impressed by its amiable natives, their farms, houses and pearl necklaces. But after he had sailed for two days into the Gulf of Paria, he wrote that he had found either paradise on earth, or a continent big enough to contain a huge river the likes of which he had never seen. Pressed for time, however, he and his men never entered the Orinoco Delta.

On the shore a bronze statue of Columbus is almost the tallest structure in Macuro. It formerly stood on the steps of El Calvario in Caracas and was presented to Macuro in 1968. Few dilapidated wood and plaster houses remain from the port's heyday in the 1930s. There was a governor in residence then and the town was the country's head customs office (Dictator Gómez wished to sidestep a debt agreement giving the British in La Guaira rights to collect customs fees).

The **Museo Macuro** occupies an old house dating from the Gómez era when an escapee from Devil's Island painted a mural showing the harbour full of ships. The museum has been put together by Eduardo Rothe out of fossils, pre-Columbian pottery, even a handmade aeroplane. Rothe calls Macuro 'the first and last town in Venezuela'. Most of its 2,300 inhabitants subsist on fishing and small farm plots. There is said to be illegal trading with Trinidad, and the area is a natural route for cocaine traffic and parrot and macaw smuggling through the Delta.

Macuro has a preschool and medical aid post, but no sewer, street lighting or telephones. The town consists of no more than a dozen streets. The beach is not idyllic because the water is brown from the Orinoco Delta. Macureños go up to a little rocky river for swimming. Aside from fishing, the only stable source of employment was for decades a nearby gypsum mine. But the plant is closing down.

Where to stay

Posada Reyes Católicos has four clean simple rooms with bath and ceiling fan; $10 per person; meals provided for $5. Four small houses on concrete stilts were built in the village to house dignitaries for Columbus' 500th; they were designed in wood by architect Fruto Vivas, and they are intended for use as a *posada*. Other lodging consists of rooms for rent in two or three houses; look for a place where you can use the kitchen. You can ask for Doña Angelina, Doña María or Señora Rodríguez who makes good food (chicken, fish). Or you can camp with a tent or hammock. There's plenty of firewood on the little beach and you can buy fresh fish from fishermen. Don't buy the meat or eggs of turtles – *tortugas* – which are an endangered species. Other food supplies should be brought with you since they are very expensive in Macuro.

Macuro to Uquire

The paths in the forest above Macuro are worthwhile. As there are no marked trails and the paths constantly change course to new plots or *conucos*, you will need a guide. The park guard can locate guides. None is better than a local farmer (*conuquero*), who is usually expert with a machete and knows how to deal with snakes. Paria is known for its bushmasters or *cuaimapiña*, and fer-de-lances or *mapanares*. Give him $10 for a day on the trails. Best to set off before 07.00 to make time before it gets hot. Water is available in mountain streams. Use insect repellent.

Two trails lead from Macuro in about six hours' hard walk to the north coast where there are crystal clear waters, rocky shores and two villages: **Uquire** and **Don Pedro**. Uquire is a large village with a fantastic beach, good snorkelling and palm trees. Don Pedro, two hours by trail from Uquire, is smaller, like a village abandoned by time. You should be able to return to Macuro by boat.

From Macuro, you walk up through shady coffee and cacao plantations to enter the wilder national park. You will probably hear, if not see, the red howler monkeys, among the few noisy wild animals. The tail end of the Serranía de Paria is here not much over 1,000m altitude. On the way down you see signs of the woods having been disturbed by hunters. The trail divides: east for Don Pedro, and west for Uquire. Choosing Uquire, you thread through plantations of cacao, mango, avocado and banana as the path, and a little river, come down to the sea. Nestico, the park guard, lives in a house under palm trees, one of about two dozen dwellings. Prepare yourself for an idyllic half-moon bay, backed by forest, edged by beach. At either end, there are cliffs. And in the cliffs there are sea caves, the first in Venezuela known to harbour guácharos (the same oilbirds that live in the Guácharo Cave).

Uquire has little in the way of supplies, except for a well-patronised bar. The boat ride back to Macuro takes two hours in an open *peñero* or fishing boat.

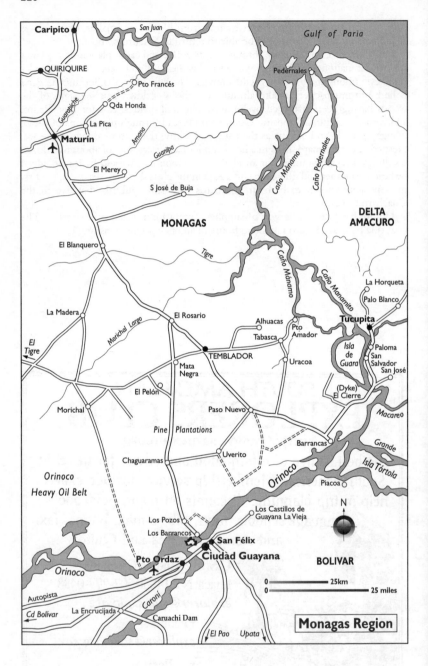

Monagas Region

Monagas and the Orinoco Delta

From its mountain border with Sucre, Monagas State slopes to lowlands and the Orinoco. Guácharo Cave, famous for its nocturnal oilbirds, is located in the hilly north. Rivers run east into the Gulf of Paria and the Orinoco Delta. Monagas provides the main route to Tucupita, capital of Delta Amacuro State. In the south, once empty plains are now green with vast pine plantations. The capital, Maturín, is the boomtown of Venezuela's great eastern oilfields. More than ten thousand reservoirs have already pumped 4,000 million barrels of crude, although few derricks are to be seen. The Furrial field near Maturín is expected to produce 500,000 barrels a day.

CARIPE

Just across the Monagas border is a small mountain town, the centre of an area producing coffee, citrus fruit and vegetables. At 900m elevation it is Oriente's mountain retreat. The pace is slow and the people are relaxed and friendly. Jeep roads climb through coffee plantations to the forest with its birdsong, giant tree ferns, and festoons of orchids and bromeliads. Trails criss-cross the area and local guides can lead you to hidden waterfalls or to the peak of **Cerro Negro**, at 2,400m the highest around. The mountain climate is a welcome relief from the heat of the coast.

Caripe is best known for the **Guácharo Cave** (see below, *Parque Nacional El Guácharo*). The cave is located about 10km northwest of the town, above the village of El Guácharo.

Getting there and away
By *bus*

The distance from Cumaná to Caripe is 127km, to Guácharo Cave 117km. The road forks at Cariaco Gulf just past Villa Frontado (Muelle de Cariaco) and climbs into very pretty mountains. Buses depart at 07.15 and 12.30 from **Cumaná**, and take about three hours. In **Caripe** the bus depot is behind the market; departures for Cumaná at 06.00 and 12.00 (check times); buses can be flagged on the highway as well. A night bus goes to **Caracas** by way of Maturín. Buses and *por puestos* leave throughout the day for Maturín, 105km.

Where to stay/eat
The area telephone code for Caripe is (092)
Caripe

In town there are three recommended hotels. **Hotel Samán**, tel: 51183, No 29 Av Enrique Chaumer; has a solar heated pool, good restaurant and cake shop; 34 rooms (some with no exterior windows), about $18 double. A short walk west of

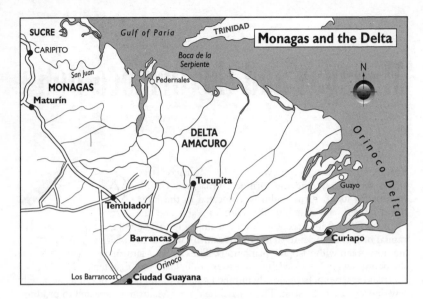

town, on the route to the cave, is **El Guácharo Hotel**, tel: 51218; with a restaurant, pool with bar, 40 rooms with TV and hot water, double $20. A good choice for its restaurant is the small **Venezia**, tel: 51875, Av Enrique Chaumer near the gasoline station; 16 clean rooms, double $14. **Hotel Caripe** is a budget hotel on the main street, double about $8; restaurant.

La Casona Vacation Rooms, north of Guácharo Cave at San Agustín fork, tel: (016) 6912719, (091) 427642; has six basic rooms with hot water, $12.

El Guácharo

Hospedaje Pomareda, tel: 51134, off highway, near the cemetery; is a house with four rooms, hot shower, plus a two-bedroom cabin with kitchen, and a garden *caney* for morning hot chocolate; double $10, three to four people $12. The owner speaks some English. **Hospedaje Mostaza**, (014) 9915938, behind Restaurant Mostaza, leaving El Guácharo; five rooms with hot shower, TV; $12 for two or three; $16 for four. Mostaza is owned by Beatriz and Frank Gómez who have another good restaurant, La Solana (same phone) and adjacent cabin for up to five people, $15, on the way to Guácharo Cave.

Fincas

Many pleasant country *cabañas* give good value with private bath, hot water, and cooking facilities for four to six people, at about $30; rooms with double bed, $15. The latest trend is 'agroturismo', inviting travellers to lodge at fruit farms (*fincas*) and coffee plantations. Accommodation is comfortable and the food is home cooked, farm fresh. The places listed below have restaurants. As the Caripe area is a popular family vacation spot, facilities are booked solid during school holidays. Reservations are recommended.

Cabañas Bellermann, tel: 51326, 7km from the caves on San Agustín–Caripe road. On a working coffee hacienda at 1,200m elevation, six spotless bungalows for two to six people; double bed $36. Their shop is famous for cakes, jams, hot chocolate and coffee liqueur, all made on the spot. The Bellermann also runs a good restaurant, **Las Delicias del Valle**, farther on.

Hacienda Campo Claro, tel: 551013, 70ha farm in the hills of Teresén-Santa Inés; 12 rooms and eight stone cabins for five. Owners Francisco and Nery Betancourt show guests the steps of coffee making and orange cultivation and processing. There are horses for hire and trails to nearby haciendas. Breakfast for guests and non-guests: coffee, orange juice, bread and jam, butter, cheese, milk and eggs, all from the farm.

Finca La Coradeña, tel: (016) 6912236, 3km southwest of El Guácharo (pueblo); a 60ha farm with ten rooms for two to three people, cabins for six. Restaurant serves hearty breakfasts, fresh country food. Owners Lesbia and Corado Machuca make renowned liqueurs of rose petals, orange, passionfruit and coffee. They take guests to waterfalls and woods.

Hacienda La Cuchilla, tel: 51331, 51469 (evenings), 3km beyond La Cuchilla. Mariflor and Luis Leopardi run a fruit and coffee farm where they have built ten cabins and double rooms. Their country restaurant is open to all at breakfast. The coffee farm is open to visitors during harvest season, Nov–Jan. Horses, trails.

PARQUE NACIONAL EL GUÁCHARO

The highway crosses the national park and dips down from the mountain crest, passing in front of the park office. Directly opposite is the mouth of **Guácharo Cave** which faces west. The cave was named Venezuela's first Natural Monument in 1949 and 627km² were declared a national park in 1975. A dawn or dusk visit will be rewarded by a view of the clamorous entry or exit of thousands of nocturnal guácharos. It is possible to camp overnight for a park fee of $2.50, when the park closes.

There is a restaurant and museum. The **Speleological Museum** displays findings from over 40 years of underground explorations in Venezuela, including spectacular crystals, fossils, Indian bones and archeological pieces. The upper floor is dedicated to Alexander von Humboldt, his maps, drawings and works.

The cave is open daily, 08.00–16.00; entrance charge is $12. It gets chilly so bring a jacket. You may take a camera but are not permitted to use a flash in the birds' roosting area. Visitors enter in guided groups of ten for an hour's tour. The

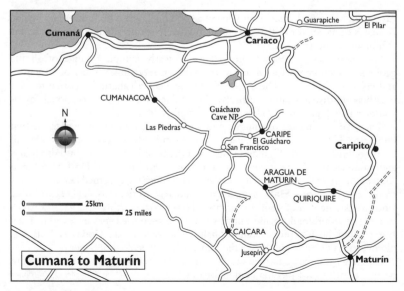

Cumaná to Maturín

THE CAVE OF THE GUACHAROS
Chris Stolley

The Cueva del Guácharo is named for, and is home to, approximately 18,000 guácharos or oilbirds (*Steatornis caripensis*). The Spanish name refers to one who sobs or laments, as they do. The English name refers to the fact that the young birds were once hunted and rendered for their tremendous fat content. The adult bird weighs about one third that of the young, the difference being solid fat. The young fatten on oil-rich nuts of seje palm, and at adulthood purge the oil by eating the fruit of the cobalonga tree.

This unique bird, which has a wingspan of a metre, has several features found in no other bird. It is the only bird known to fly in complete darkness, finding its way like a bat by the echo of sounds made by clacking its beak. You will hear this sound in the cave. It is the only nocturnal bird that is not carnivorous and it eats only on the wing, grabbing food in its beak. There has been much speculation, often conflicting, about the habits of the guácharo. The birds were once thought to fly as far as Brazil in their nightly search for the 32 kinds of fruit that make up their diet. It is now thought that they fly no more than 50km. Guácharos live in a number of other caves, 30 to 87 by various counts, and share their home with other cave-adapted creatures, including fearless smooth-furred brown rats. Bats, unable to manage a peaceful coexistence, live in their own part of the cave. This is the **Hall of Silence**, so named for the abrupt absence of bird sounds. The entrance is a bottleneck through which the birds cannot pass.

The cave has been known to Europeans since 1660. In 1799 Alexander von Humboldt, the famous German explorer, visiting the cave, described and named the oilbirds. His Indian guides would only permit him to go as far as the entrance to the Hall of Silence, to them the entrance to the world of the dead. In 1953 electric lights were installed. The birds abandoned the cave in great numbers, and only returned when the lights were removed.

cave guides are poorly paid, so if you get a good one, please tip him. A good guide is Carlos Luna, son of a 30-year veteran guide. He speaks adequate English and is a fountain of information.

Guácharo Cave is considered to have a nearly complete range of all the geological phenomena found in caverns, with an incredible variety of structures and crystals of all sizes. These are found in its deeper galleries, reported to have breathtaking displays rarely seen elsewhere. The cave is also exceptional for its complex fauna: pink fish, rodents, spiders, millipedes and bats.

The cave has 10.2km of galleries and visitors are allowed to penetrate the first kilometre. The entrance cavern, named after Humboldt, is a vast chamber 40m tall where oilbirds roost on high dim ledges and the floor is thick with bird droppings and palm seeds. The next part is a tunnel of 759m called the **Hall of Silence** (because there are no birds); stalactites and stalagmites have formed here. After this comes the **Precious Hall**, named for wonderful formations. The **Humboldt Pool** marks the end of your exploration. To penetrate farther you have to pass a channel of water 2m deep and a semi-siphon and then use ropes up an 80m slope. But beyond lie the most fabulous halls. The spectacular **Codazzi hall** was discovered as recently as 1967 by the Venezuelan Speleological Society.

Cavers wishing to go farther should contact the speleological groups and secure written permission from the National Parks head office. (See *Chapter 3, National*

Parks.) Include passport details of the whole group, take photocopies of everything and allow six weeks.

Modern speleology in Venezuela began in 1952 under the umbrella of the Venezuelan Society of Natural Sciences. Their cavers formed the Venezuelan Speleological Society to continue field investigations. According to these, the three longest caves in Venezuela are: Cueva El Samán in Zulia, 18,000m (really the tunnel of an underground river); Cueva del Guácharo in Monagas, 10,200m; and the Cueva-Sumidero La Retirada in Zulia, 6,080m. For information, fax: (02) 746436, 2429001; email: chico_wilmer@yahoo.com, and carlosb@usb.ve.

MATURIN

The state capital, long the area's trading and oil centre, offers travellers broad, tree-lined streets and pleasant parks, but little reason to linger. The Guarapiche River, on which it was founded in the 18th century, was then navigable to the Gulf of Paria by way of the San Juan. In 1797 a British force from Trinidad actually occupied Maturín. For 200 years Maturín traded mainly with the island, only 100km away by boat, until oil companies built a road link from El Tigre. Now a large oil terminal is planned for the old river pueblo of Puerto Francés, named after French buccaneers.

Today, there is a frenzy of activity, result of the government's opening of the oil industry through concessions to foreign companies for the first time since oil nationalisation in 1976. You see drilling rigs, contractors setting up camps, service trucks. For Maturín, this has meant explosive land development in suburbs, particularly north of the city. Going up are residential areas with names like Laguna Country Club, Altos de Golf, Monagas Country Club. These are accompanied by shopping malls: Centro Comercial Petroriente and Monagas Plaza in the north; CC Bolívar in the center, and CC Cascada in the south. The first, already known as the CCP, is near the headquarters of British Petroleum and PDVSA, in tract of 12 hectares.

Population today is about 315,000 and growing fast. Maturín, often called the new oil capital of Venezuela, is just 25km from El Furrial, centre of the largest oil discovery since 1970. At night, driving west, you pass scores of lighted drilling towers and producing wells with flares of burning gas. These are deep wells, 5,000 to 6,000 feet.

Getting there and away
By air
The international airport is 2km east of town, reached via Av Bolívar. There are eight daily flights and four on weekends from Caracas ($70), two from Barcelona, Barquisimeto, Carúpano, Ciudad Bolívar and Puerto Ordaz; 4–5 each from Maracaibo, Porlamar ($30). The airlines are: Aeropostal, Aereotuy, Aserca, LAI and Rutaca. Rutaca, (091) 421635, flies to Trinidad on Mon, Wed, Fri ($115); and Avior, (091) 432626, also takes charters.

By bus
Buses leave from the Terminal de Pasajeros on the opposite side of town where Avenidas Orinoco and Libertador intersect. Caracas is served by *expreso* and *ejecutivo* coaches; you can count on them for night departures. Buses and *por puestos* go to Tucupita (4 hours), Ciudad Guayana (3½ hours), Caripe (3 hours) and Carúpano (3½ hours). The Aeroexpresos Ejecutivos terminal, tel: (091) 513695, is on Av Libertador near Calle Principal Los Guaros; departures at 08.30, 22.45 for Caracas; 21.00 for Maracay and Valencia.

Where to stay

The area telephone code for Maturín is (091)

Due to the area's economic boom, accommodation in this business city can be expensive and hard to come by, but holidays and weekends can offer bargains. Out of town 3km west via La Cruz is the 5-star **Morichal Largo**, tel: 516122/4222, fax: 515544, reservations 800 52746; 210 rooms, two pools, gym, tennis; double $230 weekdays, $140 weekends. Executives go to the **Stauffer**, tel: 430622, fax: 431455, Av Alirio Ugarte Pelayo; 240 rooms and pool. A Best Western hotel is to open late 1999: the **Casa Grande Suites** with two pools, spa and heliport, 500 suites with Internet access, located in the Petroriente shopping centre.

A moderate downtown hotel is the **Perla Princess**, tel: 432579/2754, fax: 414008, Av Juncal near Av Bolívar; double $40. In the same range is many people's favourite for its location and service, the **Colonial**, tel: 421183, Av Bolívar near the Cathedral. More moderate hotels are located in western Maturín, not far from the very active bus terminal. With three floors, air conditioning and restaurant are: the **Hotel Friuli**, tel: 414162, Calle 30 at Carrera 9; the **Emperador**, tel: 414182/85, Av Bolívar Oeste-Bicentenario, around the corner from the Friuli; and the **Hoja Dorada**, tel: 517198, Av Libertador near Plaza El Indio and the bus terminal. More expensive is the **Monagas Internacional**, tel: 518811, fax: 518727, on Av Libertador by the bus station; double $74, weekends $55.

Near Plaza Bolívar is the cheap **Iruna**, tel: 429486, Carrera 7 No 64. There are more inexpensive hotels near Plaza Ayacucho at about $12 a double: the **Mallorca**, tel: 427064/8650, Carr 6 at Calle 17; **Europa**, tel: 428292; **Galicia**, tel: 413080; **La Trinidad**, tel: 429356.

RIO MORICHAL LARGO

At the bridge over the Río Morichal Largo, 82km south of Maturín, you can hire a boat from the Warao people selling crafts on the east side. On the west, where cars park, are some of the boats of tour operators. The river flowing to the Delta has an abundance of wildlife including troops of howler and capuchin monkeys, and the remarkable hoatzin. This bird, called *chenchena* or *guacharaca de agua*, is distinguished by its raucous call and disagreeable strong musty odour. They are clumsy fliers and are easily heard as they flounder about in the trees. Several features single them out among birds: their diet (leaves), digestive process (two stomachs, like a cow) and the presence of a hook at the 'elbow' of wings in fledglings which allows them to escape predators by dropping into the water then climbing back to their nests, using these hooks and their strong feet. You may see cayman or *babas*, the infamous anaconda and piranhas or *caribes rojos* as they are locally called. (No swimming in the river.)

On its way to join the Mánamo the river runs through gallery forests and *morichales*, stands of mauritia palms. This palm yields food and fibre for rope, baskets and hammocks for the Warao natives who live there. You will see them in their stilt houses (known as *palafitos*) along the bank, and in their canoes. For those who do not have the time, endurance or money to go on a full-fledged river expedition, this is a good chance to see this type of country.

Sergio Córdoba leads day tours and overnight trips staying at **Campamento Boral** which has doubles with private bath and solar lighting. Prices run from $60 per person for the lowest-priced day tour, to $115 for 2 days/1 night. All food and drink are included, and transfer from Maturín. Córdoba's company is in downtown Maturín, tel: (091) 414122, fax: 426647; Of 3A, Edif Banco Unión, Av Juncal. Other Maturín agencies doing this trip are Quintero Tours, tel: (091) 512775, and Centro del Mundo, tel: 413533.

Campamento La Tigra, about 40km west of Maturín, is a well-run lodge on a dairy and fruit farm: large swimming pool, four *churuatas* for open dining, and air conditioned cabins with hot showers, all set in neatly trimmed lawns. On a 4-day/3-night plan designed for European tourists, excursions include the Guácharo Cave, coffee hacienda, and Río Morichal Largo. The price of $300 includes transfer from Maturín airport. For information about arriving by car, tel: (092) 32842, tel/fax: 36576.

ROUTE TO THE DELTA

South of the Río Morichal bridge the highway forks at El Rosario. The right-hand route goes southwest to the Orinoco River (82km) where a ferry crosses from **Los Barrancos** (not to be confused with Barrancas on the left fork) to **Ciudad Guayana**. On the way you drive through vast Caribbean pine plantations around Chaguaramas. Intended for a pulp and paper plant, the pine trees cover 3,000km² and have converted arid sandy plains into a greener, cooler ecosystem now supporting a variety of birds as well as animals such as deer.

Off the southeast route, 30km east of Temblador (motel with pool, restaurant), there is an excursion and bathing centre called **Río Selva de Tabasca**. In the middle of 'nowhere' between Tabasca and Uracoa this surprising place has a lovely large pool (you pay a small fee for the day), bar and lunch shelters. The operators offer day trips on tributaries flowing into the Delta: to **Tucupita**, three hours via the Tabasca River and Caño Mánamo; and to Warao communities such as **El Pajal** and **Santo Domingo** where craftsmen make toy animals and baskets. With advance notice it is also possible to take a boat all the way to the Morichal Largo River, via the Uracoa, Mánamo and Tigre rivers. Trips require four passengers minimum. For information in Río Selva, tel: (087) 91599; in Maturín, ring Sergio Córdoba (see above, *Río Morichal Largo*).

From Uracoa, you can make a circle back to the Barrancas/Tucupita road.

THE ORINOCO DELTA

The Orinoco Delta is the newest of Venezuela's wilderness travel destinations. Now Venezuela's 21st state, it is called the Delta Amacuro after a river flowing from the eastern border near Guyana. Inhabitants are few and services are primitive in the hot, humid estuary. The vast maze of changing rivers and islands was previously negotiated by travellers who could get around with the locals, stop where they stopped and sling a hammock at night. The people who have been doing this for many centuries are the Warao or *Guaraúno* in Spanish. Excellent fishermen, the Warao have kept intact their way of life as the 'canoe people' (*wa arao*), safe in the outer delta marshes.

Using trunks of mauritia palm, the Warao build riverside communities on stilts, linking dwellings into villages. These *moriche* palms also give them food, wine and fibre for ropes, dugout sails and the baskets and hammocks (see box on page 179) which have made Warao crafts sought-after in Europe and North America. Numbering about 20,000, the Warao are Venezuela's largest native group after the Wayú (Guajiros). Many do not speak Spanish. Neither Carib nor Arawak, the origin of their ancient language is still debated. Today under pressure from farmers moving in, many Warao families are moving out to Monagas and Bolívar States in search of a livelihood.

Thirty-six major rivers and some 300 lesser *caños*, mostly unnamed, fan over the Delta's 40,200km². Of this area, 2,650km² were declared the **Parque Nacional Mariusa** in 1991. The park forms the core of an 8,000km² **biosphere reserve** whose boundaries are still under study. At the fan's apex by Barrancas the Orinoco spreads 22km wide. The main channel flows to the Atlantic through the

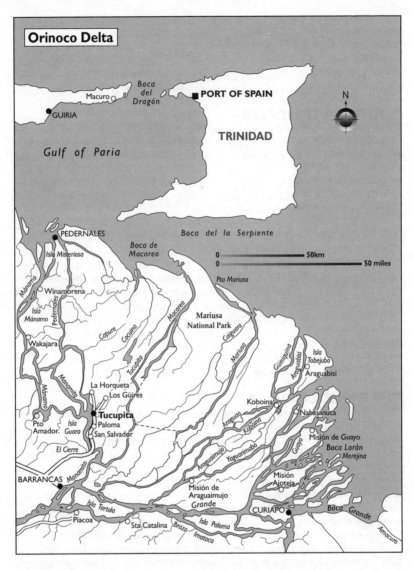

Río Grande, shipping route for Ciudad Guayana. In Warao language the name of this outlet is *wiri noko*, 'to row, place', perhaps the origin of 'Orinoco'. Less than 15km beyond the delta lies Trinidad which Columbus named on the first landfall of his third voyage. The year was 1498 and the day August 4, height of annual floods, when his ships passed through the Serpent's Mouth. Columbus was amazed by the Orinoco's freshwater 'mountain range of waves'. This outpouring has been calculated at 1.1 billion cubic metres yearly, depositing tons of silt and creating new land.

Temperatures average 26°C, cooling a little at night. Rains are often irregular, starting in April/May, pausing in July, then trailing into October and sometimes December. This is malaria country; take anti-malaria pills before arriving in the

Delta if you are travelling in the wet season. Surprisingly, there are few flying insects in the dry season.

Tucupita

The capital lies near Monagas State at a point where the east-flowing Tucupita, here quite small, breaks away from the north-flowing Mánamo which goes to the Gulf of Paria (110km). Caño Tucupita goes to the Atlantic. This strategic trading spot, traditionally used by Warao people, was settled by Juan Millán and Regino Suira of Margarita in 1848 – and was called simply '48'. There are long-rooted ties between the people of Margarita and the Warao. The settlement grew into a town with the arrival of Capuchin missionaries in 1919. Tucupita's one-storey profile is broken by the securely locked stone **Cathedral of La Divina Pastora**, looming over the early mission church of San José de Tucupita (1930) and the sultry streets.

Oil exploration by foreign companies around Pedernales and Boca de Tigre, along with tourism, is bringing new life to Tucupita. With its shady Plaza Bolívar, band concerts and esplanade called the Paseo Mánamo where people watch the river go by, Tucupita has some small-town pleasures. Businesses close from 12.00 to 15.00 so people can beat the heat with a siesta. At night there is usually music and dancing going on near the waterfront, or at Posada Delta.

Tucupita is the trading, supply and banking centre for two thirds of the Delta's 115,000 inhabitants. Public services, however, are precarious: the power supply is deficient, as is potable water; sewage is emptied untreated into the river. And, complicating matters, there is a drug problem as the Delta is a major route for running Colombian drugs to the Antilles.

The road to Tucupita crosses the Caño Mánamo over a dyke called the *cierre* that cuts off this large river from the Orinoco. Except for a few kilometres beyond Tucupita to La Horqueta and Los Güires, there are no roads. The 1969 Mánamo scheme to reclaim land for farming led to the clearing of many delta islands and shorelands for cattle. But the river was permanently changed by salt water backing up from the sea. The lack of a river current to flush the Mánamo with fresh water has brought hardship and health problems to the Warao living on its banks. Now drinking water must be delivered to villages by boat.

Some help for these vulnerable communities is coming, surprisingly, from oil companies who have teamed up with Venezuelan institutes to seek solutions to the lack of education and health services, and to diagnose environmental problems. Working in the Delta are British Petroleum, Amoco, Louisiana Land, Fe y Alegría, Tierra Viva, the Ministry of Health, La Salle Foundation, Intevep, the University of Texas and Universidad Central de Venezuela. One oil company, Benton Vinccler, cleaned up Tucupita's rubbish dump; however, several Warao families still depend on pickings, earning the equivalent of half a dollar for a kilo of aluminium beer tins.

Getting there and away

By air The airport is 3km north of Tucupita. It receives irregular flights, mainly tourism charters. There is *por puesto* service to town.

By bus Tucupita has a Terminal de Pasajeros for long-distance buses on the road 1km out of town. Many buses go to Maturín, 212km (4 hours), but you can save an hour by *por puesto*. The same is true for Ciudad Guayana, 189km, served by two departures only. As these buses cross the Orinoco by ferry, there may be delays on holidays. Two bus lines, Los Llanos and Camargüí, drive overnight from Caracas

WARAO CRAFTS

The Warao people are among the most skilled of craftsmen in all Venezuela, and some people say in all the Americas. Their tightly woven baskets of *moriche* fibre, from the *Mauritia flexuosa* palm, are found in crafts and museum collections. The women also weave hammocks of this fibre, sought as the best for comfort and long life (kept dry). Traditionally they use dyes made of *moriche* fruit, bark and other seeds although today commercial dyes are also employed. Men are the sculptors, fashioning a whole zoo of delta fauna out of light *sangrito* wood cut from the buttress roots of a large delta tree.

In every delta house, you will see these hammocks and baskets hung from roof beams. Or you may see people making them. Crafts are one of the Waraos' few sources of income. (Collecting hearts of palm is another; canneries pay the equivalent of US$0.25 for each heart, ie: felled palm.) If you can buy directly from the maker, you not only provide cash but support traditional skills. In Tucupita there is a crafts shop with an excellent selection of baskets and carvings, **Artesanía Tucán**, on the lower side of Plaza Bolívar. The house is unmarked, the closest reference being a bar; ask for Paco or his wife, the Spanish couple who have run the shop for many years.

via Maturín to Tucupita, covering the 730km in 11+ hours; fare about $14. They return to Caracas around 19.00. Local buses leave from a terminal on Calle Tucupita, two blocks from Plaza Bolívar.

Where to stay
The area telephone code for Tucupita is (087)
Prices in town are fairly standard: $12 for a double bed (*matrimonial*) with air conditioning, cheaper without. Choices of lodging are limited. The **Hotel Sans Souci** is a recent addition to Tucupita lodgings, a block south of the Cathedral on Calle Centurión, tel: 210132. The **Pequeño Hotel**, tel: 210523, Calle La Paz a block from the Paseo Mánamo, is friendly, clean and safe. The **Gran Hotel Amacuro**, tel: 210404, near Plaza Bolívar, has 25 rooms, restaurant. Much the same is the **Delta**, tel: 212467, Calle Pativilca; 16 rooms.

On the road 7km from Tucupita there is a flashy new hotel with a swimming pool, the **Saxxi**, tel: 212112/0175; air conditioning, double bed, $25. Service and restaurant are rated poorly, but there's a view at the back of Caño Mánamo and a little island. About 11km south of Tucupita in El Volcán sector there is a good small hotel on the river, the **Parque Venezia**, tel: 21558, whose management and restaurant are the best in Tucupita; double $16.

Missions, delta towns
Capuchin missionary work among the Warao began in earnest when the **Araguaimujo Mission** and boarding school were founded in 1925. These were followed by the missions of Amacuro, Tucupita, Guayo, Nabasanuka and Ajotejana. The Capuchin priests in Tucupita may be asked for permission to visit these missions (go to the Casa Parroquial). Travellers are given shelter but are reminded that donations are welcome and food is scarce, as are clothing and medicines.

A town of some 2,000 people has grown up on stilts by **San Francisco de Guayo**; it has a school, doctor, police station, and a museum of Warao crafts run by the mission Padre. Word from **Curiapo**, far down the Río Grande, reports something new: Hotel Jari, built in typical Indian fashion with 16 rooms over the river. Curiapo has electricity, a school, a library, and even a gaol.

River travel

Visitors with a hammock and mosquito net should find it easy to spend the night in any remote delta community. Ask the *comisario* or *prefecto* in each village for local orientation. These people have instructions to help visitors and tourists. Delta inhabitants are mostly open, simple people. Remember that they have only rudimentary shelter and the barest of supplies. Take some coffee and sugar. You would do well to take a long shirt and trousers/pants, hat, sunscreen, repellent, poncho or waterproof, and a plastic sheet (or bin liner) to protect your pack in the boat. A machete is essential for campers.

Most travel in the delta is by open boats with outboard motors: fishing craft called *peñeros*, faster launches, and dugout bongos (larger craft are roofed). For the northern delta by way of the Mánamo and Pedernales rivers, ask at the **Puerto Fluvial** on Paseo Mánamo, five blocks north of San José Church. There is daily service to Pedernales, 110km (five hours). There is no service to the central delta by way of the Tucupita and Macareo rivers.

Por puestos go to **Puerto El Volcán**, 22km south where the dyke closes the Mánamo. From there public launches leave for **San Francisco de Guayo**, and for **Curiapo** on the Río Grande in the southern delta, but this *transporte fluvial* is irregular. Travel time varies according to the engine used: with 40hp, the run to Guayo takes seven or eight hours; with 75hp, time is three to four hours. This also varies seasonally. During the rains the river is full and calm, making travel easier; at low water, the current, waves and trade winds are all stronger.

Bigger supply vessels to missions and towns of the eastern and southern delta leave from the port of **Barrancas**. Barrancas, although now home to an archaeological museum, has been rated as 'horrible'; travellers go there only to arrange a boat, returning to Tucupita for the night.

Ocean-going vessels navigating the Orinoco use the Río Grande. The channel is regularly dredged to allow passage of medium vessels to **Ciudad Guayana**. Where the Río Grande meets the Atlantic at **Punta Barima** there is a government station for river pilots; it has a dock and heliport. By law a foreign ship entering the Orinoco must have a Venezuelan pilot. The pilot takes the ship to its port, probably Puerto Ordaz, 270km upriver.

The Río Grande, however, is too shallow for today's large ships. Ferrominera Orinoco's iron ore exports come downriver on the Río Orinoco, carrying only 45,000 tons in the dry season, and some 70,000 tons at high water. On the conveyor belts of a 314m floating transfer station, moored in the deep waters of the Serpent's mouth, the ore is moved either to an ocean-going carrier, or to the station itself.

Tours

New services are springing up. Trips of 3 days/2 nights on the *caños* are the standard offer of local agencies; a minimum of four passengers is usual. The cost runs to $250 and up, and comfort tends to increase with price. As camps in the southern delta are more distant, the cost is higher. Most camps are native-style *palafitos* built on river banks, lit by kerosene lamps; the better ones have a generator. You may sleep in beds or hammocks with mosquito netting; toilets are rustic to say the least. There is a list of operators kept by the **Tucupita tourist office**, *Dirección de Turismo*, tel: 216852, Edificio San Juan, Calle Bolívar by the plaza.

HUMBOLDT, MAN OF SCIENCE

Alexander von Humboldt was not yet 30 in 1799 when he reached Venezuela, almost by accident. His long-planned scientific journey to the Nile had been cancelled by Napoleon, as was an invitation to circumnavigate the world. But the baron from Berlin was unstoppable. With a young French botanist, Aime Bonpland, he hoped to catch a boat to Smyrna, and they set out for Spain on foot. Handsome and single, Humboldt charmed his way to King Carlos IV. More than his talents in Spanish, biology, astronomy and meteorology, it was Humboldt's knowledge of geology and mining that won passports from the Spanish king who envisioned lucrative findings. Humboldt was ecstatic. Until then, Spanish America had been off-bounds to foreigners, a scientific *tierra incognita*.

They sailed on a ship bound for Cuba. When typhoid fever struck, the captain changed course for Venezuela. 'Had not the fever broken out on board the *Pizarro*, we should never have reached the Orinoco, the Cassiquiare,' Humboldt wrote.

His curiosity was insatiable. In the Llanos he was determined to measure the discharge of electric eels (*Electrophorus electricus* is not, in fact, an eel but is related to carp). When he arrived at Calabozo in 1800 he had 30 horses and mules driven into a pool with electric eels; some horses drowned in the frenzy as they were 'electrocuted'. But when the *tembladores* exhausted their discharge, most animals recovered and Humboldt got his wish to make the first scientific examination.

'I do not remember ever having received from the discharge of a large Leyden jar a more dreadful shock than the one I experienced when I very stupidly placed both my feet on an electric eel that had just been taken out of the water. I was affected for the rest of the day with a violent pain in the knees and almost every joint.' However, the electricity remained a mystery: it didn't register on Humboldt's electrometer, it gave off no spark of light at night, nor was there a magnetic effect. And despite dissections, Humboldt could not answer the question: why don't electric fishes electrocute themselves?

After their Venezuelan travels, Humboldt and Bonpland went on to ascend Colombia's Magdalena River and Ecuador's volcanoes, then descend the deserts of Peru before heading to Mexico and the United States. When Humboldt returned to Europe in 1804 he had such a cargo of notes, dried plants, insects and minerals, that it took him decades and most of his family inheritance to classify 6,000 new species and write three volumes of *Travels to Equinoctial Regions of America*, and *Cosmos*, his 2,000-page masterpiece examining the physical world.

The German king made a medal in commemoration of *Cosmos* showing Humboldt, a sphynx and an electric eel.

The first Warao operated company, Oriwana ('all together'), is represented by José Rodríguez, a Radio Tucupita announcer, tel: 212245. The **Oriwana Camp** is near San Francisco de Guayo; guests are transported by 'El Chino' Rodríguez, an experienced river guide, in his own *peñero*. In Caracas, arrangements may be made through Viva Trek Tours, fax: (044) 551827.

Abelardo Lara was one of the first people to organise delta tours and has had experience guiding birdwatchers. He now has his own **Campamento Maraisa** (hammocks or beds) in San Francisco de Guayo near the Atlantic. On the 7–8-hour trip passengers fish for piranha, and visit the Araguaimujo mission. Enquiries: Delta Surs, Calle Pativilca at Mariño, tel: 213877, fax: 212666. In Caracas: Orinoco Tours, tel: (02) 7618431, fax: 7616801.

By **Tobé Lodge** macaws squabble in the trees every afternoon. Guests arrive by helicopter or rapid launch from El Volcán, dine with wine and sleep Indian style in *moriche* hammocks. This upscale camp in Guayo, less than an hour from the Atlantic, is owned by Arlette and Louis Carree. *Tobé* is Warao for jaguar and the Carrees hope to make a jaguar refuge. In Tucupita, on Plaza Bolívar, tel/fax: 210709; in Puerto La Cruz, (081) 868879, (014) 9805861.

Aereotuy's 3-day tour to **Campamento Guayos** costs $525 with flight from Porlamar, or $425 from Maturín. Either way, transport from Maturín is by seaplane – you fly low over the delta's green forest threaded by winding *caños*. Guests visit the San Francisco mission and Warao village; guides are bilingual.

Tucupita Expeditions, Paseo Mánamo near San José church, tel: 210801, fax: 212986, operate the **Orinoco Delta Lodge**, two hours north of Tucupita; costs run to about $90 per day including transfer from Maturín. Built by a young American, Anthony Tahbou who married a Delta girl, the camp has boardwalks linking the dock to a dining room, sleeping area and shared bathroom. Guests explore a remoter camp near Guaranoco, birdwatching and catching *sábalo* (tarpon) and *morocoto* (damselfish) for supper. Contact in Caracas: Alpi Tour (see *Tour Operators*, page 14).

Located 1½ hours down the Mánamo, **Ubanoco** offers a plank-walled dwelling equipped with radio, rainwater tank for showers, hammocks and camp beds, dormitory style; guides speak French, German and English. Information in Margarita, tel: (095) 611622, fax: 614419.

Campamento Bujana, in the same region between Caños Bujana and Guacajara, makes the most of open native *churuatas*, one for dining and one for 20 hammocks with walkways in between; attended by Johnny Kairu and Adive Bacharo. Enquiries: Bujana Tours, tel/fax: 212776, Calle Dalla Costa near Arismendi. **Campamento Paradise**, on the Mánamo near the Gulf of Paria, is a family affair run by Daniela, Andrés and Karim Hamsi; four *churuatas* serve as cabins, and in houses of plank walls there are six rooms with showers. Guests fly to Maturín and are driven to San José de Buja, 65km, giving this delta camp competitive prices: 3 days/2 nights $240 each for two, or $210 each for three to six people. For information, tel: 210224.

Aereotuy's lodge, a converted oil camp with ten rooms and private baths, is on an island at **Boca de Tigre** (mouth of the Tigre River), in the Mánamo. Guests fly from Margarita to Maturín, then go by road to San José de Buja where they board a boat for the Delta. Cost for 2 days/1 night is $285 from Porlamar (including flight), or $185 from Maturín.

A tour led by Gilles Cros, an independent French guide, takes passengers for ten days in a wooden fishing craft navigating through the delta by way of the **Mánamo** and **Pedernales** Rivers. The *peñero*, equipped with four 65hp motors, then crosses the Gulf of Paria back to terra firma near Güiria, to overnight at the **Posada Playa Dorada** in Punta de Piedras. The boat continues around Paria Peninsula to the north coast and eventually anchors in **Carúpano**. Ring Gilles in Caracas, tel: (02) 2396213 or fax: 2354931.

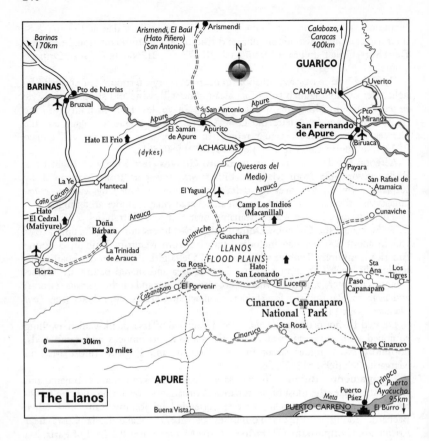

Los Llanos

The *Llanos*, or plains, stretch north of the Orinoco over 300,000km² in Venezuela and another 220,000km² in Colombia, forming one of the great natural features of the continent. It is an area poor in soil but rich in rivers, birds and animals. Life is hard for both the *llaneros* and their cattle in this environment of harsh extremes where drought and fire are followed by flood. More cattle than people live on the plains. Ranches are called *hatos* (the 'h' is silent in *hato* as in *hacienda*). Some cover many thousands of hectares. Today, instead of allowing cattle to range semi-wild in search of tender grass – the soil is so poor that each cow requires two hectares or about five acres – many ranches are modernising.

Despite technology, the image is cherished of tough *llaneros* on horseback battling drought or floods, jaguars or piranhas. And dearest to Venezuelans is the music of the Llanos, particularly the fast *joropo*. The *Alma Llanera* is an unofficial national anthem... '*Yo nací en una ribera del Arauca vibrador/ Soy hermano de la espuma, de las garzas, de las rosas/ Y del sol, y del sol...*'

The best time to move around is the dry season, from December to April. This is called *verano*, the summer. Grass withers, cattle are rounded up to waterholes, and the ground cracks in dry stream beds. It is the time when most visitors come for the drama unfolding in the remaining ponds which seethe and groan with too many fish and too little oxygen, attracting thousands of wading birds. Fishermen also take advantage of trapped fish.

Spring comes in May with the first rains. Frogs, turtles, and even fish emerge after months in a dormant state called aestivation under baked mud. New grass sprouts. Creeks turn into rivers and rivers into lakes. Fish disperse over the Llanos to spawn. Egrets and ibises congregate to nest in huge rookeries. By July, the Orinoco is in flood. On Apure's floodplains, *llaneros* give up horses and jeeps in favour of boats and aircraft. Cattle which have not been rounded up to higher ground may drown. This season is called the *invierno* or winter, well suited to water-buffalo farms.

FLORA AND FAUNA
Flora

Although the plains are quite flat, their topography is broken by communities of taller plants: evergreen gallery forests on the banks of *caños* or creeks, isolated copses called *matas,* and burned-over patches of hardy, twisted *chaparro* trees. In central Apure, floods leave a watery mosaic of *bajíos*, literally shallows. In water as deep as a frog's knees, a rapid cycle of plant and animal life develops only as long as the rains fall.

Grasslands are interrupted by dense stands of Mauritia palms called *morichales*. Among the Llanos' most distinctive features, *morichales* form in boggy hollows. At first one or two palms grow, then more as a course of clear water develops. Some *morichales* extend 50km in length and are the source of clean water year round for adjacent towns.

A whole ecosystem depends on the *esteros*, marshes whose clay bottom retains floodwaters to form shallow lakes. Then the *llanero* poles his boat along, with a harpoon at hand, seeking the shadow of a catfish moving under a floating carpet of water hyacinths. The seasonal cycle of the marsh and its animal life, water ferns and reeds, as it comes to an end with dry weather, nourishes thousands of birds and predators, until by January or February the clay bottom is exposed to the sun.

Fauna

A census in the Llanos found 323 bird species, more than 50 mammals, 354 kinds of fish, 67 reptiles and 26 amphibians. Many animals and birds on the Llanos are adapted to water. You can spot river dolphins in muddy rivers when they surface to blow. The first reptile seen is usually the spectacled cayman or *baba*, 2–3m in length. The biggest, the Orinoco crocodile, which formerly grew over 6m, has been hunted almost to extinction and is now being reintroduced in one or two areas. Both males and females defend their young and will carry

River dolphin

them to safety in their mouths. You won't see a crocodile in the wild, and the chances of seeing an anaconda are slim. Not so with piranhas, here called *caribes* (which means flesh eater and is the root of our word Caribbean, and cannibal). Caribes live in most of the plains rivers and are the easiest fish to catch. In small concentrations they do not attack water fauna unless bleeding. Nevertheless, they are one reason *not* to swim in Llanos rivers, another being the presence in muddy bottoms of stingrays, or electric eels (see box, *Humboldt, Man of Science,* page 238).

You will see family groups of what look like rotund, giant guinea pigs. These are *chigüires*, or capybaras, the world's biggest rodents. Lifting comic snouts to sniff danger, they munch plants at the water's edge. They swim and dive like beavers, weigh up to 60kg, and are hunted for food. On ranches where hunting has been banned you may see families of giant otters (or hear their snorts); they are called *perros de agua*. A mature male may measure 2m head to tail.

Shyer, solitary and rarer are the land mammals – tapir, giant anteater, tamandua, armadillo, fox, tayra and spotted cats, big and small. Peccaries run in bands, and people climb trees to avoid their ire. You can hear howler monkeys from a great distance: the *araguatos'* 'howl' is more like a roar than the jaguar's call, or cough. Venezuelans call jaguars *tigres* and they have a wide distribution, although much reduced by hunting and habitat loss. The opossum is so ordinary as to be despised, while the porcupine with prehensile tail is charming though formidable; both are nocturnal.

Birds

Water and wading birds gather by the thousands to feast at shrinking ponds. Herons, egrets, scarlet ibis, glossy ibis, roseate spoonbill, jabiru, wood storks, boat-billed herons, anhingas, cormorants, jacanas, gallinules, Orinoco geese, whistling tree-ducks, as well as many birds of prey such as hawks, falcons, kestrel and osprey, may be viewed on a single ranch. The hoatzin is a bird often seen in riverside bushes. Hoatzins digest toxic tree leaves by means of foregut fermentation rather like a cow.

Wildlife conservation

Among large mammals which have been severely endangered by hunting are the Orinoco crocodile (*Crocodylus intermedius*); giant otter (*Pteroneura brasiliensis*); manatee (*Trichechus manatus*), a 500kg relative of the seacow; giant anteater (*Myrmecophaga tridactyla*); and the nearly extinct giant armadillo or *cuspón* (*Priodontes giganteus*). The owners of Hato El Frío and El Cedral have helped to set up the **Guaritico Wildlife Refuge** along a river between their lands to protect such species.

None of these animals has suffered such loss as the large *arrau* turtle which grows to 1m in length. In 1745 Jesuit priest José Gumilla wrote in his *Orinoco Ilustrado*, 'It would be as difficult to count the grains of sand on the Orinoco's shores, as to count the immense number of tortoises.' He believed that their great number would make the Orinoco unnavigable if eggs were not taken. Stopping at Pararuma in 1800, Alexander Humboldt estimated that 33 million eggs were laid every dry season. Several hundred Indians of different tribes would assemble in late March for the egg harvest. Some tribes even came from the upper Orinoco. Turtle-egg oil was sold for lamps in Ciudad Bolívar.

Today, at low water some turtles still come to nest on the same sandy islands. The half-dozen park rangers have a next to impossible job stopping nest robbers as distances are great and the laying season covers three months.

There are other, more serious threats to wildlife habitat: a government plan to dredge and channel rivers to make a barge route for cargo, and schemes to build dykes and drain land for farming, with all the dangers of impoverishing already acidic soils and encouraging land speculation.

SAN FERNANDO DE APURE

The Apure River flows east from Colombia. San Fernando is on the south shore, 150km before the Apure joins the Orinoco. The river port is the capital and only sizeable town in this state of 76,500km^2 and about 400,000 people. As the traditional trading centre for ranchers of the lower Llanos, it is a thriving city of 90,000 inhabitants. Its main product is beef and there is a modern tannery. Cayman leather is another export. There are good roads linking the state's small towns of Achaguas, Elorza, Mantecal and Guasdualito.

San Fernando was founded in 1788 as a mission base for Franciscan monks. Today its main draw is as a travellers' base for seeing the Llanos wildlife.

Everyone gathers at San Fernando's week-long fair and agricultural exhibition in mid-April. There are bull-dogging contests (*toros coleados*) without which no fair in the Llanos is complete. Cowhands from distant ranches compete in such skills, as well as in the contest for the 'Florentino de Oro'. This prestigious award is given for the best composer/singer of couplets, a song form called *contrapunteo* at which *llaneros* excel.

The plainsmen are historically famous for bravery. On the Paseo Libertador are two monuments commemorating their part in the Independence wars, often as bareback riders with lances, as in the Monumento a los Llaneros. At the city's entrance, eight blocks north, is a statue of Pedro Camejo, known as 'Negro Primero', who died at General Páez' feet in the key battle of Carabobo. Beside it is a startling round fountain with coloured tiles, concrete crocodiles and cornucopias.

To the east stands an ornate old two-floor building with a story to tell: the **Palacio Barbarito**. In its heyday when river waters lapped at a pier in front, it was headquarters of Italian merchants, the Hermanos Barbarito, one of several large feather traders. In the 1890s San Fernando saw a boom based on feathers (pound for pound more valuable than gold) which lasted until the Audubon Society denounced the cruel fashion. A survey of heron and egret rookeries revealed that the best *garceros*, or rookeries, belonged to dictator Juan Vicente Gómez, the Barbaritos and the Lancashire Trust, a British company controlling 400 leagues.

Where to stay
The area telephone code for San Fernando is (047)
There are some passable hotels in town with air conditioning and private bath. The **Trinacría**, tel: 23578, is a newer hotel on Av Miranda near the bus station; double $14. Two blocks south on Plaza Bolívar is the **Gran Hotel Plaza**, tel: 414968, the only hotel rated as 2 star; $30 for double/triple. Hotels near the crocodile fountain at the city's northern entrance are the **Río**, tel: 23454; and **Nuevo Hotel Apure** opposite the gas station, tel: 414483; double $17. Continue two blocks on Paseo Libertador for **La Torraca**, between Carreras 3-4, tel: 22777/676, inexpensive.

Further down in price and quality but with air conditioning are **Hotel Los Llanos**, Carrera Páez between Calles 14-15, tel: 22703; and **Hotel Roma**, tel: 23652, Calle 15 between Carreras Sucre and Bolívar.

Getting there and away
By air
Las Flecheras airport is 3km east of town. From **Caracas**, San Fernando is 45 minutes by jet (about $60). At present there is only one daily flight (Mon–Fri) to San Fernando. The same plane returns to Caracas.

By bus
As you cross over the bridge into San Fernando, the bus terminal (Terminal de Pasajeros) is west, between the river and the centre, five blocks from Plaza Bolívar. From **Caracas** the distance is 400km (8 hours), and the last two hours are very hot and flat which is why buses like to travel at night. Buses go throughout the day to **Barinas** (about the same distance), and to **Maracay** (6½ hours). Expresos Los Llanos travels to **San Cristobal** at night (13 hours).

San Fernando is served by bus over a largely paved road to Puerto Páez, 210km, and Puerto Ayacucho, another 93km. As the Llanos road goes along an embankment, or *terraplén*, above the floodplain, it is an all-weather route. The journey takes eight hours with (at present) three drive-on ferries for river crossings at the Capanaparo, Cinaruco and Orinoco rivers, the last *chalana* being from Puerto Páez to El Burro. The flatbed ferries work from sunrise to sundown for a small fee.

Off-road driving
Adventurous drivers with 4x4 vehicles go south of the Apure river, *llano adentro*, in the dry season, December–April. There are no towns whatsoever. You may see some Pumé Indians (Yaruro); they fish, and carve jet (*azabache*) which they find in dunes. This is dry savannah south of the Apure, flat with beautiful dunes but no lagoons, no marshes, all the creeks dried up. Animals and even birds are scarce.

In rivers there are fat *pavón* (bass) and large *payara*, another big-game fish. You will need other food, also rope and hammocks. Take six spare fuel cans and a compass (there are places named on maps that just don't exist). The sandy tracks or *trillas* which appear most worn frequently lead to ranches, visible miles away as clumps of mango trees. When getting directions ask not how far, but how long (remembering that *llaneros* have no watches) to the next *hato* (not where you are going to, like Elorza).

North of the Apure lie the 'wet' llanos. Even in the dry season they are greener with *morichales* or palm stands, and lagoons where birds gather. However, dust is so terrible that off-road drivers wear masks. Hard ruts and runnels cut progress to 15km an hour.

CINARUCO–CAPANAPARO PARK

This tract of 5,840km² includes part of the Orinoco and several of its islands. The eastern boundary is formed by the Orinoco, the northern by the Capanaparo, and the southern by the Cinaruco. Officially it is called the Santos Luzardo National Park. The nearby Orinoco islands of Pararuma, Ramonera, Loros and Isla del Medio have been declared a wildlife refuge. It is hoped that the endangered *arrau* or Orinoco turtle and rare Orinoco crocodile will nest there.

In practice, the Orinoco is out of reach and there are no facilities of any sort, although the highway itself is an open invitation to campers. At the Capanaparo River, just beyond the old ferry crossing, a park visitors' centre is planned. Visitors will be requested to get a permit there for a small sum. Enquire about fishing season and limits at Inparques, opposite the Palacio Barbarito, San Fernando, tel: (047) 25530, fax: 413794.

The Apure grasslands are largely flooded from June to September. Two eastern lagoons, Las Mercedes and Araguaquén, are marked only by a ring of treetops when the Orinoco is in flood. The plains harbour a variety of ecosystems in gallery forests, dunes, and the 'Galeras del Cinaruco', a Precambrian geological formation like a small steppe (recalling a raised gallery).

North of the Apure you will find marshes known as *esteros*, and *morichales* in swampy hollows. In these dense palm clumps grow plants typical of Amazon and Guayana flora which here live north of the Orinoco.

Visiting the park

Local fishermen and birders like to make their own way in the dry season (during rains, the entire area is under water). There are many places good for camping. Mary Lou Goodwin shares a tip for birdwatchers (with jeep): 'One of my favourite camping spots is known as Laguna Brava. After you cross the Capanaparo, head south; count the kilometres, starting at Km 1 by the 'Welcome' sign at the junction. You will reach a sandy road going west at Km 4.6. Turn right on this road and continue for 2.2km when you veer towards the left. In 1.5km more, turn left and you will come to the lagoon in 1.3km. Here I have seen not only almost all the savannah and water birds listed for the park but also the scarlet macaw, red-bellied macaw, blue-crowned parakeet and festive parrot.' In one copse of trees, called a *mata* by locals, Mary Lou counted over 50 bird species.

Warning There are no mosquitoes in the dry season BUT chiggers await anyone on foot. By other names these microscopic ticks are called *chivacoa*, harvest mites or bête rouge because they are pink. Tuck your trouser legs into your socks or boots and spray repellent on the outside. To lessen their itch, without delay take a long bath and lather well (three minutes) with an antiseptic soap.

WILDLIFE LODGES

Several working cattle ranches have turned to ecotourism and photo safaris to support conservation (and bring in hard currency). These large private ranches all have their own radio transmitters and airfields. Most lodges accommodate about 20 people in comfort, no more. As there is great interest among birdwatchers and nature lovers in general, it's best to book well in advance in the dry season, November–April. The scenery changes totally in the wet season (take two pairs of tennis shoes or rubber sandals). Costs range between $90 and $150 per night.

Venezuelan residents often benefit from discounts. There are excursions both morning and afternoon; weekends are best. Swimming in rivers is discouraged and pools are the exception.

To meet growing demand, new lodges open every year. Of the *hatos* listed below, most are in Apure State and guests are ferried by car or plane from San Fernando or Barinas. The transfers are not always included in the package. If in doubt where to go, consult the Audubon travel service, tel: (02) 923268/2812, fax: 910716.

Hato El Frío was the first of several cattle ranches to protect its wildlife for research three decades ago when a biological station was opened. Considered a must for nature lovers and birders, El Frío's 850km^2 support thousands of spectacled cayman, deer and 13,000 capybaras, besides some 45,000 head of cattle and 6,000 horses. The four-hour excursions, morning and afternoon, take you on various trails and creeks. The lodge offers ten double rooms with bath, more under construction. Guests who find their own way to the ranch pay $120 daily for a single or $90 per person in a double during low season, July–Sept. High season, October–March, $130; intermediate months April–June. Reservations, tel: (047) 81793, fax: 81223. The entrance to Hato El Frío is at Km 187, north side, on the San Fernando-Mantecal road. The Mantecal bus from San Fernando passes the gate. Or you can call Sr Galindo, tel: (047) 21420, who provides (expensive) car service. It is a three-hour drive.

El Cedral has long been a wildlife refuge where you can see a horizonful of birds and beasts. Once the King Ranch, it was owned by the Rockefellers in the 1950s. They invested in levees which provide water in the dry season and high ground during the rains, making the ranch an excellent choice year round. Nesting time (May–Oct) is impressive as herons, egrets, spoonbills and ibises literally clothe trees in the *garceros* or rookeries. The ranch of 530km^2 has an estimated 23,000 head of cattle, 15,000 capybaras, 10,000 cayman and 300 bird species. (One section along the Matiyure River is advertised as a sanctuary but is really the same ranch.) Facilities are good: pool, bar, 25 air-conditioned rooms, some with hot water. Prices are lower in the rainy season, Apr 16–Nov 15, about $107 a night per person in a double room; high season $135. You pay extra for a single, and for road transport from San Fernando, 225km (4 hours); a car for two people costs $86; for four people, $114. They will also arrange pick-up from Barinas. The camp is located 10km south of La Ye, west of the main road between Mantecal and Elorza. By reservation only; Maso Tours, tel: (02) 2646466/4555, fax: 2641176; email: masotour@caracas.c-com.net.

Hato Doña Bárbara is part of a 360km^2 working ranch, La Trinidad de Arauca. The Estrada family has built 21 rooms, double cooled for coolness, with fan and shower. They have much to tell (in English) about the character of legend and literature called Doña Bárbara who lived and died here (her real name was Francisca Vásquez). The Estradas devote 5% of tourism income to a foundation supporting biodiversity. Costs are $90 a day May–November and $110 December–April (discount for residents). This includes excursions by jeep, river and horseback; there's an anaconda outing (largest found to date is 7m). Not included is car transfer to Elorza (4 hours) about $100 from San Fernando. From Elorza guests are taken by launch down the Arauca River. Reservations in San Fernando: Hotel Torraca, Paseo Libertador, tel: (047) 413463, fax: 412235; email: dbarbara@sfapure.c-com.net. In Caracas, Lost World Adventures, tel: (02) 7611108, 7635092, fax: 7617538.

Hato San Leonardo is in the centre of Apure State near the Capanaparo River. The 180km^2 cattle ranch is accessible by two routes: via Achaguas–Yagual, then an adventurous track from Guachara, great scenery but only dry season (4½ hours); or via San Fernando–San Juan de Payara by road as far as La Macanilla where you board

AN INQUISITIVE TRAVELLER'S GUIDE TO THE LLANOS
Edward Paine

I worked in Venezuela for four years, most of them spent between the Apure and Arauca rivers, in the heart of the Llanos, and my addiction for the area developed slowly as I worked first as a cowboy, progressing to manager of a 100,000 acre ranch. As with all the remote parts of the world, you have to work hard to get beyond initial impressions and begin to understand the local culture and traditions.

Firstly, as a transient visitor there is the problem of access: only one paved road loops its way through these immense plains and you won't see much from a vehicle. However, here are some of the ingredients that make up the Llanos.

The **cattle:** the large white ones with humps are probably Brahman. Descended from the Zebu cattle of India they have revolutionised the local cattle-breeding industry with their resistance to ticks and heat, and are replacing or being crossed with the *criollo* animals brought over from Europe by the early colonists.

The **cowboys:** still fiercely independent, the *llaneros* share with their Argentine cousin the gaucho a reluctance to go anywhere on foot when a horse or mule is available. Their main diet is, of course, meat, although as killing day is normally weekly the menu progresses through thinner and thinner *sopas* until there are a few bare bones and some spaghetti swimming around in hot water. Like all people who live by the hours of the sun and do not depend on watches, they are early risers. While you may find everyone asleep by 8pm, there will be activity in the bunkhouse several hours before dawn, soon after the cock crows. I soon learnt not to place too much trust in this natural alarm clock: one morning, after a night at one of the outlying corrals, we rose when the cock crowed, caught the horses, saddled up and set out on the eight-hour ride back to the farm centre, only to find that after five hours' riding the sun still had not risen!

The **wildlife:** by a happy chance the ranch economy has not conflicted with their habitat, so take a good guide and wonder at the bright colours and sheer numbers of birds as they fly from one lagoon to another.

The **music:** so often a shortcut to a good understanding of other cultures. You should plan to stop at any of the scruffy towns on the Llanos during the Patron Saints' fiestas, and listen to the same cowboy who that morning was up at dawn training his favourite fighting cock as he sings his heart out to his companions – companions whose agility on a horse has been converted to agile fingers moving over the strings of a harp, accompanied by the four-stringed *cuatro* and maracas.

a bongo upriver (2+4 hours). Both ways require a guide. Guests stay in seven plain cabins, each with twin beds, ceiling fan and cold-water shower; pool in an Australian tank, open national bar. Bird watching, photo safaris to caños, lagoons, gallery forest included; bass fishing on the Capanaparo extra. Daily price is $125 single, $100 double per person from May to November; $145/$120 December to April, not including transfer. In Caracas book via Ameropa, tel: (02) 5738867, 5743366, fax: 5744019; email: aventur@obm.net. English, Dutch, French and Italian spoken.

Los Indios Adventure Camp is part of Hato Macanillal, a 320km² ranch located between the Cunaviche and Cunavichito rivers. The camp is modern and complete with pool; no air conditioning. The lodge is four hours by a dry-season track south of Achaguas, or a 25-minute flight. Without transportation the cost Dec 15–May 31 is $120 a day; $100 the rest of the year. For information about transfer by vehicle, boat or aircraft, in Caracas contact (02) 2087733/933, fax: 9931983. Charter services from Caracas, such as Amazonair, are a good idea if your party is five or more; tel: (02) 2836960, fax: 2832627.

Hato El Banco, the closest and smallest (15km²) of the ranches, is 50km south of Calabozo, with an unpaved entrance road of 14km. Near the house is a lagoon with large flocks of scarlet ibis. The main house has two large rooms with single beds, fan and private bath at $106 per room; double rooms in separate building, smaller, $54 for two people, all meals. For information, ring the Audubon Society (see page 48).

Hato Piñero in Cojedes State is remarkable for its 50-year hunting ban. As a result, more fauna is seen. Owls, macaws and iguanas spy from great trees above the lodge. On a river outing the boat may be surrounded by hoatzins, ignored by passing capuchins, peered at by agoutis and curassows, and certainly preceded by herons and anhingas. Foxes, ocelots, giant anteaters and fishing bats are spotlighted at night from an open-topped safari truck. Piñero is located in the Llano Alto or upper plains and on its 800km² are varied habitats from cattle pastures and wetlands to hills, rivers and forests. Such variety combined with wildlife management has given Piñero international prestige. Five percent of net profits go to conservation, education and the biological research station. Piñero is a 370km (5–6 hours) drive from Caracas via Valencia and Tinaco; 60km before El Baúl, a sign (by Escuela Barbasco) points east. However, you must still cover 22km and pass four gates. The first-class lodge has 11 rooms with fans and hot shower. May–November $120 per person in a double, $144 single; December–April $150/$180. For transfers, not included, reservations and discounts for residents, enquire (in English) at Bio Tours GBS, tel: (02) 9911135, or fax: 9916668; email: hatopinerovzla@compuserve.com.

Hato San Antonio lies in the Arismendi basin, 66km beyond El Baúl, Barinas State. Birdlife is spectacular in beautiful untouched wetlands, habitat of capybaras, caymans and river dolphins. While it also has savannahs subject to drought, the *hato* enjoys year-round lagoons and marshes. The Calderón family (they speak English, French and Italian) emphasise the 'eco' in ecotourism on their 300km² ranch south of the Guanare River. They raise water buffalo which require no cultivated pasture, so wildlife has not been exposed to land drainage, deforestation or dykes. Cost per person, $85, includes bilingual guide, trips by boat, horseback and jeep, and meals; rooms around a patio in a handsome new lodge, with air conditioning, fan and hot water; open national bar, meals with lots of fruit, salad (vegetarian on request). In Caracas, tel/fax: (02) 9910130, (014) 9053306.

Fishing lodge

Probably the most comfortable of Venezuela's fishing options is the riverside **Cinaruco Bass Lodge** in Apure's Santos Luzardo park. It operates during the dry season only, November–May. From Caracas, fishermen are flown in for a week's sport battling large *pavón*, the peacock bass with the toughest reputation. All sport fishing is catch and release; two fishermen per boat with outboard and electric motors, plus native guide (who usually gets a big tip). The camp on the edge of the savanna has four houses, each with two doubles, hot water, ceiling fan, laundry service. There is a central dining lodge, wine with dinner, open national bar; diesel generator. Price per person, double occupancy, is about $250 a day. Alpi Tour, tel: (02) 2831433/1733, fax: 2856067.

LA GRAN SABANA
Angel Falls, at 979m the world's highest waterfall, plunges from the flanks of Ayantepui.
(EP)

WILDLIFE
Above left: *Blue and gold macaw, Amazonas* (HB)
Above right: *Yellow-banded poison frog, Gran Sabana* (HB)
Below: *Capybara. The world's largest rodent is found near rivers and wetlands. It is most easily seen in the Llanos.* (PM)

JAWS (LLANOS)
Above: *One of nine species of piranha found in South America. Not all piranhas are flesh-eaters – some are vegetarian.* (HB)
Centre: *Puma* (Felis concolor) *or mountain lion, known as 'león' in Venezuela. Weighing up to 60kg, it is smaller than the 'tigre' or jaguar and survives in a variety of habitats .*(HB)
Below: *Spectacled caiman* (Caiman crocodilus) (HB)

THE CARIBBEAN
Above: *Salt flats, Araya Peninsula* (HB)
Below: *Brown pelican* (EP)

Bolívar State

GRAN SABANA, 'TEPUIS', ANGEL FALLS

A glance at a map will show a vast area of forests, rivers and uplands south of the Río Orinoco, extending east to the Republic of Guyana and south to Brazil. Although the region loosely called *la Guayana* covers nearly half of Venezuela – the states of Delta Amacuro, Bolívar and Amazonas – you won't find its name on maps except in Ciudad Guayana, Bolívar State's largest city.

Chief attractions are **Angel Falls**, the world's highest, and **La Gran Sabana**, a huge rolling plateau crowned by sheer walled tepuis or table mountains. The ancient rainswept uplands of the Guayana Shield contain some of the oldest rocks on earth, washed by clear, tumbling rivers.

These giant *mesas* conjure images of Arthur Conan Doyle's *The Lost World*. Conan Doyle was fascinated by naturalists' reports of the walled mountains that defied ascent. When Roraima was at last climbed in 1884, members of the Royal Geographical Society packed the London meeting to hear the explorers' account. Today the tepuis are equally fascinating, and a lot easier to get to.

Gold drew the early Conquistadors to Guayana followed in 1597 by Walter Raleigh. They all searched in vain for fabled El Dorado and the golden city of Manoa. Then at last in the 19th century gold was struck in a big way in El Callao and in 1886 Venezuela was the world's largest producer. Today gold fever runs hot again as estimates put recoverable gold as high as 11,000 metric tons or 10% of known world reserves. Local and foreign companies explore concessions on the heels of some 30,000 small prospectors who scour and pit the forest, sluicing soil and mercury into rivers. Many are illegal Brazilian miners known as *garimpeiros*. Diamonds, too, are found by free miners who painstakingly wash sediments with sieves called *surrucas*, producing most of Venezuela's 300,000 carats a year.

ACCESS TOWNS
Ciudad Bolívar

Historically important as the Orinoco's major port and capital of Bolívar State, Ciudad Bolívar is colourful, lively and easy going. Shoppers jostle through arcades under balconied old buildings. Families walk in leafy shade along the Paseo Orinoco or sip juice at the new riverside market. And tourists explore jewellers for gold nuggets.

Massive boulders squeeze the Orinoco into 'narrows' – here the river is 1.6km across (1 mile); downstream by Ciudad Guayana it spreads to 5km. The Orinoco, some 2,000km long, drains a basin of over 1,000,000km² in Venezuela and Colombia. By the August flood peak, the Orinoco has risen some 15m to

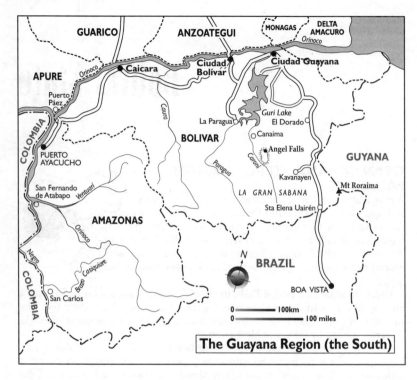

The Guayana Region (the South)

lap at the Paseo's wall. But in April passengers crossing the river must descend many steps from the Paseo to board a *lancha* at a wide beach (where no-one swims).

August is fiesta month on the Paseo, celebrating first the city's patron saint, **Nuestra Señora de las Nieves** whose day is August 5, and in the third week the **Feria del Orinoco** when everyone feasts on sapoara (or zapoara) fish, caught in circular nets called *atarrayas* cast from dugout canoes. Besides an agricultural fair, there are song sessions, food booths, arts, crafts, cultural and sports events held all over town.

In centuries past Ciudad Bolívar was port of call for traders, gold seekers, missionaries, and travellers to Indian domains. It's still like that, plus '*Lost World*' trekkers, and more and more gold miners. Diamond and gold buyers and gold workers live here. Check jewellery shops in the two *pasajes* near the Hotel Colonial; the passageways go from the Paseo through to Calle Venezuela.

Long ago, ships sailed up the Orinoco, 450km from the Atlantic, with oil, wheat and wine from Spain. Later came wood-burning paddle steamers. Dealers once bought tonka beans, copaiba oil, rubber and chicle (gum) from southern forests; and mules, hides, indigo, cacao and tobacco from the plains. But modern roads spelled the end of river trade; by the end of the 1950s, for instance, trade with San Fernando had ceased. From the Mirador on Paseo Orinoco, site of a colonial fort, you look over the river, but no ships. Look west to see the Angostura suspension bridge, 1,678m long and somewhat taller than Ciudad Bolívar (height 54m at Plaza Bolívar). Before the bridge was opened in 1967 you had to cross by ferry, like entering a different country.

The Orinoco narrows (*angosturas*) are the reason why the site was chosen in 1764 as the last home of Santo Tomé de Guayana. This settlement had been moved or burned several times, once in 1618 when Raleigh's son and the Spanish governor died in a fiasco that was to cost Sir Walter his head. Rebuilt on a rocky prominence, the new town was called Angostura. It was known in Europe mainly as the source of a medicinal bark, *Cortex angosturae*, used by Capuchin monks to combat constant fevers (and later made into Angostura Bitters).

The only town on the Orinoco, Angostura was a strategic base during Independence wars. Here arrived soldiers from England, Ireland and Germany to fight with Simón Bolívar, and from here Bolívar set out to free Colombia. The town was patriot capital of Venezuela from 1817 to 1821. In honour of the Liberator, Angostura was renamed Ciudad Bolívar in 1846. Today it is capital of Bolívar State and home to some 260,000 people.

Getting there and away
By air
Ciudad Bolívar's airport is crucial to the largely roadless interior, airtaxis providing a lifeline to distant mining camps and missions. Smack in town at the end of Av Táchira, the airport is a hive of information. Car rental agencies are here, too. There's no official money exchange desk, but you can go across the street to the Hotel Laja Real. An ATT telephone gives direct US service provided you are calling collect or have a credit card.

Adventure is clearly announced by Jimmie Angel's Flamingo parked in front of the terminal. The old monoplane put Angel Falls on the world map when the American bush pilot and prospector stranded it (the plane was borrowed) in a bog atop Auyantepui in 1937. The air force later lifted it off to restore it.

Travellers will need to produce passport or *cédula* for all flights.

Servivensa flies from Caracas daily at 11.00; this flight continues to Canaima at 12.10; $110. LAI has two flights a day, at 08.15 and 19.55. The morning flight continues to Maturín and Porlamar; for information about senior discounts, ring LAI, tel: 29091, 27531. Rutaca flies daily to Canaima at 07.30 in 12–14-seater Caravans; $57.

Airtaxis The airport thrives on gold and diamond miners, and tourism. Various airtaxi lines fly to just about anywhere that a passenger pays to go, as far away as Santa Elena de Uairén near Brazil, 2½ hours. The cost of a seat to Canaima is $50, plus $35 to fly over Angel Falls; to Kavac $60. You pay in bolívars or dollars. Weight allowance is 10kg, strictly enforced. For information, be at the airport when these flights leave, 07.00–08.00, or return, 17.00–18.00 (see below).

Rutaca is the oldest and largest local line, making both charter and scheduled flights, with a fleet of 35 planes from single-engine to twin-engine turb-props. Their office and hangars are on Av Jesús Soto just east of the passenger terminal, tel: (085) 22195, 24010, fax: 25955. They do a day tour to Canaima, plus flight over Angel Falls, for $160.

Some small companies are: **Aeroservicios Caicara**, tel: (085) 23560/463; **Aerobol**, tel: (085) 28686, fax: 28697, open 08.00–12.00, 14.00–17.00 except Sunday; and **Transmandú**, tel: (085) 21462, open 06.30–12.00, 14.00–18.00. Transmandú makes Canaima and Angel Falls flights every day. Staff are on duty very early as many flights leave shortly after 07.00, but if ticket counters are unmanned, look for employees in the Aerobar restaurant, open 06.00–19.00.

Most airtaxis are single-engine Cessnas bound for mining camps far up the Caroní River and its tributaries. Such camps are usually primitive and lack even basics; food is flown in and is scarce and costly (take provisions). Although airtaxis are insured, coverage is valid only for registered airports, not bush strips. The pilots

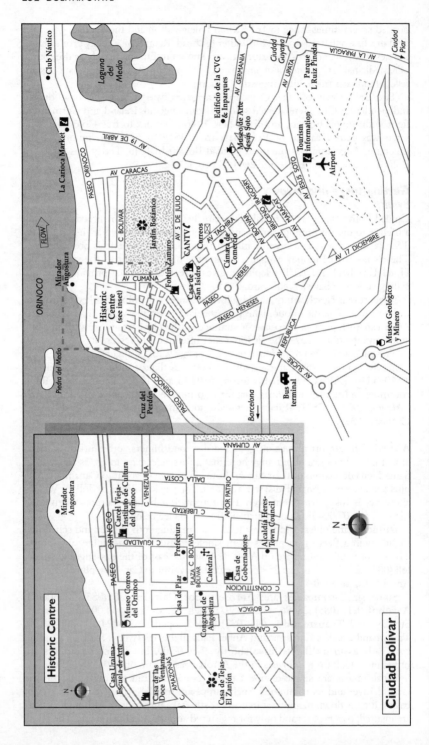

Ciudad Bolívar

are careful, but if they have engine trouble they don't make it back on time. Best flying months are in dry weather, December–April.

By bus

Ciudad Bolívar is 590km from Caracas, 780km from Puerto Ayacucho, and 760km from the Brazilian border. The bus terminal (*Terminal de Pasajeros*) is on Av República at Av Sucre, about 1.5km west of the airport. Low fares (one-sixth of air fare) and frequent service are good reasons why the bus station is always busy: some 28 daily arrivals from **Caracas** alone. Aerobuses de Venezuela, Rodovías, Tierra Firme, La Responsable, Expresos Guayana, El Callao and others cover the Caracas route. It takes anywhere from nine hours by *servicio especial* (air conditioning and curtains), to 11 hours by *servicio normal* (more local stops), $14/$11.

There is an information desk with helpful staff. Ask for connections to Puerto La Cruz, Maturín, La Paragua, Maripa, Puerto Ayacucho. Four lines go to Santa Elena and two continue to Boa Vista, Brazil. Expresos Los Llanos, Expresos Guayana, Travircan, and Línea Orinoco are among lines serving Santa Elena, $12; if you want a window that opens, avoid the *servicio especial* buses. Big Brazilian buses of the Uniao Cascavel, tel: (014) 9850933, leave nightly at 22.00 for Boa Vista, arriving at noon next day; fare $25. Travellers should buy tickets a day in advance and have passports with tourist visas. (See *Ciudad Guayana, Information*, page 260.)

Where to stay

The area telephone code for Ciudad Bolívar is (085)

Plans are afoot to restore Hotel La Cumbre, designed by Fruto Vivas and built in the 1950s; ask the tourist board (see below, *Information*). Old hotels survive downtown by the Orinoco. The riverfront is a busy district of shopping arcades, one- and two-storey dwellings and government offices. Aging hotels are mostly cheap, spartan, noisy and dimly lit.

An exception is the best waterfront choice, the ex-Gran Hotel Bolívar, a balconied building on Paseo Orinoco. It is now called the **Hotel Colonial**, tel: 24402, 20101, fax: 23080; piano bar, terrace restaurant, 60 spacious rooms with air conditioning, hot water, double $21 with a *vista al río*, without $18, triple $24.

Expensive

Top range in Ciudad Bolívar runs about $50 double. The **Laja Real**, Av Jesús Soto opposite airport, tel: 27944/55, fax: 28778; has 73 rooms and suites, swimming pool open to non-guests for a fee, full services, conference rooms, restaurants, disco, shops, car rental and travel agencies. The **Ciudad Bolívar Cumberland**, formerly Hotel Denú, is at the city's western edge, Av Menca de Leoni, tel: 512411/0662, fax: 512863; modern single-storey complex with 100 rooms, airy arches, *tasca* restaurant, large pool, spa and gym, billed as an 'executive centre' with business services.

Moderate

Opposite the airport are two plain hotels. **Hotel Da Gino** and its restaurant are located among shops on Av Jesús Soto, tel: 20313, fax: 25454; double $25, with hot water and cable TV; efficiently run. Slightly cheaper is the **Canaima**, between Av Upata and Jesús Soto, tel: 22565; a tradesman's hotel with restaurant and friendly staff.

More hotels are within walking distance in a pleasant residential district. The **Valentina**, tel: 27253, fax: 27919, has faithful clients; walk two blocks from the airport down Av Táchira, turn right on tree-lined Av Maracay. The Valentina adds a 12% tax to posted room rates: single to quadruple, $20 to $28; Il Vesubio

Restaurant serves good Italian fare. **Hotel Táchira** is 3½ blocks down Av Táchira, tel: 27489; a spacious old house with *tasca*, restaurant and 18 newer rooms in a rear wing with parking; refrigerator in room; no hot water, single/double bed $18. **Hotel Florida**, across the street on Av Táchira at Briceño Iragorry, tel: 27942; a reasonable restaurant adds attraction to this cheaper, simple hotel. **Hotel Laja City**, a three-storey business hotel owned by the Laja Real, is one more block down, on Av Bolívar near Av Táchira, tel: 29920, fax: 28778; 37 rooms with refrigerator, hot water; restaurant and piano bar. Guests may use all services of the Laja Real including fax and swimming pool.

Economy
Near the midtown bus terminal are two air-conditioned hotels; doubles $17–22. **Hotel El Jardín**, Av Bolívar, a block west of Paseo Meneses, tel: 40129; has 14 rooms on two floors and hot water; away from street behind the Restaurant Francia (haute cuisine). The **Universo** on Av República, tel: 43732, is a five-storey commercial hotel; TV, hot water, restaurant, bar.

Budget
Two blocks east at Paseo Orinoco No 131 is the bright pink **Hotel Italia**, tel: 27810, long a friendly, inexpensive standby for European budget travellers. You go through the small front door into a busy foyer and dining room which doubles for travellers as a news exchange. Some second-floor rooms overlook the Paseo, most line a rear patio; a double is $11 with air conditioning, $9 with fan. The **Ritz**, Calle Libertad No 3, tel: 23886, is around the corner from the Paseo; some rooms have air conditioning and private bath. **Hotel Unión**, Calle Urica 11, tel: 23374; has doubles with fan or air conditioning. The **Roma**, Av Cumaná near Calle El Rosario, tel: 27389; is a dingy but quiet single-storey house with parking, a short walk from the river; bottom price.

Camping
Visitors and campers in the Canaima-Angel Falls area do not require a permit from **Inparques** as you pay a parks fee on landing in Canaima. However, campers in the Gran Sabana are officially supposed to have an Inparques *permiso* costing Bs300 per day, and so far Ciudad Bolívar is the only place you can get it. Drivers will need to show insurance coverage. **Inparques** is a 20-minute tramp from the airport: Piso 1, Edificio CVG, Av Germania, tel/fax: (085) 29908.

Where to eat and drink
Sapoara, eaten baked, fried or stewed, is the fish dish in August; other river fish are bocachica, curbinata and morocoto. There's an old saying that any man who eats sapoara head will marry a local girl. *Palo a pique* is a dish of beans, rice, salted meat; the traditional *carne mechada* or shredded beef is called *trapo viejo* (old rag). Sample these at restaurants in the splendid new **Sapoara Market** at the Paseo Orinoco's east end; locals also call the market La Carioca after the district. The market bustles from 06.00 to about 13.00; its restaurants close later.

The **Club Náutico** is just beyond the market. It's nice to sit and watch the river boats cross to Soledad, and have a drink. Beer is cheap and there's a disco. Ask here for a boatman to take you for a day on the river. Alí has a *peñero* and endless stories; he's nicknamed 'El Caimán del Orinoco' because he knows more about the river than a crocodile.

Bolívar State is famous for its cashew nut praline called *mazapán de merey*. The red fleshy cashew fruit is stewed with sugar to make *merey pasado*. A warning: if you pick red fruit from a cashew tree, never put the protruding nut near your mouth. Its shell contains cardol which is very caustic. There are cashew and mango trees aplenty in **Parque Ruiz Pineda** at the east corner of the airport and Av La Paragua.

On **Av Upata** about 2–3km east of the airport, there are large informal *campestre* restaurants where grilled beef and chicken are tasty and economical: **Said Morales**, **Los Caobos** and **Marahuanta**. You can sit to eat or buy steak/chicken by the kilo to take out, also fabulous fresh cheese called *queso de mano*. This cheese is sought after in the rest of Venezuela as *queso Guayanés*.

What to see and do
In the city
History is always close at hand. Ciudad Bolívar was one of five cities in the hemisphere selected as historic world heritage during the 500th anniversary of America's discovery. Much love and labour went into restoring colonial buildings with help from Spain. Except where noted, museums are open 09.30–17.30, closed Monday.

Carcel Vieja The reconstructed colonial jail faces the Paseo Orinoco; entrance is on Calle Igualdad. Its dungeons have been transformed by the Instituto de Cultura del Orinoco into an excellent **Ethnographic Museum** which displays photographs and crafts of the region's Indian cultures: the Yekuana (Makiritare), Pemón, Kariña and Warao. The State government was the first (1990) to appoint an Indian to head the Indian affairs bureau known as DAI, Departamento de Asuntos Indígenas. Ciudad Bolívar is the seat of active Indian movements which publish a monthly paper, *Orinoco Indígena*, at Edificio Mancini, Calle Bolívar No 40.

Casa del Correo del Orinoco This stately 18th-century residence, two blocks west on the Paseo, is named after a newspaper which Bolívar created to boost the revolutionary cause. The *Orinoco Mail* (1818–30) was published in Spanish, French and English. Now the **Museo de Ciudad Bolívar**, it displays the original press, artefacts and a large art collection.

La Casa de las 12 Ventanas Boats once moored at the steps of a restored landmark another two blocks west on the Paseo Orinoco. The elegant **House of 12 Windows**, anchored atop a huge rock called the Laja de Sapoara, was the home of a patriot ship captain, José Tomás Machado, and later his son who married Cecilia Siegert, daughter of Dr J T B Siegert. The German doctor to the Liberation army marketed his Angostura Bitters formula for years in Ciudad Bolívar. The house belongs to the Universidad Nacional Experimental de Guayana and is open as a gallery; entrance on the street behind, Calle Venezuela.

Parque El Zanjón Boulder rises upon boulder up the hill. To discover this surprising park, climb the steps up Calle Carabobo to Calle Amor Patrio (top side of Plaza Bolívar) and turn west. Here the city vanishes into a maze of hot granite boulders, desert flowers and trees. A small art school functions in La Casa de Tejas. Visitors are welcome.

Plaza Bolívar Five statues in the square personify countries that Bolívar liberated: Venezuela, Nueva Granada (Colombia–Panama), Ecuador, Peru and Bolivia. To the west stands the imposing pink structure of the **Congreso de Angostura** where Bolívar was elected President of the Third Republic and proposed the creation of Gran Colombia. Guides show visitors around the well-kept building dating from 1766. Once a school, today it houses exhibitions as well as some 450,000 folios of the Guayana Historical Archives. Beside it, the state **Government Palace** functions in a colonial building where the royal treasury or Real Hacienda collected taxes for Spain; a second storey was added in 1869.

Casa de los Gobernadores Another handsomely redone 18th-century mansion, it was once occupied by Spanish governors. On Plaza Bolívar's high side, it now houses state offices. Next to it is the Parish House, also colonial.

Catedral Resplendent in pale yellow, the cathedral was begun in 1771 and took 70 years to build. It is still at the heart of city life, particularly on August 8, feast day of Our Lady of the Snows. The cathedral wall facing the plaza is pointed out as the place where Manuel Piar, a young and popular general, faced a firing squad in 1817. Piar, who had taken the city from Spaniards after an eight-month siege, rejected Bolívar's authority and was tried and executed. **Casa Piar**, the house where he was imprisoned on the lower side of Plaza Bolívar, is kept as a museum.

Alcaldía de Heres Just up from the cathedral you can't miss the aerial walkway spanning Calle Igualdad. It joins the two buildings of the mayor's office, once the city hospital. Continue south three blocks to the **Biblioteca Rómulo Gallegos**. The restored house with its stone walls and wood floors was formerly a governor's residence.

Plaza Miranda Two blocks west between Calles Progreso and Lezama, this is at the edge of the historic district. The large **Centro de las Artes** occupies a building which was variously a theatre, army barracks, police headquarters and prefecture before its restoration. Drop in for an art show or ask permission to take a rooftop photo of the city panorama.

Fortín El Zamuro You will see on a nearby hilltop a tiny colonial battery with a vulture's eye view. The little fort was pivotal during a 1903 battle when the city was taken by forces of Juan Vicente Gómez who became dictator of Venezuela (1908–35). Look for the entrance on Paseo Heres. Bronze busts of members of the Congreso de Angostura adorn the park, with Francisco Zea and Simón Bolívar at the top.

Casa de San Isidro While writing his speech for the 1819 Congress of Angostura, Bolívar stayed with a friend in what was then a coffee hacienda. The lovely house built on a huge boulder, the **Laja de San Isidro**, is on Av Táchira at 5 de Julio. Open Tue–Sun 09.00–17.00. With its tall ceilings, simple elegance, period furnishings and ample gardens it is most attractive.

Museo de Arte Moderno Jesús Soto On Av Briceño Iragorry at Av Germania, this fine museum is near the Corporación Venezolana de Guayana HQ. Soto, a leader of the kinetic art movement, was born in Ciudad Bolívar in 1923. The museum has a good collection of his large 'penetrables', smaller pieces and works by masters such as Mondrian, Kandinsky, Albers and many other international artists. In 1995 Soto was awarded France's highest sculpture prize, the *Grand Prix National de l'Esculture.*

Museo Geológico y Minero Opposite the Universidad de Oriente entrance on Av Principal de La Sabanita, the museum is 1km south of the bus terminal. In what used to be the Orinoco Mining Company guesthouse, the story is told of Guayana's gold, iron and other mineral finds. Long before the 1947 discovery of Cerro Bolívar, the iron mountain heralding heavy industries, iron was forged here. An ingot on display was made by an 18th-century Catholic missionary; even Sir Walter Raleigh saw possibilities in the iron deposits. Closed Sunday.

Money

Keep some US$ travellers' cheques in reserve, in case banks give you trouble with cash advances. Banks such as the Mercantil, Unión or Venezuela should honour credit cards. The best deal is changing US$ travellers' cheques; CorpBanca is on Avenida Aeropuerto. Do your transactions early as banks work from 08.30 to 15.30. After then, go to the Casa de Cambio in the Laja Real Hotel.

Information and tours

The Bolívar State **Dirección de Turismo** has an office on Av Táchira next to the Hotel Florida, tel: 22771, fax: 24803; weekdays 08.00–12.00, 14.00–17.30. The **airport** information booths are most useful, dispensing city maps and data on Bolívar State (closed for lunch). In the Sapoara Market (see page 254) two souvenir shops offer fair prices and there is a city tourism information booth. Smartly dressed tourism police look after travellers (they study first aid, English, local history).

Travel agents can help with tour information: **Auyantepuy**, Edificio Roke Center, Calle Bolívar, tel: 28702/84; **Di Blasio**, Av Cumaná No 6, tel: 26367; **Expediciones Dearuna**, Hotel Caracas, fax: 26089; **Kamaracoto**, CC Diamante, Av Germania at Andrés Bello, tel: 27680. **Neckar Tours** is a German-run agency based in the Hotel Colonial, tel: 28390, fax: 23080. **Soana Travel**, tel: 22536, fax: 22030, on Calle Bolívar, promotes Caura River trips. Agencies offer a spectrum of far-out destinations: Kavac by charter plane, the Gran Sabana by jeep, the Orinoco Delta by boat.

A standard day tour to Salto Angel costs around $160, starting at 07.30 or so and including a flight over the falls, meal, and a boat ride on Canaima Lagoon (choose a tour that goes to Salto El Sapo). Such all-inclusive outings are a good bet for travellers short on time or Spanish, but do not give most value for your money. (For airtaxi information, see page 251.)

At the airport enquire at Turi Express, tel: (016) 6850405, tel/fax: 28910/120; they also do a good **city tour** and have *peñeros* for Orinoco excursions. Guillermo Rodríguez speaks some English and German. Tiuna Tours have an airport desk; tel: 28686/97.

Roraima

It is probably better not to arrange a Roraima trek from Ciudad Bolívar. **Santa Elena** offers faster, cheaper excursions with local operators and guides. Or you can pack plenty of food (for the porters too) and talk in **San Francisco de Yuruaní** directly to the Indians. In **Puerto Ordaz** the Roraima professionals are Bagheera Tours; they may have a trek to coincide with your itinerary (see page 262).

Paragua expedition

The Paragua, a huge tributary feeding Guri Lake, has many small gold and diamond mines. An expedition upriver, negotiating rocks and rapids by motorised *curiara*, takes you in four days to remote **Ichún Falls**, a dramatic cataract of white foam and deep black water. On the way you fish at **Uraima Rapids**, visit diamond camps, and sling your hammock on sandy banks. Advance reservations through Viva Trek Tours, tel: (016) 6320050, fax: (044) 551683.

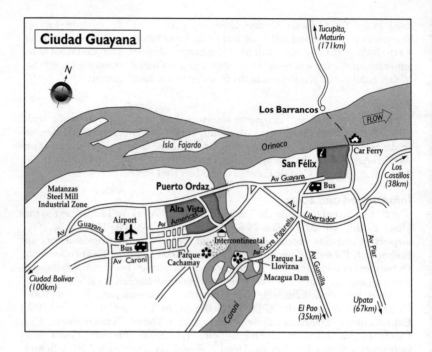

Alpi Tours represents **Camp Urayma**, a very attractive layout about two hours upriver from La Paragua; the big rapids are famous for payara fishing. Guests are flown in or driven to La Paragua. Churuata-style bungalows have beds and private bath. In Caracas, tel: (02) 2831433/5116, fax: 2856067.

Ciudad Guayana

Two disparate towns are linked by three bridges at the confluence of the Caroní and Orinoco rivers. On the Caroní's left bank is the new town of **Puerto Ordaz**, founded in 1952 as an iron ore port. On the right bank is old **San Félix**, founded in 1576, a workers' town. When they were joined in 1961 into Ciudad Guayana, the population was 40,000. Today it has 550,000 people who man Venezuela's heavy industry centre, powered by the Caroní's cheap hydroelectricity.

In practical terms such as bus and plane schedules, Puerto Ordaz and San Félix are always referred to separately.

In San Félix worker housing, mechanics' shops and small businesses spread untidily along endless highways. Rural migrants have thrown up shacks of zinc, cardboard, wood and plastic in over 100 unplanned and underserviced *barrios* spreading south of the old pueblo.

The state planning body is in Puerto Ordaz. The Corporación Venezolana de Guayana, CVG, has interests in everything from gold and hydropower to parks and pine plantations. In fact, Puerto Ordaz is a company town. It has one of the highest cost-of-living indexes in the country. Large malls in the centre have boutiques, electronic and sporting goods outlets and restaurants that reflect the tastes of a mostly middle-class population of white-collar workers. There are supermarkets, night clubs, good roads and services. But the planned city lacks something that gives most towns a heart and soul.

Getting there and away

By air Puerto Ordaz airport is 5km west of the centre on Av Guayana (road to Ciudad Bolívar). Flights specify Puerto Ordaz, NOT Ciudad Guayana. There are five daily flights to/from **Caracas** on weekdays and three at weekends ($60–80) by Avensa/Servivensa, Aserca and Aeropostal which has the best prices. Flights also serve Barcelona, Barquisimeto, Maracaibo, Maturín, Porlamar, Punto Fijo, San Antonio del Táchira and Valencia.

Canaima is served by Avensa, whose early flight from Caracas, daily at 06.00, connects with an 08.00 flight to Canaima. This DC3 flight continues for Santa Elena de Uairén, $74. (If you get off in Canaima you also pay $74.)

There's no airbus so far, but *por puestos* go to the centre along Av Guayana or Av Las Américas to the north. Those saying 'Castillito' will take you to the hotel district.

By bus There is a modern bus station in **Puerto Ordaz** on Av Guayana at Av Norte-Sur, a 20-minute walk east of the airport. This handles some through buses for the big depot in San Félix, but not all lines stop here. Service to Ciudad Bolívar is frequent, 120km (1½ hours). The Línea Caribe-Uniao Cascavel, tel: (086) 519214/8669, has a nightly coach bound for Boa Vista, departing 23.00; service from Puerto La Cruz to Boa Vista runs on Mon–Wed–Fri.

The Terminal de Pasajeros in **San Félix** on Av Gumilla, 1.5km from the old centre, is the terminus for interstate buses. Many lines go to **Caracas** throughout the day and evening, 730km (10–11 hours); some pick up passengers in Puerto Ordaz. Lines originating in Ciudad Bolívar go on to **Santa Elena de Uairén**: Línea Orinoco, Travircan, Transmundial, Turcar. Buses to **Tucupita**, **Maturín**, **Carúpano** and **Güiria** take the Orinoco ferry from San Félix to Los Barrancos. *Por puestos* link the terminal with downtown San Félix, and Puerto Ordaz.

By ferry Big car and passenger ferries cross the Orinoco from San Félix every half hour or so to **Los Barrancos**. Buses to Maturín and Tucupita go via the ferry, too, as well as heavy trucks, so there can be a queue, especially in the early morning. The new terminal is at the end of Av Manuel Piar, east of downtown San Félix. The Angostura bridge near Ciudad Bolívar is the only bridge over the Orinoco, although CVG has announced plans to build a bridge from Ciudad Guayana. To date, there are no pleasure boats on the Orinoco.

Where to stay

The area telephone code for Ciudad Guayana is (086)

In Puerto Ordaz

The expensive **Intercontinental Guayana**, tel: 222244, 230722, fax: 222253, is a class apart. Its splendid location by the Caroní bridge requires a car or taxi. It has 205 rooms, executive services, pool and tennis. Caroní river excursions leave from the hotel jetty. In Caracas call the Tamanaco, tel: (02) 2087233, fax: 2087951. Guests can use the Club Caronoco's golf links by reservation. The hotel has no direct access to Cachamay Park.

Moderate hotels, $35–48 a double, are led by the **Embajador**, at the corner of Calle Urbana, tel: 225511/91, fax: 226123; 60 rooms in an eight-floor block, good restaurant, conference and tour services. Largest central hotel is the **Rasil**, Centro Cívico off Vía Venezuela (northwest), tel: 222710/223025, fax: 227703. Its older tower has a swimming pool, disco and restaurant; 150 rooms at $36 double. Across the street the modern Rasil has 150 newer doubles at $45; car rental, tour agency, within walking distance of restaurants. **Hotel Dos Ríos**, Av México near Ecuador, tel: 220679, fax: 233092, has 82 rooms and a poolside restaurant; two blocks from the Brazilian consulate.

Inexpensive hotels with bath and air conditioning, west of Castillito, start with the **Saint Georges**, Carrera Aripao; double about $14 with bath. The **Habana Cuba**, tel: 224904, and serviceable **La Guayana Hotel** and restaurant, tel: 227375, 234866, are on Av Las Américas near Calle Turmero. **Hotel Tepuy** on Carrera Upata is a block north of Las Américas, tel: 220120/0102; restaurant, 46 rooms with hot shower, double $14; a busy commercial hotel.

Budget lodgings, passable at a pinch, are found in the river vicinity of Av Principal de Castillito. Rates are about $7 double at **Hotel Roma**, and **Portu's Hotel**.

In San Félix

Bus travellers may find central lodgings useful for an early start. There are several hotels that no taxi driver in the airport of the posher Puerto Ordaz side would know about. Or care, as they are better forgotten. Most do duty as *hoteles de cita* renting rooms by the hour, and are overpriced by comparison with hotels in Puerto Ordaz (or Ciudad Bolívar, cheaper and more interesting). Rates are $12–15. Within four blocks of Plaza Bolívar are: **Hotel Aguila**, Calle 4 near Carrera 1; the **Excelsior**, Calle 3 near Carrera 6; **Hotel Yoli**, Calle 1 near Carrera 5; **Hotel Orinoco**, Calle 2 near Carrera 3.

Information

There is a state tourism desk at the Puerto Ordaz airport, and another in San Félix facing the Orinoco at the bottom of Carrera 1 (closed weekends and lunch hours). The Corporación Venezolana de Guayana, Edificio CVG, near the Plaza del Hierro in Puerto Ordaz, prepares a useful booklet (in Spanish) about the Gran Sabana with mileages. Consult them about Ciudad Guayana sights, dams, waterfalls and parks, also the aluminium, steel and iron industries. (See below, *What to do in Puerto Ordaz*.)

The **Brazilian consulate** is located in Edificio Amazonas, mezzanine, Av Las Américas opposite Carrera Ecuador, Puerto Ordaz; tel: (086) 235243, 220537; open 08.00–12.00. Venezuelans with a passport can get an eight-day pass at the border to visit Boa Vista; visas needed for other nationalities.

What to do in Puerto Ordaz

A close look at the Caroní from **Parque Cachamay** is impressive. Here the dark river, 6km from bank to bank, races down cataracts between islands. The air is cooled by spray and deep shade. The lovely park lies between river and highway, ending at the Hotel Intercontinental Guayana. Closed Mondays, like the Loefling. Much larger, **Parque Loefling** has a zoo of native fauna including anteaters, sloths and armadillos. The larger animals such as tapirs and *chigüires* (capybara) wander free, and there is a band of capuchin monkeys in the trees.

Headquarters of state development are in Edificio CVG, tel: 226155, Calle Cuchivero, near the Plaza del Hierro, Alta Vista. This is the place to enquire about industries, dams, parks and city planning.

The big **steel and aluminium plants** in Matanzas district give free guided tours, usually on weekdays, 08.00–15.00. If you want to know what Ciudad Guayana is all about, visit one of the plants. You'll be impressed by their huge scale. The Matanzas industrial zone is the size of a small city. The enormous steel mill, **Sidor**, tel: 901165/750, occupies 87 hectares of construction, plus 27km^2 of grounds including docks on the Orinoco handling about 6,000,000 metric tons of steel a year. Some 150 buses are needed to transport its 19,000 workers. Sidor uses iron produced by **Ferrominera Orinoco**, tel: 303755, 223333, whose ore trains run here from the mines of El Pao, San Isidro and Cerro Bolívar, the astonishing iron mountain which launched Guayana's industry when discovered in 1947. If you are travelling to La Paragua, you pass the terraced mountain (see below, *Further afield*).

Venalum, tel: 993132, and **Alcasa**, tel: 992997, together produce some 650,000 metric tons of aluminium yearly. The metal is second to oil as a foreign exchange earner. Like steel, the industry is entirely integrated within the Guayana region. From Los Pijiguaos, 650km up the Orinoco, bauxite is barged down to **Interalumina**, tel: 992301, which turns the raw material into alumina.

Edelca, the state hydroelectric company, is in charge of Macagua I and II dams on the Caroní's east side. Ask the Edelca public relations office, tel: 603521, for a free guided tour. You may soon be able to walk from Parque Loefling across the Caroní by way of the dykes connecting these dams. The new Leopoldo Sucre Figarella highway follows this dramatic route linking San Félix and Puerto Ordaz.

What to do in San Félix

San Félix is properly speaking an Orinoco town. The old centre faces the Orinoco; its Plaza Bolívar is just a block from the Mirador on the riverbank. Here, you can see the Caroní's tannin-dark current flowing side by side with the muddier Orinoco waters for kilometres before mingling. With its church, noisy market, small hotels and CANTV telephone centre, downtown has a traditional air although scruffy. There are no historic buildings.

The **Castillos de Guayana**, sentinels on the Orinoco, may be visited by launch or road, a 38km trip (they are in Delta Amacuro State). Built in the 17th and 18th centuries, the forts of **San Francisco** (older) and **San Diego de Alcalá** (higher) guarded against the likes of Walter Raleigh who in 1595 made a foray up the Orinoco that led him to write *The Discoverie of the Large, Rich and Bewtiful Empire of Guiana*. In 1618 Raleigh's men returned to raid Santo Tomás, killing Governor Berrío but losing many men and Raleigh's own son. Raleigh, who had been too ill to fight, later lost his head to King James' wrath. Santo Tomás was eventually refounded upriver (today's Ciudad Bolívar).

Por puestos for this route leave from El Mirador in San Félix. If driving, take Av Guayana east through San Félix to Av Manuel Piar; go south for the signpost, then east. The Castillos are open 09.00–12.00, 13.00–17.00; closed Monday.

Salto La Llovizna is a truly lovely set of falls forming the east end of a 6km shelf of cataracts that extends across the Caroní to Saltos Cachamay in Puerto Ordaz. With the opening in 1998 of a new highway, Avenida Leopoldo Sucre Figarella, from San Félix directly to Parque La Llovizna – and over the causeways of **Macagua Dams I and II** to Puerto Ordaz – access to the park should be simpler. You can ask at the visitors' centre about guided tours of the Macagua dams which can produce up to 2,540 megawatts by means of run-of-river generators needing no reservoir. A free bus runs all day to the beautifully kept park where the Caroní thunders down a gorge between islands, throwing up spray, *llovizna*, and shaking the ground. No camping. Go early because the buses stop running around 15.00 and visitors are shepherded out. Closed Monday.

Ruins of the **Caroní Mission Church** are above the falls, 5km from the Parque Llovizna guardhouse. This was the first of a chain of wealthy Guayana missions of the late 18th century. The roofless church (restored) reveals a prosperity that was the monks' undoing when patriot armies seized thousands of their horses, mules and cattle to support the 1817 Independence campaign.

Further afield

The excursions below and others to the Delta, Gran Sabana and Caura River are offered by leading tour agencies in Puerto Ordaz. Some are: **Anaconda Tours**, CC Anto, Av Las Américas, tel: 223130, fax: 226572; they maintain their own camps and fleet of 4x4 vehicles in the Gran Sabana. **Bagheera**, tel: 529481/9171, fax: 528767; email: bagheera@telcel.net.ve; CC Gran Sabana-piso 2, Paseo Caroní; treks to Roraima, 8 days, with transfers, porters, bilingual guides $810. **Canaima Tours**, Quinta La Raulera, Calle 8, Urb Aribana, Alta Vista, tel: 6816981, 625560; **Happy Tours**, Intercontinental Guayana, tel: 232941, fax: 227748; **Karuai Tours**, CC Maripa, Calle Urbana, tel: 234785/1103, fax: 234963.

Guri Dam Waters from Roraima and Angel Falls mingle in the Caroní and flow into man-made Guri Lake. Flooding 4,250km^2, an area roughly the size of Trinidad, the lake feeds giant Guri Dam, or Represa Raúl Leoni. Its 10,000-megawatt capacity is the world's largest after Itaipu in Brazil–Paraguay. Started in 1963, Guri Dam took 23 years to complete.

A MESSAGE LEFT BY JIMMIE ANGEL

When pilot Jimmie Angel landed on top of Auyantepui, he made a mistake. Not only was there no gold, but the surface was so boggy that the plane remained stuck. Goldless (and largely foodless), Angel, his wife Marie, Gustavo Heny and his gardener Miguel, survived only because the route down had been scouted for them in advance. But before they started walking, Angel left a paper in the cockpit with a scrawled message. Their way had been previously established by Félix Cardona and Gustavo Heny. Is the fact that the escape route already existed an evidence of thoroughness, or perhaps of Angel's willingness to abandon the plane (which was not his)? Perhaps Angel was as much a publicity hound as fortune seeker. Who was the message for? An air rescue team? Years later it was found and kept by Alejandro Laime and is reproduced here.

The dam spans the Caroní River about 100km before it joins the Orinoco. Free guided tours are conducted daily except Monday by state power company Edelca, tel: (086) 603521. To drive, take the highway from Ciudad Guayana south for 75km; turn left on an access road to the main gate, 18.5km. Pick up a pass and go another 5km to the visitors' centre to reserve a tour (09.00, 10.30, 14.00, 15.30). You may have time to visit the **Mirador** for a panorama, or see the Club Náutico. In the shopping centre there are cinemas and a bowling alley.

The tour will take you below the dam face, 162m tall, and past large plazas with a huge aluminium 'Solar Tower' by sculptor Alejandro Otero and a great sundial by Esther Fontana and Lisette Delgado. You get a look in the powerhouse whose turbines supply 70% of Venezuela's electricity. Edelca even exports electricity to Colombia and Brazil.

Fishing Guri Lake is internationally famous for peacock bass or *pavón* weighing up to 25 pounds; they feed in 'wolf packs' and readily strike topwater lures. Fanged silvery payara, even larger, also slash and leap. Other sport species are caribe (piranha), aymara, coparo and curbinata. Fishing boats on the lake can be arranged for $100 a day. Guri Lodge offers sport fishing tours for $250 a day. The package includes transfers, lodging, three meals, guide and boat. In Caracas consult Jacobo Elías, tel: (02) 9530111. Another group, GG Guri Lake, offers fishermen a houseboat and 7 Ranger launches equipped with 200hp engines for speed, switching to silent electric motors for fishing. For information, contact tel: (02) 2429740; email: gigifish.com.ve.

Tours to Represa de Guri from Ciudad Bolívar or Ciudad Guayana are standard offers at about $60. The full day may also cover Cerro Bolívar.

Cerro Bolívar iron mountain In 1947 this landmark signalled the Guayana development when compasses went haywire on a prospecting plane, so the story goes. It is no longer 590m high after continuous terracing, but its silhouette is still impressive on the palm-dotted savannah as you go south to La Paragua. In the east rise San Isidro and Los Barrancos, iron mountains containing 600 million tons of high grade ore, a third of Venezuela's iron deposits. Trains haul ore to Puerto Ordaz. Capuchin monks knew the value of iron ore: in the 1750s they forged iron for tools, cart wheels and axles. This knowledge was forgotten, however, when patriot armies appropriated the Capuchins' herds and properties.

Ciudad Piar This town 10km south is the operating centre of Ferrominera Orinoco, successor to US Steel upon iron nationalisation in 1975. For a pass to the mine, go to Administration, 1km west of the centre; visits are authorised Tue–Fri. Ciudad Piar is 135km from Puerto Ordaz (bus 2½ hours); 108km from Ciudad Bolívar (bus 2 hours).

ANGEL FALLS

If one place alone draws travellers to Venezuela, it is Angel Falls, highest in the world with a 979m drop. In dry weather the falls turn to mist before reaching the ground; in wet, the 'angels' are three. After heavy rain literally hundreds of waterfalls pour off the cliffs of the giant *mesa* called Auyantepui. Consequently June to November may be the best months for a visit although clouds close in early.

The romantic name comes not from heaven but from American bush pilot Jimmie Angel. For many years Angel's abandoned plane glinted in a bog atop Auyantepui where he landed in 1937 looking for gold. All the stuff of legends. But Angel (who first saw the falls in 1935) eclipsed their earlier discoverer, a prospector and rubber hunter named Ernesto Sánchez La Cruz. As early as 1910 Sánchez reported the cascade as Churún Merú (although this fall is now said to be one at the canyon's end). This is its name (*merú* = falls) in the language of the Pemón Indians who of course knew all the time it was there. Four years after Angel (1899–1956) died, his son returned to Venezuela to scatter his ashes over the falls. Jimmie's plane (it was borrowed), dubbed the *Río Caroní*, was removed by the air force in 1970. Restored, it is now displayed at Ciudad Bolívar airport.

Angel Falls still draws adventurers who scale the canyon's face, walk tightropes, drop in parachutes... But, aside from a barricade of permits, the hazards are terrible. In 1990 French climber Jean Marc Boivin lost his life tragically in a paraglide jump over the falls.

Photographers should note that the falls face east, hidden deep in Devil's Canyon in the heart of Auyantepui. After midday they are in shade (and cloud, often as not).

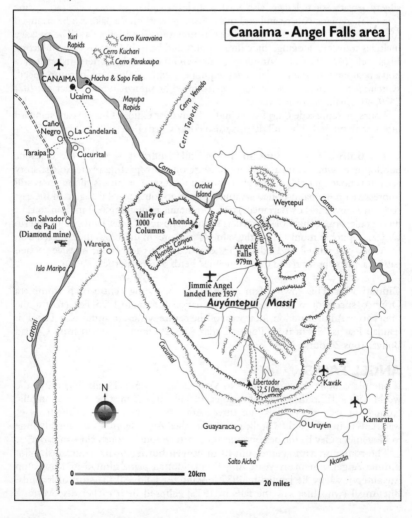

Canaima

About 50km north of Angel Falls, Canaima is located at a bend where the Carrao River spills over lovely Hacha-El Sapo Falls into a lagoon. It is the main base for trips to Angel Falls. A village of 1,000 people, mostly Pemón Indians, has grown up around the airport and Campamento Canaima where 40 years ago there was only river and savannah. Today Canaima has telephones, fax: and Internet service. Although Canaima's main lodge, restaurant and souvenir shops are more than a bit touristy, they are dwarfed by the panorama. With table mountains behind the lagoon and *moriche* palms, it's an idyllic setting.

Various excursions are offered: Salto El Sapo $25, Mayupa $45, Isla Orquídea upriver $135, and Salto Yuri downriver by jeep and boat $45.

Sapo Falls form the eastern branch of the Carrao's lovely cataracts opposite Canaima. They are beyond the Isla de Anatoly (Tomás Bernal's camp) and are reached by a short boat ride and hike. What makes the 20m falls special is a rocky passage behind the fall's curtain of water. The name comes from the *sapo minero*, a small black frog with bright yellow blotches (*Dendrobates leucomelas*). This is the perfect excursion for a hot day; good swimming.

The **Wareipa** trip takes you 45 minutes south across the savannah in a trailer pulled by a tractor, and then one hour up the Río Cucurital by dugout to Wareipa rapids, enjoying excellent views of Auyantepui's 1,000 columns, totally fascinating at sunset. (See below, *Where to stay*.)

Warning Canaima beach has stray dogs and as a result may have jiggers or *niguas*, nasty sand fleas that burrow into your feet; a week later you dig out their egg sacks with a needle. The sand used to be pure, like the clear, brandy-dark water. This is no longer true as the village lacks adequate waste treatment.

Getting there and away

Servivensa's daily jet to Canima leaves at 11.00 from **Caracas**, collects passengers in Ciudad Bolívar and arrives at 12.40, $110. Aereotuy also flies from **Porlamar**; one way, $90. There is a DC3 flight by Servivensa leaving **Puerto Ordaz** daily at 08.00, $74; it continues to Santa Elena de Uairén, but may stop over in Kavac if there are enough passengers. From **Santa Elena**, the DC3 stops in Canaima daily at 09.40; it continues to Puerdo Ordaz at 15.30. Rutaca flies daily from Ciudad Bolívar in a 12–14-seater Caravan; $57. On arrival you pay a National Parks fee ($5). If you are camping check with Inparques about a permit.

Where to stay

The area telephone code for Canaima is (086)

Ucaima, on the banks of the Carrao 3km south of Canaima, is the area's pioneer camp, built in 1958 by 'Jungle Rudy' Truffino, a river guide who died in 1994. The Dutchman's family still runs it. It has nice cabins, a bar and a library with lots of information and videos about Angel Falls. Small (20 guests maximum), rustic, and upscale: per person, double occupancy, $264 for 3 days/2 nights with meals, plus excursion to El Sapo Falls. They offer flight reservations, and 15% discount for people over 60. In Canaima, ring 622359; Caracas, tel: (02) 6930618, fax: 6930825. (See below, *River bookings*.)

Campamento Canaima is the area's biggest hotel, operated by Hoturvensa. Guests lounge in 35 bungalows, each with two to three rooms facing beautiful Canaima Lagoon and Hacha Falls. The cabins are reserved for package tours: 3 days/2 nights at $362 per person in a double (100% more for singles), slightly less during low season. This cost includes a round-trip jet from Caracas, meals in the large restaurant (open to all), a canoe outing, and a flight over Angel Falls. Book through Avensa/Servivensa, tel: 800 AVENSA, or Hoturvensa, tel: (02) 9078130/31, fax: 9078140. This package is good value as the round trip from Caracas alone costs over $200.

Tomás Bernal has an incredible camp on Anatoly's island in Laguna Canaima, now known as Tomás' Island. It has a lovely beach and view of Canaima's falls. He will rent you a hammock, but he has no spare food so bring your own for cooking. Bernal does tours to Salto El Sapo nearby and Angel Falls (see *River bookings*). Although theft has been reported as a problem in the Hoturvensa camp, your belongings should be safe when entrusted to individuals such as Tomás or others.

The native village (south) has several basic *posadas* and camps, or you can ask to sling your hammock in the house of a Pemón guide such as Matterson or Nazario. **Nazario** has a guest *churuata* providing hammocks ($5), with common bathrooms; meals can be arranged. For information on his camp and economical river trips to Angel Falls, where he and Tito Abati have built a lovely camp, send a fax: c/o Claudio Longuino, Canaima, (086) 620443, 615299.

Excursiones Churúm Vena has a *posada* by the football field; a double costs $32, hammock $6. Inexpensive meals are provided: $3.50 to $6.

Campamento Hamaca, a short distance from Hoturvensa's camp, is a large *churuata* or open-sided house offering hammocks only; it has bath houses for men and women. For information, contact Roymar Viajes in Caracas: tel/fax: (02) 5765655/5807. A 3-day/2-night package includes food, lodging and excursions to Salto Angel and Kavac by air, for a low $255. Also represented by Roymar is **Wey-Tepuy**, a modest hotel; 32 rooms with bath. Guests eat at Campamento Canaima. Open to travellers but those with agency bookings get the best deal on excursions. Roymar also books for Canaima Camp, Ucaima and Wareipa. Credit cards are accepted at a 10% surcharge. (See below, *River bookings*.)

North of Canaima's airstrip are other camps. The first, **Posada Hermanos Jiménez**, offers slightly improved lodging and restaurant: hammocks, $6; thatched bungalows with doubles and bath for about $28 per person or $75 with all meals. The Jiménez brothers run Excursiones Canaima. (See below, *River bookings*.)

Kaikusé, a small camp built by Esperanza Jiménez, is just past the Jiménez' camp: 12 rooms with bath, for up to 30 persons at $20 a night; or $45 with meals.

Gaby Truffino has opened a camp with her husband, Juan Jiménez, one of the seven Jiménez brothers. **Campamento Parakaupa** has eight rooms with bath and fan; $84 a night including airport reception and transfer, *criollo* style meals; assistance in English. In Canaima, tel/fax: 614963; email: parakaupa@ etheron.net.

Wareipa is a camp south of Canaima across the savannah and up the Cucurital (see above, Canaima). Under one large palm-thatched *churuata* are a kitchen, hammock space for 30, and bathroom. A good place to swim, explore and relax when there are few guests; about $75 a day, all inclusive from Canaima.

Camping You can also camp in Canaima beyond the Guardaparque house, on the beach with ultrafine white and pink sand, or sling a hammock. A mosquito net is recommended, although in the dry season it is not an absolute necessity. Small shops in the village carry the basics, crackers, pasta, oil and tuna. Check in with Inparques at the airport for a camping permit.

Salto Angel tours by air

Light planes make breathtaking tours to the falls, penetrating 'Devil's Canyon' which carves Auyantepui nearly in half. If your incoming flight doesn't swing by the falls, you can almost certainly fly from Canaima in one of the Cessnas providing 'Salto Angel' service. **Excursiones Canaima** offers a Cessna tour for about $40 each for four passengers. Should **Servivensa** have an empty seat on its DC3 tour for Canaima Camp guests, it will cost somewhat less.

It is possible to put together your own package, although in the end this may prove more expensive than the tours below. If you haven't a fixed length of stay, ask around at Ciudad Bolívar airport for an airtaxi flight, *traslado unicamente a Canaima*, $50. The planes are five-seater Cessnas leaving early in the morning.

Aereotuy (LTA) advertises day tours originating in Porlamar and in Ciudad Bolívar. At around $150 from Ciudad Bolívar, the day tour to Canaima includes a flight over Angel Falls (as does the **Kavac** tour). Aereotuy: in Porlamar, tel: (095) 630307/67, fax: 617746; Ciudad Bolívar, tel: (085) 25907, 24201.

Rutaca offers a day tour from Ciudad Bolívar with a flight over Angel Falls for $160. **Roymar Viajes** has a 2-day/1-night plan that includes a flight over Angel Falls and excursion to El Sapo falls. You stay at a *posada* or inn and the package costs around $200.

Amazonair takes groups of four or five from Caracas, picking up passengers from their hotel and flying them to Angel Falls direct. They picnic at Canaima or El Sapo Falls and go on to overnight at Kavac. The three-day trip takes in tepui vistas, and isolated falls such as Salto Aicha. Pilot Willi Michel (he speaks German, English and Spanish) carries all food and drink. Costs per person, including insurance, are about $720 sleeping in hammocks, or $790 staying in Ucaima. In Caracas, tel: (02) 2836960, tel/fax: 2832627.

Upriver to Angel Falls

Once on the sunny river you are on the edge of Eden. In the dry season, however, it is not usual to find anyone to take you up the Carrao River to Angel Falls. This is only because shallow rapids mean troublesome portages. Operators choose rainy weather (June–Nov) when rivers and falls are fullest. Standard craft is the native *curiara*, a long, resilient dugout powered by a 48hp outboard motor; the seats are planks and there's no roof to protect you, rain or shine. All meals and sleeping gear (usually hammock with mosquito net) are provided.

River tour operators meet the morning flights; trips lasting two, three or four days start soon after the plane lands. In the rush for tourist dollars, even one-day excursions are touted (leaving at 05.00), but not recommended: so many hours sitting on boards can be torture, particularly if it is rainy and cold. And Angel Falls receives sun only in the morning, so by afternoon the falls are in the dark.

Bernal Tours, **Excursiones Canaima**, **Tiuna Tours**, **Ucaima Camp** and **Yen Karúm** all conduct river trips. **Excursiones Churúm Vena** and **Kamaracoto Tours** are Indian-operated enterprises. The guides are usually Spanish-speaking natives; good rivermen and reliable leaders, more or less.

The cost of a three-day river trip varies from really low, $180 per person with **Churúm Vena**, to $255 with **Parakaupa** (see above, *Where to stay*). The difference lies in sleeping accommodation, meals, and bilingual guide.

Ucaima offers four days to the falls, July to early November, at about $515 with airport transfers. Guests sleep two nights in Ucaima, one night in a cabin with camp beds. Ucaima provides life jackets, insurance and bilingual guide, but not all outfits do, so check before signing up.

A cheaper alternative of boat only, at $45 a passenger (minimum six), is provided by **Excursiones Canaima** and **Kamaracoto Tours**; you bring food and camping gear.

Remember Be sure to take a hat and long-sleeved shirt for sun/insect protection, swimsuit and sun block, extra foot gear such as old canvas shoes for river and camp wear, a plastic poncho and plastic bags for yourself and belongings as it often rains (you may get chilled as well as burned). For emergencies, a torch (*linterna*), lighter and chocolates are a good idea; buy the chocolates locally as they do not melt readily. Mosquito repellent is necessary in the rainy season.

River bookings

Not all river operators work through city agencies so if you are on the spot, ask around. Six passengers is the standard group minimum. By joining a larger group you may find a better price. On the whole reservations are recommended; you may be asked to make a bank deposit in advance.

Bernal Tours contact Transmandú (airtaxi), Aeropuerto Ciudad Bolívar, tel: (085) 21462; or Canaima Tours in Puerto Ordaz.

Canaima Tours Alta Vista, Puerto Ordaz; tel: (086) 625560, 616981, fax: 690559. Also, at the national terminal, Maiquetía airport (Caracas), (02) 3552339. Canaima Tours also have a desk at Caracas' national terminal, tel/fax: (02) 3552462. The Hermanos Jiménez who operate Excursiones Canaima are a large family with two Caracas headquarters: Esperanza Jiménez, tel: (02) 5415603, fax: 5419095; and Brígida Contreras, tel: (02) 5457541/27, fax: 5419583.

Kamaracoto Tours In Ciudad Bolívar, tel/fax: (085) 27680. In Caracas, tel: 5632729, fax: 5647355.

Orinoco Tours In Caracas, tel: 7618431, 7627662, fax: 7616801; email: orinoco@sa.omnes.net.

Roymar Viajes In Caracas, tel: (02) 5765271, 5765655/5807, fax: 5766992; email: roymar@cantv.net.

Tiuna Tours Ciudad Bolívar airport, tel: (085) 28686, fax: 28697.

Ucaima Tours Truffino, Apartado 61879, Caracas 1060A; tel: (02) 6930618, fax: 6930825. Allow 4 weeks' notice at holiday time.

Kamarata to Angel Falls

One way to largely bypass Canaima where tourism detracts from the wilderness is to approach Angel Falls from Kamarata, south of Auyantepui. The mission settlement is served by airtaxis from Canaima. Aereotuy and other tour agencies make flights to nearby Kavac.

This longer, more interesting river trek skirts the eastern cliffs of **Auyantepui** and goes down the **Akanán**, a tributary of the Carrao. In Kamarata there is a group of efficient Pemón guides headed by **Tito Abati** of **Aicha Vená Tours**; he's very good and speaks English, too. Abati provides *curiaras*, outboard motors, hammocks and river guides. His Indian-built camps have amenities such as sit-down toilets. Five days to Angel Falls and then down to Canaima cost $80 a day per person in groups of six minimum. Tito does this river run from May to December. Messages sent courtesy of Rutaca's pilots, (085) 22195-Daniel Mares, will reach him at Kavac or Kamarata; also a fax: c/o Claudio Longuino, Canaima, (086) 620443, 615299. Tito can arrange food and lodging in Kamarata where there are Pemón hotels, the **Kavaikoden** (beds, bath), and other houses providing hammocks.

Going down the Akanán you pass Iguana rapids or **Iwanamerú**, a spot with lovely beaches in the drier months, and a view of the Aparamán range. The Akanán feeds into the Carrao near **Arenal**, once a miners' camp. There are good-sized rapids to pass on the Carrao before reaching the shallow Churún flowing from Devil's Canyon in Auyantepui. Tito has built a lovely camp opposite **Isla Ratoncito**, last point reached by motor craft. Then it is 1¹/₂ hours through tall forest to the foot of Angel Falls. The return journey, downstream to Canaima, takes less than a day.

To make advance arrangements for the Kamarata–Angel Falls trip, allow four weeks' notice. **Bagheera Tours** flies trekkers from Puerto Ordaz to Kamarata where they visit the mission and Kavac Falls before starting downriver, finishing in Canaima with a swim at Sapo Falls. The trek costs $740 for 5 days/4 nights; (see page 262).

Both **Cacao** and **Akanán Travel** have fixed departure dates from June to November for treks of 5–6 days, $780–930, with round-trip flight from Ciudad Bolívar. For information in Caracas, Akanán, tel: (02) 2342323, fax: 2373879; email: akanan@sa.omnes.net; and Cacao, tel: (02) 9773753, fax: (02) 9770110. Cacao also go camping up the Akanán to remote **Kamadac Falls**, five days from Kavac, December to June.

Kamaracoto Tours (see above, *River bookings*) do this route in the opposite direction: Canaima–Angel Falls–Kamarata. They take you in seven days up the Carrao, visiting Angel Falls via the Churún River, and then continue east around Auyantepui to Kamarata: a great trip.

Kavac Canyon

Aereotuy's turbo-props fly tourists daily to Kavac from Ciudad Bolívar, flight alone $40, 2 days/1 night $240; and from Porlamar $90, tour $330. Other flights and tours originate in Canaima, 15 minutes away by air. It's a wonderful flight over Angel Falls and Auyantepui, landing on a savannah strip southeast of the massif. Kavac was built for tourism by the people of Kamarata, a village two hours away. A dozen attractively thatched Indian roundhouses provide shelter. Aereotuy's camp has a restaurant, eight spartan rooms with twin beds and bathroom, and ten rooms with shared bath.

Kavac stands in open savannah with Auyantepui in the background, a splendid setting. After all the tourists have left, it is a very picturesque *pueblito*. Most of the Pemón return to their homes in Kamarata on foot, although there is a *carro* which costs a lot because petrol is so expensive. You can pay for a hammock or a bed, or you can sleep on the floor gratis. There's a shower which has warm water. At a small shop you can get a few basics, and cold beer (expensive).

To reach **Kavac Canyon** and its waterfall, you take the trail toward Auyantepui; after half an hour, there's a natural jacuzzi-type pool. Farther up the little Kavac River you swim into a canyon so narrow you touch both walls, to arrive at a dark pool where a waterfall plunges from a hole in rocks overhead. If you are not on a day trip, you must pay to join a group.

AUYANTEPUI
Peter Ireland, with notes by Nick Ziegel

Auyantepui is huge. Its 700km² top is as big as the island of St Lucia. The mesa rises from 1,000m elevation at Guayaraca savannah to 2,500m on top. In shape Auyantepui resembles a heart about 40–50km long, with a deep central gorge called Devil's Canyon; this is where Angel Falls plunges over a cliff. Rock climbers such as David Nott have scaled the face near Angel Falls. However, the only trail up Auyantepui is the southern route which was opened by Félix Cardona and Gustavo Heny in 1937, to rescue Jimmie Angel.

An expedition up Auyantepui depends on hiring Indian guides in **Kamarata**, a day from the head of the trail. Few people hike to Auyantepui because of the distance. Kamarata is a large Indian settlement where people are still genuinely very friendly. A helpful man for advice about guides is Lino, a Pemón who teaches at the school and speaks good English.

There is a well stocked shop in Kamarata, a place to eat, even 'hotels'. We camped by the volleyball court in front of the big Catholic mission. There are several taps with drinking water, and you can swim or bathe in the river.

(Nick Ziegel adds that in 1996 a third hotel was being built. He paid $6 per night, including preparation of food he bought in Ciudad Bolívar at the *supermercado* near the airport; the choice is far better and cheaper than in Kamarata. Excess baggage on a Cessna plane cost him $7 for 10kg. Nick trekked with Lino for eight days and recommends him as an extremely useful English-speaking organiser in Kamarata. Pedro, who acted as Nick's porter and had done the trek many times, received $13 per day, and Lino $17, though his experience was limited.)

We agreed with our guide Justiniano to meet in **Kavac** in the morning. The hike was said to be ten days and we agreed on $70 a day. We stocked up with plenty of food for Justiniano, too. It's a two-hour walk to Kavac, easy but hot, and there's a river halfway.

The **first day'**s hike is across savannah to begin with. It was the dry season, very hot, and the path was hard. About four hours from Kavac we bathed in the last river before the trail starts to climb; hard work in the sun. In about 2–3 hours from the river we were on top of the first level and in another hour we reached a river and campsite called **Guayaraca**. The river is beautifully refreshing (fine for drinking, as is all the water on the tepui). Some wooden frames have been constructed where you could use plastic sheeting for a roof, convenient because all other sites up the mountain were under huge rocks and so no other protection from the weather was needed. We were in the forest and saw several huge purple orchids and timid hummingbirds.

The second day's hike climbed from forest to a kind of dense tepui vegetation on a shoulder called Danto, then up more steeply to **El Peñón** (1,700m). This is a huge rock with ten 'beds' cut in the sand underneath. A perfect shelter but chilly because wind funnels through it. There's a stream five minutes away. You can see, below, the plateau and the savannah path; Kamarata and Kavac are already out of sight to the east; to the south are other tepuis.

We left behind our tent and some food, out of reach of rodents, for the return. The path goes up steeply, then over a tangle of wet tree roots, emerging at the base of a huge vertical wall. We couldn't see the top as it was cloudy. We skirted the wall, climbing steeply, using ropes (already in place) a couple of times. Scaling the final rocks to the tepui's top is great. The huge columns of rock are incredibly shaped and pitted, mysterious in the clouds. On the rock to the right as you come up is a bronze bust of Bolívar, brought up by the Universidad Central de Venezuela in 1956; hence this point (about 2,400m) is known as **Libertador**. Breathtaking views, both into and out of the tepui. There is a rock here that you can camp under, but we continued on to another rock known as **El Oso** (the bear). We walked over black rock dimpled with pools of water. Each pool is full of mosses or plants. We climbed carefully across a near-vertical slope, and jumped other crevasses many metres deep.

The water on top of the tepui is red like tea and tastes pretty good (the colouring comes from tannin, especially from the Bonnetia trees). The trail goes through some Bonnetia forest to El Oso camp. The third day we hiked four hours to **Borrachito** (meaning 'little drunkard', perhaps for the weird rock shapes?). There is a fair amount of small forest, orchids, birds. Hummingbirds darted to within a foot of my head. Borrachito is on the banks of a lovely, deep red river, the Churún, which eventually passes over Angel Falls. There is a dark cave where we slept. The fourth day was spent scrambling through forests and around crevasses, to **Boca de Dragón** where the river disappears under rocks for a space. The rock bed is 30m wide but the river covered little of it then (watch out if it should rain, however!). About an hour's walk downstream we discovered a lovely waterfall about 30m high which Justiniano hadn't seen before.

('I hired one of the only two vehicles in Kamarata for a ride as far as Uruyén. This saves four hours' hot slog across the savannah and you can reach the top of Auyantepui easily in two days and enjoy a campsite on the edge with fantastic views. We then walked on the third day to Borrachito where we camped in a cave. The fourth day was spent following the army trail cut in 1995 and trekking down the dry bed of the Churún River as far as the 30m waterfall mentioned in Peter's account. To progress further would have required a rope and climbing ability. We returned from the waterfall to our camp at Borrachito to spend a second night there.' NZ)

Return, day six. After a day exploring, we headed back. To have enough time to get to El Peñón, you need to be at El Oso by noon, Libertador by 15.00. Day seven: we got back to Guayaraca by noon. Here I set off on my own for Kavac to try to arrive in time for a flight. Although I was there at 16.00, the last flight to pick up people for Canaima at 16.30 was full. A warm shower and some beers cheered me up. The others arrived at 18.30, having come via Uruyén, a village close to the path from Guayaraca. Day eight: it seemed likely there would be planes to Porlamar, Ciudad Bolívar and Canaima. However, we took a plane to La Paragua which had just brought some cargo to Kavac: a fantastic flight below cloud level. In La Paragua everyone snarls at you. It's a gold and diamond town and we were fairly thoroughly searched at the National Guard post as we left by *por puesto*.

Flights At any airfield around the tepuis you could ask a pilot if he has places. You can cadge a lift on the daytripper planes that are not full, or on a returning cargo plane. Even if you are likely to pay a fair amount, the flight is worth it, especially in the little single-engine Cessnas which the pilots drive like cars. They fly so low the views are always spectacular. **Aereotuy** representatives in the Gran Sabana are very helpful. In Kamarata, if you want to make a reservation, you talk to **Dionisio**.

('I obtained the best information for independent travel to Auyantepui from the travel agency in **Hotel Caracas** in Ciudad Bolívar. They spoke excellent English and even tried to contact an English-speaking guide (Edmund Sonson Ray who is based in Kamarata but was working elsewhere at the time). More importantly, they did not try to sell me tours to Canaima or jungle treks or $1,000 treks. They gave out information about flights, supermarkets, public transport in Ciudad Bolívar. I paid them a couple of dollars for their trouble. Flight with **Rutaca** one way to Kamarata was standard price. The Rutaca office was 400m away from the terminal building on the airport perimeter. Flights to Kamarata depend on how many people show up at the airport on any given morning. Don't show up later than 06.30 and ask the various operators if there's a seat.' NZ)

Trail to head of Angel Falls There is now a trail to the top of Angel Falls, cut in August 1995 by a Cambridge University Officers' Training Corps expedition. The path goes up on to and right across the top of Auyantepui to where the Falls plunge off its edge into the Devil's Canyon. The 'Cambridge Route' continues from the route described by Peter Ireland.

Treks A way to save on time and gear is to join a trek for small groups led by a serious operator. **Akanán Travel** (see above, *Kamarata to Angel Falls*) leads an 8-day trek on a fixed date every month except July to September. The cost, including porters and round trip flight from Ciudad Bolívar, is $1,150.

General notes on equipment and environmental considerations
Nick Ziegel
- I would recommend gaiters and good waterproof boots in the wet season.
- A gas stove is essential as there is little firewood in places on top. (This is a national park where cooking fires are banned.)
- In the dry season there were very few mosquitoes so a net is optional.
- A fabric water carrier, 10-litre capacity, is extremely useful as we had to search for water on a couple of occasions.
- I was aware how fragile this environment is and it has to be treated with respect. The sandstone formations are very fragile and in many places had been destroyed by a thoughtless foot.
- A short scrambling rope will be of great use.
- All litter must be carried out. I had great difficulty persuading Pedro, my porter, to do this and gave him back an empty tin of tuna which he had thrown down between some rocks. All toilet paper has to be burnt. I just can't see how large numbers of people are not going to ruin this beautiful place. Roraima, as far as I'm concerned, is already ruined by litter. Auyantepui will not deteriorate so fast due to its relative inaccessibility. So please set an ecofriendly example. Please educate your guides and porters.

OVERLAND TO CANAIMA
By car and foot
Paul Rouche
During dry weather jeeps and pick-up trucks use a mining road from La Paragua some 102km south to San Salvador de Paúl, an old diamond camp. Before reaching Paúl, a track forks east to the Caroní River where it is possible to leave your car and pay the owner of a *curiara* (dugout) to ferry you across to Puerto Cucurital. From there to Canaima Camp it is a hike of about 2½ hours.

La Paragua to Caño Negro Not on most maps, this dodgy road starts opposite the old river port of La Paragua, last point for taking on petrol and supplies. I went with my wife in a Toyota 4x4 packed with food, fuel and spares as far as Caño Negro, and walked once we crossed the Caroní.

A car ferry or *chalana* over the wide Paragua River operates until 18.00 and there is a small charge for cars. We found excellent campsites by savannah creeks and in the forest (two nights along the road, then three nights in Canaima). Although it was April and the track itself was mostly dry, countless potholes, ruts and gullies kept our average speed down to 30kph.

About 21km beyond the Paragua is the **Río Chiguao ferry** (a bridge was under construction). Some distance beyond, the road deteriorated into a deeply rutted track. The mud started. And about once every kilometre the road crossed a stream or ravine, at times on a bridge of girders or felled logs. [Ed: I have had no reports of recent improvements, but plans do exist.] We saw few people along the track beyond half a dozen vehicles. At 72km from the Paragua River is the entrance to Las Bonitas, a Pemón village (1km to the left). At Km96 we spotted obscure tyre tracks veering left to **Caño Negro**: this is the best place to cross the Caroní for Puerto Cucurital and Canaima.

Because the tracks swerve through the savannah without any sign (the river is nowhere in sight) drivers should pay close attention to the kilometre reading. Jeeps can drive 6km towards the river and park by a hut at the Caño Negro. With the help of the family living there, we paddled across the Caroní River by dugout. Wide, deep and fast, the Caroní is superb, dark as steeped tea.

We tied up at a little landing on the east bank not far from the Cucurital tributary. Sightseeing tours from Canaima occasionally visit **Puerto Cucurital** by jeep. The Canaima trail began 100m to the right of a hut. Leading through forest and crossing many creeks, it emerged on to open savannah with Auyantepui's massif straight ahead. At the end of an hour's march from Cucurital, the last stretch over clear but swampy ground, we arrived at a log bridge. From here, the sandy jeep road to **Canaima Camp** led across a very hot, shadeless savannah. Half an hour brought us to a fork where we took the left hand; at the next crossing we went right, and at the third, left. The jeep road took us to Canaima airfield. My non-stop walking time from the log bridge was 74 minutes.

Crossing via Taraipa It's possible that when you arrive in Caño Negro the *curiara* owner is not at home. In that case, alternative arrangements can be made at **Taraipa**, a Kamaracoto village 14km farther south on the main jeep road to Paúl. Taraipa is a 20-minute walk from the river. Etiquette may require a consultation with the Capitán or village head about parking your vehicle and crossing the Caroní. If bargaining for a *viaje* (trip) includes your return crossing, insist on a fixed hour and day. (I know friends who were stranded anyway.) Once across the Caroní, you pick up the path northwards, skirting the river, to **Puerto Cucurital**. I'm told this stretch takes 1½ hours.

San Salvador de Paúl is 8km south of Taraipa. Its tin-roofed houses sprawl along the Caroní. There is a Guardia Nacional post with radio links to Canaima and La Paragua. Some *abastos* sell overpriced plastic canteens, hammock ropes, tinned sardines… and beer! Miners still sieve the river gravel for diamonds and pan for gold. The camp is named after a prospector called Paul whose good luck started a rush in the 1960s. Beside the airstrip is the miners' cemetery, a sad affair with pieces of tin for grave markers.

Remember Miner's tracks such as the one to Paúl may become impassable during rains. Best time would be yearend to Easter. In any event, drivers should invest in a heavy tow rope and a spade, if not a winch.

Bicycle trek
The bicycle trek to Canaima takes six days, the first by van to the mining town of **La Paragua** where bikers leave the van and cross the Río Paragua by ferry. They continue on the Paúl road (see above) to Las Bonitas and on the fourth day, at the community of **Guairarima**, put the bikes on *curiaras* to paddle across the Caroní. The last day biking takes them 10km over the savanna to **Canaima**, and a guesthouse with beds. The cost including round trip from Caracas is $850.

For fixed departures (they leave if only two people show), contact **Akanán Travel** (see *Kamarata to Angel Falls*, page 268). Akanán has led this tour for several years around Carnival, Easter and Christmas. For pleasure and now as head of his own company, Juan Carlos Rodriguez has cycled many times over trails in Bolívar and Amazonas states. His knowledge of Venezuela's outback or *interior* (and his English) grew as the logistics man on eight expeditions to tepuis, Cerro Neblina and the Siapa River, as well as helper on Steven Spielberg's *Arachnophobia* set in Canaima.

RORAIMA
'This is a brilliant walk; I've done various hikes in South America including the Inca Trail and the Torres del Paine National Park and although it's obviously impossible to make comparisons, I think that overall Roraima tops the lot.' (Huw Clough)

For several reasons, Roraima is the most important of all the tepuis. On its top is the three-way boundary marker: Venezuela to the west, Guyana to the east and Brazil to the south. The mountain called by Indians 'Mother of All Waters' drains into three watersheds: the Orinoco, the Essequibo and the Amazon. With an altitude of 2,810m, Roraima is the tallest massif (although you start climbing from the savanna at about 1,100m).

In 1912 geologist Leonard Dalton used Roraima's name to typify the tableland formation. It was also the year that Arthur Conan Doyle, inspired by Roraima, published his adventure classic about dinosaurs, *The Lost World*. However, the tepui tops are unable to support any animal larger than an opossum, the environment being extremely harsh. Not surprising since the mesas have been exposed to sun, wind and rain for over 500 million years. Clinging in crevices are mosses, lichens, tough-leaved shrubs and twisted trees. Some orchids grow on baking rocks. Of the plants, many species live only on the tepui tops, as do some birds and rodents. The small endemic black frog *Oreophrynella quelchii* which crawls clumsily and sinks in water appears to have adapted to tepui conditions by pretending to be a stone.

Roraima drew a series of explorers and naturalists in the 19th century after reports by Robert Schomburgk on a Royal Geographical Society expedition. Early parties all approached from British Guiana; all failed to scale the 600m cliffs and were driven back by storms, cold, fog and lack of food. Excitement ran high in Darwin's England, and the *Spectator* challenged in 1874, 'Will no one explore Roraima and bring us back the tidings which it has waited these thousands of years to give us?' In 1884, Everard Im Thurn and Harry Perkins finally made the ascent after a two-month expedition. It was December 18, and very wet.

Over a century later, Roraima continues to amaze spectators on foot or in helicopters. The way to the top is still Im Thurn's route (although another was pioneered in 1974 with great difficulty up the north prow in Guyana). Today, any reasonably fit person can hike to Roraima's summit in 2–3 days. Half a dozen bus lines cross the modern highway from Ciudad Guayana, dropping hikers at a roadside village where Taurepán Indians offer porters, guides and tours.

And, best of all, an amazing amount of money has been invested on bridges and road improvements to Paraitepuy, the hike's starting point. You can now drive a Chevette all the way. The village has a huge diesel generator, lights, and a 27" TV showing Kung Fu videos.

From a roadside collection of humble dwellings, **San Francisco de Yuruani** has grown into an organised minitown with tour services and a Toyota which will drive your party for a price ($50) to Paraitepuy. At San Francisco's restaurant, the **Roraima**, you can eat a hot meal, with cold beer. The **Hospedaje Minina** provides adequate, low-cost accommodation, and other houses offer beds or hammocks. Two operators compete to give guiding and porter service, **Roraima**, tel: (088) 951283, and **Arepena Tours** (no phone), both local Pemón enterprises (no phones).

For more services, see *Chapter 2, Tour operators*, pages 14–15; *Ciudad Guayana, Further afield*, page 262; and *The road to Brazil, Information and tours*, page 288.

Journey to the Lost World
Bill Quantrill with notes by Justine Freeth

How to go
The first thing to be decided when planning the Roraima hike is how to get to the Gran Sabana (see below, *The road to Brazil*) and the point from which you start walking. The best thing undoubtedly is to have a four-wheel drive vehicle, or hire

one in Ciudad Guayana. However, the driver must pay some $175 a day and be over 25. It is about 300km from Ciudad Guayana to **El Dorado** (in fact a pretty scruffy town), and another 250km to the Pemón Indian settlement of **San Francisco** just after the Yuruaní bridge. The road leading in to Roraima leaves the highway on the left about a kilometre south of San Francisco, coming back at a sharp angle and leading round the face of a range of low hills. It is not difficult to find.

From San Francisco it is about 25km (you may be lucky enough to hitch a ride) to the hilltop village of **Paraitepuy**, which is where we parked our jeep and started walking. Mark Dutton, who walked to Paraitepuy, reported his time as 6 hours 15 minutes over a very hot trail with no water for several hours. Camping was perfectly possible, but plagued with biting gnats and lots of ants.

Justine Freeth flew from Ciudad Bolívar to **Santa Elena**. She writes: 'From Santa Elena it is possible to take a jeep to Paraitepuy, but it is expensive, about $140. There are buses to San Francisco, just over one hour. At the National Guard post in **San Ignacio** my driver instructed me not to mention Paraitepuy, but to say I was going to San Francisco. This may be because the Parks Department was not issuing permits to visit tepuis; I had no trouble with permits.' This is standard advice for independent climbers. Roraima is an environmentally sensitive area and the authorities are not keen on encouraging many people to climb it. Rightly so.

Guides

It is not required that you hire a guide, although now villagers insist on it. But you are urged to do so for a variety of reasons. By taking a local guide you are doing something for the village; it is the Taurepán people who keep the track open and waymarked; it is easy to get lost when hiking on the top, and your guide will know the very few camping places. Accidents can happen and then native guides are vital for rescue in which they help whether hired or not.

The best known guides are the **Ayuso** family. Make sure you bring enough food for your guide as well as a blanket. You will need one guide for your group. If you need help to carry supplies, state you need a *cargador*, porter, and estimate for how many days. (In 1998 guides charged $40 a day, and porters $30.)

The trail

Paraitepuy is regarded as the normal starting point for the Roraima hike. You will almost certainly be greeted on arrival by the village headman who can provide a guide for you. Do not count on being able to purchase any supplies in Paraitepuy beyond the basic sardines and crackers.

'You'll need a cooker, waterproofs and warm clothes at the top. Anything you do not require for the hike you can leave in a locked hut in the village for a fee. The village is a typical Indian settlement with thatched huts but it is increasingly geared towards the many tourists going to Roraima. There are shelters specifically for hikers; there is plenty of tent space and it is even possible to hire tents in the village, but these are not of good quality.' (Justine Freeth)

The first night in Paraitepuy can be spent camping by a little river. Then you set off along an old jeep track (now closed due to erosion) down into the next valley. At the bottom you cross the stream and go through a gate. The jeep track then winds away to the right to get to the top of the ridge in front of you. The footpath cuts diagonally up across the face of the hill to the left, rejoining the jeep track at the top. You then have a lovely steady walk along the ridge, with the two tepuis of Kukenán on the left and Roraima on the right getting steadily closer as you advance. Mostly the footpath follows an old jeep trail, with occasional short cuts on the steep up and downhill bits.

After about three hours of steady walking, you come down into a valley with a slightly bigger stream than any you have come to so far, with beautiful deep, blue swimming holes. You can cross this stream dryshod, unlike the next one, Río Tek, about 15 minutes further, which has to be waded at the point where the jeep track fords it. Half an hour beyond this is the biggest river of all, the Río Kukenán. If it has been raining within the last 24 hours this can be quite a difficult crossing, especially with a full pack on your back: thigh-deep rushing water and an uneven, slippery bottom.

If, like us, you set out from Paraitepuy at around midday, you are likely to arrive at the Kukenán River in good time to set up camp, have a swim and prepare your evening meal as the sun goes down. If, however, you started in the morning, you will reach the river at about lunch time, and can continue for another three hours or so to one of the most exquisite campsites I have ever seen. Known as the **Campamento Abajo**, this is a flat meadow right under the shadow of the sheer cliffs of the Roraima massif. Two clear streams run through the meadow which is alive with birds and, at night, fireflies. The view back over the route you have come is superb. The track from the Kukenán River starts along the left-hand bank then rejoins the jeep trail until it peters out where the Roraima foothills begin; the climb up to reach the meadow is fairly stiff.

From the Campamento Abajo to the top of Roraima is about four hours' hard climb. You can see the trail winding upwards from the eastern end of the meadow. For the first two hours or so you are scrambling through the trees, over rocks, even at one point along the bed of a stream, all the time going relentlessly upwards. Eventually you come to the face of the cliff itself, at a point where an icy cold stream shoots out of the cliff face. The path changes and for the next couple of hours you work your way up a diagonal ledge on the cliff face. It is quite a broad ledge, well covered in vegetation. Most of the time you are hardly conscious of the increasingly high sheer cliff a few metres away, though occasionally you come out of the undergrowth and can get an idea of your progress. At one time you have to drop down 50m or so to get round a rock buttress. Finally you come to a point where you have to pass under a cascading waterfall (a nasty cold shower, but there is no avoiding it), then scramble up a rocky gully that eventually brings you out on to the summit.

It is not easy to move around on the summit. The surface consists mostly of huge rock formations surrounded by bog. Camping is not easy. There is one area, known as **El Hotel**, under a rock overhang sheltered from the prevailing wind, which provides space enough for two or three small tents at most. Other areas which look flat enough to camp on usually turn out to be waterlogged: if not already so, they quickly become so once the inevitable evening downpour starts. The route to El Hotel goes off to the right almost immediately after you first arrive at the summit. If this space is already occupied, the best choice is probably to find a flat rock to pitch your tent on, attaching the guys to rocks. We tried camping on what looked like a relatively dry patch of sand, but were inundated by rain running off the surrounding rocks during the night.

'Our guide knew sheltered camping spots before the top of the trail. Once on top, the walk to the triple boundary marker is not too tough, about eight hours there and back. But it is complicated and should not be attempted without a guide. Just before the marker, you walk some distance beside a huge mysterious lake, and from there you pass through a valley of crystals. This is a spectacular canyon paved with white and pink quartz crystals. (Please do not pick the crystals.) Twenty minutes beyond the marker is the most beautiful waterfall I've ever seen. Water trickles over the surface of the tepui to cascade into a pool about 10m below. The sun makes amazing rainbows in the waterfall. Just above the amber pool, pillars of rock like stalactites project into the water; between these, luxuriant plants give the impression of hanging baskets. A little further on is what is called "the great labyrinth of the north", but we didn't have time to go there.' (Justine Freeth)

Warnings Many people will be only too familiar with the pestilential little biting gnats called *jejenes*. Covering up well and using an effective insect repellent and anti-allergy cream will help to alleviate the problem but won't solve it altogether. The only place free of the little beasts is the top of Roraima where I suspect the altitude is too much for them.

The other pests are the human litterbugs now that the Gran Sabana road is paved. I am told that after Easter Week the National Guard collected over a thousand beer and soft drinks cans from the road going into Roraima. The National Guard, who are responsible for controlling the area, realise that something will have to be done and may place tighter controls on access.

Huw Clough, who took a group up Roraima without guides, would not recommend others doing the same. By using a guide you are perhaps preventing abuse of the area by hikers. Huw concludes, 'I would also appeal to campers' "green" conscience, respecting the unique ecosystem up there by keeping to the campsites. Since I first went to Roraima, there are disturbing signs of pollution (open-toilet remains by the campsites) and litter scattered all over the place. Roraima does seem to be one of the most popular hikes in Venezuela. But I hope that the authorities will impose some controls and regulations on visitors going there, before it's too late.'

Campers, remember to bring a shovel.

Roraima the quick, easy and exciting way!
Nick Ziegel

If you are short of time, and funds are not too tight, then a helicopter is an option. Instead of a 6–8-day trek the flight to the Triple Point boundary marker, calling in briefly at Paraitepuy for a porter, will cut time to three days round trip from Sta Elena de Uairén. **Aerotécnica** is on the Avenida Gran Mariscal. It is run by Raúl, who owns two Bell five-seater helicopters, and speaks fluent English. The starting price was $900 but the three of us bargained the price down to $500 for the flight. That was only £135 each.

Being dropped by helicopter on to the top of Roraima may not be the proper way to trek to a remote and beautiful place, but it was without any doubt one of the most thrilling things I have ever done. One moment I was in the cosy confines of a helicopter with modern technology all around; the next moment I found myself on 'another planet' surrounded by the weirdest rocks and plants.

From the Triple Point to 'El Hotel' via the sinkhole with the waterfall and the valley of the crystals took us seven hours. Do not pick up any crystals as souvenirs; we were searched on the way out. As it was Easter, *Semana Santa*, there were a lot of people on the trail. We counted about 60 people trekking in as we left. There appears to be no co-ordination as to how many trekking groups go up Roraima at one time. Space at 'El Hotel' is limited. There is the usual litter and fluttering toilet paper problem. Do please take all litter home and burn all toilet paper and bury your 'waste'.

THE ROAD TO BRAZIL
Beautifully graded and paved, the Gran Sabana highway is the finest in the country. Buses go regularly from Caracas and Ciudad Bolívar to Santa Elena de Uairén,

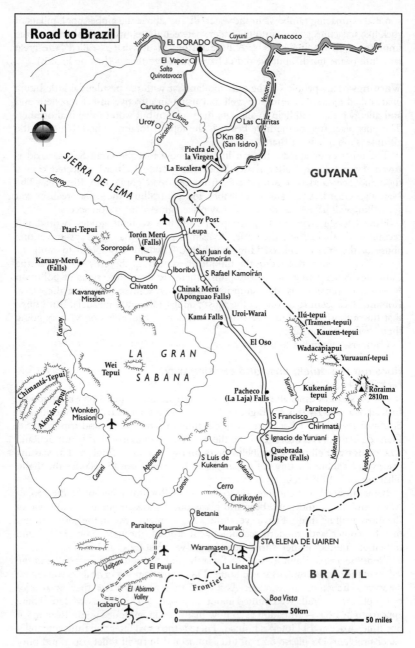

Road to Brazil

EL DORADO
Cuyuní
Anacoco
Yurián
El Vapor
Salto
Quinotovoca
Caruto
Uroy
Chivao
Chicanán
Las Claritas
Km 88
(San Isidro)
Piedra de
la Virgen
La Escalera

N

GUYANA

SIERRA DE LEMA
Carrao

Ptari-Tepui
Torón Merú
(Falls)
Leupa
Army Post
Sororopán
Parupa
San Juan de
Kamoirán
Karuay-Merú
(Falls)
Iboribó
S Rafael Kamoirán
Chivatón
Kavanayen
Mission
Chinak Merú
(Aponguao Falls)
Kamá Falls
Uroi-Warai
Ilú-tepui
(Tramen-tepui)
Kauren-tepui
El Oso
Wadacapiapui
Yuruauní-tepui

Karuay
LA GRAN
SABANA
Wei
Tepui
Kukenán-
tepui
Roraima
2810m
Chimantá-Tepui
Akopán-Tepui
Wonkén
Mission
Pacheco
(La Laja) Falls
Yuruani
S Francisco
Paraitepuy
Chirimatá
S Ignacio de Yuruaní
Quebrada
Jaspe (Falls)
Coroní
Aponguao
Coroní
S Luís de
Kukenán
Kukenán
Cerro
Chirikayén
Kukenán
Arabopo
Betania
Maurak
Paraitepui
STA ELENA DE UAIREN
Waramasen
Uaiparu
El Paují
La Línea
BRAZIL
El Abismo
Valley
Frontier
Icabarú
Boa Vista

0   50km
0   50 miles

some continuing to Boa Vista in Brazil. The road covers 330km from El Dorado's fork to the border. It goes first through the Imataca Forest Reserve and then enters Canaima National Park.

The **Gran Sabana** is a grassy plateau sloping from the north at 1,300m, down to 800m at Santa Elena. The panorama is dominated by *tepuis* or table mountains.

The basement of these giant mesas is the Guayana Shield, an igneous and metamorphic formation of some of the world's oldest rock, 2,000–3,000 million years old. The tepuis themselves are made of sandstone sediments washed from the granddaddy of all continents, Gondwana (Pangaea). Layers of these sediments are over 2,700m thick in places such as Roraima, and on the mesa tops you can see ripple marks of ancient lakes. Such isolated remnants, left standing after aeons of erosion by water and wind, are known as the Roraima Formation. Diamonds and gold may be one of Venezuela's links with the time when South America and Africa were part of the same super-continent.

In 1991, 25 tepuis were declared Natural Monuments placing them under the wing of the National Parks system. Only a few have been scientifically studied as most are remote and devoid of game or nourishment for sustaining human visitors. Soils are very poor in nutrients and high in iron and aluminium oxides; remaining forests survive in a state of continual 'stress'. Their ecosystem is fragile, vulnerable to periodic drought and man-made disasters such as mining, roads, logging and fire. Burnt stumps can still be seen from great fires that swept through the Gran Sabana in 1927–8 and 1940.

The tepui-top habitats, collectively called Pantepui, support many endemic plants found nowhere else. Plants common to the tepuis can be seen on the Gran Sabana (really an eroded tableland). In boggy areas you can spot pitcher plants (*Heliamphora*) which trap insects to obtain nitrogen, as do the tiny pink carnivorous plants called sundew (*Drosera*) subsisting in damp, sandy patches. Bromeliads come in many forms; best known member of this family is the pineapple, native to the Guayana region. The vertical cylinders of a bog bromeliad, *Brocchinia reducta*, have been discovered to trap insects and digest them, adding a new plant to the list of carnivorous species. Another bromeliad cups enough water to see it through dry periods, and has rescued travellers from thirst. Orchids growing on nothing but baking rocks must endure climate extremes, too. Temperatures on tepui tops can go down to 0°C at night.

The native inhabitants of the Gran Sabana are members of the Pemón group and subgroups, namely the Arekuna in the centre (Kavanayén), Kamaracotos in the west, and Taurepán in the south.

In the low hot country north of the Gran Sabana are vast forests, part of the 30,000km² Imataca Forest Reserve intended to regulate logging for sustainable use. When a government decree recently authorised mining concessions, on top of logging in Imataca, what resulted was little short of a war on the environment and its inhabitants.

Gold and forests

Distances are far and facilities few once you leave Puerto Ordaz. A standard simile goes: 'about as much use as a credit card in the Gran Sabana'. Better change your travellers' cheques before leaving town. It is a four-hour drive to steamy **El Dorado**, whose fork before the Cuyuní bridge is counted as Km0 for calculating distances on the highway to Gran Sabana.

Most buses do not stop in El Dorado but continue over the Cuyuni bridge. El Dorado does not face the river but its shady plaza. It offers food shops, gasoline, a hotel, and an unsavoury police station. There are many gold buyers' booths. At the confluence of the Cuyuní and Yuruari rivers, it is a major port for independent prospectors. The Cuyuní's water is clouded with mud and laced with the mercury used in gold precipitation.

El Dorado got its name during earlier gold strikes which drew steamboats of fortune hunters and supplies up the Cuyuní from British Guiana. (A century later,

El Dorado's name was dulled by the building of a penal colony on the east side of the river. Planeloads of criminals still arrive at El Dorado bound for Las Colonias.)

The big strike started in **El Callao**, 112km north of El Dorado, in its heydey one of the world's richest mines. There, on the Yuruari, gold was found in 1849. In 1855 alone the yield was eight tonnes. Today, Monarch Resources, a British–Venezuelan joint enterprise, gets some 700kg of gold yearly out of the tailings of old El Callao mines. And the descendants of miners who came from England, Corsica, Martinique and Trinidad give El Callao the country's brightest Carnival celebrations complete with steel band, calypsos and costumes, as well as its best football players.

A National Guard *alcabala* over the Cuyuní bridge checks identity papers. The road now enters the **Imataca Forest Reserve**. There are no proper towns, only farming and mining hamlets that cling to the road like a lifeline. Small holdings have been cleared by settlers. You see gardens and wooden houses built like those in former British Guayana where many settlers came from. (It's a 3-day walk on the **Guyana trail**, just south of San Miguel, Km66.)

Cars rush on by; the way is long. But take a moment to chat; the people are friendly and long to speak English. At Km33, ask for Eric Peters. He and about 100 **Akawaio** followers have a community 4km off the road, planted with shrubs, lawns, banana plants and citrus trees. There is a house for putting up guests, or you could ask to camp. You may want to buy really good bananas or coconuts. The women make pepper pots of local clay and could sell you some. Eric's pleasant compound at the back of the village consists of various houses, some raised on stilts. There is some good soil for growing peanuts.

At Km46 is **San Flaviano**, a farming community of Arawaks from the Pomeroon in Guyana. The older generation still speak beautiful Arawak. Some of the men worked for a Canadian gold mining company whose concession was annulled, bringing hardship to San Flaviano. The far-flung communities along this road struggle with poverty, malaria and water polluted by mercury from gold-mining activities. They lack medicines, clothes, farming equipment, school books. Cleer Thomas and her family at Km46 are keen on books, English or Spanish, and pencils, crayons, paper, school shirts, and clothing in general. A volleyball, or any sort of ball, is a prized gift.

Health workers in village clinics at Km33 and Km67 beg for supplies of any sort. Km67, a Pemón settlement, is the home of Padre Adriano Salvadori, a most *simpático* priest who is trying to get a clean water supply to villages. Mercury affects the whole Cuyuní basin. Tributaries from Km41 to Km88 are polluted; people cannot safely eat river fish or drink the water. This need not affect passers-by, but if you come back this way from the Gran Sabana, any suggestion or help you can give these needy people would be appreciated. Padre Adriano is the one who best knows their hard work, and hardships. He has a postal address, Apartado 1170, Puerto Ordaz 8015, Venezuela; and a telephone at the church in El Dorado, (088) 910093, fax: 911031.

The Imataca Forest Reserve covers homelands of the Arawak, Pemón, Kariña and Akawaio people. By law areas declared as forest reserves may be leased for logging under a management plan for replanting. But forestry regulations are poorly enforced, and cleared areas are open to land grabs. Loggers and miners ban the Indians from hunting and farming, leading to conflicts.

Gold is the buzz word along the highway, now called the 'billion dollar boulevard' by foreign investors. As a Canadian miner says, 'This area is one of the most important new gold discoveries in the world'.

Placer Dome, a Canadian company, and Venezuela (70%–30%) are spending $700 million to develop a find estimated to hold over 11 million ounces of gold near **Las Claritas**, Km85. The mining company, building the biggest precious metal mine in South America, displaced thousands of illegal miners who stripped the land like monstrous *bachacos* or leaf-cutter ants. Their tin-roofed community is a short distance down a right-hand road just before Km85. Previously, as much as 70% of Venezuela's gold and diamonds produced by 'free' miners was smuggled to Brazil and Guyana.

'Compro Oro' signs are painted on tin-roofed shacks in Las Claritas. It is a sad, not to say sordid, collection of market stalls, food stands, bars and brothels, but has a restaurant. Ciudad Bolívar buses stop here. Km88 or **San Isidro**, last outpost and gasoline station before the Gran Sabana, has a hotel with satellite TV, a bank, and bars overflowing with beer and mine workers.

Where to stay

Guasipati has a motel favoured by drivers from Caracas who like to break the journey halfway: **Hotel Reina**, tel: (088) 67357, on the high street through town just past Plaza Bolívar; modest, air-conditioned, convenient. There is also a hotel on the Plaza Bolívar of Tumeremo.

El Dorado has a passable hotel, the ten-room **Universo**: four doubles with air conditioning, private bath, $12; six with fan, $10; there is a locked parking lot. Other hostels let rooms by the hour and are not very clean.

La Montañita, Km70, has not only nicely kept gardens, thatched restaurant, cabins with four spotless doubles and private bath at $15, plus three new Indian-style houses, but also lovely lawns and a bathroom for tenters at $5. The Sánchez family will arrange tours to gold mines.

Campamento Anaconda, Las Claritas, Km85, is a good hotel with A-frame cabins, dining room, bar and gardens, all behind walls. A double costs $18. The package with car from Puerto Ordaz, with meals and a tour, is $250 for 3 days/2 nights. The Anaconda people know all the best Gran Sabana spots; tel: (086) 223130/0403, fax: 226572.

Campamento Gran Sabana, Las Claritas beside Anaconda, has restaurant, modern cabins, 16 doubles with bath and cold water, $18, in a large fenced area with plenty of trees and parking; tel: (086) 228820.

Barquilla de Fresa, Km84, is the home of naturalist Henry Clever who leads birdwatching tours; a cabin and six plain rooms, separate baths, cold water. Tours, $58 a day with food and lodging; reservations through Audubon de Venezuela (see *Chapter 3, Environmental NGOs*). The birds on his 35ha property and lagoon include eight different parrotlets and parrots, three kinds of cotingas, aracaris, jacamars and puffbirds. Clever knows a lot about the Gran Sabana route, 'one of the very best birding roads in the whole country'.

Canaima National Park

Shortly after San Isidro the road begins to climb **Cerro Venamo**, leaving the hot country for steep, cool mountains. At 410m altitude, the granite bulk of the Piedra de la Virgen looms at Canaima National Park's eastern boundary. The park's 30,000km^2 stretch west as far as the Caroní River, south to Roraima and the Kukenan River, and east to Guyana. It has been declared a world heritage site by UNESCO for its beauty and biodiversity.

Drivers on this national higway do not need permits. But tourists officially should carry a *permiso de Inparques* costing Bs300 per day, obtained in Ciudad Bolívar, tel/fax: (085) 29908 (unless Inparques sets up a post here). Certainly this requirement applies to commercial tours (but the companies do the dog work); the confusion lies in whether it is needed by people going to Santa Elena.

From here **La Escalera** (literally the stairway) rises sharply, gaining 1,000m elevation in 37km. Wet montane forest is the home of fabled birds such as the cock of the rock, scarlet horned manakin, white bellbird and paradise tanager, among others, and of deer and jaguar, seen occasionally.

At Km122 all persons must produce identification at a Guardia Nacional *alcabala*, and vehicles may be searched. This point on the road is only a few kilometres from Guyana's Essequibo territory disputed by Venezuela.

Temperatures drop and nights become quite cold as the road reaches the crest of the **Gran Sabana**. Campers will need warm sweaters and sleeping bags. High point of the road is the **Monumento al Soldado Pionero**, altitude 1,350m. It honours the army engineering corps who built the road, opened in 1973 by President Rafael Caldera. Simultaneously, the Brazilians opened a road from Boa Vista to the border where the two presidents met. This is still the only land link between the two nations.

By a bend in the dark Aponguao River, Km140, is the first of the Gran Sabana's many campsites, one of the few set up with outhouses. Across the road are offices of Inparques. Take this entrance for Keyla Tours' **Campamento Akopán**. The wooden cabins, bath house, hot showers, and kitchens are for tour members only. Keyla's 11-seater vans start in Ciudad Guayana and go to Santa Elena; reservations, tel: (086) 223807, fax: 229713.

The National Parks office at Km140 is followed by the army post of **Fuerte Manikuyé** or La Ciudadela. This is a frontier zone and vehicles are checked carefully, not only for firearms and drugs, but for illegal plants and rock samples. Here it is possible to buy gasoline; the pump is a necessity for people owning vehicles in Kavanayen which is often without gasoline. Kavanayen's sandy road turns right by a military landing strip at **Luepa**, Km147.

Side road to Kavanayen

Kavanayen enjoys an exceptionally beautiful setting surrounded by tablelands. You can get by bus as far as the turn-off, and continue on the sandy side road, hitching or walking. There is very little traffic, so be prepared for a night out. It is high and gets quite cold. Look for windy sites as the only drawback is the legion of gnats or biting midges in early morning and late afternoon, worst during rains.

Camping is superb by brooks and waterfalls. You can hike to your heart's desire in good weather. People with 4x4 vehicles take the rough track 17km to **Torón Falls**, off to the right at Km23. At the first ford, explore the lovely rocky creek downstream. Torón Falls, a few kilometres on, are 75m high. Please fill your rubbish bag and take it with you; there appears to be no disposal system.

Aponguao Falls or Chinak–Merú, truly spectacular, are 105m high. They drop over the savannah's edge, 11km to the south. Take a jeep track on the left at Km32, beyond the CVG agricultural station of Parupa. It leads to Iboribó, a Pemón community at the Aponguao River. Some Pemón people here make baskets and calabash bowls, some prepare simple meals, others rent hammocks and roof space, and there are bathrooms and good camping places.

A Pemón *curiara* service takes tourists downriver in 25 minutes to within 500m of the falls; price depends on the number of people. However, since the 1995 tragedy in which the river swept a *curiara* with 11 people over the falls (all died), visitors may prefer to walk. Indians will ferry you across to a savannah path (about 1 hour) for a small sum. Be sure to start early as the falls receive sun in the morning only. You can scramble down a track to the foot of the falls where the waters are safe for swimming.

Back on the Kavanayén road is **Chivatón**, long a traveller's refuge at Km47: ten stone rooms in a row with two to four beds each, private bath, cold water; generator for light; $25 per person covers room, breakfast and dinner. There's a creek for swimming if you like very cold water. Windswept Chivatón has few gnats. In Puerto Ordaz: Turismo Chirikayén, tel: (016) 6861976/4326, fax: (086) 6231435.

The **Capuchin Mission** of Santa Teresita de Kavanayén (the name means cock-of-the-rock's place) was founded in 1942 on a remote plateau (altitude 1,160m) ringed by dramatic tepuis and attendant storm clouds. From the airstrip you see, anticlockwise: NE Sororopán-tepui; N Ptari-tepui; NW Aparamán; SW Chimantá and Akopán-tepui; and S Wei-tepui, the unique cone-shaped 'mountain of the sun'. These weather makers account for one of the highest rainfalls in the country, over 3,000mm a year.

The imposing mission and boarding school, as well as village houses, are made of stone. There is public telephone service, a rural clinic or *medicatura*, a mechanic's shop, a gasoline pump sometimes in service, an airfield and a heliport. Holiday residences have been built near the heliport for the president of Venezuela, and presidents of the state oil company and Edelca.

Where to stay
The village soccer field has been used as a tenting ground. At least two houses offer inexpensive *hospedaje*; one faces **Señora Rosa's restaurant** on a deadend street opposite the Medicatura; another is on the corner of the mission block. The **Capuchin Mission** rents dormitory beds during holidays, spartan and clean with hot shower. Each room has six beds for $24 total. Tel: (086) 603763, 625200, 620800. The mission does not provide food, but there are local shops one of which will prepare food.

The **Campamento Mantopai** is a hidden surprise: ten fine Indian houses, like *churuatas* but in stone, built at the foot of Sororopán-tepui by the Calcaños, an enterprising Kamaracoto family. The road is secretive, too, running along a stream bed several kilometres over rock; you can also walk in 3–4 hours. At the end are comfortable beds, private bath, electricity, and restaurant. Each *churuata* has two beds and rents for $12 a night; enquire at the Mission, Director Mario Lanz (see above). Happy Tour includes Mantopai in Gran Sabana tours of 2–4 days; for information in Santa Elena, tel: (088) 951030. Carlos Enrique Calcaño may be reached at tel: (086) 625100 (public phone), 603762-Edelca; call once and leave a message that you will call later at a fixed hour.

Excursions
The lovely **Karuay Falls** and pools, 23km west of Kavanayen, are reached by a track so rutted that it takes jeeps over an hour in dry weather (impassable in rain). As the Karuay descends over ever bigger shelves from the Gran Sabana, it forms higher and higher waterfalls. Indian guides with *curiaras* equipped with lifebelts and jackets offer to take you downstream to **Salto Hueso** for about $4 a person. It is 2½ hours there and back plus half an hour for swimming. A trip to **Salto Techinén**, a lot higher, requires advance planning because of the distance and time involved.

Kayak Trips, tel: (02) 9453611, 9631785, offer a new wilderness trek: descending the pristine Karuay river in kayaks. An inclusive price of $1,500 for eight days covers round-trip flight from Caracas to Ciudad Bolívar and ground transport to the Gran Sabana. Once on the Karuay, trippers sleep in hammocks and Indian shelters.

Guide Carlos Enrique Calcaño leads trekkers over the old Indian trail from **Kavanayen to Kamarata**, southeast of Auyantepui. Trekkers return by airtaxi from Kamarata or Kavac to Ciudad Bolívar. Such a six-day hike is only for the really fit as the trail winds up and down across the valleys and hogbacks of the Marík, Murauri and Yromún rivers. The terrain is virtually uninhabited; there are no emergency facilities. The Calcaños provide all meals, hammocks, two porters to help carry gear, and a *curiara* for river crossing. Price per person runs at about $50 a day in a group of eight. This trek, and others up the Karuay to Ptari-tepui or downriver to Salto Techinén, can also be arranged through **Audubon** in Caracas, tel: (02) 9939262, fax: 910716.

On to Kamá Falls

Returning to the Gran Sabana highway, you see the massifs of Tramen, Ilú and Karaurén-tepui in the east; beyond them lies Guyana. Guyanese refugees of an uprising in 1969 received Venezuelan nationality as natives of the disputed area. On the right, 17km beyond the Kavanayén fork, is **San Rafael de Kamoirán**, a community of ex-Guyanese. The Kamoirán flows to Guyana where it is called the Kamarang.

A petrol tank (usually in service) at Km171 stands by a neat stone house. This is an inn called **Rápidos de Kamoirán**; reservations in Ciudad Guayana, tel: (086) 512729. It offers a quite nice restaurant and 15 plain rooms with bath; no hot water; $8 per person. The river runs over rocks behind the inn; you can ask to camp.

Watch for more waterfalls. You don't see Salto Kamá on the right at Km201, as it slips over the savannah ledge in a lovely 50m curtain. However, you will notice thatched *churuatas* which offer travellers basic shelter and food. A Pemón family rents rooms in a stone house for three or four people, separate bath. Nearer the river another family offers a cluster of nicer *churuatas* with beds, and a camping area; three people $7, tent space $2. There is also good camping at Salto Kawi, Km206, also on the right hand, but little visited.

Roraima's long silhouette rears in the east as you approach Km238. A Taurepán community here has grown up around **Quebrada Arapán** (Pacheco), also known as La Laja, where a bridge crosses the stony riverbed. It is popular among campers (despite biting 'no-see-ums' in the wet season) as there are pretty falls, **Salto Arapán**, and bigger ones downstream, seldom visited. A park employee can give you some information. Also, *churuatas* may be rented for slinging hammocks; inexpensive shelter, outhouse.

You will find (along with holiday crowds) a nearly perfect campsite at **Balneario Suruape**, 1½km west of the highway at Km244: rippling river, smooth rocks, mauritia palms. Among sunny boulders the Suruape forms several pools where people from Santa Elena splash at weekends. But on weekdays peace returns. There is also a Parador Turístico, bathrooms and an Inparques office. A number of sturdy native kiosks offer shelter for $8.

Another waterfall, wide rather than tall, is the **Yuruaní** upstream from the bridge at Km247. When waters are low, pools invite swimming and you can duck behind the falls' curtain. But this spot, reached from the south end of the bridge, is marred by midge clouds all year. Mysteriously, there is no *plaga* if you take a trail on the north side of the bridge for maybe 700m to its end, where the river has good swimming places and lovely views of Kukenán and Roraima.

San Francisco de Yuruaní, Km250, is best known as the start of the trail to Roraima (see above, page 274). This Taurepán town is growing and has a high school, church, *medicatura*, soccer field, small shops and two simple restaurants. Lodging for hikers is managed by Roraima Tours at the village entrance, tel: (088) 951283.

In **San Ignacio de Yuruaní**, Km259, a Guardia Nacional post checks all travellers. Hikers bound for Roraima are required to show a national parks permit and be accompanied by a native guide.

To find **Campamento Uruve**, a large new excursion centre in the Gran Sabana, at Km263, south of San Ignacio, turn west opposite a radio tower and go on 9km. The *churuata*-style camp is beyond **Urue Falls** whose riverbed is of red-yellow jasper. Guests sleep in hammocks in Indian roundhouses, or cots in tents. The camp has a 1,700m airstrip and serves as a base for exploring the Gran Sabana including Aponguao, Karuay, and Torón falls. Mountain biking, kayaking and paragliding are some of the tour options. The operators are SBA Nature Expeditions, tel/fax: (02) 2510990; email: sbanatureve@yahoo.com. Ask about pick-up in Ciudad Guayana.

As the highway continues over the plateau, it dips to warmer, wider savannahs studded with *moriche* palms. At Km273 the last set of waterfalls, **Quebrada Jaspe,** is famous for its red and yellow jasper bed. The creek hidden among trees is shallow and the falls are intimate, glowing as the sun strikes on wet jasper. There is good camping at Km278, east side; walk about ten minutes to a small falls, **Pozo de Agua Fría**.

Santa Elena de Uairén

Venezuelan soldiers and goldseekers of many nationalities pass through this frontier town, 15km from Brazil. Now that the highway from Boa Vista is paved, cross-border trade is soaring. Brazilian visitors stream over on their way to Ciudad Guayana and Margarita.

Santa Elena's **Capuchin Mission** and the Taurepán community of **Manakrík** lie a kilometre west of Plaza Bolívar. The mission dates from 1931, while the pueblo was founded in 1924 by one settler, Lucas Fernández Peña, and his family. He named the place on the little Uairén River after his daughter (and went on to have 27 more children). One granddaughter runs the **Cabañas Wue-Tuna** (Tukumurruku) and shop at Km303; restaurant, eight rooms with bath, $5 a person.

Booming Santa Elena packs a lot into its tiny centre. Shoppers flock from Boa Vista for clothing and appliances, miners arrive from Icabarú for supplies and weekend action, and campers and tourists come in for a decent hotel, of which there are several. Besides well-stocked supermarkets, restaurants and bakeries, there is a hospital, disco-pub with electronic piano, photo lab, two banks, three pool halls, five liquor stores, six jewellers, many pawnshops and too many gold brokers. If you appreciate a real nugget, ask at **La Casa de Los Cochanos**, Calle Roscio at Urdaneta, with this reminder: when you buy a diamond or a gold piece, get a receipt in case of Guardia Nacional checks.

You should have little trouble changing dollars in shops or hotels, but travellers' cheques will be harder, except perhaps American Express. Small exchange bureaux deal largely in Brazilian *reales*.

Getting there and away

By air The airfield is on the road to El Paují some 7km southwest of Santa Elena. The terminal consists of a waiting/control room. Across the street are a small restaurant serving would-be passengers, and a Guardia Nacional desk where you should register.

Servivensa's daily DC3 flight leaves Santa Elena at 08.30, arrives in **Canaima** 09.40 and does not continue to **Puerto Ordaz** until 15.30. From Puerto Ordaz the flight leaves at 08.00, picks up passengers in Canaima at 09.00 and arrives in Santa Elena at 11.00; fare is $74. Rutaca airtaxis serve **Icabarú** and **El Paují** ($20) all day, leaving when there are five passengers.

By bus A new terminal, on the highway about 2km north of town, receives several bus lines and *por puestos*. Buses of Expresos Guayana, Línea Orinoco, Travircan, and others leave daily for **Ciudad Bolívar** (12 hours) via **San Félix** (11 hours); you can buy tickets the day before. If you want an open window, choose a *servicio*

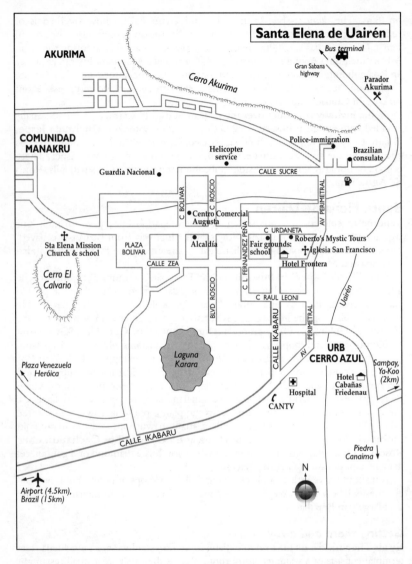

normal bus like Transvircan; it may take longer, however. The fast coaches of Turcar and Transmundial have *servicio especial* (smoked windows and air conditioning); Transmundial goes daily to **Boa Vista**. Big Brazilian coaches of the Uniao Cascavel leave daily for Boa Vista (4 hours), $10.50. (See also page 253.)

Jeeps leave at first light for El Paují, an uncomfortable two-hour ride, $10. Enquire about *por puestos* to the airport, $1.50.

To/from Brazil Travellers entering or leaving Venezuela go through Immigration not at the border but in Santa Elena. (Brazilian formalities are at the border.) Be sure to have your passport stamped in the DEX office at the back of the Prefectura, at the north end of Av Perimetral. If leaving Venezuela go to DEX as soon as you have a bus ticket, even the day before departure. Open Mon–Sat 07.30–11.30, 14.00–17.00; Sun 08.00–11.00.

Travellers in Brazil should try to get their Venezuelan visa in Manaus. The consulate in Boa Vista has been known to issue only 72-hour transit visas which cannot be extended once you get to Venezuela.

Travellers to Boa Vista or Manaus must have a passport and visa (one photo). Venezuelans visiting the border town of Pacaraima need only their *cédula*. Drivers must have proof of ownership; rented cars are not covered by their insurance outside Venezuela. The Brazilian vice consulate is near the Prefectura, opposite the petrol station; tel: (088) 951256; open weekdays 08.00–12.00, 14.00–16.00. The visa is issued on the same day. In Puerto Ordaz, the consulate is in Edif Amazonas, Av Las Américas; tel: (086) 235243.

Pacaraima, the Brazilian community across La Línea, small and colourless, depends on Santa Elena for petrol and many other necessities. In return, Venezuelans go there to buy medicines and mining gear, and eat at small restaurants. The newly paved Boa Vista road, 220km, is boosting trade and tourism. **Hotel Palace Pacaraima** lacks paint and patrons; moderate. There's a statue of Emperor Dom Pedro on the border.

Where to stay
The area telephone code for Santa Elena is (088)
At an elevation of 900m, Santa Elena is cool at night and hotels need no air conditioning. The list below is partial.

On Calle Mariscal Sucre, the first west street as you enter from the north, you will find reasonable lodgings: **Hotel Los Castaños**, tel: 951450, a 22-room motel; single or double $15; check that your bed has a blanket. **Hotel Gabriel**, tel: 951142, is a solid two-floor building with parking; clean, spacious rooms, hot water; single $12, double $17.50 with breakfast. Opposite Raúl's Helicopters is **Hotel Panaima**, tel: 951474, 24 cheaper rooms on two floors.

Hotel Lucrecia, tel/fax: (088) 951385, is south 300m on Av Perimetral: a low house surrounded by flowers; 15 twin-bed rooms, chintz spreads, hot water, TV, meals on order; double $20. Walk down to the next corner and turn west to No 187 Calle Urdaneta where you will find **La Casa de Gladys**, tel: 951171. The 15 basic rooms have private bath. Owner Gladys Bermúdez rents some camping equipment and tents. The many hikers, and Roberto of the Mystic Tour company, make this a good information centre.

In the centre are other inexpensive hotels which are possible during the week. **Hospedaje Uairén**, Calle Zea near Roscio, no phone, is enlivened by a tepui painted in vivid green; 14 dim basic rooms, single $7, double $9.50. The same family runs the small Tropicalia restaurant. The budget **Peraytepui**, no phone, on Calle Bolívar seems passable on weekdays; shared baths.

Hotel Luz, Calle Fernández Peña, tel: 951050, also draws budget travellers; 19 simple rooms with small windows and firm beds; owner Roberto Fuenmayor runs Tayukasen Tours here. The nearby **Yarima**, no phone, has the same rates and a tiny lunch place.

Hotel Fronteras, Calle Icabarú at Zea, tel: 951095, was the area's first good hotel (formerly best). Circling a green patio are rooms with three beds, $19.50; twin beds in the noisy exterior wing are $18. **Posada Tres Naciones**, around the corner on Calle Zea, tel: 951235, appears as nice and is cheaper.

The best choices for car travellers are out of the centre. In the northern Akurima suburb is **Villa Fairmont,** prospering on a formula of spacious panelled rooms, bath with hot water and popular restaurant, the Churunay Akurima; for reservations, tel: 951022; in Caracas (02) 7817302/7091, fax: 7933879. In the southeast, Cielo Azul is a district opening to the countryside. At the first intersection on Av Perimetral, cross the narrow Uairén River (east), for **Cabañas Friedenau**, tel/fax: 951353; seven quiet triples in the back, six cabins for five to nine people, all with hot water, TV, kitchens (not equipped), covered parking, $20–60. **La Posada del Mesón**, continuing on the road via Sampay, tel/fax: 951443, has 12 A-frame cabins near quiet woods; well furnished, hot water; $24 for three people.

Follow signs uphill 2km to the recommended **Campamento Yakoo**, tel/fax: 951332, built by Manfred and Xiomara Frischeisen. Yakoo certainly has the finest savannah view. Set on the hill above an open-sided restaurant are pretty oval cottages for five to nine guests; double $20, cabin for five $50; discounts Monday–Thursday. Climbing or sightseeing tours are arranged to suit needs. In Caracas, SBA Nature Expeditions, tel/fax: (02) 2510990, (016) 6343611.

Hotel Tropical at the south end of Av Perimetral is an OK motel with blue and white cabins; moderate. The clean, comfortable **Hotel Lucas**, tel: 951018, is near the highway south, on Calle La Cancha by the power station; double with hot water, $20. The Lucas, with its own well, has no water shortage.

Information and tours

To date there is no parks office. The Guardia Nacional headquarters or Comandancia is at the corner of Av Mariscal Sucre and Calle Bolívar. CANTV has a new telephone centre near the hospital (south). Aerocav, Calle Icabarú near the hospital, tel: (088) 951081, delivers private mail and cargo nationwide, also operates an international courier service. Private mail is expensive but reliable, unlike the public mails.

Local tour operators are knowledgeable and eager. **Roberto's Mystic Tours**, Calle Urdaneta 187, near Av Perimetral, tel: (088) 951171, is headed by Roberto Marrero who makes and publishes up-to-date colour maps of the area, including Roraima and the route to Boa Vista. His tour to El Paují is recommended. Ask about Roraima treks here and at **Tayukasen Tours** in Hotel Luz, Calle Fernández Peña, tel: (088) 951050; vehicle to Paraitepuy, porters and 5 nights in tents, about $50 a day; or $90 for transport only.

Caracas agencies handling Gran Sabana tours include **Turismo Colorama**. Their 'you don't have to cook' camping is a great combination of plane to Ciudad Guayana, jeep to a Gran Sabana base with hot water, kitchen and camp cots, and expert guidance to falls and tablelands. Consult their polyglot staff at CC Bello Campo; tel: (02) 2617732, fax: 2621828.

Services have multiplied enabling travellers to reach many lovely falls and viewpoints unsuspected by the ordinary driver. Day tours are about $35 without food, $65 with three meals. **Rodiske Tours**, tel: (088) 951467, at Hotel Panaima go regularly to Kavanayen, spending a leisurely three days. **Adventure Tours** is in Foto Zoom, Av Perimetral near Calle Urdaneta, tel: (088) 951371. **Happy Tour**, tel: (088) 951015/1323, fax: 951030, in Centro Comercial Trigo Pan, and **Anaconda**, tel/fax: (088) 951016, in the CC Augusto on Calle Bolívar, take groups of 4–7 around the Gran Sabana staying in the best lodges, for $50–90 a day per person, all inclusive. The complete tour of all major falls and Kavanayén is well worth the money.

Raúl Arias parks his **helicopters** at a hangar on Av Mariscal Sucre, tel: (088) 951157/049. For travellers with $1,000 to spare, this is a great way to get around. Raúl can put his Bell 5-seater 'copters on top of Roraima, by gold mines or falls, even Angel Falls. There's little Raúl doesn't know about what to see.

Road's end: El Paují, Icabarú

Icabarú is the end of the road, 121km southwest of Santa Elena. The only way to avoid the bone-jarring track up and down through forested hills is to fly in. Despite road improvements now under way, do not think of taking this route in the rainy season. Aside from road hazards, the insect pests are unbearable.

Icabarú, which began life as a 1947 diamond strike or *bulla*, is again the centre of legal and illegal mining, today mostly gold. It is a rough place, without adequate accommodation. There are stores, 'hotels', and bars with beer at nearly $4 a can. As many as 20,000 miners work this region. Large concessions are being worked by transnationals. Venezuela is South America's largest diamond producer after Brazil.

On the way from Santa Elena there are two Pemón communities, Maurak and Betania, followed by **Peraitepui**, Km55, a mixed mining community near the Surucún River. The Surucún has been known since 1931 for its diamonds. In 1941 before a road existed, when the journey from El Dorado took six weeks, a miner there named Jaime 'Barrabás' Hudson found a 154-carat diamond which had been passed over as a rock. Harry Winston bought the diamond and cut it into three stones; the largest, 40-carat 'Libertador', is part of the Winston collection. Hudson, who was driving a taxi in Tumeremo when interviewed in 1989, said he had happily 'lived' his $10,000.

El Paují, Km75, is a frontier community of perhaps 300 homesteaders, including city escapees, painters and dancers. The village is at the edge of a savannah at 860m elevation, backed by gallery forest. It is named after a turkey-sized forest bird, the *pauji*, known in English as the guan. Here in the 'monte' far from modern comforts, settlers have built houses, a school and clinic, a water system, and now a theatre and cultural centre. Some are small-scale farmers or bee keepers – El Paují's 'wild' honey is famous. Many are now also innkeepers. Modest inns and hostels put up a growing number of visitors including groups arranged by Anaconda, Happy Tour and Roberto's Mystic Tours. There is an airstrip with a regular airtaxi service to Santa Elena.

Where to stay/eat

Tenters will find campgrounds here with toilets and lighting; usual charge is $5 a tent. Ask around at the guesthouses; there are places such as **El Caminante** which let you sling a hammock or camp for $2. At **Wei Mure**, overlooking a river and falls, two painters have created their studio and, by it, two singular guesthouses; you can pitch a tent, paying $5 with facilities, even order hot breakfast for $4.

Most lodging takes the form of rustic cabins for two to four, imaginatively built and run by the owners who often cook meals, too. Prices are fairly standard: single $10, double $15, triple $20. The following list is partial.

Posada Maripak, near the airfield, has a large restaurant presided over by Marieli Gil, and three cabins with hot water; lots of camping space with lights, sink and shower; tel: (088) 951459; in Caracas tel: (02)22343661, Carmen de Gil. **Campamento Manoa**, a kilometre east, makes the international circuit with expeditions, local tours, transfer from Santa Elena; nine cabins with triples or double bed; cabin only, or package deal for $60 a head. Contact Anaconda Tours, tel: (088) 951016; in Caracas, (02) 2834603 (Yajaira).

Restaurant La Comarca is owned by beekeeper Luis Scott who serves two or three specialties each day with one of El Paují's true delicacies, his wholewheat bread. He keeps a serpentarium to extract venom for serum makers. Luis, who speaks English and German, owns the attractive **Hospedaje Chimantá** by the woods; ten doubles with solar hot water and lighting. For reservations, tel: (088) 951994, fax: 951431.

Leaving El Paují for Icabarú there are other camps: Rancho Kunebana, Cantarrana, Solonia and Jade-Luz. **Campamento Kawaik** at Km90 is a lodge by a river with a view of remote tepuis. Three cabins, again with a singular design, are built with materials rescued from gold mines; price of $75 a day includes transfer from El Paují or Icabarú, all meals, and local excursions. Charter flight from Caracas or airtaxi from Ciudad Bolívar, and a tour to Icabarú mines, can be arranged. Reservation: tel: (02) 9459806, (014) 9956135.

What to do
Ask in El Paují for a guide to **El Abismo**. From 950m elevation, the edge of the Gran Sabana falls away 400m to the upper Icabarú basin. Views are towards Brazil, the vegetation changes and squawking macaws are part of a fascinating hike (allow two days). Other, less demanding, attractions near El Paují are falls and natural swimming pools in rocky rivers: El Pozo Esmeralda, La Catedral.

CAURA RIVER AND PARA FALLS
The Caura is a mighty Guayana river, third in volume after the Orinoco and Caroní. It is doubly valued as one of the last great 'wild' rivers, its pristine waters untainted by mining or farming run-off. Racing darkly over boulders and rapids, the Caura descends 500km through virgin forests from mountains bordering Brazil to a spectacular chain of 50m falls, the **Saltos Para**, little visited as they are a day away from the nearest road. The highway running 366km from Ciudad Bolívar south of the Orinoco to Caicara crosses the Caura over a bridge at Km240.

The Caura catches some of the country's heaviest rains, averaging 3m a year, emerging as a blackwater river – coloured by a zillion fallen leaves. Black Guayana rivers run over bedrock, swiftly, and have little sediment, and as a result less insects and wildlife, as opposed to whitewater Orinoco tributaries, slow and muddy.

Best time to travel is the dry season, December to April, when rock formations, superb beaches and absence of mosquitoes contribute to idyllic camping. This is truly off the beaten track.

The people who live up the Caura are members of the Yekuana group, formerly known as Makiritares. Some speak Spanish as well as Yekuana, a Carib language. Yekuana means 'men of the river' and these Indians are indeed master makers and handlers of dugouts – durable, slim (and tippy) craft hollowed to a shell of one inch from a solid trunk. Such *curiaras* may measure over 14m. Because of the Caura's many intricate rapids, the Yekuana are the only real navigators of its changing currents. Few outsiders penetrate above Para Falls.

Maripa
Maripa is the Caura's only town. It makes a good travel base as it is also at the kilometre-long bridge on the Ciudad Bolívar–Caura highway. The pueblo is famous for making and selling *curiaras* and men can often be seen hollowing out camphorwood and sassafras trunks with axes and fire. For a riverman, however, the big investment today is his outboard motor as many of Maripa's 3,000 inhabitants depend on fishing or on farm plots up river.

In 1773 the Franciscans founded a settlement to the north called **San Pedro de Alcántara**. In the 19th century rice was widely grown and there was a rice mill nearby. At the turn of the 20th century Maripa was an export centre for rubber, balatá and tonka beans. Tonka, seed of the sarrapia tree, was used in perfume and cigarette manufacture (Lucky Strike); today the fragrant fruit is mostly left to pigs.

Maripa's wide streets are lined with government-built rural houses shaded by large mango trees. Some shops sell basics such as corn flour for *arepas*, oil, tinned

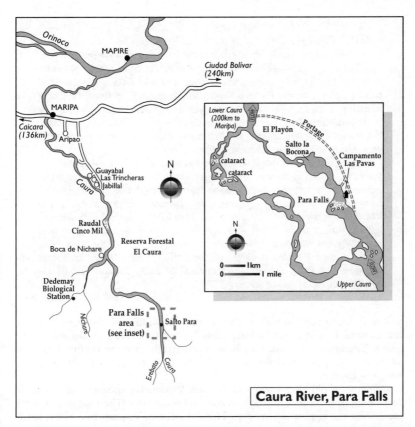

Caura River, Para Falls

sardines, soft drinks, beer, hats and rope. There is an airstrip just north of town. Telephones are at last being installed. The Yekuana community, however, maintain radio contact with Ciudad Bolívar, Para Falls and settlements on the upper Caura. The village has no doctor although there is a medical dispensary with a nurse. Because malaria is a problem in the rainy season, visitors should take preventive medicine before arriving.

Getting there and away
By bus Maripa is easy to reach by bus from **Ciudad Bolívar**, 240km (4 hours) over a good highway which continues west to Caicara, 126km. The road crosses wonderful savannahs dotted with palms. Some buses go on to **Puerto Ayacucho**. Another route, from **Caracas** to **Caicara** (8 hours), is covered by Línea Caicacho and Línea Mary. The night bus arrives at the ferry at 05.00; the crossing takes about an hour. Another line starts in **Valencia**, goes to Caicara and on to Ciudad Bolívar via Maripa.

By car/ferry via Caicara The drive from Caracas to Maripa, about 650km by way of Caicara, takes a day provided you catch the Cabruta–Orinoco ferry before sunset. The first part of the drive as far as **Chaguaramas** is mountainous and slow; the last stage over the empty Llanos to **Cabruta** is flat but speed is limited by potholes. In **Santa Rita**, the last pueblo before Cabruta, Mañino's modest chicken place makes a good break. There is also a decent motel by the road a little farther on. Cabruta has bars, small food shops and a cheap hotel.

CAURA DIVERSION

The Yekuana are among ethnic groups who have organised in self-defence. The Upper Caura, their homeland, is targeted for diversion by the state power company. Edelca has plans to build a dam at Ceiato and send half the Caura east to the Paragua River and thence to Guri Dam. Not only would this affect the forest and river ecosystems until now largely untouched, as well as the Yekuanas' trading, fishing (and tourism) activities, but the loss of water could make the rapids unnavigable six months of the year, cutting the people's access to Maripa.

The Yekuana have long had a radio system linking their villages on the Caura with Ciudad Bolívar. They are not sitting back to wait for the dam-builders. As a first step they are making maps to define ancestral lands, using satellite positioning equipment. An environmental action NGO, the World Rainforest Movement, procured them funds to buy 20 GPS sets and helped in their training. See also page 44. The next step is to claim land rights. Visitors wishing to give practical support can help through donations to the Forest Peoples Program – 'Save the Caura', World Rainforest Movement, 8 Chapel Row, Chadlington OX7 3NA, England; fax: 01608 676743; email: wrm@gn.apc.org.

The Orinoco ferry or *chalana* runs hourly, dawn to dusk, between Cabruta and Caicara. Expect to find a long queue of lorries, buses and cars waiting to board. The open barge takes an hour downstream, more returning. Cars pay $4.50 to cross; passengers do not pay. If you have no car, ask about the faster bongo or *lancha*.

Caicara, an old river town said to mark Venezuela's geographical centre, is developing new avenues, districts, depots and restaurants. The road out of town passes near the airport and modern **Hotel Redoma**. You can find older, small hotels in the centre (check to see that the air conditioning works and the shower has water): the **Miami, Cedeño, Hotel Venezuela, Bella Guayana**. A good pension is **Residencias Dina** on Calle 23 de Enero.

Where to stay/eat

On Maripa's main street a shop owner, Caramelo, has built his hotel, **Villa Maripa**, solidly room by room: a dozen with tiled shower (cold water), massive four poster beds and fans, $12 double. The property goes through to the parallel street and there is inside parking. If Caramelo's shop is shut, just hammer on the metal garage door.

Among places to eat, two restaurants in town, one at the east end and one west, serve reliable chicken, *pollo a la parrilla*; beer flows freely.

There is a good upmarket lodge, **Campamento Caurama**, with its own airfield, a few kilometres north of Maripa. Caurama is part of Hato El Retiro, a huge extension of savannah, forest and lagoons bordered by the river. Cattle and water buffalo range freely. The big mammals include otters, tapir and monkeys. A first-rate guest lodge has 18 double rooms with ceiling fan, thatched dining room, bar and swimming tank. Packages run to $112 a day including transfer from Ciudad Bolívar or Puerto Ordaz, full board, fishing and river excursions; discounts for residents. For information about the Para Falls trip, ring Ameropa, tel: (02) 5743366/3888, fax: 5744019; email: aventur@ibm.net. Or Amazonair (see next paragraph).

Caura tours

Amazonair puts its Cessnas down near Salto Para in a combined air/river plan. The charter line operated by German pilot Willi Michel picks up passengers in Caracas and flies them to the hydrology station airfield on the lower Caura (just under 2 hours). They sleep at **El Playón** beach, hike up to the falls, then go downriver to Maripa by *curiara* and return to Caracas by plane. For costs (according to days), ring: Amazonair, tel: (02) 2836960, fax: 2832627.

Various river tours to Para Falls leave from the tiny port of **Las Trincheras**, saving about three hours' river travel. The village is 52km (last part unpaved) from the Ciudad Bolívar highway, and 74km in all from Maripa. This area is part of the **Caura Forest Reserve**.

Expediciones Cacao have a fine base at the water's edge: **Campamento Río Caura**, also known as Campamento Las Trincheras. Their excursion to Para Falls leaves every Saturday, spending three nights in Las Trincheras and two in hammocks in an Indian *churuata* (roundhouse) at El Playón. The cost per person includes insurance, bilingual guide and Ciudad Bolívar transfers; $350 in hammock, $374 in double room. For information call Bernd Kroening, Cacao, tel: (02) 9773753/1234, fax: 9770110; the office maintains radio link with field bases. **Eco Posadas** also handles reservations for the guesthouse and large thatched building equipped with hammocks, shower, cold water; $45 a day covers breakfast, dinner, local excursions, insurance. They will also arrange car transfer from Ciudad Bolívar for $100; tel: (02) 9931695, fax: 9928984.

On an island in the Caura is **Campamento Yokore**, operated by a Frenchman, Philippe Lesne of Cauraventura. Passengers are picked up in Ciudad Bolívar or Ciudad Guayana and driven to **Jabillal**, the last community on the Trincheras road. From there a *curiara* takes them upriver to Yokore in half an hour. The wilderness camp offers native shelters, rustic kitchen, hammocks with mosquito nets, toilets, showers, firelight (no electricity). From Yokore it takes a full day's travel to El Playón (see below, *Up the Caura to Para Falls*). The package of 5 days/4 nights costs around $375 (minimum 4 people). In Puerto Ordaz, Philippe Lesne, tel: (086) 223121, (014) 9862495; Caracas, tel/fax: (02) 2349401, 2325390.

Gilles Cros, a French wilderness guide, is enthusiastic about the unspoiled Caura to the point of making a 12-day trek passing Para Falls and hiking over to the Paragua River. Cros picks up passengers from Ciudad Bolívar. On the river, they camp with Indians at Boca de Nichare and Soapire, sling hammocks in El Playón. Costs run about $50 a day according to group (minimum 4); tel: (02) 2396213, or fax: 2354931.

Akanán Travel has a Caura base called **Campamento Kue Kue**, after the black and yellow frog, on an island within reach of Las Trincheras. Their five nights allow leisurely camping at Para Falls. For details of monthly departure dates from Caracas (or picking up passengers en route), see *Tour operators*, page 14.

Emilio Rodríguez, a native guide who helped to build the research station on the Nichare, is offering ecotourism river trips up the Caura and Nichare, to his home at Boca de Tabaru. He may be reached by radio at noon and 18.00, band USB, 6789.00. Or leave a message for Emilio, Comunidad Edowiña, tel: (085) 930001/02.

Up the Caura to Para Falls
Hilary Branch

With the help of Yekuana friends our party of four spent five days on the river and at Para Falls. Driving from Caracas we found Germán Rodríguez, expert navigator and *motorista*, at home in Maripa in his thatched roundhouse on Calle Ruíz Pineda (towards the river). He agreed to take us and we began preparations. First, we filled two drums with petrol and 2-stroke oil; next, Germán procured a large *curiara*. The hire of a *curiara* and reliable outboard motor runs at about $80 a day, with services of pilot (*capitán*) and helper (*marinero*). Germán took his flashlight and hammock or 'porsia,' short for *por si acaso* which means 'just in case'. In another plastic bag he stashed dry cassava bread. That and fishing hooks and line would cover emergencies.

Early next morning we pushed off upriver. On board were machete, lamps, food for a week, our hammocks and tarpaulin. Crocodile-coloured, the Caura slid by for three hours nonstop to **Las Trincheras**, a *criollo* pueblo, and **Jabillal**. Over the next three hours to the mouth of the Nichare, the river changed from broad and slow, to broad and fast, broken by islands and jagged rocks. Germán scanned **Mura Rapids** like a book, selecting safe passage among boulders. The *curiara* nosed up to a flat boulder by **Raudal Cinco Mil**, rapids where a man's curiara sank along with his fortune over a century ago. Kapok, or silk cotton trees, jacarandas and a huge copaiba shaded our picnic and we cooled off in brandy-coloured water.

Later, as the sun sank behind the forest wall, macaws squawked overhead in pairs and parrots carolled on their way to bed. We slung our hammocks at Germán's own settlement at the mouth of the **Nichare River**. He and his family cultivate yuca for making cassava bread, and maize, yams, sugarcane, pineapple, pawpaw, coffee and cacao. He often hires Sanemá Indians as peons.

A small research station up the Nichare supported by the Amigos del Nichare and the New York Zoological Society studies the area's birds, animals and fish. Wildlife is greatly depleted on the river, and fish are under pressure, too, due to fishermen from Ciudad Bolívar who use 100m-long nets called *trenes*, taking tonnes of peacock bass, morocoto (pacú) and cachama.

Howler monkeys, turtles, giant otters, freshwater dolphins, and cayman, once seen everywhere up the Caura, are now very shy; crocodiles have been all but eliminated. On muddy bottoms (not beaches) there may be stingrays. Germán used a stick, or simply shuffled through sediment to avoid stepping on a nasty surprise.

Giant otter

On **Day 2** Germán threaded a maze of islands and brought the *curiara* to a dwelling at **Soapire** where a Yekuana family was roasting a whole tapir and drying many rounds of cassava, preparing for year-end festivities. Birds delighted us: anhingas all aligned on a sunny boulder, toucans flapping hard to keep their beaks up, a fishing eagle, black hawks, white egrets, grey skimmers dipping to black waters...

Finally, as Germán piloted around islands and through fast water, the Caura narrowed and we approached the end of navigation on the Lower Caura: **El Playón**, a shining expanse of white beach. Here starts a 5km series of cataracts rising to Para Falls. The beach was our campsite. Exploring hot rocks by foaming water, stripping for a wash, stringing our hammocks in a great fallen tree: El Playón was idyllic. Incredibly, not a single fly or mosquito to be seen in this dry weather. Two Indians strolled to the cascades with fishing line and worms. When they returned with a pair of 4kg morocotos, Germán gave a hasty '*hasta mañana*' and went off to share a fish supper.

From El Playón the Yekuana carry all gear around the falls in a 6.5km portage to the Upper Caura. Even loaded with tanks of fuel, they climb the trail in less than two hours. However, flatlanders take closer to three hours as the trail rises 210m in altitude.

On *Day 3* we took our swimsuits and a picnic and followed the well-beaten trail. Halfway, a boat portage bisects the path; you follow straight on for **Campamento Las Pavas**, 3km. This camp at the top of the trail is a pretty surprise: prefabricated cabins set in a neat park. Engineers making a dam feasibility study built the 'temporary' camp and helipad in 1975. Today it is maintained by the Yekuanas for tourism; a small contribution is requested from visitors for upkeep.

It is possible to stay at Las Pavas camp for about $4. Germán's nephew showed us around a dispensary, study hall, radio room and bunk house. If you need shelter, this is it, although creaking with age; no bedding provided, and the generator is broken, so no electricity. However, the Yekuanas will help portage visitors' gear up to the camp. Ask for the *encargado* and settle all prices with him. There is always a family in residence and radio contact is maintained with Maripa.

Salto Para breaks into a dazzling array of 50m falls, followed by smaller cataracts and a gorge called La Bocona. From the foot of the main falls we contracted a young boatman to take us closer in his *curiara* and had a wonderful swim.

Day 4. After a starry night, a misty dawn, and coffee at 07.00, we began an eight-hour return journey, arriving in Maripa in the evening.

Simón Bolívar

296

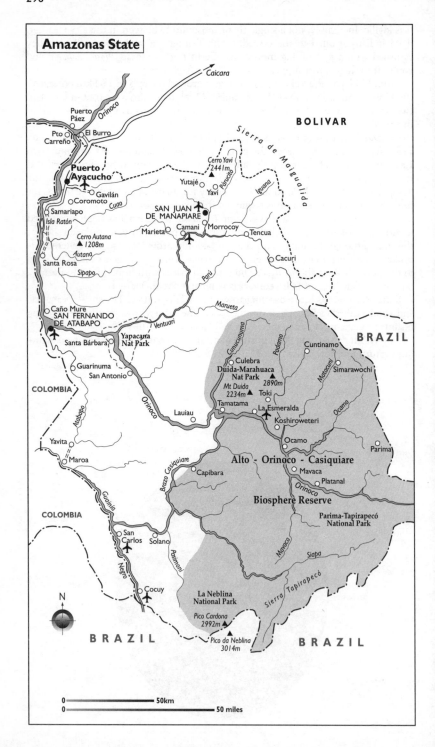

Amazonas

Amazonas is Venezuela's 22nd state. This territory of 175,750km² extends to 0°40' from the equator. Southern Amazonas was largely undisturbed by white men until gold-seeking *garimpeiros* invaded from Brazil in the 1980s. Despite this, population is still a sparse 80,000 inhabitants. The principal ethnic groups in Amazonas are the Guahibo, Piaroa, Yekuana (Makiritare), Baniva, Yanomami (Waika) and Sanemá; perhaps 40,000 people in all.

The Yekuana are admired for their long dugout canoes or the bigger bongos, and their beautifully designed communal houses. These huge conical structures accommodate several families. The Piaroa make baskets, stools, carved jaguars, anteaters and now mobiles of birds and butterflies. Their traditional roundhouse or *churuata* is also spectacular: it is like a 100-person seamless hat, 12m tall and thatched from ground to tip.

Venezuelan law requires special permits to visit Indian territory. The creation in 1991 of the Upper Orinoco-Casiquiare Biosphere Reserve (83,000km²) is intended to restrict not only mining and logging but also travel. However, the New Tribes missionaries have operated for nearly 50 years from remote airstrips. Evangelist missions in Tama Tama, Padamo and Mavaca are reached by river. Catholic missions were established centuries ago; their mission in La Esmeralda has a long history of Franciscans in the 18th century and later Salesians who have run a large school and mission since the 1940s. The Salesians also have missions in Colonia Coromoto, Isla Ratón, San Fernando de Atabapo, San Juan de Manapiare and Ocamo.

La Esmeralda has an environmental research station, the Centro Amazónico Alejandro de Humboldt. This is built on the savannah (partly funded by the German government) and is run by SADA, autonomous service for the environmental development of Amazonas.

Four national parks in Amazonas cover a total of 53,000km², protecting (mostly on paper): Duida-Marahuaca, Neblina, Yapacana and Parima-Tapirapeco. However, most of these parks fall within the new biosphere zone.

Not all Amazonas is forest. There are table mountains, too, as the area is part of the Guayana Shield. On the southern border with Brazil are two peaks: **Cardona**, 2,992m, in Venezuela, and **Cerro Neblina**, 3,014m, in Brazil. Neblina is South America's tallest mountain east of the Andes. The biggest is **Duida-Marahuaca**, 2,890m, followed in height by Yaví, 2,441m. The most spectacular is isolated **Autana**, rising vertically 1,300m out of green forest only 100km south-southeast of Puerto Ayacucho.

PUERTO AYACUCHO

Puerto Ayacucho was founded in 1924, centennial of the battle of Ayacucho. Here the great Atures and Maipures rapids divide the Orinoco: the upper headwaters lie

1,160km to the southeast; the lower Orinoco is navigable for 900km to the Atlantic. By moving the capital to this site where all travellers on the Orinoco are obliged to halt, Dictator Juan Vicente Gómez gained control of Amazonas Territory. Cargo bound for the upper Orinoco is trucked 63km south of the rapids on a road also ordered by Gómez in 1924. Across the river from Puerto Ayacucho (here at its deepest, 50m) is Colombia.

Controlling river and air traffic, Puerto Ayacucho is the regional administrative centre. The town was built on a conventional plan: the church, Salesian mission school, town council and government offices surround Plaza Bolívar. Orinoco barges once brought all the town's fuel, vehicles, beer and cement, while planes supplied perishables. But the opening of the Caicara road has changed all that. Today, large numbers of campesinos and Indians, some from Colombia, have moved in from remote areas. About half of Amazonas' population live in Puerto Ayacucho and the city is as full of vendors (and thieves) as a Turkish bazaar.

Puerto Ayacucho (altitude 115m) receives very heavy rain, over 2,300mm a year falling mostly between June and October. Depending on when you go, the weather in Puerto Ayacucho will be hot and wet (30°C) or hot and dry (26.5°C). Travellers to forests and rivers, however, may be surprised to feel temperatures drop sharply at night.

Before you go

Remember this is a malaria region; start anti-malaria medication before arriving. Bring a mosquito net, insect repellent and spirals in the wet season. Electricity is variable so always have a flashlight. At wilderness camps there's good swimming because the rivers, Orinoco included, are fast, clear and clean. Besides swimsuit, you need a cap or sun visor, rain poncho, two pairs of rubber sandals or trainers, a long-sleeved shirt, and a tracksuit top for cool nights.

Getting there and away
By air

Avensa jets fly in every morning from **Caracas** at 11.00, $80; the plane returns via **San Fernando de Apure**. Air Venezuela has a direct flight at 08.25 arriving at 9.45; $54. Taxis from the air terminal, 7km south of town, cost about $4.

Airtaxis Small lines such as Wayumi, tel: (048) 210635, and Aguaysa, tel: 210443, calculate charter costs at about $210 an hour for a three-seater Cessna, up to $260 for a seven-seater. When estimating costs for flights to jungle camps, add 50% of an hour's flying cost for every two hours the plane waits for you. Weight allowance is 10 kilos. A copy of your passport is needed in advance for the permit issued by the state government.

Single travellers may find seats on flights to remote Amazonas pueblos. For instance, Aguaysa flies to Yutajé or **Camani**, 1 hour, for $100. They operate daily service at 06.00, except Sundays, to **San Juan de Manapiare**, $60. Wayumi covers this route and also **San Fernando de Atabapo**, daily, $60; La Esmeralda, on Thursdays, $100; **Maroa** on Tuesdays, $80; **San Carlos de Río Negro** on Tuesdays and Fridays, $100. Payment may be in bolívars or dollars.

By bus

Caracas coaches such as Ejecutivos Mary, tel: (02) 5775068, take the route via **El Sombrero**. They cross the Orinoco at Caicara and from there follow the beautiful motorway 364km to Puerto Ayacucho, a journey of 16 hours. Colectivos Caicabo buses leave **Caracas** at night, arriving next day at 13.00; fare is about $18. The Terminal de Pasajeros is 6km east of Puerto Ayacucho on the highway north; taxi is the easiest way to get there.

Buses leave throughout the day for **Ciudad Bolívar** (10–11 hours) and **Caracas**. The Llanos route to **San Fernando**, **Maracay** and points west is now open; it's an 8-hour journey, crossing the Orinoco by ferry at El Burro. There are *por puestos* to El Burro, $2.50.

Where to stay
The area telephone code for Puerto Ayacucho is (048)
Two new better-class hotels have opened on Av Orinoco. At the north end near the river port is **Hotel Orinoco**, tel: 210285, air-conditioned doubles at $25; at the south end by CANTV is the **Hotel Apure**, tel: 210516, double $26, perhaps the best in town. The old **Gran Hotel Amazonas**, tel/fax: 210328, Calle Atabapo, a few blocks NE of Plaza Bolívar, now sports an unlikely new name, **Guácharo Resort**; double occupancy, $25 per person. There's a swimming pool, an off-and-on restaurant, and an unprotected parking lot.

For $8–10 a double try **Hotel Maguari**, Calle Evelio Roa near the Hotel Amazonas, tel: 210120, family-run; or **Hotel Tobogán**, Av Orinoco at Evelio Roa, tel: 210320, air conditioned.

A good choice is the **Residencias Rio Siapa**, Calle Carabobo No 39 near the Don Juan cinema; tel: 210138; about $12 double; small air-conditioned rooms give on to a pleasant garden. **Residencias Aragüita** on a side street opposite, enlarged and with air-conditioned rooms, is simple and reasonable. Both have fenced parking areas. **Residencias Internacional**, Av Aguerrevere three blocks west of Plaza Bolívar, tel: 210242; has comfortable rooms with fan; double $10 or less without bathroom; very friendly people.

Campamento Tucán, tel/fax: 211378, is a 10-minute ride south of town near the airport. Many expeditions into the interior have used Tucán as their base. Orientated to foreigners, the camp normally operates on a package basis with food, lodging and excursions; 2 days/1 night, $85. It's very pleasant: trees, a natural pool, dining room in thatched *churuata*; 20 spotless rooms with bath, air conditioning and ceiling fan. This camp is also called **Genesis** by some tour agencies. Day fishing trips are made to the Orinoco rapids where large payara are the prize; best time Jan–Apr. In Caracas, Alpi Tour, tel: (02) 2831433, fax: 2856067.

Campamento Orinoquia (Garcitas), 23km south of Puerto Ayacucho, has a wonderful setting overlooking the Orinoco by the rocky Atures rapids; it is part of a wildlife preserve. The small Indian-style camp is lovely; five *churuatas* with comfortable built-in beds. Boat excursion to Garcitas Island, photo and bird safaris, even snorkelling to see river fish. In Caracas, ring Cacao, tel: (02) 9772798, fax: 9770110; email: 73050.2614@compuserve.com.

Nacamtur, tel: 212763/4255, fax: 210325, 33km south on the Samariapo road, then left to Gavilán. Here you will find a 'Natural Camp' well managed by the owner, José Marché, who speaks English and Italian. He organises tours to local settlements, petroglyphs and rivers where you can fish. The hotel has eight large units with double, $15, and twin beds, hot showers, a good restaurant, disco, and swimming pool.

Camturama, tel: 210266, is a pricey selva resort hotel at Garcitas Rapids on the Orinoco, 20km south of Ayacucho. It has ample grounds, 50 air-conditioned doubles in thatched bungalows, hot water, restaurant, disco and pool. Basic price with meals is $75 per person; airport transfer and tours by arrangement. In Caracas tel: (02) 9418813, fax: 9435160.

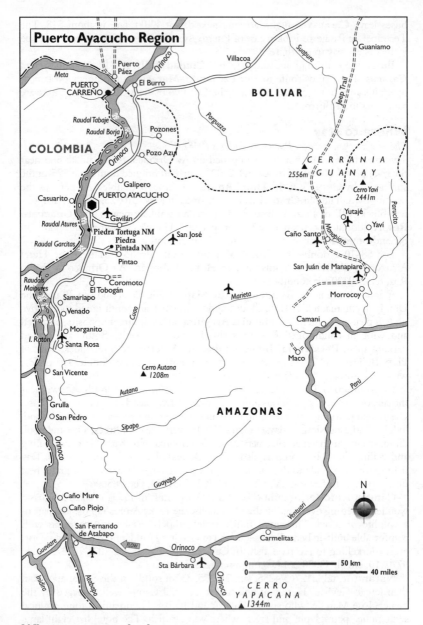

Puerto Ayacucho Region

What to see and where to eat

The **Mercado Indígena**, held on Av Río Negro a block south of Plaza Bolívar, is a fantastic mixed bag of local talents, mostly Piaroa and Guahibo. Best time to get to this crafts fair is at 06.00 or earlier on Thur–Fri; some Indians may be there at the weekend too. The early bird finds the best-made model animals, toys, pottery and baskets before the trade shoppers arrive; late-comers pick over souvenirs.

In town you can buy hammocks of any kind and mosquito nets. A good souvenir shop, **Tópico El Cacique**, is run by Vicente Barletta, Urbanización Andrés Eloy Blanco, tel: (048) 22519. Sr Vicente has been in the tourist business for over 30 years and will bend over backwards to help.

Centro CEPAI, tel: 214956, is the place to go for products made by the Yekuana, Piaroa, Curripaco and Sanema, a subgroup of the Yanomami. They have formed a distribution cooperative under the banner of self development. (For the Caracas outlet, see *Chapter 4*, page 81.) If you ask a taxi to take you to Sector CEPAI, Barrio Carinagüita towards the airport, you will find crafts including Curripaco clay pots, Arawak brooms of *chiquichiqui* fibre, hardwood benches, and baskets from all the groups. Among the organic food products are hot pepper sauce made with ants, forest honey, medicinal *seje* palm oil. By buying here you can support Indian enterprise as there is no middleman, and in this way 'give something back'.

These peoples, in scattered communities up the Ventuari, Manapiare, Paru, Orinoco and Atabapo rivers, work with the forest: planting cacao (Yekuana and Piaroa), bee-keeping (Sanema, Piaroa, Guahibo), collecting *chiquichiqui* broom fibre, and processing *seje* oil. The Yekuana also raise water buffalo on grasslands.

The **Museo Etnológico del Amazonas**, opposite the fair, is open Tue–Fri 08.30–11.00, 14.30–18.00; Sat 09.00–12.00, 15.30–19.00; Sun 09.00–13.00. Regional Indian cultures are intelligently presented; be sure to go even if you don't understand Spanish (there is a good library).

For a great sunset panorama of both Ayacucho and the Orinoco, walk to a hill called **Cerro Perico**. It is half a kilometre from the Museo Etnológico by way of Av Aguerrevere (west), then up to the left by **Restaurant La Estancia** (good steak). Another broader viewpoint, **El Mirador**, is 1.5km south of town. A parrilla place near there prepares very tasty, reasonable steak.

Delicious fried fish can be had in houses in the town. The señora puts a huge pot of oil to boil in front of her house and you sit outside as her kids bring out the table, fork and beer. Just ask '*A dónde venden pescado frito?*'

You can get the taste of Amazonas in ice-cream, too. At the **Heladería Mi Sabor**, Av Principal La Florida, seasonal palm fruits such as *moriche* and *seje* (like coconut) go into ice-cream made by Juan José Moori. Then there's *copoazú*, manioc and *túpiro*, as well as chocolate and vanilla.

Further afield

Piedra de la Tortuga Seen from the road to Samariapo, 8km south of Puerto Ayacucho, this gigantic granite boulder with its smaller 'head' looks like a tortoise. It has been declared a Natural Monument. Nearby there is an Indian cemetery, reached by river when waters are low.

Cerro Pintado South of town is a village called Pintado, 17km, referring to an immense boulder famous for prehistoric petroglyphs. Like Humboldt, one may wonder how they were carved so high up; one engraving is a 150ft-long serpent. These are difficult to discern and a guide is useful. Inparques personnel may go off for lunch and close the park between 11.00 and 14.00.

Parque Tobogán de la Selva is reached by a 6km side road, off the Samariapo highway at Km30. The 'toboggan' is a smooth, steeply inclined rock over which water slides, quite exciting in the rainy season. There are picnic tables and shelters; refreshments at weekends. The park gets crowded on holidays and maintenance is poor. But there are caretakers and it is possible to camp during the week. In the area you may visit the Coromoto community of Guahibo Indians.

Autana by air Cerro Autana, declared a Natural Monument, is seen at its most dramatic from the air. Below Autana's truncated top (1,208m) a cave big enough for a helicopter to fly through stretches from side to side. This *tepui* is sacred to the Piaroa Indians, a mythical tree of life. By helicopter or light plane, Autana is 80km away. Ask at the airport or any travel agency if there's a group you can join for an overflight.

Casuarito (Colombia) From Puerto Ayacucho's port, bongos and launches take day shoppers across the Orinoco for about $1 to Casuarito on the Colombian side, where jewellery and good leather goods are plentiful. The *pueblo* has a reputation for bars and brothels. Casuarito appears to be built on a single vast rock or *laja*. Formalities are limited to showing your passport.

Information and tours
Permits
A government agency coordinates activities in Amazonas including tourism. No travel (or mining) is theoretically permitted in the Orinoco headwaters region or Alto Orinoco Biosphere Reserve. The Servicio Autónomo para el Desarrollo Ambiental del Amazonas (SADA) has offices on Avenida Los Lirios, via Aeropuerto, tel: 210059, 210647; in Caracas, Base Aérea Francisco Miranda (La Carlota), Caracas; tel: (02) 9917853.

Tourist office
There is a government office in Plaza Bolívar, Av Río Negro at Calle Bolívar; tel: 210033; open 08.00–12.00, 14.00–17.30.

Telephones
The central office of CANTV is on Av Orinoco in the southern part of town.

Tour agencies
Specialised services are expanding rapidly, although sightseeing tours mostly go to the same places (see above, *Further afield*), adding a drive to visit native Piaroa and Guaharibo communities (photographs not recommended). Older agencies are **Tobogán Tours**, Av Río Negro No 14 south of the Museo, tel: 214865, fax: 214553; and **Yutajé** on Av Aguerrevere, a block north of Ipostel, tel/fax: 210664. They also arrange trips further afield to suit your interests: birds, fish, mountains. Ask Pepe Jaimes of Tobogán for an English-speaking guide.

Autana Adventures, Av Amazonas No 91, tel: 212619, 212237, is very professional; experienced; trips up the Rio Parguaza to visit Piaroa communities, camping and sleeping in hammocks. From Puerto Ayacucho a 2-day/1-night trip costs roughly $120; 4 days/3 nights, $200, is much more worthwhile. The managers are Henry Mora and Cesar Jaramillo, both professionals. As the agency's name suggests, they go upriver to (but not up) Cerro Autana.

Expediciones Guaharibo, Calle Evelio Roa No 39, tel: 210635/6. Alex Capriles organises travel (and permits) to far-off rivers: the Atabapo, Sipapo, Autana, Casiquiare, Río Negro. The bongo is your home by day, hammocks in a riverside camp by night. In Caracas, tel: (02) 9526996/7895, fax: 9530092.

Expediciones Orinokia, Av Río Negro No 6, tel: 210448, will arrange for passengers to get to rivers such as the Autana, $200 return. Giuseppe Bucciarelli, a biologist, went to the Piaroa community of Piedra Tonina where he hired an Indian called José at about $6 a day: trekking six days through the forest, sleeping in hammocks, fishing and hunting; in the evening they cooked the day's catch (fish, frogs, spiders) on the campfire.

Adventure tours and camps

Whitewater rafting Most breathtaking of adventures has to be rafting down the Atures rapids, a novel way to court the angels. The experts shepherd you through mammoth waves in 15ft rubber rafts. Jorge Buzzo and his wife Claudia own **Expediciones Aguas Bravas**. For $35 Jorge takes roller-coaster fans whitewater rafting down the rapids of the Orinoco, just south of Puerto Ayacucho. Their rubber raft has been especially built for these waters and is powered by outboard motor. For expert rafters the levels are three and four. It's a good thrill and the advantage of the outboard is that Jorge can return and run any rapid as often as his crew want. Wear a swimsuit. Aguas Bravas is a block south of Plaza Bolívar, on a deadend street off Av Río Negro; tel: 214458, fax: 211529.

Calypso Camp is located near Corocito, 5km north of Ayacucho by highway and a few minutes from the Orinoco River. With its own fleet of vehicles and bongos the camp conducts excursions on the Orinoco to Laguna de Las Toninas, playground of river dolphins, and to Parguaza tributary camping and sleeping in hammocks. The Swiss-run lodge has a great Indian-style roundhouse with palm-thatched roof; 54 beds, good mattresses, fans. Bathrooms are in a separate building. Price covers full board, open national bar (rum, beer), nearby excursions and airport transfer; 2 days/1 night $140. They have radio but no phone. In Caracas, tel: (02) 5450024/6009, fax: 5413036.

Tucán in Puerto Ayacucho (see *Where to stay*, page 259) offers treks of 2–10 days exploring different ecosystems by foot, plane or boat: rainforest, savannah, mauritia palm swamp, caños and rivers; also Tierra Blanca and Los Pendares communities on the Parguaza. The treks are led by bilingual guides. Costs run at about $75 a day, all-inclusive from Puerto Ayacucho. Fishing trips are also available.

More distant camps are reached by light plane. They give a real opportunity to see jungle, rivers, and sometimes Indian cultures in a short time, leaving the permits to others. The fees of such camps cover all activities and food, but not always the transfer flight.

Mawadianajodo, one of the most remote camps on the Upper Orinoco, has been run for many years by a Yekuana native, Francisco Díaz. The camp by the Cunucunuma tributary is in the Indian village (also called Culebra), not far from the impressive Cerro Duida (2,234m). You sleep in hammocks or on camp cots. It is an hour's flight by light plane from Puerto Ayacucho, or three days south by river. For information in Caracas about packages including flight with bilingual guides: tel/fax: (02) 2510990. Costs for six days run at about $1,050 per person (group of four).

Camani, on the banks of the Ventuari, is 50 minutes by light plane east of Puerto Ayacucho. By river such a trip would take five days. Trips are organised by the camp manager (who speaks five languages) to ponds where wildlife gathers, to spectacular **Tencua Falls**, three hours by launch, and to **Caño de Piedra** where there are cascades and beaches. This is a luxurious wilderness lodge with 13 elegant, spacious *churuatas* for two, with private bath and hot water. In the centre of the camp sparkles a lovely pool. The dining room serves first-class meals. Radio with phone patch. $180 daily per person, discount for residents (for plane transfer, see *Airtaxis*, page 298). In Puerto Ayacucho, tel: 210026, fax: 210443; in Porlamar, tel: (095) 627402, fax: 620989; email: camani@internet.ve.

Junglaven, located nearby, uses the same airstrip but transfers guests 12km to a more rustic lodge on the banks of **Laguna Grande**, a Ventuari tributary. Eight circular *churuatas* accommodate 26, with bath and electricity. You cross a most spectacular forest, full of birds. The owner, Capitán Lorenzo Rodríguez, is extremely interested in birders and very helpful. He compiles lists by visiting ornithologists of some 280 species such as trogon, tinamou and toucanet. From November to May fishing tours (two fishermen per boat) are offered to a field camp called **Morocoto**: payara, 10lb peacock bass and pacú, 100lb+ catfish. The price of $360 for three nights includes full board and local boat use (Tencua Falls, just over 2 hours), birding, but not the flight from Puerto Ayacucho which costs about $150 return. Fishing trips cost $250 a day. In Caracas, tel: (02) tel/fax: 9915083, (016) 6339017.

Yutajé, pioneered 30 years ago by an Italian, José Raggi, lies some 45 minutes by plane east of Puerto Ayacucho in the Manapiare headwaters. Yutajé means 'water which comes down from high', referring to lovely falls some distance from the camp. The Raggis' wilderness base offers six simple thatched cabins with two units, cold-water shower and ceiling fan, by the Corocoro River. As you go down the clear dark river herons caw and kingfishers yell 'k-k-k' in alarm, curious giant otters poke heads out of the water, and river dolphins surface, their muscular backs shining. There are lovely cascades, birds, and good bass fishing in the dry season. Current price is $70 per night with excursions, lodging and meals (you pay extra for bottled drinks, and ice 'imported' by air). Tel: (048) 213348/0664, 212550 or in Caracas, ring Amazonair, tel: (02) 2836960, fax: 2832627. Yutajé is conveniently served Mon–Sat by Aguaysa (see *Airtaxis*).

Fishing tours

Peacock Bass Safaris take you by plane to the Casiquiare watershed in southern Amazonas. Here, the Pasiba and Pasimoni tributaries are famous among sport fishermen for producing more world-record *pavón* than any other area. This is a low land of beautiful rainforest, lagoons, and dry-season beaches. Alpi's crew pick up visitors in San Carlos de Río Negro or Tama Tama, depending on river conditions, and use 16ft aluminium boats equipped with swivel seats and electric motor for catch-and-release fishing, two anglers per boat. A five-day plan, sleeping in tents with cots in a moveable camp with generator and propane refrigerator, includes 2-hour charter flight from Puerto Ayacucho. For information on rates, ring Alpiturismo, (02) 2831433/1733, fax: 2856067; email: alpisafari@compuserve.com.

The **Amazonas Peacock Bass Lodge** is a 32ft air-conditioned houseboat on the Casiquiare which started operation in 1998 for fishermen seeking the *pavón* or peacock bass, known as one of the strongest freshwater fighters. The season is October to April. To fish in various lagoons, the visitors also use a Supercub float plane (the only one in Amazonas) that previously served a Rainbow Bay Resort in Alaska. One week's fishing on the Pasimoni and Pasiba tributaries, including Caracas flights, float

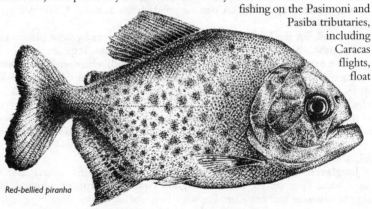

Red-bellied piranha

plane, houseboat, guides and fishing licence, comes to $3,950. For information, ring Rafael Arnal: (02) 9868685, (014) 9066586; email: panty@true.net.

UP THE ORINOCO

South to **Samariapo**, 63km, is no problem as there are buses; by *por puesto* $1.60. To travel up the Orinoco you must get a seat on a *bongo* or take the 'Expreso del Sur', a *voladora* or fast launch which covers the 180km to San Fernando de Atabapo (2–3 hours) for about $15. Transport from Puerto Ayacucho with Camani Transportes near the electricity generator costs $US14.

A river trip is always fascinating; take along your hammock and mosquito net, hat, waterproof, hammock, flashlight and food. According to SADA in Caracas, no permits are needed to go up the Orinoco as far as **La Esmeralda** (beyond this point travel is prohibited). At the *puerto* show your identification to the Guardia Nacional and state that you are an *excursionista* and wish to go only to the next pueblo. Samariapo is the embarkation port during low water and Venado, about 9km beyond, during high water. The road ends at Morganito.

You pass several islands including Morrocoy and Paloma, coming in two hours to the very large **Isla Ratón** (it has an airstrip). The village of Ratón faces Colombia. There is a Salesian Mission and boarding school where some 300 children learn to read and write.

Opposite Ratón is the Sipapo tributary, leading to the Autana River. The rivers

BRAZO CASIQUIARE FLOWS TO THE AMAZON

The name of Amazonas State is rooted not only in flora and fauna similar to Brazil's. A unique river, the **Casiquiare Canal**, in fact joins the Orinoco and Amazon basins. In Spanish it is called *brazo* or 'arm'. The Brazo Casiquiare leaves the Upper Orinoco and, depending on the season, carries off roughly one fifth of the Orinoco's waters to the Río Negro, an Amazon tributary. The Casiquiare empties near San Carlos de Río Negro (a *pueblo* with an airstrip and little else of interest). A day's journey farther is the frontier post of San Simón de Cocuy.

In 1800 Alexander von Humboldt and Aimé Bonpland started their great inland adventure. With their carriers toting trunks of instruments and boxes for plant and animal collections, they went by mule over the Llanos, and by boat to the Orinoco where their dugout was hauled through the Atures and Maipures Rapids. Then with Indians again paddling, they went up the Atabapo to its headwaters. Twenty-three Indians from the mission of Yavita dragged the bongo 11km over to the Guainía's headwaters. Continuing what is today still called 'Humboldt's Route', they went down to the Río Negro. Humboldt was at last in a position to prove the existence of the Casiquiare Canal as a link between the Amazon and Orinoco basins. His party paddled from the Río Negro up the waterway linking the two huge river systems which brought them to the Orinoco below La Esmeralda.

The Casiquiare, 320km long and about as wide as the Rhine, has an evil reputation for clouds of biting midges and mosquitoes. Humboldt and his party were distracted from insect torture only by their floating animal collection: a mischievous toucan, hyacinth macaw, parrots and several other birds, and eight monkeys. Today, travellers using outboard motors can luckily go faster than the insects.

flow from the towering tepui called **Cerro Autana**. However, the view of Autana is blocked much of the way by two mountains, and a set of large rapids halts advance by river.

San Fernando de Atabapo, next town up the Orinoco, is 12 hours by bongo from Venado or three by the Expreso del Sur launch. Here the black Atabapo River meets the brown Guaviare and lighter Orinoco. San Fernando, founded in 1759 by Capuchin missionaries, was formerly capital of Amazonas Territory. During the rubber boom it was an important centre. In 1913 Tomás Funes, the 'Terror of Río Negro', took over the town and rubber trade, killing the governor, his family and hundreds more during the next eight years. His house and the place he was executed are still pointed out. San Fernando may again see rubber exports when new CVG plantations mature. There is an airfield served by small planes from Ayacucho, 50 minutes. (See *Airtaxis*, page 298.)

TO AND FROM BRAZIL

From San Carlos de Río Negro there is weekly river service to Brazil, on a three-decker Brazilian riverboat which goes as far as San Gabriel da Cachoeira. From there passengers bound for Manaus must get another boat. The Venezuelan border post is called San Simón de Cocuy. Travellers aiming to return to Venezuela should have a multiple-entry tourist visa. If you are going to Manaus there is a consulate; or you can get a tourist card on an airline.

TO AND FROM COLOMBIA

Travellers entering or leaving Venezuela should have their passports stamped by Immigration. If this is not done, go to the DEX office on Av Aguerrevere, three blocks west of Av Orinoco.

By river, you can take the passenger ferry from Puerto Ayacucho's dock to Casuarito on the opposite bank. There you can catch a Colombian speedboat service; the *voladora* goes every afternoon to Puerto Carreño (1 hour).

By road, head north of Puerto Ayacucho to El Burro and cross the Orinoco on a ferry-barge to Puerto Páez. This small Venezuelan port lies at the junction of the Orinoco with the Meta. It has an army post and DEX office; get stamped out of Venezuela. On the Colombian side of the Meta is Puerto Carreño, a little town with the necessary DAS office to stamp you into the country; it also has a Venezuelan Consulate. Puerto Carreño is connected to Bogotá by a dry-weather road. There is air service (Satena) three times a week, however. Among various hotels is the Samanare with a genial owner, Jairo Zorro; restaurant and disco.

Venezuelan drivers go from Puerto Páez to San Fernando de Apure, crossing the Llanos on a newly finished road.

Aragua and Carabobo

Traffic courses through Aragua's valleys to the capitals of Aragua and Carabobo States: **Maracay**, 110km from Caracas, and **Valencia**, 159km. Between Maracay and the sea a large tract of mountain wilderness was declared the country's first national park, Rancho Grande, in 1937. It was enlarged to 1,078km² in 1974 and renamed **Henri Pittier** after the Swiss naturalist who worked to preserve it from axe and fire. Still threatened by flames every dry season, the park is an irreplaceable refuge for the animals and birds, trees, ferns and orchids of the Cordillera de la Costa cloudforest. There is less development on the Caribbean side where the crescent bays of Cata, Cuyagua and Choroní have beautiful beaches. Other bays such as Chuao and Cepe have no road and are reached by few outsiders.

ARAGUA STATE
Maracay

Green plantations of sugarcane border the *autopista* to Maracay, a pleasant enough city once you get through rings of factories. Maracay was founded in 1701 and prospered as the centre for cacao, tobacco and indigo plantations. Today a large

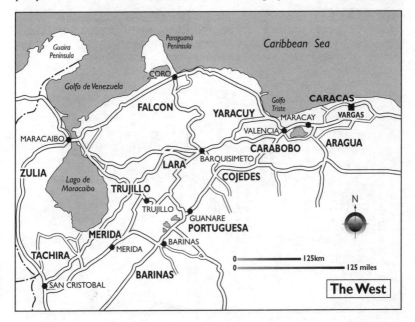

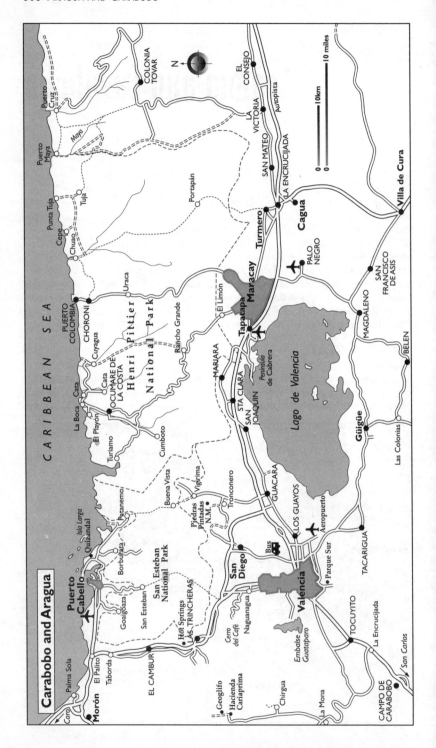

Carabobo and Aragua

CARIBBEAN SEA

COLONIA TOVAR

EL CONSEJO

Puerto Cruz

Maya

Puerto Maya

Portapán

LA VICTORIA

Autopista

SAN MATEO

LA ENCRUCIJADA

Villa de Cura

Punta Tuja

Cepe

Chuao

Tuja

Turmero

Cagua

PALO NEGRO

SAN FRANCISCO DE ASIS

Uraca

PUERTO COLOMBIA

CHORONI

Cuyagua

Henri Pittier National Park

Rancho Grande

El Limón

Maracay

Tapatapa

MAGDALENO

BELEN

Cata

La Boca

OCUMARE DE LA COSTA

MARIARA

STA CLARA

SAN JOAQUIN

Península de Cabrera

Lago de Valencia

Güigüe

El Playón

Turiamo

Cumboto

Las Colonias

Isla Larga

Quizandal

Patanemo

Buena Vista

Vigirima

Tronconero

GUACARA

LOS GUAYOS

Aeropuerto

TACARIGUA

Puerto Cabello

Borburata

Goaigoaza

San Esteban

San Esteban National Park

Piedras Pintadas N.M.

San Diego

Bus

Parque Sur

Valencia

Palma Sola

Corg

El Palito

Taborda

EL CAMBUR

Hot Springs

LAS TRINCHERAS

Cerro del Café

Naguanagua

Embalse Guataparo

TOCUYITO

La Encrucijada

San Carlos

Morón

Geoglifo

Hacienda Cariaprima

Chirgua

La Mona

CAMPO DE CARABOBO

N

10km

10 miles

0

0

part of the fertile valley has been taken over by industry. The capital has a population approaching 450,000 Maracayeros.

For visitors it is important as the take-off point for Choroní (northeast) and Rancho Grande-Cata (northwest).

Getting there and away
By air
Maracay's civil airport is in the Mariscal Sucre Air Force Base. The terminal has its own entrance 3.9km west of the Redoma Boca del Rio (Tapatapa *autopista* exit) on the old road from Maracay to Mariara. The waiting room has a view of Lake Valencia; there is a snack bar. There are two flights a day from Caracas by LAI, a line which also links Mérida–Maracay.

By bus
Maracay is a convenient crossroads for many long-distance lines. The big bus terminal is south of Av Constitución at Av Fuerzas Aéreas, a fair tramp from Plaza Bolívar. Buses go frequently to Caracas (1½ hours), Valencia (1 hour), Barquisimeto (4 hours); less often to Coro (5½ hours), San Fernando de Apure (6 hours), even Puerto Ayacucho (12 hours). Many longer journeys are at night. Buses leave hourly for Ocumare where you continue by *por puesto* to Cata. Service to Choroní–Puerto Colombia is every two hours, last bus at about 17.00.

The fast buses of Aeroexpresos Ejecutivos leave from Av Bolívar Este, opposite Ingeniería Militar, tel: 322977, 337924; service to Caracas at 06.30, 10.45, 15.00 and 18.30; Maturín, 21.00; Puerto La Cruz 22.00.

Where to stay
The area telephone code for Maracay is (043)
The larger hotels in Maracay have star-rated facilities, some with pools. Four are on or near Av Las Delicias, the route north to Choroní. Just to the west, six blocks from the Museo de Arte, is **Hotel Italo**, tel: 320522, fax: 320443; pool, sauna, restaurant, 98 rooms. The renovated **Hotel Maracay**, tel: 416211/423/623, fax: 410865, is set between the city golf course and Pittier National Park, a perfect location for golfers and birders. Its 1950s style and huge swimming pool and golf course add attraction to the 157 suites, doubles, about $63. Next on Las Delicias by the zoo is the **Byblos**, tel: 415344; a 12-storey tower with 87 comfortable rooms. The tower of 4-star **Pipo Internacional**, tel: 412022, fax:: 416298, is the farthest north; 119 rooms and suites, gym, sauna, pool.

The more moderate **Hotel Caroní**, Av Ayacucho near Santos Michelena, tel: 541817, is recommended as immaculate; doubles with air conditioning and hot water, $18; eight blocks west of Plaza Girardot. **Hotel Cristal**, tel: 540668/0246, on Av Bolívar (four blocks west of the Caroní), has large, clean rooms and low prices. The **Wladimir**, slightly higher in cost and reputation, is a block farther east on Av Bolívar, tel: 461115/2566; it has a good Italian restaurant. The newer **Princess Plaza**, tel: 332571, fax: 337929, is two blocks east of Plaza Bolívar; all air conditioned, 100 rooms; double $35.

Inexpensive older hotels with basic bed, bath and fan at about $9 double are near the Cathedral. The hotels **Central** and **María Isabel** are on Av Santos Michelena (19 de Abril). **Hotel Guayana** is a block east of the Cathedral on Av Bolívar.

What to see and do
Maracay bears the stamp of dictator **Juan Vicente Gómez** who turned the bucolic town into his private 'capital' from 1910 until he died in 1935. An

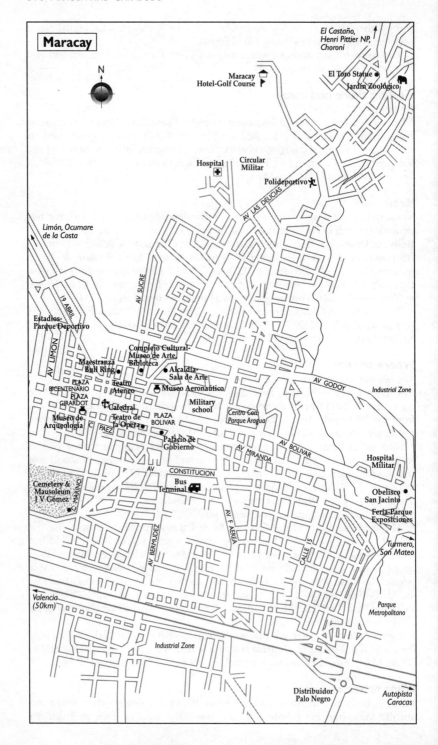

Maracay

N

El Castaño,
Henri Pittier NP,
Choroní

Maracay
Hotel-Golf Course

El Toro Statue
Jardín Zoológico

Limón, Ocumare
de la Costa

Hospital

Circular
Militar

Polideportivo

AV LAS DELICIAS

AV SUCRE

19 ABRIL

Estadios-
Parque Deportivo

AV LIMON

Complejo Cultural-
Museo de Arte/
Biblioteca

Maestranza
Bull Ring

PLAZA
BICENTENARIO
PLAZA
GIRARDOT

Teatro
Ateneo

Alcaldía-
Sala de Arte

Museo Aeronáutico

AV GODOY

Industrial Zone

Museo de
Arqueología

C/ PAEZ

Catedral

Teatro de
la Opera

Military
school

PLAZA
BOLIVAR

Centro Com
Parque Aragua

Palacio de
Gobierno

AV MIRANDA

AV BOLIVAR

Hospital
Militar

Cemetery &
Mausoleum
J V Gómez

C. MARINO

AV CONSTITUCION

Bus
Terminal

AV BERMUDEZ

AV F AEREA

CALLE 5

Obelisco
San Jacinto

Feria-Parque
Exposiciones

Turmero,
San Mateo

Valencia
(50km)

Parque
Metropolitano

Industrial Zone

Distribuidor
Palo Negro

Autopista
Caracas

illiterate, Gómez was so tyrannical that his motto of 'Paz y Trabajo' was experienced by many as 'Peace in the Cemetery and Work on the Roads'. Eldest of 13 children of an Andean farmer, he had a Bolívar fixation. He was born on Bolívar's birthday (he said) and died on the day of Bolívar's death, having already prepared his family **mausoleum**, a florid affair in the cemetery, eight blocks south of the cathedral.

Gómez erected many government buildings, the barracks opposite Plaza Bolívar, and an aviation school around the corner, now the **Aeronautical Museum**. His pride, the elegant Hotel Jardín with its Alhambra-like tiles, is today the **Palacio de Gobierno**, on the south side of Plaza Bolívar. At the southwest corner is the building he lavished most on, the fine **Teatro de la Opera**. But he died before it was opened and for 38 years it stood closed until in 1973 the city finally found the courage to finish it. Then there's the grand bull ring, **Plaza de Toros La Maestranza**, three blocks northeast of the Cathedral, designed in 1933 by Carlos Raúl Villanueva (who also had a hand in the opera house) after one in Seville.

Today the place most sought on a tour of Maracay is the Sanctuary of Venezuela's first (and only) saint, **Madre María de San José**, beatified in 1995. It stands on Calle López Aveledo, just up from Av Bolívar, and holds the sarcophagus with the saint's surprisingly intact remains. Madre María, who died in 1967 at the age of 92, devoted her life to the poor and sick, founding Maracay's first hospital. The sanctuary is closed on Mondays and at lunch hours.

Colonial Maracay grew up around **Plaza Girardot**, six blocks west of Plaza Bolívar. Here stands the white **Cathedral** or Church of San José, patron saint of the town. On and around March 19, Maracay holds its annual **Feria de San José** with parades, bull fights and an agricultural fair. The obelisk and bronze eagle in the plaza were dedicated in 1897 to the American volunteers who joined Francisco Miranda's anti-royalist expedition which landed in Ocumare in 1806. One ship was captured and the ten American officers were hanged. The statue to Atanasio Girardot who died in the battle of Bárbula, 1813, stands on the pedestrian boulevard. On Plaza Girardot's south side, two museums function in Gómez's arcaded old government house. Paintings, Bolivariana and some of the dictator's riding gear are in the **Museo de Historia**. The **Museo de Antropología** has rooms displaying local archaeological findings and pre-Columbian pots, and a basement salon housing a collection of crafts by ethnic groups including the Yanomami, Sanema, Yekuana, Panare, Guajiro and Warao.

An insurance company occupies a restored town house, the **Casa de Dolores Amelia**, north of the adjacent **Parque Bicentenario** (with underground parking). Gómez built this Andalusian mansion on Av Santos Michelena for his mistress (one of many). Although he never married, Gómez fathered many children and considered himself a family man. You can ask permission to see the tiled patio.

Walk east along the 'culture row', Michelena/Av 19 de Abril. On the next block is the restored **Teatro Ateneo**; across the street by the south end of La Maestranza bull ring is the **Café-Concert**. At this open-air *criollo* restaurant the Centro Cultural Higuaraya gives talks, poetry and music recitals on Friday and Saturday evenings. The **crafts shop**, offering fine Panare and Yekuana artifacts, is open Mon–Sat 08.00–19.00. The **Complejo Cultural** occupies an entire block ending at the foot of Av Las Delicias. Gathered here are the public library, Casa de Cultura, school of visual arts, youth orchestra and, on the east, the **Museo de Arte Maracay**. It's an active centre with classes, concerts, exhibitions and films.

Avenida 19 de Abril ends at the **Museo Aeronáutico** where two dozen planes are exhibited, mostly ex-air-force fighters. (Gómez founded Venezuela's air force.) There is a replica of Jimmie Angel's Flamingo and a wonderful 1910 French plane. Gómez was a passionate fan of films and aviation. No wonder – Lindbergh landed here in the Spirit of St Louis in 1928.

First and last, however, dictator Gómez was a cattleman who treated Venezuela as his personal ranch. There's a bronze bull, **El Toro de Las Delicias**, at the upper end of Av Las Delicias about 2km from the Aeronautical Museum. Opposite is the small **Jardín Zoológico** in an old Gómez estate. The zoo is open 09.00–17.00 except Mondays. Its animals, mostly caged, include a variety of native species such as the spectacled bear, capuchin monkey and capybara, plus a hippo, elephants, tigers, llamas. A large central lagoon has an island of nesting herons and egrets, and many iguanas, turtles, ducks, pelicans.

Choroní

From the guardpost at Parque Nacional Pittier, a mountain road spirals to cool heights then drops to the Caribbean, some 56km in all. It was built by convicts in the Gómez era as an escape to the sea where there is a fishing port, Puerto Colombia. Today it is an escape from urban chaos into enchanting forests where mists veil the ridge at 1,830m and crystal streams splash over fords on green slopes. At the bottom in the hot Choroní Valley you can see red-fruiting cacao trees under the shade of plantation giants.

Choroní conserves the nostalgic air of a colonial village isolated beyond the mountains. Beautifully painted cottages line a long street paralleling the rushing river. There are a couple of *abastos*, shops/grocers, selling supplies. On tree-filled Plaza Bolívar is the fine 300-year-old church of **Santa Clara**, Choroní's patron saint whose fiesta comes in August. Choroní became a parish in 1622.

Venezuela's first saint, Madre María de San José, was born in Choroní in 1875. As a girl she started a school for poor children here, and went on to work with the poor in Maracay until she died in 1967. She is famous for having founded Maracay's first hospital. Madre María was beatified in 1995.

Choroní's beach, **Playa Grande**, is on a lovely crescent bay a five-minute walk around the rough headland. There are snack bars and a changing room open Fri–Sun. Hammocks swing from coconut palms. But weekenders' rubbish attracts vultures, and the turquoise sea hides a dangerous undertow or *resaca* at the far end. Bathers use the west end.

Hydroelectricity for Maracay was harnessed in 1922 by a plant in Uraca at Km42 on the road. A bigger plant was installed about 4km before Choroní. It's still there, the old **Planta Cadafe**, and its turbines are now part of the Choroní Museum of Electricity; sometimes there are art exhibits, too. Open Fri–Sun 09.00–12.00; 15.00–18.00.

Puerto Colombia faces a pebbly bay, about 2km from Choroní. The village is small, although quite active since adopted by a young European crowd. Travellers are now greeted by restaurants, telephones and even a gasoline station. At night the *malecón*, seafront walk, vibrates to song (and a certain amount of drink). In the morning some fishermen haul in nets while others take visitors to solitary beaches such as Cepe or Bahía Bajo Seco for about $20 a boat, round trip.

Where to stay
The area telephone code for Choroni and Puerto Colombia is (043)
Travellers will find a range of exclusive inns, bed and breakfast pensions, and basic rooms, some in (or before) Choroní, most in Puerto Colombia.

Choroní

La Gran Posada is a small inn with a terrace restaurant, entrance opposite the Museo Cadafe (La Planta). In a lush mountain setting there are eight comfortable, spotless rooms with cold-water shower; $30 per person with breakfast and dinner. Call on weekdays tel: (043) 549307, fax: 545776.

A short way before Choroní, the road passes among enormous trees shading cacao plantations. At Km49, the lovely old Hacienda **La Aljorra** has converted nine spacious rooms with old-time furniture, hot water and private bath; $20 per person. Restaurant is open to the public. In Caracas tel: (02) 2377462/8878, fax: 2382436.

Posada Colonial Choroní, near Plaza Bolívar, encompasses two houses, the oldest dating to 1780. There's an internal patio and another behind giving on to a brook with a natural bathing pool. Five double rooms, some with private bath, others shared; $25 per person, with breakfast and dinner. Ask about car transfer from Caracas, and plan with excursions to Cepe, Chuao, and snorkelling in Valle Seco. English and German spoken. For reservations contact Cacao Expeditions (see page 14).

Posada Los Hernández, two blocks before Plaza Bolívar on the one-way street south, is a ten-room guesthouse in a low, vintage house. It was restored by SBA Nature Expeditions and serves as the base for treks to Chuao, birdwatching in the park, fishing or diving. By reservation, SBA tel/fax: (02) 2510990, (016) 6343611; email: sbanatureve@yahoo.com. English spoken.

At the **Hospedaje del Pueblo**, tel: 351756, Calle Miranda near Plaza Bolívar, you will find nine triples with bath, double and single bed, for $12 in high season.

Leaving Choroní on the way to Puerto Colombia, Calle El Cementerio enters from the west; here, in the old Hacienda El Portete, are two of the best guesthouses. The first is **La Casa de Los García**, tel: 911056, fax: 911273, a wonderfully restored late 17th-century country house with tall ceilings, walls 2ft thick and tiled roof; eight rooms have been fitted with ensuite bath and hot water; $50 for two with breakfast. The other house is the **Casa El Portete**, tel: 911255. More modern, it has been rebuilt with eight rooms and private baths; $34 per person with breakfast. Two swimming pools. By reservation, tel: 459271, 450734.

Puerto Colombia

Puerto Colombia has lots of choice. The pioneer **Hotel and Restaurant Alemania**, tel: 911036, is on the right hand at the village entrance; the river runs behind. It has a good outdoor restaurant, and ten rooms with fan, simply furnished, about $30 a double with breakfast. The Alemania has its own well water. The former German owners now operate the plain, clean **Posada Alfonso** opposite; $16 double. Down the same street, at the police checkpoint or *alcabala* is the upscale **Posada Humboldt**, tel: 911050. It's a very pretty colonial-style house around a courtyard with a fountain, trees and flowers; double $145 a day with all meals. Top class food. It has no sign and wants no casual guests; Caracas reservations, tel: (02) 9762222.

Posada La Parchita on Calle Trino Rangel, a side street by the *alcabala*, tel: 911259, has just four bed-and-breakfast rooms with bath and hot water. From Monday to Thursday the price is $10, without breakfast; reservations required for weekends when the price goes up.

Hotel Club Cotoperix did much to launch Choroní's fame. The hotel began as a charmingly remodelled old house of six rooms and hammocks. Its combination of *posada* in delightful colonial style, excellent local fish, fruit, coffee and chocolate, and beach excursions, has been so successful that the

Cotoperix now has three more guesthouses. All are by reservation only. The reception desk is in Cotoperix II on the main street, Av. Morillo. Cotoperix III is in a new 14-room house on the beach. Some of the 38 double rooms have four-poster beds, some shared bathroom with cold water; no TV or air conditioning by policy. The package includes lodging, picnics, boat to solitary beaches, excursion in the national park, and often local music at night. In view of its special services and setting, Cotoperix is good value at some $65 a person. Round trip from Caracas by car costs about $70. For information, tel: (02) 9528617/2628, fax: 9516226.

Hostal Colonial, Calle Morillo, tel: 911087, is unpretentious. Its dozen rooms are different sizes and some have ensuite shower with cold water; another has four beds, hot water and air conditioning. Prices from $15 double to $40 quadruple. For information in Caracas, call the owner at night, tel: (02) 9632155.

Posada La Montañita, Calle Morillo No 6, tel: 911132, is two doors from the sea. A second floor has been added to the pleasant old part for a total 20 rooms, with fan and cold water; double, $25 per person with breakfast and supper. Excursions are arranged by the friendly Rodríguez family. In the same range is the pretty new **Posada Cataquero**, tel: 911264, Calle Morillo No 2, built from scratch with eight doubles, hot water, patio, generous kitchen, and restaurant.

The **Posada del Puerto**, Calle Los Cocos, tel: 911239, has fully equipped apartments with kitchens, air conditioning, and a restaurant. This is a good bet for four or more people, $45.

On the cheap side is the **Hotel Bahía**, tel: 915410, above the crowded Tasca Bahía restaurant, Av. Los Cocos by the river crossing to Playa Grande, double $11. **Hotel Maitín** on a side street nearby offers basic rooms around a dark roofed patio; lacks a through breeze. **Habitaciones La Abuela** near the bus stop lack cleanliness. Lastly, **Posada Los Guanches**, near Posada La Parchita, has a quiet location near the river and nine spartan doubles with cold shower but no shower curtain.

Chuao

Chuao chocolate was long equated in Europe with the world's finest. Today some cacao plantations are being renewed (with Japanese investment). There is a trail from Choroní over the range to the east and down to the old plantation village and bay of Chuao. This is an easy hike in view of the possibility of returning via fishing boat to Puerto Colombia. In colonial times a muleteers' road linked Chuao with Turmero in the Aragua valley and it is still possible to follow this but the climb is long and hot.

Chuao's big festival is **Corpus Christi** which is the ninth Thursday after Holy Thursday, a date often falling in early June. Festivities begin on Wednesday morning, announced by drums and church bells. Many village men belong to a religious society of **'devil dancers'**, some of whom have danced since boyhood. Greatest prestige goes to La Sayona, the devils' mother figure (a man). In brightly patterned costumes and masks with staring eyes and grinning mouth, the dancers form a cross, offering themselves to God as humble servants. They advance to the church, but entry is repeatedly denied; the culmination comes with a mass in which their sins are forgiven. A small **museum** behind the church uses old plantation offices to exhibit colonial and prehistoric relics and the lurid devil masks.

The village started life in 1568 as a Spanish '*encomienda*', and became important as a cacao producer a century later. Those were slave days and today's population of 2,000 are largely descendants of Africans. Since the decline of the haciendas, Chuao has grown poorer in its isolation.

Fishermen can take you from the bay (5km from Chuao) to the next roadless beach east: **Cepe**. The news from Cepe is the opening of a guesthouse, **Posada Puerto Escondido**, four rooms with hot showers and more being built. Including boat transfer from Choroní, the package costs about $40 per person, double occupancy. For information, ring scuba divers César and Freddy Fischer, tel: (043) 414645/3614. They rent diving gear.

Hiking
Paul Rouche

Choroní to Puerto de Chuao

From Choroní there are hourly buses passing the store or *bodega* called El Mamón on the main road out of town. If you wish, ask here for someone to guide you on the first leg (about 45 minutes) up past the community of La Cesiva; beyond, there is no mistaking the single path. It's two minutes from the road, walking east through the cacao plantation, to reach a small iron bridge, the puente de metal, across the Río Choroní. The trail to La Cesiva first follows the river to an irrigation canal (right, ten minutes), passing three small stone bridges. The way is soft and shady, leading to *campesino* houses, with **Quebrada La Rinconada** on the left. After dipping, the trail crosses the Rinconada stream, now coming from the right. At a crossroads keep left and shortly there's a steep sandy ascent to the caserío of **La Cesiva**. Ask for the way to 'Sinamaica' in a northeasterly direction. From an elevation of 200m the trail rises in earnest to a fork at 680m (about 45 minutes from La Cesiva). Keep right; the way leads through a coffee plantation, then a banana plantation (this is called a *cambural*) to a point where you can see the Choroní road down to the left. Continue southeast to the ridge at 1,000m elevation (about 1¼ hours from La Cesiva).

In another ten minutes the descent begins and you will be able to see the Chuao–Cepe 'road' on the opposite ridge to the east. This side of the mountain is drier; you pass a cultivated plot or *conuco* and come to a house at the place called **Sinamaica**, 860m. Keep right at a fork below (altitude 760m); it's a steady downhill trail for an hour along a scrubby, sunny slope. Then the trail enters woods, crossing a stream bed several times, finally following it and descending to a large boulder (left, possible shelter); 15 minutes. The path may be less clear; it parallels the stream bed, crossing and recrossing it and, bearing left, finally crosses the Quebrada Sinamaica, here 5m wide (20 minutes). In the next six minutes you cross an irrigation canal three times and reach the clear **Chuao River**, 10m wide. Pick your way across among the stones, and cool your feet. The path will emerge on the entrance road to Chuao, by a small crucifix on the left.

The road to Chuao (25 minutes) is wide, and at times shaded by bamboos; it crosses the river again before reaching the pueblo of Chuao. Like Choroní, Chuao also has its long main street, *abastos*, plaza and 17th-century church painted blue and white. The church patio is often used for drying cacao beans. Chuao has been identified for centuries with the best cacao beans in the world and Venezuela's oldest plantation is here, although sadly run down.

The *pueblo* is 5km from the sea and there is still a 45-minute march to reach the **Puerto de Chuao**. However, the way is cooled by an immense cacao plantation and once you reach the bay, you can buy cold soft drinks and beer. Fishing boats pull into the river mouth. The trip by *peñero* to Choroní takes only 20 minutes, but you should make arrangements early because fishermen do not like to leave after 15.00.

From Chuao to Turmero

This is a 2-day hike with good camping in cool upper forests once you have tramped up a long, hot hill. The old trail was formerly a Spanish road linking the cacao plantations with the Aragua Valley. I consider this the most beautiful hike in Aragua State for its magnificent trees, shade and creeks.

Leaving Chuao, you pass the roadside crucifix where the trail joins from Choroní. Shortly after, the red earth road crosses the **Tamaira River** and starts to rise. From here it is a hard, shadeless walk (1–1¼ hours) up to **El Paraíso**, a hamlet on denuded slopes at an elevation of 700m. However, the road is unmistakable and wide; the noise of waterfalls down in the Quebrada Maestra (right) follows you for some distance.

Once in the sprawling hamlet of El Paraíso, ask for the camino ahead (southwest) to **Hacienda La Azucena** where some of the men work at planting and harvesting coffee and bananas. It is a relief when the path enters the old plantation; the gradient is gentler, and there is shade and water; the pipe runs to your left. In about 45 minutes walking under a beautiful canopy you come to the *quebrada* or ravine. Cross this twice; ten minutes later at a fork, take the left hand, going up.

From this point, depending on energy and rest stops, it is 1–1½ hours to the Río del Medio at 1,100m altitude. The early part is called 'La Esplanada' because it is wide and straight. This leads to forest at 1,030m and continues up and down gently, on a rocky path, reaching **La Cueva** which is a large overhanging boulder affording possible shelter. Now sunk between steep banks, the path shows its centuries of use as an eroded mule trail. Its general direction is southwest. Where the **Río del Medio** (6m wide) is joined by another creek on the left there is a possible campsite.

Sometimes overgrown by ferns, the trail continues up for two hours to a spring or *manantial* at 1,800m. There are seven fern patches which you must find your way through to the trail in the woods opposite. After passing the seventh, the path again becomes an open 'tunnel', rising to the **Quebrada Hierba Buena**, coming from the right. The small gully has a permanent spring which is the *manantial*. Apparent splits in the trail are not different paths; they join at the top.

Up to the ridge and over to the working hacienda called **Portapán** will take perhaps another 1½ hours. After leaving the spring, within 20–25 minutes the trail reaches 1,930m on the crest. It starts level, then descends. At 1,850m there is an iron cross on the left, not very tall (usually overgrown), at a spot called **El Guayabo**. The trail slants down to 1,520m at Hacienda Portapán where there is a resident caretaker, chickens and dogs.

A jeep track goes from Portapán all the way down to **Turmero**'s outskirts, a walk of almost two hours. About halfway at 1,460m elevation, a wide path enters from the left; this is the way to a ranger post, PGP **Simón Machado**. Shortly below is the crossroads for **La Mucurita** (left, an alternate route to the bottom). There are one or two gates and fences to cross, and good views of Taguaiguay Lagoon and distant Lake Valencia.

Before reaching the paving, the earth track passes an iron gate at the bottom, then a stone quarry, the **Cantera**, at an altitude of 530m. From this district, called **El Pedregal** after the stream coming from the mountain, it is 3km to **La Bodega del Chorrito** where the Turmero buses stop. Turmero has a bus service to Maracay and Cagua.

This trek is led by Akanan Travel once a month from May to December. They drive to Turmero and spend two days on the trail, arriving in Chuao on the third day in time for a swim and boat ride to Choroní. The tour is based on six hikers but goes ahead if only two show; cost with Caracas transfers is $250 (for Akanan's address, see *Chapter 2, Tour operators,* page 14).

Parque Pittier: Rancho Grande

Apart from the Choroní road, a lower and somewhat wider highway crosses in the west from **El Limón** on the outskirts of Maracay to Ocumare and Cata on the sea. In some 15km the road passes the **Rancho Grande Biological Station**. Swiss naturalist Henri Pittier (1857–1950) loved most this area of high, cool cloudforests. (You may find it wet, too: average humidity is 92%.) Pittier came to Venezuela at age 62 and, before he died at 92, had compiled a manual of 30,000 common plants, established a national botanical service and herbarium, co-founded the Venezuelan Society of Natural Sciences, and successfully urged the creation of Venezuela's first national park in 1937.

The park's ecosystems vary with altitude, starting at sea level with mangrove swamps, valleys where huge trees shade cacao plantations, and cactus and thorn thickets on dry coastal slopes, rising through deciduous forests, and climaxing in the cloudforests at 800–1,000m. Howler monkeys, ocelots, tapirs, deer and jaguars are among the larger park denizens. Over half the 136 mammal species are bats which do valuable work fertilising forest flowers and spreading seeds. Then there are 74 kinds of reptiles, 38 amphibians, and 578 bird species (over 40% of Venezuela's 1,346 species). Mary Lou Goodwin, author of *Birding in Venezuela*, has travelled widely studying the country's rich bird life. Here's some of what she says about the nation's first park.

> 'Rancho Grande at dawn is, without doubt, one of the rarest, most
> exquisite experiences a birder can have anywhere in the world. Veiled
> in mist, the rainforest emerges from the darkness and the silence at
> night's end into joyful bird songs and crystal clear light... You may
> expect to see some of the endemics, such as the handsome fruiteater; it
> is also possible to see harpy eagle (check the sky, especially around
> 10.00 to noon). Around the main grounds you should see blood-eared
> parakeets as well as white-tipped swift which nest under the
> balconies... In the mating season, February/April, it is easier to see the
> white-tipped quetzal from the terrace of the Station.'

Rancho Grande Biological Station

Rancho Grande (altitude 1,100m) is midway on the Maracay–Ocumare road. The field station is actually atop a derelict hotel built in the 1930s by the dictator Gómez but abandoned, unfinished, when he died. It's a peculiar, unforgettable place. Some people say that executions took place here and that ghosts linger. The Biological Station has been an important educational centre for the study of tropical mountain ecosystems, their dynamics and evolution, since it was created in 1966 by the Universidad Central de Venezuela's School of Agronomy. At any one time there may be as many as two dozen research projects under way by local and international scientists on everything from fauna and geology to waste management. Such studies have produced some 300 books and papers.

The station offers researchers and visitors the basics of kitchen facilities and four dormitories with bunk beds, shared bathrooms and cold showers, at a cost of $10 a night, payable on arrival. For permission to stay, contact the station chief: Jesús Manzanilla, Estación Biológica Alberto Fernández Yépez, tel: (014) 9477330, fax: (043) 453242. His address is: Instituto de Zoología Agrícola, Facultad de Agronomía, Universidad Central de Venezuela, Apartado 4579, Maracay, Estado Aragua.

For camping, you will need a good rainproof tent, sleeping bag (it gets cold at night), warm clothes, candles and food.

Trails

There is a parks fee of Bs1,000 which you pay at the entrance to Rancho Grande. Behind the station, steps lead to the Andrew Field Interpretation Trail named for an English botany student who died from a fall here while studying the huge *niño* trees. A brass plaque is dedicated to Field (1954–84) 'whose imagination, love and perseverance resulted in the creation of this trail'.

Some 150m past this plaque a trail leads left. This is the **Guacamaya trail** going up to Pico Guacamaya, 1,828m. Since you start walking at an elevation of 1,100m, the hike up is not hard. The path, at times faint, continues down a ridge north to the coast, and comes out at the village of Cuyagua.

Up the road from the station you will see on the left a fence and gate (sometimes locked). This is the trail for **Portachuelo pass**. At some 700m below Guacamaya Peak, it is a main flyway for insects and birds, including migrants from North America which begin to arrive in October, and leave again in April. At these times the Audubon ornithologists band as many as 100 birds a day.

In El Limón there are shops and places to eat. You can catch breakfast at one of the bakeries near the last traffic light before the divided highway becomes a road. Or get lunch at **Restaurant La Ternera** which specialises in grilled meat sold by the kilo: *punta trasero*, rump steak, or *lomito*, filet mignon.

Tierra Viva

Year after year the park's forests are eroded by fires and its habitats lost to farm clearing. Until now, the people living around the park have known less about it than a birdwatcher from New York. Today, this is changing. Visitors are given a colour map of the park, the first ever, detailing its life zones, animals, birds and petroglyphs. Along with it you get a trail map of the Andrew Field nature trail.

The map is an initiative of the **Tierra Viva Foundation**, an NGO that is stirring up environmental awareness. Working with people in schools, communities, companies, and government in 13 townships in Aragua and Carabobo states, Tierra Viva is helping inhabitants to raise the quality of life in the basin of Lake Valencia (heavily contaminated). The people have formed hundreds of projects, making and recuperating green zones, opening schools, recycling waste, and in the process drawing in universities, ministries and industries including a paper manufacturer, food processor, bottle maker, and margarine processor. In the park, cacao growers have a poor standard of living and a project in Cumboto, Ocumare and Cata now encourages them to improve their conditions, health and education. Tierra Viva has been asked to start a similar programme in the Orinoco Delta. For more about these 'alliances for reducing poverty', or how you can help, contact (in English) Anita Reyna, Fundación Tierra Viva, tel/fax: (02) 9512601, (045) 51406; email: tierraviva@compuserve.com. Or in England, Edgardo García, Living Earth, tel: (0171) 2423816, fax: 2423817; email: livearth@gn.apc.org.

Ocumare, Cata and Cuyagua

From the Rancho Grande pass it is 23km to the next fork; the left hand leads to Cumboto and Turiamo by another Gómez-built road. Cacao plantations along the Cumboto River are shaded by huge rubber trees; you can see incisions in the bark for collecting sap. Traffic to Turiamo is restricted as it is a naval base.

Go right for **Ocumare de la Costa**, 13km, a town dating to a Spanish settlement in 1660. It is another 3.5km to the sea at **El Playón**, a popular beach, and a village called **Independencia** in memory of Francisco Miranda's attempted landing in 1806. There are various food stores, a bakery, and restaurants.

Fringed by coconut palms, **Cata** lies 5.6km east on an almost perfect crescent bay. Almost perfect because an apartment tower looms on the beach. The west end has changing rooms, open-air restaurants, parasols, lifeguards and a paid parking lot. Tenters pay a small fee, but hanging your hammock is free. Fishing boats ferry bathers to the smaller beach of **Catita**. There are attractive two-storey bungalows with kitchens for rent, the **Balneario Turístico de Cata**; tel: (043) 458897. The Carmil's old cabins, by now decrepit, are at least cheap.

The village of Cata is inland, 4.7km. This is a very quiet place until the drums sound on fiestas such as San Juan, June 24, and Corpus Christi, ninth Thursday after Holy Thursday, when the devil dancers perform in front of the old **Iglesia de San Francisco**. Then people come from the hills around and cities far away to join in street processions.

Cuyagua is on the next tropical bay at the end of this panoramic road. Like Cata, it has a crescent beach with coconut plantation, and food stalls at weekends. The waves are big enough for surfing. But fewer people go as far as Cuyagua and the beach is wonderfully empty on weekdays (best to bring your picnic). That the beach is clean is a tribute to conservation-minded villagers who have a community action group.

Where to stay

This coast, already popular at weekends, is very crowded at holiday times, but you should have no trouble finding lodging during the week. In Ocumare there is the recommended **Restaurant and Posada María Luisa**, an 1884 house furnished with antiques, and enlarged to 19 rooms with ensuite bath and hot water; the cost including breakfast and dinner is $20 during the week, $25 at weekends and holidays. It has a swimming pool, too. The owners will arrange hikes, birding in the park, trips to La Ciénaga beach (no road), Cuyagua, even Puerto Cabello. For reservations, tel: (043) 931184, 931073.

El Playón has two inexpensive little hotels on the boulevard, the **Montemar** and the **Playa Azul**, and the better-class **Hotel Capulino** at the town's entrance. Among various guesthouses and rooms with bath for $10–12, you will find German travellers at the **Posada de La Abuela**, tel: 931187, Calle Urdaneta No 16; meals available. Another OK place is **Residencias La Coromotana**, tel: 931987, Calle Soublette; ten rooms. The **Posada Sueño Mío**, tel: 931551, on the plaza, has seven rooms without bath.

The village of Cuyagua now has two guesthouses. The **Restaurant and Posada Cuyagua Mar** has 26 rooms with bath; rates including breakfast and dinner are $24 per person, going up to $30 in high season. For information, tel: (02) 8611465, (016) 6204491. Near the plaza **La Posada de Doña Meche** offers nine simple rooms with fan and shared bath at $7 for a double bed, upstairs, as well as kitchen privileges downstairs where the family live.

CARABOBO STATE

Bypassing Lake Valencia which has pollution problems, Carabobo offers travellers a busy capital city, excellent mountain park, petroglyphs, the seaport of Puerto Cabello and beaches. The lake, which nearly halved in size during the past two centuries (it is 34km long), is now growing disturbingly as water is piped in for industries. The Valencia basin has fossils of animals such as the giant sloth, mastodon, primitive horse and the giant crocodile, megasaurus. Excavations have also revealed to archaeologists that the lake shores were thickly settled by Indian tribes.

The name Carabobo comes from an Indian word meaning 'palm from regions where water abounds'. Not really a palm, this plant (*Carludovica palmata*) has leaves

CARABOBO BATTLE BROKE ROYAL POWER

After a decade of wars for Independence, the battle which put Venezuela's reins firmly in patriot hands began on the morning of June 24 1821 on the plains of Carabobo. The adversaries were led by a Caracas patrician, Simón Bolívar (aged 36), and a Spanish nobleman, Miguel de la Torre. The two knew each other and had married Spanish girls who were cousins (Bolívar's wife died eight months after their marriage).

Holding the plains were the Royalists' 5,180 men, half of them Venezuelans. Bolívar summoned his forces: Urdaneta from Coro, Páez (who was then about 25) from the Llanos and Cruz Carrillo from the Andes, in all 6,400 men. Fighting under Páez was the British legion composed of veterans of Napoleonic wars. The Rifles Battalion, led by Arthur Sandes, was in the third division.

When Colonel Ferriar and his second, James Scott, were wounded, Captain Charles Minchin took command. The legion's resistance is credited with giving Páez's lancers the opening needed to attack the enemy's rear. At the battle's end Spanish power was broken. Triumph was not complete, however, until the battle of Lake Maracaibo on July 24 1823, and the battle of Puerto Cabello, November 10 1823.

Bolívar went on to the distant Andes with Sucre, another young (29-year-old) Venezuelan, routing the Spaniards at the battles of Junín and Ayacucho in Peru, 1824. Upper Peru formed its own state, naming it Bolivia in honour of the Liberator, and voted Sucre its president.

The **Campo de Carabobo** is 32km southwest of Valencia on the route to San Carlos. There is a large monument and Triumphal Arch, a diorama, and several restaurants and souvenir stands nearby.

resembling a fan palm, but no trunk. Natives of various countries use its fibre for weaving. It is known as *jipijapa* in Ecuador where it is made into the famous panama hats (not, in fact, made in Panama). According to historian Torcuato Manzo Núñez, the word later came to mean the place where it grew, and by extension the place where patriot armies routed Spanish forces. The State of Carabobo was, in turn, named after the Battle of Carabobo, June 24 1821, that secured Venezuela's Independence.

Valencia

Greater Valencia, a spreading city of some 1.3 million inhabitants, is the country's largest light industry centre making everything from animal feed to automobiles. It is also important historically, and was on three occasions Venezuela's capital.

The valley, 479m above sea-level and near the lake, has a climate described as pleasant with cool evening breezes from the surrounding hills. It is hard to pin down the founding date, 1553 or 1555, as all town records were burned during a 1667 attack by French pirates. By 1555 Captain Alonso Díaz Moreno had chosen the valley as a good place to live as well as a staging point for further conquest. A successful rancher, he was able to provision Diego de Losada on his expedition to found Caracas 11 years later. His family portrait (see the *Casa de los Celis*, page 334) shows seven daughters and one son. The fifth daughter married Simón de Bolívar and became one of the Liberator's early Venezuelan-born ancestors.

Valencia hung on through assaults by the tyrant Aguirre, by Carib Indians, earthquakes and, perhaps worst of all, during the wars of Independence. There were not many of Valencia's 'finest' left after 35 battles fought in the area. The year after Venezuela's Declaration of Independence on July 5 1811, Valencia served as government seat for the short-lived First Republic. In 1830 Valencia became the capital a second time when a congress met in the Casa de la Estrella to dissolve the Gran Colombian union so cherished by Bolívar (who died a few months later). Then in 1858–59 the city again became capital after the fall of president José Tadeo Monagas.

Getting there and away

By air The international airport is in the industrial area, 7km southeast of Valencia. Aserca flies to Caracas (25 minutes) three times daily, $40. There are daily flights by Aserca and Aeropostal to Barcelona, Porlamar, Maturín and Puerto Ordaz in the east, and Barquisimeto, Maracaibo, Paraguaná, and San Antonio in the west. ALM flies to Curaçao, Bonaire, Aruba, St Maarten and Jamaica; Servivensa links Valencia daily with Aruba, Bogotá and Miami.

By bus Valencia is 2¼ hours from Caracas by the *autopista*, making it a good springboard for western and central states. The large and very busy **bus terminal** lies 4km east of downtown Valencia in the Centro Big Low. This fanciful development of phoney turrets and towers has an amusement park and a huge shopping centre. Behind the shops is the Terminal de Pasajeros. Coaches leave throughout the day for Caracas and all points south and west, Barquisimeto (3 hours), Mérida (9 hours), San Antonio del Táchira (11½ hours); Tucacas is a 2-hour ride and Coro 5–6 hours.

An 'Executive' bus service to Caracas is gaining popularity. You pay more but get there faster. The air-conditioned buses have curtains sewn shut for screening videos which usually take a little longer than the ride so you don't get to see the end. Neither can you see the countryside or open a window. Aeroexpresos Ejecutivos, tel: (041) 715767/5558, will reserve you a seat on nine daily departures to Caracas; a bus at 20.00 goes to Maracay and Maturín; one at 21.00 goes on to Puerto La Cruz and the Margarita ferry terminal.

Where to stay

The area telephone code for Valencia is (041)
Hotels in this commercial city, whether expensive or modest, are less busy on weekends. All are air conditioned unless noted. Accommodation is topped by the deluxe **Inter-Continental Valencia** in La Viña district, tel: 247519, fax: 254721; golf privileges at the Guataparo Country Club, pool, six floors with 173 rooms; $250 double. The 4-star **Stauffer**, tel: 236663, fax: 234903, on Av Bolívar Norte; double $85; and **Suites Ucaima**, tel: 242281, 246355, by the CC La Viña, also have pools and are situated in northern Valencia about 4km from downtown.

Acceptable hotels on Av Bolívar, charging $25 a double, include: nearest the centre, **Hotel Palace** (former Hotel 400), tel: 218922; midtown, the **Excelsior**, tel: 214055, and **Le Paris**, tel: 216751. In the same range, **Hotel Carabobo**, tel: 588860/4467, has 42 rooms on Plaza Bolívar. Also downtown is the modern Don Pelayo, Av 101 near Calle 103, tel: 579372/78, fax: 579384; 144 suites and rooms, double about $35.

Inexpensive but still decent is **Hotel Colón**, Calle 100 a block west of Plaza Sucre, tel: 577105; double $14. Cheaper hostels are found east of the cathedral; many cater to guests by the hour.

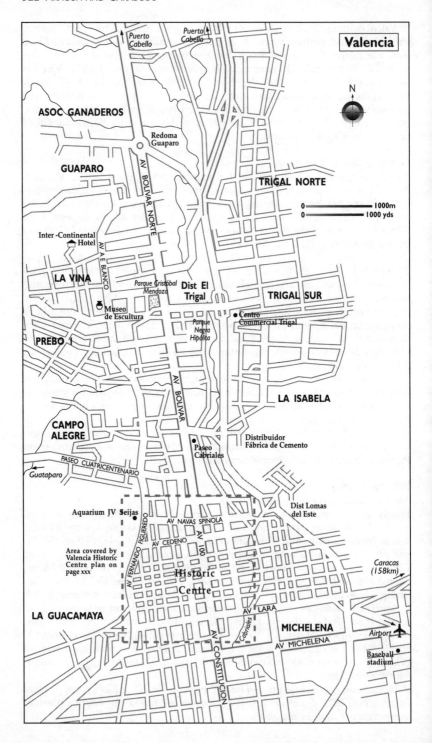

Valencia

ASOC GANADEROS

Redoma Guaparo

GUAPARO

TRIGAL NORTE

0 ————— 1000m
0 ————— 1000 yds

Inter-Continental Hotel

LA VINA

Parque Cristóbal Mendoza

Dist El Trigal

TRIGAL SUR

Museo de Escultura

Parque Negra Hipólita

Centro Commercial Trigal

PREBO

LA ISABELA

CAMPO ALEGRE

AV BOLIVAR NORTE

AV A E BLANCO

AV BOLIVAR

Distribuidor Fábrica de Cemento

Paseo Cabriales

PASEO CUATRICENTENARIO

Guataparo

Aquarium JV Seijas

Dist Lomas del Este

Area covered by Valencia Historic Centre plan on page xxx

AV NAVAS SPINOLA

AV CEDENO

AV 100

AV FERNANDO FIGUEREDO

Historic Centre

Caracas (158km)

LA GUACAMAYA

AV LARA

Cabriales

MICHELENA

Airport

AV CONSTITUCION

AV MICHELENA

Baseball stadium

N

Guataparo Royal Guest House It comes as a surprise that a 70km² ranch occupies a valley hidden among hills only 15 minutes west of Valencia. Its river feeds Guataparo Reservoir. Haciendas Guataparo operate a small guesthouse as well as raising Brahman cattle. Guests, nine in all, do indeed feel like royalty, served breakfast under the dappled shade of a former coffee patio, riding through avenues of huge trees where macaws alight. In the early 20th century the valley and coffee farm were acquired by an English company which over the years has respected the wooded headwaters and fauna. Many species of birds are close at hand. There is a pool fed by a mountain brook, and paths for riding, cycling and hiking. The charming ex-coffee-farmhouse has kitchen, dining room, four bedrooms and two shared bathrooms. The cost is $100 per person with three meals and excursions. For information about horse-riding day plans (expensive), tel: 9400679, 235271, fax: 239197. In Britain, reservations through Last Frontiers (see *Chapter 2,* page 19).

What to see and do
Historic Valencia
If you approach the historic centre from the east, you come to a leafy park by the Cabriales River, the **Parque Metropolitano**. (This park also continues north along the Cabriales to the playgrounds of Parque Negra Hipólita, by El Viñedo traffic exchange.) This used to be the terminus of the German-built **Gran Ferrocarril de Venezuela** which ran to Puerto Cabello (1888), and to Caracas from 1894 to 1960. The remodelled station houses the Inparques office. Valencianos fondly call the park 'Los Enanitos' for a large German clock in which Snow White's seven dwarfs once marked the hours. In 1986 the city at last finished the modern steel-beamed **Museo de la Cultura**, tel: 578417; open Tue–Fri 09.00–16.00, and Sat 09.00–13.00. It has a library, stage and film theatre and three galleries. There is a footbridge across the river.

If you go south to the triple-arched **Puente Morillo**, built by patriot prisoners 185 years ago, you will be on the **Camino Real**, the old entrance to the city, today Calle Colombia. It leads to Plaza Bolívar. The plaza's bronze Liberator atop a 15m marble monolith points towards the Carabobo battlefield. Streets in the small historic core have both numbers and names. Calle Libertad (Calle 101) goes along the north side of Plaza Bolívar, Colombia (Calle 100) on the south. Avenida Constitución (Av 100) runs past the west side of Plaza Bolívar; it becomes Av Bolívar when it crosses Av Cedeño. Avenidas run north–south and calles go east–west.

The **Cathedral** has parts that are 400 years old and parts such as the tower that are of later construction. The dome was added in 1955. You may want to see the 16th-century carved **Virgen del Socorro**, and three large paintings by Antonio Herrera Toro, a Valencia painter.

The restored **Casa Páez**, built by José Antonio Páez, is two blocks southeast of the Cathedral. The Bolivarian Society and community groups such as the Valencia hiking club meet here. General Páez was elected the first president of the Republic of Venezuela in 1831. He was elected again in 1839 and later refused a third term. On the patio walls he had painted murals of battles in which his armies of fierce plainsmen helped to defeat Spain. His favourite maxims ('Without virtue, there is no country') are painted on the outside walls. You can tell his rough *llanos* background from a rustic leather chair. Admired wherever he went for his zest, sense and self-taught culture, Páez spent 20 years in exile in Argentina, France, Germany and the United States. He died in 1873 in New York where his funeral cortège was accompanied by Generals Sherman and Sheridan to the docks, his remains borne to Venezuela by a US warship. The museum is open Tue–Fri 09.00–12.00, 15.00–17.30, weekends 09.00–14.00.

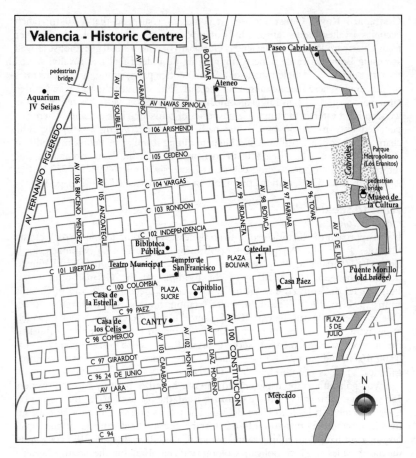

The large state **Capitol**, west four blocks on Calle Páez, was built as a Catholic hospital and later convent in 1772. It was destroyed by fire in 1795 and rebuilt as a girls' school run by Carmelites. Nuns once used cells lining the corridors, a chapel functioned in the state governor's office and the sessions chamber was a patio garden. Here you can ask to see the famous painting by Arturo Michelena of Bolívar on his white horse, Paloma. In 1874 all religious orders were outlawed by President Guzmán Blanco and their properties confiscated. The front pillars were added in 1877 when the state moved in.

Plaza Sucre occupies the next corner at Calle 100-Colombia. Opposite stands the **Templo de San Francisco** whose origins date to 1634, and next to it in a former monastery (1786), the University of Carabobo's law school. The main university is now in Bárbula. A theatre school functions on the west side of Plaza Sucre in a splendid 18th-century residence known as the **Casa Peñalver**. Across the street is the restored and modernised **Teatro Municipal**, a smaller version of the Paris Opera House. Begun in 1887, it was designed by French architect Antonio Malaussena whose son made the theatres in Maracay and Puerto Cabello. Note the splendid ceiling murals inside the large dome, painted by Antonio Herrera Toro who included his self-portrait among heroes of music and drama. For programme information, tel: 574306.

A new public library and art centre, the **Biblioteca Pública Manuel Feo La Cruz**, is on Calle Libertad, tel: 575835. Its striking three-storey columns are north of the theatre. There is a salon of Carabobo State reference works, and others devoted to crafts by local talents.

The **Casa de la Estrella**, Calle Colombia at Av 104, has been declared a national monument for its historic importance. The Congress of 1812 convened in this ex-charity hospital, writing the constitution of the First Republic and naming Valencia its capital. In 1830 another congress decreed Venezuela's sovereignty, withdrawing from Gran Colombia which included what is now Ecuador, Colombia and Panama. The state historical society functions here.

The **Casa de los Celis**, two blocks down Av 104, is one of the most beautiful colonial structures in Venezuela, declared a national monument. Now home of the **Museum of Art and History**, it was built in 1765 by the Spanish mayor who abandoned it 40 years later to the patriots. Col Pedro Celis bought it in 1837 and sold half, it was so big. Spacious, high-ceilinged rooms give on to a pair of courtyard gardens. Rooms display archaeological finds from the Valencia basin, colonial art and works by three fine painters of the late 19th century: Arturo Michelena, Antonio Herrera Toro and Andrés Mujica. Open Tue–Fri 08.00–14.00, weekends 09.30–12.30.

If you go down a block and walk east on Calle 97, in two blocks you'll see **Mi Viejo Mercado** which is a walled collection of shops around a central café. Musicians play here on Friday and Saturday evenings. The **Mercado Libre** is six blocks east between Calles 98 and 97.

Other attractions

An attraction not to be missed is the **Aquarium JV Seijas**, tel: 579815/4739, built around the city's 1877 waterworks. It is tucked at the foot of hills forming the city's western edge by Av Figueredo. Here you can spend several hours, preferably not on weekends, and eat at the soda fountain or restaurant. The large central tank (the old *caja de agua*) houses a family of freshwater dolphins. At feeding hours, 10.00, 13.30 and 17.00, these river dolphins leap and play. The aquarium tanks house an excellent collection of some 300 native species of fish, the top draw being *tembladores*, electric eels. Snakes and amphibians are in a terrarium. The small zoo, built around a ravine behind the aquarium, has a large manatee (only seen at feeding times), tapirs, peccaries, jaguar, puma and crocodiles. The aquarium not only gives courses on snake ecology but sells anti-venom serum for snake and scorpion bites. Hours are 09.00–18.00, closed Monday. Tickets cost about $0.50 and you pay separately to visit the zoo. From the bus terminal in Centro Big Low, city buses and *por puestos* take you west across Av Cedeño (Calle 105); ask to be let off at the pedestrian bridge (*pasarela*) leading to the aquarium.

The **Embalse de Guataparo** is a large reservoir about 3km west of Valencia. Its big attraction is boating; there are public changing rooms, restaurant, the private Club Internacional Guataparo, a country club and golf course. These are reached from the Paseo Cuatricentenario, a broad avenue just north of the aquarium.

The **Plaza de Toros Monumental** and the **Parque Recreacional Sur** are about 3km directly south of Plaza Bolívar. The bullring is indeed monumental, classed as one of the world's three most important along with those of Spain and Mexico. Peter Albers, who designed the bullring when it was built in 1968, was 30 years later in charge of its reconditioning for public events, with four floodlight towers, new access ramps, 4,000 seats in boxes and barriers, 38 bathrooms, and firefighting hoses and tanks. From the original capacity of 27,000, seating has been reduced to 25,000.

In March a big agricultural show takes over the extensive fairgrounds. Here you can visit the state **Museo de Antropología** at weekends, 09.00–17.00. It has a good collection of megatherium and other fossils from the Valencia basin as well as museum replicas, and pottery, ornaments and burial urns from prehistoric cultures.

Further afield
Hiking
Prebo Mountain at Valencia's western edge is a popular city target for walkers. Access is by way of Prebo suburb west of La Viña; the main Prebo road points north to the foot of the hill. Start at Avenida 24 in Prebo; the steep walk takes 30–45 minutes and gives excellent views at the top, altitude 750m. Either return the same way or take an alternative track to another part of Prebo or La Viña.

For the hike to **Cerro El Café**, northwest of Valencia, you will need to take a bus north up Av Universidad (Av Bolívar) to its intersection with the Autopista de Puerto Cabello. Start at Urbanización La Campiña in Naguanagua. It's a stiff walk up a broad road all the way to the top, altitude 1,200m. There's a pleasant picnic park with superb views over all Valencia including Guataparo Lake. Allow two hours up and one down. Best time to start is 07.00 before the day gets hot.

Campo Carabobo
En route to Tinaco is the nation's most famous battlefield, 32km southwest of Valencia. Here Venezuela, the first colony to revolt against Spain, won the battle and the War for Independence on June 24 1821 although the last Spanish troops were not ousted for another two years. There is a **Triumphal Arch** and avenue, an allegorical monument with seven steps for the seven original provinces and, on the west, a **Mirador** housing a model of the battle. The guards of honour wear period uniforms and bearskin hats, a reminder that this battle was considered so crucial by all forces that they fought in ceremonial dress. The support given by British legionnaires on that day earned them the honour of being the only foreigners permitted to bear arms in Venezuela. On the highway approaching Campo Carabobo there are several *parrillada* restaurants and large crafts shops. Also see box on page 320.

Guacara and the Vigirima petroglyphs
The **Cerro de Piedras Pintadas** poses many questions in sunny foothills north of Guacara. Shallow engravings of figures, hands and maps (places? stars?) cover dozens of weathered rocks. Who made them, and when, are matters of conjecture as such exposed glyphs cannot be dated. On the slope behind this knoll rises a wall of upright megaliths. Centuries roll back as you climb the hill and wonder at the prehistoric people who, from here, may have looked over a fuller Lake Tacarigua (now Lake Valencia). The petroglyphs are not signposted or cared for in any way. If you bring food and water this is a beautiful airy camping spot, admittedly rocky, but often solitary. The foothills are hot and grassy, not forested until higher up.

Getting there
Guacara is near the *autopista* 13km east of Valencia. From the Plaza Bolívar of Guacara, follow signs north for Vigirima. In 6.3km you will see Bodega La Esmeralda on the left; 500m beyond, turn left at Los Tres Samanes, another *bodega*. A broad road leads west in about 2km to the shady Tronconero River. After crossing the bridge, take a right fork after 500m at the Escuela Rural No 49. You are now facing north on a rough jeep track running through maize fields for 1½km towards the hills. There it veers right and passes between the petroglyph knoll and the megalith hill.

Vigirima

At the end of the main road 6km beyond the Tronconero turn-off is the village of Vigirima, built around a former colonial coffee hacienda. Its deeply shaded river and rocky pools draw many picnickers. Upstream, vestiges have been located of Hacienda Buena Vista, the residence of Valencia's founder Alonso Díaz Moreno who raised cattle and sheep in Guacara.

On the **Montaña de Mataburro** you can hike to a big *piedra pintada* in about two hours. Walk north from Vigirima's traffic circle on an earth road; you pass the Vigirima River picnic area and continue along its banks. Watch shortly for the first petroglyphs, often overgrown, left of the path opposite a fenced hut and coffee-drying patio. If you have chalk you can outline the spiral designs as they are not very clear. Keep straight (north); the path narrows and begins to climb hot grassy slopes, waterless and largely shadeless. Always go north; divided trails should join up. After an hour's climb, you pass prehistoric walls of slab rocks; these mark halfway. Near the top of Mataburro the petroglyph boulder looms on the right covered with faces, lizards, animals, perhaps a cat, spirals and designs. Some archaeologists feel that such petroglyphs marked trails over the Cordillera to salt pans near Puerto Cabello.

For information about the trail across the Cordillera from Guacara to Cumboto in Henri Pittier National Park, talk to the Audubon people in Valencia, tel: (041) 672440.

Las Trincheras Hot Springs

The **Centro Termal Las Trincheras**, halfway between Valencia and the coast (by either the old road or the *autopista*), attracts mud devotees from many parts of the world. The mineral waters are HOT. Remember Humboldt? He cooked a less-than-4-minute egg here in water over 90°C, among the hottest springs in the world. Today three pools in what is essentially the Rió Aguas Calientes are graded from warm to hot. The spring-fed river flows to the Caribbean. Whether or not you are interested in massages, steam baths or hot swimming pools, the comfortable hotel has a restaurant and gardens with macaws; 120 air-conditioned suites and rooms at $16 single, $18 double. **Hotel Spa Las Trincheras**, tel: (041) 669795. For a 3-night plan including Caracas transfers in air-conditioned car, ring Turismo Colorama, (02) 2617732, fax: 2621828.

San Esteban National Park

An old Spanish road, still cobbled in places, crosses this truly lovely part of the central range, now a 440km² park. The road was under construction in 1800 when Humboldt travelled to the coast by way of Las Trincheras. It rises from Bárbula in the Valencia valley to a pass at 1,380m before dropping down to San Esteban. The area has long been protected as watershed of the tumbling San Esteban River which supplies the seaport of Puerto Cabello with drinking water.

Hiking the Camino Real
Paul Rouche

Getting there The easiest approach to the Camino Real is from Bárbula, a *pueblo* north of Valencia. You are advised to avoid the district called **Barrio El Hospital** as the bad reputation of *barrio* thieves is based on several hold-ups. At the end of the Barrio Bárbula–Vivienda bus line, instead of turning right (east) past the chapel, go left to enter the Urbanización Carilinda by way of La Ruta del Este. You pass a police post (*puesto de vigilancia*). Then take the second street to the right; where it turns, you leave it, taking a right between two houses. The path very soon

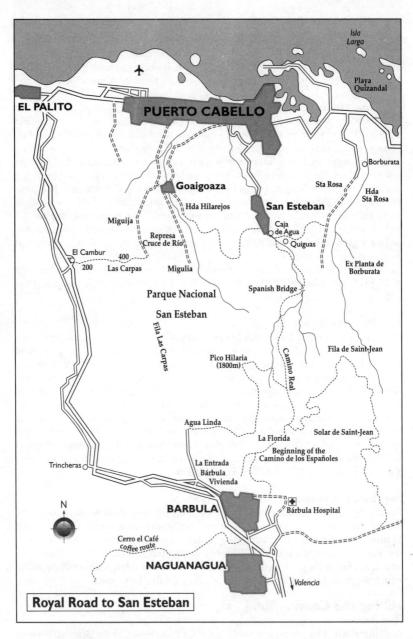

Royal Road to San Esteban

goes down to a creek. Cross a wall in the river bed and you are on the right path up. This meets the Camino de Los Españoles higher up.

Camino Real–Spanish Bridge–San Esteban
The last stop on the Barrio Bárbula–Vivienda bus route is by an Evangelist chapel. Follow the street to the right of the chapel. It will change into an earth road, make

a left/right dog-leg and dip down to cross the narrow Río Cabriales, here a creek. At the first fork beyond, go up to the right; at the second crossroads (2 minutes) go left. There's a water tank on your right; the pipeline runs along the earth road on your left, bringing water from the hills in the north. At the next fork, the **Camino Real** joins from the right. You have walked for half an hour.

The Camino Real here is well used by peasants who cultivate coffee in **Saint-Jean** near the ridge. After the coffee harvest in December, I've seen *burros* coming down from Saint-Jean loaded with sacks of coffee in a procession which seems to have changed little in 200 years. It's one thing to come down, but going up is a hard haul best begun before the sun gets hot (you feel it by 09.00). With scanty shade, the Spanish road climbs steeply. Near the cool forest at the top, you come to a level clearing known as the **Solar de Saint-Jean** (altitude 1,200m), where a path enters from Saint-Jean on the right. But keep straight on; the Camino Real is now a path. It skirts left of another solar, crosses a barbed-wire fence and narrows into a trail flanking the mountain with a precipice on the left.

At last, after winding through a bracken patch, the trail reaches the ridge forest and is joined by paths coming from Pico Hilaria (1,685m) on the left. Keep right; the path improves, leading to a fresh water spring, **Agua Fría**. The altitude here is 1,380m, highest point on the royal road. The ascent has taken roughly three hours (or longer if the heat slows you down).

Now the Camino Real is so wide that you can pitch a tent in the middle. Once over the divide, the path twists down for half an hour through cloudforests to another spring, **Los Canales**, where there are more good campsites (altitude 1,220m).

Continuing down for two hours beneath lofty forests, the royal road drops nearly 900m to the Spanish bridge. In places cobblestones can still be seen on the colonial road; more often, the sandy floor has been eroded 2–4m below its original level. Watch out for two tricky forks halfway down (do not go right). The pleasant noise of the **San Esteban River** grows nearer on the right. Turn left at a junction of leafy paths and suddenly you're standing on top of the Spanish bridge. But to really see the remarkable Gothic arch, scramble down the bank. Beyond the bridge 50m, a right fork leads to a large flat clearing (altitude 330m), good for camping, while the left fork is the true path. If you do as I did, you'll make camp up here: the temperature, the water and the forest are all refreshing.

Next day, walk down the Camino Real until it finally meets the river (30 minutes). You'll pass one false fork (keep left), followed by two real ones (go right at the first and left at the second). The river, with its gleaming boulders, crystalline water and umbrella of trees, is idyllic for a dip since you have to take off your shoes to cross it anyway. The path continues (with one left fork) to the old cacao and citrus plantation of **Las Quiguas** (altitude 200m).

To steer clear of false trails when leaving the hacienda, keep left of the house where the caretaker family lives, and head northeast through a tangerine grove. Soon you again see the San Esteban River on the right. After a 20-minute walk, the path meets a major junction. Go left, ford the river below a dyke, and you will be on a jeep road built by the waterboard, INOS. This road passes a water treatment plant at the Caja de Agua and, 15 minutes on, a bridge.

Although you soon come to many cottages, this is not San Esteban proper. Keep on between the houses for ten minutes until you find a path to the right which takes you down to a ford across the river. The village of **San Esteban** is up on the east bank.

Practical information
Time/difficulty Although the net 'marching time' for this route is less than eight hours, in practice the time doubles when you include stops for snacks,

birdwatching and rest (you'll want to cool off in the San Esteban River). The Camino Real, presenting no real difficulties, is suitable for a 2-day hike, even for less experienced walkers.

Weather Hot. Little shade on the 3-hour ascent from Bárbula. The rainy season is said to be June to November, but be prepared for showers in May and December.

Equipment Sun hat, insect repellent (a long-sleeved shirt will keep off most midges and mosquitoes), walking shoes, rain poncho.

Maps The Direccíon de Cartografía Nacional in Caracas sells accurate maps ($2.50). Sheets 6547 and 6647 (1:100,000) cover the Valencia–Puerto Cabello area. (See *Permits and Maps, Chapter 3*) However, maps of coastlines may be classed *censurada* as involving a national border, thus implying a delay for authorisation.

Permits I met no parks personnel or Guardias Nacionales, but if you are camping it is wise to get a permit from Parques Nacionales. In Valencia the Inparques office is in Parque Metropolitano/Humboldt, Antigua Estación del Ferrocarril, tel: (041) 574609.

Puerto Cabello

Although the visitor will see little of these activities, Puerto Cabello has a naval base, shipyard and large container docks. As the best harbour in the country and principal port for the industries of Valencia, Maracay and Barquisimeto, it often surpasses La Guaira in tonnage. The port and satellite districts have 200,000 inhabitants.

The port began life in the 16th century as a smugglers' anchorage. Venezuela's famous cacao, exported to Spain and illegally to Curaçao, was grown on lush plantations bordering mountain rivers such as Río Aguas Calientes, San Esteban and Borburata. In 1800 Humboldt described Puerto Cabello as 'quite modern, and the port is one of the finest in the world. A neck of land stretches first towards the north and then towards the west [which] contributes much to the smoothness of the water.' The town of 9,000 people presented 'a cheerful and agreeable aspect' despite the scourge of yellow fever. He visited the costly new aqueduct that conveyed the Río Esteban's waters to every street. At the time it was disputed whether the port's name derived from the harbour's tranquillity, 'which would not move a hair (*cabello*)', or from Antonio Cabello, a fisherman dealing with Curaçao smugglers when the port was no more than a hamlet.

Getting there and away
By air Puerto Cabello's airport is on the main road, 8km west of town. At present there are no scheduled flights but the airport handles a lot of cargo.

By bus The Terminal de Pasajeros is on Av La Paz which turns into Calle Urdaneta at Av 10/11. Buses go regularly to Valencia, San Felipe and Barquisimeto.

Take care in the bus station environs and area north to Playa Blanca where armed youngsters have held up tourists.

The terminus for local buses to San Esteban, Patanemo, El Palito and Morón is at central street corner called La Alcantarilla, about 300m from the bus station. You can't miss it as there is a large mural of a priest holding a casualty during 'El Porteñazo' (1962 insurrection). Passengers for Tucacas (1½ hours), Chichiriviche and Coro should take one of the frequent buses to Morón (25 minutes) and change to a bus coming from Valencia.

By train The Ferrocar station is on Av La Paz west of the bus terminal. This line, built by dictator Marcos Pérez Jiménez in the 1950s, covers 173km (3 hours) to Barquisimeto. The train stops at El Palito, Morón, San Felipe, Boraure, Chivacoa and Yaritagua. However, passenger service has been suspended for renovations.

Where to stay and eat
The area telephone code for Puerto Cabello is (042)
The colonial port still awaits *posadas* to complete its attractions. However, Fabio Morales who owns Restaurant La Fuente is remodelling an old house between Calles Bolívar and Lanceros for basic *hospedaje*; for information, ring him at tel: 616889. Construction of the luxury 11-floor **Hotel Marina** has been suspended on the Malecón south of the Teatro Nacional; it was to have sauna, gym, terrace with sea view, pool.

In the western suburbs (towards the airport), Puerto Cabello's first beach place has opened since the demise of the old Cumboto; it's next to the derelict hotel. On 150m of beach **Centro Vacacional La Cumboteña**, tel: 641143, fax: 640813, has a restaurant and eight air-conditioned cabins for two to seven guests; $40 a double at weekends, less Mon–Thur. Puerto Cabello's best hotel is the 3-star **Suites Caribe**, tel: 643079, fax: 643910, Av Salóm No 21 east of the airport; 66 rooms with air conditioning, TV and fridge; double $59 with sea view, less without.

Among mediocre central hotels the most acceptable is the rambling four-floor **Hotel and Restaurant Isla Larga**, Calle Miranda (La Noria), tel: 613290/3741; it is near the bus terminal and has a new pool, air conditioning, TV and maybe refrigerator, double $22. Walk east two blocks on Calle Miranda to the inexpensive **Yacambü**, tel: 610382. At the next corner, Av 9, is a better choice, **El Fortín**, tel: 612427/4356; double bed $16. In the same range are the air-conditioned **Hotel Bahía** on Av 7-Santa Bárbara at Calle Sucre, tel: 614033; and on Santa Bárbara three blocks east of the bus terminal, the Italian-run **Hotel Venezia**, tel: 614380. Two small hotels on Calle Ayacucho between Av Bolívar and Valencia are the somewhat cheaper **Capri**, tel: 615010, and **Roma**. And all the way east is **Hotel La Sultana**, Av Juan José Flores, tel: 617966/3395. It has seen better days; 39 rooms on two floors, at about $16 double with air conditioning.

Restaurant Lanceros serves good seafood every day in a lovely two-storey building on the Malecón around the corner from Calle Lanceros; popular tasca bar. **Briceño Ven** (no sign), next to the Prefectura on the Malecón, has a 35-year reputation for excellent *criollo* dishes, pork, goat and Falcón cheese; Mon–Fri 11.00–15.00, 17.00–22.00. **Da Franca's Pizzería** is to its north. Past the Iglesia del Rosario is the economical **'Lunchería' La Fuente** in a fine 18th-century house with tall ceilings facing Parque Flores; grilled red snapper at $4; fresh juices; closed Sunday. **Restaurant Venezuela**, at the end of this block in a low colonial building, has long been the seafood place; air-conditioned.

What to see
Newly restored and brightly painted after long neglect, the colonial *puerto adentro* is becoming a beacon for travellers. A seaside walk, the Malecón, has razed waterfront buildings to open broad spaces for strolling from the Concejo Municipal on Plaza Bolívar to the Monumento del Aguila. Now cherubs and fountains grace plazas where pink poui trees (*apamates*) bloom in April. Stop for

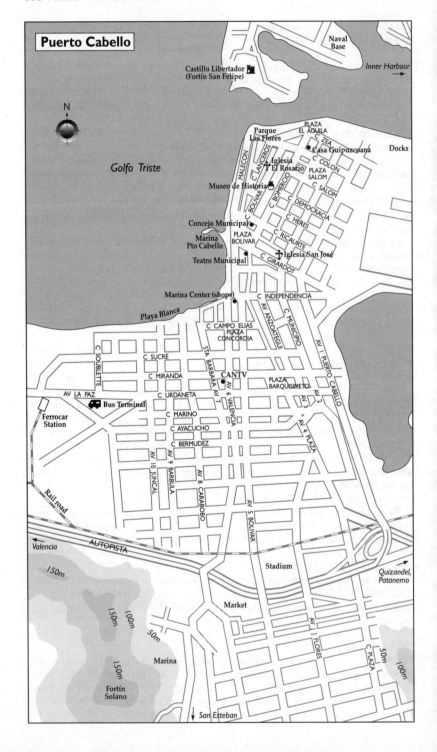

Puerto Cabello

Naval
Base

Inner Harbour →

Castillo Libertador
(Fortín San Felipe)

Golfo Triste

N

PLAZA
EL AGUILA

C. ZEA

Casa Guipuzcoana

Docks

Parque
Las Flores

C. LANCEROS

MALECON

Iglesia
El Rosario

C. COLON

PLAZA
SALOM

C. SALOM

Museo de Historia

C. BOLIVAR

C. COMERCIO

C. DEMOCRACIA

C. HERES

Concejo Municipal

Marina
Pto Cabello

PLAZA
BOLIVAR

C. RICAURTE

Teatro Municipal

C. GIRARDOT

Iglesia San José

Marina Center (shops)

C. INDEPENDENCIA

Playa Blanca

C. CAMPO ELIAS

AV. ANZOATEGUI

C. MUNICIPIO

AV. I PUERTO CABELLO

PLAZA
CONCORDIA

C. SOUBLETTE

C. SUCRE

C. MIRANDA

STA. BARBARA

CANTV

AV. 6 VALENCIA

AV. 7

PLAZA
BARQUISIMETO

AV. 3

AV LA PAZ

C. URDANETA

Bus Terminal

C. MARINO

Ferrocar
Station

C. AYACUCHO

AV. 4 PLAZA

C. BERMUDEZ

AV. 9 BARBULA

AV. 10 JUNCAL

AV. 8 CARABOBO

AV. 5 BOLIVAR

Rail road

← Valencia

AUTOPISTA

Stadium

Quizandel,
Patanemo →

150m

150m

100m

50m

Market

AV. I FLORES

C. PLAZA

50m

100m

Marina

150m

Fortín
Solano

↓ San Esteban

an ice-cream at an 18th-century house, or have juice and pizza under multicoloured awnings.

Colourful **Calle Lanceros**, first restored street behind the Malecón, is much photographed for its colonial architecture and impromptu art exhibits. Its two blocks are closed to vehicles. On this street in 1823 General Páez and his *llaneros* engaged Spanish troops for the last time; the besieged San Felipe Fort surrendered to Páez the next day. From the blue balcony of the **Museo de Historia** a second-storey walkway bridges the street; the museum actually goes all the way through to Calle Bolívar. Built in 1790, the costly mansion now houses collections of colonial weapons, antique maps, city photographs and pre-Columbian artefacts.

The small *simpático* **Templo El Rosario** with its copper dome and wooden belltower, unique in Venezuela, stands at the end of Los Lanceros. It dates from 1780 but incorporates walls of an earlier salt storehouse. The church fronts on Calle Bolívar. Follow this street, another revived by paint of many colours, north to its end (called Calle La Jeringa) at the **Monumento del Aguila**. The 'eagle' is a condor and the monument honours the American volunteers who were captured in Francisco Miranda's failed attempt to land in Ocumare in 1806; ten officers were hanged, 50 others imprisoned.

Facing the Plaza del Aguila, the public library and cultural centre occupy the imposing **Casa Guipuzcoana**. Built around 1730 it was headquarters of the Basque company given a royal trading monopoly in Puerto Cabello. To protect its interests the company constructed a fort across from the harbour channel, the **Fuerte San Felipe**, later renamed Castillo del Libertador. In the 27 years of dictator Juan Vicente Gómez the fort was an infamous prison. When closed on Gómez's death in 1935, 14 tons of chains and leg irons were pitched into the bay. Today it is part of the naval base. Visits are permitted and the navy shuttle service across the channel from the end of the Malecón is to be started again when restoration works and a Naval Museum are finished.

The **Teatro Municipal**'s former elegance as the setting for Ana Pavlova has also been rescued. This grand edifice on the Malecón, a block south of Plaza Bolívar, was designed by Antonio Malaussena and built in the 1880s.

The ungainly church looming on the east side of Plaza Bolívar is the Templo Nuevo or **Iglesia de San José**. Finished in the 1950s, it incorporated the coral-rock walls of a church begun in 1857 and left roofless for decades.

Sailboats and yachts moor at the modern **Marina Caribe** in the bay opposite the Teatro. Ask here about launch service and beach tours on the 40-passenger *Norway*. The covered launch, former lifeboat of the SS Norway, offers tours by charter as well as its regular sunset cruise of the inner harbour and docks; minimum ten passengers. It is fitted with two bathrooms, carpets, lifejackets. Office on the Paseo Marina, tel: 615066/0419.

Carnival on the Malecón is celebrated riotously with street dances, water balloons and carousing. An old custom, '**La Hamaca**', closes festivities with a mock funeral on Carnival Tuesday. Chanting a dirge and bearing a hammock with a 'dead' dummy, a procession winds to the Malecón. Drummers from the group **Tambores de San Millán** and musicians blowing horns (literally cow and deer horns) sound a lament, followed by mock battles with long poles.

The **Blessing of the Sea** on Easter Sunday fills the entire Malecón with the faithful from many parts of the coast. Some arrive at dawn for a front-row view of the fleet of fishing vessels escorting the image of the Virgin of the Valley. At 07.30 the diocesan archbishop leads the religious ceremony from a barge in the bay. Some of the faithful, not content with a distant sprinkling, dive into the bay to receive the blessing.

For the best view of the whole port, go to the reconstructed **Fortín Solano** on a hill south of the *autopista*. You start on Av J J Flores crossing south over the highway to Rancho Grande, Puerto Cabello's first suburb. Turn right after four blocks and go west towards the hill to pick up the road to San Esteban. (If you are on the *autopista*, follow signs for San Esteban.) The entrance to the fortress is close by, up a turning to the right, climbing steeply. One of the last colonial forts built in the country, it is named after the governor who ordered it built (1763–71) at great expense to the Guipuzcoana company.

The large **Mercado Municipal** is located by the *autopista* at the start of the San Esteban road. Plenty of activity on Saturday mornings.

Further afield
San Esteban
Shaded by splendid trees the old village retains a tattered elegance from the 19th century when Puerto Cabello's high society built fine estates by its cool river. One of the first walled properties on the left belongs to the family of Henrique Salas Romer. A bit further on, near the village school, stairs lead to the birthplace of patriot Bartolomé Salom, a house restored only in part, and opened to visitors. Long before this, pre-Columbian tribes also lived by the river and cut many petroglyphs on a house-sized boulder, the **Piedra del Indio**. The path to it follows above the east bank just beyond the village. Today, nostalgia is banished by weekend motorcyclists and parties of bathers who arrive with canned salsa music and beer.

In colonial times goods were transported from Puerto Cabello by way of the cobbled **Camino Real** (royal road) to Valencia. From the Caja de Agua or waterworks the 2–3-hour ascent to the arched **Puente de Paso Hondo** is a beautiful hike by the rushing river, through luxuriant vegetation of the **San Esteban National Park** (see above, *Valencia, Hiking the Camino Real*). There are fine campsites. In the late dry season, April/May, the loud 'kong, kong' of the bearded bellbird (*Procnias canobarba*) reverberates at elevations between 300 and 800m. The bellbird, whose clang sounds more like an anvil stroke, is the forest ventriloquist. You have to be very sharp to spot these birds in the high canopy.

Beaches
City beaches such as **Playa Blanca** and points west should be avoided as they are not only contaminated but unsafe (hold-ups). By contrast, the coast and islands east of Puerto Cabello have some excellent beaches. Most facilities are in **Quizandal**, about 5km on the road towards the naval base, plus 2km east through thorn scrub to the parking lot, restaurant and changing rooms of the balneario. Most bathers head for the white sands and clear protected waters of **Isla Larga**, the largest island 15 minutes east. An Italian and a German freighter, scuttled here in World War II, are now encrusted with corals, inviting snorkellers. Some *kioscos* sell food at weekends. It is possible to camp, except in windless periods when *plaga*, biting midges, make life impossible from dusk to dawn. Check first with your boatman. On weekends a seat in an open fishing boat costs about $2 round trip, leaving 08.00–13.00 and returning at 16.30. During the week fewer boats operate according to demand.

El Huequito is the beach 1km south of Quizandal. It is less developed and the entrance road is of rutted earth (no shade) from the Borburata crossroads. You can also reach this beach by walking along the seaside from Quizandal.

Borburata is the name of the next bay, valley, its river and village. The *pueblo*, about 3km south of the coast road, is the fourth oldest in Venezuela, dating to 1549. Most of the cacao haciendas which made it famous have fallen into ruins and today farmlands have become middle-class suburbs of Puerto Cabello. Every year on the Fiesta de San Juan, June 23–24, villagers rejoice in their African roots with big drums and street dances. A statue of St John the Baptist heads a procession from the church (1751), first to the river to be 'baptised'. Borburata Bay has been largely occupied by army/navy housing; to use the well-kept beach and restaurant show your passport.

Rincón del Pirata is a seaside community of little appeal but some restaurants, on the way to **Patanemo**, a beautiful curving bay backed by lush green hills, 12km from Puerto Cabello. The coastal road ends further on at the *pueblo* of Patanemo, a long street of small simple houses. On the plaza stands an unassuming little blue church with two old bronze bells. This is the scenario for masked devil dancers on the Thursday of Corpus Christi, nine weeks after Easter. The rites of submission to the church are rooted in medieval Europe. Patanemo beach is part of San Esteban National Park; you cross salty marshes 1.2km to generous coconut-shaded sands. The beach has informal fried fish stands and is popular at weekends when campers set up tents.

Where to stay

Campamento Turístico La Churuata, tel: (042) 617535, is on the main road at the fork for Patanemo beach. Its weather-beaten roofs disguise a small, pleasant retreat with a tiny bright blue pool, open-air jacuzzi, and thatched restaurant. The 14 rooms are built in spacious units of coral stone, some with air conditioning and ensuite bath, some without, for two or four people, plus a room with ten bunk beds. Including all meals and excursion, doubles cost $30–40 and quadruples $40–60. Outings include lagoons with wading birds, cascades on Río Primavera, islands, Puerto Cabello and San Esteban. For reservations in Caracas, tel/fax: (02) 9875916, 9851817; some English and French spoken. In **Los Caneyes**, a holiday community some 500m beyond La Churuata, there are inviting open-air restaurants and several signs for bungalows to let.

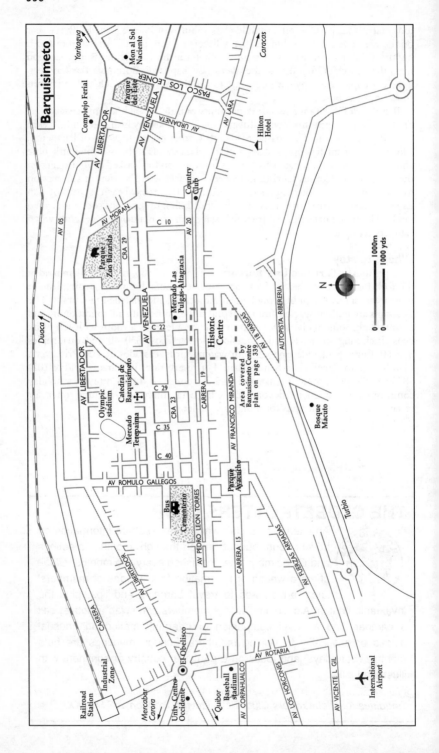

BARQUISIMETO

Barquisimeto is the capital of Lara State. A busy trading
and agricultural centre, the city is on several main routes:
to Maracaibo, to the Andes and Colombia via the
Panamericana, to Acarigua and the western plains, to Coro in
the north, and to San Felipe, Valencia and points east.

Dotted with shady parks, Barquisimeto's centre is clean and
well-kept. Streets are laid out on a Spanish pattern of *calles* which
run north–south, and *carreras* going east–west. First settled in 1552, the infant town
went through three moves before its present site by the Turbio River (altitude
566m). *Variquecemeto*, an old Indian word, means 'river of ash-coloured water'.
Because the city was shaken to its foundations by the 1812 earthquake, few Spanish
structures remain. Today's Barquisimetanos prefer to go modern.

Barquisimeto's 700,000 inhabitants make it the country's fourth largest city. The
people of Lara are practical, lively and open. They are doers: they make
instruments and play them, earning Barquisimeto the title of 'music capital of
Venezuela'. They sing in choirs, dance the Tamunangue, weave blankets, make
pots, furniture and cheese. And they grow a great variety of fruits and vegetables:
half of the country's pineapples, onions, tomatoes; a third of its sugar. Most of the
produce is sold through a giant wholesale centre in Barquisimeto called Mercabar
which covers ten acres and moves 700,000 tonnes of food yearly, fresh and
processed.

Getting there and away
By air
The terminal is about 4.5km southwest of the bus depot, 3.2km south of the
Obelisco via Av Rotaria. Servivensa, Aserca, Aeropostal and LAI have about nine
flights daily to Caracas, the cheapest being LAI, $47; fewer flights on weekends.
Also flights to Barcelona, Porlamar, Puerto Ordaz, Maturín, Coro, Maracaibo and
San Antonio. Daily international flights by Servivensa to Miami, and Santa Bárbara
line to Aruba.

By bus
The Terminal de Pasajeros is on Carrera 24 at Calle 43 in western Barquisimeto
(between Av 20-Pedro León Torres and Av Venezuela). This is a large terminus
providing quick service around most points of the compass.

Aeroexpresos Ejecutivos has departures for Caracas at 06.30, 09.15, 15.15 and
24.00, more expensive ($11), but fast (5 hours) and with curtains, air conditioning
(cold at night), bathroom, refreshments. Their terminal is at the east end of
Barquisimeto by Las Trinitarias Centro Comercial, Av Herman Garmendia, via El
Ujano; tel: (051) 546809/7907.

By rail

The Terminal de Ferrocarril is 1km north of the Obelisco traffic circle, hub of western Barquisimeto. You will see several old engines and carriages on the grounds. Ferrocar's passenger service to **Puerto Cabello** by way of Yaracuy and Carabobo states has been suspended for overhaul.

Where to stay

The area telephone code for Barquisimeto is (051)
Accommodation runs from basic hostels near the bus terminal in the west, to the 5-star **Barquisimeto Hilton**, tel: 536022, fax: 544365, in the eastern district of Nueva Segovia, very popular for its swimming pool, tennis courts, and access to golf club. The French restaurant is excellent. They have off-season plans as low as $100 a double with breakfast.

In the centre, **Hotel Bonifran**, tel: 316809/7509, Carrera 19 and Calle 31, rates 3 stars and charges $25 for a double bed. The **Principe**, tel: 312111 or 312544, Calle 23 at Carreras 18-19; has a good Italian restaurant, swimming pool and 99 clean rooms, double $30; it's worth reserving for this 4-star hotel. The **Curumato**, tel: 327349, Calle Curumato at Carrera 21, is smaller and cheaper.

Among the many downtown hotels, an inexpensive, decent choice is **Hotel Florida**, tel: 329804, Carrera 19 at Calles 31-32; doubles from $15; excellent food. The inexpensive **Hotel del Centro**, tel: 314524/5346, Av 20 at Calle 26, provides clean doubles at $10 with air conditioning, $8 without. The **Lido**, tel: 315568/5279, a block west of Plaza Bolívar, gives good value, air conditioning, double bed for $12, twin beds $15. **Hotel Villa Lara**, tel: 461621, Av Rómulo Gallegos, three blocks down from the bus station, has air-conditioned rooms with hot water for $16 a double bed and $18 for twin beds.

Various better hotels are found at the west end of town, convenient to the airport: the moderate **Gran Hotel Barquisimeto**, tel: 420511, fax: 420354, Carrera 19B at Calle 59; **Ejecutivo Canaima**, tel: 424221, fax: 423521, Carrera 19 at Calle 55; **Hosteria El Obelisco**, tel: 410311/2011, fax: 422133, Av Libertador; it has a pool. **Motel Parador El Mesón**, tel: 420421, fax: 425332, 400m west of the Obelisco, is moderate, quiet, and has a pool and small menagerie.

Where to eat

Economical meals are served at many restaurants, *arepa* and chicken places in the busy centre around Avenida Vargas; many are closed on Sunday. **Restaurant Basil** is on Calle 19 at Carreras 22-23; tasty Arab food at reasonable prices. For typical Venezuelan dishes, the **Caney de Amelia** on Carrera 17 between Calles 20-21 is a pleasant spot. **Río Mar Restaurant** on Carrera 17 at Calle 17 is an excellent seafood place which does big business for Sunday lunch; slightly more expensive than most but good value for money. **Restaurant Carlos** is an excellent downtown *arepera* on the corner of Carrera 19 and Calle 29, with an outdoor café and more tables inside.

In the more expensive east, you will find various good restaurants on Avenida Lara serving *parrilla* (grilled sausages) and steak. No place does it better than **El Llanero**.

The best ice-cream is found at **Delight Cream**, Carrera 19 at Calles 10-11; blackberry, peach yoghurt, macadamia and other flavours are made by a family who began with a pushcart.

What to see

Barquisimeto celebrates its *fiestas patronales* every January with great enthusiasm. The Virgin Mary known as the Divine Shepherdess leaves her church in Santa

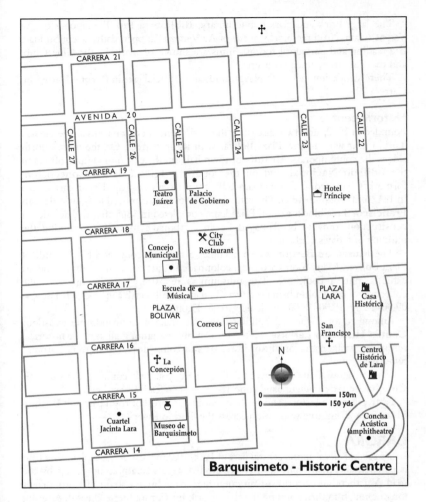

Barquisimeto - Historic Centre

Rosa and is taken in a procession to the Cathedral and then to all the city's churches. During this **Feria de la Divina Pastora**, the fairgrounds are the venue for a musical festival, sports events, and an agricultural show. This **Complejo Ferial** is on Av Libertador at the city's northeast entrance, by the circular **Monumento al Sol Naciente**, a massive sculpture in colours by Carlos Cruz Diez. Just east is the long *manga de coleo* where traditional bull-dogging events draw cowhands who compete throwing steers to the ground.

At the covered **Mercado Terepaima**, Calle 36 west of the Cathedral, the busiest day is Saturday. You will not only get the full flavour of Lara's cornucopia of fruit and vegetables, meat, cheese and beans sold at a hundred booths, but can buy cotton work-clothes and dresses. Sometimes, too, you'll see alms collectors carrying an image of their namesake, San Benito. Beating drums, the San Beniteros work their way around the market; donations go to charities.

The modern **Cathedral**, Av Venezuela (Carrera 26) at Calle 29, is a parabolic 1960s design by John Bergkamp, with blue stained glass and vaulting concrete and, inside, central stone altars and a Christ suspended from the ceiling.

The large brick and glass public library, **Biblioteca Pío Tamayo**, is on Av Vargas (Calle 20) three blocks north of Av Venezuela; open daily except Sunday. Big reading and periodical rooms. Films are shown regularly by the Cine Club, and there are free Sunday concerts.

There's a spacious zoo with playgrounds and artificial lake in **Parque Bararida**, Carrera 29.

Historic centre

Founded in 1552, after two false starts the settlement put down roots above the Río Turbio near what is now Plaza Bolívar with its great trees. On the plaza's north side is the contemporary **Alcaldía** or town hall, on the east more public offices in the **Edificio Nacional**, and on the south the **Iglesia de La Concepción**, formerly the cathedral. Dating from 1605 it was largely destroyed by an earthquake in 1812 and rebuilt in 1853. The cathedral, however, was moved to **Iglesia de San Francisco**, three blocks east on Plaza Lara, completed in 1865 after five decades of construction, only to be damaged by an earthquake in 1950 (prompting the building of today's Cathedral).

The **Museo de Barquisimeto** occupies a restored convent a block south of Plaza Bolívar. Many rooms around a colonnaded courtyard house cultural and art exhibits, plus a bookstore. The museum is repository for the fine La Salle collection of pre-Columbian pottery and images, well worth a visit. Open Tue–Fri 09.00–12.00, 15.00–18.00, weekends 10.00–17.00.

Among restored colonial buildings on Plaza Lara is the handsome two-floor **Centro Histórico Larense**. Here you can browse among all sorts of historical remnants, weapons, colonial furniture, art and coins, displayed in rooms around two paved patios.

If you follow Calle 22 downhill from here you will come to the open-air **Concha Acústica** where band concerts and dance festivals are held.

Lastly, there's a historic and really splendid old forest of royal palms in **Bosque Macuto**, a 20-minute walk south across the Turbio River.

CARORA

Lara's second city is in the central part of Lara, 102km west of the capital. The land is parched and many hills are fiercely eroded. Goats scramble up gullies by the road. Yet there are surprises. Dairymen here have bred a strain of Carora cows tough enough to thrive among the thorns (ask for Carora fuerte cheese). A recent source of pride is wine produced by the Pomar cellars (Polar and Martell). There are now 120 hectares planted with 11 varieties of French and Spanish grapes. Their quite good wines are sold under the Altagracia label; some prize years have earned Venezuela a place in the *World Wine Guide*. For a free tour of the winery in Altagracia, tel: (052) 212191.

Seek out the old town centre, northwest of the new districts lining the Barquisimeto–Maracaibo highway. Through buses bypass Carora but there is a district service from Barquisimeto. Photographers will find rewards in the **casco histórico**: several blocks of beautifully restored houses on spotless streets with patterned tiles. Carora was founded in 1569 around the Plaza Mayor, today's Plaza Bolívar. The pretty **Iglesia de San Juan Bautista** dates from the 1600s, with the addition of the tower's top storeys in 1883. Carora's *fiestas patronales* are consequently celebrated on St John's Day, June 24 or the closest weekend. Next to the church is a house called the **Balcón de los Alvarez**, a colonial residence where Bolívar lodged in 1821. On the south side of the plaza is Carora's oldest house, the **Casa Amarilla** (c1650), now a public library.

Around the corner on Calle 2 stands the **Casa de la Cultura** or **Museo de Carora** showing pre-Columbian pottery and idols from cultures which once flourished in Lara State. Continue south two blocks down this street to the single-floor **Capilla del Calvario** with its picturesque 'horned' façade. Damaged by flood in 1973, it was restored by Graziano Gasparini, who earlier restored the San Juan Bautista church and has the credit for preserving many colonial structures around Venezuela. The latest restoration job is the **Capilla de San Dionisio**, a block north of Plaza Bolívar.

Where to stay
The area telephone code for Carora is (052)
There are two motels on Av Miranda: the **Posada Madre Vieja**, tel: 212590, with good restaurant in front part; 16 plain doubles with TV, hot water, about $19; and the **Complejo Turístico Katuca**, tel: 32602, in a noisy shopping centre. Nearer downtown on Av 14 de Febrero a block or so before the bus stop at Carrera 10, there are three modest hotels. The **Bari**, hotel plus *parrilla* restaurant, charges $10 for an air-conditioned double; **Hotel Irpina** on Carrera 9, tel: 32322/62; air conditioning; decent double with bath, $15. Lastly, the **Victoria** at Carrera 8 is inexpensive but passable.

OTHER TOWNS
South and west of Barquisimeto are intensely cultivated valleys, cool premontane slopes and unspoilt old towns. Coffee, potatoes, avocados, onions, papayas, pineapples, guavas, mangos, flowers and ornamental plants are grown around Quíbor, Sanare, Cubiro and El Tocuyo.

Quíbor
Quíbor is 35km southwest of Barquisimeto. Halfway, at **El Rodeo** crossroads (west for the Panamerican to Carora), watch for signs to **Tintorero** famous for its weavers of blankets and hammocks. Many crafts shops around El Rodeo are home to makers of rustic furniture, hammocks, cuatros and other stringed instruments. Quíbor is worth a visit for its **Museo Arqueológico** which houses prehistoric pottery from excavations of an Indian cemetery uncovered near Plaza Bolívar in 1967. Huge copies of such pieces stand on the *paseo* by the church and there is a cottage industry in ceramic reproductions on sale in many shops. A small church with massive walls and a round tower, **La Ermita**, stands on Calle 13 between Avenidas 19 and 20. It is named **Nuestra Señora de Altagracia** like the church on Plaza Bolívar, but it dates to Quíbor's founding in the early 1600s.

The most popular lodging in town is the busy motel-style **Hostería Valle de Quíbor** at the eastern entrance, Carrera 5 and Calle 7; tel: (053) 42601/2; 40 rooms with hot water, TV, $20 double; swimming pool, restaurant and disco. **Hotel Gran Duque**, Av Florencio Jiménez by La Ceiba service station, tel: (053) 42149; has a restaurant and pizzeria; 27 rooms with bath, fan or air conditioning, double $8.50.

El Tocuyo
El Tocuyo, 30km southwest, is one of the oldest towns on the continent (1545) and was provincial capital of Venezuela from 1547 to 1577. The first sugarcane in Venezuela was planted in El Tocuyo, and it is still the big crop. Long ago the town was reached by boat up the Tocuyo River all the way from the coast near Chichiriviche, so that it was a natural launching point for Spanish expeditions. Sadly, an earthquake in 1950 destroyed nearly all El Tocuyo's old churches and

MARÍA LIONZA CULT

The holy mountain of the cult that draws hundreds of thousands of believers from housemaids to high officials is situated in the foothills south of Chivacoa. This small town in Yaracuy is on the highway between Barquisimeto (60km) and Valencia (110km), near the San Felipe–Morón turn-off. Believers come to seek healing or help with practical and sentimental problems, needs that in times of crisis are hard to fill elsewhere. This part of the Nirgua range was declared the María Lionza Natural Monument (117km²) in 1960, a fitting honour as María Lionza is a forest spirit of ancient origin. According to myth she is the protector of animals and spirits, and in paintings she is usually seen astride a tapir. For some, she was the daughter of an Indian princess and a Spanish conquistador.

On every street in Chivacoa the plaster images of cult figures stand in the windows of perfume shops. They are 'Las Cinco Potencias', the 'Five Powers', of which the first three are the central figures: María Lionza, the Queen or Mother; Guaicaipuro, an Indian chief who lived in the 16th century; and El Negro Miguel, a slave who led a 1552 revolt at a gold mine in Nirgua. The trio is reinforced with José Gregorio Hernández, a doctor devoted to the poor who died in Caracas in 1919; the Virgen de Coromoto, Venezuela's patron saint, or occasionally Simón Bolívar.

The big five are accompanied by a bewildering pantheon of spirits whose number and power grow with inspiration from African, Indian, Christian and now Oriental sources. If nothing else, the cult is surely transcultural. It has no higher authority and no taboos except against taking what belongs to María Lionza or killing animals without reason. From Christianity (most adepts consider themselves to be Catholics) it takes incense, candles, religious images and songs. From Africa come the drums, trances and possession by spirits. Indian sources provide shamanism, the belief in nature spirits and the use of

fine colonial buildings. The quake was withstood by an 18th-century convent on Plaza Bolívar, now the **Casa de la Cultura**. For its Spanish history and much older Indian cultures, visit the **Museo Arqueológico JM Cruxent** in the Gobernación on Plaza Bolívar, west side, and the **Museo Lisandro Alvarado** on Calle 17. The beautiful pink **Iglesia de La Concepción**, on a plaza between Calles 17 and 18, was built in the 18th century, and totally reconstructed after the 1950 quake. Its wonderfully carved wooden altar screen and the image of the Virgin (dating to 1547) are original.

Two folklore events make El Tocuyo special: on June 13 in Plaza Bolívar, the Tamunangue dancers celebrate the day of **San Antonio de Padua**; and on December 7 the **Fiesta del Garrote Tocuyano**, a mock battle and dance, marks Tocuyo's Founding Day.

Best place to stay is the two-storey **Posada Colonial** by the Casa de la Cultura on Plaza Bolívar, tel: (053) 62495; pool in rear garden, restaurant with good, plain food, 24 rooms with cold-water shower, double $12 (specify without TV which adds $2). Also **Hotel Nazaret**, Av Fraternidad at Calles 15-16, tel: (053) 62434; 14 rooms some with fan, shared bathroom; double $7.

Sanare

Sanare, 20km south of Quíbor, is the starting point for **Yacambú National Park**. Farmers in costumes come from surrounding hills (which they still plough with tobacco for healing and divining. And more recently, Cuban *santería* practices have influenced the cult with rites involving animal sacrifices and invocation of Yoruba divinities. Popular herb medicine also plays a part.

There are two main shrines by the Chivacoa River, **Quibayo** and **Sorte**, with altars to María Lionza and her court. People arrive around the clock, often in groups or 'brotherhoods', young and old, carrying fruit, flowers and particularly candles, perfume, cigars and liquor, all essential for communicating with the spirits. Tobacco is said to be holy because it has the four elements of life: carbon, oxygen, nitrogen and (very little) hydrogen. Perfume helps to attract the right deities. Rum aids in trances and is used for anointing candidates before ceremonies. Following the path uphill, worshippers make their camp and shrine by clearings in the woods or overlooking the stream.

Intermediaries or 'guides' instruct the initiates. Many of these mediums are said to have visionary or healing powers. During trances they receive the spirits who converse with the devotees. The mediums reveal omens and carry out exorcisms. Rites include bathing in the sacred river, purification by tobacco smoke and the laying on of hands.

The way to the top of Cerro de Sorte is not clear; there are many portals (shrines) and at each permission to pass must be sought through giving perfumes or rum, lighting candles or smoking cigars.

How/when to go Buses covering routes between Barquisimeto and Valencia, or San Felipe, stop at Chivacoa. There are also direct buses and *por puestos* to Chivacoa from Barquisimeto. From Chivacoa's Plaza Bolívar, Toyota *por puestos* cover the last 8–9km to the entrance sanctuaries of Quibayo or Sorte. There is most activity on weekends and holidays, in particular October 12, Día de la Raza (Columbus Day), and Easter week. You may find the crush at these times better avoided.

oxen) on December 28, Día de los Inocentes, for mass followed by the big **Fiesta de la Zaragoza**. At the northern end of this long, narrow town is a crafts shop known for its miniature nativity scenes, churches and houses, the **Artesanía Uni-Minarro** on Av Lara. La Tinaja is another crafts shop near Plaza Bolívar.

To find **Posada Los Cerritos**, tel: (053) 49016, after passing Plaza Bolívar, turn right and pass **Restaurant Yacambú** (best place in town to eat); turn left at the next corner and left again. This is a complex of 'colonial' cottages with a restaurant, 15 simple rooms with hot water and TV; double $11. Book ahead for peak holidays. **Posada Los Sauces**, two blocks farther south, has seen better days; however, rooms have bath with hot water; double $12.

TEREPAIMA AND YACAMBU NATIONAL PARKS

In striking contrast to the state's arid regions, primary forest survives in southern Lara where two national parks have been formed in an attempt to halt destruction and protect watersheds: **Terepaima**, 169km², and Yacambú, 145km². Terepaima is the lower and hotter, dropping from 1,175m to some 300m at the Sarare River. The forest here covers a third of the park only, the rest being savannah and old fields. Although animal life is severely depleted, this area is home to the ocelot and puma, deer, armadillo, agouti, opossum, monkey, kinkajou, tamandua and climbing porcupine (most of which were hunted and eaten). Turning the tables, snakes such as rattlers and corals, and ants including the infamous army ants, are feared.

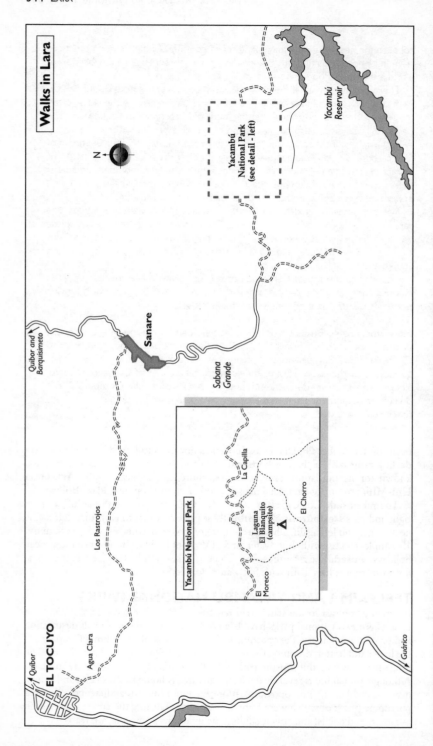

The tip of **Terepaima Park** is half an hour from Barquisimeto by road. Old earth roads climb up from Cabudare to Terepaima village providing splendid views; the Camino Real to Río Guache Seco and Caserío Los Aposentos crosses an area of pre-Columbian burial sites. Cartography map No. 6245 covers the park. For more information, check with the Inparques officer in Barquisimeto: Instituto Nacional de Parques, Parque J M Ochoa Pile, Av Libertador opposite Complejo Ferial; tel: (051) 545065, 541448.

In Yacambú, mountains rise to 2,200m along an Andean spur called the **Sierra de Portuguesa**. Flora typical of the Andes mixes with plants from the coastal cordillera and rare palms, tree ferns and local cloudforest species. Some plants grow nowhere else (like the lovely Fuchsia tillettii). Rains from April to November feed rivers such as the Yacambú. The **Yacambú Reservoir** provides irrigation for Quíbor Valley and water for Barquisimeto.

Birding

In her travels tracking the birds of Venezuela, Mary Lou Goodwin reports that Yacambú has 'what I consider to be one of the best birding roads north of the Orinoco River...wherever you stop on this road you will find birds, but my favourite spot is the lagoon. In one short day I sighted 68 species while leisurely walking this road.' Her list includes oropendula, oriole, warbler, four wrens, eleven tanagers, antpitta, redstart, parakeet, hummingbird, toucanet...

From Sanare, Paul Rouche has walked along the **Camino Real**, once the Spanish road to El Tocuyo. Today this is a questionable jeep track of some 22km, via the old and today quite dry villages of Yay and Agua Clara. His notes on a short circuit in Yacambú Park follow.

Hiking to Río Negro Canyon in Yacambú
Paul Rouche

The Yacambú National Park is little known to walkers although it has a pleasant climate, beautiful cloudforest down to about 850m, and a relatively easy trail to the **Río Negro Canyon**. This route descending by way of Quebrada El Chorro takes six hours' walking time, there and back (not counting a splash at the bottom). There is an excellent campground at **Laguna El Blanquito** at the start: picnic shelters, panorama, gardens, elegant willows and eucalyptus trees. If you make reservations through Inparques in Barquisimeto, you can rent cabins or dormitory modules for 12 people at $40; bring sheets and cooking pots. Inparques, tel: (051) 545065, 541448.

Access from Sanare

A paved road runs to Yacambú, continuing through the park to a *mirador* or lookout above the reservoir (30km). The entrance to **Laguna El Blanquito** administrative centre and campsite is well before this; stop at Km21 and walk half a kilometre from the main road. A jeep service provides public transportation from Sanare.

The earth road to **Laguna El Blanquito** (altitude 1,400m) is the start of the walk. However, do not enter the camp, but take the left fork. You pass a house, an old whitewashed chapel, **La Capilla** (the track skirts the belltower), and a great millstone. Continue on, crossing two water pipes and a fence. Just beyond a huge boulder with two crucifixes is the junction of a circle trail returning northwest to the highway via El Moreco. Keep left. Walking time to this junction is about 45 minutes.

The path descends past a hut or rancho (altitude 1,350m). In ten minutes you cross **Quebrada El Chorro**, here a small creek; 15 minutes downhill the creek is larger (altitude 1,100m). You cross again (for the last time), and bear left. Go straight (right hand) at a fork (left for Quebrada El Chorro, 15 minutes). Almost immediately, there is another fork: go left (right, two minutes up to a peasant hut called Rancho El Chorro which has an impressive view over the Río Negro).

The descent from here takes 35 minutes to the bed of the Río Negro. Cross a fence, then take a right fork. The trail, easy through forest, becomes overgrown at a large clearing invaded by bracken; bear southeast (a path comes in from Rancho El Chorro on the right); altitude 950m. Just before reaching the bottom, the path crosses a fence into a conuco or maize plot, to emerge at the lower right. Go left for the Río Negro; altitude 770m. Before exploring the rocky canyon mark your trail from the *conuco*. The **Río Negro**, when I saw it in the month of June, was a torrent. There were no pools for swimming, but we explored downstream. In ten minutes, the canyon narrowed suddenly from 100m in width to 50m, and the river appeared to rush into a dark cave.

On the return up, you may wish to take the west route for **El Moreco**; the fork is five minutes below La Capilla. Go left and stick to the main path always going up, bearing left where small trails enter. You cross the little **Quebrada Negra** about a third of the way up. At the fourth fork (five minutes before a wide earth road), take a right (the first), through a coffee plantation. This way brings you in less than an hour to the asphalt highway at El Moreco, 1.9km west of El Blanquito campsite (about 19km from Sanare).

The Andes

PARAMOS AND PEAKS

This fine mountain range is a very popular hiking area showing some of the country's best aspects: charming mountain villages, friendly *campesinos* and well-maintained trails. The world's highest cablecar (*teleférico*) runs to Pico Espejo, only 242m short of Venezuela's highest mountain, Pico Bolívar, 5,007m. The *teleférico* can save backpackers a lot of climbing, but it also deprives them of gradual acclimatisation and the beautiful path winding up the mountain below the cables.

Glaciers at one time covered the entire Mérida Valley while tongues of ice reached over to Timotes and Santo Domingo. Leftovers from this last ice age are V-shaped valleys, dark lagoons and glacier remnants such as Timoncitos (reportedly shrinking due to climate warming). Many high-country streams are stocked with trout.

TRUJILLO STATE

Trujillo State is on the northeastern approach to the Andes within easy distance of Barquisimeto. Many country roads wind over hills cultivated with coffee and pineapple to old villages such as Burbusay, Niquitao, Santa Ana and San Miguel. They are worth seeing by car. Called the 'garden of Venezuela' Boconó has pleasantly rural hotels. Flowers and vegetables grow well as farmers rely on two rainy periods, April–June and August–November.

Valera

Valera, founded in 1820, is important commercially as the state's biggest city (population 130,000). Travellers may want to lodge in this town, convenient to the airport and bus terminal. It provides various hotels, pleasant plazas and shopping malls downtown. **Plaza Bolívar** is between Calles 7-8, two blocks west of Avenida Bolívar. The **Iglesia de San Juan Bautista** is on the plaza's south side. Walk south on Av Bolívar to the new **Plaza de Los Estados** flying the banners of Pan American nations. In the attractive shopping centre are craft booths, an outdoor café, and a tourist information centre on the first floor, tel: (071) 54286.

Where to stay
The area telephone code for Valera is (071)

Hotel space, inclined to be tight on weekdays, is at a premium during the last half of August when Valera hosts the state-wide Feria Agrícola.

Topping city hotels is the **Camino Real's** 60-room tower on Av 5-Independencia, tel: 522600, 212177; restaurant, *tasca*, air conditioning, double $50. Next door is the **Albergue Turístico Valera**, tel: 55016, 56997, Av Independencia No 5, going through in the rear to the Ateneo (which built the hotel). There's a second-floor restaurant, 19 rooms, double $26.

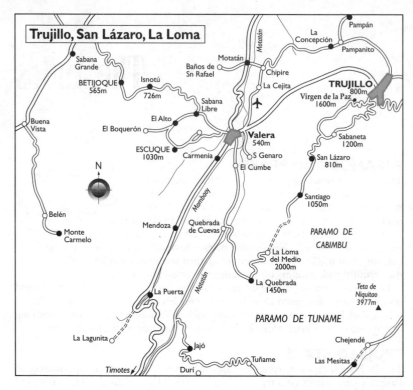

Trujillo, San Lázaro, La Loma

Hotel Flamingo Palace, La Hoyada near the airport, tel: 441063; has a restaurant, bar, and 30 motel-style rooms at about $30 double. In the centre are inexpensive hotels, perhaps the best being **Hotel Aurora**, tel: 315675, Av Bolívar at Calles 10-11; 40 air-conditioned rooms, double $18. A better businessman's choice is **Hotel El Palacio**, tel: 56769, fax: 52019, in the Miami Center, Calle 12 at Av 10-11; restaurant, 25 air-conditioned rooms, double $35. Hot springs are piped directly into two swimming pools, showers and steambaths at the modest **Hotel Hidrotermal**, tel: 92934/296, in San Rafael, 15km northwest of Valera via Motatán; informal restaurant, 21 air-conditioned rooms and one cabin; double bed $16. As non-guests may use the pool for small daily fee, this makes a pleasant outing.

Isnotú – birthplace of José Gregorio Hernández

A little town 15km northwest of Valera, Isnotú owes its fame to José Gregorio Hernández who was born here on October 26 1864. Pilgrims come to Isnotú by the hundreds at weekends and by the thousand on the anniversary of the good doctor's birth. He grew up in Isnotú where he helped his father raise six younger children upon his mother's death when he was nine. A humble, devout doctor, he is one of the best-loved figures in Venezuela for his work among the poor in Caracas. A small, neat man with a moustache, he was a familiar figure dressed in black and wearing a trilby or carrying an umbrella, hurrying on his rounds to patients and hospitals. After his death in a traffic accident in Caracas, his fame grew as a worker of miracles, and he is widely regarded as a saint. The Catholic Church has elevated him to the status of Venerable.

His statue in front of the memorial chapel in Isnotú is heaped with flowers and surrounded by candles and testimonials to cures. A small museum by the church displays his bed and personal belongings. Paintings portray his life: as a medical student at the Central University of Venezuela, as a brilliant researcher in Paris where he studied under leading specialists, and as a doctor in Caracas. A pioneer of modern medicine in Venezuela, the young doctor taught experimental physiology and bacteriology on his return to Caracas in 1891. A fervent Catholic, he twice attempted to enter the Church, once in a monastery in Italy in 1908, and again in 1913 when he entered a seminary in Rome to become a priest; both attempts were ended by poor health. He continued to receive mass daily and was known to have offered his life to God in exchange for an end to the Great War in Europe. In fact his death, on 29 June 1919, was the day after the signing of the Versailles peace treaty (see page 6).

Where to stay
The **Posada Turística Isnotú**, tel: (071) 62336, forms a complex on the plaza with restaurant, shops and a post office. There are a dozen large rooms for up to six and extra beds can be added; very plain, with bath, no hot water; $4 per person. Even cheaper are two hostels a block or two east of the church where you pay $3 per bed in dormitories: **Hospedaje Popular** and **Posada Doña María**. A better place on the road 3km east of the Isnotú turn-off is the **Posada Brisas de Isnotú** with restaurant, 12 rooms and hot water.

Trujillo
This is the state capital and was one of Venezuela's first settlements, founded in 1557 and moved seven times before reaching its final site in 1572. It is called Trujillo after the Spanish birthplace of founder Diego García de Paredes, who came to Venezuela from the conquests of Mexico and Peru where he seconded Cortés and Pizarro.

At 800m altitude, Trujillo is warm, unhurried and provincial. It is not a commercial centre like its rival Valera and has scarcely 50,000 residents. Two long streets lead up the narrow valley (Av Independencia) and down (Av Bolívar), with Plaza Bolívar in between. You can see its colonial past in low houses and the restored 17th-century **Cathedral**. The public library occupies the even older **Convento de Trujillo** dating to the early 1600s, on the corner of Plaza Bolívar and Miranda. The popular library has an audiovisual centre and a microfilm collection of Trujillo newspapers. The **Centro de Historia** on Av Independencia occupies a restored house two blocks above Plaza Bolívar, displaying arms, antiques and mementos of the Independence campaign. Bolívar vowed here to kill all enemies of the revolution including prisoners; the table he used for signing this decree, and his bed, are on view. The **Museo de Arte Popular** is near the Hotel Trujillo. The state is home to many self-taught potters, weavers and carvers; the museum organises a big biennial popular arts event in November (on even years).

Where to stay
The area telephone code for Trujillo is (072)
Reservations may be needed for the **Hotel Trujillo**, tel: (072) 33576, top end of Av Independencia, as it is pleasant and well maintained; restaurant, bar, large pool, 32 rooms on two floors, double about $30. There is a park along the river in front. On a nearby side street, the **Hotel La Paz**, tel: 34864, has 26 large clean suites with refrigerator (no kitchen), about $20 double. People eat at the adjacent **Mesón de los Cuñaos**. **Posada Valle de Los Mukas**, tel: 33148, Calle 11 at Av Bolívar,

has eight remodelled rooms around a courtyard with dining tables. **Hotel Palace**, opposite Centro de Historia on Av Independencia, tel: 31936; $9 double. With air conditioning and somewhat higher prices are **Hotel Los Gallegos**, tel: 33193, beside the Centro de Historia, and the **Centro Turístico Trujillo**, tel: 31478/224, Av Colón at Calle 2; restaurant, disco, 19 rooms in new building. On Calle 1 north of the triangle at the foot of Av Independencia, is a popular three-room guesthouse, **Posada Los Chamitos**, tel: 32898.

In La Plazuela, a restored colonial hamlet 3km north of Trujillo, **Posada San Benito** offers seven spartan rooms with bath (some have hot water) at $11 for a double bed.

Virgen de La Paz

From the top end of town opposite Hotel Trujillo, *por puesto* jeeps gather passengers for the jaunt up to the hilltop statue. At 1,600m elevation you see the now famous Virgen de La Paz landmark, erected in 1983. The concrete monument has internal stairs for those who want a view from the Virgin's knees, lap or eye. At 46m, she's as tall as the Statue of Liberty and it is said you can see as far as Lake Maracaibo.

San Lázaro to Páramo Cabimbú

A small country road, excellent for hikers or bus passengers, leaves upper Trujillo for two fine old villages, **San Lázaro** and **Santiago**. By continuing on foot or by car over an earth road up to the Páramo de **Cabimbú** and down to **La Quebrada**, this route can bring you in a circle back to busy Valera, 82km in all.

The road winds through shady plantations to **Sabaneta**, 22km, where people go to eat Trujillo-style roast chicken and large *arepas* with fresh cheese. **San Lázaro**, 8km further, is built practically atop a mountain stream, Río San Jacinto. After floods in 1986 damaged the old church, it was demolished and a new one built. Many houses were photogenically restored and the entire village was painted white and blue from top to bottom. The people are very proud of their 355-year-old village. There is a state-run inn, the **Posada Turística San Lázaro**, tel: (071) 82101, which has four plain inexpensive rooms (no hot water) in a handsome colonial house; double $10. Meals are served to order by a neighbour up the street. The **Ateneo** runs a crafts shop by the bridge where you can buy wood carvings, and baskets.

Santiago, 6km on, at the end of the paved road, is worth a stop. There is a *posada* on Calle Sucre, and beside it Señora Berta sells turnovers, *empanadas*, filled with meat or cheese. Señora Doris runs **El Buen Gusto** serving *pabellón criollo*. On the corner of Plaza Bolívar is Manuel Contreras' **curio shop**; you can buy a carving, or an old pot or machete. Santiago celebrates its fiestas patronales, like Caracas, on July 25 in honour of St James.

From here up, the mountain road lacks asphalt but at the last report it was all right for cars. Trees give way to irrigated slopes and, higher, bean and potato patches are ploughed by oxen. Above this level you see blackberry brambles, cow pastures and very few dwellings. In 12km, *poco a poco* the road reaches the crest and a ridge called **Loma del Medio** at about 2,000m elevation. The **Páramo Cabimbú**, somewhat higher, is to the east. To the west, the view sweeps over the Motatán Valley as far as distant **Pico del Aguila**.

At Loma del Medio there is a charming family-run *posada*, the **Nidal de las Nubes**, tel: (014) 9613213, 9741001, with 18 hand-built and decorated rooms. Some English and French spoken. 'Cloud's nest' is an apt name for the ridge-hugging inn. Infant clouds puff up the abyss of the Motatán gorge as hikers watch from the flower-filled terrace. Big appetites are matched by hot wheat *arepas* and homemade jam, eggs, coffee. Señora Marita, a Hungarian, and her family built the inn, which charges $32 a person in low season, with two meals. They offer excursions by horse or bicycle to the *páramo*, where local sculptor Víctor González has a 'museum'.

Now downhill, the road soon reaches the next village, **La Quebrada**, 10km, where various painters live. There is a restaurant and *posada* with window boxes, **San Roque**, (071) 82253, south of the plaza; 8 rooms, hot water, $12 double bed. The owners of **Restaurant La Quebrada** on Calle Sucre, below the church, offer six cheaper rooms with hot shower in **Pensión Urdaneta**, tel: (071) 851029. From this village the road is asphalted down to **Quebrada de Cuevas**, 9km, junction for the main Valera–Timotes highway. There remain 12km back to Valera. Alternatively, taking the highway southwest puts you on to the route for **Mérida** up the Motatán valley. (This parallels the main Transandean highway which goes along the Momboy River, past La Puerta; the two roads join near La Mesa.) In 12km you reach a left fork for Jajó (pronounced ha-HO). Buses on this route start in Valera, at the Plaza San Pedro on Av El Estadio.

Jajó

Less than 10km from the highway is a lovely, dignified village hidden many curves away from modern Venezuela. Founded in 1611, **Jajó** is set at 1,796m elevation among terraced farms, flowers and eucalyptus trees. It is still delightfully off the beaten track. Simple white houses with red roofs line cobbled streets curving down to the plaza and church built in 1990. Local lore and antiques are gathered by Pedro Sánchez at his **Museo Casa Colonial** on Calle Real. Peace and quiet are interrupted during the annual fiesta surrounding San Pedro's Day, June 29 or the nearest weekend, when locals join processions and the San Beniteros perform traditional dances such as the Sebucán.

Completing Jajó's attractions are two inns and a disconcertingly modern hotel. **Hotel Turístico Jajó** is on Plaza Bolívar, tel: (071) 57581. It has a good restaurant, plain rooms at about $11 double, but little atmosphere. In a balconied old house on the south side of the plaza is **La Pensión de Jajó**, also known as the Posada de Amparo for the lady who runs it. She rents six rooms at $9 whether occupied by one, two or three people, and will cook meals by arrangement. The **Posada Turística Marysabel** on Calle Páez (Real), several blocks north of the plaza, tel: 56999, has eight simple rooms with hot shower; double $10. Restaurant downstairs.

Jajó to Tuñame–Niquitao

A solitary jeep road crosses Páramo Tuñame (highest point 3,795m). The village of **Tuñame**, about 20km, is the supply centre for hardy but poor farm communities. It has a church, police station, basic food shops and someone who sells gasoline, but no telephones. There is a daily bus from Valera, leaving from Calle 8 at Av 4. You can overnight at the basic **Posada San Isidro** on the same street as the Ferre Finca shop. It has a restaurant and three very basic rooms behind with shared bath; double bed $5. Dormitory rooms at the restaurant and **Posada Turística de Tuñame**, by the police station, are kept busy by truck drivers who bring supplies, take produce, and sleep here because they eat well. Price per bed $2, per room (three singles, one double, two bunks) $12.

The rough *camino* continues to **Las Mesitas** (where you may find jeep transport), and from there picks up the road 13km down to **Niquitao**, altitude 1,917m, a mountain village with cobbled streets, founded in 1625 by two Spanish brothers who brought their wives. The church on Plaza Bolívar is called San Rafael de La Piedrita for a little stone that has a painted likeness of the saint. Niquitao is some 65km from Jajó. There is frequent public transportation to Boconó, 38km.

There are three small inns in Niquitao: **Posada Don Jerez** on Plaza Bolívar, 18 rooms, some hot water; **Posada Turística Güiriguay**, Calle Bolívar, a block south of the plaza, restaurant and nine rooms with hot shower; **Posada Mama Chepy**, Calle Bolívar south, seven doubles with bath and kitchen privileges.

MERIDA STATE
Timotes to Pico del Aguila
Travellers will find comfortable stopping points all along the Transandean highway. In her *Guide to Camps, Posadas & Cabins*, Elizabeth Kline lists over 80 inns on the route to Mérida here and via Santo Domingo; many moderate, some cheap and a few B&Bs.

Unless you have advance booking, avoid these routes from New Year's Eve until about January 10 or when schools reopen. It's *the* time for Andes travel.

In **Timotes** (2,020m altitude), a town founded in 1691 on lands of the Timotes Indians, there's an attractive new inn: **Posada Doña Emilia**, Av Bolívar, tel: (071) 89299, tel/fax: 89337; restaurant, seven suites of different sizes around a courtyard; double-triple $22. **Hotel Las Truchas**, up on a hill at the entrance to Timotes, tel: (071) 89158, has manicured gardens and 45 duplex cabins with fireplaces; double bed $30. Cabins with kitchens cost more.

Traffic stops in Timotes on December 29 during the feast of the black saint, San Benito. Groups of dancers, all men, are costumed as feathered Indians or negroes with blackened faces and grass skirts; others wheel and weave ribbons around a maypole.

Timotes is halfway between Valera and the Pico del Aguila pass at 4,007m. In the remaining 52km the road spirals up 2,000m in elevation, every curve giving dramatic views of the valley falling away. You will need one or two layers of warm clothing.

In **Chachopo**, 11km further, the San Beniteros also block the highway on December 29 with their procession, but here some dancers are women. On September 11 the Fiesta de la Virgen de Coromoto takes over Chachopo to honour Venezuela's patron saint. A special group of followers dressed as Indians act out the legend of the chief saved from death by the Virgin, leading to his conversion.

La Posada de Chachopo, Av Bolívar, tel: (071) 883114, is small and intimate, with a restaurant on the patio and six simple rooms with bath, hot water; single or double $15.

The last farm community before the *páramo* is **La Venta**. Here again are cabins for travellers. The **Cabañas Don Arturo** are just off the highway behind a restaurant called **Posada La Alcachofa**: four good-looking cabins painted white; fireplace, equipped kitchens, hot water; five people $50 in high season, less in low season. **Finca Santa Bárbara** has five cabins with kitchen, bath, hot water; single or double $20. Reservations are handled in Caracas by Cacao Expediciones, tel: (02) 9773753, fax: 9970110.

Pico del Aguila, often snowy, is all the more impressive when you remember that the monument marks the passage in 1813 of Bolívar's poorly equipped army on its way from taking Mérida to liberate Caracas. The roadside inn is almost an obligatory stop to catch your breath and warm up with hot chocolate. Near the restaurant is a trio of new heated cabins and a lodge with four doubles called **Posada Cueva de Los Indios**, tel: (074) 880160. Each cabin for six to eight people has three rooms, fireplace, hot water ($23); single or double $4.

Road to Piñango

This mountain is part of the Sierra del Norte, here called the Páramo de Piedras Blancas, 4,762m. The name comes from rocks split by the action of cold followed by baking sun. A lonely road, even higher than Aguila pass, winds over the *páramo* past three lagoons stocked with trout, to Piñango village, 47km. Although largely paved, the road is steep and requires 4x4 traction. Drivers may notice their car radiator appears to overheat; in fact at this great altitude water froths or 'boils' easily. The result is a notable loss of power. The Piñango *por puestos* are all 4x4 Toyotas.

Piñango is a tidy village (altitude 2,480m) in a green valley where leathery-necked farmers plough with the help of oxen. For food and lodging, ask for the house of Señora Araujo. Her husband Saturnino will provide horses for treks to the large Laguna de Piñango, to Santa Apolonia, or even for the descent by mule path to the Pan American highway south of Lake Maracaibo. **Posada Don Félix** (no phone), an old house beside the church, offers three rooms and hot showers, for one to four people, at $4 a person; meals to order.

Cartografía sheet 6042 TIMOTES covers the Piñango area, and an alternate route over a rocky jeep track from Timotes. This crosses three *páramos* in about 25km (an hour's drive), and the views are incredible. The road starts on the Transandean highway just beside Las Truchas Hotel.

Mifafí Condor Centre

Reintroducing the condor to Mérida's skies is an old dream of María Rosa Cuesta who founded this breeding station in Mifafí at 3,550m altitude. To find the centre, continue down the Transandean highway 7km from the Aguila Monument; look for a sign on the right (west). The centre is less than a kilometre up the mountain by a very rutted track. The biggest structure is an enclosure for condors born in captivity and raised for release in the wild. After the first five condors, donated by the San Diego zoo for this programme, were released in the mid-1990s, they were surprisingly joined by two wild birds. This good news was later offset by the shooting of two young females within 15km of the station, a great setback.

From the Mifafí turn-off, in another 5km the highway joins the route from Barinas at Apartaderos, and drops down to Mérida in 62km.

Barinas to Apartaderos

The route from the Llanos up to the Andes is wilder and even more beautiful than the Transandina which it joins above Apartaderos. Many people prefer it as faster although the distances from Valera/Barinas to Mérida are close, 167/163km. Following the gorge of the Santo Domingo River, the road climbs through the **Sierra Nevada National Park**. It ascends 2,000m from the Llanos to the only town of any size, **Santo Domingo**, founded in 1619. At an altitude of 2,172m, the average temperature is 16°C. The town's main livelihood is potato farming, tourism and trout. You can visit the trout hatchery 4km off the highway above the town; fish are frozen for Caracas restaurants. From here to **Apartaderos**, 26km, the road is even steeper, rising to a crest of 3,550m.

Santo Domingo's biggest fiesta is on September 30, announced by the handmade trumpets and reed flutes of the **Negros de San Jerónimo** in black face paint. They are joined by costumed groups from other villages, and together they proceed slowly from the church to a shrine by the Moruco Hotel.

Hike to Pueblo Llano and Timotes

A paved road to Pueblo Llano leaves the main highway 5.5km southeast of Santo Domingo and descends towards the Santo Domingo valley. There is a park where

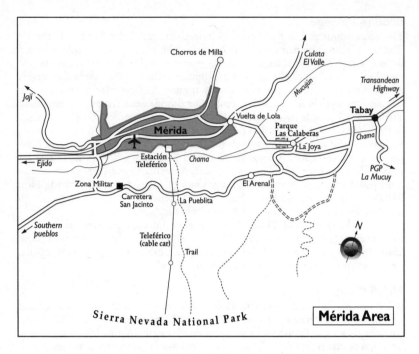

Chorros de Milla

Culata
El Valle

Jaji

Mucujún

Transandean
Highway

Vuelta de Lola

Tabay

Mérida

Parque
Las Calaberas

Chama

La Joya

Ejido

Estación
Teleférico

Chama

PGP
La Mucuy

Zona Militar

El Arenal

Carretera
San Jacinto

La Pueblita

Southern
pueblos

Teleférico
(cable car)

N

Trail

Sierra Nevada National Park

Mérida Area

you can wade in the river itself, halfway to the village of **Las Piedras**, 3.7km. On the plaza here, the new **Posada Valparaiso**, tel: (073) 88481, has 12 large rooms with hot shower; double bed $8. Beyond, the steep road to Pueblo Llano, 5km, has beautiful views. As the road was only recently paved, the farming village is quite unspoiled. You can find very inexpensive *hospedaje* for the night. An old mule/jeep track crosses the broad, fertile valley above Pueblo Llano rising to **Páramo La Estrella** (3,798m). If it is fine weather, ask the local farmers to put you on the right trail for Timotes and the Transandean highway, some 18km northwest.

Where to stay

The area telephone code for Santo Domingo is (073)
Santo Domingo is a tourist centre offering a wide choice, starting with downtown inns which are sprucing up. Best of these inexpensive places is **Posada Los Abuelos**, Calle Bolívar, in an old house a block before the church; nine simple rooms with hot water, $11 for a double bed. **La Sierra**, tel: 88110/13, fax: 88050, is a splendid addition in the centre, reasonably priced luxury brick buildings with 30 suites for two to five people, with hot water, and fireplace in larger suites; $19 for two people; restaurant with fine view. In Caracas, tel: (02) 5719845, fax: 5754835.

On the highway below town, the **Halcón de Oro**, tel: 88044/66, offers a pizzería, a restaurant, and nine rooms with hot water, for three to five people, $8 per person; English and German spoken. Nearby is the **Trucha Azul**, tel: 88066/079, fax: 88067. A 4-star resort hotel, it enjoys restaurant with view, good services, 46 spacious rooms and suites; mid-week low-season offer of $35 per person. The plain old **Hotel Santo Domingo** is 2km down from town, tel: 88144, fax: 88277; restaurant, ten rooms plus 40 cabins for up to 12 people; $30 for four. Restaurant, soda fountain, and kids' park; trout fishing offered.

On the road above town, 1¹/₂km, is the first-class **Moruco Hotel**, tel: 88070/155, fax: 88225. Set in wooded grounds the Moruco is known for its excellent restaurant and lodge with 19 rooms and 12 heated cabins with fireplace; $50 for two; best to reserve. They organise *páramo* tours and horse riding.

At the **Finca Agroturistica Páramo Maraisa**, rising to the right, farm owners Milagros and Omar Cardona take guests to private waterfalls and trout fishing, or by foot or horseback to the high *páramo*. In the farmhouse are six rooms, some with private bath and hot water, for $8. Behind their roadside restaurant are two cottages with river view and two bedrooms with equipped kitchen, plus two cabins on the opposite side of the road; $30 in high season. There is no phone, but messages may be left at tel: 88123.

You might easily skip the roadside **Las Tapias restaurant**, tel: (074) 522904, but its pleasant *posada* (lower side) offers four new doubles with hot water, $12.

Hotel Los Frailes, higher (2,850m) and colder, is on the *páramo* 12.5km from Santo Domingo. Very well run and beautifully appointed, it was designed as a mountain resort by architect Alejandro Alcega and built in 1965 (in fact, not old, the bit about a 17th-century monastery is good hype). It has become a favourite destination for its 48 heated rooms, charming restaurant, bar with fireplace, disco, gardens, babbling brook and ducks. Reserve through Avensa or Hoturvensa, tel: (02) 9078130-34, fax: 9078140; specify a room, not cabins which are across the road. Package usually includes transfer from Mérida, meals and excursions.

At the entrance to Lake Mucubají is the old standby, **Hotel Sierra Nevada**, tel: (074) 880075, a genuine travellers' inn brewing hot chocolate since the 1960s; eight rooms with hot shower and heating; double $16. **Hotel Alto Mucubají**, tel: (074) 712717, on the highway about 1km before it joins the Transandina; has six solid adobe cottages with equipped kitchen, hot water, $25 for five people; and four doubles at $15.

Laguna Mucubají

As the stunning road crests the Páramo Santo Domingo, park signs invite you to visit **Laguna Mucubají**, altitude 3,540m, 1km from the highway. You can hire horses to visit beautiful **Laguna Negra**, 2km further. Their waters give rise to the Santo Domingo, flowing ultimately to the Orinoco River. This area has some of the best walking. Just ask at the National Parks information centre by the entrance about trails and weather. Morning skies are usually brilliant and clear Dec–April, but these are the coldest months.

Apartaderos to Mérida

The Santo Domingo route joins the Transandean highway about 2km above Apartaderos, altitude 3,479m. Several hotels have been built to take advantage of the tourist trade here. The last 62km to Mérida spiral down the Chama Valley through picturesque pueblos such as Mucuchíes and Mucurubá. *Mucu* means 'place' in the old Indian tongue. Mucuchíes is the cold place, and **Mucurubá** is the place where curubas, a kind of passion-fruit, grow.

Before wheat or potatoes can be planted on such high steep slopes, children pick out stones and add them to walls. Farmers have been doing this since pre-Columbian times. The first Europeans to reach what is today Mérida reported that even the steepest, apparently inaccessible slopes were farmed by Indians who made stone terraces they called *andenes*. Here tractors are of little use, so men or oxen pull ploughs. Wheat used to be threshed using a horse and you can still see stone threshing circles. Near Mucuchíes water mills are used for grinding wheat. Today's demand for European fruit and vegetables has added new crops to the staple carrots and potatoes – apples, artichokes, leeks, brussel sprouts – and pesticides.

Life remains hard. In remote hamlets children go to one-room school houses, often unheated. Their ruddy faces are wind-burned and their clothes are too thin for warmth. To make a few bolívars, kids by the road sell flowers or woolly puppies a lot fatter than themselves (white puppies of a Great Pyrenees strain, here called Mucuchíes).

Transandean inns
The area telephone code is (074)

Colonial-style *posadas* or inns on the Transandean route to Mérida offer charm, simplicity and usually, but not always, economy. A few have meals at set hours and in some cases the price may include breakfast or two meals, *media pensión*. More are opening every month.

The place known as **Apartaderos** is a collection of hotels and souvenir shops. The actual village is called **San Isidro**, altitude 3,342m; average temperature 6°C. In peak season many roadside shops also let rooms; just enquire. **Refugio Turístico Mifafi**, tel: 880131, offers eight unheated inexpensive rooms and cabin, with hot showers, behind its restaurant and shop near the big **Hotel Turístico Apartaderos**. In a better class, **Residencias Parque San Isidro**, tel: 880012/0264, down a short driveway, has four splendid cottages for three to five people, with fireplace, nicely equipped kitchen and hot water, all with different decor; $65 high season, $40 off season. Behind a shop as you leave San Isidro, the **Posada Viejo Apartaderos**, tel: 880102/0015, is an old house with corridors around a patio where Juan Gil Sánchez offers nine basic rooms, unheated but with hot shower.

Posada San Rafael del Páramo is 4km downhill. You will see the wooden posts and white plaster of a two-storey house whose balconies overlook the valley. The moderate guesthouse (no phone) incorporates an 1868 house built by Juan Félix Sánchez' father. Twelve inviting rooms, mostly heated, have private bath and hot shower. Owners Mary and Omar Monsalve plan a restaurant with Andean dishes, too. They can arrange horse treks.

San Rafael de Mucuchíes, altitude 3,140m, 6km south, has acquired national fame for the stone chapel which Juan Félix Sánchez built at its entrance. This devout, self-taught man, already in his eighties, made the chapel and all its decorations (see page 373, *El Tisure*). At 89 Sánchez won the National Prize for Art (1989). As more people stop here to see the little chapel, San Rafael families are offering economical lodgings. Ask in the local shops about houses at: **Calle Bolívar No 1**, Calle Bolívar at Calle Miranda. **Calle Bolívar No 3** is a complete house, rented for $15 a night by the Montilla Salcedo family. **Posada El Rosal**, tel: 820331/834, is a two-floor house on the southwest high street, with eight economical, unheated but cheerful rooms upstairs, hot showers, and three basic cabins with equipped kitchen in rear. There's a *posada* near Plaza Bolívar preferred by Europeans: the **Terrazas del Sol**, also known as **Aula de las Arcas**, tel: 635439. Guests stay in seven rooms in a colonial-style heated house, while an 18th-century house provides dining and living rooms. A double is $18 per person with two meals; or $10 without; 3-day/2-night plan with all meals and excursion, $70. German and French spoken.

Another plus in San Rafael (up from Posada El Rosal) is the house where Mme Crys Fauvelle Vestrini has made her home and a French restaurant called **Folklore Crys**... paté, artichokes, mushroom sauce, spiced wine, and music by Andean talents. French travellers know all about it.

As you leave the *pueblo*, there's a nice new two-floor stone house next to Cabañas San Rafael and built by the same people: it's a restaurant with the **Posada Turística San Rafael** upstairs; wooden floors and ceilings, 11 ample rooms with hot showers, moderate prices. In Mérida ring Señora Ana Siria Alvarez, 637647, 715465, for reservations.

Mucuchíes, altitude 2,980m, is a large village 7km down the road. It was founded in 1596 and has a traditional Plaza Bolívar with church, so don't be put off by the turreted **Castillo San Isidro** in pink stone at its entrance, someone's idea of a hotel/restaurant. In the village itself, you'll find very good cooking downstairs and five plain unheated rooms upstairs at the **Posada Restaurant Los Andes**, tel: 81151, No 9 Calle Independencia which runs east. Bathrooms across the hall have hot water; $6 per person. It's worth your while to reserve early as the regulars leave little space. **Posada Doña Betty**, tel: 444277, Calle Independencia at Rivas Dávila, has six rooms for two to five people, some with hot shower, some shared, for $8 a person high season; kitchen privileges. **Posada Don Raúl**, (no phone), Calle Independencia No 38; four large rooms with double and single beds, hot shower; $6 double. Breakfast by request.

El Convite Centro Campesino, tel/fax: 81163, is at Calle Bolívar No 1, downhill. Of particular interest to hikers, this training centre puts out a list and map of local farmers and home owners who are offering guest rooms while receiving counselling in planning, administration and maintenance. This is part of a self-help programme to improve standards of living, earning capabilities, and farming techniques. El Convite (the invitation) has meeting rooms, kitchen, also bedrooms with bunk beds, bath and hot water for people taking courses. At other times rooms are open to tourists for $5 a bed. You can contribute by asking here for a guide if you are planning a hike, or by buying crafts directly from the makers.

Posada San Román, tel: (014) 9740202, a restored 18th-century hacienda house down the highway near Mucurubá, is clearly seen standing alone on the left. Five large rooms (with beds for a family) at $18 for one to four people. The restaurant provides trout in all forms and stout breakfasts; open in high season.

The **Piedras Blancas Ecological Refuge** offers an all-inclusive plan for travellers wanting to explore the Biological Reserve of Páramo Piedras Blancas that rises northwest of Mucuchíes. The Refuge was constructed of dry stone around a courtyard, with red tiled roofs, and although severely simple it has solar power and hot water. With meals, hikes and transfer from Mérida, $75 per night (discount for residents). Tenters welcome. In Mérida, tel/fax: 635633, Yves Lesenfants.

Mucurubá is about 10km south of Mucuchíes, and Escagüey 1km further. The great house of the Hacienda Escagüey, called **Casona Viva La Independencia**, was built in 1878. It really is great: there are 11 rooms from doubles to sextuples, fitted with modern bathrooms, around a large central courtyard. Restaurant and bar, too. Between the highway and the Chama River, this is more of an exclusive lodge than an inn. Also part of the hacienda is **La Cañada**, four new cabins and a restaurant, built of stone, combining country with luxury. Price per person, double $55, includes two meals. By reservation only, tel: (014) 9740712/1545, or in Caracas tel/fax: (02) 9635608, 9637951.

Take a turn around **Cacute**, just down the road, where villagers are proud of their newly restored colonial centre. Here you will find an inexpensive guesthouse, **Posada La Casa Grande**, where eight rooms occupy three sides of a quadrangle, with cane ceilings, treetrunk bedsteads, hot showers. On the other side, a restaurant serves hot *criollo* breakfasts and dinner (no lunch). Messages care of parish *junta*, tel: 742122.

Passing Los Aleros theme park you come in 2km to the restaurant and **Posada El Nidal de Nubes II**, tel: (014) 9613213, by the same Señora Marita of the renowned guesthouse in Trujillo. There are ten creatively decorated rooms with double bed and hot shower ($30) downstairs, while the restaurant featuring Andean specialities is on the second floor. A package with breakfast and dinner costs $32 per person.

The sign of a hand shows the way to **Posada de La Mano Poderosa**, tel: 523804, fax: 524031, (014) 9743304. Where the road passes La Plazuela (plaza with church), just outside Tabay, turn right at the sign of the hand and take a concrete road uphill 2km; from the end of the concrete it's a ten-minute walk to an old house with tiles on the roof, tiles on the floor and a corridor all around to take in the view. Four rooms for two to four, shared bathrooms, $5 a bed; plenty of hammock space. **La Mano Poderosa** is run by young Venezuelan and French trekking operators passionate about paragliding, biking and mountain climbing.

Tabay, the last town before Mérida, 12km, was founded in 1689 on lands of the Tabay Indians and has kept its colonial character. Red-tiled houses surround the plaza dominated by a large twin-towered church. Both Tabay and La Mucuy, across the Chama River, are famous for wood crafts and naïve sculptures, displayed at the **Casa de Cultura**. Saints and generals are favourite subjects of artesanos santeros such as Ana Rosa Parra, Mariano Rangel, Elida and María Edicta La Cruz, whose work has international demand. In the Moreno family, the father, mother and five children make a living whittling wood into bottle-shaped triptychs of saints.

Two *posadas* in Tabay are operated by the Monsalve clan. **La Casona de Tabay**, tel: 830089, is a colonial-style *posada* with patio, tiled roof, restaurant, 14 rooms, single or double $17 (Rodrigo Monsalve). The Posada Turística Tabay, tel: 830025, fax: 830121, is on the plaza, Av Bolívar at Calle Santos Marquina. Nine rooms around the central patio, and restaurant too; single or double bed $20 (Emilio Monsalve).

In **La Mucuy**, on the Sierra Nevada side of the Chama River, there are several interesting *posadas*. From Tabay's Plaza Bolívar *por puestos* run to La Mucuy, 3.5km. **Cabañas Xinia & Peter**, tel: 830454, a pretty new place, offers three equipped cottages with hot showers, for two to six people; hot breakfasts with homemade bread, jam and local cheeses. Xinia and Peter speak English and German. A 3-day tour starts with airport pick-up, and includes Jají, Mucuchíes, a hike or horse ride to Laguna Negra, Mifafi Condor Centre, the Observatory, Mérida and the Teleférico. For reservations in Caracas, ring Alpitour, (02) 2831433/6677, fax: 2856067; email: 104551.2315@compuserve.com.

At **La Joya** (5.5km south of Tabay and off to the left) a road crosses the Chama bridge. Head west 2.3km; a jeep road then climbs the last 2km to El Arenal. Here the **Posada Doña Rosa** functions in the old coffee hacienda of La Mesa which served as *teleférico* offices during the cableway's construction. Its big quadrangle has been refurbished as an inn with ten rooms with hot water. There are stables, pool and trails up to the *teleférico*. Price of $30 a night includes breakfast and supper. The owner, María Rosa Cuesta, who speaks English, is a zoologist involved in reintroducing the condor to the Venezuelan Andes. For reservations, tel: 528355, fax: 524084; in Caracas, ring the Audubon, tel: (02) 923268/2812, fax: 9910716.

Mérida

To Caraqueños, Mérida conjures up a town perched in the high, cold Andes. In fact, this highest state capital is situated on a *mesa* above the Chama gorge at a pleasant 1,625m. Far from being chilly, the climate is semi-tropical, with warm days and cool nights.

Mérida is the seat of the Universidad de Los Andes (founded 1785) known for its forestry school, and some 35,000 to 40,000 university students mingle with the city's 200,000 inhabitants. There are also five technical schools, the acclaimed Hotel School of the Andes, and several active language institutes. If you add to all these some 250,000 tourists a month during the peak holiday season (July–Sept), you get an idea of Mérida's growing importance as a cultural and travel centre. Mérida has declared the city a Cultural Free Zone to make books and educational materials cheaper. The huge Mucucharastí convention centre is another city achievement. Under such impetus, new hotels and facilities are opening constantly.

Although few historic buildings remain, the city is proud of Spanish roots dating to 1558. Mérida had two other sites before its final location where it was named Santiago de los Caballeros de Mérida. For over two centuries it belonged to the colonial province of Nueva Granada (Colombia) rather than the Captaincy General of Venezuela.

The Spaniards, clinging to a narrow foothold along the Chama, saw the advantages of co-existence with groups such as the Timoto–Cuicas. Indians planted 'roots and maize for sustenance, because the multitude of people did not allow a patch of land to lie idle, even in the cold *páramos*'. Even now, Andeans are the hardest working people in the country. They are aware that their customs are different (and their Spanish clearer), and they like it that way. Andeans pride themselves on being *gente correcta* (proper).

Getting there and away
By air
Mérida's airport is at the southwest end of the valley, just 3km from Plaza Bolívar. Buses provide service to the airport from Av 2 Lora and Calle 25. There are five flights daily to/from **Caracas** (1 hour) by Avensa, LAI and Air Venezuela, ranging in price from $75 to $53 (on Air Venezuela's Convairs). Air Venezuela links Mérida with **Maracaibo**, **Porlamar**, **Cumaná** and **Puerto Ayacucho**. As Mérida's runway is short and sometimes fogbound, the airport at El Vigía, northwest, is used in bad weather. It is reached from Mérida by 70km of road and fast *autopista* down to the lowlands.

When Mérida flights are booked solid, you can combine air to **Barinas** and bus to **Mérida**. From the Barinas airport (there is a tourism booth) it is a 15-minute walk to the bus station where *por puestos* ($3\frac{1}{2}$ hours) and buses (6 hours) depart frequently for Mérida. Best views are on the right as the road swings around hairpin bends up to Laguna de Mucubají (café stop) and Apartaderos. You will need warm clothes because it gets cold.

By bus
The bus terminal is on Avenida Las Américas, at least 3km from downtown Mérida. However, a bus service links the Terminal de Pasajeros with Av 2 Lora and Calle 25, near Plaza Bolívar. For service to Mucuchíes, Pico del Aguila and Timotes, take a **Valera** bus; for Laguna de Mucubají and Santo Domingo, take a **Barinas** bus. Buses to **San Cristóbal** (5 hours) leave every two hours during the day, via El Vigía and the lowland route. For the mountain route, take a local bus to Tovar–Bailadores. Mérida can be reached by *expreso* coach (12 hours, about $15) from **Caracas**. The main roads to Mérida are: the Llanos route via Barinas (690km from Caracas) which rises dramatically from Barinitas to Apartaderos; the scenic but slow Transandean road from Trujillo State (730km) by way of Valera and Pico del Aguila; and the Pan American highway via Barquisimeto and El Vigía (850km),

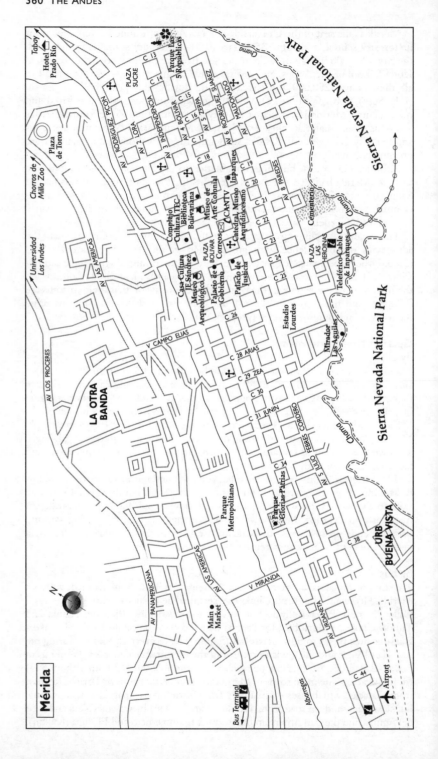

Mérida

a fast road bypassing most of the Andes. No *expreso* lines offer daytime service direct to Mérida. In order to take the Transandean route you have to go via Valera.

Where to stay

The area telephone code for Mérida is (074)

Mérida has several good hotels in splendid settings and scores of reasonable ones. Tourism booths at the airport and bus station provide lists. Try to avoid school holidays and Carnival as it coincides with Mérida's Feria del Sol. Reserve early for Christmas and New Year, too.

Among the top places, with swimming pool and doubles at about $60, are: the **Prado Río**, tel: 520704/75, fax: 525192, 150m from the northeast end of Avenida 1 La Hoyada de Milla; Mérida's first luxury hotel, 55 rooms and units, now run by the highly regarded university hotel school. The **Belensate**, tel: 663722, fax: 662823, 661255, La Hacienda district (west of the airport); has art centre, Italian restaurant, 39 rooms, bungalow. **La Pedregosa**, tel: 664295/3457, fax: 661176, Pedregosa Norte; offers 4-star facilities, sauna, disco, 104 rooms and cabins in spacious grounds with artificial lake; in Caracas, tel: (02) 9591774, fax: 9591604.

Moderate central hotels, about $26 a double, are: **Hotel Chama**, tel: 524851/1011, fax: 521157, Av 4 at Calle 29 at Av 4; **El Tisure**, tel: 526072, fax: 526061, Av 4 Bolívar at Calles 17-18; **Mintoy**, tel: 520340/3545, fax: 526005, Calle 25 No 8-130.

Inexpensive downtown choices (among many) cost around $18 a double with hot shower. They include the **Gran Balcón**, tel: 520366/4056, fax: 529055, Av Domingo Peña (west end Av 8); quiet, friendly, in the Teleférico vicinity; ask for a room with view. For a small fee they will look after your luggage while you're hiking. There is also the **Teleférico**, Plaza Las Heroínas, tel: 527370/9839; and the **Altamira**, tel: 528677/3366, Calle 25 at Av 6-7. Somewhat cheaper are the **Monte Carlos**, tel: 527335, fax: 525910, Av 7 at Calles 24-25; **Frontino**, tel: 527555/8249, Av 3 at Calle 24. The cheaper **Hotel Italia**, tel: 525737, Calle 19 at Av 2-3, is frequented by many young foreigners.

Posadas

A large number of guesthouses and pensions provide budget travellers an easy, pleasant alternative for as little as $5 a person, and some have laundry and breakfast services. A few *posadas* which have made continuous improvements have raised their rates as high as $20 a double, for example: **La Casona de Margot**, tel: 513312, Av 4 at Calles 15-16; superior furnishings, nine rooms for two to six people; reduced rates in off-season.

In the centre: **Luz Caraballo**, tel: 525411, Av 2 on Plaza Sucre; popular restaurant and *posada* of 40 rooms for one to five with hot water, double $15; book ahead. **Los Bucares** (ex Los Compadres), tel: 522841, Av 4 at Calle 15; one of the best *posadas* with ten attractive rooms, hot showers, double bed $12. **Marianela**, tel: 526907, fax: 525501, Calle 16 at Av 4-5; basic bed & breakfast, $6 per person; run by Marianela Núñez who can arrange any tour or climb as she is in the business. **Mucumbarí**, tel: 526015, fax: 529327, Av 3 at Calles 14-15; nine rooms around two patios, double with shared bath $11; laundry, breakfast to order, garden bar and grill. **Don Blas**, tel: 526755, Av 1 at Calle 17; neat, well run, 16 rooms with hot shower (ask for a new upper room), $5 a person in high season; coffee shop. **Alemania**, tel: 524067, Av 2 at Calle 18; ten rooms, most with shared bath, hot water, $10 double; breakfast by request, laundry; owner Robert Ohr runs tour agency and a guesthouse in Chichiriviche; he speaks German and English. **Posada Calle 18**, tel: 522986, Calle 18 at Av 3-4; eight pleasant rooms for two to six people, shared facilites, $12 double; laundry service, kitchen use, English spoken. **Residencias San Pedro**, tel: 522735, Calle 19 at Av 6-7; clean and spacious, eight rooms with shared bath, hot water, kitchen and laundry use; $6 high season.

In the Teleférico area: Long a favourite for simple, clean dormitory lodging at bottom rates is **Posada Las Heroínas**, tel: 522665, Calle 24 at Parque Las Heroínas. Former manager Tom Evenou has moved his tour agency Bum Bum and guesthouse to the end of the street; great view. **La Joya**, tel: 526055, Calle 24 No 8-51; rooms in four apartments with shared kitchen, bath, double $6 high season. **Encanto Andino**, tel: 526929, Calle 24 No 6-53; five plain rooms with hot shower around a patio, double $15; use of refrigerator and laundry. **Cheo's Restaurant & Hotel**, tel: 529393, Calle 24, across from Teleférico; seven rooms on second floor with phone, TV and hot water; double bed $10. **Foto Fauna**, (014) 9745227, Calle 24 No 8-265; five basic rooms, shared bath, kitchen use, $4 a person. **Finca la Trinitaria**, a beautiful farm 15 minutes from the centre of town, has a three-bedroomed colonial house for rent; sleeps six, self-catering, well furnished and equipped, US$50 per night. Contact Mary and Ian Woodward (074) 440760; bratt@ing.ula.ve.

Note The presence of many young people provides a market for drugs which are pushed in this area. Penalties for drug possession in Venezuela are heavy and lead to prison.

Where to eat

Like its hotels, Mérida's restaurants are plentiful and reasonable. There are two places a visitor should not miss. The four-storey **Mercado Principal**, Av Las Américas at Viaducto Miranda, besides providing a sales outlet for many artisans, has one large dining room (lunch only) on the top floor. Sections of tables are served by various kitchens with different menus, mostly *criollo*, plus standard pork chops, chicken for $4; try a glass of local blackberry (*mora*) wine for $1.20. Credit cards accepted. The **Heladería Coromoto**, Av 3 No 28-75, has brought fame to Mérida for an astonishing 600 flavours of ice-cream. The walls are papered with choices: after you go through all the fruits, you find vegetables such as pumpkin, carrot, even garlic; then meat, chicken, fish, shrimp; beer, whisky, liqueurs… Closed Monday.

Two hotels have excellent restaurants: the Chama's **Miramelindo Restaurant**, Av 4 at Calle 29, serves delicious Basque dishes and seafood; and Hotel Cheo's, **Calle 24** near the Teleférico, is known for *carnes a la brasa* (grilled steak), also trout. Trout, as it is raised in fish farms, is plentiful and inexpensive, although at times over-fried. At the **Exquisita Bocatá**, Av 4 at Calle 15, try something new, a *bocatá*, for a light lunch; it's like a sandwich with a filling of condimented meat. Seafood: **Marisquería Tu y Yo**, Av 4 at Calle 28. Italian: **La Trattoría da Lino**, Pasaje Ayacucho. Arab food: **Makdharma**, Av 4, 58-07. Vegetarian, the **Nutricentro Vegetariano**, Av 4 No 18-58.

Information and tours

Corporación Merideña de Turismo Cormetur has seven information booths open from Monday to Saturday. Those in the bus terminal and airport operate 07.00–19.00, and in the main market and *teleférico* 08.00–15.00. They provide maps, lists of guesthouses and tips on excursions. Headquarters of Cormetur are on Av Urdaneta at Calle 45 by the airport, tel: 800 MERIDA (63743), (074) 634701/0814, fax: 632782. Cormetur has a website: www.cormetur.com, and email address: cormetur@cormetur.com.

Money tips To change travellers' cheques, you may be requested to show their purchase slip. CorpBanca (ex Consolidado) agencies handle Amex. Otherwise, the airport exchange booth is the best place. The city has many cashpoint machines. One often mentioned as accepting Visa and giving bolívars is at the Banco Union, Avenida 4 west of Plaza Bolívar.

Inparques regional headquarters are on Calle 19 between Av 5-6, tel: (074) 529876, fax: 528785. Hours are Mon–Fri 08.30–12.00, 13.30–17.00. You may find it handy to get hiking permits, required for campers, from the Inparques office at the Teleférico station which is open Wed–Sun 07.30–14.00. All you need is a *cédula* or passport, and less than half a dollar per night's stay in the park.

Maps may be found at La Casa del Turista on Avenida 3 near Plaza Bolívar which has a selection of guidebooks, as well as souvenirs. Many tour operators sell all sorts of maps including hiking maps. Inparques has photocopies of national park maps which they sell quite reasonably.

Tour operators (See also *Mountain climbing*.) **Bum Bum Tours** is located at the end of Calle 24 past the Teleférico, tel/fax: 525879; email: raquel@bolívar.funmrd. gov.ve. Their name comes from an Andean river in Barinas State where they have pioneered kayaking and rafting. They also handle a wide variety of reasonably priced tours in and around Mérida, and farther afield to nature preserves on the Llanos. Owner Tom Evenou sells maps and runs a guesthouse, too.

Local agencies offer 3-day/2-night packages that give a pleasant introduction to Mérida. **Frontino Tours**, tel: 520955, fax: 523051, includes airport transfers, tours of the *páramo*, city and market, bilingual guide, lodging and breakfast at the first-class Hostería La Sevillana, all for $140. An off-season package offered by **Caribay Tours**, tel/fax: 634828/7596, includes airport pick-up, breakfast, tickets to the *teleférico* and Los Aleros, and lodging at Hotel Caribay, Av 2 Lora, for $85 a person in a double.

Torcaza Trails operate all-inclusive 5-day treks across the Sierra Nevada to Los Nevados, Los Rastrojos, and down to Barinas (with optional Llanos wildlife tour). Treks combine the *teleférico*, mules, jeep, and strenuous hiking (grade 3) through the full range of *cordillera* ecosystems, from cold *páramo* down to cloudforest, and deciduous woods. At Los Rastrojos (2,300m altitude), a renovated farmhouse provides three rooms with shared bath and hot showers. English, French and Italian spoken. For information, ring Rowena Hill, tel/fax: 620955, 666135; email: torcaza@cantv.net.

Paragliding Mérida has some world-class gliding country, starting at the city's *teleférico*. Tandem flights as long as 30km and lasting 1½ hours are standard; the cost is $100 per person. International competitions are held in Tierra Negra, 20km southwest of the city (tandem flights here are $60). Simon Vacker, tel/fax: 529565, and Raul Penzo, tel: 443942, of Andes en Duro give a $350 pilot's course of five or eight days, and provide cross-country fliers with radio and companion pilot for straight-line flights of about 70km. See also page 50.

What to see

A new arts complex called the **Complejo Cultural Tulio Febres Cordero** occupies the block northeast of Plaza Bolívar, Av La Lora between Calles 21 and 22. This is where the old Mercado stood until destroyed by fire. In size alone the cultural centre is one of the city's most important buildings after the Cathedral.

Fiestas

The biggest fiesta in Mérida State is the capital city's annual five-day bash, the **Feria del Sol**. This takes place in the days preceding Ash Wednesday with music, folklore, sports events and daily bullfights.

Throughout the state you may see costumed villagers celebrating traditional festivals and saints' days with street processions and ritual dances.

January (all month)	*Paradura del Niño*, a widely celebrated search for the lost Infant Jesus, with costumed Indians, angels, shepherds and dancers.
January 1	*Baile de Las Locaínas* in Pueblo Llano.
January 6	Day of the Kings in Santo Domingo, Tabay.
January, (last Sunday)	San Benito, closing fiesta in Mucutujote (near La Venta–Chachopo).
February 2	*Los Vasallos de La Candelaria* in La Punta, Bailadores.
Easter, Holy Thursday and Friday	Passion Play in La Parroquia, Lagunillas.
May 15	*San Isidro Labrador* in Lagunillas, Apartaderos, Tovar, Jají. *San Antonio de Padua* in Chiguará.
May 22	*Los Locos de Santa Rita* in Pueblo Nuevo, southwest of Mérida.
June 14–17	*San Buenaventura* in Ejido.
July 25	*Santo Apostol* in Lagunillas, Ejido, Jají.
September 24	Archangel Michael's Day in Jají and Mérida.
September 30	*Los Negros de San Gerónimo* in Santo Domingo.
October 12	*Virgen de Coromoto* in the capital of Mérida.
October 24	*Fiesta de San Rafael* in San Rafael de Mucuchíes.
December 13	*Santa Lucía* in Mucuchíes, Timotes.
December 28	*Los Chimbangueles* in Palmarito.
December 28–9	*Los Giros de San Benito* (the black saint) in Mucuchíes, Chachopo, Timotes.

There is an auditorium with 1,500 seats, crafts area, café and **Museo de Arte Moderno**, open Tue–Fri 09.00–12.00, 14.30–18.00, weekends 10.00–18.00. For information, tel: 522988, 522784.

Dominating Plaza Bolívar is the large **Cathedral**. It was begun in 1800, destroyed by earthquake, erected again between 1842 and 1867 and finally finished in 1958. The Cathedral guards the remains of a Roman soldier, San Clemente, who was beheaded as a Christian, and a 16th-century stone image of the Virgin of the Apple. Next door the **Palacio Arzobispal** has a museum of religious treasures. On the plaza's northwest side, the **Casa de Cultura Juan Félix Sánchez** provides a showcase for works by Mérida's painters and craftsmen, and salespoint for Kuai Mare books. Diagonal to the corner of Calle 23 is the **Museo Arqueológico**, part of the Universidad de Los Anges. If you read Spanish you can learn a lot about pre-Columbian cultures. Open Tue–Sun 11.00–18.00.

The **Museo de Arte Colonial**, on Avenida 4 two blocks east of the Cathedral, displays period pieces up to 1811 (Independence): furniture, artworks, including 17th-century bas reliefs. Recitals and seminars, too. Across the street is the

Biblioteca Bolivariana. Although mostly containing documents, there is also a display of Bolívar's belongings including a jewel-encrusted sword and gold sheath presented to the Liberator by a grateful Peru. If you walk to the upper end of Av 4, you will reach the **Parque de las 5 Repúblicas** where the world's first monument to Bolívar was placed in 1842.

Plaza Las Heroínas is surrounded by hotels, restaurants and a crafts market, the **Mercado Artesanal**, ending at the cablecar terminal where there is an Inparques office. To reach Las Heroínas, walk from Plaza Bolívar two blocks south to Calle 24, then go six blocks south.

The new **Museo de Ciencia y Tecnología**, tel: 713458, is located in western Mérida on Av Andrés Bello at Laguna La Rosa; Sat–Sun 10.00–18.00, adults $2. A park and artificial lake with digitally controlled 'legosaur' and 'elasmosaur' complement exhibits on Andean geology, cloudforests and fauna, all very high tech.

If you plan to stay a few days, visit **Parque La Isla** where you will find a museum about **bees** and apiculture; also the 19th-century **Febres Cordero House**, conserving regional historical documents and displaying Andean art.

The **Casa Internacional de Congresos Mucucharastí** (meaning 'meeting place' in the old Tatuy language), tel: 635918, fax: 632782, is Mérida's huge new convention centre in Parque La Isla, opposite Corpoandes. Its halls have capacity for 4,500 people, plus 2,400m^2 exhibition space, private shops and agencies.

The small, pleasant zoo at **Chorros de Milla** is another 3.5km north.

The Teleférico
Reaching 4,765m, this four-stage cableway is the world's highest. The system covers 12.5km. Understandably, it is extremely popular and reservations, tel: (074) 525080, are made well in advance. One way to avoid queues is to book with a tour group; there's one in the plaza outside the *teleférico*. On peak holidys, the *teleférico* may run daily to 15.00. Otherwise, Tue–Sun, 07.00 to 13.00 up; last car down about 14.00. The first car has been known to start up before 07.00 at peak periods. Tickets cost $17 adults, $7 children.

Because clouds often close in after midday, try to be early so as not to miss the stunning views. If you are trekking and don't want to come down, you can go up in an empty car when they start bringing people down after lunch (no reduction if you get off at intermediate stages). Make sure you have warm clothes as it is very cold up there. If you are asthmatic or suffer other breathing problems, take extra care. There is a doctor and mountain rescue team at Pico Espejo.

Note: The *Teleférico's* fourth stage to Pico Espejo, closed for some years after a cable broke and two people died, was opened early in 1999 by Corpoturismo. The third station, Loma Redonda, 4,045m, is where mules wait to carry packs or riders bound for Los Nevados village, or to take you for a ride to Laguna del Espejo; this should cost $4 or less.

Mountain climbing
Options vary from ascents of Pico Bolívar or Pico Humboldt with a guide, to hikes to Los Nevados and El Tisure by foot or mule (see reports below). According to interests (and the weather), you can spend a week on the trails without retracing your route. Mérida has many expert guides (who must be registered with both Inparques and Corpoturismo – ask to see their *carnet*) for rock, ice or mountain climbing. The two best-known climbing associations are the **Grupo de Rescate** (GAR), tel: 444666; and the **Asociación Merideña de Andinismo** (AMA), tel: 521666. Tour operators are numerous and highly competitive. Many have equipment for rent.

Climbers and hikers are required to have at least one partner and to obtain a permit from Inparques in Mérida (see above, *Tourist information*), or from the Puestos de Guardaparques (PGP) in La Mucuy, and Laguna Mucubají, open every day. Minors must show a letter of parental permission and photocopy of parent's passport/ID.

For where and how to go, consult the *montañistas* at Guamanchi Expeditions, Calle 24, a block from Plaza Las Heroínas, tel/fax: 522080; email: geca@bolivar. funmrd.gov.ve; net: www.ftech.net/~geca. Their qualified climbers will guide you up any mountain and see that you have the right support. Guamanchi runs a *posada* in Los Nevados.

Montaña is a responsible travel agency run by Jerry Keeton, an American, at Local 1, Edif Las Américas, Av Las Américas, tel/fax: 661448, 662867; email: andes@telcel.net.ve. Keeton organises Andean treks for travel companies in the USA, England, Germany and Japan, as well as tailor-made holidays. Treks to Pico Bolívar and Pico Humboldt; mountain biking circuits (with support jeeps to carry gear up the 'awesome Andes') to Pico del Aguila, Tierra Negra-San José, Jají and La Carbonera; tandem paragliding.

The people in the **Mountain Shop** opposite the Teleférico are friendly and helpful. You can hire camping equipment, sleeping bags and stoves, and they sell maps of the Sierra Nevada Park and Laguna Negra region; Tour de Montaña, tel: 526402, fax: 528309, Calle 24 No 8-107.

Natoura, Calle 24 No 8-237, is an established operator in mountaineering, rafting, biking and paragliding; run by Renate Reiners and José Luís Troconis. They also offer Amazonas, Roraima and Angel Falls, and are stretching service a bit thin. For information, tel/fax: 524216/4075; email: natoura@telcel.net.ve; net: www.natoura.com.

Further afield
Trout fishing
Ask Cormetur about the best high-altitude lagoons, stocked with trout many years ago. The season is March 15–September 30. For lagoons in national parks you will require a permit from Inparques; for others, from SARPA, Ministerio de Agricultura y Cría, tel: 632981, Av Urdaneta; bring photocopy of passport or ID, and Banco Provincial deposit slip for Bs7,400 (non-residents), or Bs3700 (residents), to the SARPA account No 027-07038-A.

Jají
Fit in a visit to Jají, a brightly reconstructed colonial village about 45 minutes from Mérida. There are restaurants, crafts and souvenir shops, and three village fiestas with processions: May 15, San Isidro Labrador; July 25, the day of Santiago Apostol; September 24, feast day of Jají's patron saint San Miguel Arcángel.

It's a quiet, pleasant place on weekdays, with cool nights at 1,780m elevation, and there are two small inns. **Posada Jaguaní**, Plaza Bolívar (no telephone); behind the Fonda, has a *criollo* restaurant and eight spartan rooms with hot water shower; single or double bed $10. The **Hospedaje Familiar** on the lower side of Plaza Bolívar (no phone) provides four rooms, only one with private bath. During off-seasons all are the same price, single or double bed $6; 50% more at holiday times, $11 with bath. **Posada Araguaney** (no phone) is in the rear part of a crafts shop on Plaza Bolívar; three rooms with hot shower. The attractive restaurant and **Posada Aldea Vieja**, tel: (074) 660072 (evenings), is half a block south of the top of Plaza Bolívar; seven large rooms on the second floor, ensuite hot showers; double bed $11, extra bed $5; ask about a plan including meals.

Theme parks
Venezuela de Antier A popular destination, the park is 12km from Mérida on the road to Jají. It is another recreation in miniature by the same man who made Los Aleros, this time featuring colourful and traditional Venezuelan sights: from Amazonas, a typical Indian dwelling; from Zulia, the bridge across the lake, and Guajira ladies dressed in long *mantas*; from Caracas, old Plaza Bolívar; weekend cockfights. Entrance $14 adults, $8 children.

Los Aleros Located halfway between Mérida and Mucuchíes, the miniature village was built in the traditional rammed-earth manner by a nostalgic Andino named Romer Alexis Montilla who looks back to the 1920s. The village is complete with working wheat mill, itinerant photographer, cinema with silent films, newpaper, bakery and restaurant. The setting is a pretty hillside at 2,150m elevation. *Por puestos* take 30 minutes from Calle 26. Open daily, except New Year's Day, 09.00–17.00; weekends 08.00–17.30. Entrance $10 adults, $6 children.

Xamú Pueblo Indígena This park is situated near Lagunillas, 25km southwest of Mérida by the highway. Again, it explores Andean customs, but from the era of the Spanish conquest, showing how the Mucujún people lived, farmed, cooked and weaved. Also, visit the **Laguna de Urao**, since prehistoric times important as a source of soda crystals, the key ingredient of *chimó*. This is a viscous black tobacco paste that is still used by old-timers (put between the lip and gum) as a stimulant and to stave off cold and hunger.

Astrophysical Observatory
At 3,600m altitude in the Sierra del Norte, the three-domed observatory has four telescopes, a Schmidt Camera with 1m-diameter lens, and a library (open for consultation). Situated near Llano El Hato, the highest town in Venezuela at 3,510m, the centre (called CIDA) is reached by a bumpy entrance road west of the Transandina between Apartaderos and Pico del Aguila. The observatory, tel: (074) 791893, 792660, is normally open to the public during summer holidays July 20–Sept 9. The entrance fee is around $3 adults, half price for children. For information about guided tours in high season, tel: 712459/3883; website www.cida.ve.

A walk off the Transandean route
Walkers have sought out the *camino viejo* which roughly parallels the Transandean route as it drops down to Mérida. Alison Vickers and Tim Wainwright write: 'A pleasant amble is to follow the old track from Apartaderos to Mucuchíes, a distance of about 14km. The old track, on the whole broad and grassy, winds down the valley through the villages, occasionally joining the main road. On the map there is no clear way. We just started walking and each time we joined the main road, we headed off on the most likely looking path, which was usually the right way. Whilst it is not spectacular in scenery or challenging in walking, it is still delightful. We passed small farms, walked along the riverbank and stopped and chatted to people working in fields who were all very friendly. At Mucuchíes we got the *por puesto* back to Mérida, but you could have walked further.'

Sierra La Culata
North of Mérida runs a parallel and slightly lower chain called **La Sierra del Norte** or La Culata (the 'butt' or rear because from Lake Maracaibo it is seen as a backdrop). Its high *páramos* are Piedras Blancas, 4,762m; Tucaní, 4,400m; La

Culata, 4,290m; and Los Conejos, about 4,200m. In 1989 2,000km² of this northern range were declared a national park in an effort to halt degradation of habitat. The park stretches from near Timotes in the east to La Azulita in the west.

In its varied ecosystems live many endangered species. The condor has vanished, although it is now being re-introduced, and the spectacled bear (*Tremarctos ornatus*) may follow if not protected. A park study by Bioma listed 59 mammal species and 61 reptiles and amphibians, including nine endemic frogs and toads. The park is also known for its endemic flora, particularly *frailejón* species. These plants range from ground-hugging velvety crowns to centuries-old trunks with tufted tops whose silhouettes reminded Spaniards of a procession of friars or *frailes*.

SIERRA NEVADA DE MERIDA

The highest Andean peaks in Venezuela rise south of Mérida's state capital. The chain culminates in **Pico Bolívar**, 5,007m (a bronze bust of the Liberator sits up there). In a cluster to the east are **La Concha** (the Shell), also known as La Garza (the Heron), 4,922m; and **La Corona** (the Crown) whose two peaks, 4,942m and 4,883m, honour a pair of 19th-century naturalists, Humboldt and Bonpland, who never saw the Sierra Nevada. Continuing east is the **Sierra de Santo Domingo** where the massif of Mucuñuque reaches 4,672m. Directly west of Pico Bolívar is **Pico Espejo** (Mirror), 4,765m, served by the world's highest cablecar system. Also to the west are El Toro (the Bull), 4,755m, and El León (the Lion), 4,740m.

These peaks form the spine of the **Sierra Nevada National Park**. The park covers 2,760km2 in Mérida State and down to some 600m elevation in Barinas State. The less freqented Barinas slopes still have undisturbed cloudforests with deer, coatis, agoutis, porcupines, pumas and even monkeys. Ornithologists have spotted the rare Andean cock-of-the-rock near cascading brooks, as well as crested quetzals, nightjars, cotingas and collared jays.

The *páramos* range from about 3,000m up to 4,300m (above this, the almost barren scree is called desert *páramo*). Like moors, *páramos* are open, windswept and largely treeless. In hollows or by lakes such as the **Laguna Negra** grow thickets of short, red-trunked coloradito trees (*Polylepis sericea*). Their twisted branches shade lichens, ferns and dark green mosses shining with dew. Evergreen coloradito forests are not hangers-on from warmer times: they like the *páramo* and are said to be among the highest-growing trees in the world, up to 4,500m. However, their ecosystem, once axed, never regenerates. This is quoted as one reason why pine trees are used for reforestation despite being quite out of place.

Weather

Snow in July Because snow clings to the 'rooftop' peaks of Bolívar, La Corona, La Concha, El Toro and El León, Merideños call them the five White Eagles. From May to November storms may buffet the *páramos* with snow which melts in a day. This season is called *invierno*, winter. Campers may find the *invierno* wet and miserable or snowy and miserable. The *verano* is the dry season or summer from about December to April. Then the Andes are at their most inviting, sunny and bright. December–February are the coldest months.

Caution Because of afternoon fog, it is best to use mornings for walking. Night temperatures may plunge to freezing above 3,500m (for every 100m rise in altitude, the mercury drops about 0.6°C). By contrast the day's high may soar to 20°C. You'll see that Andinos, even small children, have leathery faces burned by sun and wind. Sunburn occurs at high altitudes because thin oxygen permits more

THE PARAMO, AN ANDEAN GARDEN

To many plant lovers the best time to see the Andes is October to December when the *páramos* are in bloom. Bees, butterflies and even hummingbirds help to weave a bright floral tapestry. Insect pollination may seem a bit chancy at 4,000m, so perhaps the spectacular profusion of colours is a kind of over-compensation. One botanist compares the Andean *páramos* with the rhododendron belt of the Himalayas.

Some of the Andean flowers prized in Europe are the calceolaria with its yellow pouched blooms, nasturtiums, quilted-leaved gesnerias, asters, clematis, saxifrage, gentian, salvia and befaria. Lower down are beautiful begonias, fuchsias and heliconias. Dotting the *páramos* are violet or yellow tabacotes (*Senecio sp*), blue lupins (*Lupinus meridanus*) or chochos; white *páramo* chicory (*Hypochoeris*), yellow huesito shrubs (*Hypericum laricifolium*), red 'Spanish flag' (*Castilleja fissifolia*) related to the Indian paintbrush, and pale lobelias called *avenita*.

The contrasts of summer-by-day and winter-by-night require special adaptation. Some plants must resist not only sub-zero temperatures and wind but radiation so intense that moisture is sucked up, stunting growth. Many species grow in rosette or cushion form as protection. With short stems and tough roots, other plants have specially adapted leaves, thick and hard-skinned, waxy or furry.

The best example is the velvety frailejón (*Espeletia sp*), 'rabbit ears' to children, found everywhere on the *páramo*. Wool on the leaves seems to protect the frailejones against ice, sun and evaporation. Most species have rosettes of soft, silvery leaves and heads of yellow flowers. This daisy relative has 65 endemic species in Venezuela and botanists think the area was the dispersal centre for the genus. One kind of frailejón living at great elevations (4,500m) takes the place of trees. At the rate of a few millimetres a year, it reaches 3m in height and there is evidence that it lives over a hundred years.

radiation. Lack of oxygen may also cause mountain sickness, known as the *soroche* or *mal de páramo*. In the Andes to feel depressed is *estar emparamado*. And 'to cross over the *páramo*', *pasar el páramo*, means to die. So go slowly, rest often.

Hiking in the Sierra Nevada de Mérida

The Parque Nacional Sierra Nevada de Mérida provides infinite opportunities for hiking. The following are just a few. For more suggestions buy *Hiking in the Venezuelan Andes* (see *Appendix 2*, page 434).

The teleférico route and Los Nevados

Hilary and George Bradt, with further information from Alison Vickers, Rowena Quantrill and Peter Ireland

One of the most interesting aspects of our five-day walk was the vegetation changes caused by altitude, the prevailing winds, and local conditions. Between the first and second *teleférico* stations the vegetation is lush, but reaches cloudforest richness between the Montaña and La Aguada stations. Here is the 'typical' jungle scenery everyone imagines. Everything is slightly out of hand, larger than life, and competing for air, light and moisture. In this cloudforest pocket, special plant communities complement each other. We especially enjoyed this forest because

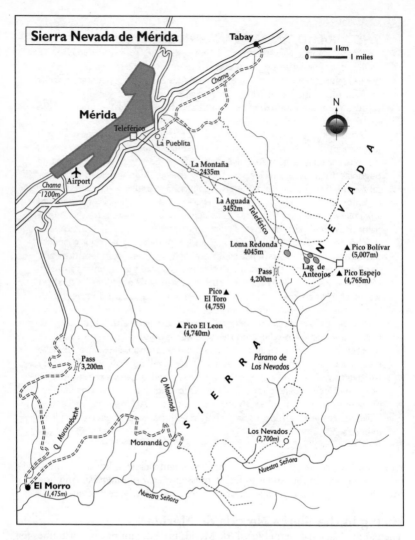

Sierra Nevada de Mérida

the path takes you not only through it, but above it as well. As you wind up the far side of the valley you're level with a fantastic array of air plants, ferns, mosses, and other bromeliads. I remember seeing the sun streaming down on an entire tree swathed in air plants. A few were blossoming, but all had bright red leaves highlighted by the sun against a hazy blue mountain. We could even look down on a group of wary guans, large tropical forest-dwelling birds.

After the humid cloudforest comes the dry, intoxicating smell of eucalyptus trees, but eventually these give way to scrub and bushes. From Redonda station we looked ahead at the bleak *páramo* in front of us, and were surprised to see a sheltered valley supporting all sorts of trees, bushes and flowers just below the pass at about 4,200m.

From the top of the pass we could see the trail winding down into the valley of the Nuestra Señora river. At first glance the landscape was devoid of anything special, but then we realised entire hillsides were covered in pink blossoming bushes. Down from the pass the mountains became drier and drier. Prickly-pear cacti were common companions bordering fields of wheat. Here on the eastern watershed, luxuriant plantlife was concentrated in the *quebradas* or stream beds. After two days of near-desert conditions it was a relief to get back on to the western slopes: bananas, grassy fields, and forests. The country folk we met along the way were friendly and always informative. Obviously construction of the *teleférico* had influenced the area enormously. Not only did many of these men help build the installations, but they could now get their produce to market more easily.

It was Christmas, and in the village of Los Nevados the padre organised a nativity play for his parish. With the help of several theological students from Mérida's university, the square in front of the church was transformed by the construction of a simple manger and signs posted over private houses, 'Pensión Rey David,' and 'Pensión Belén'. By the time we arrived, all we saw was a charmingly Andean nativity scene set up to the left of the church altar. No camels here, only typical beasts of burden: horses, donkeys and mules. Instead of the rich oriental robes, the peasants were dressed in Andean browns and greys. The stable was a typical thatched hut, and the terrain was not flat desert, but rugged, creased mountains. We met one of the students who told us the details of the pageant. Three hundred spectators had come, bringing their animals with them in case the padres needed more for the play. There were more than enough willing villagers for all the parts. What the play lacked in polish was made up in authenticity and simplicity.

Mérida–Los Nevados–El Morro–Mérida

The first thing to decide is whether to take the *teleférico* or walk up the mountain. Your decision may be made for you by the season and day of the week you make your ascent – remember the *teleférico* does not run on Mondays or Tuesdays, and may be very crowded when it is running. Rowena Quantrill recommends taking it at least to the first station. The first stretch is the most confusing (you're most likely to get lost here), and is hot and generally not very interesting.

Assuming you are walking, there are three ways down to the Chama River flowing past Mérida. The main road leaves Mérida's plateau behind the airport (west), while the two walking routes leave from beside the *teleférico* station and the eastern part of town. Each has a bridge over the river. When you get to the other side there's a road on which you turn left (north). Continue up the road until you come to telephone and electric cables strung on two sets of poles, one short and one tall. 'While still in the village, you pass a house called Villa Olga; at the next right, turn uphill; you will see a white cross 30m up the street. Just beyond, after crossing a small stream, a track to the *camino del teleférico* (just ask anyone) veers left at a fork and soon winds up to ridge. After about 15 minutes, it comes to a Rotary Club cross; keep above the Hacienda La Mesa on your left. You will soon join the beautifully contoured and graded trail. We found no yellow paint markers until nearly at La Montaña.' (Peter Ireland)

There's no water between the start of the trail and the first station (La Montaña, 2,442m) four hours away. This is a convenient stopping place: fantastic view of Mérida, and a good station café with hot food (closes at 14.00). Some hikers have reported difficulty with guards requesting a special permit to camp here, but this may no longer be required. Much better to take a lovely trail, first left of the cableway, then to the right under the lines. It follows a water pipe up the mountain.

A beautiful campsite is about 1½ hours further on; not a difficult walk and well worth the effort. It is in lush forest on a patch of grass big enough for two tents, across the Quebrada La Fría. To cross the river there's a very slippery log. We chickened out and waded. 'Make no mistake, La Fría is cold. We had spent the previous night on a bus and carried our 20kg backpacks all day; now, very soon after splashing in La Fría we had a hypothermia case; the only way we could warm him up was by zipping together a pair of bags and all three of us bundling in until nightfall.' (Peter Ireland)

Leave early the next morning so you can enjoy the scenery without hurrying. The cloudforest is at its best here as the trail climbs through ever more spectacular vistas. Be on the lookout for the only possible place you could go wrong on this trail. You'll recognise the spot because you actually pass under one of the *teleférico* pylons. ('The path to Loma Redonda starts just below La Aguada station, signposted to the right. Stick to the high side of the *teleférico* after crossing under it; the yellow markers are no longer there.' Peter Ireland)

From Quebrada La Fría to La Aguada station (3,452m) is about three hours. There is camping near the station where water is available. ('The employee was very helpful finding us a spot within the complex and invited us into his cabin for coffee.' Peter Ireland). The trail snaking up toward Loma Redonda station (4,045m) is clearly visible over the rocks, about four hours away (you may do it in less, but many people start to feel the altitude at this point). The best campsite here is five minutes beyond the station, with water available from the pumphouse. There are fine views of Pico Bolívar and the Anteojos Lakes.

The path becomes very wide at Loma Redonda because of continual use by mules carrying tourists to Los Nevados. On the third day continue up to the pass, about an hour. Before the top you will see a path to the left, bound for Pico Bolívar and the final *teleférico* station. Pause here for your last views of the mountain if you're heading for Los Nevados.

The trail to **Los Nevados** is rocky, well-used (even by the occasional jeep), and downhill with plenty of campsites and (seasonal) water. You will get your first bird's-eye view of this enchanting little village about three hours from the pass. Once you've spotted the village the easiest route down is by way of the white cross to your right as you look at the village. Or you can continue along the main trail, and double back. Don't cross the river to the east.

At Los Nevados you can buy a few basic necessities, beer, and soft drinks, and some houses offer accommodation. Or there's a lovely campsite about an hour beyond the village, by a stream. ('There are now 4–5 *posadas turísticas*. Ours was very clean and simple. For two of us in a bunk-bedded room, with evening meal and breakfast, we paid very little. Los Nevados is very relaxed and we both felt we could have spent a couple of days here.' A Vickers)

Before leaving Los Nevados have a look inside the church (1912): the Andean nativity scene described earlier is there.

The path to El Morro begins around the first row of houses to the right of the church. Walking west takes you above the Río Nuestra Señora canyon to El Morro, seven or eight hours away on a dusty track through hot, desert-like country (little shade). The trail is so well constructed that you'll positively sail along. There is water and several campsites, but the best combination is at Quebrada Mosnanda about halfway between the two villages, where the trail becomes a jeep track. An hour beyond this river is the Quebrada El Banco, your last possible campsite (only room for one tent here) and water for two hours as the road goes up and across several dry ridges.

As we climbed up from El Banco we looked down a ridge sprinkled with corrugated iron roofs, said, 'Ah, El Morro' and continued upward. However, the real El Morro then came into view far below us. It was charming, the bougainvillea shrubs contrasting beautifully with the whitewashed adobe walls and tile roofs. For accommodation ask for the *pensión* run by Señora Adriana. ('After a long, hot day, the *posada* was bliss. Señora Adriana and her grandson play a wicked game of dominoes and we had great fun playing until about midnight.' A Vickers)

From El Morro the jeep track runs to Mérida. If you go down to the village you may be able to arrange a lift. Otherwise you can take a short cut across the Quebrada Mucusabache and join the road as it climbs up a long ravine. As a relief from the rather bland road we discovered a short cut beginning on the right about halfway to a quebrada at the end of the ravine. Stones make up the roadbed which is still used by local traders because it cuts several kilometres off the jeep route.

Not long after starting up this road you should collect water as the ridge is a long dry one, taking three hours from El Morro to the top.

Once over the pass the descent is swift, the trail joining the road at a junction. The main road curves around to the right, while another older road continues down to the left. This is the shorter, steeper route. Just keep taking the right-hand forks and heading downhill to Mérida. Plenty of water and fine campsites here. When your minor road rejoins the jeep road, you'd better start hitching. It's still a long way to Mérida, and walking it could take you the best part of a day.

Practical information
Time/difficulty The hike described takes four or five days, but this can be shortened to two or three days by using the *teleférico* for the ascent to Loma Redonda. The trail itself is not difficult. It can be tackled by a fit person with a little backpacking experience in lugging cold-weather gear, and common sense to go slowly at high altitude.

Weather December to March is the dry season: clear, cold, gusty. Expect fog in the afternoon, freezing temperatures at night above 3,500m; rain, snow mostly from April to October.

Accommodation By using the *teleférico* it is possible to do this hike without a tent and other backpacking equipment. Rooms and meals can be found in Los Nevados and El Morro, but you should bring a sleeping bag.

Equipment The usual high-altitude equipment, plus insect repellent for the *bocones* (small biting insects) found at lower altitudes. Your stove is recommended as this is a national park. Suncream and lipsalve are essential.

Maps A Sierra Nevada *Mapa para Excursionistas* (photocopy, about $2.50) with reasonably accurate contours is sold by the Casa de Las Montañas in the *teleférico* square. As marked trails may be old, check any side treks with a ranger. The 1:50,000 map, sheet number 5941, made by Nacional (MARNR), is widely available in photocopy form in Mérida.

Permits You pay a nominal fee (less than $0.50) for each night spent in the park; permits are easy to obtain at Inparques office at the bottom *teleférico* station, open shortly after 07.00. The permit must be returned on completion of hike.

El Tisure – páramo and pilgrimage
Paul Rouche

High in the Andes, Juan Félix Sánchez built a chapel of rocks and peopled it with saints carved in wood. Working alone except for his wife Epifania's help, Sánchez spent years creating a Calvary of ten figures, completing it in 1976. This naïve masterpiece earned Sánchez the National Prize for Art in 1989. Since his death in

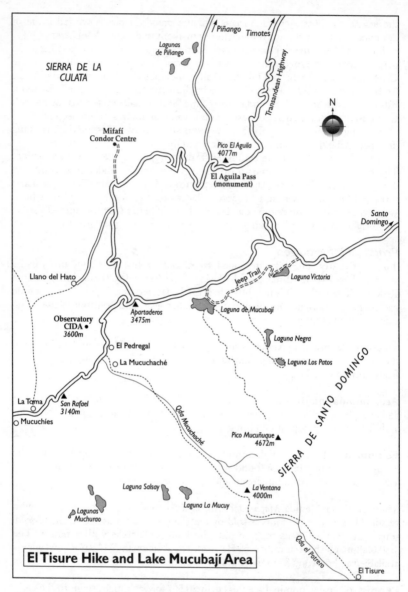

El Tisure Hike and Lake Mucubají Area

1997, at the age of 96, the saints stand on El Tisure with the clouds and wind for company, and the occasional hiker.

As an old man, Sánchez moved down to **San Rafael de Mucuchíes**. There, at the upper entrance to the village, he built a second chapel. Between this and El Tisure is a distance of some 12km or more. Mules may be hired in San Rafael (ask at the Prefectura) for the 5-hour trek to El Potrero, as the valley is known to *campesinos*. The views are enchanting at La Ventana (the window) pass, where other peasants have placed crucifixes. Despite a headstart of some 3,100m altitude and an excellent trail, many hikers will be slowed by this stiff ascent to 4,000m.

Access The path starts from La Mucuchache, a community next to El Pedregal, about 4km below the Apartaderos crossroads. The concrete road to La Mucuchache joins the Transandean highway 0.8km from Juan Félix Sánchez' chapel in San Rafael. A crucifix (dated 17.11.84) stands by the right side of this concrete road.

The Mucuchache road soon turns into earth, climbing in a southeast direction along the Quebrada La Cañada, or Mucuchache River. Still wide, the road crosses a bridge, and begins to leave behind all houses. Splendid views which open to the left over a great valley called El Pantano mark a breathing spot at 3,450m. This first stage should take 1–1½ hours walking time.

The next stage of the ascent to La Ventana Pass at 4,000m is steeper and quite hard going because of the altitude, although the path is always clear, at times cobbled, at times stepped. Walking time is 1½ hours not counting stops. The boulders framing the pass really do make a dramatic 'window'. The path widens again as it enters El Tisure Valley, south-southeast; dropping to 3,500m altitude at a stone bridge by a sign 'Valle El Tisure'. This point is midway between La Ventana and the house of Juan Félix Sánchez: a 50-minute walk either way.

The path crosses over Quebrada El Potrero (the pasture) on a stone bridge (20 minutes) and continues generally level until the first farmhouse (deserted) of El Tisure (20 minutes); altitude 3,250m. You come to a place with a stone-walled field on either side. Just afterwards, on the right you see Sánchez' farm and low house. The path itself continues another 15 minutes until ending at the chapel. There is plenty of tenting space around, and water from streams, but little protection against wind and cold. When we left the next day, the return to La Ventana pass took double time, but from there down to Mucuchache was just two hours without stops. Alternatively, old paths do exist (via El Castillo) which go east from El Tisure and behind Pico Mucuñique to eventually join the highway to Santo Domingo, but these require more exploration.

Hiking in the Laguna Mucubají area
Forest Leighty
Lying some 50km east of Mérida, this Laguna (a shallow lake or pond) at an altitude of about 3,500m is one of the largest in the Venezuelan Andes. Because of its relatively low elevation it is a good place to get acclimatised while still not being too far from help if severe altitude sickness should develop. There is some pleasant walking in the area.

Getting there Buses run between Mérida and Barinas (to the east of the lake). Get off at the Restaurante Mucubají on the pass between the Barinas and Mérida watersheds. From the restaurant it is a short walk to the Park Guard Post (PGP) where a camping permit can be obtained (no charge). If entering by vehicle just for a day hike no permit is needed but it might be a good idea to check in anyway.

There is a paved road from the PGP to near an abandoned house (now a café and visitors' centre) which is about a kilometre downhill from the PGP. Just before the house there are two areas marked for camping.

Warning You cannot leave any gear, even as big as a tent, unattended if you wish to see it again. Also gear left in a locked vehicle cannot be counted as safe unless, perhaps, the vehicle is parked at the PGP.

Laguna Negra
From the visitors' centre pass the fence that closes the jeep road, and head east. The jeep road has a slight upgrade and just as you are to leave it, the Laguna is visible

below and to the left. On a clear, calm day you may have to look hard to see it. After leaving the jeep road, the trail drops down some 150m until rising a bit to Laguna Negra which lies at about 3,475m, nearly 4km from Laguna Mucubají. Laguna Negra is a beautiful sight on a clear, calm day. The black water forms such a perfect mirror that it essentially disappears and is replaced by the reflection of the trees on the mountainside above the lagoon. Just as the trail reaches the lagoon there is a flat area much used for camping – it even has a trash basket. The trail to this point is passable to horses and many Venezuelan tourists use horses which are available for rental across from the Restaurante Mucubají.

Laguna Negra to Laguna Los Patos The trail continues on the right (west) side of the lagoon. The best trail stays slightly above the lake but there are numerous tracks that follow the edge of the lagoon, usually to have a steep exit back to the upper trail. When the head of the lagoon is reached, there are additional campsites. To continue, you must search out the trail which enters the woods without crossing the stream feeding the lagoon. Very shortly after leaving the lagoon there is a clearing with the ruins of an old house. The trail continues fairly steeply upward on a rocky path which occasionally skirts the cascade coming down from Laguna Los Patos. There is a total elevation gain of 275m and then a drop of about 60m. After reaching the amphitheatre of Laguna Los Patos, the main trail turns to the left – there is also a faint trail circling the lagoon basin to the right. There is still a bit of distance before actually reaching the lagoon which has a rather small water area.

Laguna Los Patos, lying at 3,688m, is named for the small Andean ducks (*patos*) which will usually be seen here. Near the mouth of the lagoon there is a rather uneven campsite with an existing fire area, but do not count on cooking on a fire. (It is illegal to cut trees and brush which do not regenerate at this altitude.) Somewhat further away from the lagoon (north) there are numerous campsites.

As a diversion while camping here, there is an unnamed 4,200m peak directly east of the Laguna that can be climbed as a tough scramble. Although this requires slight care in route finding, it does yield a good view.

Pico Mucuñuque area

Pico Mucuñuque at 4,600m is one of the highest peaks in the northern end of the Sierra Nevada Park. The northwestern slope of the peak forms a giant bowl which provides considerable mountain scenery and a possible route to the peak itself. A good trail leads to this area.

From the visitors' centre near the shore of Laguna Mucubají, take the trail due south that dips down through the small ravine alongside the house. There is also a trail to the west that circles the lagoon. Shortly after leaving the house a trail junction will be reached: take the right-hand fork which leads up the flat meadow-like stream course of the lagoon feeder. Cross the stream twice, heading toward the head of the stream at the Cascades where the trail begins its climb. Permission can be obtained (at the entry PGP) to camp at the Cascades area (about 3,627m) or at various higher campsites (request permission for '*campamento arriba de las cascadas*').

From the Cascades the trail climbs steadily and usually not too steeply until it reaches a large headwall which is distinguished by a white gully coming steeply down the middle of it. During this climb a couple of pleasant potential campsites will be passed. Just before the headwall at about 4,023m is the last good campsite at which water is readily available.

Until the headwall is reached, the trail is very distinct and easy to follow, but here it splits with one branch going very steeply up the white gully. By searching, you can find the other branch going around to the left of the headwall, up the stream course valley. Part way up, it turns to the right to rejoin the branch up the gully. In the morning this way is dry to pass because it is frozen but by afternoon it is wet and so it is probably preferable to descend via the gully straight ahead.

From here you are really in the mountains and have left most vegetation and flat spots below you. However, there is still a reasonably well-defined trail, although rather steep, heading generally southward – do not wander to the west. Eventually, after some steep climbing, the trail ends in a saddle at 4,540m between two false summits of the Pico. The true summit can be seen some 120m higher and a bit over a kilometre off to the left. On a clear day there is an excellent view of Picos Humboldt and Bolívar to the southwest.

Although it is only 7km from Laguna Mucubají to Pico Mucuñuque (according to a signpost at the abandoned house), the steep and rough trail and the elevation makes this an exceptionally long hike to consider doing in a one day, particularly since the park rules call for exiting by 18.00 when the entry gate is locked.

Laguna Victoria

This lagoon was originally formed behind a glacial moraine which later broke open. This gap has now been dammed, restoring the pretty lake. It is used as a trout hatchery so no fishing is allowed.

To reach Laguna Victoria from Laguna Mucubají, start as to Laguna Negra past the fence headed east on the jeep road. Very soon, 0.5km or so, there is a road leading down to the left whereas the Laguna Negra route continues on the road slightly upward and to the right. This jeep road continues downward almost all the way to Laguna Victoria which is at about 3,260m, thus a descent of around 335m. The road goes in switchbacks and is never steep. It is generally within a forested (reforested) area with various views of Laguna Victoria, but near the lake the road turns to a trail which in one spot is not too clear. Alternatively, the Laguna can be reached via the road from Laguna Mucubají toward Santo Domingo (via Barinas route) by parking near the Km10 post and hiking up (with about 60m of elevation gain) to the lagoon.

Crossing the Sierra Nevada to Barinas
Paul Rouche

A long, hard trek but very varied, this exceptionally rewarding hike takes you through two states, Mérida and Barinas, starting from Mucuchíes at 3,000m elevation and ending on the southern slopes of the Sierra Nevada at about 400m. Because of the initial altitude and the very long descent, it must be considered a hard walk of some four days. The trail follows a road to Gavidia, then an old Spanish mule path over the Andes, down to Caño Grande and the Barinas highway.

In my view this little-known trek is one of the best because of the open *páramo*, abundant streams, magnificent cloudforests on the Andes' southern slopes, and absence of people. Once you leave Gavidia, there are at most a dozen farmers' cottages along the way, and many of these are uninhabited. April, the month I chose for this trek, is not the rainy season, and although higher elevations were cold, the lower slopes were hot, dry and short on shade, making the last day's hike extra tiring.

Getting there Buses and *por puestos* to Apartaderos leave from Mérida several times daily, stopping at Mucuchíes on the way. If you have a car, ask for the *camino* to Mocao and Gavidia, leaving the Transandean highway between Mucuchíes and San Rafael. The road is steep but serviceable year-round by jeep.

The first stage, from Mucuchíes to Gavidia, takes about 2½ hours walking, not counting stops. From Mucuchíes' central square where there is a hospital, a

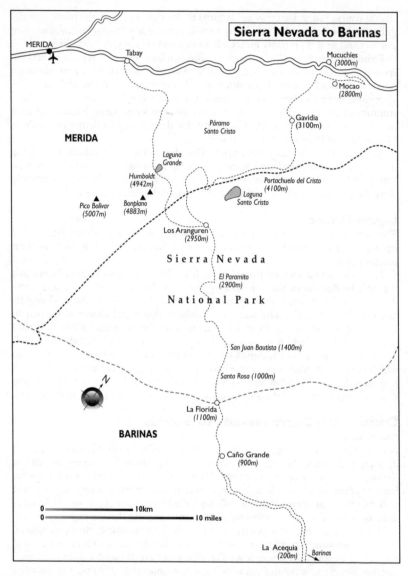

cobbled road goes down, bordering the cemetery, to the Chama River, here more like a stream. It is a short walk on cobblestones from the bridge up to the village of Mocao, altitude 2,800m. Go through Mocao, passing the chapel and straggling houses. The road parallels the valley for another 35–40 minutes. You will see the small Gavidia River coming down from the left; it passes under the road. At this point, the road winds steeply up the Gavidia *quebrada* or ravine. A hike of 1¼hrs brings you to Gavidia, taking the right fork at a high roadside chapel. At 3,100m altitude, Gavidia's main crops are potatoes, carrots and garlic. Small fields, stone terraces and hilly pastures are shaded by stands of tall trees. The narrow valley is watered by Las Piñuelas creek, crossed by a bridge.

Allow some three hours for the second stage up to the Portachuelo or pass. From Gavidia, follow the jeep track for half an hour to its end at a steep rise. The trail to the *páramo* now borders stone walls and barbed-wire fences; you go through log gates three times. Many small watercourses cross the path, the way is rockier, the trees fewer and the temperature colder. A lonely cowherd is probably the only person you'll meet.

At the top a stone wall marks the pass of Portachuelo del Cristo (over 4,100m). Without crossing the wall, keep right and a few metres higher you will find a track heading southwest among the low shrubs and velvety *frailejón* plants. The *páramo* invites tenting during the dry season, December to April, although temperatures drop to freezing. We found frost when we woke up. This is fine country for stretching your legs: you can wander in any direction over the moor-like hills.

Beginning the descent southward, allow 3½ hours down to Los Aranguren where there is shelter. First, the sandy *páramo* track passes a large lagoon on the left; altitude 3,800m. This is just one of many glacial *lagunas*. Small streams cross the path from the right; they flow south, ultimately to the Orinoco basin as this is a watershed. At the first fork in the path (about an hour), go right; steep slopes alternate with a few level spots. After another hour, for the first time the trail crosses a small river from the left; the path soon comes to cobblestones, then drops sharply along a ravine. The next fork (left) leads to a log bridge and below is the cottage known as 'Altico de Los Aranguren'. From here down to the bridge at Los Aranguren ravine is a pleasant walk of about 1¼ hours. The way, at times cobbled, follows the river closely. If you are in need of shelter, you will be glad to see the deserted house which was once Los Aranguren Inn; altitude 2,950m. In the meadow above the bridge are stone corrals, perhaps once used for mules.

Cloudforest to Santa Rosa

The next good stopping point is at El Puente, a log bridge (about 3–3½ hours). The path leads southeast from Los Aranguren between two boulders; it crosses many watercourses including the Sinigüís, and at least three field gates. At El Paramito (altitude 2,900m), where there is an inhabited house, for a change, go through two more gates. Below are splendid views of the Sinigüís Valley. In half an hour the trail suddenly enters cloudforest (2,600m) and skirts a small cascade. The forest track is uneven underfoot but the ferns, trees and orchids are of constant interest. There is a plank bridge over a clear, rocky river (2,000m altitude) and, just beyond, a clearing which makes a useful campsite. Nearby is a small waterfall called El Chorro.

Continuing down (another 4 hours), the next stage goes to Santa Rosa community. For the first 2 hours you go up and down through the forest, crossing ravines, emerging into patches of bracken only to re-enter the forest. At 1,400m altitude there is a grassy spot (suitable for a tent) called San Juan Bautista, and an abandoned *rancho*. Overgrown by bracken, the path leads to the right of the hut (southeast) and comes shortly to a Y; take the left-hand path. This reaches the hamlet of Santa Rosa in about 1½ hours, crossing *quebradas* and fences and skirting cottages four times. Take no forks until a right hand at a Y less than ten minutes above Santa Rosa, a hamlet of about eight houses and one street. There is a field on the outskirts which has space for tents. At 1,000m elevation, the air is now hot.

Mule path to Caño Grande

The path onward to La Florida takes about 3 hours, and from there to Caño Grande another 2 hours minimum. Passing *conucos* or plots of maize and yuca, the mule path dips and then rises, for a change. The countryside is less wild and you will see coffee bushes. At the first fork (30 minutes), keep right (up); at the second in another 12 minutes, go left; just before a house on a rise among coffee bushes (La Loma, 1,250m), go right, still climbing; 35–40 minutes beyond is a small ravine with water; altitude 1,280m. Since no people live nearby, the water is clean. I recommend you fill your canteens here because in dry weather you may not find water for another 3½ hours, until you reach Caño Grande. Shortly, the trail dips through a tall and very beautiful deciduous forest, only to rise steeply to a level clearing (good tenting) at 1,280m where there is a hut. This is Los Pozos, which means water holes, although I found them dry.

My walking time down to the next deserted hut called La Florida was 70 minutes without stopping. Shortly after leaving Los Pozos, the trail re-enters the woods and meets another path; take the left hand, going down. Within five minutes at a second Y, go left along a ridge, and then zigzag down. Half an hour later, the trail, still dropping through woods and climbing again, meets a third fork; go right for La Florida.

Allow 2–2½ hours for the drop from 1,100m to Caño Grande at 900m. The trail traverses deforested slopes in a southeast direction. With its ups and downs, hot sun and skimpy shade, it is wearying, although wide. You can see the Caño Grande road below on the flat. A single farmhouse marks Caño Grande.

Down to Barinas

The final stage to La Acequia on the Barinas highway is a mostly level march of at least 4 hours but there are shade trees and streams – although the water is no longer pure because more people live here. Follow the old mule track past Caño Grande and continue through gates, entering a coffee plantation (there is a spring in the woods up to the right). The track meets other watercourses, the occasional house, and in 50 minutes comes to a wider cart track which becomes a proper earth road; go to the left along this (600m altitude). In 15 minutes it fords a wide ravine, the Quebrada La Magdalena.

The next farmhouse, on the right at the top of a rise, for me marks Civilisation with a capital C because it has electricity and the owners, who grow oranges, have a car which I once hired as a taxi. (I also camped in their field.) From there, the road continues wide and flat for another 13km to reach the paved road. This, following the Acequia River, finally gets to La Acequia village (200m) on the national highway. You are 58km west of Barinas, the state capital, and there should be both buses and por puestos.

Back country roads to 'pueblos del sur'

Continuing west of Mérida, the Transandina descends the Chama gorge to Estanques, hot and dry, then rises to Páramo La Negra before going to San Cristóbal, a distance of 235km, some 5 hours by bus.

South of the Transandean highway, roads rise from the Chama gorge and cross the *páramo* to remote *pueblos del sur* where distances are better gauged by hours than by kilometres, and rustic guesthouses greet walkers and bikers. The country people are hard-working farmers; you have only to ask for help to be given shelter. (Map 5941 of Mérida State.)

Mérida–El Morro–Los Nevados

Por puestos from Mérida to El Morro cost $5; they leave by the bridge over the Río Chama at the west end of the city, from Santa Juana district south of the airport. The *por puestos* to Los Nevados ($10) leave from Plaza Las Heroínas. All go by the same route south of Santa Juana where there is a petrol station. The paved road rises steeply on arid slopes to the forest proper at 2,400–3,000m elevation. Beyond the pass the southern road is hot and dry, descending to the farming village of El Morro at 1,700m. (Ask in El Morro about another jeep road leading west to **Acequias** and the **San José** road.) There are two humble guesthouses in El Morro. A road continues south of El Morro to Aricagua, 6 hours.

Those continuing to Los Nevados by jeep face another 3 hours on a precarious track, passable only in the dry season. In Los Nevados almost every other house offers bed and one or two meals at very low cost (shared bathroom, some with hot water). The best *posadas*, the **Bella Vista** and **Guamanchi Expeditions**, cost $9–$10. Many travellers make the circle back to Mérida by taking a mule to the *teleférico*.

La González–San José–Mucutuy

This is a very steep road up from the *Transandina* at La González, 20km west of Mérida. The first part parallels the Tostós ravine. On a high ridge there is a place called Tierra Negra, a famous launching point for paragliders. (Higher, a rutted road joins from the left, coming from Acequias and El Morro.)

The road improves with trees for shade as it reaches the tiny, neat village of San José, its two dozen white houses and church set around the plaza. **Posada San José** has eight plain rooms with bath and hot water. It is run by Alonso who also organises the muleback excursions to Tostós, 7–8km. His brothers left San José to live in Mérida; for reservations you can call Alonso's sister Siuly, tel: (074) 639782. By crossing a stream beyond the end of the main street, you will come to **Posada Mochabá**, where the owner Martín has two rooms for guests in his home and a diminutive, steep-roofed cottage, also with bath; $5 a person. Martín fishes trout in the nearby lagoon, and cooks them for guests.

Higher, at about 3,500m elevation on the cloudy, cool Páramo de San José, plants make a colourful carpet of many species of *frailejón*. The road then descends the cordillera's southern side by way of La Veguilla hamlet and continues to the well-kept village of **Mucutuy**. Guest rooms (and meals, given notice), are very cheap in old houses with shared bathrooms: **Pensión La Estancia**, beyond the church; **Pensión Mucutuyana**, a bit farther, four rooms, hot showers. **Posada La Urbina** is a fine old house with eight guest rooms and a new part with six more. The road does not end here; 22km farther is the next *pueblo del sur*, **Mucuchachí**, but it is bigger, hotter and as yet has no guesthouse.

From Mucuchachí, a village of 2,000 people but few charms, a dodgy road leads west 22km to **Canaguá** (see *Estanques–El Molino–Canaguá*).

Pueblo Nuevo del Sur

The road to this village, 7km, crosses the Chama River at Puente Real, about 12km west of La González. The corkscrew ascent is not for the faint of heart as the narrow road climbs above the eroded Chama gorge. A 'rain shadow' in these mountains keeps the land arid. Far from a new village, Pueblo Nuevo appears quite old, with cobbled streets and tiled houses huddled round the church. There are one or two *abastos* selling basic supplies and beer. One señora makes meals, and one guesthouse, **La Posada Doña Eva**, offers four simple rooms at $4 on two floors around a patio.

A special date in Pueblo Nuevo is May 22, the fiesta of the 'Locos de Santa Rita' in which costumed men perform a ritual battle in front of the church.

From this route going south over the *páramo* eventually to reach **Chocantá**, another high road has been opened east to **San José**.

Estanques–El Molino–Canaguá

The gorge of the Chama drops dramatically to 442m at Estanques, quite a hot *pueblo*. Here the Chama turns north to Lake Maracaibo. To the south, slopes are heavily

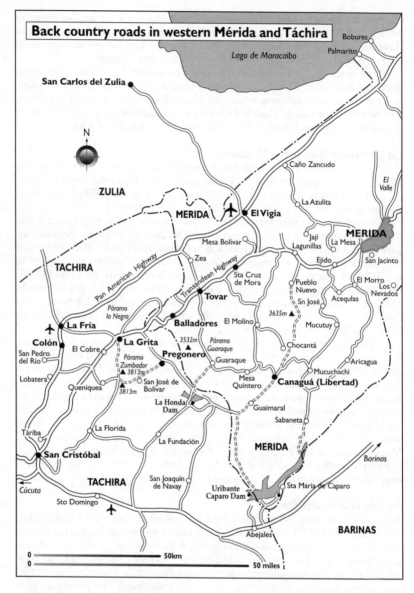

Back country roads in western Mérida and Táchira

Lago de Maracaibo

Bobures
Palmarito

San Carlos del Zulia

N

ZULIA

Caño Zancudo

El Valle

La Azulita

MERIDA

El Vigia

MERIDA

Mesa Bolívar

Jají
Lagunillas   La Mesa

San Jacinto

TACHIRA

Zea

Ejido

Pan American Highway

Sta Cruz de Mora

El Morro
Los Nevados

Pueblo Nuevo

Transandean Highway

Tovar

Sn José   Acequias

3635m

Páramo la Negra

Balladores   El Molino

Mucutuy

La Fría

3532m   Páramo Guaraque

Chocantá

Colón   El Cobre   La Grita

Páramo Zumbador ▲ 3813m

Pregonero

Guaraque

Aricagua

San Pedro del Río

Mucuchachí

Lobatera

Queniquea

3813m   San José de Bolívar

Mesa Quintero   Canaguá (Libertad)

La Honda Dam

Guaimaral

Táriba   La Florida

Sabaneta

La Fundación

MERIDA

San Cristóbal

Barinas

Cúcuta

TACHIRA

San Joaquín de Navay

Uribante Caparo Dam   Sta Maria de Caparo

Sto Domingo

BARINAS

Abejales

0 ———————— 50km
0 ———————————— 50 miles

eroded where a 'rain shadow' keeps the land arid. In Estanques look for a paved road up behind the little colonial chapel. Asphalted as far as El Molino, the road (which is joined by the Santa Cruz de Mora route) ascends through four climate zones: baking scrubland with cactus; subtropical slopes cultivated with bananas, coffee and pineapples, evergreen cloudforest, and *páramo* often chilled by dense fog.

El Molino is so small it has scarcely three streets, a church and spotless white houses. Beyond El Molino some distance you pass El Rincón de los Toros where black bulls are bred for bullfights. **Canaguá** (Libertad) is about 75km from Estanques in an attractive and prosperous coffee-growing area, pleasantly cool.

District capital, the town is the most important of the *pueblos del sur* having some 2,500 inhabitants, as well as a hospital, cultural centre, gasoline pump, bakery on Plaza Bolívar, and a number of *posadas*. The best one is 2km beyond town: **Posada Turística Canaguá**, tel: (075) 681055, five rooms with bath. From here you can circle back to the north via Mucuchachí and San José.

You can go west on yet more country roads to reach **Mesa de Quintero** (two guesthouses), and then north to **Guaraque** (one guesthouse) where there are two routes: west to **Pregonero** in Táchira State, and north to **Tovar** to rejoin the Transandean highway. The last part of this route is paved, crossing beautiful cloudforests on the Páramo Guaraque, 3,523m.

TACHIRA STATE

Between Bailadores (altitude 1,750m) in Mérida State and La Grita (altitude 1,457m) in Táchira rises beautiful **Páramo La Negra**. The Transandean Highway is an entertainment in itself as it loops up to 2,800m. At the crest, the road splits into two routes, both to La Grita: the left, lower and faster, and the right (the Transandean) across the 3,000m high *páramo*, in an exhilarating series of zigzags with spectacular views and little villages. Either way, it is worth an early start to beat the fog.

La Grita, a prosperous farm centre of some 15,000 inhabitants, was founded in 1578 on a *mesa* above fertile alluvial terraces. La Grita is 83km from San Cristóbal.

Entering by the Transandean highway, you come first to the large **Liceo Jáuregui**, a nationally known military prep school. Of La Grita's three plazas, the uppermost is Plaza Sucre. Here a two-floor colonial house, the **Balcón de La Grita**, is noted as the place where Bolívar began his Admirable Campaign in 1838. Next is Plaza Jáuregui surrounded by a convent school and the twin-spired **Iglesia de Los Angeles**, built on the earthquake ruins of an early monastery. The **Iglesia del Espíritu Santo**, dating from 1836, has been remodelled after various earthquakes. Its 17th-century image, the **Santo Cristo de La Grita**, is venerated as miraculous, specifically during August 6–10 festivities.

Drop by the **mercado** to see all the farmers' vegetables, plus wood crafts and pottery. Near Plaza Jáuregui, the market is open morning and afternoon but the earlier you go the better, especially on Saturdays.

Hostería Los Naranjos is recommended as a clean, simple place to stay, Calle 2 No 371, tel: (077) 82854, 82678.

San Cristóbal

Many roads lead to San Cristóbal. The capital of Táchira State sits on a *mesa* at the western edge of Venezuela's Andes at 825m altitude; its river, the Torbes, flows to the Orinoco. This city of some 300,000 people owes its growth as a centre of commerce to roads from the southern plains, the Andes, Zulia, central Venezuela, and Colombia, only 40km away. Indeed, San Cristóbal's flavour is reminiscent of Colombia: industrious, orderly, clean and quiet in comparison with most Venezuelan cities.

The annual **Feria de San Sebastián** changes all this. For two weeks following January 20, the city's saint's day, there are processions, parties, bull fights, folklore and cultural events, also an agricultural show and bicycle races. If you plan to visit at this time, be sure to be in place well ahead.

San Cristóbal is different in many ways. It was never sacked by pirates or racked by Independence wars. There are few colonial structures (the Iglesia San Sebastián and other buildings fell victim to earthquakes). It had no powerful citizens, no *latifundistas* or holders of huge estates. For 200 years after it was founded in 1561 as a station between Pamplona and the Sierra Nevada, little happened; the poor

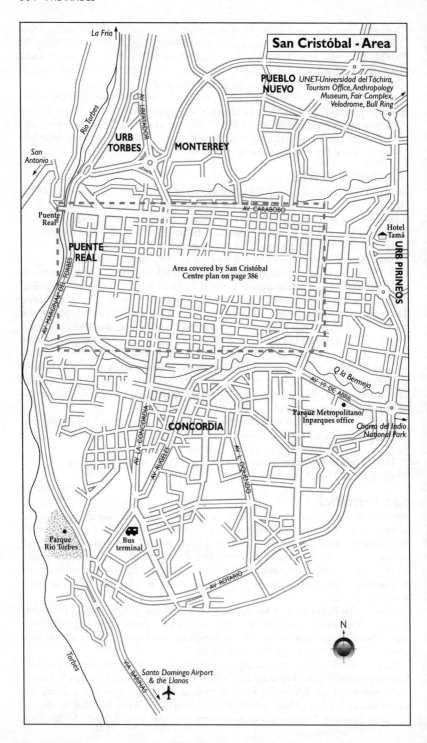

San Cristóbal - Area

La Fría

Río Torbes

AV LIBERTADOR

San Antonio

PUEBLO NUEVO

UNET-Universidad del Táchira, Tourism Office, Anthropology Museum, Fair Complex, Velodrome, Bull Ring

URB TORBES

MONTERREY

AV CARABOBO

Puente Real

Hotel Tamá

PUENTE REAL

URB PIRINEOS

AV MARGINAL DEL TORBES

Area covered by San Cristóbal Centre plan on page 386

Q la Bermeja

AV 19 DE ABRIL

Parque Metropolitano/ Inparques office

AV LA CONCORDIA

CONCORDIA

Chorro del Indio National Park

AV RUGELES

AV L OQUENDO

Parque Río Torbes

Bus terminal

AV ROTARIO

N

Torbes

VIA BARINAS

Santo Domingo Airport & the Llanos

agricultural village remained subject politically to Nueva Granada, today's Colombia. The introduction of coffee in the late 18th century was Táchira's biggest pre-Independence event.

The Spanish settlement on Indian lands was closer to Bogotá and had no road communication with Caracas. The journey to Caracas took many days by way of the Táchira, Zulia and Catatumbo rivers to Lake Maracaibo, then by sea. This was the route for coffee exports (from Colombia, too). A small railway was built to the Catatumbo in 1894. In 1925 the first road linking Caracas with Táchira, the Transandean route, was opened; by 1960 paving was still incomplete. In 1955 the lowland Pan American highway was built south of Lake Maracaibo, and the Llanos highway came soon after.

Táchira, the country's leading coffee producer, has one of the country's highest rural ratios with villages widely scattered among hills. This accounts in part for the big Colombian immigration as coffee growers hire migrants for picking. Besides coffee, the state grows much of its own food starting with rice and sugar cultivated around Ureña, bananas, papaya and other fruit near Lake Maracaibo, and potatoes and dairy products in the mountains.

Two presidents of Venezuela and two dictators came from Táchira: Dictator Cipriano Castro (1899–1908), born in Capacho; Dictator Juan Vicente Gómez (1908–35), born in La Mulera; President Eleazar López Contreras (1935–41), born in Queniquea; and Carlos Andrés Pérez, born in Rubio, president in 1974–79 and 1989–93.

Getting there and away
By air
Although the official airport is Santo Domingo, about 40km southeast on the Llanos highway, at press time it had only one daily flight to **Caracas** by Avensa, $85, and another to **Bogotá**. The San Antonio airport near the border offers many daily flights on weekdays to **Caracas**, and local connections to six other cities. The drive to San Antonio, 40km, takes an hour.

By bus
The big concrete and brick **Terminal de Pasajeros** is at the south end of Av 5 which becomes Av La Concordia, towards the Barinas exit from town. Buses to Mérida via the Panamericana leave throughout the day, until 18.00. The Llanos route is preferred by coaches going to **Caracas**, 825km (13 hours). Expresos Bolivarianos leave every half hour for **San Antonio** and **Cúcuta** in Colombia. Be aware that *servicio ejecutivo* in fast air-conditioned coaches means windows are shut and curtained. Expresos Los Llanos has started a 'buscama' or 'busbed' service on new coaches with air conditioning, toilet, carpets and telephone; for information, tel: 461035. Remember that air conditioning on express buses may make a sweater or jacket necessary.

Where to stay
The area telephone code for San Cristóbal is (076)
High rates prevail during the Feria de San Sebastián, in the last half of January.

San Cristóbal's leading hotel, **Hotel Tamá**, is in Los Pirineos district at the foot of the mountain, tel: 558366, fax: 561667. It has ten floors, gardens, olympic pool, spacious rooms, and restaurants. Single, double $65.

A dozen comfortable hotels in the $20–30 range (double) are strung along Av Libertador, paralleling the Río Torbes on the way north to the Transandean and Pan American routes. **Hotel Jardín**, tel: 431555, 434293; restaurant, quiet *cabañas*

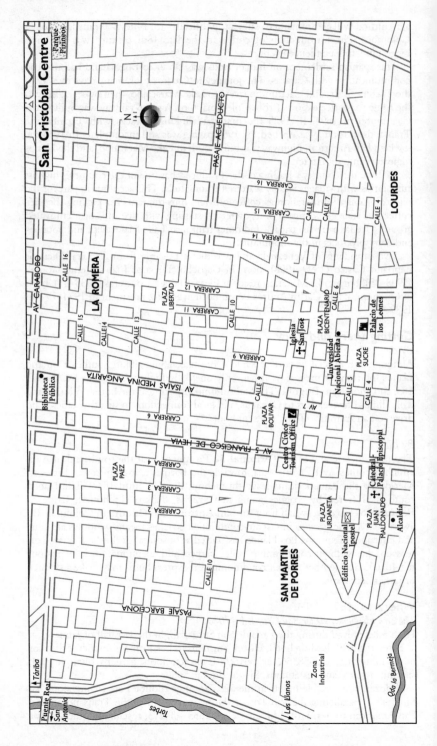

on the upper side. **Motel Las Lomas** on the river side, tel: 435775; 60 units, restaurant, pool. **Hotel Palermo**, tel: 439809; pool, restaurant, disco, air conditioning. On the river side, **Hotel Hamburgo**, Av Libertador, 50m north of Redoma del Educador, tel: 432922; single $15, double $18. Opposite, **Hotel Incret** via Urb Las Lomas behind the Casa Sindical, tel: 431794; double $20.

Respectable downtown hotels all have bathrooms with hot water. The **Bella Vista**, Calle 9 at Carrera 9, tel: 437866, has 40 standard rooms; single $14. The **Horizonte**, Carrera 4 at Calle 7, tel: 430011/5794, fax: 430492, is a ten-storey commercial hotel which has been kept up well; restaurant, 70 rooms, single $9, double $11. The restaurant and hotel **Parador del Hidalgo**, Calle 7 between Carreras 9 and 10, tel: 432839, has simple, clean rooms; single $7, double $12. **El Cid**, Carrera 6, two blocks north of Plaza Bolívar, tel: 435380, is seedy but slightly back from the street, serviceable; double $9. Among old, cheap hotels near the Cathedral is the **Hotel Ejecutivo**, Calle 6 at Carrera 3, tel: 446298, adequate; and the **Andorra**, Carrera 4 near Calle 5, basic; single $7.

Near the bus terminal is **Hotel Korinu**, Carrera 6 just up from Av. La Concordia, tel: 463706; restaurant, 70 rooms; double $20. In La Concordia, south of the centre, is **Posada Don Manuel**, tel: 478082, No 1-104 Carrera 10 at Calle 1-Av 19 de Abril; in a family home, two rooms with bath and hot shower and two with shared bath; $10 single, $12 double; kitchen privileges.

Where to eat

La Vaquera is one of the best steak restaurants in San Cristóbal and perhaps the country; follow Av Libertador north just past Motel Las Lomas. Nearby is another good steak house, the **Casa Pueblo**. You get good beef also at **La Posada del Leñador**, a bit fancier, on Pasaje Acueducto, an uphill street between Calles 10-11.

You will be in ice-cream heaven in **El Che-Lito**, Carrera 16 at Calles 20-21. On Carrera 20, there's **El Tostonazo**, good for Mexican food. On Carrera 24, **Restaurant Brocoli** is great on eggplant and mushroom dishes; it's in the Centro Comercial San Cristóbal by Iglesia El Angel. These places are about ten blocks from Hotel Tamá.

Information

Ask for a city *plano* or map at the state tourism booth on entering San Cristóbal from the Llanos. If you miss their working hours go to the National Guard checkpoint, *alcabala*, at the highway turn for Rubio. Or call the **Oficina Regional de Turismo**, Complejo Ferial, tel: (076) 562421/2805. They have a booth in Plaza Bolívar.

The **CANTV** telecommunications centre is on Calle 11, a block down from Plaza Libertad. This is the place to make overseas calls, or send and receive faxes.

Inparques HQ are in Parque Metropolitano near the top of Av 19 de Abril, tel: (076) 465216.

What to see

Main streets run parallel to the Río Torbes. Downtown *avenidas* and *carreras* run north–south and *calles* east–west. The **tourist office**, tel: 449171, is on Plaza Bolívar, ground floor of the Centro Cívico, a graceless modern structure overwhelming the plaza. Also, the state **Cámara de Turismo** has a desk in Oficina 5-13, piso 5. On the north side of Plaza Bolívar is a handsome old (1907) building, now the **Ateneo**, a cultural centre with a library, art galleries and theatre.

The imposing twin-spired **Cathedral** is at the heart of historic San Cristóbal on Plaza Maldonado, Carrera 3 at Calle 4. Built of brick in 1688, the church was destroyed by earthquake and rebuilt circa 1908; look inside for the statue of **San Sebastián**, martyred by arrows. The plaza is dedicated to city founder Juan de Maldonado. On its north side the aging **Edificio Nacional** is occupied by courts of law and public offices. It takes up a whole block, also giving on to Plaza Urdaneta. Lawyers occupy many fine old houses nearby.

If you walk up seven blocks you come to **Plaza Sucre** and the block-long **Palacio de Los Leones** named for its rooftop lions, favourite icon of Eustoquio Gómez who finished this government palace circa 1920. He was appointed president of Táchira by his cousin and dictator Juan Vicente Gómez and was, if possible, more tyrannical.

The city's newest plaza is really a double square, **Plaza Libertad**. It has an amphitheatre and a pantheon, designed by Fruto Vivas, containing the remains of citizens who fought for freedom.

The **Complejo Ferial**, the spacious fairgrounds, sports and exhibition complex, are at the city's top near the foot of the mountains, reached by way of Av. España and Av. Universidad. It is worth a trip to the Oficina de Turismo headquarters, tel: (077) 562805/2421, to ask for the latest pamphlets, maps or information on *posadas*. The **bull ring** is here, also the stadium and velodrome for cyclists.

The **Museo del Táchira**, several kilometres from the centre on Av Universidad north of the fairgrounds, is housed in the newly restored Hacienda de Paramillo, opposite the Corporación Desarrollo del Suroeste. The one-floor colonial building, formerly a convent school, devotes salons to Andean archaeology, folklore, history and art. Open Tue–Sun 08.00–12.00, 14.00–17.30.

Further afield

What makes the mountains of Táchira so interesting to botanists and birders is a break dropping to 200m between the Venezuelan and Colombian Andes. As the international border lies west of this depression, flora and fauna in the **Parque Nacional Tamá**, an extension of the Colombian cordillera, differ significantly from eastern sierras. This makes the park fantastic for birding. In addition, the park guards are the nation's best. The park is reached via Rubio, Las Delicias, and finally the remote village of Betania in the southwest. Buses travel this route, paved as far as Las Delicias, twice daily from San Cristóbal. Campers should come prepared for cold or wet weather; dry season is best.

Hills surrounding San Cristóbal make almost any direction a panoramic route. Averaging 800m elevation, a southwest road passes the first oil well in Venezuela, and the first and best coffee area in Táchira.

Santa Ana, Alquitrana, Rubio

Head south on the Llanos route to a secondary, unpaved road at Km21.7: turn southwest by the Inparques sign for Balneario Río Negro and cross the river. If it is a sunny day, take your swimsuit. This dirt road continues to **Santa Ana** (good birding everywhere). First, in 7km an old sign on the right indicates La Palmacera, an area of 'unbelievably rich' biodiversity. Walk up 2km to the Inparques house (where it is possible to stay with prior permission).

Take the short detour to Santa Ana along slopes clothed with green coffee bushes. The ripe red beans, called *cerezas*, are sun-dried in yards or on the road. The entrance to Santa Ana is marked by a cross and a little walled park with a bronze deer, hunter and dogs telling the story of how this site was found 150 years ago. The town church is surprising for its painted ceiling, walls and intricately decorated pillars.

Rejoining the road to Rubio, in 10km you come to a small but nationally known site, the first oil well drilled in Venezuela, in **Parque La Petrólea** or La

Alquitrana. Here a coffee grower formed a company in 1878 and for years exploited an oil seep on his plantation; it still seeps today. An old pump, truck and the 19th-century drilling rig are curios surrounded by a beautiful park with forest, meadow, stream, picnic shelters and toilets.

La Petrólea, part of Parque Nacional Tamá, is one of the best-kept small parks in Venezuela. There is a suspension bridge, *puente colgante*, where people swim, and the remains of a Spanish road, the old Camino Real from Bogotá which is said to go to Santa Ana following the Río Chiquito. The road's entrance is opposite the Restaurant La Petrólea.

Rubio, 11km further at the confluence of three rivers, is the place where coffee was first grown in the region. The town is named after the coffee planter, Gervasio Rubio, who came here in 1794. The picturesque colonial part of Rubio is called Pueblo Viejo where the Caparo and Capacho rivers join; altitude 830m. Across a series of bridges and up cobbled streets, charming old houses and shops with wide eaves are being restored. Rubio is a market town and Saturday is the big day as hundreds of shoppers crowd the marketplace by Plaza Urdaneta.

There are hotels in Rubio: in the centre, **Hostería Roma**, tel: (076) 623112, and **Hotel Carlama**, tel: 624770, are standard choices.

From Rubio a good road continues west then north 29km to San Antonio. Also, a more direct road goes northeast back to San Cristóbal, 20km; still another road leads north to Capacho.

San Pedro del Río

The popularity of this immaculate village in its beautiful valley has soared since the opening of the new freeway north of the capital, putting it at less than 45 minutes from San Cristóbal. San Pedro, between San Juan de Colón and Michelena, is a few kilometres west on the road to Ureña. The rivers of its name are two: Quebrada Chirirí and Río Lobaterita. On weekends San Pedro is invaded by people from the capital who come to eat or dance at two capacious *criollo* restaurants.

What makes San Pedro unique is not its restoration but the dedication of a local doctor, Pedro Granados, who saw his village decline from a prosperous coffee centre, founded in 1840, to a petroleum-age derelict. He called in the colonial-era expert, Graziano Gasparini, to plan its rebirth. The whole village pitched in, and today San Pedro is an example that *Tachirenses* take pride in.

Two cobblestone streets run up and down, and the plaza and church are tranquil oases. There is a small museum, library, a music school and as a consequence a children's band and a student band. Kids also use a basketball court, football field, even a stadium.

Easter is an especially solemn event. Nightly processions begin a week before Holy Thursday, culminating with an all-night vigil; on Holy Friday the stages of the Cross are enacted. A procession and mass mark the annual *fiestas patronales* of St Peter and St Paul, central day June 29, followed by competitions such as the *palo encebado* or greased pole, sack races and *novilladas* in which youths tackle young bulls or cows. Christmas is observed with crèches, carols, hot spicy *calentado* (alcohol) and *candela*, literally fire: a football of kerosene-soaked rags, or a bull-mask lighted in the same manner and borne by a runner in a hurry. On December 30 there is a big fireworks display.

Where to stay

Prices may rise a bit in high season. **La Vieja Escuela**, tel: (077) 93664/720, Calle Real No 3-61, is a two-level house which formerly served as a school; today there are 12 simple rooms with hot water; double bed $12, triple $16. A restaurant provides breakfast. **Posada Paseo La Chiriri**, reservations (076) 449403, Calle Los Morales, above a crafts shop, has four rooms with hot showers; $14 single or double bed, bunk bed $4 a person. **Posada Valparaíso**, tel: (077) 911032, on the mountain sloping down to San Pedro from Route 1, is in a pretty flower-filled enclave with small waterfall and pool. Six rooms with hot showers, for two to four people, $14–$17; meals by request.

In Lobatera, a nearby town on Route No 1, there's an old two-floor house on Plaza Bolívar where **La Posada de Tía Conchita**, tel: (077) 22629, has 11 simple rooms with hot water for $8 double bed, $10 two beds. The family's restaurant is in the patio. Around the corner is the modern **La Piedra del Indio**, tel: (077) 22770, which is small but not typical in the least. Swimming pool, nine rooms with double and single bed, no hot water, $10. There's a large ballroom next door.

Libertad, Independencia (Capacho)

Maps will tell you that two sister towns 18km and 15km west of San Cristóbal are called Libertad and Independencia. In practice, however, people use their old names, **Capacho Viejo** and **Capacho Nuevo**, evidence today of the strong original culture. The Capacho Indians resisted conquest until 1647 when Spaniards gathered some natives to settle this mountain ridge. An earthquake destroyed old Capacho (Libertad) in 1875 and the inhabitants moved 3km east to build a new town (Independencia). They chose new names honouring the Revolution but in fact were stubborn royalists. The geological fault crosses in between.

Route No 1 to the Colombian border follows the pretty, mountainous road through Independencia and traffic can be heavy. Stop right away at the **Plaza Bolívar**, altitude 1,272m. Facing the plaza's lower side, a curious pair of bronze French peasants guard the *cuartel* or army barracks; they have been dubbed La India and El Indio. Like the bronze lions atop the covered market nearby they were brought from France in the early 1900s. At that time dictator Cipriano Castro, who was born in Independencia, ruled Venezuela, having set out from Capacho in 1899 to take control of the government. Castro's museum and mausoleum, an odd cone-shaped monument, is on a lower street to the right. Open Wed–Sun 08.00–12.00, 14.00–17.00.

Take a look at the twin-towered **Iglesia de San Pedro** on the upper side of the plaza. After seeing its wonderfully carved wood pulpit and doors, completed in 1958, you will understand the prevalance of woodworkers in Capacho today. A large crafts school on the main street gives courses in everything from carpentry, ceramics and sculpture to raising earthworms. Just beyond it is the handsome public library.

Crafts and souvenirs of all sorts are sold beside the Intercomunal road running into old Capacho, Libertad, altitude 1,346m. If you miss the **Mercado Artesanal**, open mornings only, take a drive 3km from the church north to Barrio de los Hornos. This is where potters make everything from bricks and tiles to pots and mugs.

Hotel Paraiso, Ranchería de Capacho, tel: (076) 83136, is a reasonable place to stay. It is 10km outside of Independencia on the southeast road to San Cristóbal. Set on a hillside above the road, plain white and blue bungalows have mountain water, hot showers, TV; double $9.

From Libertad it is 21km to San Antonio through increasingly drier and lower hills. Of note is the birthplace of Juan Vicente Gómez, La Mulera. The man who ruled Venezuela as his private ranch for 27 years was born, he said, on July 24 1857, anniversary of Bolívar's birth. The eldest of 13 children (four died early) and with no schooling but his wits, Gómez grew up working the mules and cattle of his family, at 26 taking over the hacienda and businesses on his father's death. He is buried in Maracay where he died in 1935 on December 17 (again the day is subject to controversy), anniversary of the death of his life-long hero, Bolívar.

TRAVEL TO/FROM COLOMBIA
San Antonio
On the east bank of the Táchira River, San Antonio is hot and low (438m). Although the pueblo was founded in 1730, there is little to see here. Most people come to shop, in particular Colombians who get bargains such as subsidised corn flour, gasoline, and some appliances. Buses from both countries go as far as the International Bridge and you just walk across. However, if you are carrying a backpack be advised that you are a target for thieves working in teams. San Antonio is not the only place to cross the frontier but has the best communications, being only 12km from Cúcuta which has a busy airport.

Venezuelans may go as far as Cúcuta and, like Colombian shoppers, need only present identification. Drivers must have car ownership papers.

Getting there and away
By air
San Antonio's busy airport is just north of town on the road to Ureña. Servivensa, Aserca and Aeropostal have a total of eight flights daily (six at weekends) to Caracas. Aserca and Aeropostal also fly to Barcelona, Barquisimeto, Maracaibo, Porlamar, Puerto Ordaz, Valencia. Servivensa's early morning flight from Caracas to Medellín, and afternoon flight from Caracas to Bogotá, make a stop at San Antonio.

Travel agencies, all on San Antonio's main street to the bridge, are helpful if you are travelling in Venezuela but do not sell tickets for Colombian carriers.

By bus
Long-distance coach lines go under the name of *Expresos*. Look for their offices on the main street leading to the bridge. The new Terminal de Pasajeros is located a kilometre down the airport road. Four lines go to Caracas, 825km, leaving in the afternoon; most through buses take 14 hours via the Llanos route. For travel to Mérida, Maracaibo, Barquisimeto, take a bus to the San Cristóbal Terminal de Pasajeros; *por puestos* go there from Calle 5 at Carrera 4.

Where to stay
Half a dozen central hotels provide adequate lodging, topped by **Hotel Don Jorge**, Calle 5 a block east of Plaza Bolívar, tel: (076) 711932, 714089; single $18, double $20, air conditioning. In the same price range is **Hotel Adriático**, Calle 6 and Carrera 6, tel: 713721. **Hotel Colonial**, Carrera 11 near Calle 3, two blocks southwest of Plaza Bolfvar, tel: 713123; fans, double with bath $7. The **Terepaima**, Carrera 6 at Calle 2, tel: 711763, is pretty basic; $4 per person; inexpensive restaurant.

Crossing the border
Leaving or entering Venezuela, travellers need to get passports stamped at the DEX office, Carrera 9 near Calles 6, open from 06.00 to 20.00. Remember that when it is noon in Venezuela the time is 11.00 in Colombia. Tourists of most countries do not need visas for Colombia; on crossing the bridge go to DAS (Immigration) to get stamped in; open 07.00–19.00. DAS also have an office in Cúcuta, 6km, and at Cúcuta airport for air passengers only.

Frequent buses to Cúcuta and *por puesto* taxis, called *colectivos*, leave from the centre of San Antonio, Calle 6, two blocks east of Plaza Bolívar.

Ureña

Ureña, 14km north, is also on the banks of the Táchira River and has a border crossing. The Colombian road also goes to Cúcuta. Ureña is basically a farming town in the midst of irrigated rice and sugarcane plantations. A paved road links Ureña with the Pan American highway at San Juan de Colón.

The **Hotel Aguas Calientes**, 7km along this route, is a good reason for taking this road. Three kinds of thermal waters are piped to 34 rooms, each of which has a walled patio, tub and private garden; there are four rooms without. Gardens with a large pool help to make the spot a pleasant oasis, and you can have a thermal soak for about $1 even if you're not staying. Single $36, double $40, extra bed $4. Book ahead: tel: (076) 872450/58, fax: 871391.

Falcón and Zulia

THE FAR WEST

Falcón State has much to recommend it to travellers.
The island beaches of Parque Nacional Morrocoy attract
Venezuelans and foreigners alike. (For the park, and the
towns of Tucacas and Chichiriviche, see *Chapter 7, The Marine
National Parks*.) The highway continues through hilly country,
mostly hot and increasingly dry, to the state capital of Coro at the
foot of the long isthmus and peninsula of Paraguaná. Coro is the
most important and best conserved of all colonial cities in Venezuela. Following
west, Zulia is the next state and the same highway leads to the bridge across Lake
Maracaibo, the world's richest lake (from oil). On the far side is Maracaibo, state
capital and the country's second largest city. Zulia is home to the Guajiro people,
the nation's best organised ethnic group.

Coro

Founded in 1527, Coro competes with Cumaná as the oldest Spanish city on the
continent. Apparently it was the oldest continuous settlement and, when King
Carlos of Spain signed a decree creating the Province of Venezuela in 1528,
Coro became its capital. Cumaná's founding followed the discovery of pearls on
Cubagua; Indians outraged by slavers forced its removal three times. In Coro,
on the other hand, founder Juan de Ampiés got along well with the local
Caquetíos. They brought water to their village and crops by aqueduct from the
small Coro River. The land, though arid, was healthy and pleasant. *Coro* comes
from the Arawak word for wind. The Pope made Coro South America's first
bishopric in 1531, thus its church became the first cathedral. The missing
ingredient was money.

The first overland expeditions from Venezuela in search of fabled wealth set out
from Coro. Extraordinary in scope and hardship, as well as barbarity, most ended
in death. These gold-seekers were not Spanish but German. By the time Ampiés
founded Coro, Carlos V had made a deal with the banking house of Welser, leasing
them the Province of Venezuela to cover his debts as he had borrowed heavily to
buy the titles of Holy Roman Emperor.

Upon arrival in Coro, Welser's agent, Ambrose Alfinger, arrested Ampiés and
deported him to Curaçao. He then explored Lake Maracaibo and founded the
settlement of Maracaibo. A ruthless killer, Alfinger pursued his golden idol as far
as the Magdalena in Colombia where he was killed by a poison arrow. The next
German governor, Georg Hohemuth of Speier (Jorge Spira) set out with 361
men and got as far as the Río Meta in the Llanos but missed the kingdom of El
Dorado and, starving, returned with a few survivors. Nicholas Federmann got all
the way to Bogotá, only to find Jiménez de Quesada had arrived before him.
German efforts ended in 1545 when Bartholomew Welser and Phillip von

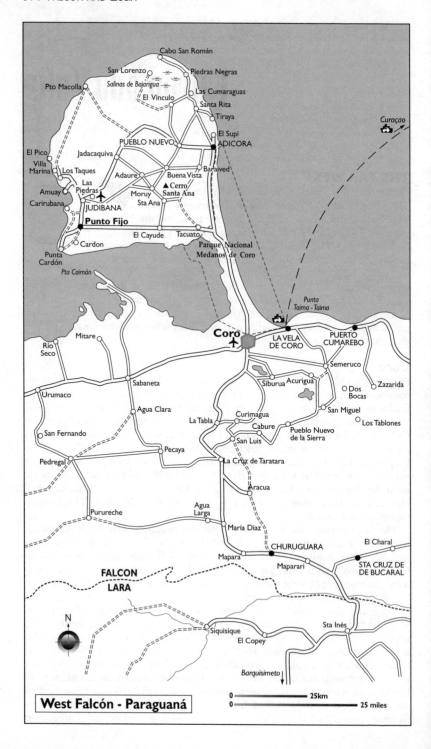

West Falcón - Paraguaná

Hutten were assassinated by Juan de Carvajal who had forged governor's credentials.

Coro, failing to produce wealth, struggled to survive. Some inhabitants, coerced by Carvajal, left with him to founded El Tocuyo (where justice caught up and he was hanged). In 1578 the governor moved to Caracas, in effect taking the capital with him. The bishop did the same in 1637. An English privateer, Christopher Mings, looted and burned Coro as late as 1659, leaving it in smoking ruins. Small wonder it appeared on some maps as 'destroyed'.

Gradually Coro took hold as a supply centre for Curaçao and Aruba through its port, La Vela. Exports were mainly cacao, tobacco, horses and mules. Such commerce continued despite being illegal and the town began to prosper. Most of its important buildings and houses date from the 18th century.

Falcón State is named after Juan Crisóstomo Falcón who was president of Venezuela in 1863–68. General Falcón and his brother-in-law, Ezequiel Zamora, led the federalist cause against the centralist party.

Coro has some 130,000 inhabitants. Average temperature is 28°C with highs over 40°C and minimum under 14°C.

Fairs and folklore Shops in Coro shut on January 2, as well as New Year's Day; this holiday is called **Día del Comerciante** when shopkeepers and merchants organise music, parties and contests on the streets. February 2 is Federation Day; most state offices are closed. The last week in July is filled by Coro's *fiestas patronales*. November is the month of the annual Falcón Exhibition and Fair at the Feria Industrial grounds east of town. In early December the **Feria del Pesebre** stirs high interest in Coro. Competition for the best Christmas crèche includes a live enactment. Choirs, theatre groups, carollers and musical groups vie for honours. Food, arts and crafts are sold.

Information The Tourist Office of Falcón State is on Paseo La Alameda; tel: (068) 511132; fax: 515327; email: sectufal@funfle.org.ve. They publish a folding colour map of the state with information in English on beauty spots, history and hotels.

Getting there
By air
If the airport were any closer to the centre planes would land on Calle Zamora. 'I walked from the airport to the colonial zone, right past Hotel Miranda. When I got off the plane the first thing that struck me was the strong, warm wind, synonymous with Coro, and the clear blue sky.' (Marco Crolla). Avensa flies daily to Caracas by way of Barquisimeto. Aero Falcón, an airtaxi line, tel: (068) 517884, flies to Curaçao, Aruba and Bonaire for $100–120–140 return; higher rates on weekends.

Las Piedras airport about 90km away in Punto Fijo, Paraguaná, has four flights daily to Caracas, others to Maracaibo, Porlamar, Barquisimeto, Santo Domingo. Avensa flies daily to Aruba and Curaçao.

By bus
The Terminal de Pasajeros is on Av Los Médanos, six blocks south of Calle Falcón. Frequent buses to Valencia via Morón, 290km (5 hours); Caracas, 450km (7 hours); and Maracaibo, 255km (4 hours). Less frequent service to Mérida and San Cristóbal (12–13 hours). For the Paraguaná Peninsula, a choice of Adécora on the east coast at 06.00, 08.00, 10.00 and noon, then 15.00 and 18.00; or Punto Fijo on the west, service all day.

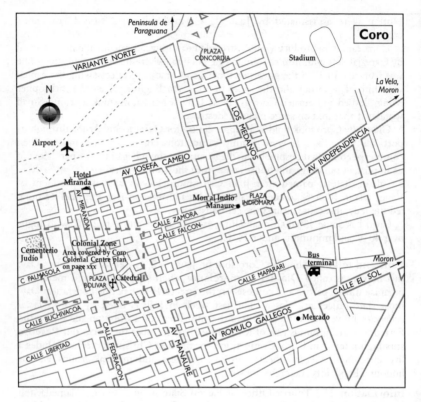

By ferry

Falcón Ferrys have reopened the long-closed route to Curaçao and Aruba with the refurbished *Lusitania Express*, for many years a ferry in Scandinavia and Poland. It offers restaurant, bar, money change, gaming tables, duty-free shops and air conditioning. Coro office: tel: (068) 530520, fax: 531481; also Posada Coro Coro Rico, Intercomunal La Vela; tel: 78517/37; email: ferry@telcel.net.ve. In Caracas, tel: (02) 7628352, fax: 7622864. In Maracaibo, tel/fax: (061) 988892.

From La Vela de Coro the crossing takes 5–6 hours to Curaçao. Sailings leave Venezuela for Curaçao Tuesday, Thursday and Saturday at 08.00, return at 17.00; to Aruba on Wednesday and Friday. Either round trip costs $85 first class, $65 tourist, passengers over 64 years, $68/$52. This does not include 4.5% sales tax or a $14 exit tax. Passengers should be at the port at least three hours before sailing time. You need a valid passport. Cars ($100) require police inspection or *experticia* and international civil insurance.

Where to stay/eat

The area telephone code for Coro is (068)

Coro has a wide range of small hotels, plus the 3-star **Miranda Cumberland** opposite the airport, tel: 523022, fax: 513096; complete with pool, gardens and central air conditioning; 91 rooms at $60 single/double, slightly more for triple.

Downtown a good central hotel is the two-storey **Venezia**, Av Manaure at Zamora, tel: 511811/44, fax: 511434; pool, restaurant, 70 modern rooms; single $20, double $33. Around the block on Calle Toledo is the **Hotel Caracas**, tel:

512465; a charming colonial house newly remodelled with 20 rooms, 20 baths, air conditioning. Cheaper is the **Hotel Zamora**, Calle Zamora, two blocks east of Av Manaure, tel: 516005; 37 rooms above a bank, air-conditioned single $10, double $13. At the same price level but better run is **Hotel Coro**, Zamora near Av Los Médanos, tel: 510387, 513421; ask for a room at the back. There are several moderate hotels on Av Los Médanos. Businessmen seem to like **Hotel Falcón**, Av Los Médanos near Av Josefa Camejo, tel/fax: 516076; restaurant, 22 modern rooms with hot water, fridge; double $28.

Coro's pioneer guesthouse is the **Posada Manena**, tel: 516615, Calle 18 Garcés near Calle 42; five clean rooms with bath; $10 double with fan, $15 air conditioned. Expect basic beds at the **Colonial**, Calle Talavera behind the Cathedral (no phone); restaurant, fan, double bed $7; two beds, $10. The **Posada Corocoro Rico**, tel: (068) 78517, on the highway east of Coro, has a restaurant and 22 plain air-conditioned rooms with bath and cold water, for $14 single or double. Falcón Ferrys have an office here.

Among restaurants, the **Aero-Club** at the airport gives good value for full meals served in style, even real chateaubriand with tarragon sauce. **Los Jarrones**, in an old house on Calle Colón, offers inexpensive local dishes such as goat, fish fillet and *pabellón*, plus music played by Coro's guitarist Eloy Chirinos. Another recommended place, also not expensive, is **Taco Taco**, a Mexican restaurant on Av Josefa Camejo. Nothing special on the outside but inside you are served tasty *tostadas* almost too big to hold, *enchiladas*, or *carne a la tampiqueña*.

Strangers should not leave Coro without tasting specialities made of goat's milk: *queso coriano* or fresh cheese, *nata*, a delicious cross between butter and salty cream, and *dulce de leche*, like a soft fudge made of milk and sugar. These can be bought at a house called **Virgen del Carmen** on Av Manaure, on the same side of the street as Hotel Venezia.

What to see

Colonial centre Coro was declared a city of World Cultural Heritage by Unesco in 1993 for its historic colonial structures. Between the plazas today called Bolívar and Falcón, the 60 or 70 families of early Coro had their homes of adobe brick. Beside them were the mud and thatch houses of the Caquetío Indians whose village predated the Spaniards. On the main plaza, the first primitive Cathedral was being rebuilt in masonry in 1595 when it was burned by Amyas Preston just 18 years after a French attack. Finally completed in 1632, the imposing white structure has massive walls and gun slits like a fortress enclosing round pillars. It is one of Venezuela's oldest churches.

Two blocks north on Calle Zamora stand the **Iglesia de San Francisco** and adjacent **Museo Diocesano de Coro**, in former times a Franciscan monastery and in the recent past, the state government seat. The original structures were burned by pirates and rebuilt in 1620. A century later the church was reconstructed in adobe; then the single nave was expanded to three; finally in the early 1900s the tower was demolished and the neo-Gothic façade added, rather detracting from its age. The museum is large, very well done and covers two floors of religious art in gold, silver, glass, tapestry, as well as colonial bells, furniture, paintings, sculpture. Guided visits on Tue–Sat 09.00–12.00, 15.00–18.00; closes Sun at 13.00.

Walk west on Zamora; it's the colonial street. The **Cross of San Clemente**, as old as the city itself, is in the next block. Sadly, it has been locked in a dismal shelter since the time of President Falcón. According to tradition it is made from the very *cují* or mesquite tree under which the first mass in the new Province of Venezuela

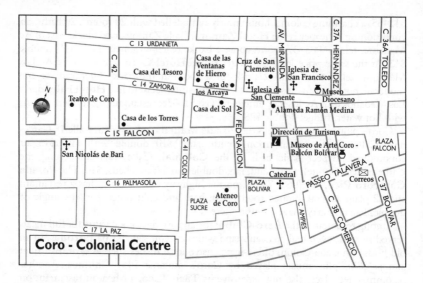

Coro - Colonial Centre

was held. The hardness of this wood makes its great age quite possible. Above the door of the yellow Iglesia de San Clemente are two window niches with painted colonial sculptures. The early church was destroyed by pirates in the 16th century and rebuilt about 1750. Go inside to see the richly painted blue, red and gold altar screen, and the ceiling anchor of Saint Clement, an early bishop of Rome who was martyred in the Crimea.

The corner house on Zamora at Calle Federación is the **Balcón de Los Arcaya**, recognised by its full balcony. Built in the 1740s, the fine mansion was acquired a hundred years later by the Arcaya family. Today it houses the **Museo de Cerámica Histórica y Loza Popular** which contains much more than china collections, native earthenware and pre-Hispanic pots. Open Tue–Sat 09.00–12.00, 15.00–18.00; closes Sun at 13.00.

The **Casa de las Ventanas de Hierro**, on the same block, has a fantastic plaster doorway considered the finest of its kind in the Caribbean, nearly 8m tall. It was built in 1764–65 by the mayor of Coro, Don José Garcés, and has never been sold, a rarity among colonial structures. The heirs, the Tellería and Zárraga families, have restored bedrooms, library, chapel, coach yard, kitchen and slave quarters as the **Museo de Tradición Familiar**. Don't miss the family daguerrotypes, swinging cradle, four-post mahogany bed, toilet chair and polychrome ceilings. Columns with 'bellies', *panzudas*, surround a breezy patio where mockingbirds sing. Open Mon–Sat 09.00–17.00.

The **Casa del Sol** on the south side of Zamora is a single-storey house of the early 18th century, one of the oldest in Coro. The name comes from the sun above the door, symbol of God. The fine residence belonged at one time to José Garcés, who built the Casa de las Ventanas de Hierro. It later served as a school and courthouse.

The stately **Casa del Tesoro** on the corner of Zamora and Colón was built in the 1770s for Andrés de Talavera, a Coriano whose wealth disappeared when he died, giving rise to tales of buried treasure (hence the name). Many generations have dug for, and even found, tunnels, but no gold has surfaced. Mariano de Talavera y Garcés, orator, intellectual and bishop of Guayana, was born here so the house is also known as the Casa del Obispo. At the time of writing, neither this house owned by A Zárraga Tellerfa nor the Casa del Sol was open to the public.

If you still have energy, walk four blocks west on Zamora to the **Cementerio Judío**, declared a national monument as the oldest Jewish cemetery functioning in South America. To see the cemetery, usually locked, ask for Pedro Roberto García who lives opposite; best after 17.00 or weekends. When the Sephardic Jews were banished from Spain many looked to the New World. They found a haven in Curaçao which was Dutch and also close to Venezuela. Joseph Curiel, who came from Curaçao, even travelled to Ciudad Bolívar to offer patriots Jewish support. After Independence, however, those who came to live in Coro had to overcome discrimination serious enough for Holland to ask reparation for damages. Curiel built the cemetery; the oldest grave, dated 1832, is that of his young daughter.

A block southeast on Calle Falcón there's an unadorned colonial church, **San Nicolás de Bari**, with a door into the old Catholic cemetery. The façade shows what San Clemente and other churches looked like before sundry remodellings. Below the roof is the date 1741.

Calle Talavera, a short and lively street in the heart of Coro, links the Cathedral with Plaza Falcón. Here you will find the **Museo de Arte de Coro** in the house called Balcón de Bolívar, or Casa de Los Senior for the Curaçao merchants who bought it in 1896 for a warehouse. The mansion is known to have stood here since at least the 1750s when it was being enlarged. During the Revolution it was confiscated as Spanish property and turned into barracks, acquiring fame when Bolívar stayed here in 1826. Now restored complete with balcony, the mansion doubles as the Coro branch of the **Caracas Museum of Contemporary Art**, holding top-notch exhibitions. There is a fine crafts shop. Open Tue–Sat 09.00–12.30, 15.00–19.30; Sun 09.00–16.00.

Further afield
Jardín Xerófito León Croizat
On the road from Coro to La Vela, this botanical garden of desert plants has a fascinating array of cacti, palms, shrubs and flowers on its 32 hectares, as well as laboratories and salons for study and teaching and visitor installations. Open Tue–Sun 08.30–11.30, 14.00–15.30.

Inparques, the National Parks Institute, has its regional headquarters here; tel: (068) 78582; tel/fax: 78451.

La Vela de Coro
Until modern highways arrived, Coro depended on its little seaport, 12km northeast, for transportation to Paraguaná Peninsula as well as for all trade, particularly with Curaçao. The ferry service between La Vela and Aruba/Curaçao has woken the quiet town once more. La Vela continues a programme to restore its old houses and beautify the historic centre with trees, benches and statues. Dating to 1527, La Vela has been declared a national monument. The biggest structure is the 17th-century **Aduana** or customs house, now home to a Museo Marítimo. There is a monument to the 1806 landing of Francisco Miranda, when the red, blue and yellow flag he designed was unfurled for the first time on Venezuelan soil. A sandy bay some 2km long provides Coro's nearest beach. Although the waves are often rough and the water turbid, the beach is crowded at weekends.

Médanos de Coro
The largest of Falcón State's four national parks covers 912km² on the isthmus of Paraguaná and the sea on either side, with the highway in between. On the windward side the sea is rough and not good for swimming. The famous sand

dunes shift over the road at the city's edge, whipped by constant trade winds. They are a short hike from Coro up the highway from Plaza Concordia. Take the bus which runs along Calle Falcón to Avenida Los Médanos and change to a northbound bus.

Warning It is important to be aware that tourists of any nationality stick out like a penguin on a sand dune. Groups of kids with knives have mugged tourists here, so be on your guard.

Taima Taima mastodon kill site
About 7km east of La Vela and north of the highway, an exhibition is being prepared at the site where a mastodon was killed 13,500 years ago by paleo-Indians. A stone spearhead was found in the body, and cutting marks indicate that hunters separated its head. This site and one in Muaco, located by José María Cruxent in 1961, have also yielded remains of glyptodon, megatherium (giant sloth) and the early horse. Burn marks have provided some 50 radio-carbon datings establishing hunters' presence here in the late Pleistocene age.

THE PARAGUANA PENINSULA
On the map Paraguaná rears on its narrow neck like a giant's head. It is easy to see that the peninsula was once an island. Indeed shifting dunes effectively blocked the 30km isthmus until a modern highway was built. This and an aqueduct bringing water from the Sierra de San Luis have transformed the semi-arid land. Villages have multiplied and farms raise melons, tomatoes, onions and aloe where before only cactus grew. An oil pipeline paralleling the aqueduct gives you the clue to the peninsula's importance as site of two of the largest oil refineries in the world.

The most northern point of Venezuela, Cabo San Román was named in 1499 by Alonso de Ojeda on his way to discover Lake Maracaibo. For the next 450 years Paraguaná's few settlers lived as the natives, from fishing, hunting rabbits, even deer; during times of drought, people left. The biggest change (good and bad) was the introduction of goats which eat cactus and can in turn be eaten. Those people with boats earned cash in the smuggling trade with Curaçao.

Then in 1947 the first oil refineries came to the west coast, bringing electricity, roads and, in the 1950s, houses and gardens to Amuay and Cardón.

Make sure to see the charming colonial churches of **Santa Ana**, **Moruy** and **Jadacaquiva** – each one quite different – the singular mountain of **Santa Ana**, and the beach town of **Adícora** which has excellent surfing and places to stay. All are easily accessible by local buses. Unless you can get a 4x4 vehicle or have a lot of time on your hands, forget about exploring the wilder north where roads are not sign-posted and may disappear altogether among scrub, thorns and rock. There are plans to make a road around the northern coast, but this may take years.

Cerro Santa Ana
Seen from afar, Santa Ana mountain rises in the middle of the peninsula. Surrounded by dry scrub, its cone is an ecological island of cloudforest topped at 830m by low windswept shrubs. Declared a natural monument in 1972, Santa Ana is a refuge of plants, birds and animals including rabbits, foxes and ocelots. It has three peaks, called Moruy – the highest and most northern, Santa Ana or 'picacho en medio', and Buena Vista, easternmost. The main way up is from the village of Moruy, but there is a trail from Santa Ana, longer and less frequented. In either case, be prepared for rain showers from September to January, and for cold wind and fog at the top.

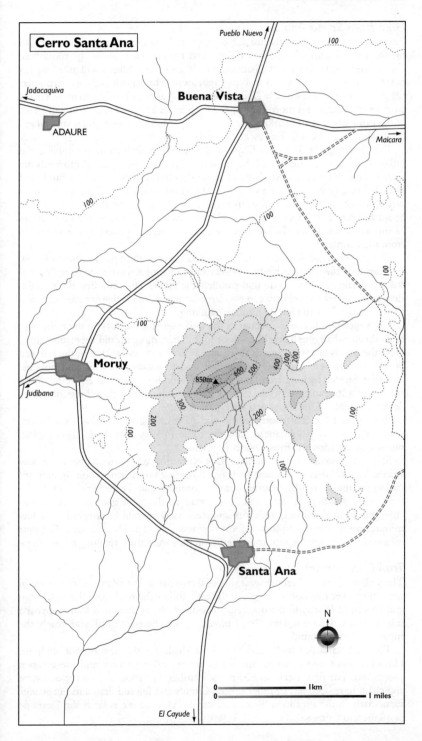

Cerro Santa Ana

Pueblo Nuevo

Jadacaquiva

Buena Vista

ADAURE

Maicara

100

100

100

100

Moruy

Judibana

850m

600 500 400 300 200

300

200

200

100

100

100

Santa Ana

El Cayude

N

0   1km
0   1 miles

Hike from Santa Ana

For information about trails and camping grounds go to the Inparques office; it's on the street leading from Plaza Bolívar and the church towards the mountain. Once camping facilities with bathrooms are complete, hikers will need to get permits. As it is, you can start walking right away. The asphalt ends at a triangular plaza and from here it's nearly 2km to the camping area. Follow the main jeep road past smallholdings and thorn bushes and keep left at all crossroads. You will arrive at the camp ground and parking area. There is a Monumento Natural sign where the trail starts to the left. The ascent is a hike of less than 3 hours.

The first stage leads to the **Caja de Agua** which for centuries supplied the village with water; 25 minutes. It begins hot and rocky, leading straight towards the Cerro. The trail reaches the shade of some deciduous trees, begins to climb and bears left (west); you will see a spiny mat of ground bromeliads, pineapple relatives called *caracuey* which turn scarlet in the dry season, and soon the first trees with Spanish moss. The Caja de Agua is a closed concrete tank fed by the pure waters of the Santa Ana River. Today, however, the village is supplied by the waterline from the mainland.

The second stage following the Santa Ana River is through deciduous forest. You can hear the songs of birds: seed-eaters and fruit-eaters such as troupials, red siskins, parakeets, doves. The trail parallels the ravine, climbing first on its right, then crossing left to pass between two large boulders. You arrive at a clearing ideal for camping near a rivulet; 20 minutes' walking.

The vegetation becomes greener as the trail rises (the creek is on the right) and leads through hanging lianas like a door to the next, more humid vegetation zone. Here the trail is not very clear as there appear to be two watercourses; the remains of the old concrete aqueduct on the left lead to another clearing and possible campsite. Shaded by huge trees, the trail skirts muddy spots by the aqueduct, more runnels of water, and goes to the right of a big boulder, then left, seeking the Piedra de Agua, source of the Santa Ana River; 20 minutes.

Bearing east the trail continues up and passes a big rock (*peñón*). In the dry season the cliff is visible ahead, and the route follows at its feet. Lianas, ferns, mosses, bromeliads and mushrooms flourish.

Someone once lived on a flat place, **Los Naranjos**, where an orange tree is now shaded by second-growth forest with red-flowering bromeliads. Soon the upward trail opens into a circular clearing, another camping spot. From here a path to the right leads down to Misaray, while the trail to the peak goes upward, at last emerging from the forest, with a magnificent view stretching eastward. In a few minutes more, the *picacho* looms above a grassy shoulder. Dwarf palms, *Geonoma paraguanensis*, grow at the top among ferns, orchids and shrubs recalling *páramo* flora.

Trail from Moruy

The well-trodden trail on the west side of Cerro Santa Ana takes you to the top in something over two hours. To get to the trail, follow the road from the little town and church of Moruy to the main north-south highway and cross to the opposite side towards the mountain, 2km, passing many houses, until you reach the Inparques camp ground.

The trail starts out rocky and with little shade for the best part of an hour. However, once above 500m, the forest makes hiking cooler and views open southward. The final ascent to 830m is a scramble over roots and up rocks; a rope and chain have been left by other hikers. Clouds and fog add drama to the *picacho*, particularly in the afternoon. But on a clear day you can see as far as the Sierra de San Luis and Curaçao.

Colonial villages
Santa Ana

The isthmus highway, 32km, ends at a Y; the east arm leads to Adícora, 27km, the west to peninsular roads and Punto Fijo, 45km. Go west for the turn to Santa Ana, 35km, at the foot of the cone-shaped mountain. This spot watered by a mountain stream was inhabited long before the arrival of Spaniards who for once kept on good terms with Arawak natives. The 17th-century **Iglesia de Santa Ana** was strongly built to impress the converts and resist pirates. It's a dazzling white church with a unique tower of concave faces added in the 1750s. If it's a Sunday, you may be one of the few lucky enough to see the gilt altar piece with its naïve carvings, complete with saints, angels, St George and dragon, and at the top a charming oil painting of Santa Ana herself, reading the good book to the young Virgin. The church is usually locked.

There are various '*ambiente familiar*' restaurants in town although no hotels. The **Bello Monte** serves good, inexpensive chicken, yuca and beer.

Moruy

Seven kilometres northwest of Santa Ana, Moruy is just as old. Humble houses are dwarfed by the domed church tower of the **Iglesia de San Nicolás**. Colonists from Spain brought with them the image of San Nicolás de Bari whose feast day is December 24. The original church, dating from the 1760s, was enlarged by two 19th-century naves, and the whole sparkles with fresh paint.

Two kilometres before the next town of Buena Vista, there's a particularly fine colonial house off to the right, **La Casa de Las Virtudes**. Now that it has neighbours the owners no longer show the 250-year-old property. Descendants of John Hill who fought in the Battle of Carabobo, the Peña family raise melons and vegetables, relying on their own well. Everywhere that the mainland aqueduct reaches (it hasn't failed in 30 years), new houses are going up and farmers are clearing plots to plant tomatoes, onions, aloe vera. Cactus is stacked to make thorny fences. Organ cactus or *cardón* grows quite slowly and in theory receives the same official protection as trees do elsewhere. But the peninsula is changing swiftly, and farming and cactus do not mix.

Craftsmen and women must look harder every year for cactus to make the attractive *cardón* chairs. In San Nicolás near Moruy there lives an extraordinary family of chair makers, the Díaz family. The two daughters and four sons are all blind and have learned their skills through careful measurements taught by their father Victoriano, who learned the trade from his father. And where did he learn it? 'I think chairs have been made here for about a century,' Victoriano says. 'A Dutchman came to live at a place called Guaracara with two other brothers from Holland. Two took up farming and the other made chairs of *cardón*. At first he wove the seats of maize leaves, like they still use over at El Vínculo, then he found *carruaja* on the mountain…that's how many people saw and started to make chairs. Today you can't get such wood… that piece comes from Pedregal. Some people cut *cardón* since they need it, and hide the wood because if the Guardias find it they confiscate it.' Hardwoods such as *poui* are also brought in from the mainland.

Jadacaquiva

Dutch influence pops up on the peninsula in many spots. Take the road from Buena Vista west across scrubland to the open, windswept point where it joins the Judibana road. A stark white church, 250 years old, stands here. It has no tower; the bells hang in a frame outside. Inside an old painting on the altar shows a Venezuelan sailboat entering Willemstad harbour in Curaçao. Note, also, the elaborately carved original altar piece.

Pueblo Nuevo

From Jadacaquiva it is 24km via a circle road to Pueblo Nuevo, an old town now the biggest peninsular focus of farm development. The church, although genuinely colonial, has been remodelled more than once. Houses near the plaza have been restored. There's a new bus terminal. Cottage industries include soaps, creams and shampoo made of *zábila* or aloe vera, *dulce de leche* made of goat's milk, and *cardón* chairs. Restaurants and pensions are beginning to appear. A good economical lunch place is the **Restaurant del Pueblo** on Plaza Bolívar: plain but satisfying *criollo* dishes such as stew, fried fish, liver and chops.

A splendid new **Josefa Camejo Cultural Complex** with library, auditorium and rehearsal rooms is named for the Independence heroine of Paraguaná who was born in 1781 in the village of Aguaque, 7km north of Pueblo Nuevo.

Reserva Biológica Monte Cano While in Pueblo Nuevo, enquire about the reserve's offices (formerly Bioma) at Av Arévalo González near Calle Páez, tel: (069) 81048. The reserve itself is 7km away via San José de Cocodite, west of the Pueblo Nuevo–Buena Vista highway. There's a visitor centre and gift shop where you can buy T-shirts and posters. You can hike the trails, or go birding. Among cactus and mesquite you can spot orioles, red siskin, spinetail, antwren, partridge, parakeets and hawks. Monte Cano protects some of the peninsula's last deciduous forest, home to threatened flora and fauna, including species found nowhere else but Cerro Santa Ana. Over-cutting and grazing by cattle and goats endanger many wild habitats on the peninsula. The ridge takes its name from *cana*, meaning grey hair, prompted by trees draped with Spanish moss (*Tillandsia*); one species is endemic. This epiphyte and many orchids live on moisture-bearing air.

Biologists also study a rare bat, found in the Cueva del Guano in the vicinity of Moruy. People call it *bigotudo* for its moustaches. Bats have lived in the 118m cave for so long that the bat dung was exploited and sold to Aruba and Curaçao in the early 1900s. Bats are important pollinating agents on the peninsula.

In Agua Sabrida, yet another biological reserve south of Miraca, Bioma investigators have found the world's smallest lizard measuring no more than 30mm, a little over an inch. Called *Lepidoplepharis paraguanensis*, it adds another species to the growing list of endemic plants and animals.

EAST COAST
Adícora

Adícora is shaping into an interesting beach and windsurfing destination. In part this is because it is close to colonial towns such as Pueblo Nuevo, Baraived and its neighbour Miraca (where almost everyone seems to be a potter), as well as to the much bigger northern beaches of Buchuaco, El Supí and Tiraya. More important, the little port has mended its streets and restored old buildings, working up much charm, and Adícora has a variety of *posadas* serving windsurfers and bathers. At holiday times, however, these rooms are too few as Adícora appears to be the only place to stay between Coro and Punto Fijo.

The old fishing village occupies the only headland along the whole east coast and was for centuries Paraguaná's principal port of trade with Curaçao. Salt was its big export, as well as guayacan (*lignum vitae*), a wood so hard the Dutch sent it home for windmill gears. Some of the original coral stone structures have been restored, little houses with Caribbean Dutch influence, painted pink, blue, yellow, mauve, green and brown. An old *faro*, lighthouse, stands by a tiny plaza. Stroll down the pretty waterfront boulevard to the small, rocky beach protected by a breakwater. The better sandy beach is through the town to the south; plenty of informal restaurants there serve fried fish. Another beach lies north of Adícora, where city people have built summer homes.

The wrecks of two French galleons lie on the seafloor facing Adícora, dating from the time when pirates and smugglers used Paraguaná as a refuge. There are nearby coral reefs for scuba diving.

Where to stay
The area telephone code for Adícora is (069)
Adícora has no jet set, but family-style places provide good lodging at moderate rates. **La Posada Casa Rosada** on the seafront boulevard is run by Franz and Alba Kitzberger. They have a charming old house with hammocks around a green patio and a small, good restaurant. Rooms are light and large with a double plus three small single beds; starting at $20 with shared bath. They also rent a large apartment with three bedrooms, $35, and a house on Calle Comercio. No phone; tel: 88049 to leave a message with Rosa García.

Posada La Carantoña, Calle Comercio near public telephones, tel: (069) 88173. In a large house a block from the waterfront, ten triple rooms with bath, no hot water, $20; clean, basic, friendly. The manager organises tours of Paraguaná, rents windsurfing sails and boards, and can contract fishing boats.

The same surfer of Náutico Moustacho runs various lodgings, all near beaches; **Vacaciones Moustacho**, tel: 88271, fax: 88054. Hardinghaus, whose nickname is Moustacho, speaks English and German. He offers first-class furnishings, kitchen, refigerator, hot water and air conditioning in independent rooms and suites for two to five people, in five different houses, for about $35 double; and a converted fisherman's cottage with fan and shared bath, at $20 double. Breakfast at waterside café, $6.

Windsurfing Adícora rents a couple of plain bungalows by the beach, usually to surfers: kitchen, three double rooms, shared bath, $25. For information in Caracas about international airport reception or transfer from Las Piedras to Adícora, equipment rental, tel: (069) 88045.

Hotel Montecano, tel: 88174, is on the south side of the Pueblo Nuevo road, 500m from Adícora. A large central octagonal room with tin roof serves as a restaurant where the friendly owner Francisco Palmese and his family make simple meals; eight cramped basic rooms with bath on the outside of the octagon are overpriced for what you get: single $8, double $10.

Hotel Bar Casa Blanca, on the main road entering town, appears to be the last choice. Its main virtue is that the Punto Fijo buses stop opposite it four times a day.

What to do
Paraguaná, famous for its winds, is gaining international repute for windsurfing. Foreign surfers have discovered the right conditions at Adícora where the same on-shore trade winds that keep temperatures at a pleasant 28°C provide dependable breeze and waves. Winds are strongest between January and May; most afternoons velocity reaches 4–7 on the Beaufort Scale. Waves, too, are big. 'We have 2–3m waves for training and 3–5m waves for crack surfers,' says the local enthusiast and promoter Nicolás Hardinghaus. 'And practically on the doorstep, there's calm water for making speed.' The period of calmest wind is July to October.

Equipment is rented by Hardinghaus' **Náutico Moustacho** centre on the waterfront beside the Guardia Nacional post; sailboards cost about $170 per week. They also arrange surfing classes, deepsea fishing and snorkelling excursions. The last word was a plan for a dive centre in Adícora. Carlos Cornielles operates

Adícora High Winds, (014) 9680660, in a house near the plaza. Carlos, who speaks English, gives classes and provides windsurf packages and gear, as well as renting some cabañas for surfers.

Buchuaco, El Supí Although only 3km from Adícora by water, Buchuaco is reached by the road from El Supí, 6.7km. Both are largely summer home developments. Their beaches are protected by coral reefs which act as natural breakwaters.

Boca de Caño Wildlife Refuge or Laguna Tiraya This is 10km north of Adícora. Flamingos gather here to feed on shrimp in the shallow waters separated from the sea by reefs. But the sun is merciless and the birds are often distant; best season to see them is November to January. (Another larger lagoon attracting very big flocks of flamingos is the Salina de Bajarigua, inland from Las Cumaraguas. But you may have to get a guide to find the way.)

Tiraya This bare-bones beach community is reached by a paved causeway over the lagoon's north end. It's a popular swimming place on weekends but shuttered and without shade or facilities on weekdays.

Further afield
A hard-packed sand road (there are plans for paving it) parallels the coast northward past the **Salinas de Cumaraguas**, a series of lagoons exploited for salt. Their evaporating waters shimmer in lavendar-rose hues, edged by brilliant salt crystals; it's an amazing sight. On the sea side, reached by a dyke over the lagoon, a large resort was built on **Bahía Mata Gorda**, with many signs announcing the Médano Caribe. However, as the hotel went bankrupt and the place has been closed for some time, all you see are its 3-floor mansions deserted among the sands.

A better road via Pueblo Nuevo–El Vínculo joins the coast road and continues further north where you reach another grand abandoned project, the erstwhile **shortwave radio station** of La Voz de Venezuela. The coast just south is called Piedras Negras for its bluffs of jagged black rocks. There are dunes and some bungalows.

The best comes in 4km, a lobster (*langosta*) restaurant or marisquería among the fishermen's little houses of Puerto Escondido. The informal seafood place is called **Restaurant Cabo San Román** (although some kilometres southeast of the cape). There are benches, plank tables and today's menu chalked on the blackboard. The star is lobster in season (October through April); or prawns, squid, roe and grouper (*mero*), all straight from the sea outside the door. Huge plates are served by the owner in shorts and flapping shirt, as sunburnt as the other fishermen who eat here.

Cabo San Román with its lighthouse, another 10km or so, is the northernmost point of Venezuela, named for the saint's day when Alonso de Ojeda touched here on August 9 1499. The seas of the upper peninsula are calmer than the east coast and despite sharp black rocks you can find quiet beaches, even trees, and lots of washed-up shells. Aruba is on the northern horizon.

WEST COAST
One day a road will continue around the still wild peninsula (more than twice as big as Margarita), but at present there's a long way to go on tracks that can lead off-road drivers up the proverbial path to nowhere. However, supposing you could continue west and south, the first place of interest would be **Punta Macolla** where an old lighthouse is said to stand.

At **Playa El Pico** the main shore road picks up. The sea is clean and inviting. Long shadeless beaches line the shore and at holidays people from Punto Fijo pitch tents. There is a large inexpensive restaurant, empty during the week.

At **Villa Marina** you begin to see fishing craft, *peñeros*, in the bay. On the northern point a quiet beach is known for its array of seashells. In the seaside village you can find economical fried fish if you don't mind loud canned music as accompaniment. On the same bay further south is **Los Taques** which is economically dependent on urban centres such as Amuay.

The integration of Amuay and Cardón refineries into the Paraguaná Refining Centre makes this the world's largest refining complex with a processing capacity of 940,000 barrels a day. Amuay, started in 1950 by Standard Oil, is a skyscraper complex of pipelines, boilers and cracking plants. Giant tankers berth at its port on Amuay Bay. Cardón, about 20km south, was built by Shell Oil.

Judibana, Punto Fijo and Cardón

After travelling through the peninsula's interior of goats, cactus and centuries-old *pueblos*, the speedways and urban sprawl on the west coast come as a shock. In fact, refineries are Falcón State's engines of development and **Punto Fijo** its biggest city. Today, secondary industries have grown up: a shipyard which makes and repairs steel boats, and a shrimp processing plant. A fishing fleet operates out of Carirubana, going after shrimp in the deep Gulf of Venezuela.

Judibana, a suburban centre near the airport, has banks, restaurants, hotels, trees and parks. Pleasant enough, it is easy to drive around but offers little to do. The town was planned by Amuay refinery to accompany an oil workers' camp.

Punto Fijo is the central city. Horns blare and cars and people shove on its main streets, Av Bolívar and Av Colombia. Its growth, and that of all towns on the peninsula, is tied to the freshwater aqueduct from the mainland. Calculations for the city's sewer treatment plant built by Maraven estimate that the area's population will be about 200,000 by the year 2000. The plant has brought cleaner beaches, and recycled water for irrigating some parks, as well as for refinery use.

Cardón, immediately south, merges with Punto Fijo (the refinery itself is some 4km further down the coast). The ex-oil camp is an open, agreeable district of homes near a golf club, zoo and park, with a hospital, schools, cultural and social centres. Opposite the zoo is the new Paraguaná Natural Science Museum. There's a good marina and sailing club.

Getting there
By air
The Josefa Camejo International Airport is generally referred to as Aeropuerto Las Piedras. It is 12km northeast of Punto Fijo. There are three flights daily to Caracas by Avensa/Servivensa, and another five flights daily to Caracas by Servivensa and Aserca, two by way of Maracaibo. Intercity routes also link Las Piedras with Barcelona, Maracaibo, Maturín, Porlamar, Puerto Ordaz and Valencia.

Servivensa has two flights a day to Curaçao and Aruba; Aserca flies to Aruba daily.

By bus
Peninsular buses stop at Calle 89 Perimetral, north of the public market in Punto Fijo. They go to Pueblo Nuevo, to Santa Ana and other towns. From here, there is also service to Coro throughout the day. Service to Barquisimeto is provided by Transporte Federación; to Maracaibo by Transporte Bucaral and Expresos Guasa.

As there is no Terminal de Pasajeros in Punto Fijo, long-distance coaches depart from individual line headquarters. Expresos Alianza is located at Calle 85 and Av 18 Colombia; Expresos Occidente, Calle 78 Comercio at Av 21. Expresos San Cristóbal is on Av Colombia at Calle 87. There are various night departures to **Maracaibo**, 14 hours; **San Cristóbal**, 14 hours; **Valencia**, 6 hours; **Caracas** 8 hours.

Airport buses leave from Av Bolívar and Calle 82.

By ferry

In 1998 **Falcón Ferrys** started up service to **Curaçao** and **Aruba** from La Vela de Coro, but had no immediate plans to include Punto Fijo in its itinerary.

Where to stay
The area telephone code is (069)
Downtown Punto Fijo

All these hotels are air conditioned, but most do not have hot water. Three central choices in the $15–20 range are: **Hotel Caribe**, Calle 78 Comercio, tel: 450321, 456354, 450421, a three-floor business hotel; **Hotel El Cid**, Comercio at Av 17 Bolívar, tel: 451967, 455245, not quite so noisy, restaurant; and **Hotel Presidente**, Av 14 Perú at Calle 78A Cuba, tel: 458964. **Pensión San Jorge**, Av Perú and Calle 81 Falcón, has doubles for $12. **Hotel Venecia**, Calle 81 Falcón near Av Bolívar, tel: 455743, 467798; single/double $14.

Closer to the centre hotels become cheaper. **Hotel Miami**, Falcón near Bolívia, tel: 458335; singles as low as $8 with fan, $11 with air conditioning. **Los Balcones**, Bolivia at Calle 84 Zamora; tel: 479939. **Hotel Latino**, Calle 88 Ayacucho, tel: 452776; near bus stops. Even cheaper is the **Euzcalduna**, Av 19 Ecuador at Falcón, tel: 451534; single with bath $9; without $8.

Better hotels are further away. Two are: the modern **Peninsula**, Calle Calatayud, tel: 459734/76, with a pool; and the **Villa Real** on Av Coro, Santa Irene, tel: 451421, 450213, fax: 454171; an apartment tower and a motel.

Cardón

The **Cardón Motel**, shore road near the Club Miramar, tel: 74795, 54655; quite popular for its gardens, seafront balconies; also trailers. Pool courtesy of the Miramar, and beach at the foot of the bluff. Book ahead as this small attractive hotel is usually full.

Judibana

The **Hotel Jardín**, Centro Comercial Judibana, tel: 460613; new wing of the two-floor building has 38 rooms with double bed, $35; old wing has 46 rooms, single $15, double $25. There are two restaurants, pool, barber. **Motel Luigi**, north of Plaza Bolívar and church, tel: 460970; 28 rooms, single or double bed, $23; well-known restaurant. Also, Motel La California, Barrio Libertador, tel: 461365.

ZULIA
Lake Maracaibo

First known by its Indian name of Coquivacoa, Lake Maracaibo is the greatest lake in South America (13,000km²), and is unique in its direct outlet to the sea. Alonso de Ojeda, leading four Spanish ships in 1499, spent nine days in the lake and found the Indians so amicable that they gave him a beautiful girl. Isabel, as she became, went back with him to the royal court and spent the rest of her life at his side. With their three children they lived in Santo Domingo where Ojeda died and was buried in 1516.

AMERICA, OR WHAT'S IN A NAME?

If honours for discovering the New World go to Christopher Columbus, then how did the continents get labelled America?

In 1499, before Columbus returned from his third voyage, an expedition set sail from Spain under Alonso de Ojeda. Map-maker Juan de la Cosa who had twice accompanied Columbus was official cartographer. Also along was Amerigo Vespucci, a Florentine merchant in the service of the Medicis and a friend of Columbus who had helped him with supplies. He had the Medicis' backing and commanded two of the four ships. The fleet was sent by King Ferdinand and Queen Isabella for the specific purpose of checking up on Columbus and finding new lands in Terra Firma (as Venezuela was called) as Columbus had rights to a tenth of royal income from his discoveries and their royal highnesses were unhappy.

When the ships sighted land (near the Guianas) Vespucci explored southeast along the coast as far as about 5° before turning back. They passed the mouths of the Essequibo and Orinoco, and next followed the coast west the entire length of Venezuela, discovering the Paraguaná Peninsula, Curaçao, Lake Coquivacoa (Maracaibo) and a large gulf which they named Gulf of Venezuela, or 'little Venice' after native villages built on stilts over the water. In 1500 Juan de la Cosa made his celebrated *Mapa Mundi* on which the New World appeared with the name Venezuela, for the first time.

Vespucci's letter to Lorenzo di Medici describing new lands, translated and published as *Mundus Novus* in Augsburg, 1504, made him famous throughout Europe and went into 50 editions. Vespucci was the first to announce that the lands were not Asia but a new continent and did not call its inhabitants Indians. He even proposed a trade route to the East Indies, going south and west around the continent (anticipating Magellan).

In 1507 a German professor, Martin Waldseemüller, at the Saint Dié university in Lorraine, was about to publish a new cosmography. He was the first to put forward the name of America for the New World and added Vespucci's letters relating four voyages as an appendix. Although historians have found proof of only two of these reputed voyages, they admit Vespucci sailed the breadth of Venezuela in 1499 and sailed to Brazil for the Portuguese king in 1501. He went up the Amazon for four days, continued south to Guanabara Bay, and was the first to go as far as Río de la Plata and beyond (50°) reaching a cold land, possibly Patagonia, which would make him the discoverer of Argentina. It was Vespucci who described the Southern Cross as a navigational guide. Pedro Alvares Cabral had already landed on April 23 1500, on the coast of Bahía State, and has the credit for discovering Brazil.

Ironically, it is Columbus who is most honoured in Venezuela although Ojeda and Vespucci discovered the entire coast from Margarita west to Lake Maracaibo and even named the country and the continent.

Historically, the lake served Spaniards as the most direct route inland to the Andes. They went south up rivers entering the lake: the Motatán to Trujillo, the Chama to Mérida, the Escalante to Táchira. All Andean exports and imports went via Lake Maracaibo. Zulia State takes its name from an important southwesterly trade route from Colombia via the Zulia–Catatumbo rivers. In the days of steamboats (*estimbotes*) people and produce travelled on a small railway from

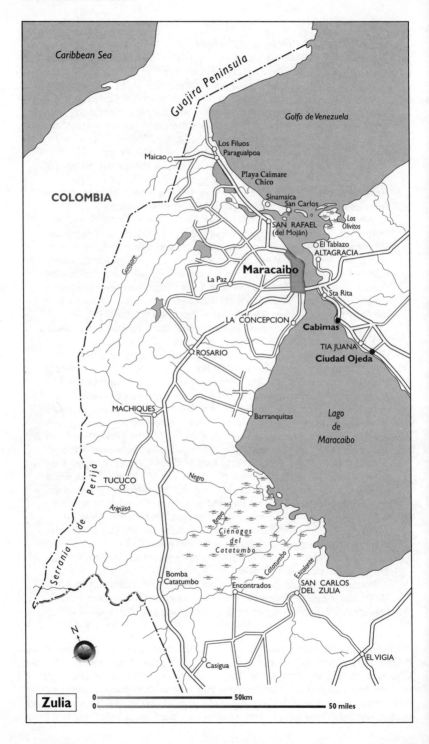

Caribbean Sea

Guajira Peninsula

Golfo de Venezuela

Los Filuos
Paragualpoa

Maicao

COLOMBIA

Playa Caimare
Chico

Sinamaica
San Carlos

Los
Olivitos

SAN RAFAEL
(del Moján)

El Tablazo
ALTAGRACIA

Maracaibo

La Paz

Sta Rita

LA CONCEPCION

Cabimas

ROSARIO

TIA JUANA
Ciudad Ojeda

MACHIQUES

Barranquitas

Lago
de
Maracaibo

TUCUCO

Negro

Ariguisa

Ciénagas
del
Catatumbo

Bomba
Catatumbo

Encontrados

SAN CARLOS
DEL ZULIA

N

Casigua

EL VIGIA

Zulia

| 0 | 50km |
| 0 | 50 miles |

Táchira to Encontrados, went down the Catatumbo and transferred on to paddlewheelers for the trip to Maracaibo. Steamboats faded when the Pan American highway opened in the 1950s. Little lake ports linger on: La Ceiba (Trujillo State), Boscán, Gibraltar, Bobures, Palmarito, Puerto Chama.

Fed by more than 135 rivers, the lake began life with such low salinity that in places the water served for drinking and irrigation. All that changed with oil, however. Seawater has more than tripled the lake's salt content since a channel was dredged in 1954 to allow passage of bigger ships into the lake.

Oil also makes the lake the richest in the world, with more than 10,000 wells producing over 700,000 barrels a day. Over 400 major deposits have been found in the lake and on shore. Some wooden derricks from the old days still stand. At night huge gas compression plants, pumping stations and gas flares light up the southeast. Underwater there lies a maze of 24,000km of pipelines, half carrying oil, half gas and oil-well water which today is reinjected into wells. A 235km surface line transports oil to the Paraguaná Peninsula, feeding the large refineries of Amuay and Cardón.

Fertile lands south of the lake have been cleared and drained by farmers and ranchers. The **Sur del Lago** is one of the country's big fruit, vegetable, milk and beef producing areas.

The Environment Ministry, oil industry and universities all work together on lake conservation (paid for by the state oil company). Saline waters increase corrosion so the risk of oil spills is ever present. Computer techniques and sophisticated detection methods have been developed including the use of satellite images. However, the worst contamination comes from agricultural runoff, industrial and human waste. It is hoped that before the year 2000 AD Maracaibo and all other towns will have their sewage treatment plants fully working. At present there is no safe swimming in the lake.

Maracaibo

Maracaibo is a colourful city spreading northwest of the lake. It is hot (average 30°C/85°F), but a lot drier than southern Zulia. As the nation's second largest city, metropolitan Maracaibo encompasses nearly two million people, over half the population of Zulia State. Here you will see businessmen, stevedores, joggers, street vendors, smugglers, musicians, artists and Guajira women in traditional flowing mantas. The people here are known for their good humour, quick wit, and knack for giving everything a nickname. They call themselves *Marabinos*, although outsiders often say *Maracuchos*. Their city is fascinating to visit for its lake, bridge and oilfields, also its *gaita* music, markets, downtown historic buildings and cultural centres.

Maracaibo has been linked by road to the rest of Venezuela only since 1962–63 when a bridge was built. The **General Rafael Urdaneta Bridge**, one of the local sights, stretches 8.6km over the neck of Lake Maracaibo and is said to be the longest prestressed concrete bridge in the world. Before the bridge, you had to take a plane, boat or ferry to reach Maracaibo. The road circling west via Machiques–La Fría was built ten years later.

Long isolation did not bother the ebullient Marabinos, many of whom would like their city to be capital of 'La República del Zulia'. After all, Zulia produces most of Venezuela's dried milk and plátanos, as well as sugar, top grade beef, tons of fish, excellent beer... and half of the nation's oil. Maracaibo's port ranks third in the nation.

The town's first settlement in 1529 by German Ambrose Alfinger was an expedition staging post; it lasted six years. Founded again by Pedro Maldonado in 1574, Maracaibo took hold as the trading centre for the entire Andean region, including the eastern part of what is now Colombia. Until San Carlos Fort was built in 1683, however, the little port was a magnet for pirates of the Spanish Main and

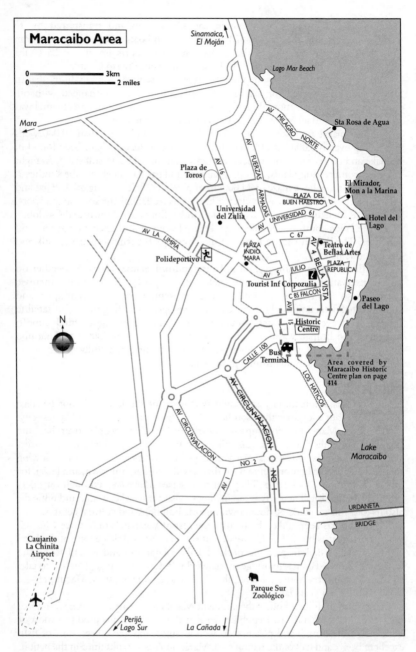

Maracaibo Area

0 ⊨⊨⊨⊨⊨ 3km
0 ⊨⊨⊨⊨⊨ 2 miles

Sinamaica, El Moján

Mara

Lago Mar Beach

AV MILAGRO NORTE

Sta Rosa de Agua

Plaza de Toros

AV 16

AV FUERZAS ARMADAS

PLAZA DEL BUEN MAESTRO

El Mirador, Mon a la Marina

Universidad del Zulia

UNIVERSIDAD 61

Hotel del Lago

AV LA LIMPIA

C 67

Teatro de Bellas Artes

Polideportivo

PLAZA INDIO MARA

PLAZA REPUBLICA

AV 4 BELLA VISTA

Tourist Inf Corpozulia

AV 5 JULIO

C 85 FALCON

AV 2

Paseo del Lago

N

AV 15

Historic Centre

CALLE 100

Bus Terminal

Area covered by Maracaibo Historic Centre plan on page 414

AV CIRCUNVALACIÓN

LOS HATICOS

Lake Maracaibo

AV CIRCUNVALACIÓN

NO 2

NO 1

AV 1

URDANETA

BRIDGE

Caujarito La Chinita Airport

Parque Sur Zoológico

Perijá, Lago Sur

La Cañada

was repeatedly set back by attacks. Three times pirates burned and sacked Gibraltar, the southern lake port for cacao and sugar growers: in 1665 Juan Manuel Nim, a French pirate; in 1669 Henry Morgan; and in 1678 another Frenchman, d'Estees.

The Battle of Lake Maracaibo, on July 24 1823, ended Spanish control. General Morales had taken Maracaibo a year after Bolívar won the great independence Battle of Carabobo, and it was not without a fleet raised in Colombia, a 10-week blockade and various land actions that Venezuelans won Zulia back. The date is celebrated today as Armed Forces Day (as well as Bolívar's birthday).

Maracaibo flowered as a coffee exporting centre in the mid-1800s, attracting German, Italian and Curaçao merchants whose names are still active today in Venezuela: Blohm, Steinvorth, Zingg, De Lima. Venezuela's first private bank, the Banco de Maracaibo, was established in 1882 by shareholders including leading families such as the Belloso, D'Empaire, Troconis, Urdaneta. After coffee came oil. And now, in northwest Zulia, mixed enterprises are exploiting gigantic coal reserves, proven at 938 million tons.

Getting there
By air
Caujarito, or La Chinita International Airport, is 12km southwest of downtown Maracaibo, a taxi run of $10–12. It is the country's second largest airport.

Airlines making a total of 15 flights daily to Caracas and Porlamar are Aserca, Avensa/Servivensa, Aeropostal, and Laser. Aserca and Aeropostal also fly to Barcelona, Maturín, Puerto Ordaz and Valencia. Mérida is served by Santa Bárbara, Oriental and Air Venezuela. Santa Bárbara is a local line named for a town in southern Zulia which as a result enjoys daily service to Maracaibo. Punto Fijo is linked by a morning Servivensa flight; San Antonio is served by Servivensa's flight at 07.50 daily except Sunday.

By bus
The Terminal de Pasajeros is large, busy and conveniently located downtown, 1.5km southwest of Calle 100-Libertador. Buses depart all day to Cabimas and eastern towns, to El Moján and the Guajira including Maicao in Colombia (5 hours), departing at 05.00. The fastest route to San Cristóbal goes west of Lake Maracaibo, 445km (8 hours). To Caracas, 745km (11 hours), about $17. To Valencia, either via Coro, 533km, or Barquisimeto, 511km (6 hours). Frequent service to Valera, 4 hours, start of the Transandean route.

Por puesto cars cover many destinations and charge much more. Within Maracaibo these shared taxis often have fixed stops or *paradas* and follow set routes along various main streets such as Av Milagro. The *por puestos* serving Altagracia on Lake Maracaibo's east coast via the bridge leave from Av 100 Libertador at the foot of Av 10.

Lake launches
The launches crossing to Altagracia on the eastern shore of Lake Maracaibo leave from the *embarcadero* on Av 100 Libertador at the foot of Av 10. The ride costs about $1.

Where to stay
The area telephone code for Maracaibo is (061)
Hotels in Maracaibo run the gamut from flophouse to luxury, and most better places are some distance from downtown. All except the lowest price have air conditioning and private bath, but not always hot water (given the prevailing heat). In cases of shortage, some may have no water.

Downtown
The classiest hotel near downtown is the 3-star **Cumberland** (formerly Cantaclaro), tel: 222944, fax: 213826, Calle 86A; doorman, Trafalgar Restaurant,

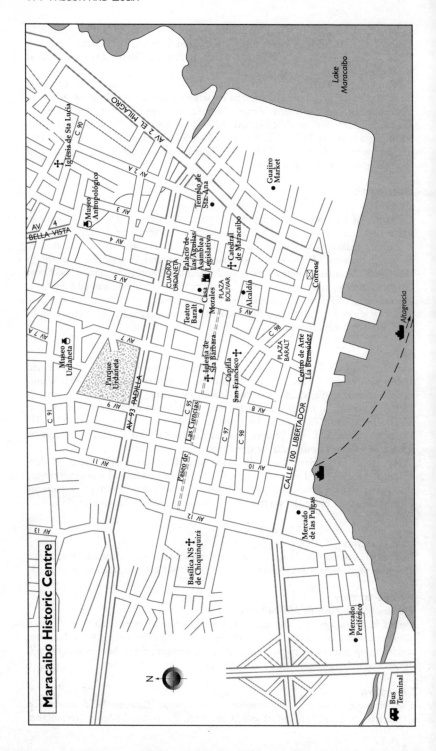

Maracaibo Historic Centre

Lake Maracaibo

Iglesia de Sta Lucía
C 90
AV 2 EL MILAGRO
Museo Antropológico
AV 2
AV 3
Templo de Sta-Ana
Guajiro Market
AV 4
BELLA VISTA
AV 4
AV 5
Palacio de Las Águilas
Asamblea Legislativa
Catedral de Maracaibo
CUADRA URDANETA
Casa Morales
PLAZA BOLIVAR
Correos
Teatro Baralt
Alcaldía
Museo Urdaneta
AV 7
C 96
AV 7A
Parque Urdaneta
Iglesia de Sta Bárbara
Capilla San-Francisco
PLAZA BARALT
Centro de Arte Lía Bermúdez
C 91
AV 93 PADILLA
AV 6
C 95
Paseo de Las Ciencias
AV 8
Altagracia
AV 11
AV 12
C 97
C 98
AV 10
CALLE 100 LIBERTADOR
AV 13
Basílica NS de Chiquinquirá
Mercado de las Pulgas
N
Mercado Periférico
Bus Terminal

Piccadilly Bar; 90 rooms, single $48, double $54. In the same range is the new **Hotel Tierra del Sol**, just south on Av Bella Vista No 87-125; tel: 230521.

In a mixed residential-business area east of Av Bella Vista is the **Astor Hotel**, tel: 914510/30, Calle 77, south side of Plaza República; real value in a two-floor Italian-run hotel with a restaurant filled every night by regulars; good food, economical. The rooms are small and mattresses aging; $11 double. A nearby hotel, the **Mansión**, tel: 912653, Av 5 de Julio, four blocks east of Av Bella Vista, is over a noisy bar/restaurant; $24 double. **Hotel Unión**, tel: 924068, is in a pleasant old-style house on Calle 84 No 4-60, a block east of Bella Vista; tall ceilings and tiled floors, 14 rooms; $15 double and usually full. A similar place, the **Nuevo Montevideo**, tel: 222762, is a block west of Bella Vista on Calle 86A, a quiet street, just before the Cumberland.

In the centre are aging hotels, passable at $11 single, $13 double. **Hotel Caribe**, tel: 225986/2159, Av 7 near Calle 93. The once imposing **Victoria** on Plaza Baralt, tel: 229697, is still OK if you get a balcony on to the plaza.

Avenida Milagro

In the south are cheap hotels, in the north expensive. **Hotel El Milagro**, tel: 228934, Av 2 opposite Templo Santa Ana, 228934, is a busy salesman's hotel with small plain rooms; $15 double.

In 2km is **Hotel del Este**, tel: 918511; 17 spartan rooms, hard mattresses, one to four people for $7–12. Two doors beyond is **Su Hotel**, tel: 927539; front parking under mango tree, dark restaurant; six rooms, single or double bed $17. A vast apartment complex on the lake, Residencias San Martín, serves here as a halfway landmark. To the north is the expensive **Hotel El Paseo**, tel: 924084/94, fax: 919453, Av 1B and Calle 74, 12-storey tower with a revolving restaurant on top, small pool; 54 suites with refrigerator. Maracaibo's best-known hotel, the 5-star **Del Lago**, is operated by the Inter-Continental chain, tel: 924022/222, fax: 914551; gardens, poolside barbecue, restaurants, shops, gym, sauna, golf and tennis; 366 rooms with mini-bars, $80–100.

There are several less expensive good hotels. Two are: **Kristoff**, Av 8 at Calle 68, a block west of Av Bella Vista, tel: 972911/17; gym, turkish baths, hairdresser, shops, pool, 307 rooms; and **Gran Hotel Delicias**, Av 15-Las Delicias at Calle 70, tel: 976111/14; small pool, restaurant, bar, 108 rooms, about $55.

Where to eat

Many of Maracaibo's restaurants are closed on Sundays. You only have to see the many workers, oilmen and upper crust eating at **La Matera** to be aware of its 30-year position as Maracaibo's leading *criollo* restaurant. Although located in a northern residential area at the first entrance to Urb La Floresta, it is rustic, tree-shaded and very reasonable, serving specialities such as coconut-bean soup, *mojito* of coconut and shredded fish, curried goat, crab with fish sauce, *huevos chimbos* – not eggs but a rum-pumpkin dessert. Tel: 548236; midday only.

El Tinajero is another Zulia restaurant with specialities such as kid-and-coconut, *chipichipi* (clam) soup, *lisa* (roe). It's on Av 3C near the Hospital Coromoto, tel: 915362.

For excellent steak, recommended no-frills restaurants are: **Mi Vaquita**, Calle 76 at Av 3H, by now an institution near Plaza La República, tel: 911990; **El Gaucho**, Av 3Y at Calles 77-78, tel: 82110; **Mi Ternerita**, Av 3Y at Calles 74-75. More restaurants in the area include Brazilian, Spanish, seafood, Swiss houses: **Casavieja**, Calle 72 No 3F-29, tel: 919961; all the pork, beef, chicken you can eat, straight from the spit as they serve it in Rio de Janeiro; closed Mon. The **Toledo**,

Calle 76 at 3H, tel: 74665; speciality is paella. **Delfín**, Calle 75 at 3H, tel: 913349; try the seafood here and at **Casa** (and bar) **Paco**, Av 4 at Calle 70, tel: 77040, a late-night place. **Chalet Suizo**, Calle 78 between Av 3G-H, tel: 914370; the place for many fondues, except Mon.

Downtown, enjoy a break at the charming **El Zaguán**, Calle 94 at Av 6, open 12.00–15.00, 19.00–24.00; also coffee and snacks outside under great bombax trees.

Teppan-yaki is prepared by the Japanese knife expert as you watch, at the new **Gran Samurai**, Av 29 at Calle 69, tel: 518806, 523043; open every day except Wednesday. And don't forget the restaurant with the best lake view: the revolving **Girasol** atop Hotel El Paseo, Av 1B at Calle 74; expensive but it's a treat.

What to see
Old Maracaibo

Within a small downtown area near the docks you can catch the city's lively spirit. Avenues go north–south, *calles* east–west. The lakeside drive, Av 2 El Milagro, ends in a right angle with the Malecón or south waterfront boulevard. This street is Calle 100-Libertador. The cavernous post office, **Ipostel**, is near the corner. Three blocks west stands a wonderful metal and glass structure dating from 1928. Now the **Centro de Arte de Maracaibo** (CAM), it was prefabricated in England and served as the public market until outgrown; the meat, fish and vegetable stalls were closed in the mid 1970s. Now elegantly restored, CAM has a museum, drama, dance and concert hall, information centre, reading room, arts and crafts shop and cafeteria.

Everything under the sun is sold at the open-air marketplace, called **Mercado de las Pulgas** or 'flea market', by the lake four blocks west on Calle 100. In the daily kaleidoscope of its hubbub, you will see many Guajira women. They come at dawn by bus, do their shopping and selling, then vanish homeward. However, this is not the place to buy crafts; with luck you may find a few baskets outside. For crafts go to the **Mercado Guajiro** stalls on Av El Milagro at Calle 96, east side. For fresh produce and staples, explore the very big covered market, **Mercado Periférico**, about five blocks southwest of Las Pulgas.

Plaza Baralt opens behind the Arts Centre. Closed to traffic, the next three blocks north on Av 6 teem with vendors hawking almost everything in loud competition: bargains in hair clips, shoes, books, shirts, watches, paintings, cassettes. Before the oil boom this plaza was the classy business and shopping centre, presided over by the statue of Rafael María Baralt, 19th-century writer and historian who wrote a Castillian dictionary, edited the *Gaceta de Madrid* and was elected to Real Academia of Spain where he died in 1860. At the plaza's north end is the restored **San Francisco Chapel**.

At Calle 96 a green swath called **Paseo de Las Ciencias** stretches between Maracaibo's two main churches: the **Cathedral** at the east end on Plaza Bolívar, and the **Basílica de la Chiquinquirá** in the west. In between is the **Iglesia de Santa Bárbara**, the only building not razed to make the Paseo. Many picturesque little houses of El Saladillo district were demolished in 1973 to give the city this splendid setting for historic buildings, museums, art works, gardens, band concerts and processions. Some of the old houses remain on Calle 96. The modern Municipal Council or **Alcaldía** stands south of Plaza Bolívar; it houses a **Museum of Graphic Arts** which is really an exhibition room.

In good Zulia fashion both the big churches have miraculous local images. Maracaibo's oldest church is the **Cathedral** whose records go back to 1610 although its construction date is not documented. It shelters the **Cristo de Gibraltar**, a crucifix rescued from fire 400 years ago when the southern lake port of Gibraltar was destroyed by Indians. Maracaibo clergy later refused to give it back, so the decision of where it belonged was left to the charred image revered as the Black Christ. Placed in a boat on the lake it first drifted towards Gibraltar but then turned to Maracaibo.

The pride of Zulia's faithful, however, is the miraculous little painting of **La Virgen de Chiquinquirá**. She is enshrined in the large yellow Basilica. The structure is older than it looks; in 1770 it replaced an earlier thatched church. As the cult of Chiquinquirá grew, so did church expansion. The final rebuilding as a Basilica took 20 years and was ready in time for crowning the Holy Image as Zulia's patron saint in 1942. Inside, it is fantastically overdecorated and has to be seen to be believed. The Virgin's gold crown is much larger than her image. Every year on November 17 followers of La Chinita, as the Virgin is nicknamed, gather outside the church at midnight to serenade her. Singing *gaitas*, they wait through the night to celebrate mass on November 18, La Chinita's Day. (See below: *Festivals, Feria de La Chinita*.)

La Chinita's legend begins in the early 1700s when a humble woman went to the lake shore where boat builders used to make *piraguas*. Among the pieces of wood she found was a small smooth plank floating in the lake. She took it to her home at No 5 on the street known today as El Milagro and used it to cover the water jug. One day after washing it she saw old traces of a religious image so she hung it on the wall. A year later on November 18 1709, she was working at her trade grinding cacao when she heard three knocks from the board; the knocks were repeated. When she went to see, a great light shone from the board which glowed with the image of Our Lady of Chiquinquirá, the same Virgin as one cherished in Colombia. Today's theory about the oil painting, measuring 26 by 25cm, is that pirates took it from a church on the Colombian coast and, when raiding Maracaibo, threw it out or lost it overboard. In any case, no one knows how long it floated in the lake before it was picked up.

Neither La Chinita nor the Christ of Gibraltar, however, has the honour of being Maracaibo's patron saint. That goes to St Sebastian as it was on his day, 20 January, that Maracaibo was said to have been founded. The day is marked with special masses in the Cathedral at 08.00 and 17.00 followed by a procession bearing the saint's image, and a concert in the Plaza de La República.

North of the Cathedral stands the **Legislative Assembly**, built in 1888. The **Casa de Gobierno** or Palacio de las Aguilas nearby was begun in 1841 and its main floor of 24 columns was completed 25 years later, followed by the upper storey in 1890. The condors or 'águilas' on the roof were added in 1929. To its west is another historic building, **Casa Morales**, famed as the place where General Morales signed his surrender following Spanish defeat in the Battle of Lake Maracaibo, 1823. The city's last remaining colonial mansion has been restored today as headquarters of the Bolivarian and historical societies; open Mon–Fri 08.00–17.00. On the next corner is the handsomely restored **Teatro Baralt**, first opened in 1883.

Lovely **Santa Ana Church** was built in 1602 at the east end of Calle 94 by a devout couple, Doña Inés del Basto and Francisco Ortiz, who then added to it Venezuela's first hospital. The chapel is one of Maracaibo's few colonial structures, enlarged in 1774 with a wonderfully baroque altar screen and pulpit. There is still a city hospital next door although not attached and not beautified.

Walk along Calle 94 to the **Museo Arquidiocesano**, a house on the corner of Av 4. The Cathedral's museum offers cool rooms, restored kitchen, antique books, silver and gold chalices; open Mon–Sat 09.00–18.00. A few steps up Av 4 is the tiny **Templo Bautismal Rafael Urdaneta** where Maracaibo's Independence hero was baptised. His words, engraved in the corner Plaza de la Herencia, refer to the statue and bas relief of his family there: 'I leave only a widow and 11 children in the greatest poverty'. To visit the **Museo Urdaneta** go west three blocks and cross Av Padilla (Calle 93) to Parque Urdaneta; the museum is another three blocks north on Av 7A. The house where he was born (1788) no longer exists; in its place is a 1936 building containing many of Urdaneta's belongings, and period weapons and paintings. There is a good historical library. Open Tue–Fri 09.00–12.00, 14.00–17.00; weekends 10.00–13.00.

For the **Museo Antropológico** continue northeast to No 91-37, Av 4 Bella Vista. Before it was converted into a museum, apparently this odd-looking structure was a gaol. You will find photos and artefacts of native cultures, particularly Guajiro and Paraujano. Open Sun 11.00–15.00; Mon–Fri 09.00–18.00; closed Sat.

Santa Lucía district, also known as El Empedrado, overlooks the lake to the east of Av 4. Topped by a church on a hill, Santa Lucía is worth exploring as one of Maracaibo's last neighbourhoods of brightly painted typical houses. Steps lead down from the plaza to lower streets. *Gaita* music, trademark of Zulia, apparently originated here as the *gaita* bands traditionally started up on St Lucia's day, December 13. The beat is insistent, pervasive; words are irreverent, satirical or devout but rarely romantic. Instruments are basically four: *maracas*, the *cuatro* or four-stringed guitar, *charrasca* (a scraped instrument); and the *furruco* whose deep notes come from rubbing an upright pole on a drumhead.

Midtown, north Maracaibo

Corpozulia is on Av Bella Vista at Calles 83–84, several blocks north of Santa Lucía. The state development agency's headquarters has a tourism office. They will tell you what's new and provide city maps, folders and a schedule of local events. Ring (061) 921811/35. Open Mon–Fri 08.00–12.30, 14.00–16.00.

The **University of Zulia** (LUZ) and its enormous campus lie several kilometres to the west where Calle 77-Av 5 de Julio meets Calle 61-Av Universidad. The university has a 600-bed general hospital, a maternity hospital, nursing and medical schools. There are schools of agronomy, engineering, law, economics and humanities. Sports tracks, stadiums, olympic pools and gyms surround the campus, and north of Av Circunvalación 2 is the Plaza de Toros, bull ring.

The new **Museo de Arte Contemporáneo** is on Av 61-Universidad, sector Fuerzas Armadas. On land donated by the University of Zulia, the museum has some 5,000m² of exhibition space for art of 'every medium'. The first stage, comprising salons, gardens, cafetería and gift shop, was opened in 1998. One exhibition hall (there are five) is three floors high; it is so big that the Contemporary Art Museum of Caracas would fit inside.

The British Council has opened a centre in Maracaibo near Avenida 15-Las Delicias, mainly for teaching English. It has a library and video collection. The address is: Av 14B, No 66A-40, between Av 67-Cecilio Acosta and Calle 66; tel: (061) 983169, fax: 984047; website: www.britcoun.org/Venezuela.

The **Centro de Bellas Artes**, Av 3F at Calle 68A, is three blocks east of Av Bella Vista; to reach it take a bus up Bella Vista and get off at the Iglesia Corazón de Jesús (3.5km from Plaza Bolívar); walk east from the corner. Since its opening in 1954, this cultural centre has presented art and theatre festivals, craft fairs and concerts. The Maracaibo Symphony Orchestra performs here. Art films are screened on Monday nights at half price. An English-language stage group, the Maracaibo Players, uses its theatre. The Players donated the **Guajiro tapestry** by Luis Montiel which forms the theatre curtain, an amazing work 16m long by 7m high. Here also, a fine little crafts shop, **Taller Mali Mai**, represents Guajiro artists; open Mon–Fri 09.00–12.00, 14.00–18.00; Sat 08.00–12.30. For times of exhibitions and concerts, also the Cine Club, ring (061) 912950, 912860. The **Alianza Francesa**, down the street on Av 3F at Calles 70-71, tel: (061) 912921, also gives exhibitions and shows films. Ask about Guajiro-style mantas designed for dress wear by Lupe Faria at her nearby shop, **Kai Kai**, Av 3E at Calle 72.

Avenida Bella Vista swings northeast to join Av El Milagro at the lake. There are adjacent parks here, the Plaza del Buen Maestro and Parque La Marina with a monument to the Battle of Lake Maracaibo. **El Mirador**, a 50m tower, provides a great lookout over the city. If it is closed there's a spectacular view to be had 1km south, from the revolving rooftop restaurant called **Girasol** at Hotel El Paseo on the lake. The entrance road is about four blocks south of Hotel del Lago, Av 1B at Calle 74.

Santa Rosa de Agua, today part of Maracaibo, is a lakeside village on stilts. It is located about 2km north of Parque La Marina and lies some distance from Av Milagro Norte so that you do not see it from the road. People, imagining that perhaps this was the village that inspired Amerigo Vespucci to name the area Little Venice, have placed his bust in the plaza. Certainly Vespucci saw villages similar to today's, although Santa Rosa is a *criollo* fishing village, not an Indian community. Here the houses or *palafitos* are built of planks with boardwalks linking one to another. This construction over the water makes houses cooler, but the lake is contaminated and drinking water must be supplied from land. For true Indian *palafitos*, take a trip to **Sinamaica**.

Festivals

Zulia's popular saint is La Virgen de Chiquinquirá and the whole state turns out for the big **Feria de La Chinita** leading up to religious observations on November 18. The fair starts out with a parade of floats on Av 5 de Julio headed by the Fair's Queen. She also presides at the opening of a bike race and a bullfight. Children's games are held in each parish with clowns and puppets. Folklore groups enliven Plaza Baralt and Av Padilla with music and dance. Rollerblade races take place on Av Milagro and Fuerzas Armadas, car races at the autodrome, baseball at the Luis Aparicio stadium. There are concerts and exhibitions at the Centro de Bellas Artes. There's an arts and crafts fair, even a nighttime lake cruise, the 'Feria del Ferry'. All to the rhythm of *gaita* bands resounding night and day.

Christmas The repetitive *gaita* beat in no way resembles a carol but this peculiarly Maracaibo music takes over not only Zulia but the entire country at Christmas time. In every district, almost every street, *gaitero* groups compose and rehearse songs. Downtown, Maracaibo's streets become a big bazaar as stalls go up along the Paseo de Las Ciencias, Plaza Baralt, Av Padilla and Calle 100.

Festival de San Benito December 27–31 is observed by the people of El Moján, Altagracia, Cabimas, Lagunillas, Gibraltar, Bobures and San Antonio with processions and costumed dances honouring the black saint. In Sinamaica, the native Paraujanos proceed in launches around 17.00 on December 27 to the opening ritual; each group is led by an image of San Benito held high. Around an altar in a thatched hall, drummers beat to a solemn dance by men of the various groups, still carrying their own San Benito.

In El Moján, celebrations on the main street are livelier, again with competing groups. South of the lake, fiestas in Bobures and Gibraltar are famous for their conical African drums, costumed *vasallos* and *esclavos* (vassals and slaves), and the all-night vigils to fulfil promises made to the saint who is also believed to enjoy a good party.

Further afield
San Carlos Island

San Carlos, a headland rather than a true island, is being groomed for tourism for its good beaches and restored fort. The star-shaped **Castillo de San Carlos** guarding the entrance to Lake Maracaibo was built in 1680–88. The fort last saw action in 1903 when its guns repelled warships sent by European powers to blockade Venezuelan ports for non-payment of foreign debts. Although the watch tower has disappeared, the Castillo's massive walls have withstood centuries of sun, wind and surf. Strong winds at times sweep the gulf, raising huge waves and blowing ships off course or worse, on to land. The fortress was put to use by Dictator Juan Vicente Gómez as a political prison and some cells still bear the scratched names of occupants. Gómez's death in 1935 freed hundreds of unfortunates here, in Puerto Cabello's fort and in Caracas.

The dazzling beach facing the Gulf of Venezuela is broad, sandy, mostly deserted, and worth the short trek for bathers. However, it is shadeless and as the sun is white hot you will be well toasted in half a day. The more popular beach is on the south side where food stalls serve snacks. This beach is near the pier.

San Carlos village now has streets, a new church and a small museum. People in the community are beginning to offer rooms for rent and Corpozulia has opened an inn. The **Posada de San Carlos** has air conditioning, terrace, beds and bunks for 12 people. For reservations ring Corpozulia in Maracaibo, tel: (061) 921811, 921840.

Getting there Launch ferries run frequently from El Moján to Toas Island and San Carlos. El Moján is a growing town at the mouth of the Limón River. It is not very pretty, but has a new bus terminal with fast service to Maracaibo, 40km.

Coaling port

Not only San Rafael del Moján but the whole area is changing swiftly under the impact of mining in the huge Guasare coal deposits, some 70km west. Once again Petróleos de Venezuela has control through its subsidiary Carbozulia. The open pit mines of Paso Diablo and Socuy, currently exporting five million tonnes yearly, are aiming for 20 million tonnes by the year 2003. Shell and Ruhrkohl of Germany have invested in mixed companies. Coal from Guasare is of good quality, having high calorie and low sulphur content. Zulia's proven reserves are nearly 1,000 million tonnes (out of an estimated 8,000 million tonnes).

A new port will be built somewhere along the Gulf of Venezuela; both Boca de Paijana at the west end of San Carlos Island and Pararú further north have been discussed as possible sites. Meanwhile, lorries move coal to the small port of Santa Cruz de Mara on the lake.

Sinamaica Lagoon

A network of marshes and lagoons including Sinamaica drains into the Limón River. This is the territory of some 1,800 Paraujanos, fishermen and their families of mixed *criollo*-Indian culture. Their villages on stilts form one of the biggest tourist attractions near Maracaibo. The main embarcation point for tourist launches (six passengers) is **Puerto Mara**, just down to the right before the Río Limón bridge, 5km from El Moján. The big time is weekends. If you go on a weekday (barring holidays) there will be little activity and you may have to hire the whole *lancha*, $25, for an hour's outing. You can eat well at one of the two large open-sided restaurants and the alcohol list is almost longer than the menu. There are public phones and bathrooms.

The second port, **Cuervito**, is on the lagoon 5km from the village of Sinamaica (60km from Maracaibo). There are *por puestos* linking the two villages. If you arrive early on Wednesday you will see boats bringing people to market. There are usually many launches here all day to take you to lake communities such as Pueblo Barro, about 15 minutes away, or Caño Morita, La Boquita and Boca de Caño. Most visitors stop for refreshments at the **Parador Turístico** built for the purpose in the lake.

Shops, schools, even a church and police station, are all built over the water *palafito*-style, some linked by boardwalks. Dwellings have walls made of *esteras* or reed matting, and roof of reeds or palm-thatch. The traditional one-room house has hammocks for sleeping but few chairs and no door; ceiling beams provide storage and hanging space. Beside their canoe, a Paraujano family's most prized possession is the TV set. Onshore, houses are often built with planks, tin roofs and room dividers. These may be the homes of Paraujanos who earn wages in oil and coal, coconut plantations, or shrimp farms. Besides being outside the money economy, the lagoon has other drawbacks for living: poor sanitation, lack of fresh water in the dry season when the lagoon becomes salty, and mosquitoes in the rainy season.

Endless kilometres of beach and shallow waters lining the Gulf of Venezuela have long attracted bathers from Maracaibo where the lake is contaminated. Most popular is **Caimare Chico**, developed with restaurants, two pools and 76 not-very-private bungalows; lively Saturday nights. Reservations at Hotel El Paseo, Maracaibo: tel: (061) 919744. The side road is signposted, about 12km beyond Sinamaica.

The Guajira Peninsula

The road north enters arid lands where Guajira women dress Arab-wise in billowing *mantas* and Guajiro men clad in shirt, sash and loincloth tend their cattle. Guajiros represent Venezuela's largest indigenous group: 168,000 out of the total of 197,000 natives (1992 census).

Both the Guajiros and Paraujanos belong to the Arawak language family and they are properly called Wayúu and Añú, meaning 'people'. Many of the Wayúu grow up learning Spanish as a second language in school. At the same time a large number live in Maracaibo and have done well in city life, graduating from university and, as Nemesio Montiel, teaching anthropology and entering politics as congressman. The Guajiro district of Ziruma in Maracaibo is quite near the university campus.

The Wayúu are perhaps the only New World natives who successfully took advantage of the Europeans' arrival with cattle and horses and soon developed a cattle-centred economy unique in the Americas. As early as 1550 they already had cattle which quickly replaced subsistence hunting and gathering. Formerly semi-nomadic, moving with cattle from well to watering hole, today most have houses in scattered communities. They are also quite adept at smuggling (either to or from Colombia) as they recognise no border.

That the Wayúu remain independent herders is a tribute to their complex and highly structured society. Families are tightly organised in *castas* or clans where authority rests with the matriarch's brother. Clan lines, including chieftains, descend through women. A bride's worth is calculated by the number of cattle the groom pays, and negotiations are long. If cattle cannot compensate for offences or injuries (even miscarriage and suicide are causes for blame), long and bloody feuds may ensue.

Although living very close to the gulf, Guajiros are not fishermen or navigators. For them, the gulf is fun and safe, the hard sand great for bicycles, the beach for children as the world over. Swimming is limited by shallow waters but near Paraguaipoa you can see Guajira ladies wade coolly into the waves, *mantas* and all (*para* means 'sea').

Paraguaipoa, 95km from Maracaibo, is the area's only sizeable town. It has grown, first as a business and barter centre for people as far away as Maicao and Ríohacha in Colombia, then as a funnel for contraband goods arriving by sea on the long coast. However, electricity, health services and personal security are all precarious. The army has a post and car checks are frequent.

Los Filuos market draws lines of *plátano*-laden trucks, herdsmen with goats and sheep, and hundreds of Guajiros coming by jeep and truck from the dusty Alta Guajira or upper peninsula (mainly Colombia) to do their bartering. Held early Monday, the market is located just beyond Paraguaipoa. Although this is not a tourist market, you may find for sale some Guajira sandals with soles made of tyre rubber, hats, bags crocheted in many colours and sizes, sashes and mantas of cotton, nylon or dacron.

The artists who make these bags and the by-now famous Guajiro tapestries live in villages not far from Paraguaipoa. One of the top names is Tere González who lives by the Laguna del Pájaro; she is now in her 80s. Luis Montiel, who died in 1998, was the grand master of tapestries (see *Centro de Bellas Artes*, page 418). His workshop is called **Mali Mai**; it is located 7km north of Los Filuos, plus 1.5km southwest by a side road at Yagusirú. Many craftsmen execute his designs and the place is always active. In Maracaibo, ask about their work at the Mali Mai shop, Centro de Bellas Artes. The village of **Ulerí**, where celebrated leader Torito Fernández lived and where Luis Montiel was born, sponsors an intercultural centre, **Alitasa**. Many of the inhabitants are descendants of El Torito. Near the plaza with its busts of Torito Fernández and Rómulo Betancourt, fringed hammocks in bright colours set off carved gourds, bags and tapestries for sale.

Between Paraguaipoa and Maicao in Colombia there is a 26km road and before the border you must stop at the army post of Paraguachón for passport control. As the whole area is reputed to be a hotbed of drug runners or *narco traficantes*, authorities are understandably paranoid. This border crossing is not recommended as a travel route.

WESTERN ZULIA
Sierra de Perijá

Much of the territory between Lake Maracaibo and the Sierra de Perijá was colonised and cleared after the 1960s. Farmers and ranchers spread south from Machiques into a frontier zone where since the time of the Spanish conquest the much-feared Motilones had defended their homeland with 6ft arrows. In 1961 an Indian reservation of 1,887km^2 was created to halt attacks by ranchers who set fire to native villages from the air. Today, the remaining 1,500 Motilones have either withdrawn further up the mountains or live on the reservation. They are now known by their own Carib name of Bari. These people are still harassed by colonists crossing the border from Colombia, and by the army pursuing Colombian guerrillas. Loggers, coal miners and oil companies exploit the reservation, often with government concessions.

In the early 1970s the Perijá road west of the lake was completed from Maracaibo some 370km to La Frfa in Táchira State. Although pretty enough, it is still a lonely road. The last gasoline station is important enough to be marked on maps as the **Bomba Catatumbo**. About 1km beyond, the welcome restaurant and hotel **El Andino** stands in the middle of nowhere. A series of bridges over the big southern rivers, the Arigüisa, Catatumbo, Socuayo and Zulia, are all guarded by soldiers who inspect vehicles and check identity papers.

Machiques is the only sizeable town on this route, 130km south of Maracaibo. As the centre for prosperous dairy cattle farms and dried milk industries,

Machiques has a good little hospital, schools, housing developments and places to stay and eat. The Motel Tukuko has a restaurant, soda fountain, and air conditioned rooms with hot water.

Tucuco Mission

Efforts to pacify the warrior Motilones and their more passive neighbours, the Yukpa, began with the founding by Capuchins in 1945 of the **Misión de Los Angeles de Tucuco** in the Perijá foothills, 50km southwest of Machiques. The Capuchins, using army or oil company planes, 'softened' the Indians with gifts of food, tools and cloth dropped by air.

Today a village of 90 houses built by the state flanks the mission. The main residents are Yukpas, mostly subsistence farmers. Besides the church, the mission has vocational workshops and a school for 350 Yukpa and Bari children. A museum exhibits photographs, tools and artefacts of the two cultures, and models of indigenous houses.

Parque Nacional Sierra de Perijá

A band stretching along the Colombian border roughly from Machiques to El Rosario was declared a national park in 1978. The park covers 2,950km^2 of the Serranía de Los Motilones, named for the once-fierce natives who today call themselves Bari, the 'people'. The mountain chain rises abruptly from the basin of Lake Maracaibo to 3,500m at Pico Tetarí, west of Machiques. This part of the Sierra de Perijá in the Andean range is thickly covered by undisturbed forest and is likely to be left a 'wild' barrier on the border. Ecosystems vary from natural savannahs to tropical rainforest, premontane forest and páramo on the crest. Heavy rainfalls, more than 2,700mm yearly, feed mountain torrents.

In 1991 another large wilderness area was declared **Parque Nacional Ciénagas del Catatumbo**. A *ciénaga* is a swamp; these wetlands bordering Lake Maracaibo extend south to the Catatumbo River. For centuries goods and travellers from the Andes (Colombian and Venezuelan) reached Maracaibo by riverboat via the Catatumbo and the lake. Now that the Perijá highway runs west of the lake, traffic is local. There are no visitor facilities.

A strange phenomenon, the **Faro del Catatumbo**, illuminates skies above the Catatumbo basin with flashes of lightning (no thunder). This silent, intermittent *relampagueo* has occurred for centuries and is seen from as far away as the Andes. It is thought to be diminishing as a result of climate changes and human activities.

Cueva del Samán

Measuring more than 18km in length, the Cueva del Samán in the forested Guasare region of the Sierra de Perijá is Venezuela's longest. However, it does not compare with the Gúacharo cavern, as it basically follows a long underground river. It was first explored in 1990 by an expedition of the Venezuelan Speleological Society. They reported 15 galleries, some over 1km in length, and a big river forming pools 300m across. The river forms part of a system connecting at least 15 caves. White crabs, eyeless fish, centipedes and scorpions were found in the cave, while outside were tracks of pumas and jaguars. (See also page 49.)

THE EASTERN LAKE COAST
Los Puertos de Altagracia

One of the easiest and best outings while visiting Maracaibo is to take a fast ferry (for less than $1) across the neck of the lake. On the opposite shore there is a charming colonial town, Altagracia. Before the bridge people travelling from Coro to Maracaibo took a boat from one of several old ports around Altagracia. As the distance is a fifth of that by road, launches continue to ferry workers to jobs on either shore. The *'flechas'* (arrows) leave from the old pier at Calle 100-Libertador from dawn to dusk on the half-hour, returning on the hour.

Altagracia is a pleasant town with brightly painted typical houses. Around Plaza Miranda stand several 200-year-old structures including the **Museum of History**, finest house of its era. The Battle of Lake Maracaibo was planned here in 1823 and in 1826 Bolívar stayed on his fruitless journey to save the union of Gran Colombia.

Altagracia's beach, **El Vigía**, is considered to be one of the lake's best. Trouble is, the huge oil terminal of Puerto Miranda lies a few kilometres north, followed by the giant El Tablazo petrochemical complex managed by Pequiven, another arm of the state oil company. Pequiven has formed an enterprise called Produsal to supply a sodium chloride plant.

Controversially, 800,000 tonnes of salt a year is to come from nearby coastal wetlands of the Ciénaga de Olivitos. This is the home of otters and a hundred bird species including the pink flamingo. In theory, the flamingos are protected by a wildlife preserve established in 1986. In practice, however, the Environment Ministry sees no threat to the delicate habitat which is a breeding ground for much of the lake's fish as well as the flamingos.

Your best way of seeing the mangrove canals of Los Olivitos, and the flamingos while they remain, would be by boat. The fishermen of **Sabaneta** on Tablazo Bay fish by night and during the day their boats ride at anchor. They have joined conservation forces fighting to save the wetland ecosystem.

Santa Rita racetrack

Built in 1988 just east of the lake bridge, the big **Hipódromo de La Rita** has everything that Maracaibo's racing bettors could desire: roofed seating for 8,000 (jackets required for the grandstand, Jockey Club); closed circuit TV, a good breeze and a view of the lake. Computerised monitors receive bets from the capital. In nearly every Zulia town cheers greeted the arrival of the national *pari-mutuel* races called the 5 & 6, run here on Wednesdays from 17.30 (in Valencia on Fridays, in Caracas on Sundays). The oval track has a 1,000m straight and stables for 600 horses.

The *pueblo* of **Santa Rita** is south of the bridge; many of its little houses are in the multi-coloured Maracaibo style.

Oil towns: Cabimas to Mene Grande

Following the eastern shore of the lake, a highway goes south through a series of oil towns: Cabimas, Tía Juana (Lagoven HQ), Ciudad Ojeda, Lagunillas (Maraven HQ), Bachaquero and Mene Grande. As you will see by the 'donkey' pumps nodding non-stop, these towns spring from intense oil activities in the Bolívar Coastal Field, both on land and in the lake. In over 80 years Zumaque No 1, the first country's commercial well, has produced over half a million barrels of oil and is still pumping steadily. This well, declared a national monument, is on Cerro La Estrella in the area of Mene Grande. It is famous also as the place where the ceremony nationalising the oil industry was held on January 1 1976.

Imagine, if you can, how the area looked before oil, before highways and supermarkets. Drilling equipment, shipped down the lake, was transported in an open bongo up the Motatán River, then carried by mule and oxen over uninhabited, thickly forested terrain. Drilling was hard work in adverse conditions, under temperatures as high as 45°C. Drilling had scarcely started on Zumaque No 1 when a fire destroyed the derrick and work began again.

OIL, THE 'BLACK GOLD'

For over 65 years Venezuela has been among the world's biggest oil exporters. The state company **Petróleos de Venezuela** (PDVSA) is listed as the second largest oil corporation (1993, 1994), behind Saudi Aramco and ahead of Royal Dutch/Shell. World attention was rivetted by the 1922 blow-out on Lake Maracaibo's east coast of a well called Barrosos No 2. For nine days the well spewed out a million barrels of oil before it was brought under control. Four years later oil took over as the country's leading export.

Even before the Conquest, Indians around Lake Maracaibo caulked their canoes with oil and used it as a curative. They called the oil seeps *menes*. Spaniards used oil for lamps as well as boat repair. As early as 1539 a barrel of oil was exported to Spain 'to alleviate the gout of Emperor Charles V'. It was shipped from Cubagua which then had a seep. Then in 1878 a local Táchira company, La Alquitrana (*alquitrán* means tar), first exploited oil near Rubio (operations finally closed in 1934). It was not unil 1914, however, that Venezuela entered the oil age with the first commercially important well, Zumaque No 1 in the Mene Grande field. Shell subsidiaries brought in this well and Los Barrosos.

From a primitive agricultural country, Venezuela rocketed into an oil economy. For the people, used to haciendas bossed by a *patrón*, the new system was just bigger and easier. Some wealth filtered down from the top, and a centralised government controlled all power. For a long time there was a great deal of money and work. Three quarters of the population moved to cities. But oil dependency was too great; when prices fell the economy crumbled. By this time corruption had riddled the administration and public services were bankrupt. Despite democracy mayors and state governors were appointed, not elected, until 1989.

Oil fields extend north of the Orinoco from the Maracaibo and Apure basins in the west, to the Orinoco Delta in the east. In Monagas State a big discovery was made in 1986 in El Furrial. Such new finds bring proven reserves up to 58,500 million barrels, placing Venezuela fourth in global terms. And these figures do not include the Orinoco Tar Belt, the world's largest reserve of heavy crudes or naphthenes with 26,000 million barrels recoverable by traditional methods, and 148,000 million barrels by enhanced methods. Bypassing the cost of moving oil as thick as molasses, a new technology mixes bitumen and water to make a cheap boiler fuel called Orimulsion (exported to Canada, England, Denmark, Taiwan).

Today Japanese, American and European companies have been awarded contracts to exploit concessions for the first time since oil was nationalised in December 1975. Then, crude production averaged 2.2 million barrels per day. Current output by state company PDVSA is 3.2 million barrels daily. PDVSA is also a holding company for petrochemicals (Pequiven), coal mining (Carbozulia), bitumen (Bitor), a Curaçao refinery (Isla), fertilisers, and shipping. Its many foreign interests include shares in activities such as Ruhr Oel in Germany, Nynas Petroleum in Sweden and Belgium, and Champlin Refining, Unocal and Citgo (100%) in the USA, and, recently, a chain of petrol stations in the UK.

In the 1920s when concessions were given on the lake itself, oilmen pioneered offshore techniques to erect rigs on concrete piles. Today there are thousands of wells in the lake. On the drive from Cabimas to Tía Juana, there's an amazing view at Km5 of this horizon of oil derricks. You can get this sight from the lakeside dyke in Tía Juana, Lagunillas or Bachaquero. So much oil continues to be pumped out of the ground that the eastern shore has sunk as much as nine metres and a dyke 50km long keeps the lake from flooding coastal towns. As modern technology improves, new oil deposits are being discovered deeper under the lake.

The biggest city is Cabimas with about 175,000 people, followed by Ciudad Ojeda with 100,000. Ojeda's centre was laid out in the 1940s using Washington, DC, as a model, and its streets radiate like spokes from a single plaza.

Where to stay
Puente Urdaneta
If you are arriving at night and are reluctant to face a strange city, it is possible to stop at the **Hotel Riviera** just before the entrance to the bridge over the lake. Its security guards, much too secluded entrance and very private bungalows give away its use as a *hotel de citas*, but also make it a quiet safe hideaway on weekdays. Good beds, double $18. There are informal roadside restaurants nearby.

Cabimas
The **Cabimas Internacional**, Av Andrés Bello, tel: (064) 45692/94/95, is expensive. You pay for lake view and top-class facilities; poolside bar-restaurant, bank, car hire; 221 rooms. Among cheaper places, all with restaurants, are **Hotel Girasol**, tel: 42551; **Paraíso**, tel: 41578; **Remanso**, tel: 513214; **El Viajero**, tel: 42720.

Ciudad Ojeda
It's hard to find a good moderate place on this stretch. The 11-storey **Hotel América** on Calle Trujillo at Av Bolívar, tel: (065) 25522, is modern but its 178 rooms are pricey. 'We were happy to find a tiny, clean place with *nevera* (fridge), air conditioning, the motel-style **Hotel Lago**, Av Bolívar near Plaza Ojeda circle, tel: (065) 27742, 23628; rooms are a quarter of the price of the América. Stay away from '*tiradero*' motels like the one in Bachaquero; they want clients by the hour.' (Eirwen and Carlos Rodríguez)

Lagunillas
The **Hotel Lagunillas**, Centro Comercial Maraven on the highway, tel: (065) 21432, 24050 (Maraven); at least half the 50 rooms are taken up by Maraven employees so it's best to book ahead for this well-kept, busy hotel.

Appendix 1

LANGUAGE
English-Spanish glossary

A brief list of commonly used words and phrases with Spanish equivalents, including weekdays, months and numbers. Phonetic pronunciation is given for each word. The list gives a visitor with no knowledge of Spanish enough to get around, find luggage, ask the time, look for food and communicate other basic needs.

English	Español	Pronunciation (accent on underlined syllable)
hello	ola	<u>oh</u>-la
goodbye	adiós	ah-dee-<u>oss</u>
how are you?	¿como está usted?	<u>coh</u>-moh eh-<u>stah</u> ew-<u>stayd</u>
see you later	hasta luego	<u>astah</u> lew-<u>aygoh</u>
good day	buenos dias	boo-<u>eyn</u>ohss <u>dee</u>-ahs
good afternoon	buenos tardes	boo-<u>eyn</u>ohss <u>tarr</u>-dayz
good evening	buenos noches	boo-<u>eyn</u>ohss <u>noh</u>-chayz
morning	mañana	man-<u>nya</u>-na
afternoon	tardes	<u>tarr</u>-dayz
evening	noches	<u>noh</u>-chayz
very good	muy bien	mwee bee-<u>en</u>
thank you	gracias	<u>grah</u>-see-ahs
please	por favor	pohr fah-<u>vor</u>
excuse me	perdóneme	pehr-<u>dohn</u>-ay-may
many thanks	muchas gracias	<u>moo</u>-chas <u>grah</u>-cee-yahs
yes	sí	see
no	no	noh
what is your name?	¿como se llama?	<u>koh</u>-moh say <u>jah</u>-mah
my name is...	mi nombre es...	mee <u>nohm</u>-bray ays
I don't understand	no comprendo	noh cohm-<u>prayn</u>-doh
do you speak...	Habla...	<u>a</u>-blah...
...English	...Inglés	...en-<u>glays</u>
I'm hungry	tengo hambre	<u>ten</u>-goh <u>am</u>-bray
how much?	¿quantos?	<u>kwahn</u>-tohss
that's expensive!	¡está caro!	eh-<u>stah</u> kar-oh
that's too much!	¡está todo mucho!	eh-<u>stah</u> toh-doh moo-cho
I want	quiero	kee-<u>eh</u>-ro
I don't want	no quiero	noh kee-<u>eh</u>-ro
I would like	quisiera	kee-see-<u>eh</u>-ra
I am lost	estoy puerde	eh-<u>stoy</u> <u>pwehr</u>-day
to the right	a la derecha	ah lah day-<u>ray</u>-chah
to the left	a la izquierda	ah lah eez-kwee-<u>ehr</u>-dah
where is...	¿donde está...?	<u>dohn</u>-day eh-<u>stah</u>...
restaurant	el restaurante	el reh-staw-<u>rahn</u>-tay
bathroom	el baño	el <u>bahn</u>-yo
hotel	el hotel	el oh-<u>tehl</u>
bedroom	la habitación	la ab-ih-tas-<u>yon</u>
towel	la ropa	la <u>roh</u>-pah
soap	el jabón	el zhah-<u>bohn</u>
telephone	el teléfono	el tay-<u>lay</u>-foh-noh

currency exchange	la casa de cambio	la kasah deh cahm-bee-oh
bank	el banco	el bahn-coh
river	el río	el ree-oh
forest	la selva	la sehl-bah
airport	el aeropuerto	el ahy-roh-pwahr-toh
Indian village	el pueblo de los Indios	el poo-weh-bloh day loss een-dee-oss
boat	la barca	la bar-kah
bus station	stación del autobús	stah-see-ohn dehl ow-too-boos
street	la avenida	la ah-vehn-eedah
house	la casa	la cah-sah
guide	el guía	el gee-yah
luggage	equipaje	eh-kee-pah-hey
what time is it?	¿que hora es?	kay orah ays
what time is...	¿que hora...	kay orah...
the meal	la comida	la koh-midh-ah
breakfast	desayuno	day-say-ooh-noh
lunch	almuerzo	ahl-moo-ehrt-soh
dinner	cena	say-nah
what is your...	que es su...	kay ays soo...
phone number?	número de teléfono?	nume-eh-row day tay-lay-foh-noh
address	dirección	dee-rek-shee-yon

Weekdays Días laborables

Sunday	domingo	doh-min-goh
Monday	lunes	loo-ness
Tuesday	martes	mahr-tess
Wednesday	miércoles	mee-ehr-coh-less
Thursday	jueves	hoo-ay-bess
Friday	viernes	bee-err-ness
Saturday	sábado	sah-bah-doh

Months   Meses

January	Enero	ay-nay-rho
February	Febrero	fay-bray-roh
March	Marzo	mahrso
April	Abril	ab-reel
May	Mayo	my-oh
June	Junio	hoo-nee-oh
July	Julio	hoo-lee-oh
August	Agosto	ow-go-stoh
September	Septiembre	sayp-tee-aym-bray
October	Octubre	ock-too-bray
November	Noviembre	noh-bee-aym-bray
December	Diciembre	day-see-aym-bray

Numbers Números

zero	cero	zay-roh
one	uno	oo-noh
two	dos	dohs
three	tres	trayss
four	cuatro	kwat-roh
five	cinco	seen-koh
six	seis	says
seven	siete	see-aytay
eight	ocho	oh-cho
nine	nueve	noo-ay-bay
ten	diez	dee-ayz
eleven	once	ohn-say
twelve	doce	doh-say
thirteen	trece	tray-say
fourteen	catorce	kaht-ohr-zay
fifteen	quince	keen-zay

sixteen	*diez-y-seis*	<u>dee</u>-ayz ee <u>says</u>
seventeen	*diez-y-siete*	<u>dee</u>-ayz ee see-<u>ay</u>tay
eighteen	*diez-y-ocho*	<u>dee</u>-ayz ee <u>oh</u>-cho
nineteen	*diez-y-nueve*	<u>dee</u>-ayz ee <u>noo-ay</u>-bay
twenty	*veinte*	bay-<u>ihn</u>-tay
twenty-one	*veinte-y-uno*	bay-<u>ihn</u>-tay ee <u>oon</u>-o
thirty	*treinta*	<u>trayn</u>-ta
forty	*cuarenta*	kwahr-<u>ehn</u>-ta
fifty	*cincuente*	seen-<u>kwen</u>-tay
sixty	*sesenta*	says-<u>ehn</u>-ta
seventy	*setenta*	say-<u>tehn</u>-ta
eighty	*ochenta*	oh-<u>chen</u>-ta
ninety	*noventa*	noh-<u>ben</u>-ta
one hundred	*cien*	<u>see</u>-ehn
two hundred	*doscientos*	dhos see-<u>ehn</u>-toss
one thousand	*mil*	meehl
one million	*millón*	meeh-jee-<u>ohn</u>

At the restaurant

à la carte	*del menú,* or *de la carta*
banana	*cambur;* tasty varieties are the small, plump *cambur manzano,* finger bananas *titiaros,* cooking bananas *plátanos*
beans	*caraotas.* Black beans, *caraotas negras,* are a national staple. Larger red and brown varieties are called *frijoles.*
beef	*res;* steak *bifstek* (often tough); better cuts are – rump *punta trasera,* sirloin and churrasco *solomo de cuerito,* tenderloin *lomito*
bill	*la cuenta*
bread	*pan;* toast *pan tosdado*
breakfast	*desayuno*
butter	*mantequilla;* you are often served *margarina*
chicken	*pollo;* boned *deshuesado,* roast *al horno,* broiled *a la parrilla*
dining room	*comedor*
delivery service	*servicio a domicilio*
dinner	*cena*
drink	*bebida, trago;* non-alcoholic *bebida natural, refresco.*
egg	*huevo,* boiled *pasado por agua,* scrambled *perico*
fish	*pescado;* Brazilian mullet *lebranche,* hake *merluza,* mackerel *sierra* and *carite,* red snapper *pargo,* shark *cazón,* sea bass *mero*
garlic	*ajo*
grapefruit	*toronja*
grill	*parrilla,* mixed grill *parrilla mixta,* grilled *a la plancha*
ham	*jamón*
juice	*jugo;* freshly made *jugo natural,* processed *de cartón o de botella.*
lettuce	*lechuga*
lobster	*langosta*
lunch	*almuerzo*
maize	*maíz;* on the cob *jojoto.*
meal	*comida*
milk	*leche,* sour milk *leche ágria* or *pasada* (off)
mint	*hierba buena, menta*
orange	*naranja*
omelette	*tortilla*
pancake	*panqueca,* also *crepe*
pineapple	*piña*
pork	*cochino;* chops *chuletas,* roast pork leg *pernil*
potato	*papa;* fried *frita,* mashed *puré,* baked *al horno*
prawn	*langostino*
rare	*medio crudo, poco cocido;* medium *término medio,* well-done *bien cocido*
salad	*ensalada;* fruit salad *ensalada de fruta*
salt	*sal;* over salted *exceso de sal*
sandwich	*sandwiche, emparedado*
shellfish	*mariscos*

shrimp	*camarones*
snack	*merienda*
soft drink	*refresco*
squid	*calamares*
stew	*guisado*
sugar	*azúcar*; brown sugar *azúcar morena*, sugar loaf *papelón* or *panela*
sweet potato	*batata*
take-out	*comida para llevar*
tasty	*sabroso*; tasteless *desabrido*
tea	*té negro*; when ordering a cup, specify *leche aparte*, milk on the side, or you may get a cup of hot milk with a teabag. Iced tea (*té frío*) or Nestea is popular. Herb tea is *té de hierbas*
tip	*propina*
tunafish	*atún*
turkey	*pavo*
vegetables	*vegetales*, *legumbres*. The word *verduras* covers roots, not greens
vegetarian	*vegetariano*
water	*agua*; drinking *agua potable* or *pura*, boiled *agua hervida*, filtered *agua filtrada*, tap water *agua del chorro*. Bottled water is sold as *agua mineral*, either carbonated (*con gas*), or plain (*normal*).

Medical

ache	*dolor*
altitude sickness	*mal de páramo, soroche*
bite	*mordedura* snake, dog bite; *picada* insect, bird bite, peck
blood	*sangre*, blood test *examen de sangre*
broken bone	*fractura del hueso*
dehydration	*deshidratación*
diarrhoea	*diarrea*
doctor	*médico*
earache	*dolor de oído, otitis*
faint (v)	*desmayarse*, fainting spell *desmayo*
fever	*fiebre*, yellow fever *fiebre amarilla*
first aid	*primeros auxilios*
headache	*dolor de cabeza*
heatstroke	*insolación*
ill	*enfermo*; illness, disease *enfermedad*
pain	*dolor*
poisonous	*venenoso*, snake *ponzoñoso*
rape	*violación*
unconscious	*sin sentido, desmayado, inconsciente*
vaccination	*vacuna*

Vernacular

Venezuelan speech is often colourful and incisive. The words below are listed for two reasons: their importance to travellers, and their colloquial usage perhaps not found in phrasebooks.

alcabala	police or army road checkpoint. It is an offence to be found without identification or passport.
arma blanca	weapon made of steel, especially concealed knife. Police may legally confiscate a penknife with blade longer than 4cm. A machete is justified as a work tool, *arma de trabajo*.
arrecho	very difficult, tough, angry; or fantastic, terribly good.
avisparse	to keep a sharp eye out, as in Avíspate! Look lively!
balneario	beach or bathing spot with parking and food, but not always changing room.
barrio	originally, neighbourhood; a district of poor homes (*ranchos*) often built on invaded land lacking basic services.
bicho	insect, general word for thing, being, specially crawlies.
bochinche	uproar, commotion, disorder.
bomba	water pump, petrol station, bomb.
bonche	a party with alcohol (from 'punch').

bongo	large river craft hewn from single trunk, with raised sides, outboard motor.
bulla	racket, confusion, row; a diamond or gold rush.
caney	shelter with thatched roof.
caño	small tributary or side channel of river, at times drying up; a delta channel.
cardón	columnar type of cactus growing on Paraguaná Peninsula.
caribe	piranha. The original Carib word meant meat-eater, whence 'cannibal'.
catire	blond or fair-skinned, a foreigner from the North.
chalana	flatbed river ferry, sometimes propelled by a launch.
chamo/a	boy/girl, kid (informal).
chévere	great, fine.
chimbo	of poor quality, makeshift, imitation.
chinchorro	hammock made with an open-net weave; fishnet. See *hamaca*.
chivacoa	microscopic red ticks, the harvest mite; also called bete rouge, chiggers in the West Indies, USA.
churuata	thatched Indian round house, sometimes open sided; now, loosely, any house or shelter with thatched roof.
cola	tail; queue, as at the bank or in traffic. Also, a ride as in hitch hiking, *pedir cola*. A third meaning for *cola* is glue.
colgadero	rope for slinging hammock.
conuco	plot for subsistence farming, usually cleared by slash-and-burn.
criollo	creole, native-born, but not indigenous.
curiara	dugout canoe hollowed from a single trunk.
excursionista	hiker, trekker. *Estoy de excursión*, 'I'm on an outing.'
falca	capacious dugout for carrying cargo, 15-18m long, with roof and outboard motor.
fila	mountain ridge; *filo*, sharp edge of knife.
fino	good quality, as clothes, musical instrument, beverage.
franela	T-shirt, from the English 'flannel'.
guachimán	watchman or gatekeeper (taken from English).
habilitar	to enable, to cause an office to open for work in off-hours (a charge is made for issuing visas on weekends).
hato	large cattle ranch; *hatillo*, little ranch.
hay	there is/are. *Hay comida*, there is food; *no hay agua*, there is no water.
invierno	winter: the rainy season, May to October.
jefatura	police headquarters.
jején	gnat with a very irritating bite, infesting certain grassy areas, river banks.
ladilla	literally, louse; tiresome, a bore.
limpio	clean; without money, as in *Estoy limpio*, I'm broke.
liquiliqui	man's cotton suit with button-up neck, worn without shirt; traditional in the Llanos.
Llanos	the great plains of the Orinoco (ll is pronounced as y); *llanero*, cowboy.
malandro/a	rogue, scoundrel, bad lot, wrong doer, lawbreaker.
marico/a	homosexual
mata	generally, a plant; in the Llanos, a lone copse of trees.
mecate	rope for hauling, or for hanging hammock etc.
molestia	trouble, inconvenience. *No es molestia* means 'It's no trouble'. But take care, officials get angry when you say *Estoy molesto*, 'I am upset, offended'.
moreno/a	person of brown or dark skin, part Negro. It is not disparaging, and may be a term of affection.
morro	a rounded peak, promontory.
mosca	literally, a fly; colloquially, beware, as in *Mosca con los malandros!* Watch out for the bad guys!
motorista	operator of a boat, engine driver.
nailon	fishing line, monofilament (from the English).
nigua	sandflea, jigger (US), chigoe (West Indies).
palafito	a lake dwelling raised on posts, as houses on Lake Maracaibo that inspired the name of 'Little Venice' or Venezuela.

palanca	lever; by extension influence, strings. *Tiene palanca*, he's got influence.
palo	a stick, tree; a drink or shot of alcohol (from the era when plantations gave workers wooden chits instead of money, so they bought a '*palo de ron*').
pana	friend, chum (from 'partner').
páramo	high moorlike Andean terrain with low vegetation, from about 3,000m to the snow line.
peñero	wooden or fibreglass fishing boat with outboard engine.
pica	trail cut by machete. *Picar*, to cut, slice; to sting (insects).
pirata	a car operating illegally as a taxi or *por puesto*.
plaga	general word for biting insect pests.
por puesto	pay-by-the-seat cars (*carritos, colectivos*) or small buses (*busetas*) run privately.
prepotente	overbearing, bossy, macho attitude.
puri-puri	nocturnal biting gnats so small they pass through the finest netting.
ranchos	shacks. *Ranchos* are often erected on someone else's property by migrants to cities; they may be enlarged into multi-storey houses. *Ranchería*, a group of shelters used by fishermen or Indians.
ratón	hangover; *enratonado*, hung over.
raya	sting ray. The spotted marine ray is called *chucho*.
real	*real* has two meanings: money, the 50 cent piece. *Cuesta mucho real*, It costs a great deal. *Real* also means royal, also real.
rumba	swinging party.
rústico	any 4x4 vehicle.
sifrino/a	of superficial values, member of consumer society.
tepui	tablemountain of the Guayana Shield (from the Pemón); also *tepuy*.
tigre	jaguar. *A tigra* is a poisonous snake of the Bothrops family, *mapanare*.
toros coleados	competition among cowhands to throw the bull by its tail, bulldogging, practised in a *manga de coleo*.
verano	summer: the dry season, occurring not at midyear but at the end of the year.
zamuro	vulture. *En pico de zamuro*, in the vulture's beak; to be in mortal danger. *Estómago de zamuro*, the digestion of a vulture, able to eat anything.
zaperoco	uproar, disorder

Appendix 2

FURTHER READING

Everyone's heard of *The Lost World* by Sir Arthur Conan Doyle and *Green Mansions* by W H Hudson. Here are more factual books:

Birding in Venezuela by Mary Lou Goodwin, Sociedad Conservacionista Audubon de Venezuela, Caracas, 1997. The fourth edition covers the haunts of more species than most ornithologists could hope to see and in the bargain is an excellent guide for wilderness travel. Practical spiral binding.

Birds of Venezuela by Rodolphe Meyer de Schauensee and William H Phelps Jr, Princeton University Press, New Jersey, 1978. The 52 colour plates make this book an invaluable companion on travels, especially in the Llanos region where so many of Venezuela's 1,340 bird species are seen in the open.

Churún-Merú, the Tallest Angel by Ruth Robertson, Whitmore Publishing, Pennsylvania, 1975. The expedition that measured Angel Falls and put it on the world map in 1948. Some good details on jungle travel, Jimmie Angel and old-timers.

Climb to the Lost World by Hamish MacInnes, Hodder & Stoughton, London, 1974. Lively account of the expedition which climbed Roraima's north prow from Guyana. Good background on Everard Im Thurn's 1884 ascent, climbing techniques.

Diccionario de Historia de Venezuela, edited by Fundación Polar, Caracas, 1997. Four volumes give the essential history of people, towns, states, important geographical features, as well as political and literary figures. A CD ROM *Diccionario Multimedia*, produced by Videodacta, is updated annually by Polar: www.fundacionpolar.com.

Ecotourism Guide to Venezuela edited and published by Miro Popic, Caracas. Updated in English and Spanish this book covers national parks, natural monuments and over 500 camps and inns, emphasising higher quality (and price). Also route maps, useful data and seasonal changes in fauna and flora.

Guide to Camps, Posadas & Cabins by Elizabeth Kline, published by the author, Caracas, 1997. Invaluable original research gathering under one cover some 900 Venezuelan guesthouses, inns and remote camps, with prices, services, personal comments, and some pretty colour photos. Third edition.

Guide to Venezuela by Janice Bauman and Leni Young, Ernesto Armitano, Caracas, 2nd edition 1987. An irreplaceable background source on history and geography, as well as roads, sights, churches and customs. The first Venezuelan guidebook written by people who actually went to the places themselves. Clear maps. A Spanish edition is being published in regional sections by a state oil company, distributed and sold through PDV gasoline stations. The first three updated books of the *Guia de Venezuela* are: *Caracas and Los Roques*; *Miranda, Carabobo and Aragua*; *Oriente including Margarita*.

Hiking in the Venezuelan Andes by Forest Leighty, Venezuelan Andes Press, Danbury, CT, 1992. A small, practical book written by a long-time hiker who has graded the trails for difficulty. Many maps. Available in Caracas and Mérida.

Mamíferos de Venezuela by Omar J Linares, Sociedad Conservacionista Audubon de Venezuela, Caracas, 1998. The definitive mammals book of 327 species, with descriptions of nine biogeographical regions, and illustrations by Josu Calvo, Michael Le Coeur and Víctor Pérez. In Spanish.

Humboldt and the Cosmos by Douglas Botting, Michael Joseph Ltd, London, 1973. This is a fascinating biography of Alexander von Humboldt, perhaps the last 'universal man': geographer, botanist, geologist, explorer, diplomat and writer. He reached Venezuela's Casiquiare Canal, fixed the height of mountains and latitude of rivers, and collected thousands of new plant and animal specimens.

Los Aborígenes de Venezuela, Walter Coppens, editor, Fundación La Salle de Ciencias Naturales, Caracas. In Vol. III (1988) anthropologists write about seven contemporary ethnic groups including the Warao, Yanomami and Piaroa. Clear maps. Vol. II covers six groups, among them the Paraujano and Pemón. In Spanish.

Los Caminos del Avila by Paul Rouche with Jocelyne L Rouche, Oscar Todtmann Editores, Caracas, 1994. A series of walks on the Avila in a trio of pocket-size books, graded by difficulty, with meticulous elevation notes, walking times and route sketches. The ambitious hiker who wants to go from the Avila to Naiguatá and Los Caracas on the coast will need this book. In Spanish.

Out of Chingford by Tanis and Martin Jordan, Coronet, 1989. Subtitled 'Round the North Circular and up the Orinoco', this is an entertaining account of the Jordans' travels in an inflatable boat. Angel Falls area was one major expedition.

Personal Narrative of Travels to the Equinoctial Regions of America 1799-1801 by Alexander von Humboldt. Translated from the French by Thomasina Ross, London, 1852. The second of three volumes details explorations in Venezuela: Cumaná, Guácharo, the Apure, Orinoco, Atabapo and Casiquiare rivers. Humboldt studied everything he could see or touch: electric eels, curare. It's all here, and still valid today.

The Explorers of South America by Edward J Goodman, Collier-Macmillan, London, 1972. The journeys, sometimes quite fantastic, of Columbus, Vespucci, Ordaz and Raleigh in Venezuela, and later naturalists Humboldt, Bates, Spruce. Plus the famous Andean and Amazonian explorations. Concise reference work.

The Last Great Journey on Earth by Brian Branston, Hodder & Stoughton, London, 1970. A British hovercraft expedition crossed from the Amazon via the Casiquiare to the Orinoco in 1968 and rode the great Atures rapids.

Venezuela in Focus by James Ferguson, Latin American Bureau. Excellent economic and political background.

Venezuela's Islands in Time by Uwe George, National Geographic, May 1989, pp 526-561. Travel among tablelands, with spectacular photos and illustrations of how the Guayana Shield came to be. For those with 'tepui fever'.

Venezuela: World Bibliographic Series by DAG Waddell, Clio Press, Oxford and Santa Barbara, California, 1990. An annotated listing of 815 books concerning Venezuela. The source for anyone studying a particular aspect of the country.

WEBSITES
Fishing
Alpiturismo www.alpiturismo.com
Gigi Charters www.gigifish.com.ve
Venezuela Big Game Club www.Venezuelamarlinsafari.com.ve

Organisations

British Council www.britcoun.org/venezuela
British-Venezuelan Chamber of Commerce www.britcham.com, www.energyven.com
Centro Venezolano Americano www.cva.org.ve
Provea (human rights) www.derechos.org.ve
US Consular Affairs (travel warnings) www.travel.state.gov.
US National Trade Data Bank-NTDB (country commercial guides) www.stat-usa.gov
Venezuelan American Chamber of Commerce www.venamcham.org

Regions

Amazonas Camp Calypso www.vzla.com/calypso
Hato Piñero (Llanos) www.branger.com/pinero.html
40 Cosas para hacer en Margarita www.geocities.com/The Tropics/Shores/3454
Merida Travel Web www.merida_travel.cptm.ula.ve
Peninsula de Paraguana www.une.edu.ve/paraguana
UNE-Coasts (beaches of Aragua, Carabobo) www.une.edu.ve/costas
Venezuela Tuya www.venezuelatuya.com/gransabana
Venezuela Virtual - www.venezuelavirtual.com/pais/info_geo/info_geo.html Los
Roques, Margarita, Playas Falcon, Morrocoy, Choroni, Tacarigua, Mochima,
Medina, Turuépano

Travel companies and services

Akanan Travel www.caracasnet.com/akanan
Alpiturismo www.alpiturismo.com
Last Frontiers www.lastfrontiers.co.uk
Lost World Adventures - lwaccs@cantv.net
Margarita Online www.margaritaonline.com
Montaña Adventure Travel www.venadventure.com

Windsurfing

Caribe Winds www.enlared.net/caribewinds
Casa Viento www.sni.net/windsurf
Surfven www.geocities.com/pipeline/dropzone/2514/page4.html
Windsurfing Margarita www.enlared.net/the_loft

COMPLETE LIST OF GUIDES FROM BRADT PUBLICATIONS

Africa by Road   Bob Swain/Paula Snyder   £12.95
Albania: Guide and Illustrated Journal   Peter Dawson/Andrea Dawson/Linda White   £10.95
Amazon, The   Roger Harris/Peter Hutchison   £12.95
Antarctica: A Guide to the Wildlife   Tony Soper/Dafila Scott   £12.95
Australia and New Zealand by Rail   Colin Taylor   £10.95
Belize, Guide to   Alex Bradbury   £10.95
Brazil, Guide to   Alex Bradbury   £11.95
Burma, Guide to   Nicholas Greenwood   £12.95
Cape Verde Islands   Aisling Irwin/Colum Wilson   £11.95
Central America, Backpacking in   Tim Burford   £10.95
Central and South America by Road   Pam Ascanio   £12.95
Chile and Argentina: Backpacking and Hiking   Tim Burford   £11.95
Cuba, Guide to   Stephen Fallon   £11.95
East and Southern Africa: The Backpacker's Manual   Philip Briggs   £13.95
Eastern Europe by Rail   Rob Dodson   £9.95
Ecuador, Climbing and Hiking in   Rob Rachowiecki/Mark Thurber/Betsy Wagenhauser   £12.95
Ecuador, Peru and Bolivia: The Backpacker's Manual   Kathy Jarvis   £13.95 (winter 1999)
Eritrea, Guide to   Edward Paice   £10.95
Estonia   Neil Taylor   £11.95
Ethiopia, Guide to   Philip Briggs   £11.95
Galápagos Wildlife   David Horwell/Pete Oxford   £14.95   (summer 1999)
Georgia   Tim Burford   £13.95 (autumn 1999)
Ghana, Guide to   Philip Briggs   £11.95
Greece by Rail   Zane Katsikis   £11.95
Haiti and the Dominican Republic   Ross Velton   £11.95
India by Rail   Royston Ellis   £11.95
Laos and Cambodia, Guide to   John R Jones   £10.95
Latvia   Stephen Baister/Chris Patrick   £11.95
Lebanon, Guide to   Lynda Keen   £10.95
Lithuania   Gordon McLachlan   £12.95 (spring 1999)
Madagascar, Guide to   Hilary Bradt   £12.95
Madagascar Wildlife   Hilary Bradt/Derek Schuurman/Nick Garbutt   £14.95
Malawi, Guide to   Philip Briggs   £10.95
Maldives, Guide to   Royston Ellis   £11.95
Mali   Ross Velton   £13.95   (autumn 1999)
Mauritius, Rodrigues and Réunion   Royston Ellis/Derek Schuurman   £12.95
Mexico, Backpacking in   Tim Burford   £11.95
Mozambique, Guide to   Philip Briggs   £11.95
Namibia   Chris McIntyre   £12.95
North Cyprus, Guide to   Diana Darke   £9.95

Peru and Bolivia: Backpacking and Trekking   Hilary Bradt   £11.95
Philippines, Guide to   Stephen Mansfield   £12.95
Poland and Ukraine, Hiking Guide to   Tim Burford   £11.95
Romania, Hiking Guide to   Tim Burford   £10.95
Russia and Central Asia by Road   Hazel Barker   £12.95
Russia by Rail, with Belarus and Ukraine   Athol Yates   £13.95
South Africa, Guide to   Philip Briggs   £11.95
Southern Africa by Rail   Paul Ash   £12.95
Spain and Portugal by Rail   Norman Renouf   £11.95
Spitsbergen, Guide to   Andreas Umbreit   £12.95
Sri Lanka by Rail   Royston Ellis   £10.95
Switzerland by Rail   Anthony Lambert   £10.95
Tanzania, Guide to   Philip Briggs   £11.95
Uganda   Philip Briggs   £11.95
USA by Rail   John Pitt   £12.95
Venezuela   Hilary Dunsterville Branch   £13.95
Vietnam, Guide to   John R Jones   £11.95
Your Child's Health Abroad   Dr Jane Wilson-Howarth/Dr Matthew Ellis   £8.95
Zambia, Guide to   Chris McIntyre   £11.95
Zanzibar, Guide to   David Else   £11.95

Bradt Guides are available from bookshops or by mail order from:

Bradt Publications
41 Nortoft Road
Chalfont St Peter
Bucks SL9 0LA
England
Tel/fax: 01494 873478
Email: bradtpublications@compuserve.com

Please include your name, address and daytime telephone number with your order and enclose a cheque or postal order, or quote your Visa/Mastercard card number and expiry date. Postage will be charged as follows:

UK: £1.50 for one book; £2.50 for two or more books
Europe (inc Eire): £2 for one book; £4 for two or more books (airmail printed paper)
Rest of world: £4 for one book; £7 for two or more books (airmail printed paper)

Index